PROFESSIONAL
SHAREPOINT® 2013 ADMINISTRATION

PROFESSIONAL

SharePoint® 2013 Administration

PROFESSIONAL

SharePoint® 2013 Administration

Shane Young
Steve Caravajal
Todd Klindt

A Wiley Brand

Professional SharePoint® 2013 Administration

Published by
John Wiley & Sons, Inc.
10475 Crosspoint Boulevard
Indianapolis, IN 46256
www.wiley.com

Copyright © 2013 by John Wiley & Sons, Inc., Indianapolis, Indiana

Published simultaneously in Canada

ISBN: 978-1-118-49581-0
ISBN: 978-1-118-49580-3 (ebk)
ISBN: 978-1-118-65504-7 (ebk)
ISBN: 978-1-118-65471-2 (ebk)

Manufactured in the United States of America

10 9 8 7 6 5 4 3 2 1

For general information on our other products and services please contact our Customer Care Department within the United States at (877) 762-2974, outside the United States at (317) 572-3993 or fax (317) 572-4002.

Wiley publishes in a variety of print and electronic formats and by print-on-demand. Some material included with standard print versions of this book may not be included in e-books or in print-on-demand. If this book refers to media such as a CD or DVD that is not included in the version you purchased, you may download this material at http://booksupport.wiley.com. For more information about Wiley products, visit www.wiley.com.

Library of Congress Control Number: 2012955720

I dedicate this book to my wonderful wife, Rosemary. I'm not sure I understand how or why you put up with me, and the writing of yet another book. Words cannot express my appreciation. I love you a lot!

—Steve

I would like to dedicate this book to my beautiful wife, Jill. Just today she reminded me that after the last book I told her to never let me write another book, and here we are. I would not have been able to hold it together long enough to finish this book without her support. Thanks, babe, I love you.

—Todd

This book is dedicated to Baby Luke. Howdy. Funny enough, you are nine months old as I write these words. I have doubts that by the time you are old enough to read this book that paper books will even exist anymore. Either way, take a look at this old relic and smile and know all things are possible with your friend hard work. Dad got a D- in English and yet this is book number six for him. You and your brother better get better grades than me. Your mother and I love you.

—Shane

ABOUT THE AUTHORS

 STEVE CARAVAJAL is director of productivity solutions and lead architect with the Microsoft Corporation. Steve has 25+ years' experience in technology leadership, strategy, product development, consulting, and training. Dr. Caravajal works with large enterprise companies, and his focus includes architecting solutions that include SharePoint, enterprise social computing, business intelligence, search, and cloud-based applications. He also advises several local companies on Enterprise strategy. Steve holds a bachelor of science degree in chemistry and mathematics, and a doctoral degree in chemistry and computer science. He is an adjunct professor at a couple of local universities in the Cincinnati area, teaching Enterprise Architecture, public and private cloud technology, and software development. In addition to holding several patents and speaking at conferences, Steve has written four books: *SharePoint 2007 and Office Development Expert Solutions, Inside SharePoint 2007 Administration, Professional SharePoint 2010 Administration*, and *Professional SharePoint 2013 Administration.*

 TODD KLINDT has been a professional computer nerd for nearly 20 years, specializing in SharePoint for the last 10 years. His love affair with SharePoint began one slow day at the office when he discovered SharePoint Team Services 1.0 on the Office XP CD that was holding up his coffee cup, and he decided to take it for a spin. The rest is history. Since then, he has had the pleasure of working with SharePoint farms both large and small. In 2006 he was honored to be awarded the MVP award from Microsoft for Windows SharePoint Services, and he has written several books and magazine articles on SharePoint. Todd has presented sessions on SharePoint at many major conferences both in the United States as well as Europe and Asia, and does the user group circuit, SharePoint Saturday events, and the occasional children's birthday party as well. He chronicles his SharePoint adventures on his blog, `www.toddklindt` `.com/blog`. Because his chosen career as a Hollywood stuntman didn't pan out, he is currently working his dream job as a SharePoint consultant at Rackspace, where he spends his days fixing broken SharePoint environments and bringing new SharePoint environments into the world, along with the occasional nap at his desk. If you're bored, you can follow him on Twitter @toddklindt.

 SHANE YOUNG is just your average SharePoint nerd who has been doing nothing but SharePoint for a long time now. Microsoft has been kind enough to award him MVP status for eight years running now, so you know he is the outspoken type. Thankfully, his newest employer, Rackspace, appreciates that about him. If you are wondering what happened to SharePoint911, don't worry; the band is still together, we are just flying the Rackspace flag these days, bringing fanatical SharePoint to the open cloud. You can contact Shane on Facebook, LinkedIn, Twitter (@ShanesCows), via e-mail (`shane.young@rackspace.com`), his blog (`http://msmvps.com/shane`), or through his company's website (`www.SharePoint911.com` or `SharePoint.Rackspace.com`). Shane lives in Cincinnati, Ohio, with his wife, Nicola, his two sons, Grant and Luke, and their two dogs.

ABOUT THE TECHNICAL EDITORS

BRIAN CAAUWE is a SharePoint 2010 MCM and has been working with the SharePoint platform since 2007. He typically walks the tightrope between administration and development as a senior SharePoint consultant, with a focus on systems architecture, security, migrations, and integration strategies with Avtex Solutions.

Brian came to the SharePoint world from a network administration background working with Active Directory, SQL Server, Exchange, Citrix, and many other proprietary applications. Armed with this administration baseline, and a pre-existing passion for web development, his skills were a perfect match for SharePoint.

SEB MATTHEWS is a Microsoft architect with over 20 years' experience working with mid-tier and enterprise organizations. He is currently providing consultancy services to businesses that want to utilize Microsoft technologies in big-data, cloud, and business-critical scenarios, architecting information repositories, portals, and business process management platforms.

A frequent speaker at conferences and community events, Matthews is also an active member of the SharePoint community in Europe, Africa, and the U.S.A. When he isn't SharePointing, he enjoys the outdoors, being a geek, and spending time with his wife, young son, and Barney the dog.

STEPHEN WILSON has worked as a technical resource in a number of industries such as retail, financial, and higher education. Over the last six years he has been devoted to training and consulting on SharePoint and related technologies. He has extensive experience with presenting, developing documentation, and training programs. As a consultant, his focus has been on installation and infrastructure. Recently, Stephen has become more involved with presenting at SharePoint events.

CREDITS

ACKNOWLEDGMENTS

THANKS, NICOLA! Yes, once again you are up for the wife of the year award for putting up with another book writing — and this time we have two kids. How crazy is that? Grant and Luke are lucky to have you for a mommy! I would feel bad to again forget mentioning the other two boys, so just in case Tyson or Pugsley learn how to read: Hello, doggies.

To my fellow authors: Good job, guys. We once again managed to get a masterpiece out the door without killing each other. That is some kind of miracle. I am certain one of you will want to write another book sooner or later, so I will go ahead and start getting an outline together. *Ugh.*

Hey, all of you contributors: Good work! I know it is annoying trying to work with us but hopefully the result is worth it. I know that Todd, Steve, and I really appreciate it and the book wouldn't be nearly as good without you guys. One person I want to call out specifically is Stephen Wilson, who carried multiple torches with his content creation and tech editing. Thanks, Stephen. You are a heck of guy; I don't care what Todd says. The key point here is Rackers rule!

Wiley folks! Thank you. I know we are a pain in the butt to work with but the end product looks great. Ami and Mary, I feel the worst for you two because you have to battle us and then work with us at the same time. Sorry. And Jim? Yeah. Not sure how many grey hairs you have with our names on them but I am certain they are many. Thanks for continuing to love us.

I love you, little Sparky!

—SHANE

WELL, THIS BRINGS US to the close of another SharePoint book. I guess I should thank my partners, Shane and Todd, but since they didn't do any of the writing — oops sorry, one chapter each — thanks guys, you are a big help! One of the best experiences in the world is writing a book, but unfortunately one of the worst experiences is writing a book. So, I should definitely thank our Wiley task masters, Mary and Ami, who worked to keep us in line and productive. If you've ever tried to herd cats, you'll know what their experience was like, so thank you very much; we couldn't have done it without you. As always, the technical editors and the contributing authors played a very big role, so thank you very much for all your help! And last, but definitely not least, I want to thank my beautiful and wonderful wife, Rosemary. I know that I tell you I'm not going to do this again, and yet I continue to do it again. Thank you so much for your support and patience.

—STEVE

MY PORTION OF THIS book would not have been possible without the support of my lovely wife, Jill. Thanks again. You endured another year of me writing a book, and even worse, a year of me whining about writing a book. You kept the kids clothed and fed, and the house running. I appreciate it. You're my rock.

I am contractually required to thank my coauthors. Thanks, Shane and Steve, for putting up with me for another book. Once again, we all vowed to never do this again, and once again the lure of fame and fortune ruled out over common sense. Now it's time for the supporting tour and movie deals. I hope you're both ready. I know I am.

This book would not be as awesome as it is without the help of some very dedicated contributing authors. They did a great job writing chapters and keeping us on our toes. Thanks, guys.

Finally, this book would have stalled multiple times if it weren't for the tenacity and nagging of Wiley folks. Many times they had to bring us kicking and screaming back on task. A special shout out to Ami and Mary, who put up with a lot of missed deadlines. Sorry about that. It's all in now, though.

—TODD

CONTENTS

INTRODUCTION

THE THREE AMIGOS ARE BACK together to write another SharePoint Administration book. It feels kind of crazy to know we are done with this process for a third time. With the 2007 edition we had almost no clue what we were doing but we knew that the topic was important. The 2010 edition was painful but a great adventure; when we started I never imagined we could fill that many pages. Now, with the 2013 edition, you will find the same voice and humor, but many changes and updates relevant to the newest version of SharePoint.

This book, like our other two, is written from the point of view of real administrators who perform the tasks it describes; it is not an academic exploration. This is the same way we teach training and give presentations at major conferences around the world — focusing on real-world SharePoint. We are often asked, "Will this book/training/presentation help me prepare for the SharePoint certification exams?" — and we always have the same answer: "Does that matter if you cannot do your job well?" This book is focused as much as possible on helping you administer SharePoint effectively and efficiently. If you do a good job learning and using SharePoint, things like passing the exams will follow naturally. In case you are wondering, two of us have already passed some of the exams and one of us is a slacker and hasn't taken any yet.

Some of the changes in this edition of the book include the following:

> ➤ Coverage of the new features, obviously. Highlights are found in the Office Web Apps chapter, since they are now for everyone, and Search is 100% all new so that chapter requires some studying. The App model is also interesting; as admins we aren't creating apps but there is some work required to get the pieces in place. I wish I could tell you the jokes are all new but we like to be green so you will see some "recycling" of material. Don't worry they aren't all repeats but don't be surprised when it happens.

> ➤ More focus on step-by-step. For example if you look at Chapter 8, where we cover Business Intelligence, it is almost entirely instructions for configuring the different tools and then the examples so you can confirm everything is working. Readers from the 2010 book really pushed us for more of this level of content.

> ➤ Less focus on features that rolled up from 2010 mostly unchanged. A great example is Managed Metadata. With SharePoint 2010 this feature was new so it got broad coverage. In this edition, Managed Metadata is mentioned where appropriate but no deep dive. You might notice there is no longer a chapter on navigation and governance, because we tried to spread out the governance love so it is embedded in all of the chapters instead of bringing all of those thoughts into one place.

WHO THIS BOOK IS FOR

Although we are seasoned pros who have been dealing with SharePoint for 10 or more years, we don't make such assumptions about you. We cover topics with a wide-enough brush that if you are new to SharePoint you can connect the dots. If you are an old pro, you can still find the nuggets new to 2013 that you crave thanks to organization and headings. The sweet-spot reader for this book is someone who has read our book *Professional SharePoint 2010 Administration* (Wrox, 2010) and has *some* hands-on experience with SharePoint administration, although that isn't required. If you are new to our style of writing you will just have to learn to appreciate the personality of the book while you learn to love SharePoint — and by personality we mean Shane's really funny jokes and comments, and Todd's and Steve's weak attempts at humor. The book has some "Easter eggs" too, so be sure to look at those screenshots closely.

WHAT THIS BOOK COVERS

SharePoint 2013 administration!

Oh, you wanted more detailed information? OK then. This book is primarily focused on traditional SharePoint administration topics, but it also includes other topics that might not seem related to administration per se. Yes, you should read those too. Topics like using Office 2013, branding, and development are covered in such a way that you will learn the key components and be able to speak intelligently about them. You might not finish the business intelligence chapter ready for a career change, but you will leave it knowing the full power of the BI stack and what you need to do as an administrator to enable that functionality. So, read all of the chapters, pretty please.

HOW THIS BOOK IS STRUCTURED

The book is divided into chapters, but not parts. In general, you can read them in any order you want, because they are mostly self-contained, with plenty of cross-references added when needed. There are a few things to consider, though, while you think about which chapters to read when. Although all the chapters stand on their own, Chapters 2 through 4 are very complementary for understanding and building a new 2013 SharePoint farm. Chapter 7 covers Windows PowerShell for SharePoint, and that is one you should read early and often. Almost every chapter in the book includes some PowerShell, so if you are unfamiliar with it then jumping ahead to that chapter will be helpful. Other than that, each chapter's title makes it clear what is covered.

WHAT YOU NEED TO USE THIS BOOK

The only thing you need to read this book is a comfy chair and some free time. If you want to follow along with the examples, some virtual machines would probably be handy to build out your farm. Of course, if you are the brave (or reckless) type, you can always just test on your production farm. Let's hope that isn't the case, though. Try this stuff out somewhere else first.

This book is written to show you as much of SharePoint 2013 as possible. That means topics range from SharePoint Foundation to SharePoint Server Enterprise. We also cover Office Web Applications, SQL Server Reporting Services, PowerPivot, and PowerView. Some of those are pretty pricey, but because they are either in use or being evaluated in many farms we see in the wild, we thought they were important to cover. The best thing we recommend to fully enjoy this book? A TechNet subscription. Then you would have all of this software at your fingertips to follow along.

CONVENTIONS

To help you get the most from the text and keep track of what's happening, we've used a number of conventions throughout the book.

> **WARNING** *Boxes like this one hold important, not-to-be forgotten information that is directly relevant to the surrounding text.*

> **NOTE** *Notes, tips, hints, tricks, or asides to the current discussion are offset and placed in italics like this.*

As for styles in the text:

➤ We *italicize* new terms and important words when we introduce them.

➤ We show keyboard strokes like this: Ctrl+A.

➤ We show filenames, URLs, and code within the text like so: `persistence.properties`.

➤ We present code in two different ways:

```
We use a monofont type with no highlighting for most code examples.
```

```
We use bold to emphasize code that's particularly important in the present context.
```

SOURCE CODE

As you work through the examples in this book, you may choose either to type in all the code manually or to use the source code files that accompany the book. All the source code used in this book is available for download at `www.wrox.com`. Each chapter that has companion code will indicate that at the beginning of the chapter. Once at the site, simply locate the book's title (either by using the Search box or by using one of the title lists) and click the Download Code link on the book's detail page to obtain all the source code for the book.

> **NOTE** *Because many books have similar titles, you may find it easiest to search by ISBN; this book's ISBN is 978-1-118-49581-0.*

Once you download the code, just decompress it with your favorite compression tool. Alternately, you can go to the main Wrox code download page at `www.wrox.com/dynamic/books/download.aspx` to see the code available for this book and all other Wrox books.

ERRATA

We make every effort to ensure that there are no errors in the text or in the code. However, no one is perfect, and mistakes do occur. If you find an error in one of our books, such as a spelling mistake or a faulty piece of code, we would be very grateful for your feedback. By sending in errata you may save another reader hours of frustration and at the same time you will be helping us provide even higher quality information.

To find the errata page for this book, go to `www.wrox.com` and locate the title using the Search box or one of the title lists. Then, on the book details page, click the Book Errata link. On this page you can view all errata that has been submitted for this book and posted by Wrox editors. A complete book list, including links to each book's errata, is also available at `www.wrox.com/misc-pages/booklist.shtml`.

If you don't spot "your" error on the Book Errata page, go to `www.wrox.com/contact/techsupport.shtml` and complete the form there to send us the error you have found. We'll check the information and, if appropriate, post a message to the book's errata page and fix the problem in subsequent editions of the book.

P2P.WROX.COM

For author and peer discussion, join the P2P forums at `http://p2p.wrox.com`. The forums are a web-based system for you to post messages relating to Wrox books and related technologies and to interact with other readers and technology users. The forums offer a subscription feature to e-mail you topics of interest of your choosing when new posts are made to the forums. Wrox authors, editors, other industry experts, and your fellow readers are present on these forums.

At `http://p2p.wrox.com` you will find a number of different forums that will help you not only as you read this book, but also as you develop your own applications. To join the forums, just follow these steps:

1. Go to `http://p2p.wrox.com` and click the Register link.
2. Read the terms of use and click Agree.

3. Complete the required information to join as well as any optional information you wish to provide and click Submit.

4. You will receive an e-mail with information describing how to verify your account and complete the joining process.

> **NOTE** *You can read messages in the forums without joining P2P but in order to post your own messages, you must join.*

Once you join, you can post new messages and respond to messages other users post. You can read messages at any time on the Web. If you would like to have new messages from a particular forum e-mailed to you, click the Subscribe to this Forum icon by the forum name in the forum listing.

For more information about how to use the Wrox P2P, be sure to read the P2P FAQs for answers to questions about how the forum software works as well as many common questions specific to P2P and Wrox books. To read the FAQs, click the FAQ link on any P2P page.

1

What's New in SharePoint 2013

WHAT'S IN THIS CHAPTER?

➤ The installation process

➤ Changes to service applications

➤ Introduction to Apps

If you feel like you only just got your head wrapped around all the improvements and new features that SharePoint 2010 offered, you may also be feeling a bit dismayed by the appearance of SharePoint 2013. When will the madness end? Clearly, SharePoint 2010 was a huge leap forward from SharePoint 2007 — its improvements and enhancements were massive. It introduced us to the service application infrastructure that was a much needed improvement to the SSP model that SharePoint 2007 used. It was a great time to be in the SharePoint business. At this point, you are probably all cozy and comfortable with your SharePoint 2010 farms. You have them built and humming along just the way you want and now Microsoft has released SharePoint 2013!

Don't worry; it's still a great time to be a SharePoint administrator. SharePoint 2013 is new and improved, but it's nothing you can't handle, especially with this trusty book by your side. This chapter provides a brief overview of some of the more exciting new features of SharePoint 2013, and what has changed since SharePoint 2010. It is meant to pique your interest in the SharePoint 2013 journey that lies ahead of you, both as you explore this book and as you work with SharePoint in real-world scenarios. Each abbreviated description includes a reference to the chapter in which you can get the full scoop. Of course, you'll want to read this delightful tome from cover to cover, certainly before the movie comes out, but this chapter enables you to jump ahead to the juicy parts.

INSTALLATION CHANGES

Familiarizing yourself with SharePoint 2013 might seem daunting, but you'll be pleased to hear that the installation process is not radically changed from the SharePoint 2010 installation process. If you can install SharePoint 2010, with a little effort and a small amount of stumbling, you can install SharePoint 2013, too. The following sections break it down, hitting the main points.

System Requirements

SharePoint 2013 is a little more demanding than SharePoint 2010 when it comes to hardware requirements. Gone are the days of squeezing by on 8GB of RAM and a measly 80GB C: drive. SharePoint 2013 does big things, and it needs big iron to do them. For a production SharePoint Server 2013 box, you need at a minimum 12GB of RAM and four 64-bit cores. In truth, you can still get by with that 80GB C: drive. If you want to run everything on a development or evaluation box, you'll need to crank that RAM up to 24GB in order to handle SharePoint and SQL Server. Keep in mind that these values are minimums. The Windows 8 minimum RAM requirement is a miniscule 1GB, but no one would seriously consider running it in production that way. A Windows 8 box with 1GB of RAM is how an IT department would punish users who pester them too much. Don't punish your users by running your SharePoint servers on the minimum requirements either. They remember that kind of stuff when they're buying holiday gifts.

SharePoint 2013's software requirements are very reasonable. It requires a database back end that's running 64-bit SQL Server that's either SQL Server 2008 R2 with Service Pack 1 or SQL Server 2012. If you want to use some of the advanced business intelligence (BI) features or the new Access Services service application of SharePoint 2013, you'll need Service Pack 1 on SQL Server 2012. SharePoint itself must be installed on a server running Windows Server 2008 R2 Service Pack 1 or Windows Server 2012. It does a good job of bridging the old and the new both with SQL Server and Windows.

The Installation Process

As shown in the setup dialog in Figure 1-1, the SharePoint 2013 installation process looks nearly identical to that of SharePoint 2010.

In addition to Windows Server and SQL Server, SharePoint 2013 requires a few other software pieces, but most of them are installed with the Prerequisite Installer, another similarity to SharePoint 2010. The SharePoint 2013 splash screen is nearly identical to its older sibling, which is a good thing. The links are the same; only the background has been updated to match the new color scheme. The links take you to

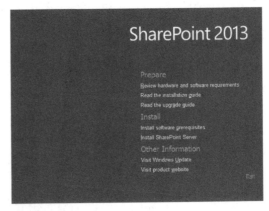

FIGURE 1-1

documentation you should read before installation (but after this book, of course), as well as links to the Prerequisite Installer and the SharePoint installer. It's your one-stop shop to get started with SharePoint 2013. Chapter 3 is the authoritative chapter on it. Well, at least the most authoritative chapter in this book.

Upgrading from SharePoint 2010

Any successful upgrade begins with plenty of researching and planning. That hasn't changed when upgrading to SharePoint 2013. As with each successive version of SharePoint, the upgrade story has gotten better. In SharePoint 2013 in general, the focus is on site collection owners, and upgrade is part of this focus. SharePoint 2013 enables site collection owners to decide when their site collection is upgraded, and when they would like an eval of how it will look when it's upgraded. Site collection owners can also test their site collections to see how well they will upgrade, and see the actual upgrade logs for their site collection when the upgrade is performed. Lazy SharePoint administrators world 'round are cheering at the thought of this. Because site collections aren't actually upgraded when SharePoint 2010 databases are attached to a SharePoint 2013 server, those database attaches go very quickly. This means less downtime for users when the upgrade happens, and less time that administrators need to spend working nights and weekends. The only real losers here are those pizza delivery folks who fuel late-night IT workers.

The "bad" news in SharePoint 2013 isn't really that bad. Consider it "less good" news. Upgrading from SharePoint 2003 to SharePoint 2007 provided three options: side-by-side (also known as gradual) upgrade, in-place upgrade, and database-attach upgrade. Upgrading from SharePoint 2007 to SharePoint 2010 eliminated the gradual option, leaving only in-place upgrades and database-attach upgrades. SharePoint 2013 has voted another upgrade method off the island. This version's upgrade victim was in-place upgrade. In other words, the only way to upgrade SharePoint 2010 content to SharePoint 2013 is to attach your SharePoint 2010 databases to a SharePoint 2013 farm. This will work with content databases and many service application databases. If it sounds confusing and maybe a little scary, don't worry — it's all demystified in Chapter 5, "Upgrading to SharePoint 2013." After reading it, or maybe even just thumbing through and looking at the figures, you'll be well prepared to upgrade even the fussiest of SharePoint 2010 farms to SharePoint 2013 with ease.

Patching

You can't talk about upgrading without mentioning patching. Whereas an upgrade is considered a *version-to-version*, or V2V, upgrade, patching is considered a *build-to-build*, or B2B, upgrade. Although upgrading and patching might seem like different activities, the plumbing in the background is the same.

There are three types of patches for SharePoint 2013: service packs (SPs), cumulative updates (CUs), and hotfixes. Service packs aren't on a set schedule, and are typically released every 18 to 24 months, whenever they're good and ready. They fix all the bugs that have been identified since the last service pack or RTM. They're thoroughly tested, and in some situations not only fix bugs, but introduce new functionality. Service Pack 1 for SharePoint 2010 introduced some new features, such as sending deleted webs to the Recycle Bin. When a service pack is released, it should be introduced into your test environment sooner rather than later; and it should be made part of production as soon as possible, as service packs can dramatically affect performance and security.

CUs are released on schedule — roughly at the end of every even-numbered month. Each CU contains all the bug fixes of the previous CU, plus whatever has been fixed in the last couple of months. CUs are tested but not as thoroughly as service packs. The general recommendation is to install a CU only if it fixes a problem that your farm is experiencing. Several CUs for SharePoint 2010 broke things, and some were so troublesome that Microsoft removed them until they worked properly. Don't let your farm be the one that identifies a problem CU. If a CU does provide a fix for a problem your farm is having, be sure to test it in your test environment first, and wait a few weeks before unleashing it on production. Patches cannot be uninstalled, so if a CU has a regression (something that used to work but is broken by the patch), you're stuck with it until the next CU is released. In short, be careful with CUs. They aren't as dangerous as playing with fire, but they're close.

The last type of patch is the hotfix, or security patch. These little devils usually sneak on to your SharePoint server undetected through Windows Update. Hotfix patches are released to address urgent security issues in SharePoint. Therefore, it is very important to get them onto your servers, although they tend to be the least tested of all the patches because of the need to release them quickly. In most cases you have to bite the bullet and install them. When you do, don't forget to run the Configuration Wizard afterward to complete the installation. It also wouldn't hurt to give the nearest homeless person a couple of bucks for breakfast. Every bit of good karma helps.

CENTRAL ADMINISTRATION

The Central Administration site is like home base for SharePoint administrators. No matter how bad your day is, or how badly broken SharePoint is, if you can get to Central Administration, often called just Central Admin, there's hope. Central Admin, shown in Figure 1-2, is one of the first dialogs you see after installing SharePoint; and as we all know, you only get one chance to make a first impression. As you can tell from the numerous links, Central Admin provides easy access to every aspect of SharePoint's behavior. Central Admin in SharePoint 2013 bears a very striking resemblance to Central Admin in SharePoint 2010. They look so much alike, in fact, that SharePoint 2013's Central Admin could probably use SharePoint 2010's Central Admin's ID to get into bars if it had to.

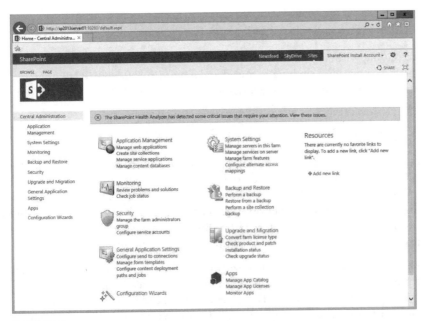

FIGURE 1-2

There are some differences, however, the main ones being the branding and layout changes that are universal to SharePoint 2013. These include the flat look and the location of the Site Settings gear, which is cleverly hidden in the top-right corner of the page, directly under the Internet Explorer settings gear. With one exception, the links on the home page of SharePoint 2013's Central Admin are identical to the links in SharePoint 2010, right down to the red bar across the top alerting you that your farm has critical errors. If you could find it in Central Admin in SharePoint 2010, you can find it in SharePoint 2013.

The aforementioned exception, which you may have noticed, is the newly added Apps link in the left-hand navigation. Apps are new to SharePoint 2013, so no link was needed for them in the SharePoint 2010. Other than that, all those Central Admin navigating skills you honed in SharePoint 2010 transfer directly over to SharePoint 2013. Want to create a new site collection? It's still available by selecting Application Management ➪ Create Site Collections. Want to set up incoming e-mail? You can still find it using System Settings ➪ Configure incoming e-mail settings. Administrators of SharePoint 2013 will be glad to find that Central Administration retains its familiar style of being wide rather than deep. Everything you need is typically two or three clicks away.

SERVICE APPLICATIONS

SharePoint has always been both show pony and workhorse. It's pretty, and it's easy to use, but it also works hard behind the scenes to ensure that all the functionality you're looking for is available. In recent versions of SharePoint, much of that functionality has been powered by service applications. This section spends some time looking at service applications in SharePoint 2013, and how they evolved into their current form.

In SharePoint 2003 the architectures were very rigid, and were based around machine types. As your farm grew, you needed to follow specific configurations in order to scale components such as search and your job server. If having servers in those specific roles didn't work for your situation, you were out of luck. Those restrictions were relaxed with the release of SharePoint 2007, which introduced the concept of a shared service provider (SSP). Although the servers and services in the SSP were rigid, the server roles were not. It was possible to add another Search Query server, or an Excel Calculation server, whatever you needed; there were limits, but it was more flexible. However, there was still room for improvement. You couldn't consume services from more than one SSP in a single web application, and the SSP was provided as one solid block of functionality. If you wanted a second Business Data Connection Service, you could only get that by creating a second SSP, which gave you a second Search instance, a second User Profile service, and so on — better than SharePoint 2003, but not quite ideal.

SharePoint 2010 finally fixed most of these issues. You no longer have to fight with a monolithic SSP; instead you have flexible, friendly service applications. If you want a second Business Connectivity Service, you just create one; there is no need to create another entire SSP. In addition, you can mix and match web applications and service applications in any way imaginable. If you feel you are lacking in imagination, see Chapter 2, "Architecture and Capacity Planning."

SharePoint 2013 carries on in the same tradition. The service application architecture hasn't changed, as shown in the Manage Service Applications dialog in Figure 1-3. At a glance, it could be easily mistaken for its counterpart in SharePoint 2010 Central Administration.

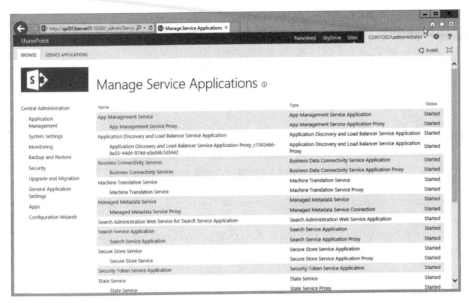

FIGURE 1-3

There are some new faces, however. Here is a list of the new service applications in SharePoint 2013:

➤ Access Services

➤ App Management

➤ Machine Translation

➤ Work Management

➤ PowerPoint Conversion

For those of you who are thinking that Access Services existed in SharePoint 2010, that's true. However, the Access Services in SharePoint 2013 bears little resemblance to its SharePoint 2010 counterpart. In fact, the SharePoint 2010 version lives on in SharePoint 2013 as Access Services 2010. For more detailed information, see Chapter 4, "Understanding Service Applications," which explains each of the new service applications and the functionality they provide.

The Search service application in particular has received some improvements in SharePoint 2013, rebuilt to be better and stronger. Shortly before SharePoint 2010 was released, Microsoft bought a search company called FAST. The purchase didn't happen soon enough for FAST to be properly integrated in SharePoint 2010; but in order to take advantage of the FAST Server product, Microsoft awkwardly bolted it on to SharePoint 2010 — the equivalent of strapping a jet engine on top of a Toyota Corolla. It was a kludged solution at best.

In SharePoint 2013, Microsoft rebuilt the SharePoint Search service application and properly integrated FAST technology into it. They also consolidated Search so it is the same service app, with different levels of functionality, regardless of whether you're running SharePoint Foundation or SharePoint Server. The interface in Central Admin is roughly the same, so if you're comfortable with it in SharePoint 2010 you'll feel right at home in SharePoint 2013. Figure 1-4 shows the new SharePoint 2013 Search Administration interface. There are additional links for the new functionality that was added, but for the most part you configure it the same way.

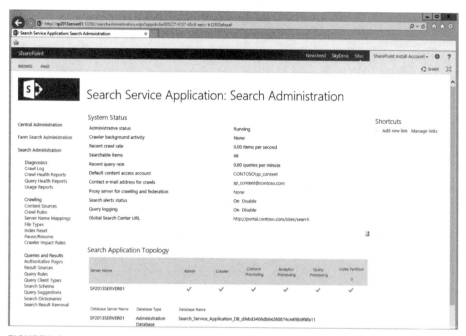

FIGURE 1-4

Under the hood, however, Search is a completely different beast. It's still based on roles, like Search of the past, but now each role is more clearly defined, manifesting itself as a `noderunner.exe` process on your SharePoint boxes. Here is a list of the six search components and what they do:

➤ **Index** — Stores and replicates portions of the search index

➤ **Query Processing** — Responds to user search queries and provides results

➤ **Search Administration** — The Search ringleader, this component controls the other components. There can be only one Search Administration component per Search service application.

➤ **Crawl** — Crawls the content sources and passes on their contents to the Content Procession components

➤ **Content Processing** — Processes the documents retrieved from the Crawl component and writes the results to the Index component

➤ **Analytics** — Creates usage analytics and search analytic reports

Most of these are old familiar friends, but new to the list is the Analytics component. If you think of the usage logs as content sources, and the usage reports as queries against that source, you can see how it works together. The new features have introduced some complexity. For instance, changing the Search topology can no longer be done in the comfort of Central Admin. That's now a task that only PowerShell can accomplish. Search is a powerful capability, which is why it has been given its own chapter. For more information, see Chapter 13, "Configuring and Managing Enterprise Search."

The Managed Metadata and User Profile service applications have also received some minor improvements in SharePoint 2013. Managed Metadata was expanded to include support for custom navigation. This capability enables you to design and store complex global navigation structures in the Managed Metadata service application. These navigation structures are stored like regular metadata, making it easier to work with them. Not to be outdone, the User Profile service application now supports quicker synchronization with Active Directory. Microsoft has added back the Active Directory Import connection that was used in SharePoint 2007. It's just read-only, but it's faster than the FIM-based profile synchronization of SharePoint 2010, and it supports LDAP filters, as SharePoint 2007 did. This is great news for smaller shops that aren't ready to take advantage of all the functionality offered by the User Profile service. What is all the functionality, you ask? Chapter 14, "Configuring User Profiles and Social Computing," explains all the wonders of this service, and how you can best take advantage of it in your environment.

At this point, you've looked at both the new service applications and the changes made to existing service applications. One last service application to note is one that has gone away — sort of. In SharePoint 2010, you needed to install the Office Web Apps (OWAs) on your SharePoint servers and expose them as service applications. In SharePoint 2013, the OWAs are now their own product, and they must be installed on their own, non-SharePoint server. Although many SharePoint users have reacted to this change with dismay, the news isn't all bad. The OWAs have increased functionality, even in SharePoint. They can give you document previews right in your document libraries, for instance. You can also use the OWAs to render Office documents in Outlook Anywhere in Exchange 2013. Chapter 15, "The Office Web Applications for SharePoint," covers installation and configuration of the OWAs.

CLAIMS AND AUTHENTICATION

One of the more significant changes in SharePoint 2013 is the emphasis on claims-based authentication (CBA). CBA was first introduced in SharePoint 2010; and to say it was a little rough around the edges would be generous. Even as a version 1.0 product, Microsoft recommended using CBA as the default authentication method for all web applications. In practice, though, very few SharePoint administrators jumped on the CBA bandwagon, unless they needed it for forms-based authentication or they just enjoyed pain. Change is tough, and classic-mode authentication worked fine in almost all situations. On top of that, many things didn't work with CBA. The combination of CBA's complexity and its incompatibility issues were a one-two punch against its adoption.

Despite its faults, CBA is important. It is the cornerstone of federated authentication in SharePoint, and in SharePoint 2013 Microsoft has upped the ante. CBA is no longer just recommended, it's the default authentication provider for SharePoint. When a new web application is created in Central

Administration, classic-mode authentication is no longer even an option. Figure 1-5 shows the Create New Web Application dialog. Note that the option to choose between classic or claims-based is gone. You can use any authentication type you want as long as it's claims-based. However, classic-mode authentication, while discouraged, is still available using PowerShell cmdlets.

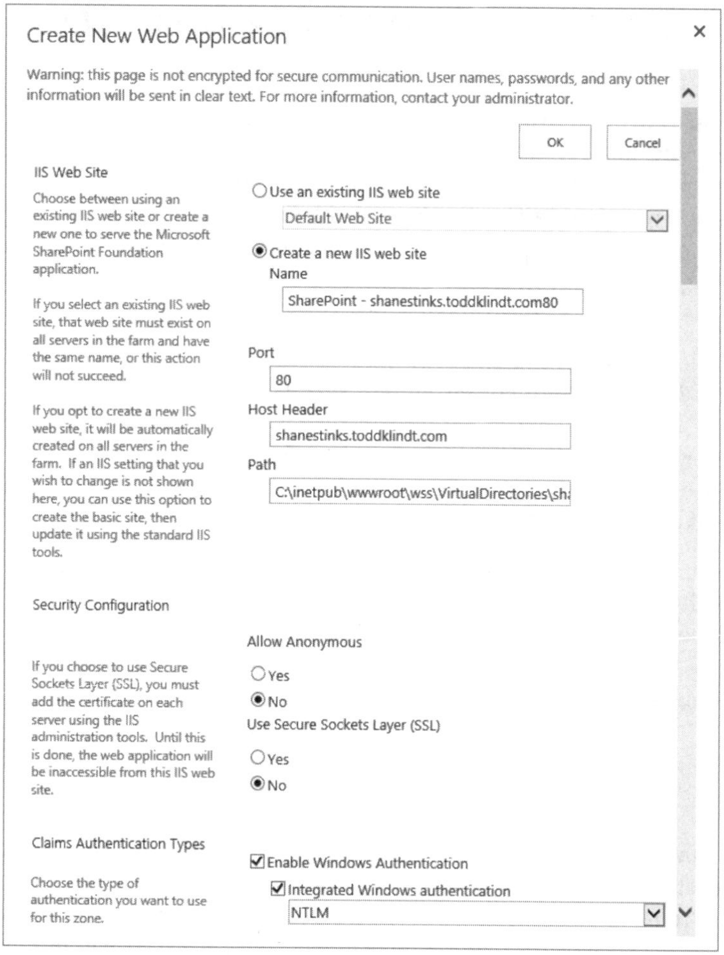

FIGURE 1-5

The extra complexity of claims-based authentication is offset by several benefits. For one thing, SharePoint can now easily use non-Active Directory authentication stores. Or perhaps you want to give users logins for SharePoint but not add them to your corporate Active Directory. No problem, CBA can do that. Your users can use any authentication store that supports Security Assertions Markup Language (SAML) claims. Examples of this include Microsoft's Live ID and OAuth, which is used by Google and Facebook. This flexibility enables you to give users access to SharePoint without you having to manage their accounts, and without them having to remember yet another username and password. You can also feel safer using CBA with SharePoint 2013, as most of the problems SharePoint 2010 had with it have been resolved. Chapter 6, "Claims Identity Management and Security," explains in detail how CBA works, and demonstrates how you can get the most out of it. Claims-based authentication can be daunting, but don't let that stop you from digging in and getting comfortable with it.

MANAGING SHAREPOINT 2013 WITH WINDOWS POWERSHELL

Another thing that Microsoft got right in SharePoint 2010 was moving to PowerShell for the command-line administration tool — a move not immediately appreciated by SharePoint administrators. PowerShell's learning curve is steep. With all its objects, methods, and properties, PowerShell is more than most administrators are used to working with, and if you're not careful, you end up looking like a developer when you're using it. Nobody likes that, not even developers. That said, most administrators familiar with PowerShell would agree that it is a great tool, even if it's a bit unwieldy and unforgiving at times.

SharePoint 2013's command-line interface continues to be PowerShell, though now it is based on PowerShell v3. There aren't a lot of radical changes to PowerShell in v3, but there are a few improvements, which SharePoint 2013 leverages. For instance, PowerShell has an improved integrated scripting environment (ISE) that is much improved over its v2 version; it's actually usable! PowerShell v3 also includes PowerShell Web Access, which provides a way to execute PowerShell commands in a web browser. Also included is a bevy of commands and syntax improvements that SharePoint administrators can take advantage of.

As SharePoint matures, each new release increases the number of tasks that can be performed from the command line. Following a SharePoint Server installation, you can find more than 770 cmdlets in the SharePoint Management Console, which includes nearly 300 new cmdlets for SharePoint 2013. Chapter 7, "Administrating SharePoint 2013 with PowerShell," shows you all the magical things you can do from the command line using PowerShell.

SHAREPOINT APPS

Probably the most significant change in SharePoint 2013 is the addition of SharePoint apps. Brand-new to SharePoint 2013, apps provide another way to add functionality to your SharePoint farm. They are intended to extend, not to replace, the existing ways of adding functionality — farm (full-trust) solutions and sandbox solutions — which still work fine but have not been sufficient in some situations. SharePoint 2013 apps were added to address those needs.

Farm solutions have existed since SharePoint 2007. They require someone with farm administrative rights to log onto one of the SharePoint servers and add the solution to the farm. Then they must deploy to the farm or a web application. This method gives developers the most flexibility, but it poses the most challenges for administrators; and there are security and stability concerns because the code is running on the SharePoint servers themselves, and could potentially have full access to the server, depending on how well the security options are locked down.

To address some of these liabilities, sandbox solutions were introduced in SharePoint 2010. Instead of requiring farm administrators to load them, sandbox solutions can be uploaded and activated by site collection administrators. In addition, farm administrators can control the resources a sandbox solution can consume, as well as which SharePoint server consumes them. This has brought us closer to administration nirvana, but not close enough. The sandbox worked almost too well. Developers complained that it was too restrictive, and the throttling would sometimes disable solutions that weren't impacting server performance. It was a step in the right direction, but there was room for improvement. Enter SharePoint 2013…

SharePoint apps address the concerns administrators had with the methods previously available to extend SharePoint functionality. With SharePoint apps, the apps can run on SharePoint, another server entirely, or even in the client browser. If the code isn't running on the SharePoint servers, it is much tougher for it to bring down a server by consuming resources. It also makes it tougher for the code to create any security problems, or exploit any that might already exist. All this increased stability and security does come with a small price, in the form of a complex setup, but once the App Management and Subscription settings service applications are created and configured, it's smooth sailing.

As administrators, we aren't the only ones who benefit from the new app model. Developers stand to gain a lot from it, too. In addition to reducing the number of times innocent developers are blamed for taking down SharePoint servers, there is another benefit: money. The new app model also includes a public SharePoint App Market where developers can publish and sell their apps to users who want to add them to their farms. Their apps can also be sold on Office365. Although we probably won't see a lot of developers quitting their day jobs and buying big houses in the Caribbean from the proceeds, it should be worth their time — and it increases the number of apps to which the rest of us will have access. Everybody wins!

Chapter 10, "Managing SharePoint Developer Solutions and Features," and Chapter 11, "Managing Apps and the New App Model," cover different aspects of this new feature. They include how to configure SharePoint to use the app model, and how to write apps for it. There's something for everyone.

WORKFLOW MANAGER

Workflows have been in SharePoint since the 2007 release, and they have proven to be a capable and popular feature for modeling business processes. Out of the box, SharePoint 2013 supports all workflow functionality that existed in SharePoint 2010. This means that the workflows in content databases you upgrade from SharePoint 2010 will function without any extra work afterward. However, if you have SharePoint Server, with a little extra work, you can take workflows up another notch. Heck, another two notches! Sorry SharePoint Foundation users, the Workflow Manager requires SharePoint Server.

While SharePoint 2013 natively supports SharePoint 2010 workflow, there are two additional workflow options: SharePoint 2013 workflows and Project Server 2013 workflows. The SharePoint 2013 workflows are available after you install the SharePoint 2013 Workflow Manager, which is an additional download. The Workflow Manager doesn't need to be installed on a SharePoint server, and for performance reasons it probably shouldn't be. After you have successfully installed the Workflow Manager, you're only one carefully crafted PowerShell cmdlet away from being able to use the SharePoint 2013 workflows. If you install Project Server 2013, you'll obtain even more workflow options.

After installing the SharePoint 2010 Workflow Manager, and optionally Project Server 2013, you can open SharePoint Designer 2013 and enjoy your handiwork. If all the components are installed and configured correctly, when you create a new workflow, you'll see a drop-down with three workflow platforms. The fun doesn't end there; you can also use the new workflow functionality in Visual Studio, if you're a developer type.

What does all that effort buy you? SharePoint 2013 adds some useful enhancements to SharePoint Designer. You'll be able to use Visio 2013 to develop workflows, and you'll be able to easily create and start SharePoint tasks with workflows. Significant improvements have also been made in scaling workflows and making them work better in highly dense or multi-tenant environments. We could go on and on, but Chapter 16, "Installing and Configuring Azure Workflow Server," explains it all in detail. If this section has whet your appetite to learn more about what's new with workflow, that's the place to satisfy your curiosity.

NEW USER EXPERIENCE

One of the first things you notice after installing SharePoint 2013 and Central Admin pops up is that it looks different — not radically different, but different nonetheless. And while it will take some getting used to (for those of you used to the old color scheme), the new interface has a lot to offer, addressing two of the most common issues raised by SharePoint 2010 users: "Why is it so slow?" and "How can we make SharePoint not look like SharePoint?" The following sections describe how SharePoint 2013 has resolved those burning questions.

Faster

One of the goals of the new user experience (UX) was to make it faster. No one likes to wait for web pages to load. If a web page, any web page, takes more than a couple of seconds to load, our impatient little brains are distracted by something shiny and we lose interest. SharePoint has a lot going on in the background — many components have to come together in order to render a page. In the past, SharePoint hasn't been the most efficient in its page load size, and it wasn't afraid of a postback or two. That resulted in some slow page loads, sometimes many of them.

SharePoint 2013 has made great strides in speeding up page loads. New to SharePoint 2013 is the Minimal Download Strategy (MDS), which takes advantage of the fact that most SharePoint pages have a lot in common, so it's inefficient to download redundant material every time you load a new page. As you move between pages that have MDS enabled, SharePoint sends the browser only the changes that occur in the content areas of the page. The parts in common, such as the global navigation and the branding, are reused. The MDS is enabled by default, but it can be disabled. It doesn't work well with some page types, such as publishing sites, so disabling it on them will improve performance. After you read Chapter 12, "Branding SharePoint" and you start making your own master pages, make sure they are designed to take advantage of MDS, too.

If MDS were the only performance improvement in SharePoint 2013 we would still be in great shape, but Microsoft didn't stop there. Also added is a new feature called Distributed Cache service, which caches frequently requested information and makes it quickly available to all the servers in the farm. The Distributed Cache service is used for both read and write operations, so it contributes to fast page loads and fast submissions. This is primarily used to facilitate Search and the new social features of SharePoint 2013, both of which require fast access to vast amounts of information. The Distributed Cache service enables both features to cache this information and get it back to users as quickly as possible. If your farm leverages these features heavily, you can increase the amount of RAM each server allocates to the Distributed Cache service, or dedicate servers entirely to it. Chapter 2, "Architecture and Capacity Planning," provides more guidance about how Distributed Cache service figures into designing your farm's architecture.

Prettier

As SharePoint administrators, we've all heard the following: "Can we make SharePoint not look like SharePoint?" This has to be tough on SharePoint's self-esteem. Fortunately, thanks to some changes and Design Manager, it is easier than ever to customize SharePoint and make it as non-SharePointy as you want, although SharePoint 2013's out-of-the-box look has been updated from SharePoint 2010, so you might decide it doesn't look so bad after all.

To match Microsoft's UX changes in its other products, SharePoint has adopted the Modern UI, formally known as Metro. It has a flat look and uses the Metro-style boxes we are accustomed to seeing in Windows 8 and Windows Server 2012. Links to help pages and documents, as well as templates in picker screens, now all resemble tiles. These tiles are active, meaning they reveal useful information when users hover the mouse over them. The new look is very clean and crisp. Figure 1-6 shows an example of the Modern UI, in this case the dialog used when creating new lists or libraries.

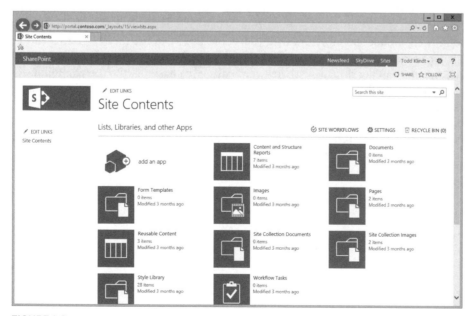

FIGURE 1-6

The content pages in SharePoint have received the majority of the facelift. The settings pages in the /_layouts directory haven't been changed too much from SharePoint 2010. Earlier in this chapter it was mentioned that Central Admin hasn't changed. It includes the new branding, but the navigation is identical to SharePoint 2010. Central Admin is prettier, but just as easy to use as before.

To make it easier for admins to gussy up SharePoint, SharePoint 2013 comes with a new feature, the Design Manager. This feature brings SharePoint branding more in-line with the techniques used to brand other types of websites. Designers are no longer forced to use SharePoint Designer to brand SharePoint sites. They can use industry standard tools to create their new designs. With these tools designers can create an HTML file that they will upload to the Design Manager. The Design Manager will walk them through converting it to SharePoint Master pages and other supporting files. Being able to use industry standard tools will open up SharePoint branding to a larger crowd, and hopefully result in more SharePoint sites that don't look like SharePoint.

GETTING SOCIAL

If the introduction of apps was the biggest change to SharePoint 2013, changes to the social platform have to be a close second — or maybe third, behind Search. Even a quick glance at the new social features makes it obvious that this was one of Microsoft's main areas of focus; and from the looks of it, their effort has provided major dividends for users.

Although SharePoint 2010 had some social features, they didn't come close to what users were accustomed to on the Internet. SharePoint 2010 has been a great collaboration platform, but it always felt lacking because of these missing social features we have all come to expect.

SharePoint is no longer lacking in this area. The enhancements made to the social experience in SharePoint 2013 not only put it on par with what public sites offer, it exceeds them in a lot of cases. Of course, SharePoint does the easy stuff. Much like Facebook, users can post status updates to let coworkers know what they're up to. Are you curious when Jack down the hall is making a trip to the copy room? Well, wonder no more. As with Facebook, users can use the @ sign to mention coworkers, which makes it easy to find out who is talking about you. These status updates can become threads, and you can tag threads with keywords using the hashtag (#). You can follow fellow users and trends, and all this traffic is integrated into Search results. Figure 1-7 shows a sample conversation between two coworkers. SharePoint also supports users posting pictures to their newsfeed, so if you like that picture of someone's dog eating a shoe, go ahead and "like" it, and SharePoint will be all over it. It has even worked the newsfeed into regular SharePoint sites, like team sites. Again, SharePoint can do the easy stuff.

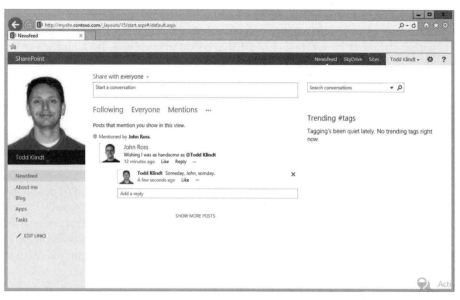

FIGURE 1-7

Now let's take a look at some of the not so easy stuff SharePoint 2013 can do. In addition to following your coworkers, you can also follow individual documents. You can also post comments and create threads about individual documents. These are just a couple of the advanced social features that SharePoint 2013 provides. We're all used to the public social functionality that Internet sites offer, but with access to your Active Directory information and your work documents, SharePoint 2013 takes it up another level: The social features of SharePoint are fully integrated into a user's workflow. Social in SharePoint isn't just fun, it's actually useful! Chapter 14, "Configuring User Profiles and Social Computing," explains how to set up all this social business, and how to configure it to get the most out of it for your organization.

SUMMARY

This chapter's purpose was to get you whipped into a lather about SharePoint 2013. It covered some of its major improvements, such as the shiny new app model that not only makes SharePoint more stable and secure for administrators, but also gives developers more flexibility (and the opportunity to become independently wealthy and buy a private island by selling SharePoint apps in the public store). This chapter also introduced you to all the big changes made to Search, in terms of both architecture and functionality. You have also seen how SharePoint's social features have been improved and extended in SharePoint 2013, and how your company can leverage them. All the new functionality provided in SharePoint workflows will be a welcome change to companies that heavily use them.

SharePoint 2010 got a lot of things right, so those aspects didn't change much in SharePoint 2013. This chapter covered those as well. The service application infrastructure, for example, hasn't changed much. Neither has using PowerShell to bend SharePoint to your will. If you have a good grasp on them now, you'll feel very comfortable using SharePoint 2013.

Finally, you looked at a few components that received overhauls in SharePoint 2013. Claims-based authentication (CBA) existed in SharePoint 2010, but it wasn't a big player and wasn't taken very seriously. That's all changed in SharePoint 2013. CBA is now front and center — the primary authentication mechanism. Branding also got some welcome improvements that will make your SharePoint 2013 experience both faster and more aesthetically pleasing. The best of both worlds, brains and good looks too.

SharePoint 2013 has a lot to offer and this book covers all the information you need to get the most out of it. It is the culmination of many months of hands-on experience with SharePoint 2013, which included making almost every mistake possible with it. Mistakes can be painful, but they're also usually a good way to learn. As you're reading the book, you are encouraged to follow along in SharePoint 2013 and try things. Sure, you're going to break stuff, but you'll have fun and learn a lot while you're doing it. Keep this book by your side and we'll get you through it.

2

Architecture and Capacity Planning

WHAT'S IN THIS CHAPTER?

- ➤ SharePoint products and licenses
- ➤ Critical non-SharePoint servers
- ➤ Hardware specifications
- ➤ Terminology
- ➤ Tools for controlling your deployment

SharePoint 2013 has greatly expanded its functionality from previous versions. New features include the following:

- ➤ An enhanced social experience, including microblogging, enhanced social experience, communities, and the capability to "follow" people, items, and sites
- ➤ More flexibility regarding how web applications consume services through service applications
- ➤ The Distributed Cache service, which helps relieve the workload on SQL, increase performance, and ease the technical networking complexity of multi-SharePoint server farms
- ➤ A new Request Management service that helps to distribute specific workloads

Applications that have undergone significant change include the following:

- ➤ **Office Web Apps** — Is now required to be installed on a separate server and is a shared service between SharePoint 2013, Exchange 2013, and Lync 2013.

> ➤ **FAST Search Server** — No longer exists as a unique product (or SKU) which can be purchased from Microsoft – it has been fully integrated into SharePoint.

> ➤ **2013 Workflow** — While all the goodness you came to know and love in SharePoint 2013 is still available to you, SharePoint 2013 Workflow contains new capabilities that require the Azure Workflow Manager.

Those and numerous other new features in SharePoint 2013 are reasons why people are so excited about the product. Of course, all that new functionality means that users will deploy SharePoint for more tasks than ever before — and that increased traffic leads to increased demands from a hardware perspective. To complicate matters, the Office Web Apps and SharePoint 2013 Workflow services have now been spawned into their own application, which is a shared service between multiple Microsoft products that connect to SharePoint through the service application proxy. (Don't get excited about a new GUI to explore – these server applications install and are configured completely through PowerShell.)

As a result of all these changes, administrators can anticipate a large increase in the number and size of servers in their farms. You can anticipate that the same user from SharePoint 2010 will make far more requests per second (RPS) to a SharePoint 2013 farm. In addition, the Office Web Apps service is designed to take requests from both Lync 2013 and Exchange 2013. Therefore, you have to consider the entire "collaboration" scenario of these services in planning your SharePoint infrastructure.

In terms of scaling your hardware, you can apply the same general benefits and rules used for SharePoint 2010. SharePoint service applications not only provide the capability to build unique servers in the SharePoint farm that provide a single service, they can be built into unique farms that provide a *published* service, to which farms can *subscribe*. Most service applications can coexist with one or more other service applications, just as they did in SharePoint 2010. There is one notable exception found in OWA. Here are a few curious facts about OWA:

> ➤ It requires its own server.

> ➤ It cannot be installed on a SharePoint server.

> ➤ It doesn't need to reside in the same Active Directory (AD) domain as the SharePoint server.

> ➤ It can be shared as a resource between more than one SharePoint farm which *could* reside in different AD domains.

> ➤ It can be consumed by both Exchange 2013 and Lync 2013 to provide in-browser Office document editing.

> ➤ It is free for all read-only scenarios but requires a license for edit capabilities.

> ➤ It can't be installed on a server that already utilizes Port 80, 443, or 809.

This chapter begins with a primer on the different versions of SharePoint 2013 you can expect to see, including an overview of SharePoint in the cloud. If you have spent any time with SharePoint 2007 and 2010 (and who wouldn't want to), you will find the consolidation of the product and licensing model riveting! There are some significant changes. Then, because a SharePoint DVD isn't good for much more than a coaster until you have the supporting servers on which to install it, you will learn all the software requirements you need to bring to the table.

Armed with the necessary software knowledge, the discussion turns to hardware, including the amount of metal you will need, ways you might consider scaling up versus out, and where virtualization might come into play. The chapter also delves into the misty atmosphere of cloud-based computing and how that might fit into your architecture decisions. Finally, the chapter describes some of the clever new tools available that will help you keep SharePoint running smoothly in your environment.

While this might not be as exciting as a blockbuster Hollywood movie, it will turn you into what every good summer blockbuster needs: a superhero. Therefore, read carefully and make sure you pick up your cape with the "S" on it from the dry cleaners — you will look much better as you soar through the clouds.

NAMES, NAMES, MY KINGDOM FOR A CONSISTENT NAME!

In terms of the core SharePoint naming convention established in SharePoint 2010, nothing has changed. Don't get too comfortable, however, there are other changes. Specifically, the products formally known as Search Server, Search Server Express, and FAST Search Server no longer exist. Search Server and Search Server Express have been discontinued as an available product. Fast Server technologies have been fully integrated into SharePoint.

SharePoint Foundation

SharePoint Foundation will continue the legacy that SharePoint 2010 Foundation and WSS have established over the years, including that friendly price point that makes it so attractive. The name SharePoint Foundation is a perfect match for what the program brings to the table. As an administrator, it is easy to think of the product only in terms of the features you readily see in the browser — such as creating team sites and collaborating on content within lists and libraries, or features such as blogs, wikis, RSS feeds, alerts, and easy browser-based customizations.

Yet underneath all that great functionality is where some of the true power of SharePoint is hidden. Here, the foundation provides developers with a great platform on which to build. Out of the box, it handles storage, web presentation, authorization, user management, and has an interface into the Windows Workflow Foundation — and because all this functionality is easily accessible through the object model, APIs, and web services, it can greatly accelerate a developer's job.

At this point, you might be thinking, "Wait. I thought you said that SharePoint 2013 Workflow required a new server; so why are you talking about Windows Workflow Foundation?" Simple. Windows Workflow Foundation continues to exist. If you don't want to install and configure the SharePoint 2013 Workflows, that's fine. You only need to install Azure Workflow Manager / Client applications if you want to use workflow capabilities. To help keep you out of trouble in SharePoint Designer 2013, the workflows are kept separate.

Therefore, rather than build all those infrastructure pieces for every web-based product, developers can leverage SharePoint Foundation and concentrate on just building the solution. Many companies have utilized these core SharePoint collaboration capabilities for many years. It is actually most advantageous to start with SharePoint Foundation, as these core collaboration capabilities generally meet the requirements of most new SharePoint users. This enables you to avoid additional licensing costs until features associated with those licensed versions are actually *required* by users.

SharePoint Server 2013

SharePoint Server 2013 is considered the premium SharePoint product. Compared to SharePoint Foundation, it offers additional collaboration and social capabilities and extends the use-case scenarios. Its robust tools enable better aggregation and displaying of content, which makes building grandiose thing, such as, portals much simpler, while better enabling end users to create specific line-of-business solutions for their departments. It also introduces additional web content management tools that enable developers to use Server as a platform for building Internet-facing websites.

This is achieved by building on the capabilities introduced by SharePoint Foundation. Anytime you install SharePoint Server, the Foundation product is installed automatically as well (though you will not see SharePoint Foundation installed in Programs and Features). Keep this in mind as you manage your environments, making sure you keep current regarding both Foundation and Server issues, as you really have both products. As you perform tasks such as applying service packs or adding third-party applications, this knowledge might affect how you go about these tasks.

Standard and Enterprise

As in the past, SharePoint Server 2013 is available primarily in two flavors, Standard or Enterprise. Standard introduces core functionality such as social, search, and advanced web and enterprise content management. Enterprise focuses primarily on adding functionality through new service applications, business intelligence, line-of-business integration, reporting, and some Office client services such as Visio and InfoPath Forms services.

This functionality is provided through one of two licensing models: a *client access license (CAL)* or a *subscriber access license (SAL)*. A CAL is an individual license that you buy for a single user to access SharePoint. The person who buys it owns it forever. Also available is an option to pay an additional yearly fee for what is called *Software Assurance* (SA). Software Assurance grants the licensee the permission to use any version of SharePoint that is currently supported by Microsoft. A Software Assurance License (SAL) is an individual license that is rented, or leased, from a service provider, usually a hosting provider. A SAL includes Software Assurance by default but is not owned. This can be useful for scenarios in which a "lifetime" license isn't necessary. For example, a contractor might require access to SharePoint for a defined period of time for a specific project. Table 2-1 summarizes SharePoint 2013 licensing options.

TABLE 2-1: SharePoint 2013 Licensing Options

LICENSE TYPE	PURCHASE LOCATION	PURCHASE METHOD	SOFTWARE ASSURANCE
Client Access License (CAL)	Licensing Reseller	Owned	Optional (Extra)
Subscriber Access License (SAL)	Service Provider	Rented	Included

You only need to run one setup program, which puts all the binaries on the server; and based on the license key you enter, either the Standard features will be available or both the Standard and

Enterprise features will be available. You are required to have an appropriate CAL or SAL for each user accessing SharePoint Server 2013. To be clear: these licenses are for individual *named users*, not *concurrent users*.

> ### A BRIEF NOTE ON LICENSING
>
> SharePoint licensing is a notorious black hole and it cannot be covered completely in this book for several reasons. The most important reason is that Microsoft reserves the right to make changes to how they license their products, which can rapidly make any published information obsolete. This chapter provides some additional guidance on the types of licenses that are available and who can use them after covering all the different types of server use cases available in SharePoint.

Hosted SharePoint aka SharePoint for Internet Sites (FIS)

SharePoint first added the capability to host public Internet sites in SharePoint 2007, with the integration of Content Management Server. A few brave souls ventured to trust their sites to this *new* technology. With the release of SharePoint 2010, many more companies began using this platform — some for single, public Internet sites, and some for an intranet site publishing platform for many brands. It was clear to Microsoft that companies wanted to use its technology in this way, as most of their intranets were running on SharePoint — a logical extension of their approved tools and technologies.

As the conversation about SharePoint 2013 continues, it becomes evident that Microsoft had two obstacles to overcome in relation to SharePoint for Internet Sites:

➤ It was clearly too expensive. A company with licensing requirements for a "medium-size" farm that included four SharePoint servers, for which the per-server license fee is in the neighborhood of $45K per server, would be facing a $180K fee for SharePoint licensing alone.

➤ With the rise of SharePoint Online, as delivered by Office365, Microsoft had to clean up its product naming conventions.

As a result, Microsoft has changed the way it charges for "purchased" licenses (CAL model) and changed the naming of the product. What was once called "SharePoint for Internet Sites" is now called "hosted SharePoint."

Another change related to the SharePoint FIS license is the removal of hosted SharePoint Standard Edition. It's all (Enterprise) or nothing with hosted SharePoint now.

One very important thing to understand about hosted SharePoint is *where* it is applicable. Remember that everyone authorized to access the SharePoint Server site needs a CAL. When building an intranet portal, it is easy to count how many employees you have and to purchase a CAL for each one of them; but when you stand up http://www.company.com and make it available to the world, now how many CALs do you need? There are roughly 1.8 billion people on the Internet, and potentially every one of them can visit your website. That's a lot of CALs to buy.

Luckily, this is where hosted SharePoint comes into play. It allows unlimited non-employee access to your SharePoint Server. The reason why *non-employee* is emphasized is because this license does not cover any company employees, which has caused a lot of confusion in the past. The proper hosted SharePoint license can help you control the cost of your SharePoint Server deployment, but great care should be taken to use it properly.

You might be thinking to yourself, "That says *non-employee* when talking about my Internet site. Does that mean I could extend my intranet site into an extranet site, keep an authentication mechanism in place, and use the hosted SharePoint license?" The answer is a resounding *yes*! There is no reason to get all worked up about whether users will authenticate into the farm or not. Hear me now: authentication has *nothing* to do with the license that is required. Licensing has everything to do with *who the users are*. If they are employees (in the U.S., receiving a W-2 tax form at the end of the year), then only one licensing vehicle is available to them: the CAL or the SAL. If they are non-employees, then they can use either the per-user model or the per-server model. You choose the one that makes the most financial sense to you. Note one point that is relatively new to the SharePoint licensing story: if a "non-employee" is a contractor or agent using SharePoint as any of your employees would use SharePoint, he or she must have a CAL. The Hosted license will not work for you.

When you are licensing SharePoint in the traditional "on-premises" fashion, you actually require two licenses: one license for each user authorized to use SharePoint and one license for each server instance on which SharePoint is running. This second license is called, oddly enough, the *server license*. You can now use this server license as the licensing vehicle for any "extranet" users of SharePoint; impressive — a price drop from Microsoft. This is also the license that you would use for an on-premises deployment of a public-facing web page. Taken together, these changes enable Microsoft to delve deeper into the WWW space and simplify the jungle we have known as SharePoint licensing.

Search Server Express

In 2008 Microsoft introduced a product called Search Server Express. It was all of the good of SharePoint Server 2007 Search bolted on top of WSS v3 for the same price of WSS, free! This carried over to the SharePoint 2010 product cycle as well. It was a very popular flavor of SharePoint because who doesn't like more free stuff?

With the SharePoint 2013 product cycle there is no more Search Server. You may think you need to go to your Congressman and complain for such an injustice but you don't. The reason Search Server Express existed was because WSS/Foundation search was awful so Microsoft was compelled to offer the enhancements. Fortunately they solved the problem differently with SharePoint 2013. This time around Foundation has the same great Search architecture as SharePoint Server. No need for a product to bridge the gap so no more Search Server. Check out Chapter 13, "Configuring and Managing Enterprise Search," for all of the fun details on Search.

FAST Search Server 2010

Oh, the casualties just keep coming. In 2008 Microsoft bought the Norwegian company FAST Search. With the release of SharePoint 2010, Microsoft took its first steps in integrating the product. As such, it was only half-baked into SharePoint. In SharePoint 2013, FAST is now been fully integrated, and no longer available as a standalone product.

SharePoint Online

Another push for SharePoint from Microsoft is SharePoint in the cloud, hosted by Microsoft. If you are interested in deploying SharePoint using this model, then you can probably stop reading the book at the end of this section because in SharePoint Online, the entire server infrastructure is hosted and maintained for you. This model removes the administrative overhead of SharePoint, enabling a business to focus on using SharePoint's out-of-the-box power. (While this might be great for the business, it does eliminate the need for a SharePoint System Administrator, so many of us will consider this license option the enemy.)

Microsoft has made so many improvements to the usability, functionality, and application model of SharePoint, they would probably argue that you don't need no stinking servers! For many use cases this is true. Software as a Service (SaaS) is a strong model that takes managing SharePoint out of the equation, enabling the business focus previously mentioned. Noble, for sure, but not necessarily practical in the long term for all customers. There are still certain payloads and use cases that make the Software as a Service model impractical, including the following:

➤ The need to deploy farm-level solutions. This will never happen in a traditional SaaS offering.

➤ Business intelligence solutions often require fast and secure access to back-end data warehouses or line-of-business systems.

➤ True Active Directory integration doesn't currently exist in SharePoint Online in a non-synchronized implementation. That means a time lag between when you change your personnel in your AD and when those changes are available in SharePoint Online.

➤ External data connections. As with BI, fast and secure access to back-end data systems is required. While this can be done in part in SharePoint Online, many companies aren't willing to allow this type of access to systems in their data center from a SaaS provider.

➤ Limited support. At the time of this writing, SharePoint Online (and Office365 for that matter) does not offer the escalation path to Premier Support that other product lines have.

This is not to say that SharePoint Online isn't a great platform. It absolutely is and meets a strong need in the greater SharePoint community; one where you just need out-of-the-box SharePoint in a collaboration scenario. If this is your only goal of SharePoint, then Online is probably the way to go.

There are actually two models to consider with SharePoint Online: shared and dedicated. The shared model provides you with a slice of a shared farm and enables you to use SharePoint out of the box. Server-deployed code and customizations are not permitted but sandbox solution and the new app deployment/consumption are available to developers. The dedicated model enables you to run your own farm, and you are allowed to make *approved* customizations to the server. Any change must be packaged in a solution package and validated by Microsoft before being deployed to the server. All licenses are bought per user.

This offering still contains some newer licensing options added in 2010. One of these is the concept of the "deskless worker." These are users you can add at a lower price point, and they have mostly read-only access to SharePoint. This is called the Kiosk subscription option. Also available are models that support hosting a partner collaboration site and public-facing Internet sites.

An interesting point to make around SharePoint Online and On Premises SharePoint is that Microsoft has been doing a lot of work around their ability upgrade and enhancing SharePoint

Online *on the fly.* The promise here is that upgrades and enhancements could come to hosted SharePoint at Microsoft before they are made available to the general public. This could provide a distinct advantage with regards to receiving either fixes to SharePoint or new features before they are received by on-premises customers.

> **NOTE** *This chapter covers SharePoint Online because it is an additional available SKU in this product cycle, but you have other notable options if you are looking at a hosted scenario. Companies such as RackSpace.com and Fpweb .net offer hosted SharePoint environments that you may find a little more flexible than SharePoint Online. Of course, hosting internally can still be the most flexible and full-featured option, but it is good to know your enemies.*

ADDITIONAL SERVER PLANNING

As a SharePoint administrator, you are also now responsible for a whole host of software. Because SharePoint isn't an operating system (yet!), you need to have the right OS in place in order to deploy it. Additionally, SharePoint stores 99% of its content and configuration in a database, so SQL Server has to enter the conversation sooner, rather than later. Finally, most deployments want to take advantage of SharePoint's ability to send notification e-mails, and some even take advantage of its ability to receive e-mail. Even though you may not directly be responsible for these products, they will affect your livelihood. Users don't call to complain that SQL Server isn't working; they call to complain that they cannot access SharePoint, that SharePoint isn't sending alert e-mails, or that the data in the BI Portal of SharePoint is out of date. It is your job to determine whether that is because SQL Server (or any other server or service) isn't responding. This section covers the ins and outs of these various components.

Windows Server and Required Additional Software

SharePoint is available only as 64-bit software (it's been exclusively 64-bit since 2010), so by extension it can only be installed on servers with 64 bits or more. (Don't bother looking — there is no 32-bit "test" version hiding out there. The authors have looked under every rock on the Internet and inside Microsoft; and like unicorns, it doesn't exist.)

For production deployments, you will be installing on the 64-bit edition of Windows Server 2008 R2 Service Pack 1 (SP1) Standard, Enterprise, or Datacenter, or the 64-bit edition of Windows Server 2012 Standard or Datacenter.

Noticeably absent is the Server Core installation of Windows, which unfortunately does not allow all the components necessary for SharePoint's operation to run, so it is not supported. In addition, the Web Edition is not supported, which is probably a good thing — thanks to its limited memory capacity, it would not perform very well.

After installing Windows Server, the server needs to be included as a member of an Active Directory (AD) domain. SharePoint does not support local machine accounts for any type of farm deployment, and the configuration wizard will issue an error if you try to use a local account.

Most administrators realize that something like IIS needs to be installed on the Windows Server in order for SharePoint to render web pages. They are often tempted to install this manually, which is safe to do but probably a waste of time. The server also has roughly a dozen other prerequisite software packages that need to be installed, including the Web Server (IIS) role. Thankfully, you can use the SharePoint Products and Technologies Preparation Wizard, aka the prerequisite installer, to install and configure all these components when the time comes. That tool, and all of its intricate details, is covered in Chapter 3, "Installing and Configuring SharePoint." Please note that an active Internet connection is required by the server to use this tool. If one is not present then you will need to download all prerequisites and install them manually.

BUT I ALREADY DID "X" TO MY SERVER!

Don't worry if you already installed IIS, PowerShell, or one of the other prerequisites. The prerequisite installer tool will determine that. If you successfully installed and configured one of the requirements, the tool will skip it and move on to the next one. In the case of IIS, if you enabled the role but didn't configure it the way SharePoint requires, the prerequisite installer will make the necessary changes. So keep that chin up; all is good.

Another common mistake to avoid is adding the server to a domain, or even promoting it to a domain controller (typically only done on a test virtual machine) after your SharePoint farm has been configured. Programs such as IIS and SQL Server don't always take too well to these changes. SharePoint makes references to these specific names in the Configuration database when SharePoint is installed. If you make these changes after SharePoint is installed, you will find a lot of aspects of SharePoint break immediately. Make any computer name changes (which adding to a domain causes) as soon after installing Windows as possible. Then you can safely continue with getting it ready for SharePoint. Think of these types of activities as laying the foundation on which to build your SharePoint house. SharePoint is painfully picky about server names as it installs SharePoint. It takes crazy notes about what you chose and gets very mad if you change that later after the installation.

Windows Vista, 7, and 8

In order to appease your friend the developer, Microsoft has introduced the capability to install SharePoint using a standalone install, for development purposes, on certain versions of Windows Vista x64 and Windows 7 or 8 x64. In these instances, a Developer Site must be created. The editions that are supported are:

➤ Windows Vista SP1 and later:

  ➤ Business edition

  ➤ Enterprise edition

  ➤ Ultimate edition

➤ Windows 7 RTM and later:

➤ Professional edition

➤ Enterprise edition

➤ Ultimate edition

➤ Windows 8 RTM and later:

➤ Professional edition

➤ Enterprise edition

➤ The N and KN editions of the preceding software will also work.

Absolutely not supported is using a standalone installation for a production farm. Standalone installations should only be used for developers who wish to do SharePoint development locally on their own machine. If development is done in these environments, then it is highly recommended that developers have a test environment to validate their solution before deploying to production. These types of deployments are a little more tedious in the initial configuration and are discussed in more detail in the next chapter.

SQL Server

Get used to it: SQL Server just became your best/worst friend. Because everything inside of SharePoint, including all your content, lives inside a SQL Server database, as SQL goes so does your farm. Specifically, an unhealthy SQL Server means an unhealthy SharePoint farm. For example, the most common performance bottleneck in SharePoint is SQL Server. Therefore, in order to do your job effectively, at a minimum you need to understand what is going on in SQL Server. Ideally, you will start sucking up to your resident database administrator (DBA) to ensure that your SharePoint databases are well cared for.

As with the Windows Server requirement, SharePoint also requires 64-bit SQL Server; 32-bit SQL Server is not supported. The 64-bit editions of SQL Server that are supported are the 64-bit edition of Microsoft SQL Server 2012 or the 64-bit edition of SQL Server 2008 R2 Service Pack 1. In case you are considering trying to sneak an unsupported edition of SQL Server by SharePoint, know that SharePoint checks before you attempt to create your farm.

E-mail Servers and SMS Options

SharePoint comes with a handy piece of built-in functionality that enables it to send e-mail. This is often used to notify users that they have been granted access to a particular site. Users can also subscribe to an alert whereby they are notified when items are modified on a particular list or library. Additionally, with a little extra work, SharePoint workflows (2010 or 2013) can be configured to e-mail users as necessary.

In order for SharePoint to send this e-mail, it needs to be configured with an outbound e-mail server. The SMTP server you point SharePoint at needs to allow anonymous relay from SharePoint. Unfortunately, SharePoint cannot be configured to provide authentication information when sending e-mails. (Also unfortunately, this hasn't changed since 2010.) In most environments, anonymous relay is not permitted, because for years evil spammers have used anonymous relays to avoid detection as they flood you with offers for low-cost medicines and opportunities to invest in dubious banks. In this case, you can ask the e-mail administrator to add the IP addresses (or subnet) of all SharePoint servers to the list of servers that are allowed to anonymously relay mail. If this is not acceptable, then your second option is to install the SMTP service on one of your SharePoint servers and then configure it as necessary. You need to ensure that it can correctly send outbound e-mail and that it allows all anonymous relay from all SharePoint servers in the farm. This isn't difficult for a Windows admin, as it just involves adding a role to one or more of the Windows Servers.

Another requirement for outgoing e-mail is that port 25, the default SMTP port, is *not blocked* between the SharePoint servers and your e-mail servers. Such a blockage can happen at the firewall level or at the local server level. Some antivirus vendors configure their software to block port 25 outbound on all machines. This will stop SharePoint from sending e-mail, so be on the lookout. This also emphasizes the need to have a thorough understanding of what SharePoint is doing, what e-mail is doing, what the networking environment is doing, and how to troubleshoot all those components. In the end, if "Bob" doesn't get his announcement, it's not SharePoint's fault. It's your fault!

A lesser-known feature of SharePoint is its ability to receive incoming e-mail and then route that e-mail to the appropriate list or library based on the To: address. This enables scenarios such as having salespeople in the field e-mail their expense report to a special e-mail address. That e-mail would be routed to the SharePoint server and then the attachment could be extracted and uploaded to the appropriate document library. From there, whatever business process needs to take place could be invoked. Yes — this means workflow. A simpler scenario might be setting up an e-mail address for a discussion forum. Then, anytime you send an e-mail to that address, the e-mail becomes a discussion item in the list, enabling a conversation that begins in e-mail, which is notoriously poor for capturing intellectual property, to be forwarded to SharePoint. Once in SharePoint, it is easily indexed so it can be discovered later; and because it is now a normal list item, the discussion can continue, as all good SharePoint users would expect.

Configuring this functionality requires the help of the e-mail administrator; note, however, that it does not require the use of Exchange. This is a multi-step, complex process that touches several pieces, but the core steps are as follows:

1. Install and configure one of your SharePoint servers to run the SMTP service. This server will then need to be set up to accept e-mail for the domain you define for SharePoint. Typically, it would be something like @sharepoint.company.com.

2. Configure your corporate e-mail server to route mail for the @sharepoint.company.com domain. The idea is that when your corporate e-mail server receives that e-mail, it just passes it over to the SharePoint server.

3. Go to SharePoint Central Administration and enable incoming e-mail. You need to tell SharePoint that it is looking for e-mails in the @sharepoint.company.com domain.

4. Now someone with the manage list permission level can go into his or her list and associate an e-mail address with the list — for example, doclib1@sharepoint.company.com.

5. This associated e-mail address would now need to be configured as a valid contact on the e-mail server.

With these steps completed, e-mails will be sent to doclib1@sharepoint.company.com. Your corporate e-mail server will relay that mail to the SMTP service running on the SharePoint server. The SMTP service then takes that e-mail and puts it in a mail-drop folder. The SharePoint timer service checks that folder once a minute by default, looking for e-mail. When it finds a message, it routes it to the appropriate list or library based on the address.

While that is a simple scenario, many configuration options are available. You can, for example, configure Exchange Server and Active Directory to allow users to create their own e-mail addresses. This is done through the creation of an additional organizational unit in your domain. This is a more complex scenario, but it eliminates the administrative burden of having to set up e-mail contacts each time a new list or library requires mail functionality.

You can find detailed configuration information, with multiple scenarios and troubleshooting steps, on TechNet (`http://technet.microsoft.com/en-us/library/cc262947(office.15).aspx`).

Sending messages via e-mail isn't the only way to inform SharePoint users. SharePoint has become so cool that it can even send text messages; and because SharePoint still isn't old enough to drive, you don't even have to worry about it texting and driving. Once the service is configured, users can choose to have alerts sent to e-mail or text message or both.

The service is pretty straightforward to set up from within Central Administration and can be scoped at either the farm or the web application level. You will need to provide the URL of an SMS sending service. If you don't have one handy, you can click the link on the page to find one based on your preferred wireless provider. Just watch out for this functionality: it can easily become a runaway cost depending on the expenses incurred from your SMS provider for each message.

HARDWARE REQUIREMENTS

Build it and they will come. Underpower it and they will complain. (No user has ever complained that SharePoint is too fast.) Of course, with budgets being very tight, you will feel the pressure to keep hardware costs as low as possible. This tension between functionality and cost creates a fine line to walk.

Perhaps the easiest way to start thinking about hardware is to do a comparison of the minimum recommended requirements from MOSS 2007 through SharePoint Server 2013 (see Table 2-2).

TABLE 2-2: MOSS 2007 versus Server 2013 Recommended Minimum Hardware Requirements for a 2-tiered farm

	MOSS 2007	**SERVER 2010**	**SERVER 2013**
Processor	2 Core/3 GHz	4 Core/2.5 GHz	4 Core
RAM	2GB	8GB	24GB

Note that part of the wide gulf between minimum server requirements from 2007 through 2013 indicates that Microsoft has done a better job of setting the minimum bar this time. Note also that the need for SharePoint resources is growing exponentially. It could be argued that attempting to run a single server with all SharePoint resources running on that one server isn't practical anymore for a full production installation of SharePoint.

Why show SharePoint 2007 requirements in a book about SharePoint 2013? Simple — there is still a ton of SharePoint 2007 running in production; and if it's still running in production, it could be running at the original hardware specifications from Microsoft. That's why it is incredibly important that you — our trusty SharePoint administrator — understand what will be required of your new farm in order to run SharePoint 2013.

Experience has shown that SharePoint farms tend to range from vastly undersized desktop-class machines running thousands of users, slowly, to supercomputer-class machines that on their best day use 20 percent of their resources to serve 100 users. Therefore, if you are going to make hardware assumptions at least in part based on your 2007 or 2010 environment, make sure you understand how that hardware is used today. The next few sections describe the different server types and how their hardware considerations vary.

Web Servers

Often referred to as web front-end (WFE) servers, these are the machines ultimately responsible for rendering of the SharePoint pages. They typically do not have a high CPU load because they attempt to cache as much content as possible to avoid doing the same work repeatedly (there are a lot of configuration capabilities here). To do caching properly, the server consumes quite a bit of RAM, so be sure to dedicate a substantial portion of your spending on this server to RAM.

A key consideration when determining how much memory you might need is the number of application pools you plan to have. Application pools are a deep topic, but in a nutshell they comprise the various IIS processes that listen for incoming web traffic and then handle it accordingly. In Task Manager, you will see each application pool as `w3wp.exe`. For example, when you create a new SharePoint web application and choose a new application pool, a new instance of this process runs. Now when you access SharePoint, this process is actually receiving your request and coordinating with SharePoint to render your page. When SharePoint is caching content in memory, it is being stored in RAM associated with this process.

Part of this consideration, though, is that every application pool has a certain amount of overhead associated with it, the process, and the memory it needs to do its job. Therefore, for each new application pool you create, your RAM requirements will increase, so plan accordingly.

RAM is also affected by the "search-based nature" of all things SharePoint 2013. In SharePoint 2013 you can configure the SharePoint Index process to index content *at the time it is uploaded into SharePoint* — known as "Continuous Crawl." If this is done you have two primary results:

➤   Content shows up in search results nearly immediately

➤   Your memory requirements on the server increase (aka: thank you NodeRunner.exe)

This role requires very little local storage and does not need to be optimized in any way. The only storage this machine is handling is the SharePoint root, all the local ULS and IIS logs, and possibly some disk-based BLOB caching. In other words, don't get carried away here and create a 500GB C: drive. SharePoint occasionally needs to have extra space for temporary files, maybe to unpack a solution or to deploy a service pack, so an 80GB or 100GB C: drive is reasonable for your WFE. Microsoft recommends that you allow for five times the amount of free space as RAM on the SharePoint Server. Not only do they recommend it, they have set a health analyzer rule to help remind you of the fact (it's a nasty red warning).

> **NOTE** *SharePoint* root *refers to a folder structure:* `C:\program files\common files\Microsoft shared\web server extensions\15.` *In SharePoint 2010, the* `\14` *folder was called the* 14 Hive, *so you may hear some people refer to the SharePoint root as the "15 Hive." If you do, try not to make fun of them.*

Application Servers

Application server is the generic name for any server that is responsible for providing resources for the various service applications. These are servers that have the SharePoint code installed on them. They are added to the farm using the configuration wizard or PowerShell. They *could* take SharePoint customer traffic if the load-balancer were configured that way. The tricky part of sizing these boxes is that each service application has a different usage profile, so the requirements vary according to what is running on the box and how heavily that functionality is being used. In addition, when building out an application tier, you should consider scaling out versus scaling up: Is it better to have one large application server with a lot of resources but a single point of failure, or several smaller boxes running the same services that provide fault tolerance but require more administration? The following sections describe some of the key types of application servers and their individual considerations.

Search Server

This section begins with the term "Search Server" as opposed to either Query Server or Index Server because there is so much new to Search in SharePoint 2013. These additional components are the result of fully integrating FAST Search into SharePoint. Of particular interest is how SharePoint consumes everything related to FAST's inclusion. For instance, nearly the entire web content management experience is one that is served by SharePoint Search. That same story continues to other areas of SharePoint with the addition of the Content Search Web Part (CSWP). Each CSWP is associated with a search query and shows the results for that search query in a way that is easy to style. The CSWP can be used to display any content that is stored in the Search Index.

Search is divided into the following component parts:

➤ **Crawl Component** — Crawls content sources to collect crawled properties and meta data from crawled items and sends this information to the content processing component.

➤ **Content processing component** — Transforms the crawled items and sends them to the index component. This component also maps crawled properties to managed properties and interacts with the analytics processing component.

➤ **Analytics processing component** — Analyzes the crawled items and how users interact with the search results. The analyses are used to improve the search relevance and to create search reports and recommendations.

➤ **Index component** — Receives the processed items from the content processing component and writes them to the search index. This component also handles incoming queries, retrieves information from the search index, and sends back the result set to the query processing component.

➤ **Query processing component** — Analyzes incoming queries, which helps to optimize precision, recall, and relevance. The queries are sent to the index component, which returns a set of search results.

➤ **Search administration component** — Runs the system processes for search, and adds and initializes new instances of search components.

To support these new components of Search in SharePoint 2013, the following databases are created:

➤ **Crawl database** — Stores tracking information and details about crawled items such as documents and URLs. It also stores information such as the last crawl time, the last crawl ID, and the type of update (add, update, delete) during the last crawl.

➤ **Link database** — Stores unprocessed information that is extracted by the content processing component and information about search clicks. The analytics processing component analyzes this information.

➤ **Analytics Reporting database** — Stores the results of usage analysis, such as the number of times an item has been viewed. It also stores statistics from the different analyses. These statics are used to create the usage reports.

➤ **Search Administration database** — Stores the settings for the Search service application, such as the crawl rules, topology, query rules, and the mapping between crawled and managed properties.

Needless to say, a lot of planning goes into an architectural plan for a SharePoint farm. Gone are the days of putting the Query Server on the SharePoint Web Server and using a dedicated Index Server. Microsoft's guidance for server specs for the Search components are described in Table 2-3.

TABLE 2-3: Minimum Search Server Requirements by Role

SEARCH COMPONENT ON THE SERVER	RAM	HARD DISK	PROCESSOR
Index Component	16GB	500GB additional disk space, preferably a separate disk volume/partition	All components: 64-bit, 4 cores minimum, 8 cores recommended When hosting virtual machines on Windows Server 2008 R2 SP1, a maximum of 4 cores are possible.
Analytics Processing Component	4GB for developer or evaluation use 8GB for production use in a single server or in a multiple-server farm	300GB additional disk space, preferably a separate disk volume/partition	
Crawl Component Content Processing Component Query Processing Component Search Administration Component	4GB for developer or evaluation use 8GB for production use in a single server or in a multiple server farm	80GB for system drive You must have sufficient space for the base installation and for diagnostics such as logging and debugging, for creating memory dumps, and for other operations. For production use, you also need additional free disk space for regular operations. For production environments, maintain twice as much free space as RAM.	

Table 2-4 summarizes the requirements for the database server hosting search databases:

TABLE 2-4: Database Server Minimum Hardware Requirements

COMPONENT	MINIMUM REQUIREMENTS
Processor	64-bit, 4 cores for small topologies 64-bit, 8 cores for medium topologies
RAM	8GB for small topologies 16GB for medium topologies
Hard Disk	80GB for system drive Hard disk space depends on the amount of content

Table 2-5 summarizes Microsoft's guidance for the volume of items that trigger breaking Search components onto their own servers.

TABLE 2-5: Search Volume Thresholds

NUMBER OF ITEMS	ACTION
Any number	If high availability is a requirement of all features of your farm, then a duplicate of each server component must be running somewhere either in your farm or in a different failover domain in your farm. Don't forget to ensure that the databases are running in a redundant server configuration.
Up to 10 million items	All Search roles can coexist on one nonredundant server or on two servers.
From 30 million items and upward	Add one crawl database per 20 million items. Add one index partition per 10 million items. Add up to two query processing components.
From 80 million items and upward	Add one crawl database per 20 million items. Add one index partition per 10 million items. Add up to four query processing components. Add one link database per 60 million items. Add one analytics reporting database for every 500,000 unique items viewed each day or every 10–20 million total items.

You need to keep a close eye on these servers for utilization. So much of the overall "SharePoint experience" is bound to the performance and health of Search that this single set of component services needs to be monitored and managed on a frequent basis.

Managing the Search service involves three primary tasks:

➤ Managing the default search topology

➤ Managing search components

➤ Managing the index component

Be aware that any buttons you used to click in SharePoint 2010 for these tasks, such as Manage Search Topology, are gone. No more pretty GUIs. PowerShell is used nearly exclusively to manage SharePoint. Repeat the following mantra after me: *I will learn PowerShell, I will learn PowerShell, I will learn PowerShell….*

> **NOTE** *Many of the metrics for this section came directly from Microsoft. You can review these metrics and many others by visiting the Microsoft TechNet site:* `http://technet.microsoft.com/en-us/library/jj219628.aspx`.

Distributed Cache

The Distributed Cache service provides in-memory caching services to several features in SharePoint Server 2013 to provide fast retrieval of data, and it has the subsequent effect of lowering the load on SQL Server. Like so many other new features in SharePoint 2013, Distributed Cache is a feature that will be used mostly by large SharePoint farms such as those found at large hosting companies. Because the Distributed Cache service holds context- and application-specific information in memory, it eliminates the need to set the "sticky session" (or server affinity) flag on the network load balancer for SharePoint farms that have many SharePoint web Servers.

The Distributed Cache service in SharePoint is actually an extension of the AppFabric of the underlying Windows.

Following are some of the features that use the Distributed Cache service:

➤ All social features

➤ Collaboration features

➤ Authentication

➤ OneNote client access

➤ Security trimming

➤ Page load performance

Note that the Distributed Cache does not replace other "caches" within SharePoint, such as BLOB cache and Output cache.

Servers that are running the Distributed Cache service are termed *cache hosts*. A cache host can be joined with other cache hosts to create a *cache cluster*. A cache cluster has a "total cache size," which is the sum of the memory allocated to the Distributed Cache service on each cache host. Note that while the data in the cache is stored in memory on any one of the cache hosts, the cache host or cluster can't be made highly available. There is only ever one copy of an item in the cache.

When you plan to implement the Distributed Cache service, consider that it can be deployed in two modes: dedicated mode or collocated mode. In dedicated mode, all services other than the Distributed Cache service are stopped on the application server that runs the Distributed Cache service. In collocated mode, the Distributed Cache service runs together with other services on the application server. Dedicated mode is the recommended mode in which to deploy the Distributed Cache service.

As you can imagine, the Distributed Cache service is a memory-intensive service. It is recommended that the following services *not* run on the same server that is functioning as a cache host:

➤ SQL Server

➤ Project Server

➤ Excel Services

➤ Search Services

When SharePoint is installed the Distributed Cache service assigns 10% of the total memory for the server. If additional memory is added, administrators have to manually adjust the memory assigned through PowerShell: Update-SPDistributedCacheSize -CacheSizeInMB <CacheSize>. If a cache host's server utilization reaches 95%, it will throttle itself by no longer accepting new read/write requests until the utilization falls below 70%. This doesn't mean that customers don't get their data — it just means the request times out and SharePoint then requests the information from the SQL server.

Because there is never more than one copy of any item in the cache, it is very important to carefully add and remove servers from the Distributed Cache cluster. To join or rejoin a server to a cache cluster, use the SPDistributedCacheServiceInstance cmdlet. To remove the Distributed Cache service from a server on which it was running, don't simply remove the service. It is recommended that you first shut down the service, and then remove it using the following two PowerShell cmdlets:

```
Stop-SPDistributedCacheServiceInstance -Graceful
Remove-SPDistributedCacheServiceInstance
```

Please take note of the -Graceful tag shown in the cmdlet above. The "graceful shutdown" of a Cache Server in a Cache Cluster transfers any cache data to another Cache Server in the Cache Cluster from the server being removed.

Request Manager

The Request Manager is another new bit of functionality in SharePoint 2013 and represents another feature that will only be used by extremely large farms or more specifically large hosted SharePoint farms. The purpose of this feature is to help SharePoint understand more about the requests that it receives and how to handle or throttle them. This feature allows additional "intelligence" (or rules) to be applied to specific types of traffic. In SharePoint farms with multiple servers which are hosting all web applications, a network load balancer would be used to distribute the traffic across all servers with the intent of creating a "balanced" load across all servers as well as avoiding servers which are unavailable. Figure 2-1 shows how these components are arranged in a network and how traffic flows through the environment.

The Request Management service creates a request routing bus between SharePoint web servers to ensure that specific types of traffic go to a specific server or collection of servers. Examples of the advanced routing capabilities available for various SharePoint requests include the following:

➤ Based on Server Health Score

➤ Specific HTTP elements (e.g., host name, service type, etc.)

➤ Source IP

➤ Type of traffic (user vs. service)

➤ Resource availability

SharePoint WFE 1   SharePoint WFE 2

FIGURE 2-1

An interesting use of this service can be to aid with troubleshooting. As an administrator, there is nothing worse than the error that is received "sometimes." The "sometimes" is usually associated with one server in a large group of SharePoint servers that is experiencing issues. Using rules to direct specific traffic to just one server enables the SharePoint engineer to observe an issue as it is being experienced, which helps with its identification and resolution.

One other important activity that the Request Manager performs is using rules to identify harmful requests to SharePoint. Should the service encounter traffic that fits that specified pattern, the Request Manager doesn't route that traffic at all, enabling SharePoint to avoid activity that could jeopardize the health of the farm. It should also be noted that the Request Management service is intended to work with Host Header site collections as the service changes the request header when redirecting traffic (e.g., http://portal.contoso.com to http://spwfe1).

Why not just use a network load balancer for all of this, you ask? Well, an NLB is great at more generic requests. To be fair, the NLB generally has no idea what SharePoint is, let alone what specific types of traffic it receives. The Request Management service adds additional intelligence to direct traffic. Please note that this doesn't mean it *replaces* traffic management of the NLB. The NLB is still very much a required component of your large-farm architecture.

To take this to the level of absurdly sized use cases, it is even possible to build dedicated request management farms. These farms are used to direct traffic (based on rules of your choosing) to their own unique farms. This is obviously a relatively unique scenario and one that applies only to large hosting companies. For example, say that you are a hosting company that continuously builds multi-tenant SharePoint farms as the previous one reaches a certain level of utilization. Such a hosting company could manage a database of users and their associated farms. In this case, all customers are directed to the request management farm when logging into SharePoint. The Request Manager determines, based on the customer, to which content farm they should be sent. An enterprise scenario for which this might be a good fit is when the legal department for a company needs to access SharePoint and store their data uniquely separate from all others. A resource management farm could evaluate the user's identity based on their credentials and direct them to the correct content farm. Very cool, if complex, stuff!

There are three main functions of the Request Manager:

➤ Throttling and routing

➤ Prioritization

➤ Load balancing

These features run as part of the Request Manager, which runs on SharePoint Servers in the farm, which in turn are running the SharePoint Foundation Web Application Service (SPFWA). This is the core SharePoint service that runs on every web server in the SharePoint farm.

The Request Manager configuration includes five elements that determine how the rule logic is evaluated and applied before these elements are routed and to which server they are routed:

➤ **Routing targets/servers** — A routing target (or machine) is any server running the SharePoint Foundation Web Application Service. Targets have a weight applied, which grades them as a viable target for traffic. This weight can be a static amount and/or a health weight.

➤ **Machine pool** — A collection of routing targets

➤ **Routing rules** — A definition of the criteria by which traffic is routed (or abandoned)

➤ **Throttling rules** — Rules used by a routing target to evaluate whether it will refuse a request

➤ **Execution groups** — A collection of routing rules that controls the precedence of rule evaluation and that manages routing rules in batches. There are three groups (0, 1, 2) that are evaluated in order. If the rule isn't associated with an execution group, then it is evaluated with those in Group 0.

In the context of the Request Management service, throttling rules are the natural evolution of the throttling introduced in SharePoint 2010, which provided the capability to throttle the amount of content returned from large lists. This myopic approach only considered the current farm. Conversely, request management in SharePoint 2013 allows for "servers based on load" to be avoided to help ensure the perception of a happy-healthy SharePoint farm for your users. For instance, assume it is the first of the month and the new sales figures have been posted via Excel Services. Every salesperson and executive is going to log into SharePoint to see how the company did, thereby putting the servers that serve Excel Services under extreme load. A load balancer can distribute all users across all servers; but in terms of ensuring that the Excel Services servers are providing data quickly, the Request Management service helps balance the Excel Services traffic — and the server can throttle new requests if it starts to struggle under the load.

One last comment about administering the Request Management service: it's all handled with PowerShell. There is no GUI in Central Administration or anywhere else for that matter that will assist with configuring Request Management. Repeat after me: *I will learn PowerShell, I will learn PowerShell, I will learn PowerShell....*

Excel Services

Excel Services and the other service applications that are focused on Office client tasks and compatibility features are generally more CPU heavy. This is because they typically do not have any storage and are only being used to offload processing from the clients to the server. Business units utilize these services much differently than other services with SharePoint. Consider the server load when a user opens a Word document on his or her computer from SharePoint to edit. SharePoint only has to work when the file is opened or saved. In the context of Excel Services, when the user opens the file and every time the data is refreshed, the server application has to "compute," or work. This work all occurs in memory with little to nothing going to disk. To that end, it's important to consider how your users (or if your users) will use Excel Services. Therefore, don't overscale for this functionality until you confirm that business adoption will accelerate demand. The three keys to success in managing the scaling of service applications such as Excel Service or Search Query Service? Monitor, monitor, monitor.

Shredded Storage

Despite its unfortunate name, Shredded Storage may turn out to be your favorite new feature in SharePoint 2013. The purpose of Shredded Storage is to bring to SharePoint item *versioning* the behavior a lot of us thought was there from the beginning. For example, suppose you spend weeks creating a wonderful 10MB PowerPoint presentation that surpasses anything you have ever done before. Unfortunately, your manager likes to get his hands into everything and wants to provide "his input." In order to ensure that your artistic integrity isn't damaged, you turn versioning on in your document library so you can easily see what was changed and roll back anything that isn't to your liking. After several changes on both your parts, you have 10 versions of your 10MB file. In all versions of SharePoint up through 2010 that support versions, you would have consumed 100MB of SQL Server storage. That's because every version that is saved is a complete copy of the entire document. The magic behind Shredded Storage is that when a version is saved to SharePoint 2013, only the delta (or change) is saved.

It's time for a quick primer of how SharePoint stores documents. When a file (of any type) is stored into SharePoint, it is actually housed in SQL Server. The way SQL Server accomplishes this is by converting that file into what is called a binary large object, or BLOB. The advent of Shredded Storage doesn't change this other than saving the BLOB that represents the delta from the last version, which might be only a small portion of the entire file.

A lot is going on behind the scenes to capture all these fragments of files in order to keep track of them and reassemble them upon request by a user (or Index service). We won't cover all those details here — that's what TechNet is for — but we will describe the methodology employed to accomplish this Herculean feat.

In SharePoint 2010 Microsoft introduced the Cobalt protocol, or file synchronization via SOAP of HTTP. This was introduced into SharePoint and the Office Client applications with the purpose of limiting the amount of bandwidth required to send incremental changes of Office documents back to SharePoint. Cobalt did a great job of this and end users everywhere rejoiced in the network performance (sarcasm included free with the purchase of this book). Even though in SharePoint 2010 the incremental change was sent from the Office client to SharePoint, the SharePoint server still reassembled the entire document before committing the document back to SQL Server. The reality is this was the building block for Shredded Storage.

Welcome to SharePoint 2013 and Shredded Storage, which now has the ability to only save the delta to SQL Server. A lot of additions were made to the DocStreams table in the Content Database schema inside of SQL Server to facilitate the storage, tracking, and reassembly of various Office documents into one complete document for you to enjoy and show to your friends and neighbors. The goal of Shredded Storage is to limit the amount of data that needs to be transmitted between the client and SharePoint, as well as limiting the amount of data that needs to be stored in the SQL Server content database(s).

Back to the example of the PowerPoint document that began at 10MB and underwent 10 edits and saves. If those edits were just text or slide ordering, then the total amount of storage consumed would be less than 11MB. This feature alone doesn't significantly change your SharePoint configuration from a service or feature perspective. You won't be building Shredded Storage resource farms in support of rich document editing. That's just silly. What you will do as you plan storage for your farm(s) is include much less SQL Server disk space, as the version storage requirements for Office documents will be dramatically less.

One last point before moving on: notice that the preceding refers to Office document storage. Because Microsoft chose to implement this feature on top of Cobalt, it only affects Microsoft documents *out of the box*. If you are using SharePoint for other document or image types that don't have Cobalt implemented, then every version saved of that document will consume the total size of that document in SQL Server.

Usage and Health Data Collection

The Usage and Health Data Collection service application might be the most data-intensive Service in SharePoint. It enables the collection of all the diagnostic and usage data from your entire SharePoint farm into the logging folder and the logging database. This database can then be used for reporting, and it is even flexible enough to accommodate custom reporting. Interestingly enough, this service application can be configured in partitioned mode — meaning it is configured for multi-tenancy. The benefit here is that all the reporting information is gathered and can be reported on *by tenant*. These tenants could be individual companies consuming a hosted SharePoint offering or they could be departments within a large enterprise that are consuming SharePoint in a "charge-back" model.

Results have shown that in large environments, this feature creates a very large SQL Server load. Therefore, in order to fully utilize it, you may want to consider putting it onto its own SQL Server or at least creating a mirror of the reporting data so that you can pound against it with your reporting tools and not create contention for the active database. Check out Chapter 20, "Monitoring and Analytics," for full details, but be sure to factor the amount of usage of this functionality into your farm planning.

> **NOTE** *For more information, see the following TechNet article on configuring Usage and Health Data Collection:* `http://technet.microsoft.com/en-us/library/ee663480.aspx`.

SQL Servers

There are entire multi-book series on this one topic, and even if you read all of them you still wouldn't have a definitive answer about sizing your SQL Server. Therefore, as you approach sizing this particular box or boxes, don't be afraid to ask your friendly neighborhood DBA for help. In addition, keep in mind that over the years, the main bottleneck in most SharePoint farms is SQL Server performance. As a side note, this has been true since SharePoint started saving all of the user data in SQL Server. If anything has changed, it has changed for the worse as more service applications are created that rely on SQL Server to store their information.

The key thing to remember is that all the standard SQL Server hardware best practices are important. SQL Server loves memory and will utilize every bit it can get its hands on, so you should plan accordingly — 16GB of memory should be the absolute minimum you consider, and 32GB or even 64GB might be appropriate in a heavily used production environment. CPUs require the same consideration; a quad-core processor might get you started, but boxes with multiple hex-core processors are more common.

Even if you buy enough CPU and RAM, you still are not out of the woods. Disk configuration has as much, if not more, to do with performance. You need to plan for the number of spindles your SQL Server has access to and how they will be configured; and to do this properly, you must consider the amount and shape of data you plan to store in SharePoint. You should be following the SQL Server best practices specifying that the data (*.mdf) and log (*.ldf) files are on different disks, and that the log files are optimized for write. When you are considering which databases to optimize first, the order is as follows:

1. Tempdb (a SQL System database)
2. Search databases
3. Content databases

While tempdb should clearly always be the first database optimized, your needs for the Search databases and content databases will vary according to your specific scenario. For example, if you have created a content database for collaboration that is excessively large (greater than 200GB), then in order to minimize locking issues you may need to move that database to optimized disks instead of the typical content database that performs adequately on a basic RAID 5 volume. The key here is to make sure either you understand all your SQL Server disk requirements before you purchase the box or you have access to a flexible solution, such as a SAN, for storing your databases.

If you are dealing with an inordinately large amount of users and/or WFEs, consider having more than one SQL Server (or cluster). This enables you to spread your content databases across multiple SQL servers and helps to limit the bottleneck of a single SQL server. Bear in mind that this solution is for the extreme scenario of tens of thousands of users in a single SharePoint farm.

> **NOTE** *The TechNet SQL Server TechCenter at* `http://technet.microsoft` `.com/en-us/sqlserver/default.aspx` *is full of additional guidance on planning and sizing a SQL Server deployment.*

Finally, when it comes to SQL Server, SharePoint doesn't really care how you set it up. As long as SQL Server is running a supported version and can serve databases back to SharePoint, it doesn't matter whether SQL Server is dedicated to SharePoint or is shared with other applications in the company. Nor does SharePoint care whether SQL Server is clustered or doing database mirroring or even transparent encryption. SharePoint simply calls to a SQL Server instance for a database, and if data is returned it is happy. Your users just might not be happy with the responsiveness of SharePoint if SQL Server is architected incorrectly.

Mixing and Matching Servers

Now that you have an understanding of the different types of servers, you need to consider how they will be deployed onto actual hardware. As you combine them, you need to consider the hardware profile of each, and how the server will need to support the aggregate of SharePoint roles.

One Server

This is a configuration you will typically see only for demonstration and evaluation purposes. In the example shown in Figure 2-2, all SharePoint server roles and the SQL Server are configured to run on one machine.

Microsoft's recommendation for a "one box wonder" whereby SharePoint and SQL are installed on a single machine is as follows:

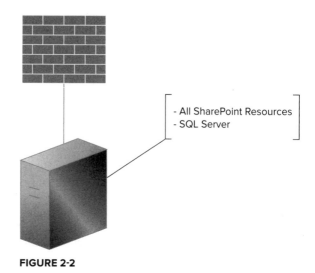

- All SharePoint Resources
- SQL Server

1. Install a single server with a built-in database or one that uses SQL Server.

2. Deploy a development or evaluation installation of SharePoint Server 2013.

FIGURE 2-2

3. Confirm the following hardware requirements are met: 24GB RAM, a 64-bit 4-core processor, and 80GB system drive on the hard disk.

Two Servers

A two-server configuration is generally considered the minimum point of entry for a small SharePoint deployment. In this scenario, shown in Figure 2-3, all the SharePoint services run on one server, and SQL Server runs on a separate server.

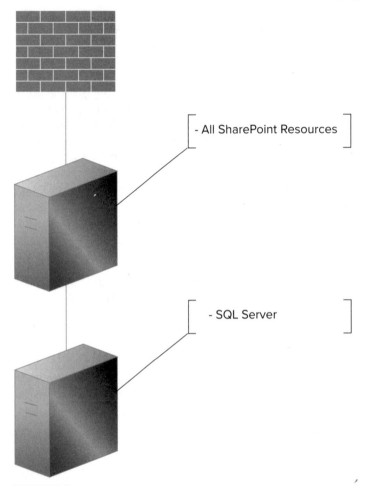

- All SharePoint Resources

- SQL Server

FIGURE 2-3

Following are Microsoft's recommendations for installing SharePoint as a standalone server. Note that these are minimum requirements. As mentioned previously, memory is cheap compared to angry users because SharePoint is slow. Do yourself a favor: double the memory.

1. Install a web server or application server in a three-tiered farm.

2. Follow a pilot, user acceptance test, or production deployment of SharePoint Server 2013.

3. Confirm the following hardware requirements are met: 12GB of RAM, a 64-bit 4-core processor, and 80GB system drive on the hard disk.

Three Servers

Adding a second server with SharePoint installed enables the creation of a high-availability solution (see Figure 2-4). By putting some type of network load-balancing (NLB) device in front of SharePoint, you can ensure that the WFE services are fault tolerant. Then, by configuring the service applications to run on both machines, you can avoid one server crashing and ruining your day. Note that everything you add to the SharePoint farm affects the performance of that farm. It was just pointed out that by adding a second WFE to the farm you increase the fault tolerance of the farm. Conversely, putting a substandard NLB in front of SharePoint might lower its performance even though you have increased the farm's resiliency. When a quality NLB (and it is suggested that you use a hardware-based NLB dedicated to the single role of load balancing) is placed in front of your SharePoint farm, performance can actually increase. The NLB manages the traffic coming through itself and balances the load across each WFE.

In terms of hardware requirements, as a general rule they remain the same for the two-server configuration described in the preceding section.

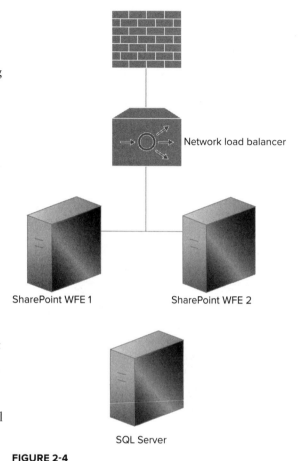

FIGURE 2-4

Four or More Servers

This is where you start making choices. Figure 2-5 shows a scenario in which the environment has been optimized for performance and availability for WFE and Query, but the downside is that the application tier does not provide high availability. This is generally not a good idea, so you may want to jump straight to introducing a fifth server to the farm in order to bring high availability to the other service applications. You will not need another NLB device because service applications handle their own load balancing.

At this point, you probably get the idea that you can scale out any of the various service applications as necessary to meet your needs, which leads to our next topic: server groups.

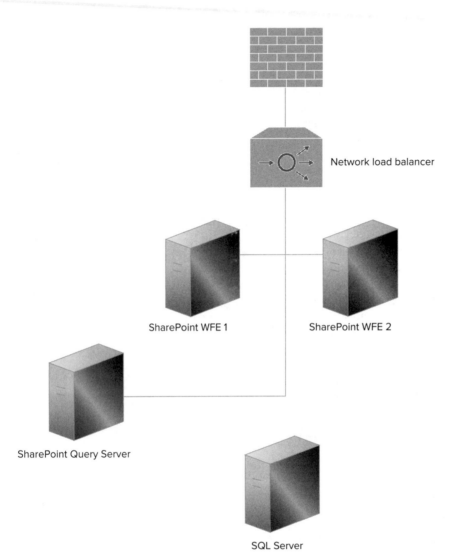

Network load balancer

SharePoint WFE 1

SharePoint WFE 2

SharePoint Query Server

SQL Server

FIGURE 2-5

> **NOTE** *The Search service application architecture remains the most complex and demanding of all the service applications. For many administrators, the majority of their farm architecture will be based on meeting the demand of this feature. Please see Chapter 13, "Configuring and Managing Enterprise Search," which explains all the components of the Search architecture in detail, including additional farm topologies for optimizing the Search service application.*

Server Groups

Server groups refer to the logical concept of grouping similar SharePoint service applications together on the same logical server. This enables you to add servers, which means additional capacity, to each tier as demand increases. This also segregates the performance impact of the various service applications. Figure 2-6 shows an example.

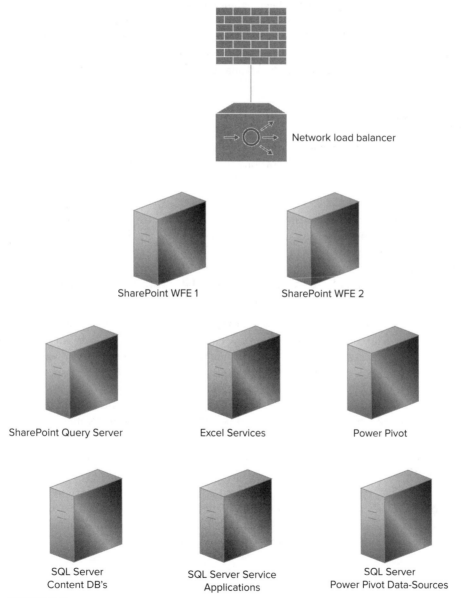

FIGURE 2-6

This example isolates the web, search, business intelligence (BI), and all the other service applications. Now, if business adoption of the BI increases beyond the current capacity, it will not affect the performance or stability of the rest of the farm. It is also simple to purchase another server, install SharePoint onto the box, and then add it to the farm. Once it is a member, you would then add it to the BI group by configuring it to run only the Excel and PowerPivot services. Note that you will not see the term "server group" in Central Administration anywhere; it is only a logical concept.

Notice also in Figure 2-6 that SQL Server has been extended into various logical groupings. The performance characteristics and demands of different databases can vary greatly, and in large environments it can be very helpful to configure and manage each one separately. It should be noted that for every SharePoint and/or SQL server added to a farm, you increase your licensing exposure. Carefully choose server additions based on verified demand by your business units within your company.

Other Hardware Notes

Now that you are familiar with the hardware and server configuration options, the following sections describe a few more important considerations as you plan your farm's architecture.

The Network

Network connectivity between the servers in your farm is hugely important. At a minimum, all servers in the farm should be connected through gigabit connections. The hard requirement here is that each server should be connected by a gigabit connection with less than one millisecond of latency. *Can* you have greater latency between servers? Yes. Will your users like you for this? No. This precludes most companies from having a SharePoint farm with servers in multiple, geographically dispersed data centers attempting to act as one farm.

For many companies, the sheer volume of network traffic generated between the members of the farm is overwhelming. In order to better control this traffic, they move all inter-farm traffic to a dedicated virtual local area network (VLAN). This is like the server groups discussed earlier. Grouping all this traffic makes it easier to monitor and administer in the case of any issues. A dedicated VLAN is not a requirement for SharePoint, but in a large farm it is often recommended. This is also a way to create a secure boundary between the SharePoint environment and the rest of your network — provided it is a requirement by your security department to create that level of server-based isolation.

Network Load Balancers

In order to achieve high availability of the SharePoint web applications, it is necessary to introduce a tool to do network load balancing. This can be either a hardware-based tool, such as an F5 device, or an external software solution, such as Microsoft's reverse proxy server solutions, or even something as simple as the built-in Windows Network Load Balancing (NLB) feature.

Hardware-based solutions are generally best, as they offer the most configuration options and usually the best performance, but they are also typically very expensive. The software-based solutions such as TMG provide a happy middle ground, especially if you are already using them in your environment. They include just enough options and monitoring to make the cut. Although using the Windows NLB is free because Windows provides it out of the box, it is a very rudimentary feature. It cannot do tasks such as confirm whether the server is serving valid pages, and instead only confirms that the server responds to ping traffic. For mission-critical scenarios this is not an ideal solution. At the end of the day, SharePoint is a web-based application. It is generally recommended that you use whatever standard your company has for NLB solutions.

Prior to SharePoint 2013, SharePoint cached too many requests and didn't share that cache across WFEs, so if users were constantly moving from server to server, it was possible for them to have erratic results. In the bright shiny morning of 2013 and the new reality of distributed cache — specifically, by caching the FedAuth token — it is no longer necessary to use "sticky session" on the load balancer.

If you are adding an NLB to your farm because a high-availability solution is required for your environment, then ensure that you make every aspect redundant — including the NLB! Having redundant WFEs is of no benefit if your NLB fails, thereby blocking network traffic to your SharePoint servers. The NLB provides additional value in that it is listening /verifying a server is "alive" and can also monitor additional HTTP headers like the SharePoint Health Score, or listen for 503 errors that are produced in the event of an unhealthy server.

Server Drives

When you configure SharePoint, it is generally a good idea to remove everything possible from the C: drive. For example, navigate to Central Administration and change the diagnostic logs to be hosted on the E: drive instead of the C: drive. Remember that this is a farm-wide setting, so all servers in your farm must have an E: drive or they will get errors and stop logging. This is inconvenient but not the end of the world. The end of the world happens if you try to add a server without an E: drive to this farm after changing this setting. You will get file I/O errors running the configuration wizard and it can take a long time to figure out the cause. That is why it is recommended that all the SharePoint servers in your farm have standard drive letters. A simple design choice like that can greatly reduce your headaches going forward. It is also very important to configure your disk drives with some form of redundancy, such as mirroring (also known as RAID 1). This gives your data security should one of the hard drives fail and also has the ability to provide performance increases on reads and writes to the drive.

Virtualization

Now that you have learned about hardware considerations, the question that logically follows is, "Which servers can I virtualize?" After looking at some of those server groups, it is very easy to see some opportunities. Typically, when it comes to virtualization, it is recommended that you start at the top of the farm and work your way down. Web front ends have almost no disk requirements and generally are consuming RAM and some CPU. They virtualize very well. How well application servers virtualize depends on what service applications they are hosting. For example, if you have a server group that is hosting only services such as Office Web Apps or the Managed Metadata service, they would virtualize easily — again, because they have almost no disk requirements.

Your query and index servers can be virtualized but the benefit will depend on your performance expectations. Crawling 10 or 20 thousand items once a day is a pretty light load, and will virtualize without issue. However, trying to crawl 100 *million* items virtualizing and still getting the performance you need would be extremely difficult; but just because it's difficult doesn't mean that it can't be attained. If your implementation is one that has a user community in the same geographic location, then you can assume that your farm will sleep for half of the day. If this is the case, then you can be a little more liberal about virtualizing the index server. Just make sure you configure the indexing to occur when no one is using the farm. You will also want to work with your virtualization engineers to have that server configured to be allowed to use additional physical resources if they aren't being consumed by other processes.

The moral of the story when it comes to virtualizing SharePoint servers is that you should first understand how hard that server is working and where its first bottlenecks occur. If you can safely virtualize without reducing performance, then do so. Also, if you are building test and development environments for which performance is not a critical factor, then virtualization is the way to go.

Should you virtualize SQL Server? That question generates almost as much passionate debate as Mac versus PC. Virtualizing SQL Server and achieving acceptable performance is possible; unfortunately, your average virtualization administrator, in partnership with your average SQL Server database administrator, cannot do it well. It is too complex a configuration for someone to stumble through. As a SharePoint administrator, you already know that SQL Server is going to be the factor holding your farm's performance down; do you really want to gamble with virtualization, which is likely to further decrease that performance? Remember disk I/O on the SQL server is king.

One other point to make about virtualizing SharePoint server is the impact it can have on hosted (remember FIS) licensing. Hosted licenses license the entire "processor socket" in a Services Provider License Agreement (SPLA) model. That socket has many cores that can be divided up among several SharePoint servers. For instance, in a traditional on-premises installation for which you had two SharePoint WFEs for a Hosted (FIS) site, you would be required to purchase two separate licenses even if these were virtualized. In a hosted SPLA model whereby the license is applied to the processor socket and not the server, one license could be applied to two SharePoint VMs that each had four virtual CPUs (cores) of an 8-core processor.

TERMINOLOGY

One of the biggest challenges for SharePoint administrators new and old is the vocabulary. SharePoint is littered with words, such as "site," that have about a dozen different meanings (no one is ever really sure what a site actually is, and many consider it apt that site is a four-letter word). To clarify this confusion, Figure 2-7 is here to save the day. Once you can speak to the entire hierarchy from top to bottom your job is half complete, you have practically conquered SharePoint — so study hard.

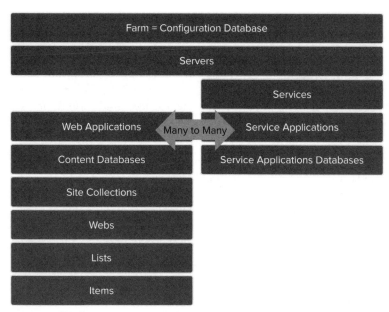

FIGURE 2-7

Starting from the top you see "Farm = Configuration Database." This means that each SharePoint *Server* can belong to only one farm. A farm can be a single server (refer to Figure 2-2) or something as complex as what is shown earlier in Figure 2-6. A farm refers to all the servers using the same configuration database. When you run the configuration wizard, you choose to connect to an existing configuration database (join a farm) or create a new configuration database (create a farm). All servers in a farm, therefore, share everything, including the Central Administration site that controls all servers in the farm.

WHY DOES THIS LOOK FAMILIAR?

Some of this material on terminology is repeated verbatim in Chapter 3, "Installing and Configuring SharePoint." That isn't a mistake. These concepts are too important to overlook, and because some people skip around we wanted to double the chances that you read it.

Below this, in the column on the right, is "Services." These are the actual services on the server that run to provide functionality to the "Service Applications." For example, the Excel Service Application you create in Central Administration from Manage Service Applications is a Service Application Connection point. That Service Application Connection point is the proxy to the instances of the Excel Service that are running on the server(s) in the farm. Don't worry if that isn't completely clear; Chapter 4, "Understanding Service Applications," is dedicated to the inner workings of service applications.

Finally, at the bottom of the right-hand column is "Service Application Databases." Some service applications require database(s) to store information in order to work, while others do not. This is just one of the many reasons why using SharePoint 2013 means you will be getting to know SQL Server.

"Web Applications," at the top of the left column, are the actual SharePoint websites you visit. Because they appear in IIS, you will hear people refer to them as sites, websites, IIS sites, and other creative things. However, it is very important that you refer to them as *web applications,* or *web apps* for short, as everything in the SharePoint management interface and all the documentation always refers to them as web applications. Examples are http://portal.company.com, http://www .company.com, https://extranet.company.com, or http://team.

Between Web Applications and Service Applications is a double-headed arrow labeled "Many to Many." This is your reminder that this is the only place on the hierarchy with a many-to-many relationship — in other words, one web application can consume multiple service applications, and service applications can also service multiple web applications. This is one of those seemingly infinite configuration options that makes SharePoint so much fun to architect.

Every time you create a new web application, SharePoint automatically creates a new "Content Database" for you and associates it with the web application. This will be the default location for storing content from the web application. You can also create additional content databases to associate with the web application. This is done to help scale. Two unique web applications cannot share a content database.

That brings you to the most important concept in SharePoint: the site collection. Site collections are the unit of scale in SharePoint. The easiest way to think of a site collection is as a bag, because they are really just a boundary or container. They are not actually content users can touch. The reason why this "bag" is so important is because it determines a lot about how your information is stored.

Site collections are a storage boundary and are stored in one and only one content database. They cannot span multiple databases. When you create a site collection it is created in a database and that is where it stays unless you manually move it. If, for example, you want to limit all your content databases to 40GB because that is the largest size you are comfortable with, then you need to ensure that no site collection is larger than 40GB. Similarly, if you have multiple site collections (and everyone does), then you would need to apply quotas to those site collections to ensure that the sum of the site collections doesn't exceed your 40GB database limit. For instance, if you have 10 site collections, then you set your quotas to 4GB per site collection.

Normally we would state that the strongest security boundary (other than a new farm) would be at the Web Application layer. When your farm is deployed in multi-tenant mode, the site collection is also a security boundary. In this mode a customer (or tenant) is assigned a subscription ID. This ID becomes the identifier for everything that stores data in SharePoint. From content DBs to Search DBs to managed meta data — all of that data is segregated inside of the common databases by this subscription ID. This way, content from one tenant doesn't "leak" into another tenant's site or search data or term store.

Site collections are the only objects in SharePoint to which you can apply a storage quota. If you want to limit a user to storing only 10GB of content in a particular document library, there is no way to do that. You would have to set that entire site collection to a 10GB limit. If you have two document libraries and you want to give each one 10GB of storage, then you have to ensure that each document library is in its own site collection.

Even if you have no intention of holding users to limits, quotas are generally recommended for all site collections, as they serve as a checkpoint and help prevent runaway site collections. When users call to say that they are getting warnings or errors because they have met their quota, it is a simple process for you to increase the quota, and it gives you a chance to ask, "So what are you doing with SharePoint that you need so much storage space?" It would be good to know if someone is just backing up an entire MP3 collection to SharePoint.

Site collections also serve as an administrative boundary. Site collection administrators are a special group of users who have complete power over the site collection without necessarily having any access to other site collections. The Site Settings page contains an entire menu of configuration options that only a site collection administrator can modify (see Chapter 8, "Configuring SharePoint for Business Intelligence"). For example, suppose you have two groups, such as HR and Accounting, in the same site collection. If one of them comes to you because they need to administer one of these special settings, you will have to do some rearranging. If you make Nicola from Accounting a site collection administrator, then she can fully administer the account site as needed, but she also has full control over the entire site collection, including the HR web. You need to instead move the Accounting web to its own site collection and then make Nicola an administrator there.

Site collections are also boundaries for out-of-the-box functionality such as navigation and the various galleries. This can be a drawback of many site collections. Out of the box, it is impossible to enforce consistent, self-maintaining navigation across site collections. The galleries such as the themes, Web Parts, lists, and solutions are all scoped at the site collection level. For example, if you need a list template to be available to multiple site collections, then you have to manually deploy it to each.

Site collections also serve as security boundaries. The All People list and the various SharePoint groups are all scoped at the site collection level, and are not accessible for reuse outside of the site collection.

> **NOTE** *Developers and Windows PowerShell refer to a site collection as an* spsite, *so when you hear that word you can equate it to site collection.*

Inside of site collections are one or more *webs*. A web is the object that is referred to throughout the user interface as a site. It can also be called a subsite or a subweb. Again, because the term "site" can be very confusing, whenever possible refer to these as webs. This is the first object users can actually touch. You can apply security to it, and it contains all of the user content. Each web has its own *lists* (libraries are just a special type of list). and all those lists store *items*, which refers to the actual content, such as documents and contacts.

As you look at the hierarchy from web applications to items, remember that it is a one-to-many relationship going down but a one-to-one relationship going up. That is, an item can belong to only one list, a list can belong to only one web, a web is part of only a single site collection, a site collection lives in only one content database, and a content database can be associated with only one web application.

Still a little fuzzy? Try this analogy to understand how these pieces work together: Web applications are the landfill. Content databases are giant dumpsters. A site collection is a big, black 50-gallon garbage bag. Webs, lists, and items are pieces of trash. Your users spend all week creating garbage, continuously stuffing it in the garbage bags, with each piece of trash occupying only one garbage bag at a time. Each garbage bag can hold only 50 gallons of trash (quotas) before it is full, after which the user has to either ask for a new garbage bag or get a bigger garbage bag. That full garbage bag is placed in a dumpster, and it is not possible to put a garbage bag in more than one dumpster without destroying it. Dumpsters are serviced only by one landfill but that landfill can handle thousands of dumpsters without issue. How was that? Clear as mud?

CONTROLLING DEPLOYMENTS

SharePoint 2013 ships with more than a handful of tools that help you keep it under control. First take a look at the different throttling capabilities of SharePoint and then things to consider when it comes to SharePoint's recycle bin. With all of those tools in hand you then you can review the primer on the boundaries of SharePoint to make sure you keep performance in check.

HTTP Throttling

A potential challenge SharePoint administrators have faced in the past and are certain to see again is lack of resources and the odd behaviors it produces. One scenario is an overworked WFE server. As a WFE is processing requests, it can reach a point where it is not immediately responding to a request due to a lack of resources. It will then begin to queue the requests, but it has a limited capacity for storing requests also. If the queue fills up, then it will just start indiscriminately dropping requests until it catches up. While this is not a big deal for a typical GET request, what if you are a user who has just spent an hour taking a survey or filling out an application? If that PUT request is dropped, your hour was spent in vain and you will have no option but to start over.

To avoid this issue, Microsoft introduced HTTP throttling to protect a server during peak load. By default, this feature monitors the available memory in megabytes and the ASP.NET requests in queue. As it monitors these counters, it generates a health score for the server on a scale from 0 to 9, with 0 being the best. The monitor checks every five seconds by default. If the score is 9 for three consecutive tests, then the server will enter a throttled state. In this throttled state, SharePoint will return a 503 server busy message to all GET requests, including the crawler if you happen to be indexing. In addition, all timer jobs are paused, which enables the server to concentrate on finishing existing requests and hopefully makes room for anyone doing a PUT request, like that user who just spent an hour filling out a form. The monitoring continues every five seconds, and throttling is disabled after one occurrence of a score below 10.

You can configure this feature using Central Administration, to be enabled or disabled per web application. Using Windows PowerShell, you can go a step further and view and edit the thresholds using the following cmdlets:

➤   `Get-SPWebApplicationHttpThrottlingMonitor`

➤   `Set-SPWebApplicationHttpThrottlingMonitor`

> **NOTE** *You can introduce your own counters, but that requires object model code, a topic outside the scope of this book.*

The health score is exposed to all HTTP requests. If you use a tool that enables you to inspect your web traffic, such as Fiddler (www.fiddler2.com), you will see in the header under Miscellaneous the value X-SharePointHealthScore. Where this truly comes into play is with the Office clients. The Office 2010 and 2013 client programs are aware of the score and can use it to adjust their behavior. For example, Word uses it to determine how often updates should be requested when handling live co-authoring of a document.

Large List Throttling

Compared to SharePoint 2010, a few refinements have been made to throttling in SharePoint 2013. SharePoint 2013 supports lists of up to 30 million items. Previous versions of SharePoint did recommend not exceeding 2,000 items in a list view because of the strain it put on your farm's performance. Think about what happened behind the scenes when a user tried to view 3,000 items in a list. First, the SQL Server had to generate a query to return all 3,000 items at once. Next, that information had to be sent to the WFE server and added to the page. Finally, the user had to download the page with its 3,000 items and wait on Internet Explorer to render all that content. It could literally take minutes to return the page. Sadly, there was no way to stop users from doing this or even to monitor that activity until now. SharePoint 2013 improves this scenario.

SharePoint 2013 provides controls that you can configure to prevent the bad behavior listed previously. Figure 2-8 shows the Resource Throttling screen in Central Administration. You can access this screen by navigating to Application Management ➪ Manage web applications. Then select your web application, click the drop-down for General Settings, and select Resource Throttling. All default settings are shown.

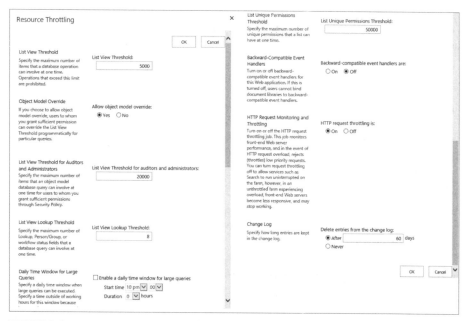

FIGURE 2-8

The List View Threshold, which is set to 5000 by default, represents the maximum number of items a standard user can return in a view. As users approach the limit, they will see the dialog shown in Figure 2-9, which indicates how many items they have and where the throttling limit is set.

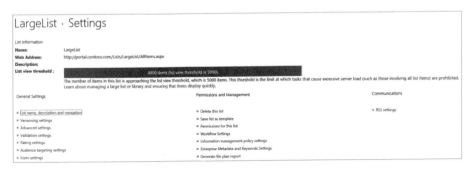

FIGURE 2-9

The following relevant settings are available:

➤ **Object Model Override** — This setting specifies whether a developer can override the throttling through the object model code to allow their code to run.

➤ **List View Threshold for Auditors and Administrators** — This setting is used to grant special power users a larger threshold. You can set a user up as an auditor through the Manage web applications screen. You first add a permission policy and enable the Site Collection Auditor permission policy level. Then, using User Policy, also on the Mange web applications Ribbon, select the new permission level you created.

➤ **List View Lookup Threshold** — This setting controls the number of lookups that can be specified.

➤ **Daily Time Window for Large Queries** — This setting is also referred to as *happy hour*. It allows you to set a time of day when throttling is disabled and views are unrestricted.

➤ **List Unique Permissions Threshold** — This setting limits the number of unique permissions a given list can have. This is a good idea, as you can run into performance problems if a list has too many unique permissions coupled with too many items. Security trimming is a great but sometimes expensive feature.

The remainder of the settings are not part of the list-throttling feature.

When users exceed this limit, they will see a warning message in the browser stating, "Displaying only the newest results below. To view all results, narrow your query by adding a filter." This will show the last 1,000 modified items.

Recycle Bin Architectural Implications

The Recycle Bin? Are you serious? Isn't that like designing a kitchen around the garbage can? Not really. When a site is deleted in SharePoint 2013, it isn't truly deleted — it's sent to the recycle bin.

The implication for you, our dazed SharePoint administrator, is that you have to account for SQL Server disk storage of potentially very large sizes. If a user deletes a site that contains 100GB of storage, your SQL server still has to store that data. It will of course be removed when the recycle bin flushes itself or you manually remove it.

One key with the Recycle Bin is keeping its scope in mind. If you delete a list item, folder, a whole list, or even a web (aka subsite), those items will all appear in the site collection Recycle Bin and can be recovered using your browser. If you delete a site collection then you have to go to the SharePoint server and use your friend PowerShell. The cmdlet `Get-SPDeletedSite` will help you get started. Or better yet go take a look at Chapter 9, "Configuring SharePoint for High Availability Backups," for the full scoop on the Recycle Bin.

Software Boundaries and Limits for SharePoint 2013

Trying to keep up with all of the boundaries, thresholds, and limits for SharePoint is probably very similar to keeping up with the US tax code from year to year. Everything you could ever hope to know is there right beside bizarre things you don't even understand why you should care about. All of the information is there, but generally speaking you should focus on the information most relevant to you.

As you dive into these different considerations for SharePoint one key piece of advice is try to think about why a specific threshold might be in place and what they are trying to tell you with that limit. Some examples:

➤ **5 zones per web app** — SharePoint has been this way since SharePoint 2007 and isn't configurable or exceedable. SharePoint law!

➤ **20 managed paths per web app** — The idea is to have as few as possible because SharePoint has to check the whole list every time you make a web request. If you introduce 3 or 4 to meet a specific need, you open Pandora's box. All of the sudden 3 or 5 becomes 50 and all of SharePoint suffers. So even though the threshold is 20 really just using the out-of-the-box managed path might make the most sense.

➤ **10 application pools per server** — This one is trying to protect you from having 1TB of RAM. If money is no object and you feel like your server has too much RAM stretch this limit as far as you want.

➤ **Database size limits** — Is it 200GB or 4TB or infinite? The answer is it depends. 200GB works well if you don't like to think. But the more important question is not how big of a database can SharePoint support but instead how big of a database can you support? Can you really back up, maintain, and move back and forth to test a 1TB database? If not then why are you worried about SharePoint's upper bounds?

Keep the preceding in the back of your mind as you read through the limits of SharePoint. Some limits are financial, some are because SharePoint cannot handle it, and some are trying to keep you out of trouble. Also, if you do try to test a limit with your initial solution consider the possibility that growth over time might cause you to blow by the limit and create problems in the long term.

This topic is really a doozy. Microsoft has a great article on TechNet that offers guidance on all things related to the boundaries and limits of SharePoint. This document is also updated on an ongoing basis based on new findings, patches, and service packs. Therefore, instead of killing trees to copy and paste content that will be changing over time, here is the link to the web page: `http://technet.microsoft.com/en-us/library/cc262787.aspx`.

The key point is: don't ignore this page. You cannot build a farm with a 10-terabyte site collection and then be mad at SharePoint when nothing works. If you read this page early and often you can avoid known issues.

SUMMARY

Wow! What a fun ride. As you can see now, SharePoint's architecture is a vast topic that seems to get more vast with each version and even each patch. After reading this chapter you should feel confident in laying out a farm topology and all of the components that go into that decision. Those components are everything from the role of SQL Server and email to how distributed cache and Request Manager allow you new flexibility.

And of course as you plan all of that out don't forget that maybe Cloud is part of or even your whole solution. A few years ago that conversation wasn't even on the table but in today's world it is very real. So make sure you run it up the flag pole. The same way virtualization used to only be for testing yet today almost every SharePoint farm has some portion virtualized. Cloud is coming and the more you know the better off you are.

All set? Great. Now that you know the pieces of the puzzle dive into the next chapter and start assembling the puzzle.

3

Installing and Configuring SharePoint

WHAT'S IN THIS CHAPTER?

> ➤ SharePoint prerequisites
> ➤ Installing SharePoint 2013 Enterprise
> ➤ Creating and configuring the farm
> ➤ Creating web applications and site collections

Just as we urged in the 2010 edition of this book: Please read this chapter! After many years of reviewing SharePoint farms, we can count on one hand the number that were built correctly. It isn't because SharePoint is especially hard to install and configure, it's just very particular about numerous settings.

The focus of this chapter is installing SharePoint Server 2013 Enterprise — using the *least-privilege security model* and meaningful database names. This approach is the opposite of the two most commonly used approaches. The first is to use an account for everything, assign it super administrator privileges, and then use all of the wizards, which results in a train wreck. At the other extreme is the second approach, which is to just download a PowerShell script and run it to magically create a SharePoint farm. While that is undoubtedly handy, you don't learn anything from the process, so the first time you hit a bump in the road you are stuck. No train wrecks or magic occur in this chapter, just a clear, production-level install done in a slow, deliberate fashion that explains all the steps.

PREPARING THE ENVIRONMENT

Before starting the SharePoint installation and configuration for this environment, several servers were built with dedicated roles to make it easier to translate to your environment. There is a dedicated domain controller, a dedicated SQL Server, and a dedicated SharePoint server.

All machines are running Windows Server 2012 Standard with the GUI. All current Windows Server Windows Updates have been applied.

The domain controller, named DC, is a single-processor machine with 1GB of RAM. A new Active Directory (AD) forest was created for the domain Contoso.com. DC has all the AD roles and hosts DNS for the domain.

The SQL Server, named SQL, is a four-processor machine with 8GB of RAM. It is running SQL Server 2012 Standard RTM. The machine is a member of the Contoso.com domain. SQL was installed using the blog post at `http://msmvps.com/blogs/shane/archive/2012/09/17/` `a-simple-install-of-sql-server-2012-for-sharepoint-server-2013-or-2010.aspx`. Even if you have SQL Server already installed, confirm that you have changed the Max Degrees of Parallelism setting to 1 and have set up the permissions correctly. Both of these steps are covered in the blog post as well. For this environment the AD account Contoso\sp_install has been given the SQL Server roles of dbcreator, public, and securityadmin.

The SharePoint server, named Server, is a four-processor machine with 8GB of RAM. It is a member of the Contoso.com domain. The AD account Contoso\sp_install has been made a local administrator on the SharePoint server. Nothing else has been done to the machine. Tasks such as adding the Web Server (IIS) role will be handled by the prerequisite installer included with SharePoint.

For a better understanding of the supporting servers, the hardware requirements, and all the software you need in place to make SharePoint happy, please see Chapter 2, "Architecture and Capacity Planning," which covers all of these topics in detail.

LOGGING IN AND MOUNTING THE FILE

In order to install SharePoint you need to login to the SharePoint server with an account that is a local administrator on that server. Therefore, in this example you will use Contoso\sp_install to remote desktop into Server.

Once you are logged into the server you need to get a copy of SharePoint Server 2013. Whether you download the trial version from the Internet or have the official DVD copy, when you run setup .exe the same thing happens. You are prompted for a license key, and based on that key you get your version of SharePoint.

To ensure an experience consistent with the examples in this chapter, download the SharePoint Server 2013 trial from `http://technet.microsoft.com/en-us/evalcenter/hh973397.aspx`. For some reason, the download for this version is an IMG file. If you are using Windows Server 2012, then you can right-click the file and mount it, which works the same as inserting a DVD. If you aren't using Windows Server 2012 or are otherwise having problems working with the file, then check out `http://www.slysoft.com/en/virtual-clonedrive.html`. This handy free utility enables you to mount IMG and ISO files natively in Windows. This is quite handy, especially if you used TechNet's download, which is in the form of an ISO file. Thank goodness for consistency.

RUNNING THE PREREQUISITE INSTALLER

The prerequisite installer is a wonderful little tool that you are likely already familiar with, as Microsoft uses a similar tool with several other Server products. As the name suggests, it handles the download and installation of any programs that you need to install before you install SharePoint. Otherwise, you must manually download and run at least 11 different programs from `http://technet.microsoft.com/en-us/library/cc262485(v=office.15).aspx`. There's useful information on that page, but if you're interested solely in the prerequisite installer, here's the direct section link: `http://technet.microsoft.com/en-us/library/cc262485(v=office.15).aspx#section5`. The prerequisite installer will also install and configure the Windows Server roles and features you need, such as IIS.

This section uses the prerequisite installer but it is quite possible that your SharePoint server will not have access to the Internet, which makes it hard to automate the process. In that case, you have a couple of options. You can either download the programs from the preceding link and then manually install them individually or you can script the process. The latter method isn't really scripting, but running the program with a whole bunch of parameters. If you run `prerequisiteinstaller.exe /?` from a command prompt, the screen shown in Figure 3-1 appears, displaying all your available options. You need to download all of these bits, place them in a directory and then create a command line that tells SharePoint where to find them. If you decide to go the route of creating your own command line, be sure you save all your work for future reference, as it will prove extremely helpful if you will be installing a lot of SharePoint servers without Internet access. If not, this is a lot of work with very little gain. TechNet has a nice article at `http://technet.microsoft.com/en-us/library/ff686793(v=office.15)` with additional details if the command line is your chosen path.

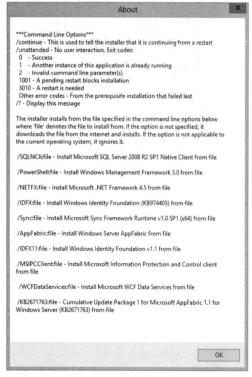

Whatever you decide, you must still run the prerequisite installer to ensure that installation is complete. In other words, even if you manually install and configure everything you still need to run the tool to confirm you did everything successfully. It only takes a couple of minutes and prevents any unpleasant surprises later.

It isn't unusual for the prerequisite installer to require rebooting your machine once or twice as it runs. Don't fight it; instead, go get something to drink while it reboots. When you log back in to Windows, the prerequisite installer will automatically restart — that is, assuming it can get to the file. If you had to previously mount an IMG or ISO file, that mounting often doesn't survive rebooting, so when you log back in you get an error. Not a big deal. Just click OK, mount the file again,

FIGURE 3-1

and then manually run prerequisite installer again. It will skip the steps it has already completed and continue. Just keep running it until the Installation Complete message appears.

Use the following steps to run the prerequisite installer on the SharePoint server. You can be logged in as any local administrator on the server. The account type isn't important until you are ready to install SharePoint in the next section.

1.   Open the folder containing the SharePoint install files. If you downloaded an IMG or ISO file, then you have to mount that first.

2.   Double-click `prerequisiteinstaller.exe`.

3.   At the Welcome screen, click Next.

4.   Read all of that license goodness and select "I accept the terms of the License Agreement(s)," then click Next.

After several minutes the install will do one of three things: complete successfully, prompt you to reboot so it can keep going, or error out. If it prompts you to reboot, just click Finish and the server will reboot. When you log in after the reboot, the installer will automatically resume. If it does not, you may need to remount your ISO or IMG file. See the Login and Mount the ISO section if you need to troubleshoot the error message seen in Figure 3-2.

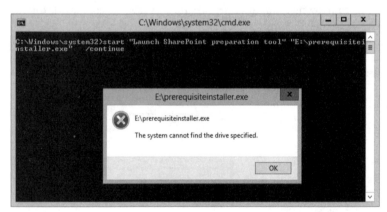

FIGURE 3-2

If you get an error, it will contain a link to the error log. The log file is relatively readable, so you should be able to determine the cause of the failure. Usually it is an Internet connection issue. Also, sometimes it doesn't hurt to just try again before troubleshooting. SharePoint 2010 had a bad habit of just wanting to be run twice. When you get the Installation Complete message, click Finish.

ADDING FORGOTTEN PATCHES

As great as the prerequisite installer is, ensure that you install any appropriate additional patches, depending on your OS. Hopefully, in the near future such patches will be rolled out as Windows Updates, but currently you need to handle this yourself.

Windows Server 2008 R2

If you are using Windows Server 2008 R2, not Windows Server 2012, you need to manually request, register, download, and install the following patches:

➤ KB 2554876 at `http://go.microsoft.com/fwlink/p/?LinkId=254221`

➤ KB 2708075 at `http://go.microsoft.com/fwlink/p/?LinkID=254222`

➤ KB 2759112 at `http://go.microsoft.com/fwlink/p/?LinkId=267536`

Windows Server 2012

For those of you using Windows Server 2012, Microsoft didn't leave you out of the fun:

➤ KB 2765317 at `http://go.microsoft.com/fwlink/p/?LinkID=268725`

RUNNING SETUP

Now that your environment is primed and ready to go, you can use the following steps to install SharePoint:

1. Remote desktop into the SharePoint server as your install account — Contoso\sp_install for this example. See the earlier section, "Preparing the Environment," if you need a reminder about what permissions this account needs.

2. From the folder in which the SharePoint files are mounted, run `setup.exe`.

3. At this point, SharePoint will confirm you have installed all the prerequisites and that there are no pending reboots. If you get any setup error message here, then you need to either reboot or note which prerequisite you did not install. Assuming you did everything correctly, you will see the Enter your Product Key dialog. Enter your key and click Continue. Remember that if you use the trial key, it is valid for 180 days only. Also, if you are having a hard time finding the trial key, it is located at the bottom of the page on which you started the process of downloading the trial version, in a very light font.

4. Read the license terms (don't you always?), select "I accept the terms of this agreement," and click Continue.

5. Stop! When people screw up installs, this is where it happens most frequently. When the dialog shown in Figure 3-3 appears, choose Complete! If you choose Stand-alone, then SharePoint will automatically install SQL Express on this machine and configure everything with a bunch of crazy defaults. Don't do it.

   After choosing Complete, click Install Now. If you want to change the default file locations you can, but note that this doesn't install all of the SharePoint files to that new location. You will still have the files in the `c:\program files\common files\Microsoft shared\web server extensions\` folder no matter what. This is why the previous chapter emphasized that you need at least 100GB of space for your C: drive. Even if you accept the default for the Search files location when you configure the search service application, you can still specify the location of those Search files.

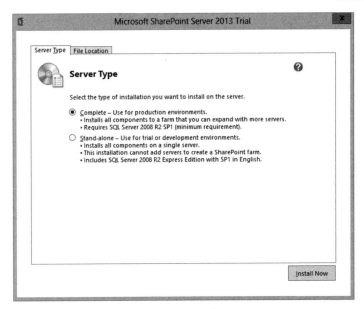

FIGURE 3-3

6. When setup finishes, the Run Configuration Wizard window will appear. SharePoint is offering to kick off the wizard to help you create or join a farm. Say, "No thank you!" by deselecting "Run the SharePoint Products Configuration Wizard now." Then click Close.

You don't want to run the configuration wizard because it is recommended that you do some of the initial configuration steps using PowerShell in order to avoid having the Central Administration content database created with a GUID in its name.

AUTOMATING SETUP

If the preceding steps seem too complicated or you build so many SharePoint farms that you would like to automate that process, SharePoint provides that capability through the use of a `config.xml` file. If you look in the folder where you mounted the SharePoint install files, you will see a folder called files. This folder contains several other folders, each of which contains a different `config.xml` preconfigured to its scenario; and because it is just an XML file you can make changes as necessary. At the time of writing, Microsoft has not released a 2013 guide to using `config.xml`, but the 2010 guide, located at `http://technet.microsoft.com/en-us/library/cc261668.aspx`, should work fine in its absence.

Another option to consider is more radical: all the steps in this entire chapter could potentially be automated. If you flip over to Chapter 7, "Administering SharePoint 2013 with Windows PowerShell," it describes several different scripts you can leverage to really add some flavor to your installs. While that is great fun, those scripts assume a certain comfort level with installing SharePoint. The best way to attain that comfort level is to keep reading this chapter, which breaks down the whole process without using any magic.

CREATING THE FARM

Now that SharePoint is installed you need to create a SharePoint farm. If you are going to have only one SharePoint server in your farm, then simply follow the steps in this section. If you are going to have several SharePoint servers in your farm, then you need to follow these steps on one server to create the farm, and then all the other servers will follow a slightly different process to join the farm. The server on which you run these steps will be the server that hosts Central Admin by default, so determine which lucky server will have that role and then solider on:

1. Make sure you are still logged into the SharePoint server as your install account — Contoso\sp_install in this example.

2. Open the SharePoint 2013 Management Shell.

3. When the window opens you will see an error message at the top: "The local farm is not accessible. Cmdlets with FeatureDependencyId are not registered." This is expected, as you have not yet created the farm. Although you can ignore this error for now, keep in mind that it should not appear after you create the farm.

4. At the prompt, run the following PowerShell command and press Enter. You need to change the DatabaseServer parameter value to your server's name. In this example, the SQL server is named sql, so that is what is used. You can also use Figure 3-4 to check your work.

```
New-SPConfigurationDatabase -DatabaseName SharePoint_Config -DatabaseServer sql
-AdministrationContentDatabaseName SharePoint_Admin_Content
```

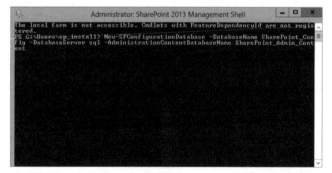

FIGURE 3-4

> ### PINNING THE SHAREPOINT 2013 MANAGEMENT SHELL TO THE TASKBAR
>
> You will be using the SharePoint 2013 Management Shell constantly throughout your SharePoint career, so here is a trick to make your life easier: Pin the Management Shell shortcut to the taskbar. To do so, right-click the file in the Start menu and select Pin to Taskbar. After doing that, you need to set the shortcut to always run as administrator. You will never do anything with the SharePoint 2013 Management Shell that doesn't require you to run as an administrator. After it is pinned, hold down the Shift key and right-click it to expose the properties option. When the properties panel opens, click Advanced. Now you have the option to always have the program run as administrator.

5. A dialog will appear in which you enter your Windows PowerShell credentials. A common mistake is entering the wrong account here. It doesn't want your username and password; it wants your farm account's username and password. This needs to be a dedicated account, as it is the most fragile in the farm. For the book example, use **Contoso\SP_farm**. This account needs to be created in AD, and at this point it only needs to be a domain user. Enter the domain\username and password and then click OK.

6. Now you are returned to the Management Shell to enter the farm passphrase. This passphrase is used to allow servers to join and leave this SharePoint farm. In order to qualify as a secure passphrase, it must meet the following guidelines:

> ➤ It must contain at least 8 characters.

> ➤ It must contain at least 3 of the following 4 character groups:

>> ➤ English uppercase characters (A through Z)

>> ➤ English lowercase characters (a through z)

>> ➤ Numerals (0 through 9)

>> ➤ Non-alphabetic characters: "! " # $ % & ' ( ) * + , - . / : ; < = > ? @ [\ ] ^ _ ` { | } ~

Type in your passphrase and press Enter. Be sure to make note of it, as you will need it later if you add more servers.

Now would be a good time to take a break. This will run for a while, as it is doing a lot of heavy lifting behind the scenes, such as creating your configuration database and the Central Admin database.

7. When the commands are done running, your Management Shell will return to the slow blinking cursor and in typical PowerShell fashion you will not see any messages, which is a good thing. Open the SharePoint 2013 Products Configuration Wizard from the Start menu.

8. At the Welcome to SharePoint Products dialog, click Next.

9. A pop-up will appear warning you that some services will be stopped or restarted. That's fine; just click Yes.

10. In the Modify server farm Settings dialog, leave the default of "Do not disconnect from this server farm," and click Next. Seeing any other screen at this point is a bad thing and means something went wrong in steps 1-6.

Most likely the farm failed to create and you got an error message. You will need to go back and work through that error message. If any databases were created when you got the error message, you will probably need to delete those from the SQL server on your own.

11. In the Configure SharePoint Central Administration Web Application dialog, click Specify port number and enter any number you can remember.

12. Under Configure Security Settings, use the default of NTLM. Keep in mind that this is asking if you want Central Administration to use NTLM or Kerberos. It is not asking if you want Kerberos anywhere in your farm. You always want NTLM for Central Administration. Confirm your settings using Figure 3-5 as an example. If everything looks good, click Next.

13. On this screen quickly double-check all of your settings and then click Next to finish creating this fabulous farm. You might notice the progress bar goes straight to step 4 of 9. This is because you did the earlier steps using PowerShell.

FIGURE 3-5

14. After a couple of quick minutes you should get a Configuration Successful screen. Click Finish.

After a few moments Internet Explorer will open and the Central Administration website will load. Don't get trigger-happy and start pressing buttons. You'll explore how to configure your new farm after a brief message about multi-server farms.

Adding More Servers to the Farm

One of the great things about SharePoint is its ability to scale. As described in Chapter 2, it is easy to create some extremely flexible topologies with multiple SharePoint servers. Obviously, before you can start scaling, you first need to install SharePoint on those servers. That means following the steps outlined in the earlier sections to run the prerequisite installer, add the forgotten patches, and setting SharePoint up as you did on your first server. It is completely safe to perform those steps on all your servers at once.

After deploying all the necessary bits, you would create the farm on one server only, keeping in mind that this server will have Central Administration installed on it by default, and therefore planning accordingly. With that step completed on the first server, you are ready to add the other servers to the farm. Repeat the following steps on all additional servers in your farm:

1. Remote desktop to the server using a local admin account. It should be the same account you used to do the first server. For this example, that is Contoso\sp_install.

2. From the Start menu, run the SharePoint Products and Technology Configuration Wizard.

3. At the Welcome to SharePoint Products screen, click Next.

4. A dialog will appear warning you that some services will be stopped or restarted. Click Yes.

5. For the Connect to a server farm dialog, select "Connect to an existing server farm" and click Next.

6. For Database server: enter your SQL Server name and click Retrieve Database Names. In this example, the SQL server name is sql.

7. After a moment the screen will refresh. In the drop-down database, select your configuration database name. It should be SharePoint_Config unless you changed it when creating your farm initially. Also, if you have multiple databases listed, ensure that you choose the correct one. Click Next.

8. In the Specify Farm Security Settings dialog, enter the passphrase you specified when creating the farm. For this example, use **pass@word1**. Click Next.

9. In the Completing the SharePoint Products Configuration Wizard dialog, click Next to join the farm. The Advanced button is used for configuring this server to also host the Central Administration website. If you are the curious type, it is safe to click; and if you would like to have this server host Central Administration, you can select the option. This example assumes you do not.

10. When these steps are completed, click Finish to close the configuration wizard.

11. After a moment Internet Explorer will open and take you to Central Administration. Note that Central Administration is running on the first server you provisioned. Close the window.

That's it. At this point you would return to the first server and continue building out your farm and following these exact steps on all your additional servers. As mentioned earlier, it is safe to run these steps on all the servers at the same time. Unlike Black Friday shoppers, the servers will take orderly turns adding themselves to the farm. If they could get you one of those fancy $99 TVs, life would be perfect.

Configuring the Farm

You have a farm but it isn't very helpful yet. You still need to configure the core services of SharePoint. SharePoint provides these services through the service application framework. Check out Chapter 4, "Understanding Service Applications," for a deeper dive of how service applications work. Each of the various services — such as Search, User Profiles, and Excel Services, to name a few — are offered in an a la carte fashion. As you create each service application, you can connect your various SharePoint web applications to it to consume it. In this section, you will do the initial configuration of the core service applications. You will do this in a scalable fashion, in order to avoid some of the goofiness that tries to sneak in along the way.

The following sections describe all the service applications and outline the steps to create and configure each one. While it is not necessary to create the service applications in the following order, it is recommended because some of them automatically register themselves with other service applications if they are present, saving you extra configuration steps. Note that the service applications appear in Central Administration in alphabetical order. In addition, as you work through the list, some of the service applications are considered "required" or "highly recommended," while others are optional. They are identified as such as you work through the sections.

> **NOTE** *You might also notice that an initial farm configuration wizard, or* white wizard, *is available to do all of this configuration for you. Although you are welcome to use it, this chapter avoids it because the wizard automatically does a lot of little things that are less than ideal, such as adding a GUID to all your database names and setting up My Sites to run on a web application named after the server. We highly recommend skipping the wizard and following along to configure your service applications the way the cool kids do.*

1. Make sure you are still on the first SharePoint server with Internet Explorer open logged in as your install account.

2. You should see a pop-up dialog asking whether you want to Help Make SharePoint Better. Make your selection and click OK. (You might be surprised to know that the authors recommend you select Yes. Microsoft actively monitors any feedback you provide and prioritizes fixes based in part on this information — so if they are looking for problems to fix, wouldn't you like them to fix yours?)

3. From the Welcome dialog, choose, "No, I will configure everything myself," by clicking Cancel.

Now you will find yourself at the home screen of Central Administration. You can create most of the service applications from here by clicking through and providing some basic information. Unfortunately, some don't work that way, such as the State Service and the Usage and Health Data Collection Service. Never fear, however, as where there is a will there is a way, and PowerShell is that way. Before you do anything else, you need to open the SharePoint Management Shell.

1. From the taskbar, click the SharePoint Management Shell link you created earlier.

Creating a Managed Account

Before continuing, you need to create a *managed account*. This is an Active Directory (AD) account you register with SharePoint, which you can use to run services and application pools. This enables you to manage one account's password in a central location from which SharePoint can update all the places it is used in the farm. SharePoint can even automatically change the password for you. It's a great feature, but it isn't optional, so you have to follow along in this section.

To get started you will need two AD accounts, sp_serviceapp and sp_webapp. If you are creating these two accounts in Active Directory, for now they just need to be domain users with no special permissions at all.

1. Open Central Administration.

2. From the right-hand side of the page, click Security.

3. Under General Security, click Configure managed accounts.

4. From the menu bar, click Register Managed Account. You may notice that sp_farm is already registered. SharePoint did this for you automatically when you made it the farm account.

5. In the Service account credentials section, enter **Contoso\sp_serviceapp** in the User name field if you are following the example. Remember to always add **Domain** in front of your account name.

6. For Password, enter your password. In the example, pass@word1 is used.

7. Ignore the other check boxes and click OK.

8. From the menu bar, click Register Managed Account.

9. In the Service account credentials section, enter **Contoso\sp_webbapp** if you are following the example. Remember to always add **Domain** in front of your username.

10. For Password, enter your password. In the example, pass@word1 is used.

11. Ignore the other check boxes and click OK.

Now you have three managed accounts registered, which you will be able to use as you continue configuring your farm.

Creating the Service Application App Pool

Each service application has a service application proxy, which is really just a web service. Those proxies, when created, have to run within an IIS application pool. By default in SharePoint, all your service applications should run in the same application pool unless there is a specific reason to otherwise handle them.

> **NOTE** *For more details on service applications, check out Chapter 4, "Understanding Service Applications."*

When you create your first service application using Central Administration, you can use that page to create an application pool. Alternately, if you are the enterprising type, you can create the app pool using the SharePoint Management Shell. To simplify the instructions, use the following steps to create it using PowerShell:

1. Open the SharePoint 2013 Management Shell.

2. Type the following and press Enter:

    ```
    New-SPServiceApplicationPool -Name "Default SharePoint Service App Pool" -
    Account contoso\sp_serviceapp
    ```

3. Confirm your work using the screen shown in Figure 3-6.

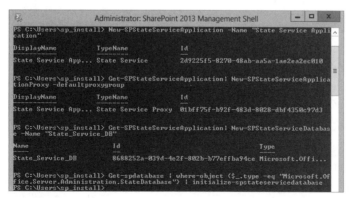

FIGURE 3-6

Provisioning the State Service

The State Service service application is used to maintain state. This is one of those goofy .NET developer things which is the equivalent of writing on your hand. It holds the information temporarily while you use it and then it goes away. Some people assume this isn't necessary but even out-of-the-box features use it so just go ahead and provision it to save looking up the error messages later. Because there is no GUI to do you will be using the SharePoint Management Shell.

1. At the prompt, type the following and press Enter:

```
New-SPStateServiceApplication -Name "State Service Application"
```

2. At the prompt, type the following and press Enter:

```
Get-SPStateServiceApplication| New-SPStateServiceApplicationProxy
-defaultproxygroup
```

3. At the prompt, type the following and press Enter:

```
Get-SPStateServiceApplication| New-SPStateServiceDatabase -Name
"State_Service_DB"
```

4. At the prompt, type the following and press Enter:

```
Get-spdatabase | where-object {$_.type -eq
"Microsoft.Office.Server.Administration.StateDatabase"} |
initialize-spstateservicedatabase
```

5. Confirm your work using the screen shown in Figure 3-7.

FIGURE 3-7

Success. Now you have created the State Service application.

Usage and Health Data Collection

Monitoring the status of your farm's health is a critical aspect of SharePoint administration. This service application collects the various logging information stored in SharePoint and writes it to the logging database. This service application should always be created.

1. At the prompt, type the following and press Enter:

```
New-SPUsageApplication -Name "Usage and Health Data Collection"
```

2. At the prompt, type the following and press Enter:

```
$proxy = Get-SPServiceApplicationProxy | where {$_.TypeName -eq "Usage and Health Data Collection Proxy"}
```

3. At the prompt, type the following and press Enter:

```
$proxy.Provision()
```

4. Review Figure 3-8 to confirm your work.

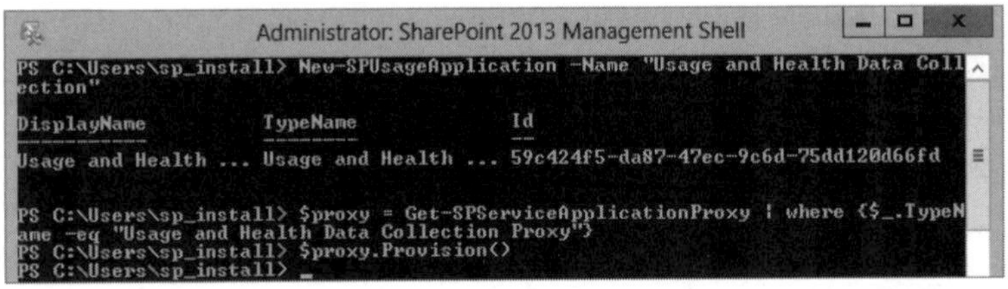

FIGURE 3-8

That will do it. Now you have created the Usage and Health Data Collection service application.

Checking Your Available Service Applications

Your list of available service applications varies according to what version of SharePoint you have and what, if any, third-party service applications you have installed. This walk-through assumes that you have SharePoint Server Enterprise with no third-party service applications installed. If you are using SharePoint Server Standard, your list will be slightly shorter:

1. From the left side of Central Administration, click Application Management.

2. Under Service Applications, click Manage service applications.

3. From the Ribbon, click New. Figure 3-9 shows the list of service applications for SharePoint Server Enterprise.

These are the service applications covered in the following sections. One additional "secret" service application, called the Subscription Settings Service, will be created with PowerShell.

FIGURE 3-9

Access Services

The Access Services service application is used to create some very powerful applications and publish them through SharePoint. Called, appropriately if unimaginatively, Access apps, they are a new type of database that you build using Access 2013 and then access through SharePoint using a web browser. Business users are very excited about this functionality. SharePoint and SQL Server administrators do not share their enthusiasm. For one thing, each app creates its own database, which must be hosted on SQL Server 2012. The instance of SQL Server that hosts those databases must have some scary changes made to it, such as enabling SQL Server Authentication and named pipes.

Because of all of these requirements, Access Services are not considered part of a standard SharePoint server build, so feel free to skip it. No, this isn't a total cop-out. Readers who are interested in configuring this service application can jump to Chapter 8, "Configuring SharePoint 2013 for Business Intelligence," which contains a section dedicated to all of the chaos.

Access Services 2010

This is your old friend from SharePoint 2010. Another downside of the Access app model described in the preceding section is that there is no standard way to convert an Access Services 2010 service application to the new 2013 model. Therefore, if you are bringing over any Access applications from 2010, you would attach the service application database from Access Services in SharePoint 2010 to this service application to continue to host those applications. Note also that if you are using any of the reporting functionality of Access Services 2010, then SQL Server Reporting Services must be installed and configured, just as it was with SharePoint 2010. For more information on installing and configuring Reporting Services, see Chapter 8. After that is complete, you can follow these steps to create the Access Services 2010 service application. Access Services 2010 is a completely optional service application and should only be created if you have a specific purpose for it.

1. From Central Administration, select Application Management ➪ Service Applications ➪ Manage service application, and then click New.

2. In the drop-down menu, select Access Services 2010.

3. In the Create New Access Services Application dialog, enter **Access Services 2010** for the Name field.

4. For Application Pool, select Use existing application pool.

5. From the drop-down, select Default SharePoint Service App Pool.

6. Leave the check box selected for "Add this service application's proxy to the farm's default proxy list."

7. Confirm your settings against Figure 3-10 and then click OK.

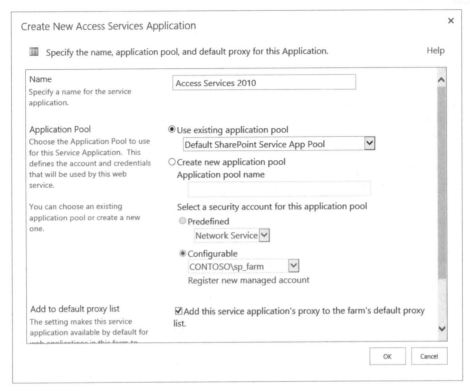

FIGURE 3-10

Starting the Service on Server

Now that you have created the service application you need to start its corresponding service on server on the appropriate server. If you just have one server, then the choice is clear; but if you have a lot of servers, then you need to balance out your load and determine which server should host the given service. For more details on server topologies, please see Chapter 2, "Architecture and Capacity Planning." For the steps in this section, one server is assumed.

Because you will alternate between creating a service application and then starting its corresponding service on server, to make your life easier it is recommended that you open a second tab in Internet Explorer. Leave that tab on the Services on Server page while your first tab stays on Manage service applications. That way, you can avoid navigating around a lot and instead just move from tab to tab.

1. In Internet Explorer, create a new tab. If you are unfamiliar with that process, just press Ctrl+T on your keyboard.

2. From the new tab, open Central Administration. In this example, the URL is http://server:5555 but yours may vary.

3. From the homepage of Central Admin, click Application Management.

4. Under Service Applications, click Manage services on server.

Now you are all set to move back and forth and quickly start the corresponding service for each service application you create. If in the previous section you created the Access Service 2010 service application, then start that service.

1. On the Services on Server page, find Access Database Service 2010.

2. To the right of the name, click the Start link. After a moment you should be returned to the Services on Server page, and the status should now be Started.

If your farm has multiple servers, you can use the Server: link at the top of the page to specify the server for which you are starting the service. If you click the displayed server's name, you can then click Change Server. From the pop-up window that appears, you then select the server whose services you want to manage.

Configuring the App Management Service

The App Management Service is the service application that brings apps and the SharePoint and Office store in SharePoint to life. Chapter 11, "Managing and Configuring Apps," covers all the fun that apps brings to the table and the different ways you can use the functionality. As part of building a smoothly functioning farm, you need to configure this application, so the steps are included in this chapter. Chapter 11 repeats the steps but with a different spin, explaining more details along the way. Note that configuring this service application also requires creating the Subscription Service application and making some changes to DNS.

Creating the Subscription Service Application

The Subscription Service application in SharePoint 2010 was used only for multi-tenant environments. It is still used for that purpose in SharePoint 2013, but now it also plays a key role in the delivery of the App Management service as well. As such, you must create it before you continue. Also, to keep you on your toes you have to do it from the Management Shell.

1. Make sure you are in the Management Shell.

2. Type the following and press Enter:

```
$sa = New-SPSubscriptionSettingsServiceApplication -ApplicationPool "Default
SharePoint Service App Pool" -Name "Subscription Settings Service" -
DatabaseName "Subscription_Settings_Service_DB"
```

3. Type the following and press Enter:

```
New-SPSubscriptionSettingsServiceApplicationProxy -ServiceApplication $sa
```

4. Type the following and press Enter:

```
Get-SPServiceInstance | where{$_.TypeName -eq "Microsoft SharePoint
Foundation Subscription Settings Service"} | Start-SPServiceInstance
```

5. Confirm your work against the screen shown in Figure 3-11.

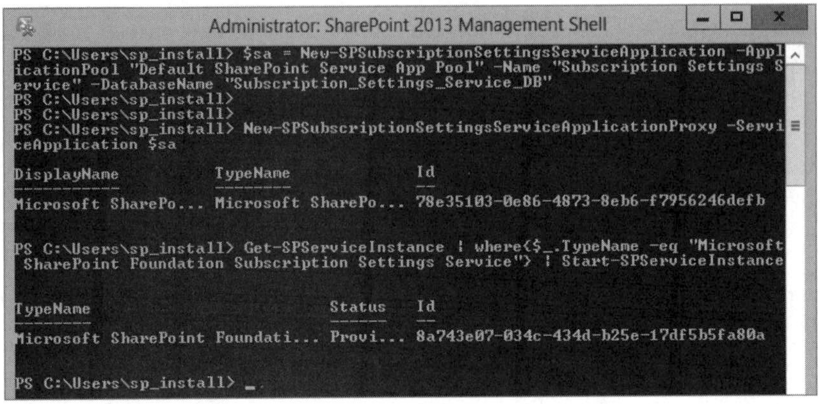

FIGURE 3-11

Configuring DNS for the App Management Service

Each app that you publish is published to its own URL. To facilitate this across your farm, these apps are created either as a subdomain of your current domain or as a new, unique domain. The subdomain route is easier but it opens the door to cross-site scripting vulnerabilities, so this section walks you through the more secure option. To learn more about the two options, check out the TechNet page at `http://technet.microsoft.com/en-us/library/fp161236(v=office.15)`.

Because these changes are domain wide, your company's DNS administrator may need to make these changes. The following section assumes you are the person with the required permissions, and it steps through the most typical scenario. There are hundreds of variables in play here, of course, so your steps may vary for your production environment. For example, you might use a Linux DNS server making the how-to below, useless. Regardless, you will need to create the DNS records.

As a reminder, the example primary domain name is Contoso.com. The domain controller name is DC, the SharePoint server name is Server, and you will be creating a new DNS Zone called ContosoApps.com:

1. Log onto a Domain Controller as a Domain Administrator.

2. From the Start menu, open DNS Manager.

3. Double-click the server name so you see Forward Lookup Zones in the main pane.

4. Double-click Forward Lookup Zones.

5. From the right pane, right-click Forward Lookup Zones (see Figure 3-12).

6. From the fly out, select New Zone to start the wizard.

7. At the Welcome screen of the New Zone Wizard, click Next.

8. For the Zone Type, accept the default of Primary zone and click Next.

9. For Active Directory Zone Replication Scope, accept the default and click Next.

10. In the Zone Name dialog, enter **ContosoApps.com** for the zone name and click Next.

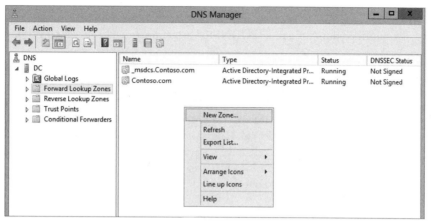

FIGURE 3-12

11. For Dynamic Update, accept the default and click Next.

12. At the Completing the New Zone Wizard screen, click Finish.

13. From the right pane, double-click ContosoApps.com.

14. Right-click ContosoApps.com and select New Alias (CNAME)..., as shown in Figure 3-13.

> **NOTE** *The official guidance from Microsoft is to use a CNAME record, but most other DNS recommendations are to use a HOST (A) record instead of an Alias. In some load-balanced environments there is not a registered DNS entry for the load-balancer and other DNS entries reference the IP address of the load balancer, which would cause additional confusion here.*

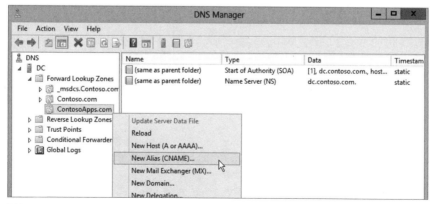

FIGURE 3-13

15. For Alias name, enter *.

16. For Fully qualified domain name (FQDN) for target host:, enter **server.contoso.com**.

POINTING YOUR NEW DNS ZONE

The example assumes you have only one SharePoint server, so it is clear where you point your new DNS Zone. If you have more than one SharePoint server serving web traffic, then you most likely have a network load balancer. If so, then you would point your alias at the load balancer. No trickery going on here. You just want to ensure that all the web requests for apps go to all your SharePoint web servers.

---

17. Check your work against the dialog shown in Figure 3-14 and click OK.

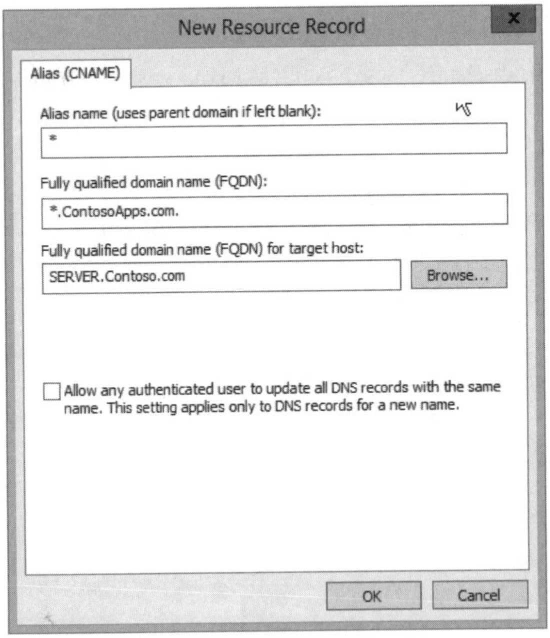

FIGURE 3-14

18. Close DNS Manager and log off the domain controller quickly, before you break something.

That completes the configuration of the new DNS zone. Assuming you don't change your farm configuration drastically, you should never have to modify the settings made here.

WEB APPLICATION CONSIDERATIONS

Later in this chapter you will learn about web applications and how to create them; but to ensure that you get the whole story about the App Management service application, note the following: if you are going to use path-based site collections with a host header named web application, as 99% of admins did with SharePoint 2010, then in order to make the App Management service work you must also create a SharePoint web application with no host header, listening on port 80 (or 443 if you are using SSL). For this web application you also need to create a site collection at the root, which enables SharePoint to get the App requests. If you are using host header–based site collections, then you can ignore all this fun. If you are confused, don't worry; later in this chapter you will create a web application and site collection for portal.contoso.com. Just run through the steps in the Web Application section, and for step 5 leave the host header blank.

Creating the App Management Service

Now that you have configured all the ancillary pieces, you can create the actual service application:

1. Make sure you are still on the Manage service applications page in Central Administration.

2. Click the New button in the Ribbon.

3. From the menu, select App Management Service.

4. For Name, enter **App Management Service**.

5. For Database Name, use **App_Management_DB**. The key here is to get rid of that nasty GUID on the end.

6. For Application pool, select Use existing application pool.

7. From the drop-down, select Default SharePoint Service App Pool.

8. Leave the default of Create App Management Service Application Proxy and add it to the default proxy group. Click OK.

After a minute the displayed message "This shouldn't take long," should go away and you are returned to the Manage service applications screen. Now you need to start the service instance:

1. Switch over to your Internet Explorer (IE) tab for Services on Server.

2. Find App Management Service and click Start to the right of it.

After a moment the screen is refreshed and the status should be set to Started. If so, you are doing great and are in the home stretch.

Configuring the App Management Service

The final step is to configure the App Management Service to use that awesome Contosoapps.com DNS Zone you created in DNS earlier:

1. Switch back over to the Manage service applications tab in IE.

2. From the left-hand menu, click Apps.

3. In the App Management section, click Configure App URLs. The page may take a minute to load, so be patient.

4. In the Configure App URLs dialog, for App domain: enter **ContosoApps.com**.

5. For App prefix:, enter **app**. Click OK.

6. Navigate back to the Manage service applications page by clicking Application Management ⇨ Service Applications ⇨ Manage service applications.

That's all, folks. You are now ready to use apps. For more information about how to do that, remember to check out Chapter 11, which provides all the details, including how to verify that you have everything set up correctly. From an administrative standpoint, however, you are done. Move on to the next service application on your list.

Configuring the Business Data Connectivity Service

The Business Data Connectivity (BDC) service application facilitates connecting SharePoint to external data sources such as web services and databases so that information can be exposed within SharePoint. This useful tool can be used by developers or power users, so as an administrator configuring the farm you just need to create the service application, start the service, and you are done:

1. From the Manage service applications screen, click the New button in the Ribbon.

2. From the menu, select Business Data Connectivity Service.

3. For Name, enter **BDC**.

4. For Database Name, enter **BDC_Service_DB**. Remember to get rid of that evil GUID.

5. Scroll down to Application Pool and select Use existing application pool.

6. From the drop-down, select Default SharePoint Service App Pool.

7. At the bottom of the page, click OK. Then click OK again in the Success pop-up window.

To start the service:

1. Switch to your IE tab for Services on Server.

2. Find Business Data Connectivity Service and then click Start to the right of it.

Before users can begin creating models, external systems, and external content types, however, you need to give them the appropriate permissions. You can do that by opening the BDC service application and selecting Set Metadata Store Permissions from the Ribbon. In the dialog that appears, you can assign permissions for Edit, Execute, Selectable in Clients, and Set Permissions.

Creating the Excel Services Application

The Excel Services Application enables you to host and publish Excel workbooks within SharePoint so users can consume and even work with the information without using the Excel client. For example, you could create an Excel chart that is displayed on the home page of your team site for all visitors. This shouldn't be confused with the Excel Office Web App, which is used to create and edit workbooks in a browser version of the client. In the grand scheme of things, the Excel Services Application is optional. Chapter 8 covers how to really use Excel Services in nerdy detail, including examples, if you are interested.

To create the service application, follow these steps:

1. From the Manage service applications screen, click the New button in the Ribbon.

2. From the menu, select Excel Services Application.

3. For Name, enter **Excel Services**.

4. Scroll down to Application Pool and select Use existing application pool.

5. From the drop-down, select Default SharePoint Service App Pool.

6. Leave the default of "Add this service application's proxy to the farm's default proxy list." Click OK at the bottom of the page.

To start the service:

1. Switch to the IE tab for Services on Server.

2. Find Excel Calculation Services and then click Start to the right of it.

That will do it. Excel is up and running.

THE MACHINE TRANSLATION SERVICE

This service application enables SharePoint to provide automatic translation of content through the use of an external translation service. Microsoft has a service called Microsoft Translator that will probably be the go-to provider for these translations. However, because configuring and using this service application is a complicated proposition, and not considered part of a typical farm build, it is not included in this book. For more information, see `http://technet.microsoft.com/en-us/library/jj553772(v=office.15).aspx`, where you will find details about the various configuration steps.

Configuring the Managed Metadata Service

The managed metadata service application is an old friend from SharePoint 2010 that has even more of a starring role in 2013. You can use it to manage terms in order to create a structured corporate taxonomy, but it is flexible enough to be used for a user-driven folksonomy. It also supports terms in multiple languages, and if you want to define enterprise content types you can do so through the use of its content hub feature. New in 2013, now you will see some WCM solutions using managed metadata to create new types of navigation, a topic discussed in Chapter 21, "Configuring and Managing Web Content Management and Internet Sites."

Several service applications, such as Search, User Profiles, and even the Machine Translation Service, depend on the managed metadata service application being provisioned, so you should consider it required. For now, you just need to concern yourself with creating the service application:

1. From the Manage service applications screen, click the New button in the Ribbon.

2. From the menu, select Managed Metadata Service.

3. For Name, enter **Managed Metadata Service**.

4. For Database Name, enter **Managed_Metadata_Service_DB**.

5. Scroll down to Application Pool and select Use existing application pool.

6. From the drop-down, select Default SharePoint Service App Pool.

7. Leave all the other defaults. If you wanted to use the Content Type Hub, you would edit the Managed Metadata Service later to provide the location.

8. Click OK at the bottom of the page.

This service application doesn't provide any "working on it" messages, so don't be alarmed when nothing happens after you click OK. Just wait a minute or two and you will be returned to the Manage service applications screen, where you will see your new service application.

Now start the service:

1. Switch to the IE tab for Services on Server.

2. Find Managed Metadata Web Service and then click Start to the right of it.

Although your service application is ready to go, there is one more configuration task to perform if you want to use all of its features. One of the useful features enabled by the managed metadata service application is the capability to save your custom navigation to it; but before you can play with that feature you need to set your service application to be the default storage location:

1. From the Manage service applications page, locate the Managed Metadata Service you just created but this time click to the right of the *second* listing of the name. If you click the name it will open the Term Store Management Tool. That is not what you want; you need the Properties option to be enabled in the Ribbon, as shown in Figure 3-15.

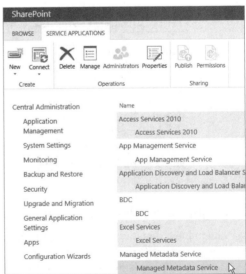

FIGURE 3-15

2.   Click Properties from the Ribbon.

3.   The dialog shown in Figure 3-16 should appear. Select the option "This service application is the default storage location for column specific term sets," and click OK.

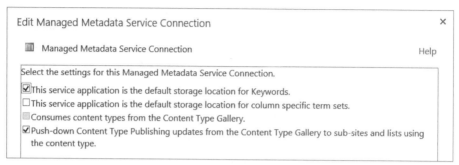

Edit Managed Metadata Service Connection   ✕

▦ Managed Metadata Service Connection   Help

Select the settings for this Managed Metadata Service Connection.

☑ This service application is the default storage location for Keywords.
☐ This service application is the default storage location for column specific term sets.
☐ Consumes content types from the Content Type Gallery.
☑ Push-down Content Type Publishing updates from the Content Type Gallery to sub-sites and lists using
    the content type.

FIGURE 3-16

Configuring PerformancePoint Services

PerformancePoint Services (PPS) is a SharePoint Server 2013 Enterprise feature that is used for building dashboards. It is particularly useful for integration with SQL Server Analysis Services. This section describes how to get the Service application going. This service application is optional. The service application is also covered with great fanfare in Chapter 8 with working examples.

Note that in order to properly connect this service application to SQL Server Analysis Services, you must also install ADOMD.NET v11 (which is interesting because the SharePoint prerequisite installer already installed v9 for you, and some situations require v10). In any case, install v11 before continuing. No reboot is required:

1.   Download the 64-bit version from `http://go.microsoft.com/fwlink/?LinkID=239662&clcid=0x409`.

2.   Run the download MSI.

3.   At the Welcome screen, click Next.

4.   Read the license, select "I accept the terms in the license agreement," and click Next.

5.   At the Ready to Install screen, click Install.

6.   At the Completing screen, click Finish.

Now that v11 is installed, create the service application. This part should be very familiar at this point:

1.   From the Manage service applications screen, click the New button in the Ribbon.

2.   From the menu, select PerformancePoint Service Application.

3.   For Name, enter **PerformancePoint Service**.

4.   Check the box for "Add this service application's proxy to the farm's default proxy list."

5. For Database Name, enter **PerformancePoint_Service_DB**. This time you are getting rid of the GUID and the spaces in the name. Spaces are even worse than GUIDs.

6. Scroll down to Application Pool and select Use existing application pool.

7. From the drop-down, select Default SharePoint Service App Pool.

8. At the bottom of the page, click Create.

9. After a minute a screen will pop up indicating that the service application was created successfully and specifying the additional steps you need to perform. Click OK.

Now start the service:

1. Switch to the IE tab for Services on Server.

2. Find PerformancePoint Service and then click Start to the right of it.

The service application is up and running. The last step you need to perform is to set up the unattended service account. To do that, however, you have to create the Secure Store service application first. Therefore, jump ahead to "Configuring the Secure Store" and do that. When you are done, come back here. Don't worry; this page will wait.

> **NOTE** *It might seem odd to have you jump ahead; the editors are very uncomfortable right now! However, I have taught it this way for years; alphabetical order is the correct order. You may just want to mark this page to return to after you've finished Chapter 8, as PPS is worthless without completing Chapter 8 anyway.*

You're back? Great. To set up the unattended service account, follow these steps:

1. From the Manage service applications page, scroll down and click PerformancePoint Service from the list of service applications you have created. Note you must click the top one in the list.

2. From the Manage PerformancePoint Services: PerformancePoint Service page, click PerformancePoint Service Application Settings.

3. For Unattended Service Account:, enter the User Name for the account you want to use for data connections. Typically you would create a regular domain user account dedicated to this role. In this example, use **Contoso\SP_PPS**. As you build out PerformancePoint applications, you will give this account permissions to your data sources as appropriate.

4. Enter your account's password for Password:.

5. Click OK.

That takes care of everything. If you want to confirm that the new application has been created, you can navigate back over to the secure store service. When you are done poking around, navigate back to the Manage service applications page.

Configuring the Search Service Application

Search is still the most awesome feature SharePoint provides — and while lucky Chapter 13, "Configuring and Managing Enterprise Search," is devoted to all things Search, before you can have fun with those things you need to create the service application. However, before creating Search, which is a required service application, you should be aware that there is an easy way and a right way. The easy way is to use Central Administration. If you go that route, you just specify a name and some application pools and it will provision it. The downside is you are left with databases with some nasty names, which are not readily fixable. It does work, however, so if you don't care about awful names go for it.

We disdain databases with bad names, however, so to create Search the "right" way you have to do everything with PowerShell. The following code example represents the mother of all scripts to perform the necessary magic. It should be run as administrator from the SharePoint 2013 Management Shell. The version shown here has been modified slightly from the script that Todd Klindt has made available at www.toddklindt.com/createsearch2013, which is based on work done by Spence Harbar, whose blog is at www.harbar.net. You can either download this script from Todd's SharePoint blog or type it all in. If you prefer to type it, note the following tips:

➤ You can skip any line that starts with a #, which is the PowerShell symbol for a comment.

➤ Make sure the second line of the following script contains your service application pool name. If you have been following along with this chapter, then the script is correct.

➤ Run this script on the server you want to be your primary search server. This script uses a variable to set the server name.

```
# Get App Pool - Make sure that is what your farm uses.
$saAppPoolName = "Default SharePoint Service App Pool"

# Search Specifics, we are single server farm
$searchServerName = (Get-ChildItem env:computername).value
$serviceAppName = "Search Service Application"
$searchDBName = "SearchService_DB"

# Grab the Appplication Pool for Service Application Endpoint
$saAppPool = Get-SPServiceApplicationPool $saAppPoolName

# Start Search Service Instances
Start-SPEnterpriseSearchServiceInstance $searchServerName
Start-SPEnterpriseSearchQueryAndSiteSettingsServiceInstance $searchServerName

# Create the Search Service Application and Proxy
$searchServiceApp = New-SPEnterpriseSearchServiceApplication -Name $serviceAppName
 -ApplicationPool $saAppPoolName -DatabaseName $searchDBName
$searchProxy = New-SPEnterpriseSearchServiceApplicationProxy -Name "$serviceAppName
 Proxy" -SearchApplication $searchServiceApp

# Clone the default Topology (which is empty) and create a new one and then
activate it
$clone = $searchServiceApp.ActiveTopology.Clone()
$searchServiceInstance = Get-SPEnterpriseSearchServiceInstance
New-SPEnterpriseSearchAdminComponent -SearchTopology $clone -SearchServiceInstance
 $searchServiceInstance
```

```
New-SPEnterpriseSearchContentProcessingComponent -SearchTopology $clone -
SearchServiceInstance $searchServiceInstance
New-SPEnterpriseSearchAnalyticsProcessingComponent -SearchTopology $clone -
SearchServiceInstance $searchServiceInstance
New-SPEnterpriseSearchCrawlComponent -SearchTopology $clone -SearchServiceInstance
$searchServiceInstance
New-SPEnterpriseSearchIndexComponent -SearchTopology $clone -SearchServiceInstance
 $searchServiceInstance
New-SPEnterpriseSearchQueryProcessingComponent -SearchTopology $clone -
SearchServiceInstance $searchServiceInstance
$clone.Activate()
```

The script takes several minutes to run, but when it is done Search is set up and ready to rock. Note that you should make two changes now that the service application is created: change the default content access account to a dedicated account and define a Global Search Center. Both changes can be made from the home page of Search Administration and are covered in Chapter 13, "Configuring and Managing Enterprise Search."

Configuring the Secure Store Service

The Secure Store Service is used for storing credentials for service applications such as PerformancePoint and by developers who need to make external data connections and need a location to map user credentials to other accounts. As an administrator you don't do much here, but this service application is required, so this section demonstrates how to create the service application and then generate an encryption key so it is ready to be used by service applications and developers.

Follow these steps to create the service application:

1. From the Manage service applications screen, click the New button in the Ribbon.

2. From the menu, select Secure Store Service.

3. For Name, enter **Secure Store Service**.

4. For Database Name, enter **Secure_Store_Service_DB** (again knocking that GUID off the end of the name).

5. Scroll down to Application Pool and select Use existing application pool.

6. From the drop-down, select Default SharePoint Service App Pool.

7. Leave the check box for Audit log enabled selected.

8. At the bottom of the page click OK.

9. After a minute a dialog will pop up indicating that the service application was created successfully. Click OK.

To start the service:

1. Switch to the IE tab for Services on Server.

2. Find Secure Store Service and then click Start to the right of it.

With everything up and running there is still a final task: you need to generate a key. Ensure that you keep track of this key, because if you ever restore the database you will need it.

1. Switch back over to the Manage service applications tab in IE.

2. In the list of service applications, click Secure Store Service. You should get in the habit of clicking the top one when two are listed, but in this case it actually doesn't matter which one you click.

3. You can ignore the red warning on the page, which is normal. From the Ribbon, click the Generate New Key button in the Key Management section.

4. Here you will be prompted for a new key. Enter the key twice and then click OK. In this example, pass@word1 works well. Like the farm passphrase, the key must meet certain requirements:

   ➤ It must contain at least eight characters.

   ➤ It must contain at least three of the following four character groups:

      ➤ English uppercase characters (A through Z)

      ➤ English lowercase characters (a through z)

      ➤ Numerals (0 through 9)

      ➤ Non-alphabetic characters: "! " # $ % & ' ( ) * + , - . / : ; < = > ? @ [\ ] ^ _ ` { | } ~

5. After a moment the screen will refresh and the New button will be an option. Success! Switch back to the Manage service applications screen by clicking Application Management ⇨ Manage service applications.

That does it. Your Secure Store is up and running. If you created the PerformancePoint service application earlier, now is the time to complete its configuration.

Configuring the User Profile Service

The user profile service application is the life blood of the user and social experience in SharePoint. Even if you feel tempted to skip this service application because you think you don't need it, every SharePoint farm should have the user profile service set up and configured. As described in Chapter 14, "Configuring User Profiles and Social Computing," there are numerous fun reasons why you should be excited about what this service application brings to the table. Although you need to perform a lot of little steps in order to get the service application provisioned properly before you can import profiles, if you did this with your SharePoint 2010 farm the process remains the same.

Before you provision the service application, you need to create a My Site web application and a My Site host site collection. You will create the web application as http://my.contoso.com:

1. In Central Administration, click Application Management from the left-hand menu.

2. Under Web Applications, click Manage web applications.

3. From the Ribbon, click New.

4. Ensure that the port is 80.

5. For Host Header, type in **my.contoso.com.** Remember that whatever you use for a host header needs to resolve in DNS.

6. For authentication, leave the defaults of Integrated Windows authentication and NTLM.

7. Scroll down to the Application Pool section and select Create new application pool.

8. For Application pool name, set it to Default SharePoint Web App Pool or any other fancy name you like.

9. In the Select a security account for this application pool, select Configurable.

10. From the drop-down menu, select Contoso\SP_WebApp. If that name doesn't appear in your list, then you need to return to the section, "Creating a Managed Account," as you skipped a step.

11. Scroll down to Database Name and set it to **WSS_Content_My.**

12. Leave everything else at their default, scroll to the bottom of the page, and click OK.

We'll defer a detailed explanation of those steps until later in the chapter when you create another web application. For now you just need to perform the preceding steps to get the user profile service application going.

Now create the host site collection:

1. When the Application Created page pops up, don't click OK. At the bottom of the window, in blue, is a link to Create Site Collection. Click that.

2. In the Create Site Collection dialog, enter **Contoso My Sites** for Title.

3. For URL, accept the default of http://my.contoso.com.

4. For Select a template, click the Enterprise tab.

5. From the list of templates, select My Site Host.

6. You should always have both a primary and a secondary site collection administrator. In this example, for primary User name: enter **Contoso\sp_install.** For secondary site collection administrator User name:, enter **Contoso\Administrator.**

7. Scroll to the bottom of the page and click OK. Then click OK again when the Site successfully created window appears.

For the web application, you need to also enable self-service site creation to allow users to create their own personal site:

1. In the list of web applications, click SharePoint - my.contoso.com80.

2. From the Ribbon, click Self-Service Site Creation.

3. For Site Collection, click On.

4. Leave all the other settings at their default and click OK.

Now that the web application and site collection are ready to go, you can create the actual service application. The main point here is to ensure you don't end up with ugly database names.

1. Return to Manage service applications (Application Management ➪ Manage service applications).

2. Click the New button in the Ribbon.

3. From the menu, select User Profile Service Application.

4. For Name:, enter **User Profile Service**.

5. For Application Pool, select Use existing application pool.

6. From the drop-down, select Default SharePoint Service App Pool.

7. Scroll down to Profile Database section and for Database Name enter **User_Profile_DB**. The purpose of this step is to eliminate spaces (which break your DBA's scripts) in your database names. Putting User_ in front of all the database names keeps them together in SQL Management Studio. This isn't required but it will prove handy.

8. Scroll down to Synchronization Database, and for Database Name enter **User_Sync_DB**.

9. Scroll down to Social Tagging Database, and for Database Name enter **User_Social_DB**.

10. Scroll down to My Site Host URL, and enter the URL of the site collection you created previously. In this example, use http://my.contoso.com.

11. Accept all the other defaults and click Create.

12. When the Site successfully created window appears, click OK.

Now start the service:

1. Switch to the IE tab for Services on Server.

2. Find User Profile Service and then click Start to the right of it.

For now you can ignore the User Profile Synchronization Service. That monster is covered in Chapter 14, "Configuring User Profiles and Social Computing." You will need to complete the steps in that chapter to import users into the profile store.

At this point you may be wondering how to disable the creation of personal sites by your users. It's a fair question, because personal sites can be a breeding ground for craziness if left unchecked. You don't want users using their personal site for work that should be stored and managed in a departmental location. For most new SharePoint deployments, this feature is best left to phase 2. Keep in mind that if you do disable personal sites, users will not be able to use the social features of SharePoint. If disabling the user's capability to create a personal site sounds like a good idea to you, then follow these steps:

1. From the Manage service applications page, click User Profile Service. Remember to click the first one in the list.

2. It is very likely you will get an error, depending on your farm topology and SharePoint's mood. If you do, then you need to do an IISReset on the SharePoint server hosting Central Administration. If that's unclear, then rebooting that server works also.

3. Now that you have found your way to the Manage Profile Service: User Profile Service page, find the People section and click Manage User Permissions.

As shown in Figure 3-17, by default Authenticated Users have the permission of Create Personal Site. To disable My Sites you would deselect that permission for both user groups and click OK. Note that this action also disables personal storage, which is what you likely wanted, but it also removes newsfeeds and followed content. Therefore, weigh this decision before doing anything rash.

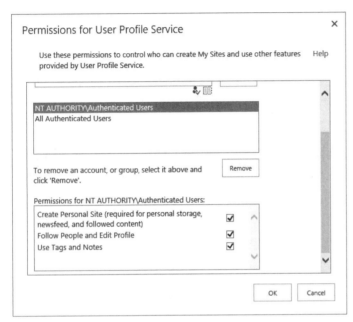

FIGURE 3-17

Again navigate back to the Manage service application page. Only three more service applications to go.

Visio Graphics Service

This fabulous service application enables users to embed Visio diagrams on the page so they can be viewed by someone without Visio and also provides for those diagrams to have external data connections that can be refreshed. This service application is considered one of the many SharePoint BI tools. It is not required in your farm unless you plan to use it, but is covered in Chapter 8.

Follow these steps to create this service application:

1. From the Manage service applications screen, click the New button in the Ribbon.

2. From the menu, select Visio Graphics Service.

3. For Name, enter **Visio Services**.

4. Scroll down to Application Pool and select Use existing application pool.

5. From the drop-down, select Default SharePoint Service App Pool.

6. Leave the "Create a Visio Graphics Service Application Proxy and add it to the default proxy group" checked and click OK.

Now start the service:

1. Switch to the IE tab for Services on Server.

2. Find Visio Graphics Service and then click Start to the right of it.

Now you are ready to use Visio services. Note that there are a few settings for tuning the diagrams you display and such like. In addition, if you plan to work with data connections, you will need to look at the Trusted Data Providers section and possibly provide an unattended account. Chapter 8 has an example and walks through the additional configuration.

Word Automation Service

The Word automation service is used to automate the conversion of Word documents into other formats. This isn't something that just magically happens; it generally requires developer involvement to make it all run well. As an administrator, you just need to create the service application, letting other people handle the automation. This service application is considered highly optional in your farm.

Follow these steps to create the service application:

1. From the Manage service applications screen, click the New button in the Ribbon.

2. From the menu, select Word Automation Services.

3. For Name, enter **Word Automation Service**.

4. Scroll down to Application Pool and select Use existing application pool.

5. From the drop-down, select Default SharePoint Service App Pool.

6. Check the box for "Add this service application's proxy to the farm's default proxy list."

7. At the bottom of the page click Next.

8. For Database Name, enter **Word_Automation_DB**.

9. At the bottom of the page click Finish.

Now start the service:

1. Switch to the IE tab for Services on Server.

2. Find Word Automation Services and then click Start to the right of it.

Work Management Service Application

This final service application, new to SharePoint 2013, is used to combine the tasks throughout your farm and beyond and then expose them on your My Site. The beyond might include Exchange 2013 or Project Server 2013. This cool feature enables users to keep track of all of those pesky tasks they have been overlooking (or ignoring).

Even better, no real configuration is required by the administrator; just create the service application as follows:

1. From the Manage service applications screen, click the New button in the Ribbon.

2. From the menu, select Work Management Service Application.

3. For Name, enter **Work Management Service**.

4. Scroll down to Application Pool and select Use existing application pool.

5. From the drop-down, select Default SharePoint Service App Pool.

6. Leave the box checked for "Create a proxy for this service application?" and click OK.

Now start the service:

1. Switch to the IE tab for Services on Server.

2. Find Work Management Service and then click Start to the right of it.

CREATING WEB APPLICATIONS AND MORE

Woo hoo! You have everything installed and a fully functional farm. Before you can invite users to the party, however, you need to create something for them to access — web applications, site collections, and webs. The first subsection takes a brief detour to ensure that these terms are clearly understood. Then you will walk through the steps to create these items.

Terminology

Don't skip this section. Even if you are quite certain you know all the terminology, humor us by reading this material. Even the most seasoned SharePoint "professional" can lack an understanding of exactly what each part of the SharePoint hierarchy represents.

Figure 3-18 is the SharePoint containment hierarchy. The main thing to understand as you look at the items is that a one-to-many relationship is reflected as you work down the list, whereas a many-to-one relationship is reflected as you work up the list. For example, a content database can (and often does) contain more than one site collection, but a site collection can only be located in one content database.

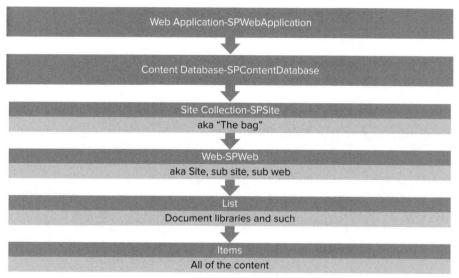

FIGURE 3-18

The most commonly misunderstood term is *site*, which end users often use when they actually mean web, and which developers often use when they actually mean site collection. This leads to utter chaos when it comes to troubleshooting or scaling your farm because they represent totally different things. As a best practice, never use the word "site," and take every opportunity to encourage your fellow SharePoint admins to do the same if you catch them using it. Remember site is a four letter word and should be treated as such.

Web Applications

It's easiest to think of a web application as the thing that lives in IIS. This is the address that your users will enter in their browser. Because it is something users will work with on a regular basis, you should try to choose a short, meaningful name. Names like http://portal.contoso.com or http://intranet.contoso.com work much better than a name like http://scificharacter.scifiplanet.scifigalaxy.local. You want to choose a name that is both memorable to your users and easy to type. Also, the temptation is to only use the NetBIOS name http://portal, but that can cause confusion in different ways later. Best practice is to use a fully qualified domain name from the beginning.

SharePoint 2010 introduced claims-based authentication, although many users continued to use the classic Windows authentication because they had no idea what the new method was or why they should care about it. In SharePoint 2013, claims-based authentication is now the standard. Indeed, when creating a web application using Central Administration, it's the only available option. The three seemingly different options — Windows claims, forms-based authentication (FBA), or Trusted Identity provider — are just different flavors of claims. Fortunately, this important topic is covered in detail in Chapter 6, "Claims Identity Management and Security."

Use the following steps to create the web application http://portal.contoso.com:

1. Return to the home page of Central Administration.

2. Under Application Management, click Manage web applications.

3. From the Ribbon, click New.

WHEN THE NEW BUTTON IS GRAYED OUT

On the Manage web applications page, generally speaking things work as expected; but every now and then SharePoint will throw you a curveball. For example, you might find the New button is grayed out. There are a couple of reasons why this might be the case. One is if you are not a local administrator on the SharePoint server but you are a farm administrator. In this case, you can access central admin but you don't have the Windows rights to create a new web application so SharePoint doesn't display the option. The second reason is harder to catch and happens only when you are opening Central Administration from the server itself. When you launch Central Administration using the shortcut on the Start menu, it actually runs psconfigui.exe, which launches IE and disables all the lockdown behavior. If you open IE and type in the URL for Central Administration, there is a good chance that the scripts you need run to enable the button will be grayed out. Moral of the story? Anytime you are troubleshooting the New button being grayed out, you should RDP into the SharePoint server and run the shortcut. That is the solution most likely to resolve the problem.

4. For Port, enter 80. You could use a different port but users often don't understand URLs with ports, so use the default of 80.

5. For Host Header, enter **portal.contoso.com.** You want to have more than one web application using port 80, so you have to make them all unique by using host headers.

6. In most scenarios, all the defaults until you get to Application Pool will be fine. For this section, select Use existing application pool.

7. From the drop-down, select Default SharePoint Web App Pool (Contoso\sp_webapp). If you don't have that application pool, return to the section, "Configuring the User Profile Service." In that section, you created the my.contoso.com web application, which should create the application pool.

8. In the next section, change the Database Name to **WSS_Content_Portal.** The idea here is to ensure that anyone looking at the list of database names can easily identify the purpose of each web app. A simple naming convention saves a lot of headaches later.

9. Accept all the other defaults and click OK.

10. After a moment you will get a pop-up window indicating that the application has been created. Click OK to close the window.

Now your web application and content database have been created. Because you just created the host header portal.contoso.com, you need to ensure that you have a DNS entry that resolves portal .contoso.com to your SharePoint server. As a word of caution, use a host or a record in DNS. Don't use an alias or CNAME, as those just lead to trouble.

Because you are using portal.contoso.com to access the server named Server, if you try to open that URL from the SharePoint server itself you will get an authentication error. This is because of a security mechanism called the *loopback check* that protects you from reflection attacks. There are two ways to work around the issue, both of which are covered at http://support.microsoft .com/kb/896861. You can review the article and choose which method you prefer. Method 1 is very specific and disables the check just for names you specify, whereas method 2 turns off the security feature entirely. The choice is yours but you need to select one for SharePoint to be happy.

To make it easier to manage SharePoint in a multi-server farm, it is recommended that you modify the hosts file on each machine so that each web application points to the local server. You can find the file in c:\ windows\system32\drivers\etc\ and it is named just hosts with no extension. Using Notepad, modify it to add an entry to point 127.0.0.1 to portal.contoso.com as shown in Figure 3-19. If you have a problem trying to save the file, that is because you have the user access control still enabled. In that case, you need to run Notepad as an administrator.

For an automated way to change both the hosts file and the loopback setting using a PowerShell script, see Todd Klindt's blog post at http://www.toddklindt.com/ edithosts.

```
File  Edit  Format  View  Help
# Copyright (c) 1993-2009 Microsoft Corp.
#
# This is a sample HOSTS file used by Microsoft TCP/IP for Windows.
#
# This file contains the mappings of IP addresses to host names. Each
# entry should be kept on an individual line. The IP address should
# be placed in the first column followed by the corresponding host name.
# The IP address and the host name should be separated by at least one
# space.
#
# Additionally, comments (such as these) may be inserted on individual
# lines or following the machine name denoted by a '#' symbol.
#
# For example:
#
#      102.54.94.97     rhino.acme.com        # source server
#       38.25.63.10     x.acme.com            # x client host

# localhost name resolution is handled within DNS itself.
#      127.0.0.1       localhost
#      ::1             localhost

127.0.0.1             portal.contoso.com
127.0.0.1             my.contoso.com
```

FIGURE 3-19

Site Collections and Webs

Now that you have a web application sitting there, you need to create a site collection so it has something to serve up. Site collections are the unit of scale in SharePoint. The easiest way to think of a site collection is as a bag, because it is really just a boundary or container. It is not actually content users can touch. The reason why this "bag" is so important is because it determines a lot about how your information is stored.

Site collections are a storage boundary and they are stored in one and only one content database. They cannot span multiple databases. When you create a site collection it is created in a database, where it will stay unless you manually move it. If, for example, you want to limit all your content databases to 40GB because that is the largest size you are comfortable with, then you need to ensure that no site collection is larger than 40GB. Similarly, if you have multiple site collections (and everyone does), then you would need to apply quotas to those site collections to ensure that the sum of the site collections doesn't exceed your 40GB database limit. For instance, if you had 10 site collections, then you would set your quotas to 4GB per site collection.

Site collections are the only objects in SharePoint to which you can apply a storage quota. If you want to limit a user to storing only 10GB of content in a particular document library, there is no way to do that. You would have to set that entire site collection to a 10GB limit. If you have two document libraries and you want to give each one 10GB of storage, then you have to ensure that each document library is in its own site collection.

Even if you have no intention of holding users to limits, quotas are generally recommended for all site collections, as they serve as a checkpoint and prevent runaway site collections. If a user calls and says that he is getting warnings or errors because he has met his quota, it is a simple process for you to increase his quota, and it gives you a chance to ask, "So what are you doing with SharePoint that you need so much storage space?" It would be good to know if he is just backing up his MP3 collection to SharePoint.

Site collections also serve as an administrative boundary. Site collection administrators are a special group of users who have complete power over the site collection without necessarily having any access to other site collections. The Site Settings page contains an entire menu of configuration options that only a site collection admin can set. If you have two groups — such as HR and Accounting, for example — in the same site collection and one of them approaches you because they need to administer one of these special settings, you have to do some rearranging. If you make Nicola from Accounting a site collection administrator, then she can fully administer the account site as needed but she also has full control over the entire site collection, including the HR web. You need to instead move the Accounting web to its own site collection and then make Nicola an administrator there.

Site collections are also boundaries for out-of-the-box functionality such as navigation and the various galleries. This can be a drawback of many site collections. Out of the box, it is impossible to enforce consistent, self-maintaining navigation across site collections. The galleries such as the themes, Web Parts, lists, and solutions are all scoped at the site collection level. For example, if you need a list template to be available to multiple site collections, then you have to manually deploy it to each one.

Site collections also serve as security boundaries. The All People list and the various SharePoint groups are all scoped at the site collection level and are not accessible for reuse outside of the site collection.

Inside of site collections you have one or more "webs." A web is the object that is referred to throughout the user interface as a site. It can also be called a subsite or a subweb. Again, because the term "site" can be very confusing, whenever possible refer to these as webs. This is the first object users can actually touch. You can apply security to it, and it contains all the user content. Each web has its own *lists* (libraries are just a special type of list) and all of those lists store *items*, which refers to the actual content, such as documents and contacts.

All of that is said to remind you not to take site collections lightly. Create them deliberately and often because they will keep you out of trouble down the road.

Follow these steps to create that first site collection:

1. Return to the home page of Central Administration.

2. Under Application Management, click Create site collections. Avoid the temptation to make fun of the fact that the link says Create site *collections* even though you can only create one site collection using the link.

3. Confirm at the top of the page that Web Application says http://portal.contoso.com; if not, you can click the link to change web applications.

4. For Title and Description, enter something helpful or creative. In this example, use Contoso Portal for Title and leave Description blank.

5. For URL:, you need to choose the root site collection by selecting the / from the drop-down. Creating this site collection first is a requirement.

6. The Select experience version drop-down is interesting. You can choose 2013 or 2010. For this example, choose 2013. Keep this setting in your memory bank. It is a new twist to SharePoint that you might find handy down the road.

7. In the Select a template section, choose Team Site.

8. For Primary Site Collection Administrator User Name, enter **Contoso\sp_install.** In a real-world environment you would use an account that makes sense for the site collection you are creating.

9. For Secondary Site Collection Administrator User Name, enter **Contoso\administrator.** Again, in your environment use a better account. The key point is that every site collection should have both a primary and a secondary owner.

10. While every site collection in the world should have a quota, you haven't learned about them yet so you can leave this at No Quota for the moment.

11. Double-check all your settings and click OK.

After a minute or so you will get a message indicating that the site collection was successfully created. Click the link to dive into the awesomeness that is SharePoint 2013.

SUMMARY

What a fun ride. If you made it through this whole chapter then congratulations are in order. You now have a properly configured SharePoint farm that you can build on for years to come. Hopefully with enough practice working through this chapter you will become more comfortable with how the farm works. This will make your life of supporting and troubleshooting SharePoint much easier. Speaking of understanding how things work that is what the next chapter is all about. Digging into the underpinnings of those service applications you just created.

Understanding Service Applications

WHAT'S IN THIS CHAPTER?

➤ The history of services in SharePoint

➤ Service application basics

➤ Administering service applications

➤ Multi-tenancy in SharePoint 2013

Beginning with Microsoft SharePoint 2010, services in SharePoint have been provided by service applications. SharePoint 2013 utilizes the same services architecture, though some of the services are new or modified. Service applications seem simple enough on the surface: The installation wizard deploys them for you in most cases, and the services are automatically available within your farm. Harnessing the full power of this architecture takes a little more effort. Consider, for example, Search, which you can make available in your farm simply by clicking through the wizard but can also be offered as a service that can be consumed by other farms.

In order to truly understand how the different parts of SharePoint's architecture interact, you need to first understand the terminology used, which includes familiar words such as *application*, *service*, *proxy*, and *proxy groups*. Mastering the terminology is critical to getting the most out of SharePoint, so pay close attention to the figures in this chapter, which help to put the terms and concepts in context.

This chapter provides the fundamental information you need to understand in order to implement this flexible architecture, including the basics of Central Administration as well as the deeper options exposed by PowerShell cmdlets, which have their own unique lingo.

Once you have mastered SharePoint's terminology and PowerShell has become an old friend, you will tackle the topic of multi-tenancy, which enables you to set up an instance of a service application in a way that enables each site collection to behave as though it is using a dedicated service, rather than a shared resource. It might sound overwhelming at this point, but working through the examples will help you grasp these important concepts in SharePoint. Sometimes the most challenging things are actually the most fun.

A HISTORY OF SERVICE APPLICATIONS IN SHAREPOINT

To truly understand the purpose and function of service applications it is helpful to look at the way services used to be provided in SharePoint. Microsoft Office SharePoint Server 2007 (MOSS) used a different service model called the Shared Service Provider (SSP). As the name implies, this provider hosts multiple services, such as Search, User Profiles, My Sites, the Business Data Catalog, and so on. The problem with this model was that each SSP contained the whole set of services, and a web application could only be associated with one SSP. In practice this meant that in order for a company's department or group to have an independent Business Data Catalog, that group had to have its own SSP, which in turn meant duplicating all the services. In terms of resources, maintaining two SSPs in a large environment was very resource expensive.

For example, imagine you have an intranet for your entire organization at `http://intranet`. Human Resources determines that it needs to isolate its Business Data Catalog from everyone else for security and privacy reasons. With the SSP model, the only way to do this is to create a new web application for HR, such as `http://hr`, and a new SSP to which it can be associated. This means HR can no longer use the other services provided by the SSP associated with the intranet web application, such as Search. HR now has its independent BDC, but in order to use search in the `http://hr` web application, you also have to configure Search in the HR SSP. As described earlier, that's because each SSP contains an instance of each service, and a web application can only be associated with one SSP at a time, as shown in Figure 4-1.

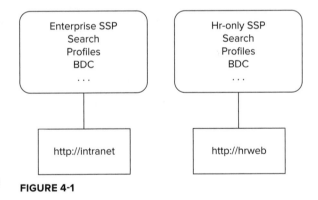

FIGURE 4-1

The introduction of service applications in SharePoint 2010 eliminated that constraint. Individual services were able to stand on their own as service applications. Using service applications, meeting a requirement such as HR's in the preceding example is a snap: Create a new BDC service application — named HR-Only BDC, for example, create the HR web application at `http://hr`, and associate it with all the service applications used by the intranet *and* with the HR-Only BDC. That's right; HR can continue to have access to the same BDC as the rest of the intranet and access to its own private BDC as well, as shown in Figure 4-2.

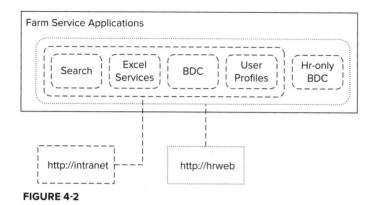

FIGURE 4-2

Another important change was made along with the introduction of service applications. SharePoint 2010 Foundation was included in the service model, whereas previously Windows SharePoint Services (WSS) had no SSPs for sharing services at all. Foundation had fewer service applications available, but the mechanisms were the same. This is the same for SharePoint 2013, with all versions from Foundation to Enterprise sharing the same service application architecture but different product levels having different service applications available. Having all versions of SharePoint using the same structure is a big benefit for administrators because it eliminates inconsistencies between products.

Service applications can be thought of as shared service providers that have been divided into their individual components. This creates a much more flexible architecture that can be configured in nearly infinite ways. The cost of flexibility is usually complexity, and service applications are no exception. On the bright side, this chapter provides all the details you need to manage and understand that complexity.

SERVICE APPLICATION FUNDAMENTALS

The preceding section is just a simplified overview of how services work in SharePoint, of course. Before you can effectively put service applications to work, it is important to understand the connections and relationships of services to web applications. The following sections explore the glue that binds service applications. While conceptually it is easy to see that service applications provide capabilities to the web applications, in reality there is a lot going on to make those connections work. To effectively troubleshoot and support the SharePoint farm going forward, you need to learn those details.

TOMATO OR TAMAHTO?

There are some key pieces of service applications that use different terminology depending if you are looking at TechNet, Central Administration, or PowerShell. The key to it is not to over think things. For the sake of this conversation anything that refers to a group is the same thing, anything that refers to a connection is just that. For example:

➤ Service application connection group = proxy group = group

➤ Service application connection = proxy = connection

The best plan is don't think too hard; the obvious answer is the right answer.

The Connection Structure

Service applications are not offered directly to web applications, as you might have assumed from the preceding section. Instead, a series of connections and associations determine how services are offered, as shown in Figure 4-3.

SharePoint web applications are associated with service application *groups*. These groups are composed of one or more service application *connections*. Service application connections act as a bridge, admitting the service applications into the service application groups. A service application consumes one or more service application *services*, some of which may have databases for storage. If this sounds confusing, the following sections should help clarify how these components are integrated.

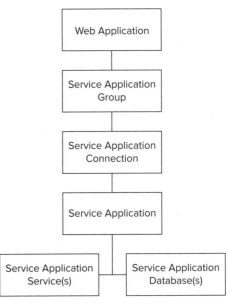

FIGURE 4-3

Service Application Groups

You already know what a web application is at this point. The service application *group* specifies how services are associated with a web application. When you created the web application in the example in Chapter 3, you used SharePoint's default service application group (see Figure 4-4). Notice that all the check boxes are grayed out when the default group of connections is chosen. You cannot edit the default group in this dialog as you create a web application.

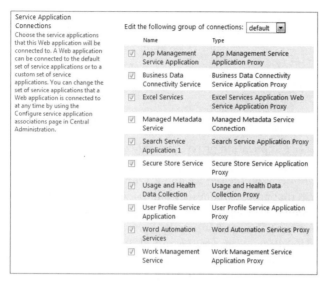

FIGURE 4-4

The default group is automatically provisioned for you. If you used the initial Farm Configuration Wizard, then all the service applications are part of this group. When you manually create a service application, you can choose to include it in the default group or not by using the check box shown in Figure 4-5.

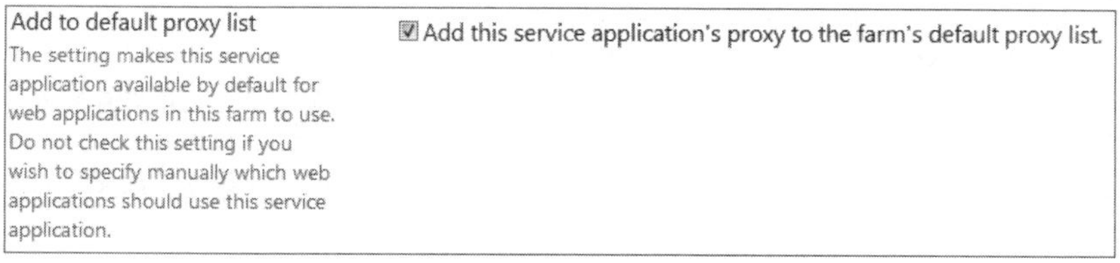

FIGURE 4-5

This group enables you to associate a web application with a collection of service applications. If the default group doesn't meet your needs, you can you can use the [custom] option to specify which service applications you want to use for the web application. Keep in mind that although [custom] appears in the group drop-down menu, you cannot reuse this "group." When you create a web application and specify [custom], you choose the service applications available to that web application. If you then create a second web application and select [custom], you will not see the service applications you chose for the first web application selected. Each usage of [custom] is a unique instance, and not reusable.

Proxy groups or *application proxy groups* are other terms you may hear used for service application groups. This is how they are referred to in the SharePoint 2013 Management Shell and in the object model (OM).

> **NOTE** *To create a group you can reuse, you need to use the SharePoint 2013 Management Shell and run the* `New-SPServiceApplicationProxyGroup` *cmdlet. You will learn more about this cmdlet in the section "Service Application Administration" later in the chapter.*

Service Application Connection

The *service application connection* (or service application proxy; remember tomato/tamahto) is what most users are thinking about when they create the service application from Central Administration. This connection is the path between the service application, along with its web service(s), and the service application group that accepts requests from the web application. In other words, the web application is associated with a service application group that in effect is saying, "Here are all the service applications you can use." When the web application wants profile information, for example, it knows what User Profile web services to call. If you look in IIS, you will see a website named SharePoint Web Services. If you drill through this list, you can find these service application connections and their web services. They will be named and listed as a 32-character GUID, not a logical name.

Like the service application group, the service application connection is known by a few other names, including *proxy* and *application proxy*, especially when dealing with the SharePoint 2013 Management Shell and the SharePoint object model. Recall from the preceding section that service application groups are sometimes referred to as proxy groups. Avoid using these older terms, as "proxy" is one of those ambiguous, overused IT words that often cause confusion.

Service Application

The destination of this complicated connection matrix is the *service application*, which provides the service you need. The service application *groups* and service application *connections* serve to organize and access the service applications. When you create a service application, the accompanying service application connection is created with it. Some service applications require storage; the databases they use are covered next.

Service Application Database(s)

As mentioned earlier, not all service applications have a storage requirement, For example, Excel Services does not store data; it only facilitates the display of data stored somewhere else, so it doesn't need a database. Conversely, Search has intensive storage needs, so it has multiple databases. The Managed Metadata service needs only one database to do its job.

Of special note for SharePoint 2013 is the new Access Services. Access Services as they existed in SharePoint 2010 still exists as a separate service application named Access Services 2010. The new Access Services (without the year suffix) is used by creating individual Access sites, also called *apps,* in SharePoint 2013. Each Access app stores its information in a SQL database, so if you create 20 Access apps you will have 20 databases. Note that you must have a SQL Server 2012 server to host these Access app databases. These databases don't need to be on the same SQL Server as the rest of the SharePoint databases. See Chapter 8, "Configuring SharePoint 2013 for BI," for more information on configuring Access Services.

When a service application needs a database, you are prompted to provide a name if you are manually creating the service application; for some service applications, such as Search, the databases will be automatically created and named. Each database is unique to an individual service application. For example, if you create an Enterprise BDC service application and an HR-Only BDC service application, you will have two unique databases. You can use a single database and service to host data that needs to be kept logically separate, but it requires additional planning and the use of PowerShell cmdlets. You'll learn more about that later. Given a choice, don't create a database name with an ugly GUID on the end.

Table 4-1 shows the service applications that require a database or databases.

TABLE 4-1 Service Applications Requiring Database(s)

SERVICE APPLICATION	HAS DATABASE(S)	CROSS-FARM CAPABLE
Application Management Service [new in 2013]	Yes	
MachineTranslation Services [new in 2013]	Yes	Yes
Access Services [new in 2013]	Yes	
Access Services 2010		
Business Data Connectivity Service	Yes	Yes
Excel Services Application		
Managed Metadata Service	Yes	Yes
PerformancePoint Service Application	Yes	
Search Service	Yes	Yes
Secure Store Service	Yes	Yes
State Service	Yes	
Subscription Service	Yes	
Usage and Health Data Collection Service	Yes	
User Profile Service	Yes	Yes
Visio Graphics Service		
Word Automation Services	Yes	
Work Management Service		

Service Application Service(s)

Sometimes called services, *service application services* are located in Central Administration on the Application Management page. Under Service Applications, click the Manage services on the server link. The link is also on the System Settings page.

The services are the true workhorses in the stack. When you make a request to Excel Services, for example, the request goes through the groups, connections, and applications we have already discussed to finally get to the service application service. The service application deals with the hand off of the request, but all the actual processing and work is done by the Excel Calculation Services running on one or more servers in your farm.

These services are one of the key ways you scale service applications. If, due to heavy usage, you find that you need more performance from Excel Services, then you could start the Excel Calculation Services on another server in your farm. That way, when you make requests of the Excel service application, it will distribute the request between both of the servers running the services. You can continue to add servers running the service until you achieve your performance target.

Each service application handles this load balancing of the services in its own way. Excel Services has a setting to control the load balancing. Managed Metadata just does the load balancing on its own.

> **NOTE** *Search load balancing is covered in Chapter 13, "Configuring and Managing Enterprise Search."*

Tying It Up with an Example

This section looks at an example using two scenarios that incorporate the default service application group and a custom application group, respectively. Figure 4-6 provides a schematic diagram of these scenarios, which apply the concepts described in the preceding sections.

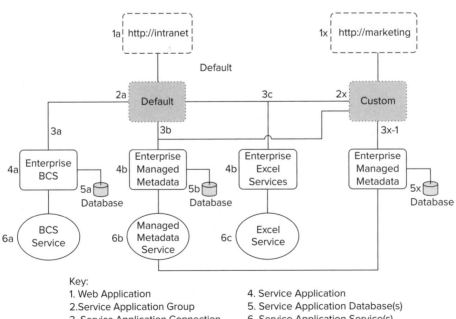

Key:
1. Web Application
2. Service Application Group
3. Service Application Connection
4. Service Application
5. Service Application Database(s)
6. Service Application Service(s)

FIGURE 4-6

Looking first at the left side of the diagram, this company has a SharePoint web application, `http://intranet` (1a), that is associated with the default (2a) service application group. The default service application group contains three service applications: Enterprise BDC (4a), Enterprise Managed Metadata (4b), and Enterprise Excel Services (4c). These are connected to the default service application group by the three service application connections (3a, 3b, 3c). (Note that these connections are not something that administrators can actually touch through Central Admin; they are created when the service application is created and they enable the web applications to talk to the associated service applications.) The Enterprise BDC stores its content in its database (5a) and uses the Business Data Connectivity service (6a) running on the server. You can also see that the Enterprise Managed Metadata service application has a database (5b) and a service (6b). Finally, Enterprise Excel Services does not have a database but is using the Excel service (6c). This process is relatively straightforward.

Now consider the slightly more complicated scenario on the right side of the figure. The company has a second web application at `http://marketing` (1x). That web application is using the [custom] (2x) service application group. Now for the twist; there are still three service application connections, but the connection (3b) to the Enterprise Managed Metadata (4b) and the connection (3c) to the Enterprise Excel Services (4c) are reused, demonstrating that a service application can be connected to multiple service application groups. Enterprise Managed Metadata continues to use the same database (5b) and service (6b) as before, because it is the same service application. The same is true for Enterprise Excel Services and its service (6c).

Note one final twist: Marketing has a unique service application, Marketing Managed Metadata (4x) that is connected (3x) to the [custom] group. This service application has a unique database (5x) for its storage, but it uses the same Managed Metadata service (6b) that the Enterprise Managed Metadata service application did.

If you grasp these relationships, then you understand the essential behavior of service applications — maybe not everything, but you are certainly off to a solid start.

Connecting Across Farms

Once you understand the service applications and all their proxies in your farm, the next logical step is to add more connections. Some service applications are capable of being published and then consumed across different SharePoint farms. Even more impressive is the fact that none of the service applications except the User Profile service application require the two SharePoint farms to be in trusted active directory domains. In fact, a SharePoint 2010 farm can even consume services from a SharePoint 2013 farm, though this capability is limited to the service applications and features available in SharePoint 2010, of course. For example, SharePoint 2010 can't consume the App Management service from SharePoint 2013.

Before you can publish or consume the service applications between two farms, you have to establish a farm *trust*, which is done by using the SharePoint Management Shell to create and register certificates between the two farms. This is covered in greater detail in the section "Service Application Administration" later in the chapter.

After the farm trust is configured, you can access the publishing farm and select the service application you want to publish. Once it is published, you get a URL for accessing the published service.

From the consuming farm, you simply connect to the published service by providing the URL. Then the connected service application can be added to a service application group, and it will provide services just as if the service application were part of the farm. Figure 4-7 shows an example of four farms at work.

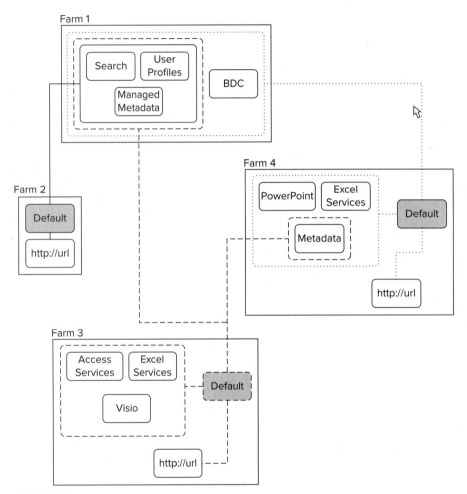

FIGURE 4-7

Farm 1 introduces a concept that hasn't been discussed yet: the *enterprise services farm*. The enterprise services farm highlights the advantage of the service application architecture over the monolithic SSP model. Typically used only in large companies, this type of farm is created and maintained exclusively to provide services to other SharePoint farms throughout the organization. This way, the services farm can be optimized for hosting services and can be maintained in the same manner. For example, a Search index might contain several million items, requiring several days to do a full crawl, and hours to do an incremental crawl. In order to do this efficiently, you need to optimize your hardware for Search. If you have three SharePoint farms and each maintains its own Search service application, it would be very expensive to do a lot of repetitive crawling of content. Instead, a much better solution would be to maintain the index in one farm and just consume the service from the other farms.

Farm 2 is a simple farm for publishing content, maybe hosting just informational websites or similar content. In this farm, the demand for service applications is low, and all the service applications it does require are provided by the enterprise farm. Therefore, this farm actually has no local service applications and is just optimized for displaying SharePoint content.

Farm 3 is a collaboration farm, and a busy place. This farm has demands for all types of service applications — some are consumed from farm 1, and others are hosted locally. The locally hosted service applications are those not capable of being published across farms, so they must reside in the farm where they are needed. Note that the Managed Metadata service application from farm 4 is being consumed. Other than that, there is nothing special about this scenario other than the flexibility of consuming service applications from multiple farms.

Farm 4 is very similar to the collaboration farm in terms of purpose. It is hosting its own web applications and consuming local and remote service applications. Additionally, it has published the Managed Metadata service application for consumption by farm 3. Although all three farms are using the default group in this example, this isn't a requirement. You very well could have configured the [custom] group in any of the farms to consume the cross-farm service applications.

Service Applications As a Framework

You have probably noticed by now that all the service applications act slightly different. This is because service applications are really a collection of individual services built to plug into a framework. The advantage of this framework is that anyone can plug into it. Third-party vendors and developers can use it to add their functionality to SharePoint 2013 just as they did with SharePoint 2010; but instead of needing to create a custom third-party application to administer their added SharePoint functionality, developers just plug right into Central Administration, providing administrators with a consistent experience. From an administrator's perspective, there is no difference between these service applications and one provided out of the box with SharePoint 2013.

SERVICE APPLICATION ADMINISTRATION

Now that you have a working knowledge of the fundamentals, it is time to put that knowledge to work. In this section, you will learn how to operate all the knobs and switches that enable you, as a SharePoint administrator, to do your job. Your job encompasses everything from actually creating service applications to managing their security and properties with the GUI or PowerShell. Sounds like a grand time.

Creating a New Instance of a Service Application

In Chapter 3, you set up your farm and included all the service applications needed to get it off the ground. That was a great way to quickly get up and running; but now you are ready for prime time, and HR is screaming for its own instance of the Managed Metadata service application. They would like to name it HR-Only Metadata. The following steps describe how you would create it for them:

1. Open Central Administration.

2. In the Application Management section of the home page, click the link to Manage service applications.

3. Here you can see all the service applications currently available in your farm. In the Ribbon, click the New button and select Managed Metadata Service, as shown in Figure 4-8.

4. For Name, enter **HR-Only Metadata**.

5. Confirm you have the correct database server listed.

6. For Database Name, choose something that will help you identify it, like HR_Only_Metadata_DB. (Remember that it is best to avoid spaces in a database name.)

FIGURE 4-8

WHEN EVERYONE WANTS THEIR OWN MANAGED METADATA SERVICE

If other divisions in the company also request their own Managed Metadata service, you can use what Microsoft terms a *partitioned service application*, which keeps data and processing separate despite being in a single process and database. This is discussed in greater detail later in the "Multi-Tenancy in SharePoint 2013" section.

NOTE *If you want to host this database, or any other database, on a different SQL Server, you merely need to ensure that permissions are set up. Once that is done, you can just enter the new server's name. Typically, the permissions you need are found in your farm administrator account. This is the account you specified when you ran the SharePoint Products and Technologies Configuration Wizard (the gray one) when the farm was first configured. The SQL Server rights this account needs include dbcreator and securityadmin on the existing or new SQL Server that you are trying to use. In addition, the SQL Server needs to meet the minimum SharePoint requirements for SQL Server.*

7. Most of the time you will choose the "Use existing application pool" radio button. From the drop-down menu, select your default app pool, as shown in Figure 4-9.

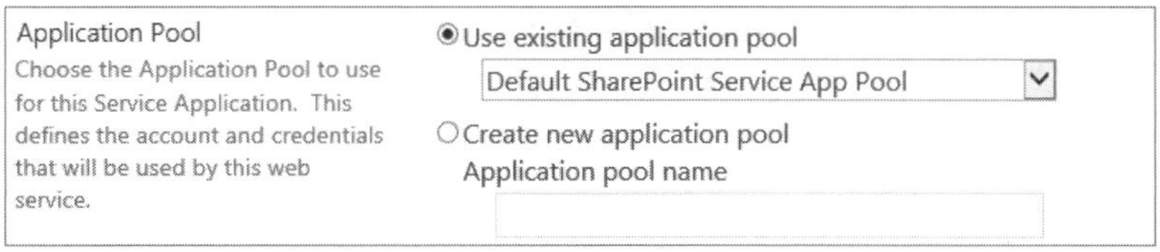

Application Pool

Choose the Application Pool to use for this Service Application. This defines the account and credentials that will be used by this web service.

⦿ Use existing application pool

Default SharePoint Service App Pool ▾

○ Create new application pool
Application pool name

FIGURE 4-9

> **NOTE** *For optimal performance, the current best practice is to keep all your service applications in one application pool. This may change as the product evolves, but it makes the most sense for now. Application pools consume a great deal of resources, and performance testing has shown that you get the best results when all your service applications are in one application pool.*

8. At the bottom of this dialog are two options regarding the content type hub and reporting syndication errors. Leave these two options alone for now.

9. The last check box, "Add this service application to the farm's default list," is checked by default. For clarity's sake, they mean Default Proxy Group. Leave it as is. Later in the "Managing Service Application Groups" section you will learn how to change this setting after the fact, if necessary.

10. Leave all the other settings at their default and click OK. After the service application is created, you will be returned to the Manage service applications page.

Using the Ribbon to Manage Service Applications

Service applications are built by developers and then bolted into SharePoint through the service application framework, which enables developers to use the Ribbon to manage their service applications. However, because there is no hard set of rules about how the buttons on the Ribbon must be used, you will see a variety of behaviors. This section describes the primary uses of the various Ribbon commands.

When looking at the various management screens and options, you will see that some service applications use all the Ribbon buttons, while others use almost none. This is the power of flexibility at work. After reading this section, you will be able to apply the information provided here to each service application in order to determine exactly how it works.

The Operations Group's Buttons

Now that you have your HR-Only Metadata service application, you need to be able to administer it. The first thing to take a look at is its properties. To do that, click once to the right of the service application to highlight it, which enables the available options on the Ribbon, as shown in Figure 4-10. (If you are taken to the Manage service applications screen after clicking, then you accidentally clicked the name of the service application. Press the Back button in your browser and try again.)

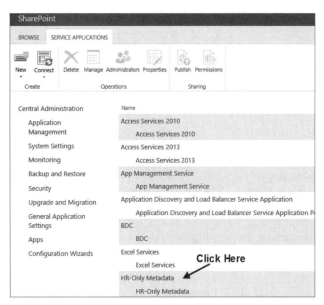

FIGURE 4-10

Now click the Properties button on the Ribbon. That invokes a window showing the settings you specified when you created the service application. Most service applications allow you to access this screen. Here, you can check information (such as what database name you used) or adjust settings if you change your mind about something (such as the application pool). When you are done looking around, click Cancel to return to the Manage service applications screen.

Click the Manage button on the Ribbon. This will take you to the page for managing the actual service application. In the case of HR-Only Metadata, you are now taken to the screen for defining terms and all those other fun things you can do with managed metadata. All the service applications that have something to manage have their own manage interface. This is just another piece of the framework.

In short, use Properties to look at or change settings you configured when creating a service application. Use Manage to access the service application and do whatever it is your service application was designed to do.

Setting Up a Delegated Administrator

Now that you have found this awesome screen for managing the managed metadata terms, wouldn't it be great if you could give someone in HR access to add all of them? Well, you are in luck. You can easily add someone as a delegated administrator:

1. Ensure that you are still at the Manage service applications screen in Central Administration.

2. Click to the right of HR-Only Metadata.

3. Click Administrators from the Ribbon.

4. Enter the name of the HR user and click Add (for example, Contoso\NicolaY). You will then see the user's name in the middle section. Make sure the name is highlighted.

5. In the bottom section, click the box to the right of Full Control and click OK. Figure 4-11 shows an example.

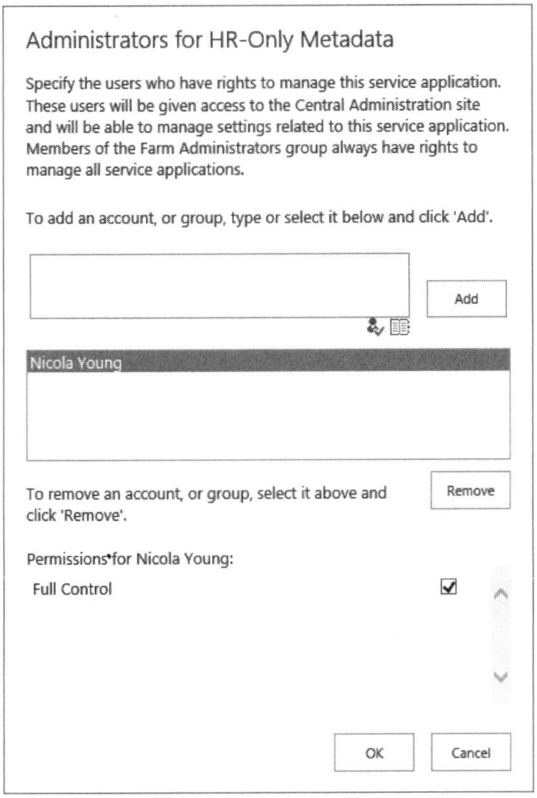

Administrators for HR-Only Metadata

Specify the users who have rights to manage this service application. These users will be given access to the Central Administration site and will be able to manage settings related to this service application. Members of the Farm Administrators group always have rights to manage all service applications.

To add an account, or group, type or select it below and click 'Add'.

	Add

Nicola Young

To remove an account, or group, select it above and click 'Remove'.   Remove

Permissions for Nicola Young:

Full Control   ☑

OK   Cancel

FIGURE 4-11

Now the HR user is a delegated administrator. Delegated administrators can access Central Administration, but they will see only those service applications to which they have been granted permissions. If Contoso\NicolaY logs into Central Administration, she will see something similar to what is shown in Figure 4-12.

That's a lot of white space. Security trimming has removed everything to which she doesn't

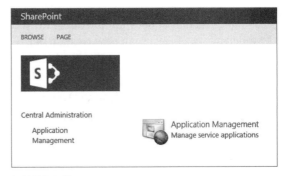

FIGURE 4-12

have access, which is clearly most of page. If she clicks the Manage service applications link, she will see what is shown in Figure 4-13.

As a delegated administrator, she can see only the one service application to which she has access; and when she clicks on it, she only has the option of Manage. This level of trimming enables you to delegate the management of specific components without compromising security.

FIGURE 4-13

If you were to log back in as the real administrator and check the permissions, you would see that the user has been added to a special site collection security group called Delegated Administrators. This makes it simple to find everyone who has been granted access. Note, however, that even if you remove users from managing all the service applications, they are not removed from this Delegated Administrators group. Therefore, be sure to do a little cleanup from time to time if you often change delegated administrators.

Managing Service Application Proxy Groups

Now that you know how useful these groups are, this section demonstrates how to manage and consume them. After a brief walk through the GUI tools, we'll take a look at some of the hardcore things you can do with the SharePoint 2010 Management Shell.

Using Your Mouse to Manage Groups

Put that mouse to work with the following steps:

1. Open Central Administration.

2. Click Application Management.

3. In the Service Applications section, click Configure service application associations.

The Service Application Associations page displays a list of all your service applications and the application proxy group with which each one is associated. This is where all that terminology you studied comes in handy. You already know that application proxy group means service application groups, and that application proxies really mean service application connections. The nice thing about this page is you can now click on one of the proxy groups to change its connections if necessary. For example, if you wanted to remove HR-Only Metadata from the default group, this is how you would do it:

1. Click on the proxy group Default.

2. Deselect HR-Only Metadata.

3. Scroll down the page and click OK.

Now all the web applications associated with the default service application group will no longer have access to the HR-Only Metadata service application.

When you first accessed the Configure Service Application Associations screen, you may have noticed that because you have multiple Managed Metadata service applications in your farm, one appears as [default] and the other(s) appear as [set as default], as shown in Figure 4-14.

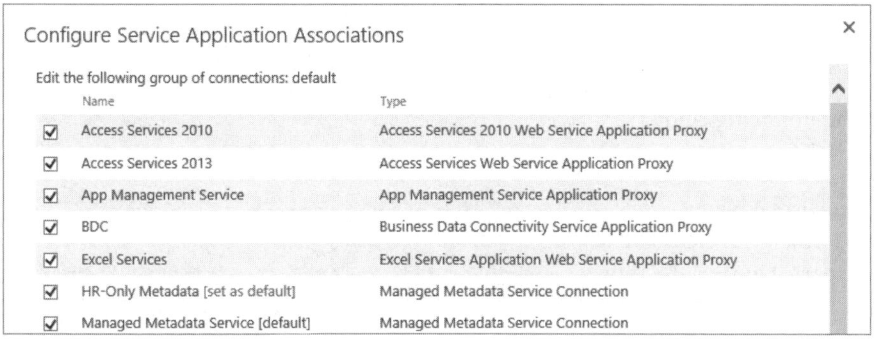

FIGURE 4-14

This is because you can associate multiple Managed Metadata service applications with one connection group, so you need to specify which one should be the default. Both are equally accessible; one of them just needs to be presented to the user first. You will see the set as default option with other service applications, as applicable.

The interface for manipulating the service application connections in a connection group is the same whether you are modifying the default, [custom], or even a custom connection group created with the SharePoint 2013 Management Shell.

Using the Keyboard to Manage Groups with PowerShell

As with just about everything related to SharePoint 2013 administration, anything you can do in a GUI you can do better with Windows PowerShell cmdlets in the SharePoint 2013 Management Shell. This section covers some of the key cmdlets you can use for service applications, but it skips over all the details about using the SharePoint 2013 Management Shell for administrative tasks, as Chapter 7 contains that information. If you are new to Windows PowerShell, you might find it easier to put this section on hold until you have had a chance to dig into Chapter 7.

Depending on which components you have installed, there are more than 100 different cmdlets related to service applications. Because it would be impossible to cover all of these without doubling this book's page count, this section takes a look at a few of the more important ones. To discover most of the cmdlets, run the following command from the Management Shell:

```
Get-Command *serviceapplication*
```

Have fun with the list that is returned. You will notice that each service application, such as Excel Services, has its own cmdlets, which you can use to provision a new service application without the need to use Central Administration.

Creating a New Service Application Group

After spending all that time learning about service application groups, you were no doubt dismayed to learn that you cannot create reusable groups in Central Administration. As you might guess, you can create your own group using PowerShell.

The cmdlet you need is `New-SPServiceApplicationProxyGroup`, for which you just need to provide the `-name` property. The command is as follows:

```
New-SPServiceApplicationProxyGroup -name YourCustomGroup
```

Now you have a group called YourCustomGroup. The group is empty, of course, so now you can add a connection to it. To do so, you first need to get the ID of the connection you want to add. To achieve that, run the following cmdlet:

```
Get-SPServiceApplicationProxy
```

This will return the DisplayName, TypeName, and Id, which is a GUID. The Id is the important part. Figure 4-15 shows example output. Keep in mind that your GUIDs will be different. (At least they should be; if they are not, you have bigger problems than this book can solve.)

To add the Excel Services connection to the group, you would run the following command:

```
PS C:\Users\sp_install> Get-SPServiceApplicationProxy

DisplayName              TypeName              Id
-----------              --------              --
Business Data Con...     Business Data Con...  4178678e-2e49-4228-b42c-7c4617186832
Word Automation S...     Word Automation S...  f949078e-a588-4380-9aa3-cc0f88fa0870
HR Only Metadata         Managed Metadata ...  7db3e4fb-4f2e-4997-96fd-c0eb00680090
Managed Metadata ...     Managed Metadata ...  f98711eb-e85d-4b9e-8faa-a4326faa8472
Secure Store Service     Secure Store Serv...  82fb729b-46c9-414e-ae6f-928593aec692
Search Service Ap...     Search Service Ap...  5127fa56-7f12-446c-8635-1fa013062585
Work Management S...     Work Management S...  a6fe3afa-0d3b-425a-aa72-7b183a51cce6
App Management Se...     App Management Se...  09bafcf5-6564-41fa-ac1e-40c16e8727c1
Application Disco...     Application Disco...  bcdac5fe-aa70-49c7-9b7b-5871d551bd48
User Profile Serv...     User Profile Serv...  b3f02f2c-0c45-41c7-b8aa-529e379fadd8
Excel Services           Excel Services Ap...  f5064277-c045-4984-be7e-215752552596
Usage and Health ...     Usage and Health ...  6e6fa6db-bc97-4e9d-a88a-f63d78e7b8f7
```

FIGURE 4-15

```
Add-SPServiceApplicationProxyGroupMember YourCustomGroup -member
F5064277-c045-4984-be7e-215752552596
```

Remember that you need to enter the GUID for your service application proxy. If you are thinking that was a very long process to merely add a service application connection, you're right.

An Easier Way to Add Connections

Let's cheat. Now that you have the new group, you can return to the GUI and do a little clicking to add the other connections to it. Navigate back to Central Administration ➪ Application Management ➪ Configure service application associations. Confused? When you get to that page, you will not see YourCustomGroup. You won't see it on this page until you associate it with a web application. To change a web application's service application group association, follow these steps:

1. From the Application Management page, select Manage web applications.

2. Select the web application for which you want to change associations.

3. From the Ribbon, click Service Connections.

4. From the drop-down, select YourCustomGroup. Scroll down the page and click OK.

Now go back to Configure Service Application Associations. You should see YourCustomGroup. Click it. A simple web interface will appear for selecting the service application connections you want to include in the group.

Publishing a Service Application

Now it's time for some more fun with Windows PowerShell cmdlets. Publishing a service application and consuming it isn't too terribly difficult and can mostly be done through the UI. The tricky part is setting up the farm trusts and properly securing the Application Discovery and Load Balancer service applications. Once you knock out those two pieces, the rest is a breeze.

Setting Up the Farm Trust

Follow these steps to set up the farm trust:

1. On the publishing server, create a folder at `c:\PubCerts`.

2. From the publishing server, open the SharePoint 2013 Management Shell. To get the certificate, type the following line and press Enter:

   ```
   $rootCert = (Get-SPCertificateAuthority).RootCertificate
   ```

3. To export the certificate, type the following line and press Enter:

   ```
   $rootCert.Export("Cert") | Set-Content C:\PubCerts\PublishingRoot.cer
   -Encoding byte
   ```

4. Copy the `c:\PubCerts` folder from the publishing server to the consuming server.

5. On the consuming server, create a folder at `c:\ConsumerCerts`.

6. From the publishing server, open the SharePoint 2013 Management Shell.

7. To get the certificate, type the following line and press Enter:

   ```
   $rootCert = (Get-SPCertificateAuthority).RootCertificate
   ```

8. To export the certificate, type the following line and press Enter:

   ```
   $rootCert.Export("Cert") | Set-Content C:\ConsumerCerts\ConsumingRoot.cer
   -Encoding byte
   ```

9. To get the STS certificate, type the following line and press Enter:

   ```
   $stsCert =
   (Get-SPSecurityTokenServiceConfig).LocalLoginProvider.SigningCertificate
   ```

10. To export the STS certificate, type the following line and press Enter:

    ```
    $stsCert.Export("Cert") | Set-Content "C:\ConsumerCerts\ConsumingSTS.cer"
    -Encoding byte
    ```

11. Copy the `c:\ConsumerCerts` folder to the publishing server.

12. Still on the consuming server, to load the publishing server's certificate, type the following line and press Enter:

    ```
    $trustCert = Get-PfxCertificate "C:\PubCerts\PublishingRoot.cer"
    ```

13. To set up the trust using the certificate, type the following line and press Enter:

    ```
    New-SPTrustedRootAuthority PublishingFarm -Certificate $trustCert
    ```

14. Return to the Management Shell on the publishing server.

15. To load the consuming server's certificate, type the following line and press Enter:

```
$trustCert = Get-PfxCertificate "c:\ConsumerCerts\ConsumingRoot.cer"
```

16. To set up the trust using the certificate, type the following line and press Enter:

```
New-SPTrustedRootAuthority Collaboration -Certificate $trustCert
```

> **NOTE** *If you have multiple farms you want to trust, make sure in steps 13 and 16 that you use unique names for each farm for PublishingFarm and Collaboration. Those names are used to identify the actual trust so you cannot reuse them when setting up other farms to trust this farm. If you are only setting up one trust you can just ignore this.*

17. To load the consuming server's STS certificate, type the following line and press Enter:

```
$stsCert = Get-PfxCertificate "c:\ConsumerCerts\ConsumingSTS.cer"
```

18. To add the STS certificate to the trust, type the following line and press Enter:

```
New-SPTrustedServiceTokenIssuer Collaboration -Certificate $stsCert
```

19. Return to the Management Shell on the consuming server.

20. Type the following line and press Enter:

```
Get-SPFarm | Select Id
```

21. Record that GUID for use later.

22. Return to the Management Shell on the publishing server.

23. To get the security object for the Application Discovery and Load Balancer service application, type the following line and press Enter:

```
$security = Get-SPTopologyServiceApplication |
Get-SPServiceApplicationSecurity
```

24. To get the farm's claim provider object, type the following line and press Enter:

```
$claimProvider = (Get-SPClaimProvider System).ClaimProvider
```

25. To set up the new claim principal for the consuming farm, type the following line and press Enter:

```
$principal = New-SPClaimsPrincipal -ClaimType "http://schemas.microsoft.com
/sharepoint/2009/08/claims/farmid"
 -ClaimProvider $claimProvider
 -ClaimValue <Type the ID from Step 21, don't include the <>>
```

26. To give that principal permission in your publishing farm to the Application Discovery and Load Balancer service application, type the following line and press Enter:

```
Grant-SPObjectSecurity -Identity $security -Principal $principal
-Rights "Full Control"
```

27. To set the access just given, type the following line and press Enter:

```
Get-SPTopologyServiceApplication | Set-SPServiceApplicationSecurity
-ObjectSecurity $security
```

That completes the process of establishing a trust between the two farms so that the publishing server can serve up service applications to the consuming farm. If you want to look at the trusts or possibly remove one, you can do that through the GUI by navigating to Central Administration ➪ Security ➪ Manage trust.

Publishing a Service Application

For this task, you could dive back into PowerShell or you could use the GUI in Central Administration. Let's be "efficient" (i.e., lazy) and use the GUI. For this example, you will publish a Managed Metadata service application:

1. On the publishing server, open Central Administration.

2. Navigate to Application Management ➪ Manage service applications.

3. Click to the right of the service application you want to make available.

4. In the Ribbon, click Publish.

5. On the Publish Service Application page, check the box for "Publish this Service Application to other farms."

6. For the Publish URL, copy all of the string that begins with "urn:" and ends with ".svc." For example, it will be similar to the following:

```
urn:schemas-microsoft-com:sharepoint:service:ac40e8f87daa43d9bec93f9fa99360c7
#authority=urn:uuid:de389296913c4f00b7970f50ea298fd4&authority=
https://server:32844/Topology/topology.svc
```

7. Scroll down the page and click OK.

8. Click to the right of the service application.

9. From the Ribbon, click Permissions.

10. Enter the farm ID of the consuming farm (refer to step 21 in the previous section, "Setting Up the Farm Trust"). Click Add.

11. Highlight the remote farm: <Your Farm ID>.

12. For permissions, check the box to assign the permissions you wish to give to the remote farm. The permissions available will vary according to the service application being published.

13. Open Central Administration on the consuming farm and navigate to Application Management ➪ Manage service applications.

14. From the Ribbon, click Connect.

15. Enter the URL for the service application you want to access from step 6 in this section. Click OK.

16.   Click the service application name so that it is highlighted in yellow.

17.   You can specify whether this service application should be included in the default service application group. When you are done, click OK.

18.   Either accept the default connection name or enter your own. When you are finished, click OK.

19.   At the Success screen, click OK.

You can now work with the service application just as if it were part of your farm. The first time you work through this process, take your time; it is easy to make a small mistake that results in hours of troubleshooting.

MULTI-TENANCY IN SHAREPOINT 2013

No discussion about service applications would be complete without digging into the multi-tenant capabilities that have been improved from SharePoint 2010. Under normal circumstances, the multi-tenant discussion usually pertains to hosted environments where a SharePoint farm is providing services to any number of different companies; but as you will see in this section, the concept of multi-tenancy applies directly to the enterprise as well.

Managing Service Application Groups

In SharePoint 2007, the walls of security and the isolation of data and services went along the lines of web application to site collections to webs. If you need a refresher, check out the terminology section in Chapter 3, "Installing and Configuring SharePoint 2013." Beginning with SharePoint 2010, it became possible to create a new segregation layer of data and services between the application layer and the associated site collections. This segmentation is possible through the use of *site subscriptions*. Site subscriptions enable you to group together site collections that are part of the same web application. Site subscriptions are a logical group of site collections that can share settings (in the Subscription Settings database), features, and service data. Site subscriptions are identified with a subscription ID. The subscription ID is used to map services, features, and sites to tenants, and to partition service data by tenant. Note the following characteristics of site subscriptions:

➤   A site can be a member of only one site subscription at a time. This prevents any conflicts with licensing schemas.

➤   There is no Central Administration interface for managing site subscriptions. Management must be handled through PowerShell, including creating, managing, and removing sites from a site subscription.

➤   A site can only join a site subscription(s) in the same web application. Sites can't join a site subscription(s) associated with other web applications.

➤   Site subscriptions can span multiple content databases.

Once you have a site subscription associated with site collections, the site collections can consume data from service applications. While this concept is not necessarily new, what is new is that some of these service applications can be provisioned such that their functions and data are kept separate from other site collections (tenants) that may be consuming that service application. SharePoint 2010 and 2013 refer to this type of service application as a *partitioned service application*. For instance, if Enterprise Search were provisioned as a partitioned service application and associated with two site subscriptions, then search results from subscription A would never be returned to subscription B. Note also that no changes or additions were made to the number of databases required to support this capability. SharePoint merely segments the content within the single database (see Figure 4-16).

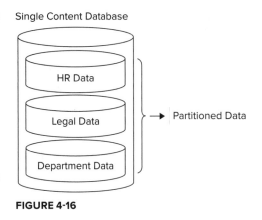

Single Content Database

HR Data

Legal Data

Department Data

→ Partitioned Data

FIGURE 4-16

Although non-partitioned service applications can be created with Central Administration or PowerShell, the latter is required to provision a partitioned service application. When creating a partitioned service application in PowerShell, you only need to add the `-Partitioned` or `-PartitionMode` switch depending on the service application.

Some service applications do not lend themselves to being partitioned, such as those that do not store user-specific data. Table 4-2 shows which service applications within SharePoint 2013 can be partitioned.

TABLE 4-2 SharePoint 2013 Service Application Partitioning

CAN BE PARTITIONED	CANNOT BE PARTITIONED
User Profiles (using Profile Synchronization)	User Profiles (using AD Import)
Managed Metadata	Excel Services
Business Data Connectivity	Access Services
SharePoint Search	Access Services 2010
Secure Store Service	Visio Service
Search	State Service
Machine Translation Service	Work Management Service
Word Automation Service	PerformancePoint
	Usage and Health
	App Management Service
	Subscription Settings

Another set of capabilities that was previously managed at the web application layer was Features. When a feature was installed and activated at a web application layer, it was automatically available for activation at the site collection level. Beginning with SharePoint 2010, you can group features together into what are called *feature packs*. Feature packs are logical groupings of features that are then made available for activation to a site subscription by an administrator of that site subscription.

SharePoint 2013 is smart enough to prevent the use of web parts that are part of a feature that is not part of a site subscription.

Once a site subscription is created and sites are associated with it, the sites are managed through a site template called a Tenant Administration site. It's called this because a hosted customer (or department) is referred to as a *tenant*. The Tenant Administration site gives the tenant administrator full administrative rights over the site collections, including permissions to create new sites if self-service site creation is enabled.

Creating a Site Subscription

When you are ready to start working with SharePoint in the hosting mode, keep in mind that nearly all your system administration will be done through PowerShell, as these new features are not built into the SharePoint Central Administration console. This is true for creating site subscriptions, feature packs, and partitioned service applications, and provisioning Tenant Administration sites. The PowerShell cmdlet to create a new site subscription is as follows:

```
New-SPSiteSubscription
```

When building your site subscriptions, using variables for your commands enables them to be reused and/or nested within other cmdlets. For example, to create and view a new site subscription, use the following:

```
$SiteSub = New-SPSiteSubscription
```

Once you have the subscription, you need to get the site collection or site collections you want to add to the subscription into a variable.

To add a single site collection to a variable, use the following:

```
$TargetSite = get-spsite http://portal.contoso.com/sites/marketing
```

To instead add all site collections within a web application to a variable, use this:

```
$TargetSite = Get-SPWebApplication http://portal.contoso.com | Get-SPSite
```

Now that you have your site collection(s) in a variable, use the following to add their subscription:

```
$TargetSite | ForEach-Object{Set-SPSite -Identity $_ -SiteSubscription $SiteSub}
```

To view all the site collections that are now part of the site subscription, just type the name of the variable:

```
(Get-spsitesubscription $SiteSub).sites
```

From here you could create the Tenant Administration site using the PowerShell cmdlet `new-spsite`, identifying the site template as `tenantadmin#0`:

```
New-spsite –url http://portal.contoso.com/sites/tasite -template "tenantadmin#0"
-owneralias domain\username -sitesubscription $SiteSub
```

> **NOTE** *As previously mentioned, site collections aren't the only SharePoint artifacts that can be grouped; features can be grouped into Feature packs.*

Another benefit to site subscriptions is that usage analysis data and logging data are also segmented, like the user data. This enables the IT pro to troubleshoot and debug based on a specific site subscription. In addition, segmenting the usage data enables a hosting company or enterprise that's using a charge-back model for IT services to charge according to usage based on data, processes, or the number of users.

Multi-Tenant Use Cases

The use of multi-tenancy in the traditional hosted services scenario should be clear at this point. For example, suppose a hosting company decides that it would like to be able to sell SharePoint services to its customers. All the customers will be different individuals or companies that want assurance that their information is kept separate from the other sites hosted on the common infrastructure. Windows SharePoint Services (WSS) 3.0 included mechanisms to keep a customer's content separate from other customers' data, but it lacked the capability to separate processing and data from additional services such as Enterprise Search.

These customers would need to be provisioned using an STSADM command and be given site collections that would be held in shared web applications. The hosting company was also bound to using WSS because of the common shared service provider (SSP) found in MOSS. One of the challenges that the SSP created in this specific scenario was with Enterprise Search. Enterprise Search was designed to index all content associated with that SSP. The query service would then provide results to users when requested. The challenge specific to this scenario is the very real possibility of exposing customer A's data to customer B via Enterprise Search, as MOSS lacked the capability to segment the data based on site collection. Adding SSPs was not an option because the number of SSPs that can be provisioned in a single farm is limited.

The newer service application architecture fixes this through service application partitioning as discussed throughout this section. Partitioning creates secure boundaries between information and processing based on site subscriptions, making it impossible to expose customer A's data to customer B. As previously mentioned, partitioning must be done when the service application and proxy are created. Now let's apply the concept of partitioning to the enterprise.

Partitioning in the Enterprise

Just as it would in a hosted scenario, a large enterprise needs to handle data and services in a manner similar to the hosted world. Consider, for instance, managed metadata. There are terms within the organization that need to be controlled by one central group and consumed by the entire organization. Other terms ought to be defined and managed by individual corporate divisions or departments. The same holds true for Enterprise Search. A partitioned Enterprise Search service application would enable content from one department to remain wholly separate from content in other divisions, as depicted in the general council example shown in Figure 4-17.

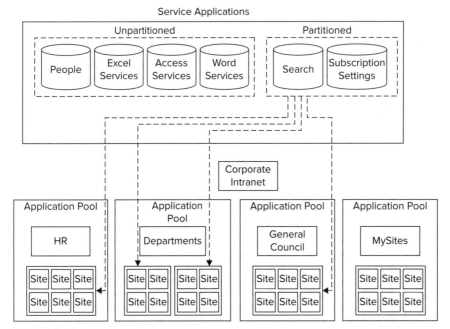

FIGURE 4-17

The capability to segment this data and to create feature packs gives both the multi-tenant hoster as well as the Enterprise customer an opportunity to offer different tiers of services to their customers. The hosting company can provision a single farm and provide SharePoint Foundation, SharePoint Server Standard, and SharePoint Server Enterprise products. To take things one step farther, they could also layer on additional third-party tools to enhance their product offering and more easily manage the provisioning and billing of those services.

From the Enterprise customer's point of view, they can provide multiple versions of SharePoint to their users on a single farm. For instance, only half of a company's 10,000 employees may need SharePoint Foundation capabilities. The remaining user community may need SharePoint Server Enterprise features. Individual SharePoint farms can now have multiple licensing schemas associated with them in a way that is easier to manage and control. In this case, only 5,000 users would need SharePoint Server Enterprise licenses, while the remaining users would use SharePoint Foundation licensing — and this solution would be perfectly acceptable to Microsoft.

The additional capabilities provided by the service application architecture, as well as the partitioning features, provide additional scalability previously not available in SharePoint. For instance, as Enterprise Search grows in content size and usage, it can now be segregated into its own SharePoint farm created for the purpose of providing Search services to the content farm(s). These types of farms, known as *service application farms*, provide services and data to other SharePoint farms; they are not directly consumed by users. Figure 4-18 shows an example.

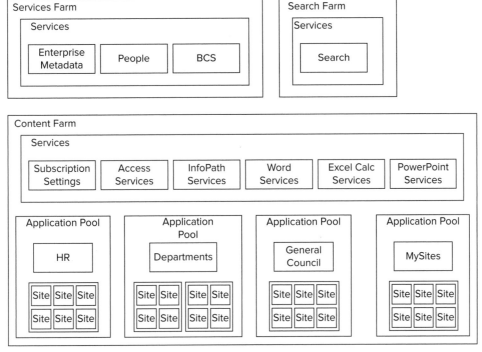

FIGURE 4-18

SUMMARY

The service application framework provides a vast improvement over the shared service provider model offered previously. This method for sharing resources and managing services is scalable, flexible, and robust. As a SharePoint administrator who needs to make your farm sing, it is relatively easy to scale from a small, simple farm all the way up to multi-server farms with just a few simple mouse clicks or keyboard taps. In addition, if you start to feel like even all of that flexibility isn't enough, you can also incorporate the use of multi-tenancy.

Now that you are familiar with all the options for connecting your web applications to service applications, even from remote farms, you can rest easy. Although you can configure SharePoint in a seemingly infinite number of ways, this chapter has demonstrated how you can harness and manage its impressive capabilities. You have Central Administration for the easy tasks, and a large set of Windows PowerShell cmdlets for taking things to the next level.

5

Upgrading to SharePoint 2013

WHAT'S IN THIS CHAPTER?

➤ Supported upgrade methods

➤ Upgrade best practices

➤ Upgrading content and services

Getting SharePoint 2013 installed and configured is a good first step, but your farm needs some content in order for your users to really fall in love with it. SharePoint 2007 and SharePoint 2010 wormed their way into most company's hearts, so you probably already have good SharePoint content out there just aching to be upgraded to your new SharePoint 2013 farm. Although the upgrade process has a lot of moving parts, with the proper planning and execution you can perform a smooth upgrade using one of the methods described here without getting any of your fingers caught in the upgrade gears. This chapter covers everything you need to know to upgrade your content from SharePoint 2010 to SharePoint 2013.

UPGRADE CONSIDERATIONS

Each new version of SharePoint presents a new upgrade experience. Some parts are better, some parts are worse. Upgrading with SharePoint 2013 is the same way. This part of the chapter covers what works and what doesn't work.

What You Can Upgrade

There are many pieces of SharePoint 2010 you may need to upgrade. It's not all about getting those PowerPoint presentations into your new farm. Here are some different things you can upgrade.

Content

Like the versions of SharePoint that preceded it, it's tougher to stump SharePoint 2013 when you're upgrading content. It handles customizations better; and in situations where it can't figure out what to do, it doesn't simply fail, it gives you a meaningful error message, and then moves on gracefully. Troubleshooting is covered later in the chapter, should you need to employ it. SharePoint 2013 is also more lenient about which version of SharePoint 2010 you upgrade from. In fact, it will upgrade from any of them. When upgrading from SharePoint 2007 to SharePoint 2010, the SharePoint 2007 farm had to be at least at Service Pack 2 (SP2). This caused some real problems for SharePoint 2007 farms that were unstable. If they weren't already at SP2, upgrading the farm to that, just to immediately upgrade to SharePoint 2010, was painful and risky. That requirement was the source of much trouble and gnashing of teeth by SharePoint administrators. Fortunately, our cries were heard by the folks at Microsoft and they benevolently omitted any restrictions regarding which build your SharePoint 2010 farm needed to be at in order to be upgraded to SharePoint 2013. These are a few examples of what's good. Now, on to what's not so good.

When upgrading from SharePoint 2003 to SharePoint 2007 you had three options: upgrade SharePoint 2003 in place to SharePoint 2007; attach your SharePoint 2003 content databases to a SharePoint 2007 farm and upgrade your content; or do a side-by-side, or gradual upgrade, whereby both SharePoint 2003 and SharePoint 2007 were installed and running on the same hardware. You would then gradually move your site collections from SharePoint 2003 to SharePoint 2007. After the last one was upgraded, you would uninstall SharePoint 2003 and you had a happy SharePoint 2007 farm. The side-by-side approach was the most popular, but there was an option for almost all upgrade scenarios.

When SharePoint 2010 came out we lost the side-by-side upgrade option, and many tears were wept. This method had been an admin favorite, as it provided a great back-out option. If the upgrade to SharePoint 2007 went awry, the SharePoint 2003 version of the site collection was still there. However, we SharePoint admins are a hearty bunch. We took our upgrade lemons and made some tasty SharePoint 2010 lemonade. After wiping our tears, most SharePoint admin adopted the database upgrade method to get SharePoint 2007 content into SharePoint 2010. It worked pretty well, but it required most companies to buy all new hardware. Great for Dell and HP, not so great for SharePoint customers. Then SharePoint 2013 was released.

We lost one upgrade option, the gradual upgrade, when SharePoint 2010 came out. We lost a second upgrade option, the in-place upgrade, when SharePoint 2013 came out. That's the bad news. The good news is you won't have to spend a lot of time deciding which upgrade method is best for you. Your only option is the database attach method. The "Upgrading Content" section later in this chapter will walk you through that process along with all its ins and outs.

Service Applications

Since you cannot upgrade your SharePoint 2010 farm, you might assume it's not possible to upgrade your service applications. For companies making heavy use of service applications, such as Managed Metadata, Search, and User Profile Service, this could be a problem. Those service apps represent a lot of information, and even worse a lot of the SharePoint administrator's time. All is not lost. There are six SharePoint 2010 service applications whose databases can be attached to a SharePoint 2013 farm:

➤ Business Connectivity Services

➤ Managed Metadata

➤ Performance Point

➤ Secure Store

➤ User Profile Service

➤ Search

Later, this chapter will walk through the mechanics of upgrading each of those service apps. This functionality is good in that it enables you to upgrade the service apps without having to upgrade the entire farm, and all the junk that comes along with that. You can pick and choose the parts to upgrade, and leave the rest behind.

Customizations

Customizations are the bane of any upgrade. If everyone just uploaded Word documents to SharePoint, upgrades would be as smooth as butter. That wouldn't be any fun, though. SharePoint is a great platform to customize, and you could make a wide range of customizations to SharePoint 2010. Some will upgrade well, some not so well. This section covers the ones that will upgrade without much fuss. The problem children are covered later in the chapter.

There are nearly an infinite number of ways to customize SharePoint, so it can be hard to determine whether it's going to cause you upgrade-related heartburn or not. As a general rule, any customization you do from the web browser should upgrade just fine. This could be a customization to a list, such as adding a column or two, or creating the view that displays your list just right. It might also be adding some pages to your site, or adding Web Parts to the Web Part pages your site already has. If you made the change inside the browser, chances are good that SharePoint knows what you did, and can handle upgrading it to SharePoint 2013.

The next step in customizing SharePoint 2010 was using the much-maligned SharePoint Designer (SPD). SPD gets a bad rap. Like any tool, whether it's used for good or evil depends heavily on whose hands it is in. Some customizations made to SharePoint 2010 in SPD are very innocent, such as tweaking the properties of a page or Web Part. Other SPD customizations are evil, such as putting Web Parts on pages outside of Web Part zones. In other words, whether your SPD customization will easily upgrade depends to a great extent on how evil is it. If your users have used SPD to customize pages in SharePoint 2010, that needs to be thoroughly tested before the site collection is upgraded in your production SharePoint 2013 farm. You can do this in a test SharePoint 2013 farm, or by using an evaluation site collection in your production SharePoint 2013 farm. Evaluation site collections are covered later in this chapter in the "Upgrading Site Collections" sections. If you determine that an SPD customization won't upgrade at all, or upgrades incorrectly, you can use the Reset to Site Definition option in Site Settings to delete the offending customizations.

The final step of SharePoint customizations involves busting the scariest tool of all: Visual Studio. If it can't be done in the browser, and it can't be done in SharePoint Designer, if you try hard enough you can probably do it in Visual Studio. As mentioned earlier, the more complicated a customization, the more likely it is to cause problems during upgrade. Like the old saying goes, "complexity is the enemy of stability"; and it doesn't get much more complex in the SharePoint world than Visual Studio.

There were two supported ways to introduce custom code in SharePoint 2010: farm solutions and sandbox solutions. Both types of solutions are supported in SharePoint 2013, so at a high level everything should work when it's upgraded. It's when you get down into the weeds that the trouble begins.

In SharePoint 2010, sandbox solutions were solutions that were uploaded as WSP files to a site collection. From there, webs in that site collection can use the functionality that the sandbox solution provides. That could be Web Parts, branding, lists, or any number of other things. Because sandbox solutions live in a WSP file that is stored in a document library, they are in the same content database as the content, and therefore come along for the ride during upgrade. You don't need to take any special steps to upgrade them, they'll just fall in line and work.

The only concern is the code they use. SharePoint 2013 does a pretty good job of understanding SharePoint 2010 API calls and translating the differences in their object models, but it is possible to stump it. There are also some things that have been removed from SharePoint 2013, or just flat out don't work. Because sandbox solutions are so seamlessly upgraded, it's easy to get complacent and not test them adequately. Don't let yourself fall into that trap or your users will be very cranky when things don't work correctly. Similarly, because SharePoint 2010 sandbox solutions are so effortlessly upgraded, it's easy to convince yourself to not spend any time looking at the code to see if there's a better way to do it in SharePoint 2013. However, after your developers or you have gone through some SharePoint 2013 development training, take some time for a good thorough code review of all your solutions. If you don't have time for formal training, at least read Chapters 10 and 11 to get a handle on the new development landscape. Then crack those sandbox solutions open in Visual Studio and see if there are ways to make them run better in SharePoint 2013.

There have been some discussions about sandbox solutions and their relationship to SharePoint 2013. To quote Facebook, "It's complicated." One of the first public announcements about sandbox solutions in SharePoint 2013 stated that they were deprecated — a fancy way of saying that they work now but might not work in future versions. This scared a lot of people, as sandbox solutions were introduced in SharePoint 2010, so it looked like they were going away as quickly as they were introduced. Later, Microsoft clarified its stance, saying that the new SharePoint App model was the recommended way for users to add functionality to SharePoint 2013, and that sandbox solutions were just deemphasized. Regardless of the official word, SharePoint 2010 sandbox solutions work just fine in SharePoint 2013. If their functionality can be done through a SharePoint app, you should consider it.

The other way to extend SharePoint 2010 was with farm solutions. Like their sandboxed brethren, they upgrade pretty smoothly for the most part. Microsoft clearly invested a lot of time to ensure that SharePoint 2013 is backwardly compatible with SharePoint 2010 code. To see how deeply it has integrated support for SharePoint 2010, you can even create a new site collection in SharePoint 2010 mode in SharePoint 2013. When SharePoint 2013 executes code, it evaluates it to determine the version of SharePoint for which it was written. After it has determined that, it looks in different locations for assemblies and other resources. This enables SharePoint 2013 to better handle SharePoint 2010 code without sacrificing flexibility in native SharePoint 2013 code.

Unlike sandbox solutions, farm solutions were not stored in the content databases of the site collections that used them. They're scoped at the farm level, so they are stored in the farm's Config database. Because you can't upgrade your SharePoint 2010 farm to SharePoint 2013, you'll need to manually install the necessary farm solutions in SharePoint 2013 . Hopefully you have all the installation files, normally WSP files, on a file share somewhere. If so, copy them over to one of the servers in your SharePoint 2013 farm and install them using the same instructions you used when you installed them in SharePoint 2010.

EXTRACTING YOUR FARM SOLUTIONS FROM SHAREPOINT 2010

If you don't have all the WSPs handy, your upgrade is not doomed. It is possible to extract all the farm solutions from your SharePoint 2010 farm using PowerShell. Of course it is!

Run the following PowerShell statement on a server in your SharePoint 2010 farm:

```
(Get-SPFarm).Solutions | ForEach-Object{$var = (Get-Location).Path +
 "\" + $_.Name;
     $_.SolutionFile.SaveAs($var)}
```

Using this statement, PowerShell will enumerate all the farm solutions in your farm and save them as WSP files in the current directory. You can copy them over to your SharePoint 2013 farm and install them there. If you have specific instructions about how to install any of them, use those. Otherwise, use the following two PowerShell statements to add all the solutions to the SharePoint 2013 solution store and then deploy them:

```
# Add all WSP files in the current direction to SharePoint
Get-ChildItem | ForEach-Object{Add-SPSolution -LiteralPath
 $_.Fullname}
# Deploy all solutions in the farm
Get-SPSolution | ForEach-Object {If ($_.
 ContainsWebApplicationResource -eq $False) {Install-
    SPSolution -Identity $_ -GACDeployment} else {Install-SPSolution
 -Identity $_ -
    AllWebApplications -GACDeployment}}
```

For more information on how these statements work, please see Shane's blog post at http://msmvps.com/blogs/shane/archive/2011/05/05/using-powershell-to-export-all-solutions-from-your-sharepoint-2010-farm-and-other-fun.aspx.

As stated earlier, your SharePoint 2010 farm solutions should install into SharePoint 2013 without any hassle, and they should work fine. However, upgrading is a great time to do housekeeping. If you or your company has written any of the solutions, take a look at them now to see what you can do to make them work better with SharePoint 2013. If you got them from a third party, check whether they have been updated for SharePoint 2013. While the solution will probably work just fine without alteration, there's a chance they can work even better.

What You Can't Upgrade

Reading the preceding pages, it's tough to imagine that there isn't anything that can't be upgraded to SharePoint 2013. Although the upgrade options are very good, there are a few things that cannot be upgraded.

Content

This bears repeating: You can upgrade to SharePoint 2013 from any version of SharePoint 2010. There is no way, out of the box, to upgrade content from SharePoint 2007 or SharePoint 2003. As long as your content or service application database is from SharePoint 2010 RTM or later, you can attach it to SharePoint 2013.

Service Applications

Earlier in the chapter is a list of the service applications whose databases can be upgraded to SharePoint 2013. Some service applications weren't so lucky. If a service application isn't in the preceding list, it can't be upgraded. In most cases that's not a big loss. The service apps that can't be upgraded didn't have databases, so they didn't have anything to bring over. They provided services to data that existed someplace else. As long as that data is upgraded, and the corresponding SharePoint 2013 service application is created, the new farm will maintain the functionality that the SharePoint 2010 farm had.

In SharePoint 2010 the Office Web Apps were installed on top of SharePoint 2010 and installed as service applications. In SharePoint 2013 the Office Web Apps are no longer installed on a SharePoint server, and are no longer service applications. Because of this architecture change, they cannot be upgraded. If the Office Web Apps are installed and your SharePoint 2013 farm is connected to your Office Web Apps server, your upgraded content will automatically take advantage of it. Chapter 15, "The Office Web Applications for SharePoint," walk you through what's new with the OWAs. It also walks you through how to install the OWAs and configure SharePoint 2013 to use them.

The PowerPoint Broadcast site template offered in the SharePoint 2010 OWAs has no equivalent in the 2013 OWAs, so if you have that site in SharePoint 2010 you'll need to delete it. You can do so in SharePoint 2010 before you upgrade, or in SharePoint 2013 after you attach your database. Either way is fine. If you forget about this and try to upgrade a PowerPoint Broadcast site, SharePoint 2013 will snicker under its breath and pleasantly remind you that it cannot upgrade that type of site.

To avoid the snickering and mocking from SharePoint, it's easy enough to scour your SharePoint farm for the PowerPoint Broadcast sites and remove them. For that, our friend PowerShell comes to the rescue. Use the following PowerShell statement, either in SharePoint 2010 or SharePoint 2013, to find all the PowerPoint Broadcast sites:

```
Get-SPSite | Where-Object { $_.rootweb.webtemplate -eq " PowerPointBroadcast" }
```

If you find any of the varmints in your farm, you can either delete them manually in Central Admin, or show off a little and use the following PowerShell statement:

```
Get-SPSite | Where-Object { $_.rootweb.webtemplate -eq " PowerPointBroadcast" } |
Remove-SPSite
```

Be very careful when automating deletions. Make sure you use the first statement to see what would be deleted. Even if you've already read Chapter 7, "Administering SharePoint with Windows PowerShell," and you understood it all, you can still make costly mistakes. Nothing takes all the fun out of an upgrade faster than deleting all the content you just upgraded. Take my word for it.

While you're deleting unnecessary site collections, keep your eyes open for the Office Viewing Cache site collections, as they are not used by the new Office Web Apps either. There will be one per web application and the URL will be /sites/Office_Viewing_Service_Cache. Like the PowerPoint Broadcast site, these can be deleted before or after the upgrade.

FAST Search Center Sites

FAST was a casualty of the move to SharePoint 2013. Microsoft bought the search company FAST in 2008 but it was too late in the development cycle to get it properly integrated into SharePoint 2010. FAST Server for SharePoint was a separate product for SharePoint 2010 that was bolted on and replaced SharePoint Server's content search. Part of that bolted-on experience was it having its own Search Center site. In SharePoint 2013 the bulk of the FAST functionality was added to SharePoint's search, and the FAST product was eliminated. Because of that, SharePoint 2013 has no need to upgrade a SharePoint 2010 FAST Search Center site. Its own Search Center is more than capable. Like the PowerPoint Broadcast site, you can delete these before or after you attach the content database to your SharePoint 2013 farm.

Don't Upgrade Crap

The upgrade process in SharePoint has always been very robust, and that continues with SharePoint 2013. However, there are a few things you can do before your upgrade that will make it go more smoothly and quickly. This section provides some guidance on things you can do to prepare for your upgrade to SharePoint 2013.

As you're planning your upgrade, it's the perfect time to take stock of your SharePoint 2010 farm and look for pieces to leave behind. This could be any part of your farm, but the biggest bang for your buck comes from pruning unnecessary customizations and unused content. Let's start with the customizations.

SharePoint is very popular and has been for several years. SharePoint 2010 was the most popular version of all and as such it enjoyed a very rich third-party ecosystem. There's a solution for almost every SharePoint need. Most SharePoint administrators tried a lot of these solutions before they settled on the ones that met their needs; but not all of the failed solutions were always properly cleaned up. In other cases, solutions are still installed for processes that are no longer being used. Regardless of why they're there, unused farms or sandbox solutions should be removed in

SharePoint 2010 before moving your databases to SharePoint 2013. It was mentioned earlier that customizations are one of the biggest problem points when doing upgrades. It makes sense to remove as many customizations as you can beforehand. You can use the following command in PowerShell in your SharePoint 2010 farm to list any installed third-party solutions:

```
Get-SPSolution
```

You can also get this information in Central Administration by clicking System Settings ➪ Manage farm solutions. Figures 5-1 and 5-2 show how this information is displayed in PowerShell and Central Admin, respectively.

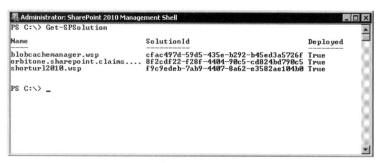

FIGURE 5-1

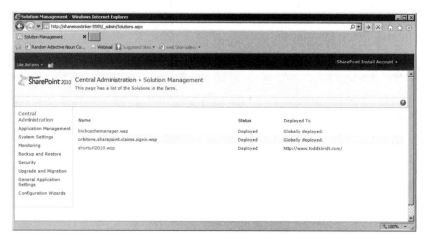

FIGURE 5-2

In this case, three farm-level solutions are installed. Each of these solutions should be evaluated to determine whether they are actively used in SharePoint 2010. If not, they should be removed. It should also be determined whether their functionality makes sense in the new SharePoint 2013 farm, and whether the new features of SharePoint 2013 replace the functionality in the solution. If a case can be made to remove them, they should be removed. The fewer moving pieces in the upgrade, the more smoothly it will go and the quicker everyone involved will get their weekend back. If the

Deployed status of a solution in SharePoint 2010 is "false" then it is a prime candidate for removal to the "farm" where all our childhood pets now frolic.

Because removing unnecessary solutions only helps if you do it on the SharePoint 2010 side before the upgrade, there is an inherent risk because it's being done to a production environment. As with any change made in production, ensure that good change control measures are in place, and remove the solution in a test environment first. The solution you are removing may seem useless, but it might quietly add the "Give the SharePoint Administrator a raise" workflow that we've all come to know and love.

Although farm solutions are the proper way to extend SharePoint 2010 functionality, there are other, back alley, ways to extend SharePoint 2010. This might be manual web.config edits, manually copying features into the Features directory, or other unsavory approaches. Regardless of how you added functionality to your SharePoint 2010 farm, they should all be evaluated before the upgrade takes place.

Features aren't the only detritus that should be cleaned up before you upgrade your SharePoint 2010 content. The content itself should be reviewed to see if it's all worthy of gracing a SharePoint 2013 farm. Just as features are often given a test drive, the same can be done with webs and site collections. Suppose some well-meaning user has a site collection or two created for a fun new project that never really takes off. Or worse yet, they create a web or site collection for the sole purpose of trying something they read on a SharePoint blog, or to try some fancy new SharePoint add-in that is supposed to make SharePoint faster, better looking, and cure ear wax, all at the same time. Whatever the case, once they are abandoned, those little sandboxes don't seem to be cleaned up very often. If your farm has any number of site collections at all, it can be tough to separate the wheat from the chaff. Fortunately, a little PowerShell will help you root out site collections that haven't had any changes made to them. The following PowerShell command will list all the site collections in your farm according to the order in which their content was last changed:

```
Get-SPSite -Limit All | select url, LastContentModifiedDate | Sort-Object -Property
LastContentModifiedDate
```

The output will look similar to what is shown in Figure 5-3.

```
Administrator: SharePoint 2010 Management Shell                                    _ □ X
PS C:\> Get-SPSite | select url, LastContentModifiedDate | Sort-Object -Property
LastContentModifiedDate

Url                                     LastContentModifiedDate
---                                     -----------------------
http://upgrade/sites/Office_Viewing_... 8/22/2010 3:29:08 AM
http://upgrade/sites/test7              8/22/2010 3:29:08 AM
http://sharepoint/sites/Office_Viewi... 10/17/2010 9:50:51 AM
http://upgrade                          10/29/2010 1:00:05 AM
http://sharepoint/sites/ross            5/9/2011 4:00:04 PM
http://sharepoint/my                    5/9/2011 4:00:05 PM
http://sharepoint/sites/blob            5/9/2011 4:00:06 PM
http://sharepoint/my/personal/laura     5/9/2011 4:00:06 PM
http://sharepoint/my/personal/todd      5/9/2011 4:00:07 PM
http://sharepoint/my/personal/shane     5/9/2011 4:00:08 PM
http://sharepoint/sites/team            5/9/2011 4:00:08 PM
http://sharepoint/sites/Records         5/9/2011 4:00:08 PM
http://sharepoint/sites/Publish         5/9/2011 4:00:10 PM
http://sharepoint/sites/test            5/11/2011 6:04:34 AM
http://sharepoint/sites/portal          9/17/2012 4:43:33 AM
http://sharepoint                       2/24/2013 3:43:00 PM


PS C:\> _
```

FIGURE 5-3

This uses the site collection's `LastContentModifiedDate` property to tell you when it was changed last. While this isn't the only way to find stale data, it's a good way to get the hunt started. If you have a site that is used for archiving, it might be very important but only infrequently updated. Also, each site collection has a `LastSecurityModifiedDate` that reflects when the permissions on a site collection were last changed. This might also tell you whether a site collection is important. Don't delete any site collections based on their `LastContentModifiedDate` alone. This just gives you an idea of where to start investigating first. If you're not sure whether a site collection should be upgraded, consider creating a new content database in your SharePoint 2010 farm for questionable site collections. Then use the PowerShell cmdlet `Move-SPSite` to move the questionable site collections there. That way, they won't slow down your upgrade of the important site collections but you still have them if needed.

Finding webs that haven't been changed recently is a little tougher, but still doable. The following PowerShell command uses a similar technique to list all the webs in the site collection `http://sharepoint/sites/portal` to see when they were last modified:

```
Get-SPSite http://sharepoint/sites/portal | Get-SPWeb -limit all | select url,
LastItemModifiedDate | Sort-Object -Property LastItemModifiedDate |
Format-Table -AutoSize
```

This output will look similar to what is shown in Figure 5-4.

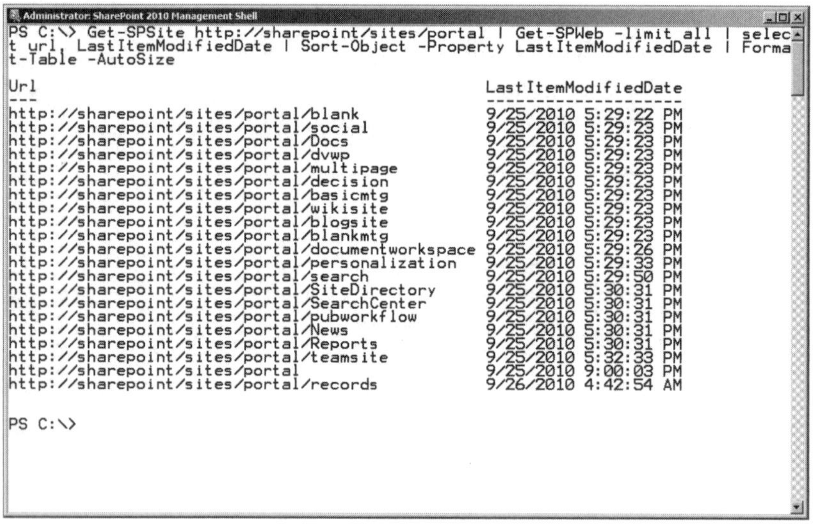

FIGURE 5-4

> **WARNING** *Both of these operations can be expensive from an I/O standpoint, so if your farm is large, be careful with them, or run them against a test or dev farm with copies of your production databases. Their I/O demands could tax your SQL Server and result in a reduced experience for your end users.*

However you determine which functions and features or content you're still using, spending a couple of hours going through it all can save you a lot of time and frustration during the upgrade to SharePoint 2013.

UPGRADING CONTENT

While there are several steps to successfully upgrade content from SharePoint 2010 to SharePoint 2013, the process is relatively straightforward. This section describes the steps necessary to attach a SharePoint 2010 database to a SharePoint 2013 farm and upgrade it.

Creating the Web Application

Recall that our only option when upgrading content to SharePoint 2013 is to attach a SharePoint 2010 content database to a SharePoint 2013 web application. Therefore, the first step is to create a web application in your SharePoint 2013 farm. This can be the web application in which the data will permanently reside, or a temporary web app used only for upgrading. This flexibility is important if your SharePoint 2010 web application uses classic-mode authentication, rather than claims-based authentication (CBA, or just "Claims"). If you're not completely up to speed on CBA, Chapter 6 is all about claims and authentication. In SharePoint 2010, CBA was an option, but a lot of farms continued to use classic-mode authentication as they had in previous versions of SharePoint. In SharePoint 2013, Claims is an integral part of SharePoint; and it is necessary for most new SharePoint 2013 functionality to work. If your SharePoint 2010 environment uses classic-mode authentication, it will have to be converted to Claims in order to get the most out of SharePoint 2013. This conversion can be done either in SharePoint 2010 before the upgrade, or in SharePoint 2013 after the upgrade. Either method works fine, so use whichever method works best for your situation. Here are some things to consider.

To upgrade to Claims in SharePoint 2010 before upgrade:

➤ It must be done in production, so that carries some risk.

➤ If the upgrade to SharePoint 2013 isn't done immediately, some SharePoint 2010 functionality may be lost.

➤ The process to convert to Claims in SharePoint 2010 is more complicated than in SharePoint 2013.

➤ You can upgrade content and authentication separately, which enables easier troubleshooting.

➤ All SharePoint 2013 functionality works immediately after upgrading.

To upgrade to Claims in SharePoint 2013 after upgrade:

➤ You must go to extra effort to create a classic-mode web app in SharePoint 2013.

➤ Upgraded content won't have full functionality in SharePoint 2013 until after authentication is switched to Claims.

➤ The process for upgrading to Claims is smoother in SharePoint 2013 than in SharePoint 2010.

If you choose to upgrade to Claims in SharePoint 2010, this is the process:

1. Use the following PowerShell to convert the web application to Claims:

```
$wa = Get-SPWebApplication http://webapplication
$wa.UseClaimsAuthentication = $true
$wa.Update()
```

2. Migrate users from classic-mode to Claims:

```
$wa.MigrateUsers($true)
```

3. Push out the changes to all the servers in the farm:

```
$wa.ProvisionGlobally()
```

Any accounts, including the Search content crawl account, that have been given web application policies in Central Admin will have to be given those policies again. If the portalsuperuser and portalsuperreader accounts have been defined, they must be reset with their claims-based version; otherwise, the web application may not render. Finally, if any alerts do not work correctly, they may need to be re-created by the user. If you choose to convert to Claims after the upgrade to SharePoint 2013, you need to create a classic-mode web application in SharePoint 2013 using PowerShell. The PowerShell you would use looks like this:

```
New-SPWebApplication -name "Classic Web App" -Port 80 -url
http://upgrade.contoso.com -ApplicationPool "ClassicAppPool"
-ApplicationPoolAccount
(Get-SPManagedAccount "domain\sp_webapps") -DatabaseName WSS_Content_Classic
```

This web app will be the one the classic-mode SharePoint 2010 databases are attached to when they're upgraded. After the databases have been attached, use the following PowerShell command to convert them to Claims:

```
Convert-SPWebApplication -Identity http://upgrade.contoso.com -To Claims -
RetainPermissions
```

The preceding command will upgrade both the web application and the user mappings from classic to Claims. If additional classic SharePoint 2010 databases are attached to the now-converted web application, simply rerun the `Convert-SPWebApplication` command to convert the user mappings in the newly attached database.

Regardless of the approach you take, make sure the web application you create in your SharePoint 2013 farm matches the authentication method used in the databases that are attached to it. It's also a good idea to create a site collection at the root of the web app before any upgrading takes place. This gives you a site collection to browse to in order to ensure that all of the underlying framework is working. This way, if there's a problem with DNS or something else, you'll know about it before you attach any SharePoint 2010 databases — and you know the problem isn't caused by the upgrade.

> **WARNING** *If you follow this advice, remember to either delete the test site collection or detach the database that was created when the web application was created. If you don't, you'll get an error when you try to attach the SharePoint 2010 database that contains the root site collection of the web app.*

Testing the Content Database

There are several steps to attaching your SharePoint 2010 content database to your SharePoint 2013. This section will walk you through each of them.

Restoring the Database in SQL Server

The first step in getting your database into SharePoint 2013 is getting it into the SQL Server instance that SharePoint 2013 is using. When testing the upgrade, your latest database backup should suffice. When you're actually doing the upgrade, you'll need to shut down all your SharePoint 2010 servers and then do full backups of all your SharePoint 2010 databases.

Whichever step you're doing, copy the database backups over to the SQL instance that SharePoint 2013 is using and restore them. Many of the database's properties are stored in the backup, and you might have to change them before you start using the database with your SharePoint 2013 farm. If the databases were not already using the Simple recovery model, it's safe to switch them to that after the restore. If anything goes wrong with the upgrade, you just revert back to your backups, so having transaction logs won't really do you any good. After the upgrade is complete, you'll start backing the databases up regularly and you can change them to the Full recovery model if that's what your disaster recovery strategy uses. Chapter 9, "Configuring SharePoint for High-Availability Backups," explains your different options and how to utilize them.

You also have to change the permissions to your databases in SQL Server. The database's permissions are maintained during the backup and restore process. Using the same service accounts in two different SharePoint farms is a bad idea — like juggling chainsaws bad. Like juggling torches bad. Like juggling chainsaws on fire bad. Your SharePoint 2013 farm should have completely different service accounts than the farm from which your databases came. This means your SharePoint 2013 farm won't be able to access the databases to test them or mount them. You'll have to give two accounts permission to your databases after you restore them.

The first account is whatever account you'll be running PowerShell as when you run the test and mount the cmdlets we'll walk through later in the chapter. Ideally, this will be a dedicated SharePoint administration account and not one of your SharePoint service accounts. The blog post at http://www.toddklindt.com/sp_farm explains why this is a good idea and how to configure it.

The second account to which you'll need to give access to your newly restored databases is whichever service account is going to access it. In the case of content databases, this will be the app pool ID of the web application to which you're attaching the database. If you followed the guidance in Chapter 3, this will be the sp_webapp account. If the database is a service application database, then that service application's app pool ID will need access to it. In Chapter 3 that account is sp_serviceapps.

Each of these accounts needs the db_owner role on the database. You can give this permission in SQL Service Management Studio (SSMS). Open SSMS and navigate to Security ⇨ Logins in the Object Explorer. Find the account to which you want to grant access to the new database. Right-click it and select Properties. When the Properties dialog appears, navigate to the User Mapping page and find the restored database. Select the db_owner roles and click OK. Figure 5-5 shows giving the CONTOSO\sp_webapps account the db_owner roles for the WSS_Content_tk_com database.

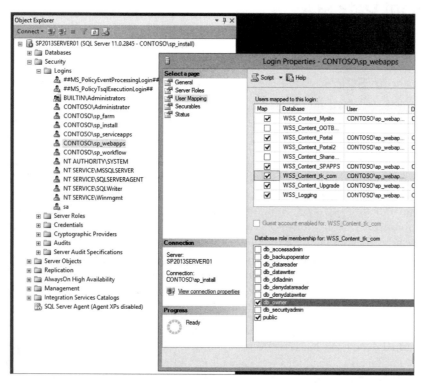

FIGURE 5-5

Do this for all the databases you restore. If you forget this step you will probably get the following error message in PowerShell when you try to test or mount the database:

```
Cannot open database "wss_content_tk_com" requested
by the login. The login failed.
Login failed for user 'CONTOSO\sp_webapps'.
```

If you don't get an error like that, then the account you're running PowerShell as has permissions to that database through a server role.

Running Test-SPContentDatabase

Now that the databases are restored and configured correctly, you can start testing them to see how nicely they'll play with SharePoint 2013. When upgrading from SharePoint 2007 to SharePoint 2010, you had a great way to assess the challenges that lay ahead of you: the preupgrade-check operation in STSADM.EXE. It would inventory your SharePoint 2007 environment and point you to any problems you might have before you upgraded. Unfortunately, this tool is not available when upgrading to SharePoint 2013, but there is a suitable replacement in `Test-SPContentDatabase`. You can run this cmdlet on either SharePoint 2010 or on SharePoint 2013 before the database is attached. It needs the name of the database you want to attach, and the web application to which you want to attach it. When it executes, it goes through the database and compares it to the farm and the web application to ensure that all the pieces needed to render the content in the database are in place. Some databases are more cooperative than others. Figures 5-6 and 5-7 show the output from the following statement:

```
Test-SPContentDatabase -Name WSS_Content_tk_com -WebApplication
http://upgrade.contoso.com
```

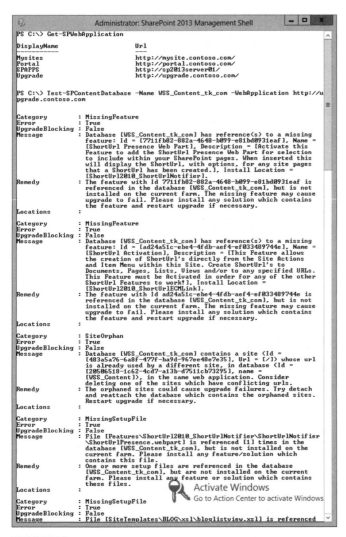

FIGURE 5-6

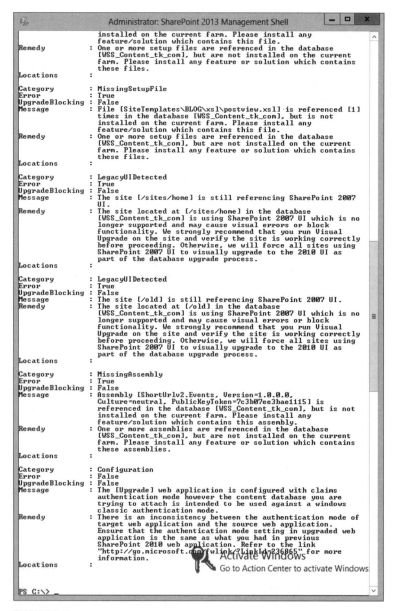

FIGURE 5-7

These figures show a few things. The first line is Get-SPWebApplication, which returns a list of all the web apps in the SharePoint 2013 farm by name and URL. When using Test-SPContentDatabase you can use the web app's URL or its name. Without any additional parameters, Test-SPContentDatabase simply lists the objects in the content database that the web application or the farm cannot support. Figures 6 and 7 show a few errors in the content database. Before addressing each issue, however, let's look at some techniques you can use when you have a particularly troublesome database like the one shown here. Chapter 7 covers a cmdlet, Start-Transcript, that writes all the input and output on the screen to a file. When you have a database with a significant number of issues, they can fill the screen buffer and you miss the issues at the top. If you run Start-Transcript before you run Test-SPContentdatabase, all of its output will be written to the transcript file saved in your Documents folder. You can reference that file if any issues scroll off the screen. You can also pipe the output through the more command so that it only shows one page at a time, like this:

```
Test-SPContentDatabase -Name WSS_Content_tk_com -WebApplication
  http://upgrade.contoso.com | more
```

Press the spacebar to see the next page.

When mounting a database, you'll end up fixing an issue or two, then rerunning Test-SPContentDatabase to see how much progress you've made. If your database has a lot of issues, like the one in the figures, it's easy to lose track of how many issues you've cleared and how many you have left. You can use the count property to get the number of issues. As you clear up issues, you will see the number go down. To get only the number of issues in the database, use the following syntax:

```
(Test-SPContentDatabase -Name WSS_Content_tk_com -WebApplication
  http://upgrade.contoso.com).count
```

Your only output will be a number; the smaller the better.

Now let's walk through each issue and see what can be done to address it.

Fixing the Issues

When you're looking at the output of Test-SPContentDatabase you should start at the top, because fixing issues there will oftentimes fix issues downstream.

The first two reported issues refer to missing Features. Although SharePoint 2013 can't tell you the name of the missing Feature, it does provide the Feature's ID and its description to help you figure it out. In this case, the Feature is referenced in the database, but the files for the Feature do not exist on the SharePoint 2013 farm being tested against. Depending on what the Feature does, that may or may not be a big deal. While the message indicates what the Feature is, it doesn't indicate where it is referenced. That will help you figure out what needs to be installed, or determine if the web or site referencing the Feature can be deleted. Test-SPContentDatabase has an optional parameter, -ShowLocation, which provides the GUID of the web or site collection that references the Feature. You can take that information back to the farm from which the database came to find the Feature reference. Note that on large databases, the -ShowLocation parameter may significantly increase the amount of time Test-SPContentDatabase takes to run.

After you've either installed the missing Feature or deleted the web or site collection that references it, run Test-SPContentDatabase again. In this case, installing the ShortURL Feature will clean up the MissingFeature issues, as well as the MissingSetupFile and MissingAssembly issues later in the output.

If you can't figure out which Feature is missing, or aren't able to install it into your SharePoint 2013 farm for whatever reason, don't worry, all is not lost. While SharePoint is unhappy about these issues, it's not terribly concerned. Notice that each issue has an `UpgradeBlocking` property. This is SharePoint's way of waving the white flag and admitting that it can't handle the issue it found. In the case of the two issues reported here, neither of them has `UpgradeBlocking` set to true. Therefore, although SharePoint has found a problem, it's not anything it can't handle, so you can go ahead and attach the database. Again, depending on what the missing Feature did, the content in the database may or may not render correctly. As you're fixing issues, keep your eye on the `UpgradeBlocking` property.

The next issue is one that you were warned about earlier in the chapter. It says it will not be able attach the site located at /. This is because the Upgrade web app already has a site collection in its root. This is the site collection used to verify that DNS and everything is working correctly. Because that site collection is no longer needed, you can either delete the site collection or detach the content database that was created along with the web application.

The issue is in the category MissingSetupFile. In this case the setup file is part of the ShortURL Feature mentioned in the first issue. This is why you start at the top. If all the MissingFeature issues are addressed and you still have MissingSetupFile issues, then you can troubleshoot them individually.

Figure 5-6 indicates some issues that are not part of the missing Feature. Instead, they were caused by customizations that were made to a blog in one of the site collections. Clever readers may have already figured out that the database in the figures is from `http://www.toddklindt.com`. It's had a few bad things done to it. The blog MissingSetupFile issues are probably related to those bad things.

The next two issues in Figure 5-7 have the category LegacyUIDetected. This database was originally created in SharePoint 2007, and not all of the webs have been visually upgraded to the SharePoint 2010 interface. Like the Remedy section says, the recommended approach is to go back to your SharePoint 2010 farm and switch the UI to the SharePoint 2010 mode and make sure everything works. Then attach it to your SharePoint 2013 farm. If you don't do that, all the webs will be automatically changed to the SharePoint 2010 UI. While that will probably be fine, it's better to control that change yourself.

The next issue refers to a missing assembly, which is part of the ShortURL Feature that was missing in the first issue. Again, fixing the issues from the top down can keep you from chasing your tail on little issues like missing files and assemblies. When the list of issues is so long that it scrolls through the scrollback buffer it's tempting to start with the issues you can see. Always start at the top. You'll save yourself time, and possibly even pull out less hair during your upgrades.

The final issue that `Test-SPContentDatabase` found is an authentication mode issue. The database tested came from a SharePoint 2010 web application that was using classic-mode authentication, but the web application it was tested against uses Claims. This is the issue discussed earlier in the chapter.

Additional Parameters

Before attaching this database and upgrading site collections, there is one additional parameter of `Test-SPContentDatabase` to cover, `ShowRowCounts`. This parameter gives you the row count for each table in the content database before it reports the issues. Figure 5-8 shows example output.

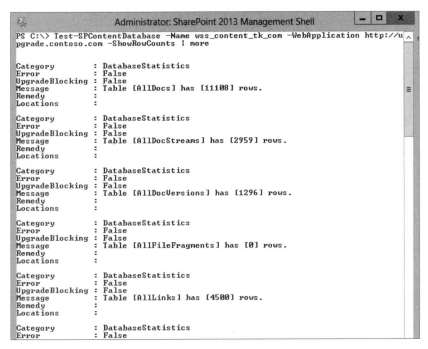

FIGURE 5-8

Here you can see the row counts for the first five tables in the content database. Getting this information in not necessary in most cases. It can help in scenarios where the upgrade process is taking longer than expected. It exposes issues such as an excessive number of document versions. Even if you don't need the information, it's interesting to see.

Now that the database is tested, it's time to attach it.

Attaching the Content Database

After you have tested your content databases and fixed as many issues as you can, it's time to attach the database. Use the PowerShell cmdlet `Mount-SPContentDatabase` to mount the content database to the web application that will serve its content. The syntax for `Mount-SPContentDatabase` is similar to `Test-SPContentDatabase`, and if you aren't using any of the optional parameters when testing your database, you can usually just press the up arrow in PowerShell, replace "`test`" with "`mount`" and press Enter. Here is the command used to mount the database that you tested earlier against your upgrade web application:

```
Mount-SPContentDatabase -Name wss_content_tk_com -WebApplication
http://upgrade.contoso.com
```

Figure 5-9 shows the output returned from running that command. While it might be tempting to run screaming out of the room when you see all that red error text, it's not so bad. You know from running `Test-SPContentDatabase` that there will be some issues.

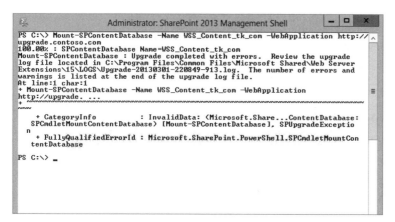

FIGURE 5-9

To satisfy your curiosity about what happened during the upgrade, SharePoint 2013 does a thorough job documenting the process. Each time a database is upgraded it creates two log files. One contains all the events associated with the upgrade, good and bad. The other is a subset of the first, containing only error information. If you just want to see what went wrong, skipping all the back-patting for what went well, go right to the error log. Both logs are in the 15 Hive (`c:\program files\common files\microsoft shared\web server extensions\15`) in the Logs directory. The full log will have a name like Upgrade-YYYYMMDD-HHMMSS-MMM.log, where YYYY is the four-digit year, MM is the month, DD is the day, HH is the hour in 24-hour format, MM is the minutes, SS is the seconds, and MMM is the milliseconds when the upgrade was started. The errors-only log has the same name with "-error" at the end. They're both text files, so they can be read with any text editor. They also have the same schema as the ULS logs, so you can use the MSDN ULS Viewer to view them as well. You can find out more about the ULS Viewer in Chapter 19, "Troubleshooting SharePoint."

The Upgrade log contains a tremendous amount of information, so if problems are reported during the upgrade it's more efficient to start your troubleshooting in the error log, then work back into the full log if you need more information. The full Upgrade log is a good way to determine how long it took to complete a particular mount. All the lines are time stamped, or if you're bad at math you can search for "Elapsed time" at the end of the log to see how long it took. Keeping track of these times in your test environments will help you plan your production upgrades.

If you prefer to consume your error logs in a civilized manner, you can also view them in Central Admin. On the Upgrade and Migration page there is a link to "Check upgrade status." Clicking that will take you to the `/_admin/UpgradeStatus.aspx` page where you will find all the tales of previous upgrades. Some upgrade stories have happy endings, some don't; they're all available on this page, shown in Figure 5-10. You can click each upgrade's status to load its details on the bottom. If you want to read the full log, its location is listed as "Log File" at the bottom.

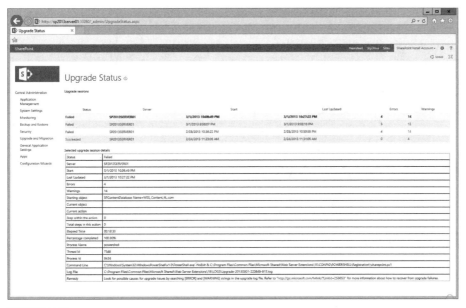

FIGURE 5-10

After the database is attached you should verify how things look. The following PowerShell cmdlet returns the site collections in that database, so you know where to start looking:

```
(Get-SPContentDatabase wss_content_tk_com).sites
```

Figure 5-11 shows the command's output, which contains a couple of notable things. First, notice there's an Office Viewing Cache site collection in there. As you'll read in Chapter 15, the Office Web Apps have been completely redesigned for SharePoint 2013, and they no longer use a caching site collection. Because of this, the Office Viewing Cache site collection has no SharePoint 2013 equivalent and cannot be upgraded. You can either delete them in SharePoint 2010 before you upgrade, or in SharePoint 2013 afterward.

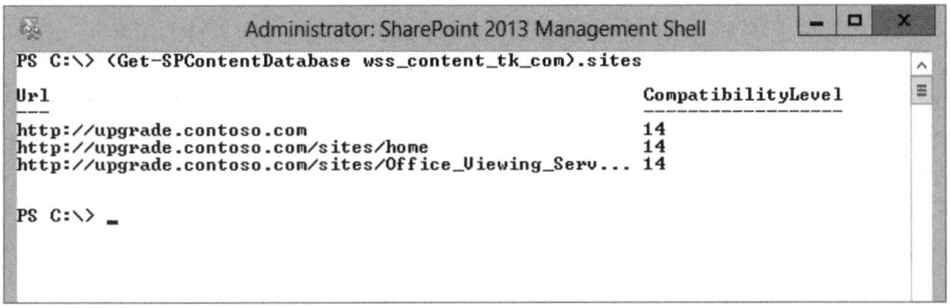

```
Administrator: SharePoint 2013 Management Shell

PS C:\> (Get-SPContentDatabase wss_content_tk_com).sites

Url                                               CompatibilityLevel
---                                               ------------------
http://upgrade.contoso.com                        14
http://upgrade.contoso.com/sites/home             14
http://upgrade.contoso.com/sites/Office_Viewing_Serv... 14


PS C:\> _
```

FIGURE 5-11

All the site collections in this content database have the CombatibilityLevel 14, which is SharePoint 2010. By design, it is not possible to have the site collections upgraded to the SharePoint 2013 compatibility level when a SharePoint 2010 database is attached. The team that owns the upgrade process planned the upgrade around one guiding principle, "Do no harm." Because some site collections might not render after being upgraded, they decided that none of the site collections can be upgraded without a deliberate action on someone's part. Because this database is attached but none of the site collections have been upgraded, the following section walks through upgrading the site collections.

UPGRADING SITE COLLECTIONS

After restoring your content database in SQL, testing it against your SharePoint 2013 web application, and mounting it in SharePoint, you're in the home stretch. You're so close you can almost smell that newly upgraded SharePoint 2013 site collection.

Another difference between the upgrading process in SharePoint 2010 versus SharePoint 2013 is that it is no longer scoped at the web level, but at the site collection level. The upgrade process can also be delegated to site collection administrators, or it can be done by farm administrators. This section mainly covers how the site collection administrators can upgrade their site collections in the browser, but the PowerShell is also included so farm administrators can join in on the fun on the back end.

When you browse to any of the site collections in newly mounted SharePoint 2010 content databases you're likely to feel a little underwhelmed. OK, a lot underwhelmed. As shown in Figure 5-12, it looks and acts almost exactly like SharePoint 2010. The only exception is the red bar at the top begging you to upgrade it. Not a lot of payoff for all that work you've done. This is expected, however. As mentioned earlier, SharePoint goes out of its way to not upgrade SharePoint 2010 site collections to SharePoint 2013 when the databases are attached. You must upgrade them deliberately.

Site collection administrators have three upgrade-related options they can run for their site collections: run a heath report, create an eval site, or upgrade the site collection to SharePoint 2013. Each option is an important cog in the upgrade wheel.

Before SharePoint 2013 can upgrade your SharePoint 2010 site collection, it runs a health check looking for seven things that it hopes you didn't do in that earlier version. You can manually trigger that health check to get a heads up on potential issues before you're ready to run the upgrade. Log into your SharePoint 2010 site collection as a site collection administrator and select Site Actions ➪ Site Settings. Toward the bottom of the Site Collection Administration section is a link to Site collection health checks. This page is pretty simple; there's one button, Start checks. Click that button to have SharePoint 2013 run the health checks on the site collection and let you know if it found any issues. Figure 5-13 shows the health check from the database we attached earlier.

FIGURE 5-12

FIGURE 5-13

You can see SharePoint checked for the following seven things:

➤ Conflicting Content Types

➤ Customized Files

➤ Missing Galleries

➤ Missing Parent Content Types

➤ Missing Site Templates

➤ Unsupported Language Pack References

➤ Unsupported MUI References

Our site collection didn't do too badly. It got passing grades on the last five items. It has a conflicting content type of Video that should be removed before upgrade. SharePoint 2013 was also kind enough to indicate that several pages have been customized and they might cause problems after upgrade. There's even a link provided to convert them to their default. How handy is that? Running the health check is completely optional. SharePoint will run it before it does an upgrade. Running it manually gives you the chance to get the jump on any potential issues you might have before you do the actual upgrade.

If you're a farm administrator you can use the PowerShell cmdlet `Test-SPSite` to do the same tests. Of course, because it's in PowerShell it's easy to script and loop through many site collections at once. In typical PowerShell fashion, the output isn't pretty but it's serviceable. Figure 5-14 shows an example of what you can expect.

FIGURE 5-14

`Test-SPSite` also has an optional parameter, `-Rule`, that you can use to run an individual rule if you don't want to run all seven.

After clearing up any health errors, it's time to see what this site collection will look like with a little SharePoint 2013 shine on it. Unlike SharePoint 2010, you don't have a Visual Upgrade option. A site collection is either in SharePoint 2010 mode or SharePoint 2013 mode. In place of the Visual Upgrade mode available when upgrading to SharePoint 2010, you now have the option to create upgrade evaluation site collections. When creating an eval site, SharePoint 2013 creates a copy of your SharePoint 2010 site collection and appends its path with "-eval." You should always upgrade the site collection at the root of a web application first. When you do, its eval site is created at `http://webapp/sites/root-eval`. Then it upgrades the -eval site to SharePoint 2013. You can use this eval site to see how well the upgrade went and to look for issues. Figure 5-15 shows the dialog for creating this eval upgrade from the browser. To access this dialog, log into a SharePoint 2010 site collection as a site collection administrator, where you should see a red bar at the top extolling the virtues of upgrading. Clicking the "Start now" option takes you to the upgrade page, where you can click the option to upgrade the site collection or click the Try a Demo Upgrade link on the right to take the upgrade for a test drive. We'll do that first.

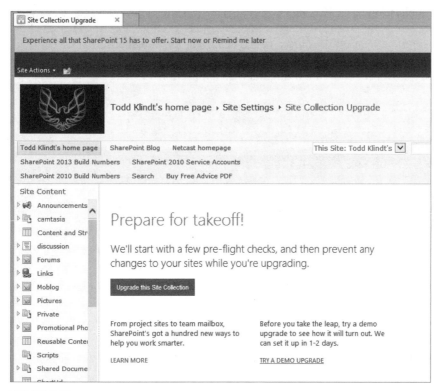

FIGURE 5-15

Clicking the demo upgrade link brings up the dialog shown in Figure 5-16. You have to love the casual wording in SharePoint 2013. "Before you take the leap" they want you to try the upgrade. How very nice of them. The eval sites are not created immediately. As the dialog says, it will take a day or two before it's created.

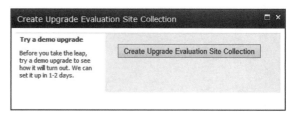

FIGURE 5-16

Upgrading site collections is a very expensive operation in terms of SQL I/O. Copying an entire site collection and then upgrading it is even worse. To prevent an eval upgrade from making your servers less responsive for normal SharePoint traffic, the eval sites are created by a timer job, which runs once a day at 1:00 a.m. As shown in Figure 5-17, you'll get an e-mail when your eval site is ready for you to kick the tires.

FIGURE 5-17

I don't know about you, but I'm pretty impatient. I think even Minute Rice takes too long to cook. I certainly don't want to wait two days for my eval site collection to be created. Fortunately, you can give that eval timer job a kick in the pants and run it before it is regularly scheduled to run at 1:00 AM. Each web application has a "Create Upgrade Evaluation Site Collections job" timer job. From Central Admin, select Monitoring ➪ Review job definitions, find that job, and click the Run Now button in its definition. Figure 5-18 shows the job definition for web application we're using for upgrade. Clicking the Run Now button will fire off this timer job, which will start a series of events that results in an -eval site for the root of our upgrade web application.

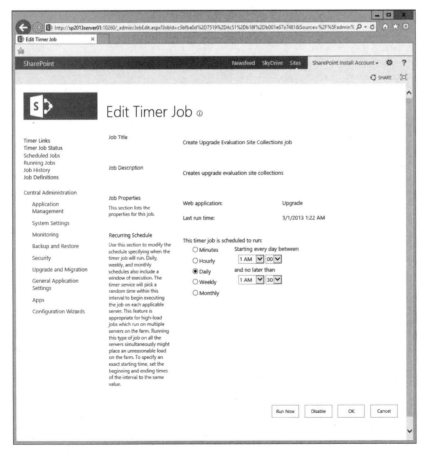

FIGURE 5-18

You can also do this in PowerShell. The job's PowerShell name is "job-create-upgrade-eval-sites," so some quick PowerShell can filter that out of the list of timer jobs in the farm and execute it. The first line of the following PowerShell will find all the eval site timer jobs in the farm; the second line will execute them:

```
Get-SPTimerJob | Where-Object { $_.name -eq "job-create-upgrade-eval-sites" } |
    select name, WebApplication
Get-SPTimerJob | Where-Object { $_.name -eq "job-create-upgrade-eval-sites" } |
    Start-SPTimerJob
```

Figure 5-19 shows this PowerShell masterpiece at work.

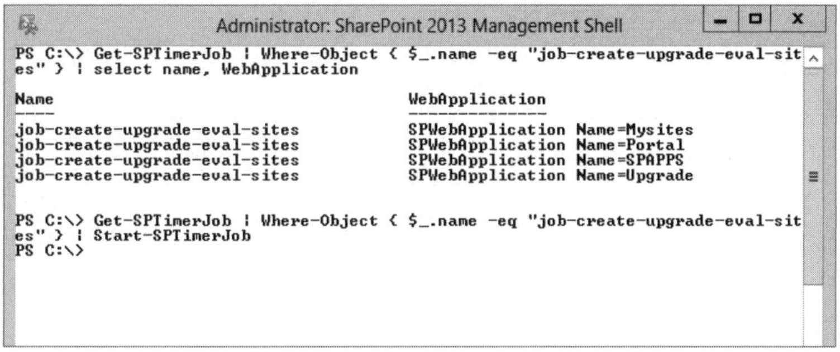

FIGURE 5-19

If you don't want to run it for all the web applications in the farm, you can filter by web application as well.

After the timer job runs, it will create a copy of your site collection and then run the upgrade process on that copy. The time this will take varies wildly according to the size of the site collection, the makeup of the site collection, and the horsepower of your SQL server.

After the eval site collection is created and you have received your congratulatory e-mail, fire up your browser and take it for a spin. This is your chance to see things the upgrade might screw up. Be sure to test things such as workflows, content types, and fancy SharePoint magic you've shown off to your buddies. Those are the kinds of things that will give the upgrade some heartburn.

It's *very* important to understand that the eval site is temporary. It *will* be deleted in 30 days. Don't do anything in this site collection that you'll miss. Unlike the Visual Upgrade in SharePoint 2010, you can't switch back and forth. Continue to use the SharePoint 2010 version of your site collection until you do a proper upgrade. If you prefer to use PowerShell to request an eval site collection, you can use the `Request-SPUpgradeEvaluationSite` cmdlet.

Eval site collections are typically created by site collection administrators, and they're the best people to verify that their site collection upgraded correctly. When planning your upgrade, ensure that good documentation is in place specifying who is responsible for testing what. You should also have a list of things to check. Make sure new webs can be created, make sure documents can be uploaded — common tasks like that. In addition, ensure that any third-party software you have is functioning correctly. After you have poked around the eval site and you think everything is in good shape, go ahead and upgrade the site collection to SharePoint 2013.

Site collection administrators can upgrade their site collection by starting the same way they did the eval. Click the link in the red bar or select Site Actions ➪ Site Settings ➪ Site Collection Upgrade. Both paths will lead you to the screen shown previously in Figure 5-15. Instead of clicking the link for the demo upgrade, click the Upgrade this Site Collection link to do the actual upgrade. After you do that, you're greeted with the friendly dialog shown in Figure 5-20.

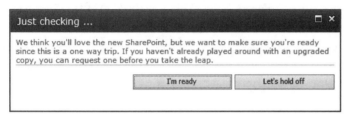

FIGURE 5-20

Assuming you didn't click it by accident, click the "I'm ready" button. If you lose your nerve and need to get back to the SharePoint 2010 version, click the "Let's hold off" button. These buttons have street cred, that's for sure.

When you click "I'm ready," your site collection is added to the list of site collections to be upgraded. There's no one- or two-day waiting time now. Now you're in the big leagues. The next page you'll see is shown in Figure 5-21.

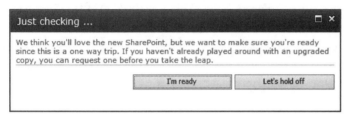

FIGURE 5-21

You can stay on this page to see the status of the upgrade, or, if you're impatient like me, you can browse back to the site collection and see the upgrade in action. If you get there quickly enough you might get a page like the one shown in Figure 5-22.

You can see SharePoint swapping out the sprites and generally making a mess of things. It sorts itself out, though. If you wait long enough it turns into a site like the one shown in Figure 5-23.

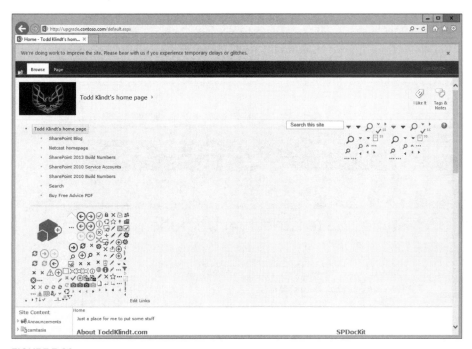

FIGURE 5-22

FIGURE 5-23

Now, as tempting as it might be to say, "The front page loaded up, it must be good," you should investigate further to verify that everything upgraded correctly. After a site collection has upgraded, the Site Collection Upgrade link no longer leads to a page offering to upgrade the site collection. Instead it takes you to a page like the one shown in Figure 5-24, containing a link to the upgrade status.

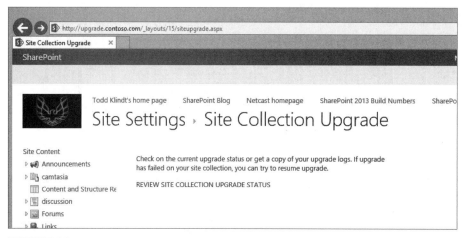

FIGURE 5-24

Clicking Review Site Collection Upgrade Status takes you to a page like the one in Figure 5-25. It gives you an overview of how the upgrade went. It also includes a link to the upgrade log file for that particular upgrade.

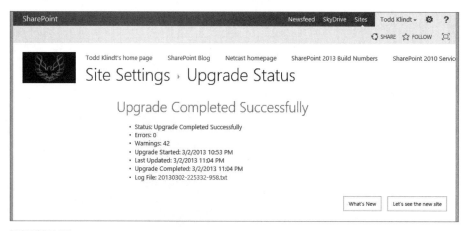

FIGURE 5-25

If you click the log file link, another tab will appear and an upgrade log file very similar to the ones you saw when you attached your content database will open. Figure 5-26 shows the first few lines from this site collection's upgrade.

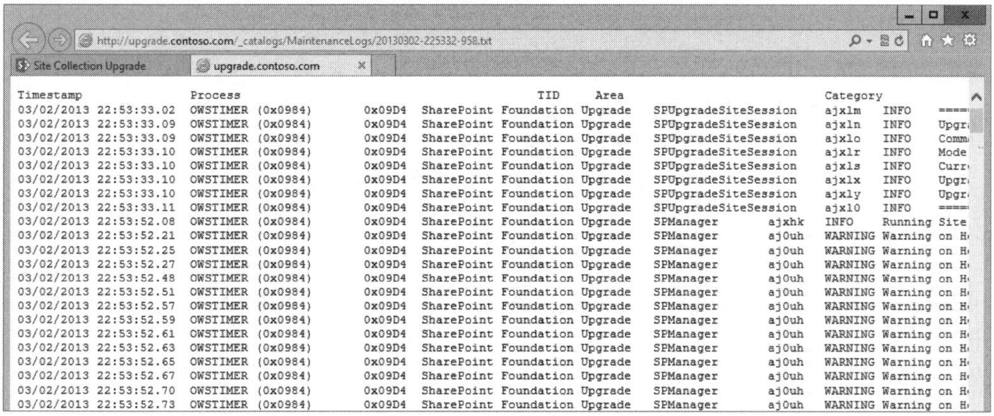

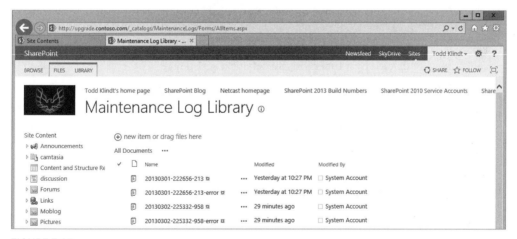

FIGURE 5-26

This log, and the logs from any other upgrade operations you've done, are stored in a hidden library in the site collection. You can get to it manually by browsing to /_catalogs/MaintenanceLogs/ in your site collection. When you do, you'll see something similar to Figure 5-27. These logs are also on the server in the 15 Logs directory. Their names all start with "SiteUpgrade-."

FIGURE 5-27

While this upgrade strategy was very clearly planned, with the site collection administrator doing most of the heavy lifting, it can also be done by a farm administrator with PowerShell. The cmdlet Upgrade-SPSite will upgrade a site collection as well. Because the Upgrade-SPSite cmdlet does both build-to-build (b2b) upgrades after a patch and version-to-version (v2v) upgrades as in this situation, you must use the -VersionUpgrade parameter to force PowerShell to upgrade the site collection to SharePoint 2013.

Throttling and Governance

Upgrading site collections is a very expensive operation when it comes to SQL I/O. Nearly the entire process takes place on the SQL server, as it runs stored procedures to make changes in the database. That's why eval site collection creation is relegated to running in the middle of the night when that burden is felt the least. Because site collection upgrades happen immediately, some other throttles have to be put in place to ensure that the farm isn't taken down by multiple upgrades happening at the same time. Site collections with less than 10MB in content and fewer than 10 webs are upgraded in the web application app pool. This is throttled to five app pool upgrades per web app. Site collections that are larger than 10MB or have more than 10 webs are upgraded via a timer job. You can adjust these values in PowerShell. They are stored in the `SiteUpgradeThrottleSettings` property of the web application. Use the following PowerShell to see a web app's current settings:

```
(Get-SPWebApplication http://upgrade.contoso.com).SiteUpgradeThrottleSettings
```

These limits are in place for a reason, so be very careful if you adjust them. Each content database is also throttled to 10 upgrades at the same time, which you can also adjust in PowerShell. Here is the PowerShell to see the current setting:

```
(Get-SPContentDatabase wss_content).concurrentsiteupgradesessionlimit
```

As a farm administrator you may want to control some aspects of the upgrade process. Fortunately, there are some other knobs and dials that can be tweaked. Web applications have three properties that apply to upgrades:

➤ **UpgradeEvalSitesRetentionDays** — Defines how many days elapse before the eval site collections are deleted by a timer job. By default it's 31 days.

➤ **UpgradeMaintenanceLink** — Creates a link to a custom upgrade maintenance page.

➤ **UpgradeReminderDelay** — Enables you to configure how many days a site collection admin can ignore the reminder bar. Its default value is 30 days. If this is set to 0 the reminder bar will say "Upgrade Required" instead of "Upgrade Available."

While this isn't strictly an upgrade issue, it is also possible to prevent users from creating fresh SharePoint 2010 mode site collections in SharePoint 2013. Any site collection that is created in SharePoint 2010 mode will eventually need to be upgraded, so preventing this can save you time down the road. Use the following PowerShell to restrict new site collections to only the SharePoint 2013 mode:

```
$wa = Get-SPWebApplication http://upgrade.contoso.com
$wa.CompatibilityRange = 15
$wa.update()
```

Not to be left out, the site collection has some PowerShell tricks up its sleeve as well. If you want to prevent site collection administrators from doing the upgrades on their own, you can specify that at the site collection level by setting the `AllowSelfServiceUpgrade` property to `$false`. Following is an example of PowerShell you could use to restrict Self Service Upgrade to all the site collections in a database you recently attached:

```
Get-SPSite -ContentDatabase wss_content_tk_com -Limit All | ForeachObject {
$_.AllowSelfServiceUpgrade = $false }
```

After that PowerShell is executed, all the site collections in the content database wss_content_tk_com will have to be upgraded by a farm admin with the Upgrade-SPSite cmdlet. While that sounds like more work, it does have a couple of advantages. First, it can be scripted, resulting in less work to upgrade multiple site collections. The following PowerShell code will walk through a content database and upgrade all the site collections at once:

```
Get-SPSite -ContentDatabase wss_content_tk_com -Limit All | Upgrade-SPSite -
VersionUpgrade -QueueOnly
```

The -QueueOnly option puts the upgrade job in the Timer Job queue which gives it some flexibility over where the upgrade takes place and can save time.

Second, Upgrade-SPSite has a parameter, -Unthrottled, that allows the site collection to be upgraded even if the throttling limits have been met. It's like a first-class ticket that allows your site collection to jump to the front of the queue and be upgraded straightaway.

Once SharePoint upgrade fever has infected your company, it can be easy to lose track of the upgrades in process and the upgrades in queue. Again, PowerShell dons its Superman cape and comes to the rescue. The cmdlet Get-SPSiteUpgradeSessionInfo will report back all the pending upgrades, eval sites, and full upgrades. To remove one from the list, you can use Remove-SPSiteUpgradeSessionInfo.

UPGRADING SERVICE APPLICATIONS

Content databases aren't the only databases that can be upgraded from SharePoint 2010 to SharePoint 2013. There is an exclusive club of service applications whose databases can also be upgraded to SharePoint 2013. Here are the members of that club:

- ➤ Business Connectivity Services
- ➤ Managed Metadata
- ➤ Performance Point
- ➤ Secure Store
- ➤ User Profile Service
- ➤ Search

In each of these cases the upgrade method is the same. Restore a copy of your SharePoint 2010 database into your SharePoint 2013's SQL instance and start the service instance. Then create a new version of the service application in your SharePoint 2013 farm with PowerShell and point it at the restored database. When the service application is created, it will see a database is already there and upgrade it. When the service application is created it will have all the settings or content from the SharePoint 2010 version, depending on the individual service app. Because each service app behaves just a little differently, let's take a look at each one.

Business Connectivity Services

If any entities were defined in your SharePoint 2010 Business Connectivity Services (BCS) service application it's easy to bring them over to your new SharePoint 2013 farm. Following are the steps to upgrade your SharePoint 2010 BCS database to SharePoint 2013:

1. Restore the BCS database into your SharePoint 2013 SQL instance. The identity that the service app app pool runs as will need to be given the db_owner role on the database. If you followed the service account guidance in Chapter 2, that will be sp_serviceapps. Also give the user under whom you're running the PowerShell the db_owner role.

2. Start the Business Connectivity Services service instance. You can do this in Central Admin by selecting Application Management ➪ Manage Services on Server, or with the following PowerShell snippet:

```
Get-SPServiceInstance | where-object {$_.TypeName -eq "Business Data
Connectivity Service"} | Start-SPServiceInstance
```

3. Create the BCS service application with PowerShell. The PowerShell assumes you have a service app app pool named "Default SharePoint Service App Pool." If your app pool name is different, adjust it accordingly. It also assumes the database from your SharePoint 2010 farm was named BusinessConnectivityDB.

```
# Start the service instance
$serviceapppool = Get-SPServiceApplicationPool "Default SharePoint Service App
 Pool"

# Create the service application
$bcsapp = New-SPBusinessDataCatalogServiceApplication -Name "Business
Connectivity
 Service" -ApplicationPool $serviceapppool -DatabaseName "BusinessConnectivyDB"
```

4. When the service application is created it creates its own proxy, so you don't need to create one with PowerShell.

Managed Metadata

While the Managed Metadata service (MMS) was new to SharePoint 2010, organizations were quick to adopt it. In order to bring all those terms over to your SharePoint 2013 farm you can upgrade your SharePoint 2010 MMS database. Following are instructions on how to introduce all those tasty terms to your SharePoint 2013 farm:

1. Restore the MMS database into your SharePoint 2013 SQL instance. The identity that the service app app pool runs as will need to be given the db_owner role on the database. If you followed the service account guidance in Chapter 2, that will be sp_serviceapps. Also give the user under whom you're running the PowerShell the db_owner role.

2. Start the Managed Metadata Services service instance. You can do this in Central Admin by selecting Application Management ➪ Manage Services on Server, or with the following PowerShell snippet:

```
Get-SPServiceInstance | where-object {$_.TypeName -eq "Managed Metadata Web
    Service"} | Start-SPServiceInstance
```

3. Create the MMS service application with PowerShell. The PowerShell assumes you have a service app app pool named "Default SharePoint Service App Pool." If your app pool name is different, adjust it accordingly. It also assumes the database from your SharePoint 2010 farm was named ManagedMetadataDB.

```
# Start the service instance
$serviceapppool = Get-SPServiceApplicationPool "Default SharePoint Service App
    Pool"

# Create the service application
$mmsapp = New-SPMetadataServiceApplication -Name "Managed Metadata Service" -
ApplicationPool $serviceapppool -DatabaseName "ManagedMetadataDB"

# Create the servce proxy
New-SPMetadataServiceApplicationProxy -Name "Managed Metadata Service Proxy" -
ServiceApplication $mmsapp -DefaultProxyGroup
```

When you open the MMS management page in Central Admin, you should see all the terms from your SharePoint 2010 farm.

PerformancePoint

The PerformancePoint service application can also be updated to SharePoint 2013. Following are the instructions for bringing it over from your SharePoint 2010 farm:

1. Restore the PerformancePoint database into your SharePoint 2013 SQL instance. The identity that the service app app pool runs as will need to be given the db_owner role on the database. If you followed the service account guidance in Chapter 2, that will be sp_serviceapps. Also give the user under whom you're running the PowerShell the db_owner role.

2. Start the Managed Metadata Services service instance. You can do this in Central Admin by selecting Application Management ➪ Manage Services on Server, or with the following PowerShell snippet:

```
Get-SPServiceInstance | where-object {$_.TypeName -eq "PerformancePoint Service" }
    | Start-SPServiceInstance
```

3. Create the PerformancePoint service application with PowerShell. The PowerShell assumes you have a service app app pool named "Default SharePoint Service App Pool." If your app pool name is different, adjust it accordingly. It also assumes the database from your SharePoint 2010 farm was named PerformancePointDB.

```
# Start the service instance
$serviceapppool = Get-SPServiceApplicationPool "Default SharePoint Service App
  Pool"

# Create the service application
$perfpointapp = New- SPPerformancePointServiceApplication -Name "Performance Point
  Service" -ApplicationPool $serviceapppool -DatabaseName "PerformancePointDB"

# Create the servce proxy
New- SPPerformancePointServiceApplicationProxy -Name "Performance Point Service
Proxy" -ServiceApplication $ perfpointapp -DefaultProxyGroup
```

Search

SharePoint 2010 contained two SharePoint Search service applications. There was the bare-bones Search that came with SharePoint Foundation, and there was the full-blown Search service application that came with SharePoint Server 2010. It is only possible to upgrade the SharePoint Services Search service application. If you're upgrading from SharePoint 2010 Foundation to SharePoint 2013 Foundation, you have to build it all from scratch. While that's a tough pill to swallow, there is a silver lining. It will be a brand-new Search service application and there won't be any cruft from the old Search messing things up. It will even have that new service application smell.

SharePoint Server 2010 had three databases in its stable; the Administration database, the Property database, and the Crawl database. Of these, only the Administration database can be brought over to SharePoint 2013. It contains all the settings and configuration, so it's the only one that offers any value to a new farm. The steps for upgrading the Search Administration database are similar to the steps for upgrading the other service applications, but they require a little more PowerShell:

1. Restore the Search Administration database into your SharePoint 2013 SQL instance. The identity that the service app app pool runs as will need to be given the db_owner role on the database. If you followed the service account guidance in Chapter 2, that will be sp_serviceapps. Also give the user under whom you're running the PowerShell the db_owner role.

2. Start the Search Service service instance. Unlike the other service instances, you cannot do this in Central Admin. It must be done in PowerShell. The following snippet will do:

```
$SearchInstance = Get-SPEnterpriseSearchServiceInstance
Start-SPServiceInstance $SearchInst
```

3. Now create the Search service application with PowerShell. The PowerShell assumes you have a service app app pool named "Default SharePoint Service App Pool." If your app pool name is different, adjust it accordingly. It also assumes the database from your SharePoint 2010 farm was named Search_AdminDB, and the SQL instance is named SharePointSQL.

```
# Get the app pool and service instance
$serviceapppool = Get-SPServiceApplicationPool "Default SharePoint Service App
  Pool"
$SearchInstance = Get-SPEnterpriseSearchServiceInstance

# Create the Search Service application by restoring the old Admin database
```

```
Restore-SPEnterpriseSearchServiceApplication -Name "Search Service Application" -
applicationpool $serviceapppool -databasename "Search_AdminDB" -databaseserver
"SharePointSQL" -AdminSearchServiceInstance $SearchInstance

# Create the service proxy
$ssa = Get-SPEnterpriseSearchServiceApplication
New-SPEnterpriseSearchServiceApplicationProxy -Name "Search Service Proxy" -
SearchApplication $ssa

# Add the proxy to the default proxy group
$SearchProxy = Get-SPEnterpriseSearchServiceApplicationProxy
Add-SPServiceApplicationProxyGroupMember –member $SearchProxy -identity " "
```

Secure Store

Upgrading the Secure Store service application for SharePoint 2010 allows you to keep all the identify mappings that you were using. These are usually used in conjunction with other service applications. Because the contents of the Secure Store database wouldn't be very secure if you could restore it without the encryption key it was encrypted with when it was created, you'll need that in order for the upgrade to work. Here are the steps to upgrade your Secure Store database:

1. Restore the Secure Store database into your SharePoint 2013 SQL instance. Be sure to give the identity under which your service application app pool is running the db_owner role in the database. If you followed the account guidelines in Chapter 2, that account will be sp_serviceapps. You'll need to give the account you're running the following PowerShell under the same permissions.

2. Start the Secure Store service instance on one or more servers in your farm. You can do this from Central Admin by selecting Application Management ➪ Manage Services on Server, or with the following PowerShell:

```
Get-SPServiceInstance | Where-Object { $_.TypeName -eq "Secure Store Service" } |
Start-SPServiceInstance
```

3. Create the Secure Store service application. The following PowerShell assumes you have a service app app pool named "Default SharePoint Service App Pool." If your app pool name is different, adjust it accordingly. It also assumes the database from your SharePoint 2010 farm was named SecureStoreDB and your passphrase was pass@word1:

```
# Get the service application pool
$serviceapppool = Get-SPServiceApplicationPool "Default SharePoint Service App
 Pool"

# Create the service application
$securestoreapp = New-SPSecureStoreServiceApplication -Name "Secure Store
Service"
 -ApplicationPool $serviceapppool -DatabaseName "SecureStoreDB"

# Create the service proxy
```

```
$securestoreproxy = New-SPSecureStoreApplicationProxy -Name "Secure Store Service
  Proxy" -ServiceApplication $securestoreapp -DefaultProxyGroup

# Restore the passphrase
Update-SPSecureStoreApplicationServerKey -Passphrase "pass@word1" -
ServiceApplicationProxy $securestoreproxy
```

You now have a Secure Store service application in SharePoint 2013 that contains all the credentials it had in your SharePoint 2010 farm.

User Profile Service

It shouldn't come as a surprise to anyone that the User Profile Service (UPS) is a little more trouble than the other service apps. It does have a certain reputation to maintain, after all. Before upgrading your UPS service application, make sure your MMS service application has upgraded correctly. The UPS uses the MMS to store terms, so they should be in place before you bring the upgraded UPS online.

The SharePoint 2010 UPS used three databases: Profile, Social, and Sync. Only the Profile and Social databases support being upgraded. The Sync database is scratch space for the UPS while it's doing imports and exports, so it doesn't contain any useful information to upgrade. Use the following steps to bring your SharePoint 2010 profile information into your SharePoint 2013 farm:

1. Restore the UPS Profile and optionally the UPS Social databases into your SharePoint 2013 SQL instance. The identity under which the service app app pool runs needs to be given the db_owner role on the database. If you followed the service account guidance in Chapter 2, that will be sp_serviceapps. Also give the user under whom you're running the PowerShell the db_owner role.

2. The UPS has two service instances: the User Profile Service and the User Profile Sync Service. You only want to start the former before you create the service application. You can do this in Central Admin by selecting Application Management ➪ Manage Services on Server, or with the following PowerShell snippet:

```
Get-SPServiceInstance | where-object {$_.TypeName -eq "User Profile Service" } |
Start-SPServiceInstance
```

3. Create the UPS service application with PowerShell. The following PowerShell assumes you have a service app app pool named "Default SharePoint Service App Pool." If your app pool name is different, adjust it accordingly. It also assumes the Profile DB from your SharePoint 2010 farm was named UserProfile_ProfileDB, and your Social DB was named UserProfile_SocialDB.

```
# Get the service app app pool
$serviceapppool = Get-SPServiceApplicationPool "Default SharePoint Service App
  Pool"

# Create the service application
$upa = New-SPProfileServiceApplication -Name "User Profile Service"
```

```
-ApplicationPool $ serviceapppool -ProfileDBName "UserProfile_ProfileDB"
 -SocialDBName "UserProfile_SocialDB" -ProfileSyncDBName "UserProfile_SyncDB"

# Create the service proxy
New-SPMetadataServiceApplicationProxy -Name "User Profile Service Proxy" -
ServiceApplication $upa -DefaultProxyGroup
```

4. The User Profile Service's Profile and Social databases should reflect the content that was in SharePoint 2010. The final step is to start the User Profile Sync service and set up your account synchronization. Chapter 14, "Configuring User Profiles and Social Computing," will guide you through that process.

USING THIRD-PARTY TOOLS TO MIGRATE CONTENT

This chapter has devoted a lot of pages to using the out-of-the-box upgrade techniques to upgrade your SharePoint 2010 to SharePoint 2013. In a lot of cases these techniques will be sufficient. In some scenarios, however, it makes sense to use third-party tools instead to get your content into you SharePoint 2013 farm. This section covers some of those scenarios.

Upgrading from Older Versions

All the upgrade options covered previously in this chapter require that the databases come from a SharePoint 2010 farm. It can be from any patch level of SharePoint 2010, but it has to be SharePoint 2010. If your current farm is SharePoint 2007, you have three options. The first is to do an in-place upgrade of your SharePoint 2007 farm to SharePoint 2010. Although that will get your content and services to SharePoint 2010, it carries significant risk.

The second option is to build a SharePoint 2010 farm solely for the purpose of getting the SharePoint 2007 databases to SharePoint 2010. Then they can be upgraded to SharePoint 2013 using the options discussed earlier. This is better than the first option but it requires a lot of time, as you're doing the upgrade twice. It also requires more machines; and while they can be physical or virtual, you still need the resources and the time to configure them. This option might work for some organizations, but it's a very manual and time-consuming process.

The third option is to use third-party migration software to bring the content from your SharePoint 2007 (or heaven forbid SharePoint 2003) into SharePoint 2010. While each of these tools has its own requirements, they are all probably looser than SharePoint 2013's. Some of this software runs on the server, and some on a client. Regardless of where it runs, you get to define source and destination content. After your SharePoint 2013 farm is built, upgrading is usually as simple as picking your SharePoint 2007 web application or site collections and pointing them to the corresponding spot in your SharePoint 2013 farm. Of course, if you want to upgrade your content from SharePoint 2010, that will work as well. That might sound silly, given that you can upgrade SharePoint 2010 content with out-of-the-box tools. The next section covers why you might want to do that. For now you have an option that enables you to easily upgrade content to SharePoint 2013 from SharePoint 2007 or earlier.

Restructuring Your Farm

When attaching your SharePoint 2010 content databases to SharePoint 2013, they arrive exactly as they were, for better or for worse. In some cases you may not want everything to be the same. You might have a large site collection that should really be several site collections; or you might have a web that's in one site collection but really makes more sense in another. Problems like that are not easy to fix in SharePoint, and because of that they can become very entrenched. When upgrading with the database attach method, you're simply bringing those problems forward.

One way to fix that is to use third-party migration software to migrate to SharePoint 2013. Instead of bringing whole databases and site collections over, you can take the time to redesign things. You can then build out the structure in SharePoint 2013 and use the migration software to bring pieces over and put them where they belong, instead of where they were. This gives you the capability to break up any large site collections, or put webs in more appropriate places.

You can also take a hybrid approach whereby you attach directly any databases that don't need to be restructured. Then you use the third-party software to migrate over the data that needs to be reorganized. This gives you the best of both worlds. You can use the PowerShell cmdlet `Move-SPSite` in SharePoint 2010 to put the problem children site collections in their own content databases. That way, you can easily attach the site collections that are fine, and segregate the troublesome content.

Choosing Third-Party Migration Software

There are a lot of good SharePoint migration tools out there, so it can be difficult to decide which one to use. Fortunately, most vendors provide free trials, so you can try them out to see how they work. Before you try any of them, make a list of the tasks you want it to perform. Is scripting migrations important to you? Will you be migrating workflows and metadata? Will you be migrating multiple languages? Each migration suite has strengths in specific areas. Making sure you know what you want before you take them for a test drive will help you choose the one that's best for you.

When you do the trial of the migration software, try to test a wide variety of content. Try publishing sites as well as blogs and teams sites. Try a heavily customized site. Make sure you test a site with a lot of workflows if they're important to your company. If you use any custom content types, make sure they are also migrated and that you can create new instances of them. Understanding what is important to your organization will help you design your testing. Also, don't be afraid to try offerings from different companies. They all have something to offer.

SUMMARY

You have put a lot of work into your SharePoint 2010 farms, and it almost seems sad to be giving all that up for SharePoint 2013. Similarly, your users have put an awful lot of content into SharePoint 2010, and you owe it to them to do the best job you can, upgrading it all safely to SharePoint 2013. This chapter covered the supported method for upgrading. Then it went into excruciating detail about how to upgrade content and service applications, should you choose to. Finally, you learned how to augment the out-of-the-box upgrade functionality with third-party software. Upgrading is complicated work, but armed with enough knowledge and enough practice it's easy, and almost fun.

Claims Authentication and OAuth

WHAT'S IN THIS CHAPTER?

➤ What's new with claims and authorization?

➤ User authentication

➤ Application authentication

➤ Server-to-server authentication

SharePoint 2013 contains several new enhancements to the claims infrastructure, and it introduces *Open Authorization* (OAuth) capability, which enables new server-to-server and application authentication scenarios.

A user authentication model called *claims-based authentication* (CBA) was first introduced in SharePoint 2010. SharePoint websites using CBA are said to be using claims authentication, or just claims. SharePoint 2013 introduces several new enhancements to the claims infrastructure and capability, and it is now the default user authentication mechanism for all SharePoint 2013 websites. As SharePoint adoption increases, users are accessing SharePoint websites from both their company's on-premise implementation and from cloud-based solutions such as Windows Azure, and SharePoint online, which is a part of Office 365. A SharePoint application may even be accessed from different organizations. This diverse set of access scenarios requires a robust authentication and authorization infrastructure, which CBA provides for applications running on-premises or in the cloud.

CBA is based on the concept of *identity* and utilizes open-source standards and protocols so that it works with any corporate identity system, not just Active Directory and not just Windows-based systems. Identity is represented by a set of information about the user, and this information is encapsulated in a security token. This token is presented to any application to which the individual is attempting to gain access. The individual's token, and therefore his or her identity, is verified by some directory service. Typically, user authentication contains username and password information. The beauty of CBA is that this token can contain a richer set of information that can be used for authorization, as well as confirming user authentication. CBA provides a trust-based system between applications and a centralized provider that issues the token. The application trusts the individual because the provider is trusted. Therefore, in addition to providing a single sign-on environment, this eliminates the need for each application to authenticate the user, enabling the application to focus on what permissions to assign, and how the application interacts with the user. CBA can be used in combination with OAuth to provide new authentication scenarios.

SharePoint 2013 also introduces support for the Open Authorization 2.0 (OAuth) standard. OAuth is an industry standard protocol that allows a user or application to temporarily access resources or information on behalf of another user, thereby eliminating the need for the requesting user to share his or her password information. SharePoint 2013 uses this capability to provide the new server-to-server authentication capability with other applications, such as Exchange Server 2013, and apps in the SharePoint Store or App Catalog.

This chapter provides an overview of the claims authentication process and the new SharePoint 2013 claims enhancements. It also covers the new server-to-server authentication process, the OAuth functionality, and how these new security processes are used.

WHAT'S NEW WITH CLAIMS AND AUTHORIZATION?

Several new capabilities are introduced in SharePoint 2013, and the following sections cover those most pertinent to the administrator. As you plan to upgrade to SharePoint 2013 from SharePoint 2010, you should be planning your strategy to migrate classic-mode websites to claims-mode websites. The user authentication infrastructure is now more efficient and effective, as login tokens are now cached using the Distributed Cache Service. SharePoint 2013 can share resources and information more securely with other applications using the server-to-server authentication process. OAuth, which is new to SharePoint 2013, is used to provide access to resources.

Migrating from Classic to SharePoint 2013 Claims

This is a very important topic for SharePoint administrators, as Windows claims authentication is the new default user authentication mechanism for SharePoint 2013 when you create a new SharePoint 2013 web application. SharePoint 2013 will continue to support classic-mode authentication, but the capability to create a classic-mode SharePoint web application is no longer available using the web browser. You can still create a classic-mode web application using PowerShell, but claims authentication is recommended and it is required to support all SharePoint 2013 functionality.

SharePoint 2013 supports three different types of claims authentication: Windows-based claims, Security Assertion Markup Language–based (SAML) claims, and forms-based authentication (FBA) claims. Organizations that used classic-mode authentication in SharePoint 2010 have the following supported options for migrating to claims-based authentication:

➤ Migrate from classic authentication to claims authentication in SharePoint 2010. SharePoint 2010 content can then be migrated to SharePoint 2013 via normal methods (database attach, etc.).

➤ Migrate the SharePoint 2010 content to SharePoint 2013 via the database attach method. Convert the classic-mode web application to use claims via PowerShell.

SharePoint 2013 introduces new PowerShell cmdlets to accomplish this migration. For a more in-depth discussion of the classic-to-claims migration, and the overall process of upgrading SharePoint 2010 to SharePoint 2013, administrators should refer to Chapter 5, "Upgrading to SharePoint 2013."

> **NOTE** *At the time of this writing, Microsoft is publicly stating that classic-mode authentication is being deprecated, and therefore is encouraging all organizations to migrate to claims in SharePoint 2010 if possible before upgrading to SharePoint 2013.*

Authentication Infrastructure

SharePoint 2013 introduces the new Distributed Cache Service (DCS), which is used to cache login tokens (also known as FedAuth cookies). This is a big improvement over SharePoint 2010, which stored the login token on each web front-end (WFE) server in the farm. In SharePoint 2010, users who are redirected to a different load-balanced WFE often need to re-authenticate when using SAML or FBA authentication if load balancer affinity, also called sticky sessions, is not enabled. Therefore, sticky sessions are no longer required with SharePoint 2013. In addition to the use of the DCS, SharePoint 2013 has much more verbose logging of the claims authentication process. The ULS logs contain much more information about user authentication, such as user redirection, token addition and removal from the cache, and so on, which helps to manage and troubleshoot claims.

OAuth

SharePoint 2013 supports and extends the OAuth 2.0 standard. As mentioned earlier, OAuth is an industry standard protocol that enables users to authorize an application to act on their behalf without sharing their username and password. This is accomplished by establishing a trust relationship between the applications, which means you don't have to assign a Windows login credential to an application. This enables users to, for example, share their resources or data (SharePoint lists, documents, photos, and videos) stored on one website with another website, or use this information as input for a custom application. OAuth is used only for resource access, not for user authentication. As you might guess, the new SharePoint 2013 Cloud App Model (also referred to as just the App Model) uses OAuth extensively to authorize apps to access resources on behalf of users.

SharePoint 2013 uses OAuth to allow applications to access SharePoint resources in one of three ways:

➤ With the combined permissions of the application and the user

➤ With only the permissions of the application

➤ With only the permissions of the user

The app is given access to these resources by defining a trust relationship between the application and SharePoint 2013. Depending on the architecture of the application, a trust relationship between SharePoint 2013 and a cloud provider such as Windows Azure Access Control Service (ACS) can also be established. These trust relationships are very similar to the trust relationships used for authenticating SharePoint users with claims authentication. We provide a more detailed discussion of the claims authentication process in the User Authentication section.

> **NOTE** *For a more thorough discussion of the new Cloud App Model, readers should refer to Chapter 11, "Managing and Configuring Apps."*

Server-to-Server Authentication

Server-to-Server (S2S) authentication, which is used to create SharePoint *high-trust apps*, is a scenario for application-to-application authentication, and OAuth provides the basis for this capability. S2S uses a Microsoft extension of the OAuth protocol to enable services or servers to share resources on behalf of a user, and this user does not have to be authenticated. S2S requires user profiles, so user profile mapping and profile imports must be configured. For all those interested in using SharePoint Foundation 2013, high-trust apps are not possible because user profiles are required and not available in Foundation. S2S allows SharePoint to share information across SharePoint 2013 farms, and with other S2S-compliant applications. For example, the following SharePoint 2013 capabilities utilize S2S:

> ➤ **eDiscovery** — The Electronic Discovery capability enables SharePoint 2013 to index mailbox content in Exchange Server 2013 and conversation content in Lync Server 2013 to include that information as part of a legal hold.

> ➤ **Task management** — Tasks created in Outlook 2013 or in SharePoint 2013 are synchronized and viewable from a user's personal site.

> ➤ **Site mailboxes** — These are Exchange 2013 mailboxes that are rendered and viewable from SharePoint 2013 websites.

> ➤ **Workflow** — As discussed in Chapter 16, "Installing and Configuring Azure Workflow Server," S2S is used by SharePoint 2013 to authenticate and share information with the new Azure Workflow Server.

That concludes a brief overview of some of the new key features, which are discussed in more detail throughout the chapter. The following section describes claims identity and the actual authentication process. It introduces several new terms and provides a basis for the rest of the chapter.

USER AUTHENTICATION

In this section, our goal is for the administrator to gain a deeper understanding of claims-based authentication, as this is the new default mechanism for SharePoint 2013. We begin by introducing the concept of claims-based identity, and then describe how to use it, ending with a high-level overview of the claims authentication process.

Claims-Based Identity

Users new to claims-based identity routinely ask the same set of questions:

➤ Why do we need yet another way to authenticate users?

➤ What is user identity?

➤ What is a claim?

➤ Why is claims authentication the default SharePoint mechanism?

The answers to these questions are associated with the key challenges related to providing users with access to information. These challenges include user identity, user access, and user information and storage. As you will see, claims-based identity presents a solution to these challenges.

User Identity

User identity is a fundamental requirement for application security, in terms of both user authentication and user authorization. Knowing who is requesting access to websites and access to object information is critical to providing a secure environment. The challenge is determining which identity technology is the right one for a specific application, and then which one is the best across the enterprise or cloud environment so that you can accommodate the needs of all the applications. The solution can become very complicated. You need to satisfy two key requirements:

➤ How users will gain access to the enterprise's applications, regardless of their location

➤ How different types of user information will be retrieved by the applications so that the applications can accomplish their required functions

---

CLAIMS IDENTITY VERSUS CLASSIC IDENTITY

Administrators are very familiar with classic user identity, which is represented by the domain\username format. Claims identity is represented by a very different format: i:0#.w|domain\username, and although there is some similarity they are very different. A given user can have a classic identity and a claims identity, and SharePoint will treat this as two totally different users.

User Access

User access to websites and information is necessary for sharing and collaborating inside and outside the organization. Providing user access in a secure manner is critical, and a key challenge. Administrators and developers need to know whether an application will be accessed by employees from within the organization, from a device outside the organization, from the public Internet, or any combination of these. One technology may not be enough; the organization may have to support multiple technologies. For example, you might use Windows integrated security for internal users, and forms-based authentication (FBA) for users outside the organization; but this introduces complexity in terms of providing a single authentication mechanism and the need for storing different user information in multiple locations. In addition, neither Windows integrated security nor FBA provide much information about the user, with the latter providing username and password information only, unless both the membership and role providers have been created and configured. In addition, suppose you need to provide access to partner or vendor employees. For that you need to implement *identity federation* using SAML so that users won't need a separate login. An example of identity federation would be using Active Directory Federated Services (ADFS). ADFS would provide a SSO experience for these non-employees, without IT having to give them a company login account. Finally, keep in mind that the application requiring login may exist in the cloud, as this scenario is rapidly gaining popularity; or you could have a hybrid scenario, with applications both on-premises and in the cloud.

User Information

How will information about users be stored and retrieved? The application can query the user for some information and look up other information. This may not sound like a big issue, but consider the number of different applications in an organization, and that each may need to store and retrieve information that is specific to its functionality. Even when your organization requires simple identity capability, such as all users across the enterprise authenticating using Active Directory, this type of login provides very little information about the user.

The Solution

The solution to user access and user information has typically been solved by each different application requiring its own login and user information. This may not be an issue if there is just one application, but when you have multiple applications this becomes a big problem for both users and administrators. Claims identity offers a different and better solution: create a single identity approach for all scenarios so that the user is authenticated once, and each application is provided with the specific information it needs. However, you may be wondering why you need to use claims; wouldn't SharePoint's classic mode NTLM and Kerberos work just fine? The following reasons may help to convince you otherwise:

➤   NTLM and Kerberos protocols haven't been significantly updated in many years.

➤   The need to federate SharePoint with other systems and to establish hybrid environments that include both on-premise and cloud resources is here and increasing. NTLM and Kerberos are not particularly well suited for interoperability with other applications outside your organization.

➤   Windows claims supports both NTLM and Kerberos.

➤   Claims alone and in combination with OAuth offers new ways to delegate authentication and authorization, and to utilize user profile information.

➤   SharePoint and SAML open new directory integration possibilities that Active Directory alone cannot meet. For non-Microsoft products and technologies, SAML is the standard, just as Active Directory is the standard for Microsoft products.

➤   You may already be using claims authentication and not realize it. For example, when you log in to Windows Live (which has been renamed to Microsoft ID) or grant access to your Facebook profile, you are using WS-Federation and OAuth.

Claims-based identity provides a common way for applications to acquire identity information from users, irrespective of whether they are inside the organization, in other organizations, or on the Internet. Now that you understand the concept of claims identity and its role as a solution for user authentication, the following section takes a look at using claims identity.

Using Claims-Based Identity

The purpose of this section is to show how claims identity is used to authenticate users. It begins with a real-world analogy that illustrates the use of claims. Then you will learn the technical requirements for implementing claims authentication. Finally, you will walk through the actual claims authentication process.

A Real-World Analogy

It's very likely that at some point, you have used your driver's license to establish or verify your identity. Your license contains a set of attributes that assert your identity, such as name, age, eye color, and so on. In order to obtain such a license, prospective drivers must furnish required credentials bearing proof of their identity. This proof might be a birth certificate, a passport, and might even include a utility bill or some other proof of residency. These assertions are verified by the state agency, and the state issues your driver's license. This list of identity assertions is used by other companies or agencies to verify your identity because they trust the state agency that issued your license.

In claims identity, this list of assertions can be considered a set of *claims*. Assertions can include a username, a role, an employee ID, and a variety of other attributes pertinent to the individual's position. The state agency represents the *Security Token Service* (STS). Users request access to SharePoint resources and are redirected to the STS. The STS verifies their identity (authenticates the user), and then issues a *security token* that encapsulates the user's claims. The STS functions as an *identity provider* (IdP) because it creates and manages security tokens. To create a security token, the STS must be able to locate valid credentials for a user in an attribute store. Active Directory Domain Services can be used as an attribute store for an STS, and would be an example of an *authentication provider*. SharePoint and other applications trust the STS and therefore do not have to re-authenticate the user. The claims can then be used to determine authorization and permission levels for access to SharePoint 2013 resources.

A *relying party* is any entity that trusts the issuer of the driver's license or, in the claims world, the STS. In the physical world, the security agent at the airport is a relying party. In the claims world, SharePoint trusts the STS (or multiple STSs) to have authenticated the users who make requests for SharePoint resources, and therefore is a relying party. In both the real world and the claims world, those who produce the security tokens often add other relevant information about the user to the tokens. In the driver's license example, address information, height, weight, and a picture are typically included. In the claims world, security tokens can include information that SharePoint can use to authorize the user's requests for SharePoint resources, such as organization information, group memberships based on geography or job role, or any other information that can be used to determine what a user can do inside of SharePoint. In our driver's license analogy, the relying party of a driver's license depend on the birthdate to determine whether a user can purchase alcohol. Note that the relying party makes this decision based on the value of the birthdate, not just the presence of the birthdate. As a relying party, SharePoint uses attributes gathered from Active Directory and other attribute stores. In the case of the driver's license and the security token, these attributes are added when the token or license is created. This addition of claims is referred to as *claims augmentation.*

Driver's licenses expire, and once expired they are no longer considered a legitimate means of providing identification. Similarly, a security token has a defined lifetime after which it is no longer valid.

Driver's licenses are also subject to being modified or duplicated to provide false information. Relying parties in the physical world (security agents at an airport, for instance) deal with this by not accepting licenses that show signs of tampering. In the claims world, the STS knows the type and number of claims specified by the relying party, and the STS token is digitally signed to protect against tampering and ensure authenticity.

Technical Requirements

To implement claims identity, SharePoint 2013 utilizes a Security Token Service (STS) defined in WS-Trust, and is configured to trust one or multiple STSs. SharePoint 2013 is claims-enabled once it is installed, but the following provides perspective on the key components. Implementing claims-based identity and using claims for authorization generally requires using and understanding a set of core technologies:

➤ **Windows Identity Framework (WIF)** — WIF provides the .NET classes required to enable claims-based authentication. All the required interactions with the security infrastructure (Active Directory, LDAP directories, cloud-based directory services such as Windows Azure Access Control Service, etc.) are enabled by WIF. WIF is based on a set of open-source standards, and specifically includes capability for WS-Security, WS-Trust, and WS-Federation. WIF is part of the SharePoint 2013 prerequisites, and it is automatically installed when you run the prerequisite installer.

➤ **Security Assertion Markup Language (SAML)** — SAML is a markup language that is the recognized standard for communicating identity information. WIF officially supports SAML 1.1, although support for SAML 2.0 is currently available via a Community Technical Preview (CTP) from Microsoft.

➤ **Open Authorization 2.0 (OAuth)** — OAuth is a protocol that enables users to authorize access to resources without user credentials (user ID and password, certificates, etc.). The user is required to authorize this access when it is first requested. Subsequent access is considered to be acceptable to the end user. Access is granted to specific resources for a specific duration. OAuth is the protocol used to allow SharePoint applications from the Office Store or an organization's application store (known as the *App Catalog*) to access SharePoint resources on behalf of the user or the application principal. OAuth is used to allow applications that are running outside of SharePoint to access protected SharePoint resources.

➤ **Active Directory Federated Services 2.0** — ADFS 2.0 provides both identity federation and single sign-on (SSO) solutions. ADFS is an STS. It uses Active Directory as its identity store; and Lightweight Directory Access Protocol (LDAP), SQL, or a custom store as an attribute store. ADFS is not required for SharePoint 2013, but it enables SharePoint 2013 to federate with other applications. ADFS also provides SAML 2.0 support, and it can be used with SharePoint 2013 to deliver this capability.

> **NOTE** *Many of the terms associated with claims-based identity and claims authentication are summarized in Table 6-1. For a deeper explanation of how WS-Trust, WS-Security, and WS-Federation work together in a claims-based authentication scenario, see "Understanding WS-Federation" at* `http://msdn` `.microsoft.com/en-us/library/bb498017.aspx.`

Claims-based authentication is user authentication that utilizes claims-based identity. Users can have identities in different directory stores and use them simultaneously to access different resources in SharePoint. Claims-based authentication is the default for SharePoint 2013. SharePoint 2013 supports Windows claims (NTLM and Kerberos), FBA claims, and SAML 1.1 claims. In order to use SAML 2.0, SharePoint 2013 must federate with ADFS, which supports both SAML 1.1 and SAML 2.0. Using claims-based authentication enables you to take advantage of all the new capabilities in SharePoint 2013.

> **NOTE** *Claims identity and the claims authentication process in WIF are based on multiple standards and specifications, some of which are listed in Table 6-1. These standards and specifications are managed by the Organization for the Advancement of Structured Information Standards (OASIS). Interested readers are referred to the OASIS website for more details* `https://www.oasis-open` `.org/.`

TABLE 6-1: Claims-Based Identity Terminology and Descriptions

TECHNOLOGY	DESCRIPTION
Windows Identity Foundation (WIF)	A set of application programming interfaces (APIs) that can be used by developers to build claims-aware and federation-capable applications. WIF provides a framework to claims-enable your applications and to create custom security token services. This enables enterprises to use a single identity model so that applications can communicate and interoperate using industry standard protocols. See `http://www.microsoft.com/en-us/download/details` `.aspx?displaylang=en&id=17331`.
ADFS 2.0	Provides both identity federation and single sign-on (SSO) solutions. ADFS 2.0 is a security token service (STS) responsible for issuing security tokens. It uses Active Directory as its identity store; and Lightweight Directory Access Protocol (LDAP), SQL, or a custom store as an attribute store. ADFS 2.0 supports both active (WS-Trust) and passive (WS-Federation and SAML 2.0) scenarios. ADFS 2.0 supports SAML 1.1 and SAML 2.0. Windows Server 2012 includes ADFS 2.1.

continues

TABLE 6-1 *(continued)*

TECHNOLOGY	DESCRIPTION
Claim	A claim is an identity assertion about the user, but in general it is any piece of information that describes a characteristic of the user.
Security token	A token, or security token, represents a collection (one or more) of claims and a digital signature. The token is digitally signed to protect against unauthorized claim changes.
Secure Store Service (STS)	Creates and issues security tokens. The STS is a web service that issues tokens as defined by the WS-Trust security standard.
Identity provider	Any organization that backs the STS, ensures that the claims are authentic, and authenticates the user.
Relying party	An application that accepts and uses a security token. The application has been configured to trust the STS and is relying on the information contained in the claims.
WS-Security	The protocol that defines a security token and how to include and/or refer to one in a SOAP message.
WS-Trust	Deals with the issuing, validating, and renewal of security tokens. It also defines the concept of a Security Token Service (STS), and how to request a security token directly from the service, including the format of messages used to request and respond.
WS-Federation	Specifies the process for sending and receiving WS-Trust messages via a web browser (passive profile) and SOAP clients (active profile).
Security Assertion Markup Language	SAML is an XML-based standard for exchanging authentication and authorization data between applications and services. SAML tokens are XML representations of claims.
SAML Protocol	Defines message patterns for requesting and receiving SAML security tokens from a Security Token Service.

Understanding the User Authentication Process and Authentication Providers

User authentication scenarios in SharePoint 2013 can be as straightforward as using Windows Integrated Security and Active Directory or as complicated as using Windows Azure Access Control Service as a federation provider. The process for user authentication with a trusted IdP and using

SharePoint's internal STS is a complex process. This process is shown in Figure 6-1, and described in the following steps. This example uses SharePoint as the relying party, but the relying party could be any claims-enabled application.

1. The process begins when the user makes a request to access SharePoint resources or a SharePoint website. In reality, a web browser or other client acting on behalf of the user makes an HTTP Get request. SharePoint checks to see if the request contains a SAML token with the user's identity. Once a valid SAML token is identified, SharePoint 2013 then inspects the target URL of the incoming request to see whether it references a standard SharePoint site or a child site associated with a specific app web. If the incoming request targets a standard site, SharePoint 2013 conducts its authentication and authorization process granting access to the requested resource. However, if the request targets an app web, SharePoint initiates an OAuth process. In our scenario, the client is requesting access to a SharePoint website, and has not yet been authenticated, so no SAML token is present.

2. Since the user has not been authenticated, SharePoint sends an authentication request redirect to the client so that it can be authenticated by its IdP.

3. The client issues an authentication request to its IdP, which can be Active Directory, FBA, or any SAML-based system, and the client is authenticated based on the user's credentials. In general, the request also contains information identifying the application to which the user wants access. The IdP performs a lookup in the appropriate user directory or database and validates the user's identity.

4. Once the client is authenticated, the IdP returns a Windows token, FBA token, or SAML token to the client.

5. The client sends the authentication token to SharePoint, and the SharePoint STS creates a new token with the appropriate claims. The SharePoint STS can perform claim transformation and claims augmentation, the former modifying the claims information while the latter includes adding additional claims information.

6. The SharePoint STS sends the new SAML token back to the client. So, at this point we have two tokens, an authentication token from the IdP and a SAML claims token from the SharePoint STS.

7. The client submits the SAML token to SharePoint, and SharePoint reviews the token, as in Step 1. SharePoint or the application verifies the token's signature, confirming that it originated from a trusted IdP, and the claims are accepted. The token can also contain claims about the user that SharePoint can use for authorization.

8. SharePoint issues a response with the requested content to the client, and the process is complete.

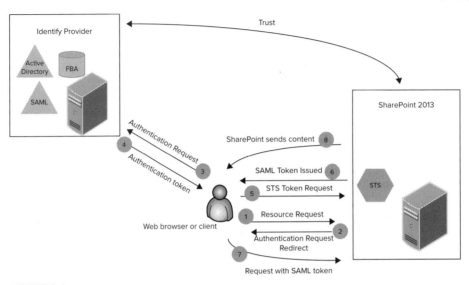

FIGURE 6-1

Claims authentication is based on delegating user authentication to a trusted STS that is backed by the identity provider. The trust is established and verifiable by the STS and the claims-consuming application (SharePoint) using the public:private key pair of a digital certificate.

A key benefit of claim identity and claims authentication is that the application does not have to authenticate the user. The application can focus on authorization because it no longer needs to authenticate the user. An application can specify exactly what claims it needs and which identity providers it trusts. Because the application doesn't have to authenticate the user, it can be deployed on-premise or in the cloud without change. The application only needs to be configured to trust the appropriate STS, and the administrator configures the STS to issue the right claims required by the relying party.

Authentication providers are the means by which users are authenticated, because they represent a directory or database containing the user's credentials. An example of an authentication provider is Active Directory Domain Services (AD DS). Other terms for an authentication provider that you may see used are *user directory* and *attribute store*. Claims authentication represents an authentication type, and it is a specific way of validating credentials against one or more authentication providers. SharePoint 2013 includes a local or internal STS and WIF to claims-enable web applications; therefore, SharePoint 2013 websites are configured to utilize claims.

> **NOTE** *Classic-mode authentication is still supported, but it is being deprecated, so organizations are encouraged to use claims authentication. Classic-mode configuration is done using PowerShell cmdlets; it cannot be implemented using Central Administration.*

Claims authentication in SharePoint 2013 supports all the authentication providers supported in SharePoint 2010: Windows authentication (Kerberos, NTLM, Basic), forms-based authentication using ASP.NET membership and role providers, and SAML token-based authentication. As demonstrated in Chapter 3, when you create a new web application, the default authentication type is claims, and the default authentication provider is NTLM. You have the option to also choose Kerberos, and this type of configuration is very important for establishing a SharePoint farm to support business intelligence, as discussed in detail in Chapter 8, "Configuring SharePoint for Business Intelligence." In general, organizations that don't use AD DS can use either FBA or SAML, as outlined here:

➤ For organizations using an LDAP directory, FBA is easier to implement than SAML, although both approaches are available. SharePoint Server 2013 has a built-in LDAP provider. FBA can utilize the default providers that are included with ASP.NET, or organizations that have very specific security requirements (and very good developers) can create their own providers if necessary.

➤ SAML is recommended for those organizations already using an authentication environment that supports WS-Federation 1.1 and SAML 1.1, which are both supported by SharePoint 2013. SAML tokens can be produced by identity providers such as Active Directory Federation Services (ADFS) and others.

➤ Utilizing ADFS and services such as Windows Azure Access Control Services (ACS) as federation providers enables end users to authenticate against many common identity providers or even another organization's Active Directory instance. ADFS 2.0 also supports SAML 2.0, so ADFS can be used to federate with SharePoint 2013 to enable integration with third-party SAML 2.0 providers.

The process for using FBA and SAML authentication providers with SharePoint 2013 is similar to that for SharePoint 2010, and is discussed in detail on TechNet. Several key references that describe the configuration are described in Table 6-2.

> **NOTE** *Claims-based authentication is Microsoft's recommendation for all web applications and zones of a SharePoint 2013 farm, as this enables you to take advantage of all the new features and scenarios in SharePoint 2013 that use server-to-server authentication and app authentication.*

> **WARNING** *The new Office Web Applications (see Chapter 15 for a detailed discussion) can only be used by SharePoint 2013 web applications that use claims-based authentication. Office Web Apps rendering and editing will not work on SharePoint 2013 web applications that use classic-mode authentication.*

TABLE 6-2: References for Configuring FBA and SAML Authentication Providers

AUTHENTICATION PROVIDER	REFERENCES
Forms-based authentication	http://technet.microsoft.com/en-us/library/ee806890 http://www.microsoft.com/en-us/download/details.aspx?id=34684
SAML authentication using ADFS	http://technet.microsoft.com/library/hh305235.aspx http://technet.microsoft.com/en-US/library/jj219641.aspx

Several scenarios require the use of additional identity capability. One such example is federated user authentication, which is discussed in the next section.

Federated User Authentication Process

As collaboration boundaries expand and need for information increases, access to resources that are not hosted by your company or an organization that knows you is needed. For example, many people want to use Internet-based resources such as Facebook, Twitter, and so on. Because accessing any computer-based resources involves some type of authentication, authorization, and user administration, this greatly complicates our access requirements, and therefore our ability to access external resources. In claims terminology, the user wishes to access an application that doesn't trust the user's STS; but what if the application that owns the resources the user wishes to access trusts an STS that trusts the user's STS? This is referred to as *identity federation*. In this scenario, an identity provider offers an STS (for example, SharePoint 2013) and another STS is offered by a *federation provider* (FP). The administrator configures the federation provider STS to trust the identity provider STS. As a result, the user is allowed to securely access the necessary resources even though the resources are outside his or her environment.

Users on the Internet typically interact with several common IdPs (e.g., Facebook, Microsoft ID, Yahoo, Office 365). If SharePoint 2013 or any claims-enabled application in general needed to accept identities from each of these (i.e., trust them), two different approaches could be used:

➤ Configure SharePoint 2013 or the application to trust each STS. Users would be presented with a list of available STSs, choose the one they want to use, and proceed to authenticate against that STS.

➤ Use a federation provider (FP) such as ADFS 2.0 or Windows Azure Access Control Service. The FP trusts each of these STSs and provides an abstraction layer between them and SharePoint or the application. In this case, SharePoint or the application is configured to trust only the federation provider STS.

The FP simplifies administration, especially if multiple applications need to be configured. FPs can also provide claims transformations that alter the type and number of claims. FPs are an abstraction layer that can shield an application from the peculiarities of each STS that the application needs to support. The claims transformation capabilities enable claims that originate from each different STS to be mapped to a consistent set of claims appropriate for the relying party application. Figure 6-2 shows an overview of the federated user authentication process with a FP, such as ADFS or Windows Azure Access Control Service (ACS), and a different IdP that is trusted by the FP. The following steps in the process illustrate two new key points: how an STS can act as a federation provider, accepting one token and producing another, and how one STS can trust another STS:

1. A web browser or other client on behalf of the user requests access to SharePoint 2013. SharePoint provides information about which STSs it trusts. In this example, SharePoint trusts only one STS, the FP STS.

2. The client contacts the FP. The FP STS offers the user a choice of identity provider STSs that it trusts. The FP STS is configured to trust multiple STSs, such as Microsoft ID, Azure ACS, Facebook, and others. Since SharePoint trusts the FP, this trust relationship allows users to authenticate against these other IdPs and gain access to SharePoint.

3. The appropriate IdP STS is chosen, and the web browser or client contacts the selected IdP STS. The necessary credentials are provided to the chosen IdP STS, and the IdP STS authenticates the user and generates an IdP security token. This token can't be used to access SharePoint because SharePoint doesn't trust this IdP.

4. The browser submits the IdP token to the FP STS, which validates the token to ensure it came from a trusted STS.

5. Once the IdP token is validated, the FP STS generates a new security token and sends the FP token back to the client. The FP STS can also transform the claims that come from any IdP STS so that the token sent to the SharePoint-relying party looks the same regardless of which IdP STS authenticated the user.

6. The client submits the FP STS token to SharePoint 2013, which verifies that that the FP token was issued by a trusted STS, the claims information is processed as appropriate, and the user is granted access. The token can also contain claims about the user that the application can use for authorization.

7. SharePoint issues a response with the requested content to the client, and the process is complete.

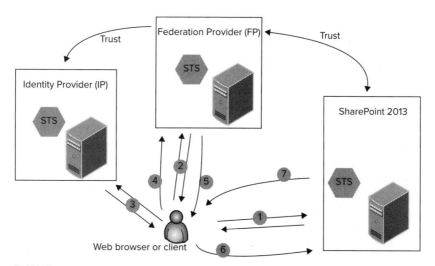

FIGURE 6-2

This process illustrates how one STS can trust another STS, and how federated identity can be used across environments and applications. ADFS 2.0 supports both web browsers and other clients, such as Office desktop clients and those built using Windows Communication Foundation (WCF). The ADFS 2.0 STS can be used entirely inside an organization, exposed on the Internet, or both. ADFS 2.0 is not required to use SharePoint 2013 claims-based identity. CBA or federated CBA can be implemented using an STS from any vendor, or even a custom-built STS.

Part of the beauty of this process is that users gain access to resources without explicitly logging into the desired application. Users log in to their familiar application, and they have *single sign-on* (SSO) with the desired application.

APPLICATION AUTHENTICATION

This section begins with a brief overview of the new Cloud App Model. Our purpose here is only to provide information pertinent to the authentication discussion, as Chapter 11, "Managing and Configuring Apps" is dedicated to this topic. This is followed by a discussion of the critical role that OAuth plays in SharePoint 2013 authentication. The section concludes with two examples that illustrate the use and process of app authentication, including a detailed discussion of the OAuth process.

Cloud App Model

The new SharePoint 2013 Cloud App Model enables developers to provide solutions, called *apps* in the new terminology, to extend the capabilities of SharePoint 2013. This new approach to creating customized solutions for SharePoint 2013 largely replaces the traditional approach discussed in Chapter 10, which is still available but no longer recommended. The new app model describes a new paradigm for a solution that is self-contained, installs and uninstalls easily, does not negatively impact SharePoint performance, is applicable to SharePoint 2013 on-premise or in the cloud, and is easy to use. Like it or not, this is the new world. This section describes the authentication and authorization aspects of the new app model because they are pertinent to a complete discussion of this chapter's subject, but other aspects of the app model are covered in detail in Chapter 11. Two key points are pertinent to our discussion:

➤ SharePoint apps refer to complete solutions for customizing SharePoint 2013 that were created using the new app model.

➤ SharePoint apps require claims authentication on the SharePoint web application.

SharePoint apps can be obtained from one of two sources: the *Office Store* (sometimes also referred to as the *SharePoint Store*), located publically on the Internet and managed by Microsoft, and an enterprise application store located inside the SharePoint 2013 farm known as the *app catalog*. An app catalog is created within a SharePoint 2013 web application. The important point here is that these app locations are installation points for the app; the app is not installed in the store. The store is where administrators and any users with the proper permissions go to install an app, or download the app for inclusion in the app catalog.

> **NOTE** *At the time of writing, the public Office Store is located at* `http://office` `.microsoft.com/en-us/store`, *and the SharePoint Store is at* `http://` `office.microsoft.com/en-us/store/apps-for-sharepoint-FX102804987` `.aspx`.

One of the key drivers for the new app model is to ensure that SharePoint apps do not negatively affect the performance of the SharePoint environment, and therefore they are applicable to both on-premises environments owned by corporations, and public, multi-tenant environments such as Office 365. This is accomplished by not allowing any of the actual code from the app to be installed inside the SharePoint environment; SharePoint does not host the app. The SharePoint app is hosted in one of three places:

> ➤ **Provider-hosted** — This type of app is hosted on a separate set of servers from the SharePoint farm. These servers can be located on-premise as part of the corporate enterprise or hosted in the cloud.

> ➤ **Autohosted in Windows Azure** — This is only available for SharePoint 2013 online, which is part of Office 365. The app runs as a web role in Windows Azure, and uses ACS to obtain the security token.

> ➤ **SharePoint-hosted** — The app is hosted in a SharePoint 2013 website that is part of the site collection where the app is installed. This has historically been referred to as a subsite, but in the app model it is referred to as a subweb or app web. In a multi-tenant scenario such as SharePoint 2013 Online, the app runs in the app catalog.

The administrator should note that apps running on-premise are either provider-hosted or SharePoint-hosted. Every authentication method is supported by on-premises apps with one very notable exception: SAML authentication is supported only for certain identity providers. For additional details, see the Microsoft plan for app authentication in SharePoint 2013 at `http://technet.microsoft.com/en-us/library/jj219806(v=office.15).aspx`.

OAuth

The flexibility of the app model means that components of an application could be in SharePoint, on an app server on the corporate intranet, or hosted on the public Internet. If these components request secured SharePoint resources, then these requests need to be authenticated. SharePoint 2013 uses OAuth 2.0 to allow applications to access SharePoint resources in one of three ways:

> ➤ With the combined permissions of the application and the user

> ➤ With only the permissions of the application

> ➤ With only the permissions of the user

Resource access is enabled by defining a trust relationship between the application and SharePoint 2013. If necessary, it also uses a relationship between SharePoint 2013 and Windows Azure Access Control Service (ACS). These trust relationships are very similar to how SharePoint interacts with an STS in the user authentication scenario. Note the following key points about OAuth's role in SharePoint authentication:

➤ OAuth enables users to approve an application to act on their behalf without sharing their username and password.

➤ OAuth is used only for access tokens that are used to retrieve data from SharePoint 2013. In the context of the app model, this means it is used to authorize app requests for SharePoint resources.

➤ App permissions are based on trust, and are granted upon initial installation of the app.

➤ Apps installed from the SharePoint Store can use ACS as its STS.

➤ OAuth is not used for user authentication.

➤ OAuth is used as part of the server-to-server authentication capability, which is discussed later in the chapter.

➤ OAuth is used as part of the "app authentication" process, which is discussed in the next section.

App Authentication

Note that some of the public documentation on TechNet and MSDN uses the terminology *app authentication* to include both authentication of the app by a trusted STS *and* authorization of both the app and the associated user when the app requests access to a secured SharePoint resource. Administrators should be aware that the first part of the process is very similar to the claims authentication of a user, while the latter part is the OAuth portion of the process. In other words, OAuth is an authorization protocol, but in some ways it is very similar to user authentication. Once users are authenticated, the next step is to authorize them, as the goal is to provide users with access to resources. Likewise with the app, app authentication should be followed by app authorization, as the goal is to provide the app with access to SharePoint content.

App authentication is required when an external component of an app needs access to SharePoint resources — for example, a SharePoint Store app or an app catalog app, such as a web server that is located on the intranet or the Internet, attempts to access a secured SharePoint resource. For instance, an app that includes a component that runs in Windows Azure is an external app. App authentication enables a new set of functionality and scenarios that can be achieved by allowing an app to include data from SharePoint resources in the results that the app processes and displays for users.

To provide the app access to SharePoint resources, SharePoint must perform app authentication. SharePoint 2013 must be explicitly configured to allow external app functionality access to resources. Specifically, this includes the following:

1. SharePoint needs to verify the identity of the app, and the user on whose behalf the app is acting. SharePoint needs to trust the app, which is accomplished by establishing a trust with the app's STS. This trust is established using the PowerShell cmdlet `New-SPTrustedSecurityTokenIssuer`.

2. SharePoint needs to verify that the app has the appropriate permissions for the type of access being requested. The app developer requests the permissions it requires, and those permissions are granted at installation. By default, you must be a site owner or tenant administrator to install an app. An app can also be granted permissions explicitly by a site owner or tenant administrator. Once the trust is established, the next step is to register the app with the Application Management service, and then configure app permissions. This is accomplished using the `Register-SPAppPrincipal` cmdlet, and then the `Set-AppPrincipalPermission` cmdlet to assign the permission. Therefore, the app requests access using the following permissions: the permissions granted at installation, the permissions associated with the user on whose behalf the app is acting, and those explicitly granted using the `Set-AppPrincipalPermission` cmdlet.

To summarize, app authentication requires the SharePoint farm to be configured with an app authentication trust, the app to be registered with the Application Management service, and app permissions to be configured. Now let's look at an example of app authentication.

> **NOTE** *In order for the SharePoint Store App Authentication example discussed in the next section to work, your SharePoint farm must be configured to host apps, as discussed in Chapter 11, and you must have an Office 365 account. The latter is necessary to access the ACS service and establish an ACS trust. In general, there are two ways to configure SharePoint 2013 for app authentication:*
>
> ➤ *Use an Office 365 subscription, which is illustrated in the following SharePoint Store App Authentication example, and configure SharePoint to trust ACS, as the app is using ACS as its identity provider.*
>
> ➤ *Use the server-to-server (S2S) authentication process, which is illustrated in the App Catalog App Authentication example. This approach doesn't require an Office 365 subscription or the use of ACS. It instead relies on a direct trust relationship between the SharePoint farm and the app. S2S is discussed in more detail in the Server-to-Server Authentication section.*

SharePoint Store App Authentication

This example demonstrates installing an app from the SharePoint Store, and using ACS as the STS. Your on-premises SharePoint farm can use an external STS, such as ACS, and in general SharePoint can be configured to trust many different token providers. SharePoint needs to be configured to trust ACS, and the example also illustrates how to grant explicit permissions to the app. The OAuth process for granting the app access to SharePoint resources is shown in Figure 6-3. In order for the OAuth process to proceed successfully, you must configure SharePoint 2013 to trust ACS. First, however, there are a few PowerShell cmdlets that need to be run to establish the ACS trust and register the app as discussed earlier in the previous section.

Step 1 is necessary whenever you want to configure SharePoint to trust an external STS. In this example, SharePoint is being configured to trust the ACS instance that corresponds to your Office 365 account. You may be wondering why you need an Office 365 subscription. Recall that app authentication requires verifying the authenticity of both the app and the user. If you already have an Office 365 tenant, then your identity is already being verified using ACS as part of your subscription. App identity verification is accomplished using ACS because the app has chosen to use ACS as its identity provider STS. Steps 2 and 3 complete the app authentication process by registering the app with the Application Management service and explicitly assigning permissions to the app. These steps are discussed in much more detail in Chapter 11 if you need additional information.

1. This step configures SharePoint to trust ACS. From the SharePoint 2013 Management Shell, execute the `New-SPTrustedSecurityTokenIssuer` cmdlet:

   ```
   New-SPTrustedSecurityTokenIssuer
       -MetadataEndpoint "<Metadata endpoint URL of ACS>"
       -IsTrustBroker -Name "ACS"
   ```

The value for `"<metadata endpoint URL of ACS>"` is `https://accounts.accesscontrol` `.windows.net/metadata/json/1/?realm=<contextID property of your Office 365` `subscription>`. This metadata endpoint URL value and the value of your `"<contextID property` `of your Office 365 subscription>"` are discussed in the document "sps-2013-config-one-way-hybrid-environment.docx," which you can download from `http://www.microsoft.com/en-us/` `download/details.aspx?id=35593`.

2. Now you register the app. From the SharePoint 2013 Management Shell, execute the `Register-SPAppPrincipal` cmdlet. The <app principal name> is based on your Office 365 tenant, and the value is based on two different IDs: the context ID and the app principal ID. This information is determined using Microsoft Online Services PowerShell, and it is fully documented in "sps-2013-config-one-way-hybrid-environment.docx."

   ```
   $spsite = Get-SPSite "https://<url_of_site>"
   $appPrincipal = Register-SPAppPrincipal
       -NameIdentifier <app principal name> -Site $spsite
       -DisplayName "My Office 365 App"
   ```

3. Finally, you assign permissions using the `Set-AppPrincipalPermission` cmdlet. This cmdlet can be used to both add and change app permissions, and it can be repeated multiple times to configure the app with the necessary permissions:

   ```
   $spsite = Get-SPSite "https://<url_of_site>"
   Set-AppPrincipalPermission -appPrincipal $appPrincipal
       -site $spsite
       -right <Level> -scope <Scope>
   ```

The `<Level>` parameter options include Read, Write, Manage, or FullControl. The `<Scope>` parameter values include Farm, Site collection, SharePoint Online, Web, Documents, List, or Library.

Now that the app authentication has been configured, the following steps walk through the OAuth process for this example:

1. An app has been installed to the SharePoint farm from the SharePoint Store. The user opens a SharePoint page in the browser that renders content from the app that was previously installed. The app is hosted on the Internet and uses ACS as its trust broker (IdP STS). Because the app is requesting SharePoint resources, SharePoint needs to perform app authentication. SharePoint must obtain a context token that it can send to the app. The context token provides "context" about the app's request, including current user, SharePoint website, etc. SharePoint requests ACS to create and sign a context token, as it is the app's IdP, and SharePoint has been configured to trust ACS. The context token is used later in the process to request an access token.

2. ACS authenticates the user via the Office 365 subscription information, verifies the app identity, and issues a signed context token to the SharePoint STS. The context token is digitally signed with a client secret that is known only by ACS and the app (the app owner receives the client secret value when the app is registered in the store). The SharePoint STS receives the context token, which contains information about the app and the user.

3. Once received by the SharePoint STS, SharePoint attempts to render the web page in the browser, which includes an iframe that references the app server URL. As part of rendering the page, it passes the context token to the iframe.

4. Because the iframe references the URL of the app server, the iframe causes the browser to request a page from the app server, and the context token is included as part of the request sent to SharePoint Store app server.

5. The app server receives the signed context token. It validates the token's signature using the client secret. Because the client secret is known only by the app and ACS, the app knows it is a valid SharePoint request. The client secret and the client ID (assigned when the app is registered) values represent the app credentials. The app passes its credentials to ACS as part of the request for an access token, and it subsequently receives an access token from ACS. The access token authorizes the app access to specific SharePoint resources for a specific duration. This token can be cached, which alleviates multiple ACS requests each time it needs SharePoint resources, or it can be configured to make a new request each time.

6. The SharePoint Store app server sends the OAuth access token and the resource request to the SharePoint 2013 server. This request, sent via the HTTP authorization header, can be for a web service call or a client-side object model (CSOM) request.

7. The SharePoint server authorizes access to the content and returns the requested information to the app server. Depending on the app security model, the appropriate combination of app permissions and user permissions are used to determine whether the app has the necessary permissions to access the SharePoint resources being requested.

8. The app server renders the iframe contents, which satisfies the user's request for the SharePoint page. This completes the process.

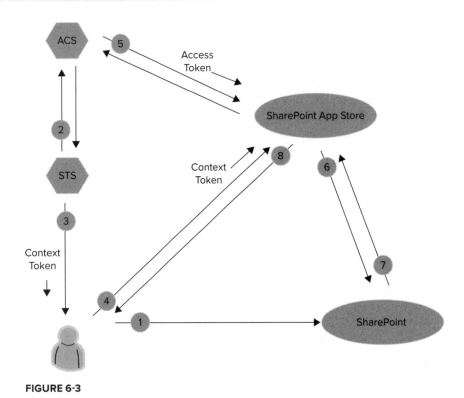

FIGURE 6-3

You might need to review the process a couple of times because it is quite involved, but it will be worth the effort.

App Catalog App Authentication

This example illustrates the second approach to app authentication. In this case, your app is hosted on-premises in servers that are not a part of the SharePoint farm, and not in the cloud as in the previous example. The app has been deployed to the SharePoint app catalog; app catalogs are deployed to web applications in SharePoint 2013. Apps in the app catalog are assumed to be more trustworthy than those external to SharePoint, so the app authentication process is different.

For this scenario, you need to configure a server-to-server trust relationship between SharePoint and the app. This type of configuration is also referred to as a *high-trust app*, which is an example of a provider-hosted app for use on the premises; it is not intended to be used in a cloud-hosted environment. Administrators should not be misled by the terminology "high trust," so the following should further clarify what this means:

➤ A high-trust app does not have "full trust" access, and must still request and be granted access to SharePoint resources.

➤ The app is considered "high-trust" because it is trusted to impersonate a user (aka "asserting a user's identity"), and it is responsible for creating the user portion of the access token.

➤ A high-trust app uses a certificate instead of a context token to establish trust.

Figure 6-4 shows the process for app authentication in this scenario, as described in the following steps. The SharePoint configuration is more involved in this scenario, so administrators are referred to Chapter 11 for details, or to `http://msdn.microsoft.com/en-us/library/fp179901(v=office.15).aspx#Configure`.

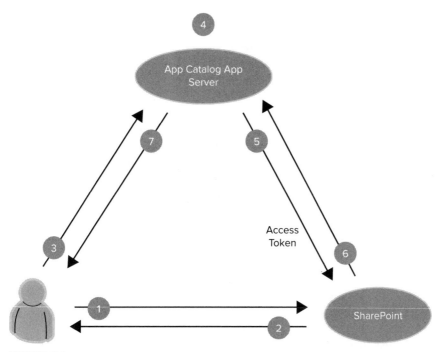

FIGURE 6-4

1. A user opens a SharePoint page that renders content from a SharePoint app catalog app in an iframe. The app is hosted on the intranet (not part of the SharePoint farm) and uses a self-signed certificate for its access tokens. The SharePoint resource that is accessed by the app requires authentication.

2. SharePoint sends the requested page and the iframe to the user's browser.

3. The user's browser requests iframe content from the app server.

4. The app server, which is hosting the app, authenticates the user and generates an access token signed with its self-signed certificate.

5. The app server sends the resource request and the access token to the SharePoint server.

6. The SharePoint server authorizes access to the content. If the app's permissions and the user's permissions are sufficient, then the content is returned to the app server.

7. The iframe content is returned to the user's browser.

As you can see, even though the actual SharePoint configuration is more involved in the second example, the OAuth process is much simpler. This should be expected, as an app that has been deployed to the app catalog should be trusted to a much greater extent than one that is hosted outside of the organization. This example was a good warm-up for the next section, which delves more deeply into S2S authentication and gives examples of how it is useful to enable different servers to share information.

SERVER-TO-SERVER AUTHENTICATION

Server-to-Server authentication (S2S) represents an example of application-to-application OAuth. This approach uses a Microsoft extension of the OAuth protocol to enable applications or servers to share resources on behalf of users, without user authentication. This is achieved using a trusted connection between applications. As you saw in the last example of the preceding section, this type of configuration can be used when deploying a developer-hosted app in a private network to avoid any dependencies on ACS or any other servers running across the Internet. The S2S process is essentially an access request and access granting process between two S2S-compliant applications or servers. The criteria to share resources between two compliant servers include the following:

➤ The application or server requesting the resources must be trusted.

➤ The application or server requesting the resources must have the proper permissions.

Do these criteria look familiar? They should, as they are exactly the same criteria you saw previously for app authentication. Just as SharePoint 2013 has a native STS for user authentication, SharePoint 2013 also has another STS dedicated to provide server-to-server security tokens. A trust established between the SharePoint 2013 STS and any other S2S-compliant server or services enables the sharing of resources. For on-premises deployments, the key step that configures the trust relationship involves establishing the JavaScript Object Notation (JSON) meta data endpoint of the other S2S-compliant service. This is accomplished using the `New-SPTrustedSecurityTokenIssuer` cmdlet.

S2S-compliant servers include SharePoint Server 2013, Exchange Server 2013, Lync Server 2013, Azure Workflow Server, or any other software that supports the Microsoft server-to-server protocol. Server-to-server authentication enables a new set of functionality and scenarios, such as the new eDiscovery capability in SharePoint 2013 and Exchange 2013. It also enables information from one SharePoint 2013 farm to be retrieved and displayed from another SharePoint 2013 farm. This is discussed in the next section.

> **NOTE** *For more information about the SharePoint S2S protocol, see OAuth 2.0 Authentication Protocol: SharePoint Profile, located at* `http://msdn.microsoft.com/en-us/library/hh631177(office.12).aspx`.

SharePoint to SharePoint S2S

The SharePoint 2013 to SharePoint 2013 configuration is the simplest S2S scenario. It requires configuring a one-way trust between the server receiving the requests and the server that will be sending them. Detailed documentation about the configuration is provided at `http://technet. microsoft.com/en-us/library/jj655400.aspx`, so here we will only show the key PowerShell command that makes it all possible, `New-SPTrustedSecurityTokenIssuer`:

```
New-SPTrustedSecurityTokenIssuer -MetadataEndpoint
    "https://<HostName>/_layouts/15/metadata/json/1"
    -IsTrustBroker -Name "<FriendlyName>"
```

The parameter `<HostName>` is the name and port of the SSL-enabled SharePoint web application of the farm that will be sending S2S requests, and the `<FriendlyName>` parameter is a friendly name for the SharePoint 2013 farm that is sending S2S requests. It is recommended that OAuth communication occur over SSL, but it can be configured using PowerShell to use HTTP for lab environments. Administrators responsible for configuring app authentication and S2S will become very familiar with this PowerShell cmdlet. Figure 6-5 shows the inter-server communication process, which is described in the following steps:

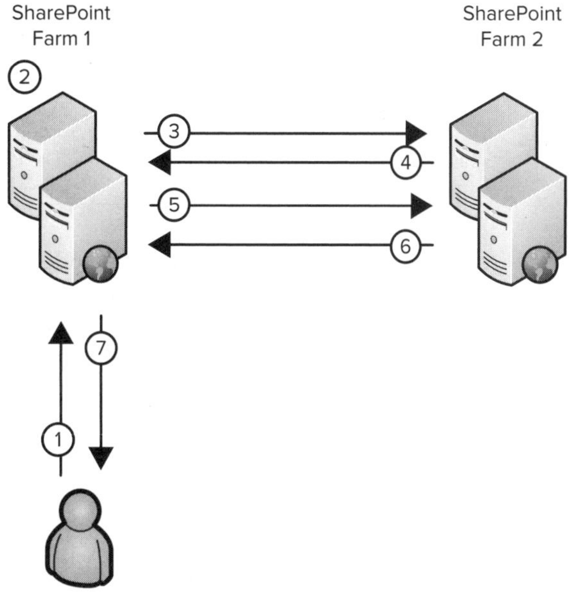

1. A user opens a SharePoint 2013 page that requires information from another SharePoint 2013 farm.

2. SharePoint Farm 1 generates a server-to-server token.

FIGURE 6-5

3. SharePoint Farm 1 sends the token to Server Farm 2.

4. Server Farm 2 validates the token from Server Farm 1.

5. Server Farm 2 replies to Server Farm 1 to confirm that the token is valid.

6. The components on the SharePoint page that need the information from Server Farm 2 access the data on Server Farm 2.

7. The page is rendered for the user.

SharePoint to Exchange and Lync S2S

The S2S process for sharing information between SharePoint 2013 and Exchange 2013, and SharePoint 2013 and Lync 2013, is the same but the configuration is more involved. Table 6-3 contains references to TechNet articles that describe the configuration process in detail, so we will not repeat that discussion here. The configuration process details the steps required to establish two, one-way trusts. These two, one-way trusts are necessary to support SharePoint consuming information from Exchange and Lync, as well as Exchange and Lync consuming information from SharePoint.

TABLE 6-3: Configuring S2S Between SharePoint 2013 and Another Server

SERVER	REFERENCE
Exchange 2013	`http://technet.microsoft.com/en-us/library/jj655399.aspx`
Lync 2013	`http://technet.microsoft.com/en-us/library/jj670179.aspx` `http://technet.microsoft.com/library/696f2b26-e5d0-42b5-9785-a26c2ce25bb7(Office.15).aspx`
SharePoint 2013	`http://technet.microsoft.com/en-us/library/jj655400.aspx`

We discuss configuring SharePoint 2013 and Azure Workflow Server (AWS) in Chapter 16, "Installing and Configuring Azure Workflow Server." AWS is the new workflow capability for SharePoint 2013. Despite the name, AWS can be used on-premises, and it can be hosted on a server that is part of the SharePoint 2013 farm or separately. S2S is a great new addition to the claims authentication capability of SharePoint, and it will provide new authentication approaches for non-SharePoint applications.

SUMMARY

The subject of claims authentication is vast, and providing all the necessary information and background would require an entire book. The overview provided in this chapter focused on the key areas and new features of interest to administrators. Unlike SharePoint 2010, SharePoint 2013 doesn't introduce a new user authentication technology, but it does include changes and enhancements. This chapter covered key definitions and terminology, and provided some insight into the actual user authentication process. It also introduced the new application authentication capability, whether that uses app authentication or S2S. SharePoint 2013 is adopting more standards with each release. OAuth is the most recent example of standards adoption, and it is at the core of the new app model and S2S authentication. Claims and OAuth open doors to many new, valuable scenarios. Bottom line: Claims authentication is here to stay, and it has become a critical player in the overall architecture and operation of SharePoint 2013.

7

Administering SharePoint with Windows PowerShell

WHAT'S IN THIS CHAPTER?

➤ Basic Windows PowerShell usage

➤ Using common SharePoint 2013 cmdlets

➤ Working with the SharePoint object model

Windows PowerShell has become the standard by which much of the administration of SharePoint takes place since its introduction in SharePoint 2010. Prior versions of SharePoint relied on the SharePoint administration tool, stsadm.exe, which dealt largely with string input and output in order to get or set any configuration options not already available through Central Administration. There were strong limitations with this, as you were limited to textual input and output of only the configuration options that the tool was designed to access. If you wanted to, say, get a list of site collections in the farm and set a different quota based on some property of each site collection, the path was much more difficult than would be considered acceptable for a toll you would likely only use once or twice.

PowerShell was available to be used in those earlier versions by accessing the SharePoint .NET Application Programming Interface (API) directly, but this remained more in the realm of development than general system administration due to complexity. As of SharePoint 2010, and continued in SharePoint 2013, SharePoint provides a Management Shell, which is essentially a standard PowerShell session with a set of snap-ins pre-loaded to add a number of SharePoint-specific PowerShell cmdlets for interacting with the SharePoint environment via the PowerShell command-line interface.

This chapter will get you up to speed with the basics of PowerShell and demonstrate how to harness it to benefit your SharePoint 2013 farm.

INTRODUCTION TO WINDOWS POWERSHELL

In general, there is no requirement to use PowerShell to administer SharePoint. The vast majority of standard configuration options are exposed in the Central Administration UI. However, more advanced features, such as partitioning service applications for multi-tenancy, creating SharePoint databases without GUIDs, as well as automating common repetitive tasks, is where PowerShell begins to really shine. Plus, once you start using PowerShell you'll wonder how you ever got along without it.

For example, creating multiple collections through Central Administration can be a time-consuming process, one at a time. However, you might find yourself in a situation where site collections in your development environment need to be reproduced in your production environment. With a little knowledge of PowerShell and the SharePoint cmdlets, you can generate a comma-separated list (.csv file) of all the site collections and supporting information in the development environment using the Get-SPSite and the Export-CSV cmdlets, and then use PowerShell's Import-CSV cmdlet with the New-SPSite cmdlet in the production environment to recreate them with a single push of the Enter key. This same process using Central Admin would potentially take a tremendous amount of time and likely result in you spraining your mousing finger. No one likes that.

MICROSOFT SHAREPOINT 2013 MANAGEMENT SHELL AND OTHER HOSTS

PowerShell has been a staple of the Windows Server operating system since it came standard in Windows 2008. Windows 2008 R2 began including PowerShell version 2, which was great for SharePoint 2010 because it relied on PowerShell version 2 as a minimum. However, SharePoint 2013 requires PowerShell version 3. If you are installing SharePoint 2013 on Windows 2008 R2, the prerequisite installer will attempt to install version 3, unless Windows Management Framework 3.0 has already been installed. Thankfully, PowerShell version 3 has been included as the standard for Windows Server 2012, which simplifies things a bit if you are using the latest and greatest software available to SharePoint 2013.

Microsoft SharePoint 2013 Management Shell

The Microsoft SharePoint 2013 Management Shell, shown in Figure 7-1, is the out-of-the-box SharePoint command-line interface. True, it's not much to look at. As a matter of fact, it looks a lot like the standard cmd.exe command-line interface. However, it's a cleverly disguised PowerShell console, with the SharePoint commands registered and ready for use. Open the SharePoint 2013 Management Shell and PowerShell at the same time. If you squint, you might see that they look pretty similar. The only obvious difference is that the SharePoint Management Shell has a black background, whereas the standard PowerShell background is blue. They may look similar, but only the Management Shell will run the SharePoint commands without further configuration.

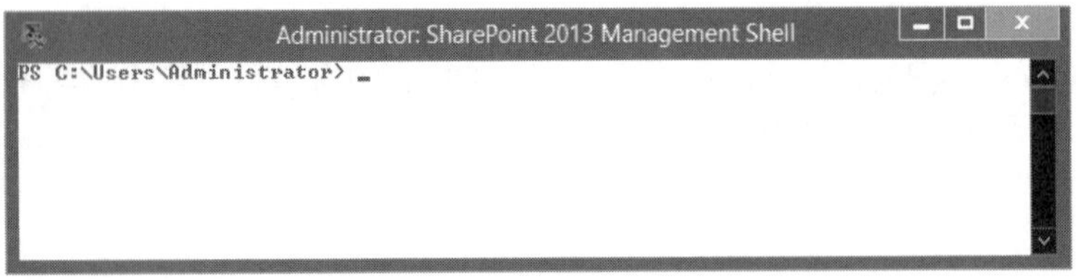

FIGURE 7-1

For example, if you run a very basic SharePoint command in both consoles, such as `Get-SPSite`, the Management Shell will happily return a list of site collections, whereas the PowerShell console won't have a clue what you want it to do and it will make its displeasure very evident.

In other words, the SharePoint 2013 Management Shell is just the PowerShell .exe with a command-line parameter that points to a PSC1 file or a console file. The PSC1 file tells the PowerShell host to register the SharePoint commands. One other minor difference is that it also has a title bar that says SharePoint 2013 Management Shell, but otherwise the Management Shell is all PowerShell. If you've learned anything about PowerShell by working with other products such as Exchange or Windows, it all works here too.

Using Other Windows PowerShell Hosts

The Management Shell is the only host that is pre-configured to run SharePoint commands, but it is not the only host that an administrator can use. Two common hosts are available to administrators with Windows PowerShell version 3: the standard Windows PowerShell console and the Windows PowerShell Integrated Scripting Environment (ISE), shown in Figure 7-2. Administrators can also use any of the third-party PowerShell hosts available free or for purchase. Many of these boast a rich graphical user interface, although the rest of this chapter sticks with the Management Shell because it is most often used by administrators, but not telling you how to configure these other hosts would be like ordering a build-it-yourself bed only to find out you got all the parts but only half of the instructions.

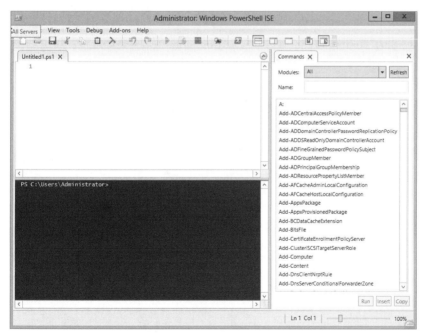

FIGURE 7-2

We will be adding commands to the PowerShell ISE host, which provides a multiline editor with breakpoints and other help for scripting. Adding commands to other third-party hosts is similar, though you might need to consult their specific documentation if you run into any issues.

The ISE is installed with Windows Server 2008 R2 and Windows Server 2012 but it is not activated by default. To activate the ISE, use the Add Feature dialog of the Server Manager. Figure 7-3 shows the Server Manager's Add Feature dialog with the ISE feature checked.

To register the SharePoint PowerShell commands with ISE, you must be working locally on a SharePoint 2013 server. The SharePoint 2013 PowerShell commands do not work from remote workstations.

> **NOTE** *SharePoint 2013 commands must be run on a SharePoint 2013 server. The commands cannot be run from a client. PowerShell 3 does provide a remoting capability whereby commands can be executed from a client to run on the server. This is a PowerShell function and not specific to SharePoint 2013, and many of the SharePoint 2013 cmdlets will not function through this remoting interface. To learn more about configuring Windows PowerShell remoting with SharePoint 2013, read the following blog post (although the article was written with SharePoint 2010 in mind, most of the content translates to 2013 seamlessly):* `http://blogs.msdn.com/b/opal/archive/2010/03/07/sharepoint-2010-with-windows-powershell-remoting-step-by-step.aspx`.

If you find yourself in the standard PowerShell console, or one of the many PowerShell hosts available, and need SharePoint cmdlet functionality, you can use the `Add-PSSnapin` PowerShell command to register the SharePoint PowerShell cmdlets:

```
Add-PSSnapIn Microsoft.SharePoint.PowerShell
```

`Add-PSSnapIn` is a PowerShell command that registers add-on modules with the PowerShell console. The Microsoft.SharePoint.PowerShell snap-in contains the registration information for the SharePoint cmdlets.

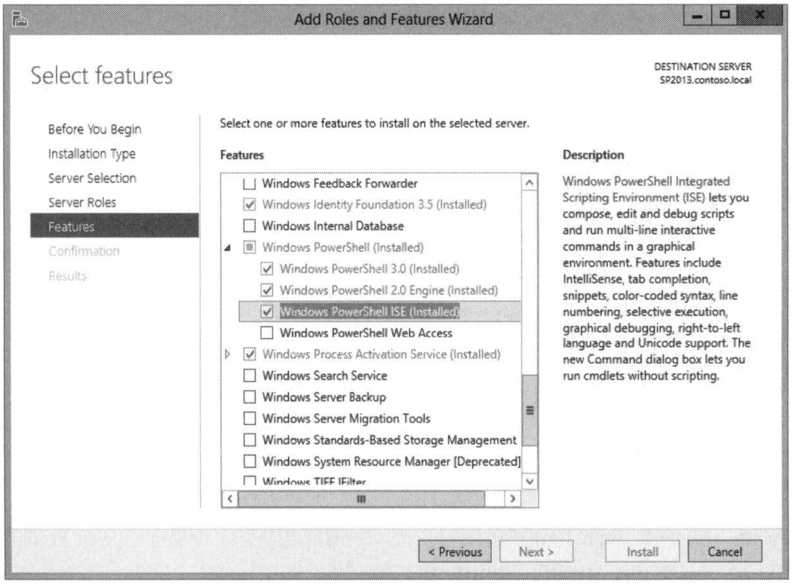

FIGURE 7-3

This will get you started. To verify that the SharePoint 2013 commands are available in ISE, simply run a SharePoint command such as `Get-SPSite`. ISE should respond with a list of site collections in the farm. Note one tiny issue: You are required to add the Microsoft.SharePoint.PowerShell snap-in every time you start the host. To avoid this, you can run the command to add the snap-in to your profile, which will run each time you start a host.

You can locate your profile by typing **$Profile** into the command line, which will return the path to your profile. `$Profile` is a variable containing the current user's profile location. The profile location may be different for each host. The ISE profile is different from the PowerShell profile, so commands for the ISE user's profile will not interfere with other PowerShell hosts. If the profile exists already, you can use the following command to open it:

```
Notepad $Profile
```

If the profile exists, Notepad will open it. If the profile does not exist but the directory exists, Notepad will prompt you to create a new file. Add the `Add-PSSnapin` command with the Microsoft.SharePoint.PowerShell value into your ISE profile and save it. You need to restart ISE to read in the profile changes. When you need a command, variable, or function to persist between sessions, you can use the profile.

If you are authoring scripts to execute SharePoint cmdlets, it is a good idea to always start your scripts by loading the SharePoint snap-in with the Add-PSSnapin command because the script may be executed in a standard PowerShell console, or third-party host, at some point in the future. This ensures the script will always be able to run in any PowerShell host on a SharePoint server. The `Get-PSSnapin` command in the `IF` statement below checks to see if the snap-in is loaded. The `-EA` parameter is short for ErrorAction, and the "SilentlyContinue" suppresses errors that occur if the snap-in is already loaded. If the `Get-PSSnapin` command does not return a value, then the `Add-PSSnapin` is executed to load the SharePoint snap-in. More code could be added to check to see if a snap-in is even registered on the server, or to display text output based on the outcomes of the `IF` statement below, but that is beyond the scope of this book:

```
If((Get-PSSnapin Microsoft.SharePoint.PowerShell -EA SilentlyContinue) -eq
$null){Add-PSSnapin Microsoft.SharePoint.PowerShell}
```

COMMANDS

PowerShell is powered by commands. Commands get things done. There are four basic types of commands: cmdlets, functions, scripts, and native commands. It is not necessarily important to know the differences between these command types to work with PowerShell and SharePoint, but it doesn't hurt. If you are just starting out with PowerShell, you can find a wealth of general information at `http://technet.microsoft.com/en-US/scriptcenter/dd742419.aspx`.

Cmdlets

Cmdlets (pronounced command-lets) are compiled commands that are installed and registered with PowerShell; they are all named using a verb-noun combination. To make them easy to remember, the noun part of a PowerShell cmdlet is always singular. The verb portion of the name should be one of the PowerShell acceptable verbs. PowerShell defines a list of these verbs and what they mean at `http://msdn.microsoft.com/en-us/library/ms714428(VS.85).aspx`. Because the verbs are "standardized," you can usually guess the verb portion of the cmdlet. An example of a cmdlet is `New-SPWebApplication`, which has a corresponding `Remove-SPWebApplication`. Although you might have expected the verb "delete" to delete a SPWebApplication, "delete" is not one of the standardized verbs, so it cannot be used.

As you might have already guessed, the SharePoint commands that we will be using are cmdlets. You saw that SharePoint installed the cmdlets on the server, and the Management Shell registered them with the host using the PSC1 file; and you now know how to manually register them in the ISE. You can also create custom cmdlets, but that is a topic beyond the scope of this book. To learn more about writing your own cmdlets, see the MSDN article at `http://msdn.microsoft.com/en-us/library/dd878294(VS.85).aspx`.

SPEED TYPING

As you'll soon discover, some PowerShell cmdlet's names can get rather long; and even after you've typed all that, you still need to add parameter names. As admins, we are accustomed to clicking "Next" buttons; we're not ready for all this typing. PowerShell has our back, though, supporting "tab completion." Once you start typing a cmdlet's name, or one of its parameters, you can press the Tab key and PowerShell will start cycling through all the cmdlets, parameters, or methods that are available based on what you have entered. This helps you save time and avoid typing out those long PowerShell lines more quickly. It also helps if you've forgotten a cmdlet or parameter name. For a cmdlet, just type part of the name and then start pressing the Tab key. Parameters are even easier; just type a hyphen (-) and then start pressing Tab. PowerShell will cycle through all the parameters for that cmdlet. Pretty spiffy.

Functions

Functions are made up of a command or a series of commands that are intended to be reusable for performing a task multiple times within the same script. Functions can accept parameters (variables that are passed to the function at the time the function is called), which enables the same code to be executed with different parameters each time. This provides the benefit of reducing the amount of duplicate code in a script. Functions are defined in PowerShell by typing the function into the host. PowerShell then parses the function and verifies the syntax. Functions can be reused for the lifetime of the host session. If you close the host then you lose the function, and you will need to enter it again when you start another session with the host. You can enter functions into your profile so they will be available whenever you start a session.

> **NOTE** *There's nothing worse than working on an award-winning function only to lose it when you shut down the host. Consider yourself warned and save your function in your profile or at least to a text file so you can copy it later. A great way to protect yourself against this calamity is to run the* Start-Transcript *cmdlet each time you open PowerShell. Heck, it would make a great addition to the* $PROFILE *file you created earlier in this chapter.* Start-Transcript *creates a text file that's a transcript of everything that happens in that PowerShell session. If you run this every time you use PowerShell, you'll never lose that important function that will finally gain you the richly deserved admiration of your co-workers.*

Functions have their place and are great for containing code that you want to call from various other scripts or commands, but space limitations prevent an in-depth treatment of them here.

Scripts

PowerShell scripts are made up of a mix of commands, functions, loops, decision trees, user input/output — basically all the methods available to PowerShell for creating reusable code with program-like functionality. General SharePoint administration will commonly result in the use of "one-liners," whereas scripts are generally reserved for larger-scale repetitive tasks, such as an automated installer for SharePoint if you find yourself doing that a lot. Aside from the amount of code involved, a primary difference between a script and a one-liner is that scripts are saved to a text file with a .PS1 file extension. Later you can run the script by typing in the filename.

Scripts, in contrast to functions or PowerShell snap-ins, survive the host shutdown and can easily be recalled. Another great benefit of the script is that once a script is created and tested, it can be saved to a script library and reused. By default, hosts do not run unsigned scripts. This is to protect you from accidentally running scripts that have the same name as common commands. In addition, hosts will warn you if you attempt to run a script that has not been signed. This prevents you from executing a script that has been modified to do something malicious, such as replacing all your SharePoint backups with pictures of the world's ugliest dog. You can modify the security setting using the cmdlet Set-ExecutionPolicy. Because you can accomplish so much using the SharePoint cmdlets, you will not be doing much with scripts in this chapter. Scripts are only necessary if you want to chain together a complicated series of cmdlets or walk through complicated loops.

> **NOTE** *For security reasons, the PowerShell application is not associated with* .PS1 *files. The default application associated with* .PS1 *files is Notepad, so double-clicking a* .PS1 *file will open the file in Notepad. This effectively prevents users from double-clicking a malicious script and running it accidentally. If you change the file association, which is not recommended, you run the risk of inadvertently running a malicious script. While this might seem very inconvenient, there were some very dark days when hackers were using VBScript to compromise machines. Microsoft wants to ensure that PowerShell is only used for good, not evil.*

Native Commands

Native commands are commands that run outside of the host process, such as notepad.exe or stsadm.exe. These commands can still be called from within the commands or scripts that you execute in the PowerShell host. This provides useful functionality that may not be provided by PowerShell directly. For example, suppose your script were logging information to a .txt file, and at the end of the execution you wanted to display that .txt file automatically. You could add a line such as the following to the end of your script to automatically launch Notepad.exe in its own process and display your log file:

```
Notepad.exe "MyLog.txt"
```

BASIC POWERSHELL USAGE

PowerShell is a huge topic to which entire books have been dedicated, and highly experienced users teach weeklong classes on PowerShell. Although a single chapter cannot cover everything there is to know about PowerShell, this section explains the key things that new users should understand. Many of the SharePoint PowerShell cmdlets can be used as one-liners or "standalone," so a comprehensive understanding of PowerShell is not necessarily required. That said, understanding a few PowerShell concepts in conjunction with the SharePoint cmdlets can greatly facilitate your work.

Listing the SharePoint Commands

The toughest part of using a command-line interface, whether it's PowerShell, the old Windows CMD prompt, or a Linux bash shell, is determining which commands you can use. You can sit a drunk koala bear in front of Central Administration and it can click around long enough to figure out to do tasks like create a site collection. If you sit that same koala down in front of a PowerShell prompt you'll get koala spittle on your keyboard but no new site collections. The learning curve to PowerShell can be steep, and discovering the right command is a big reason why.

Fortunately, PowerShell provides the Get-Command cmdlet to retrieve a list of available commands. Used in isolation, the Get-Command cmdlet will return all commands that are known to the host. Get-Command, like many commands, accepts optional parameters. Because we are interested in only the SharePoint 2013 commands, we can limit the commands displayed to just the SharePoint 2013 commands by using the optional -Module parameter. To list only SharePoint commands, execute the following command:

```
Get-Command -Module Microsoft.SharePoint.PowerShell
```

Figure 7-4 displays the output of the Get-Command cmdlet using the –Module parameter.

FIGURE 7-4

We mentioned earlier that all PowerShell cmdlets consist of a verb and a noun. All the nouns in the SharePoint PowerShell cmdlets start with "SP." The Get-Command cmdlet accepts wildcards, which you can use to get a list of all the SharePoint PowerShell cmdlets in an easier-to-remember method:

```
Get-Command -noun sp*
```

At last count, more than 750 PowerShell cmdlets were included with SharePoint 2013, which is probably many more commands than you want to list, unless you are printing them out for some kind of tree-killing reference manual. As the preceding example demonstrates, you can filter the list somewhat by using the optional -noun or -verb parameter for Get-Command. For example, if you were wondering what commands work with a web application, use the following command:

```
Get-Command –Module Microsoft.SharePoint.PowerShell -noun SPWebApp*
```

Because the SharePoint module is the only module with cmdlets using the SPWebApplication noun, you would get the same results if you omitted the –module parameter. However, it's a good idea to leave it if you're searching by verb, as the SharePoint cmdlets use the same verbs as the non-SharePoint cmdlets. If you need to know which command to use for backups, use the following command:

```
Get-Command –Module Microsoft.SharePoint.PowerShell -verb Backup
```

Figure 7-5 shows how you can control the output of Get-Command with the –noun and –verb parameters.

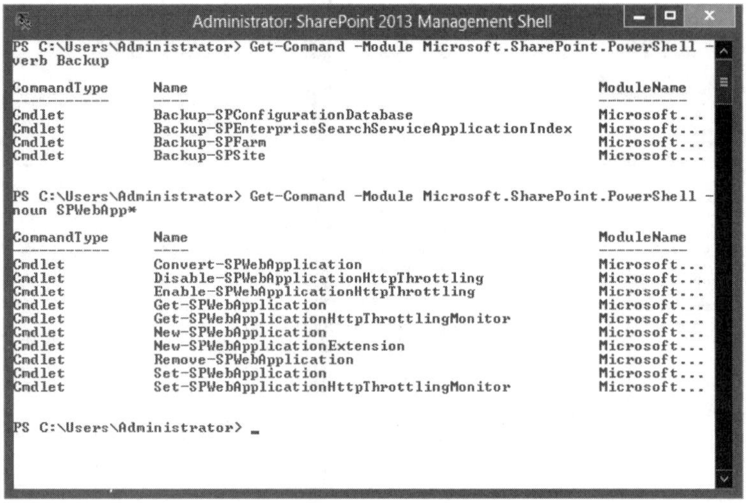

FIGURE 7-5

PowerShell Help

We mentioned earlier that one of the difficulties in mastering a command-line environment is figuring out what to type. It can be very frustrating. The designers of PowerShell were ingenious, though, providing the extremely useful Get-Help command. Whereas the Get-Command cmdlet is useful for determining which commands are available to PowerShell, you can use Get-Help to understand the *usage* of a command. The Get-Help command is a standard PowerShell cmdlet. To get help for a particular command, simply call Get-Help, passing in the name of the command for which you want help. For example, to view help about New-SPWebApplication, you would use the following:

```
Get-Help New-SPWebApplication
```

Figure 7-6 shows the help returned for New-SPWebApplication. It provides numerous details about the command, including parameters, examples, and usage. Get-Help accepts the optional parameters of –detailed, -examples, and -full. When learning how to use an unfamiliar PowerShell cmdlet, running Get-Help with the –examples parameter is a great way to quickly get up to speed on how to use it. Examples of the available options are shown under the Remarks heading (refer to Figure 7-6). To learn more about Get-Help, simply use Get-Help Get-Help — a little repetitive, but it works.

FIGURE 7-6

Note that the Windows Server product team that covers PowerShell (a subteam of Server & Tools) at Microsoft has decreed that every PowerShell cmdlet included with a Microsoft product must have help information and at least one example. That's admirable, but unfortunately not all of the examples are accurate; some of the SharePoint cmdlets have flakey examples. The good news is that you can update the help information for cmdlets by running `Update-Help`. If your SharePoint server has access to the Internet, PowerShell will check for updated help for the modules installed. This may fix some of the erroneous help entries, but be aware that some just don't work.

PowerShell Variables

It is virtually impossible to ignore variables, except in the most basic cmdlet usage. The first time you pipe the output (covered in the section "PowerShell Pipeline") of one command into another command you are already using variables. Despite what some developer "friends" might tell you, variables are not the second coming of algebra, although the similarities are uncanny. In a basic sense, variables hold information. All PowerShell variables start with the $ character, and they can hold any type of valid object.

> **NOTE** *Certain objects in SharePoint, such as* SPWeb, SPSite, *and* SPSiteAdministration, *must be properly disposed of. One-liner SharePoint commands will dispose of all objects correctly. Storing these SharePoint objects in variables can lead to performance issues and memory leaks if the variable is not handled correctly. This section on variables deliberately avoids using these SharePoint objects until the subject of disposal is addressed later in the chapter.*

In Figure 7-7, the variable $webApps is set to the output of Get-SPWebApplications. $webApps now contains all the web application (SPWebApplication) objects. You use the Count property to determine how many web applications are contained in the variable, and you can display the web applications by simply typing the variable name.

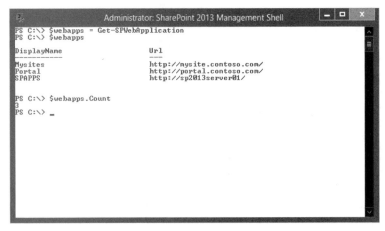

FIGURE 7-7

> **NOTE** *Wondering which commands were used to get the output displayed in the screenshots of the Management Shell? Just take a look at the top of the figures to see the commands following the administrator prompt.*

Note that the Get-SPWebApplication cmdlet does not include your Central Admin web application by default. This is helpful because it means you won't always have to check to ensure that whatever settings you are applying to your standard web applications aren't being inadvertently applied to the Central Admin site. You have to include the -IncludeCentralAdministration parameter in order for Central Admin to be included.

Because this chapter doesn't go much beyond one-liners, it doesn't dive deeply into variable usage; but keep in mind as we proceed that anytime a $ character is being used, a variable is in play.

PowerShell Objects

Understanding exactly what an object is can be complicated, but a car provides a useful analogy. Like an object, a car has properties. Properties are information about the object, such as the car's color, make, model, weight, whether it has been flooded or not, and so on. If you're given the object car, instead of the word "car," you can use those properties to make decisions. If you have a group of car objects, you can decide to view only the blue ones by checking the `car.color` property. That's one aspect of strings that lets you down. When you get a list of site collections from STSADM, you get text. If you want information that isn't in the text, you have no way to get more information; and if the information you need is hidden somewhere in that string, you have to do complicated text manipulation to get it out. Objects make this type of work much easier.

Continuing with the analogy, like objects, cars also have methods. Methods are actions you can take with your object. For the car example, a method might be start, accelerate, slowdown, rolldownwindows, driveoffcliff, and so on. Objects are treated the same way — different methods are associated with different object types. The car in your garage is an instance of the object car, and it has different properties than other instances of the car object, such as those in your neighbor's driveway. Methods are one way in which you interact with the objects. The `SPSite` object has a `dispose` method, which flushes it out of RAM. It also has a `delete` method, which is one way to delete an `SPSite` object.

You can view the available methods and properties of an object by using the `Get-Member` cmdlet, which is covered in more detail later in this chapter in the section "Web Applications."

PowerShell Pipeline

You've already seen how using objects makes PowerShell better than STSADM. The pipeline is another PowerShell feature that enables you to take your scripting up another notch. In particular, it enables you to create the aforementioned one-liners by chaining together the output of one cmdlet to the input of another cmdlet. For example, the `Get-SPSite` command returns all site collections in the farm. The `Get-SPWeb` command returns a specific web object. If you needed to retrieve all `SPWeb` objects, you could chain the `Get-SPSite` command to the `Get-SPWeb` command using the PowerShell pipeline. To get all the `SPWeb` objects on your farm (excluding any within the Central Administration web applications), use the following command (see Figure 7-8):

```
Get-SPSite -Limit ALL | Get-SPWeb -Limit ALL
```

FIGURE 7-8

What are being passed between these commands are objects. You will soon see how you can use the methods and properties of these objects to further control what is passed, and how the recipient cmdlet can filter the incoming object to get to the property on which it needs to act.

BLEEDING ON THE SCREEN

When you run the preceding `Get-SPSite`/`Get-SPWeb` one-liners, instead of getting a friendly list of all the webs in your farm you might instead get a screen full of red error messages. This is how PowerShell shows its displeasure. Several things can raise PowerShell's ire, a fact that will become very evident the more you use PowerShell. In this case, it's probably caused by a lack of permissions to the Config database or one of the content databases. PowerShell accesses SharePoint and its SQL Server databases with the identity of the user PowerShell is running as, so that user must have permission to whatever he or she is trying to access.

There are two ways to do this. First, you can make the user db_owner on all the SharePoint databases or give the user the SYSADMIN role on the SQL Server instances being used. That works, but from a security standpoint it's not great. A second, better way is to run the `Add-SPShellAdmin` cmdlet to give the user permission to the databases to which he or she needs access. This must be run as a user with db_owner rights to the database in question. The `Add-SPShellAdmin` cmdlet must be run for all users against each database they need to run PowerShell against. You can run `Get-Help Add-SPShellAdmin` to get more information.

Controlling Output

Armed with a basic understanding of the pipeline and its use of objects, this section takes a look at how to control the output of these objects. While the pipeline passes objects around, the input you provide to PowerShell and the output you expect returned at the end is always text. PowerShell handles this with ease. When an object hits the end of a pipeline, it must be captured to a variable, set to void, or formatted for the screen as text. You have already looked at using variables, so you should be familiar with the concept of capturing. *Void* is a fancy developer term for nothing, or a null value. You don't need to worry about void. Formatting, however, is something that you will likely want to wrangle control of in order to view the data you want in a form that makes sense to you.

By default, PowerShell formats the output of an object in a table, with columns representing a handful of the most useful properties of the object. In many cases it is fine to let PowerShell format your objects for display in its own default fashion. When an object makes it to the end of the pipeline, the default formatters automatically take effect, unless overridden.

Consider the default formatting for the `SPFarm` object using the `Get-SPFarm` command. In Figure 7-9, you can see that the Config database `Name` and `Status` properties are returned from the `SPFarm` object, which is the default format for output from that object. However, while those are key properties, they are not the only properties associated with the `SPFarm` object.

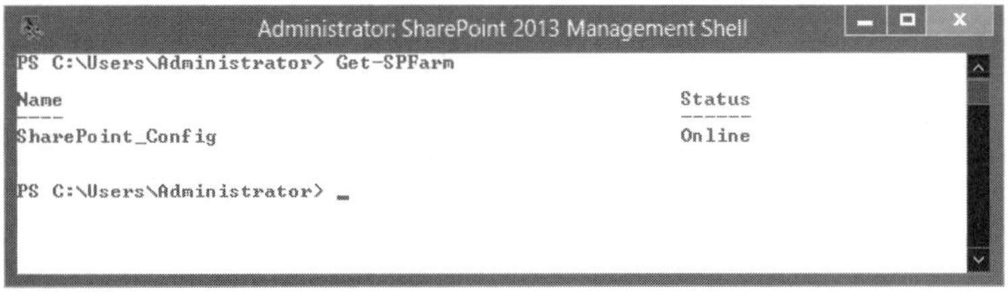

```
                Administrator: SharePoint 2013 Management Shell        [ - ][ □ ][ x ]
PS C:\Users\Administrator> Get-SPFarm

Name                                              Status
----                                              ------
SharePoint_Config                                 Online

PS C:\Users\Administrator> _
```

FIGURE 7-9

By controlling the output, you can view additional properties and specify how you want the objects formatted. You control the format using the format commands, the most common of which are `Format-List` and `Format-Table` (`fl` and `ft` are the respective aliases for these commands). There are a few others, but this section looks at only these two common formatting commands.

A WORD ABOUT ALIASES

As you're getting up to speed with PowerShell you'll probably "borrow" several PowerShell scripts from various websites. There's nothing wrong with that, as long as you properly credit your sources. It's a great way to learn how to use specific PowerShell cmdlets. However, you might see some things that don't seem to follow the verb-noun form described in this chapter, and some things won't be words at all. You'll see weird symbols such as `?` and `%`. What does it all mean?

To ease the transition from other languages, such as Windows or Linux shell scripting, PowerShell supports the use of aliases. An alias is an alternative way to reference some PowerShell cmdlets. For example, this chapter mentioned the "ft" alias for `Format-Table`, and the "fl" alias for `Format-List`. If you're ever reading someone else's PowerShell code and you see commands you don't recognize, run the PowerShell cmdlet `Get-Alias` to determine whether the unknown command is an alias for something else. Because aliases can be confusing, it is recommended that you avoid them while learning PowerShell.

`Format-List` will display object properties in list format. Each object gets one or more rows to display a property and a value. When you see text fly across the screen during some of your outputs, you can assume that you are looking at objects formatted in list style. The example shown in Figure 7-10 displays the `SPFarm` object's returned properties in List view, after using the `Format-List` command. The `Format-List` command also accepts an optional `Properties` parameter, which enables you to provide a comma-separated list of property names to be displayed. Use `Get-Member` to get a list of the properties for the object you're formatting.

FIGURE 7-10

`Format-Table` will display an object's properties in tabular fashion. Each object gets a single row and one or more columns depending on what properties should be displayed. The default format for most objects is table style, so simply piping the objects to the `Format-Table` might not get you much further. What will help is the optional `-Property` parameter, which accepts a comma-separated list of properties to display. You could choose to display all `SPFarm` properties using the following command:

```
Get-SPFarm | Format-Table *
```

If you do that, however, you will get a result that resembles The Matrix — that is, practically unreadable because you attempted to put too many columns in such a small amount of space. The `Format-List` command is better for showing a large number of properties. For example, instead of displaying all properties, you can display only the `DisplayName`, `Status`, and `BuildVersion` properties. Figure 7-11 shows an example result using the following command:

```
Get-SPFarm | Format-Table -Property DisplayName, Status, BuildVersion
```

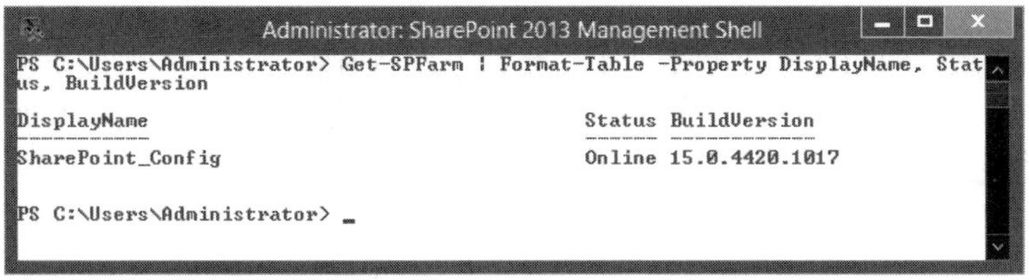

FIGURE 7-11

Additionally, the `–Property` parameter is assumed to be the default value passed to the `Format-Table` command. The following example shows the preceding command but using the short name of the `Format-Table` command and passing the desired properties:

```
Get-SPFarm | Format-Table DisplayName, Status, BuildVersion
```

Of course, the output of the preceding two commands is identical.

Due to space limitations, this chapter doesn't cover many other formatting commands or output commands to pipe content to files, including CSV. To learn more, use these two help commands:

```
Get-Help Format
Get-Help Out
```

> **NOTE** *To clear the screen, use CLS, which is an alias for Clear-Host.*

USING SHAREPOINT COMMANDS

As mentioned earlier, there are more than 750 individual SharePoint 2013 commands, so one chapter cannot possibly cover them all. This section will get you started working with some of the more common SharePoint commands for PowerShell. Readers interested in looking at a complete list should check out `http://technet.microsoft.com/en-us/library/ff678226.aspx`.

Working with the Farm

The highest-level SharePoint administration object is the farm, which contains many key properties, methods, and collections associated with the SharePoint farm. You can access many of the farm's properties using a specific SharePoint 2013 command.

For example, you can determine the farm's status, display name, and version by using the `Get-SPFarm` command (refer back to Figure 7-9). The output of this command is nothing special. The default output for the SPFarm object is to display the Status and DisplayName. However, you learned earlier how to use `Format-List` to control formatting of the objects You can also pipe the output of `Get-SPFarm` through the `Select-Object` cmdlet to display specific properties so feel free to modify the output of the SPFarm object. To add the BuildVersion column to the output, use the following command:

```
Get-SPFarm | Select-Object DisplayName, Status, BuildVersion
```

To access an individual property on the SPFarm object, use dot notation (.). You could also do this using a variable, but that has its own complications, which are covered at the end of this chapter in the discussion of disposal. For example, to access the BuildVersion property of the SPFarm object, use the following command:

```
(Get-SPFarm).BuildVersion
```

The parentheses specify that you want the BuildVersion property of the *result* of the Get-SPFarm command. The result of the Get-SPFarm command is an SPFarm object. Without the parentheses, PowerShell would interpret your command as "get the BuildVersion property of the Get-SPFarm command," which does not have a BuildVersion property. Figure 7-12 shows the result.

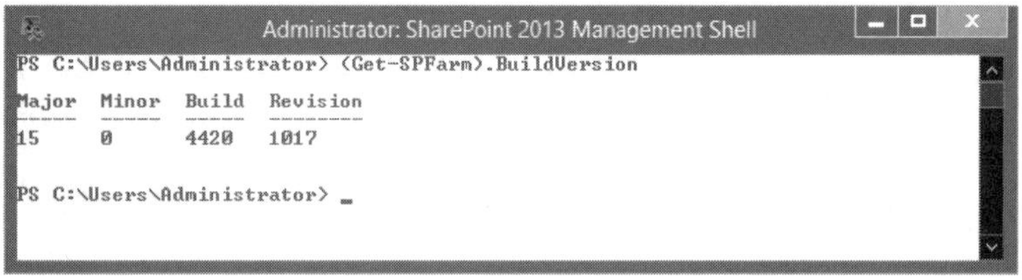

FIGURE 7-12

There are quite a few methods for the SPFarm object, such as backup and restore, but we won't cover any of these because SharePoint includes specific cmdlets for many of these methods. There's not much point spending time learning how to work with the object model when you can simply run a command that works more closely with the features you are trying to leverage.

Working with the Farm Configuration

This section touches on two useful farm configuration commands. The Get-SPFarmConfig command returns farm-level configuration information for items that are not on the SPFarm object. Figure 7-13 displays example output of the Get-SPFarmConfig command.

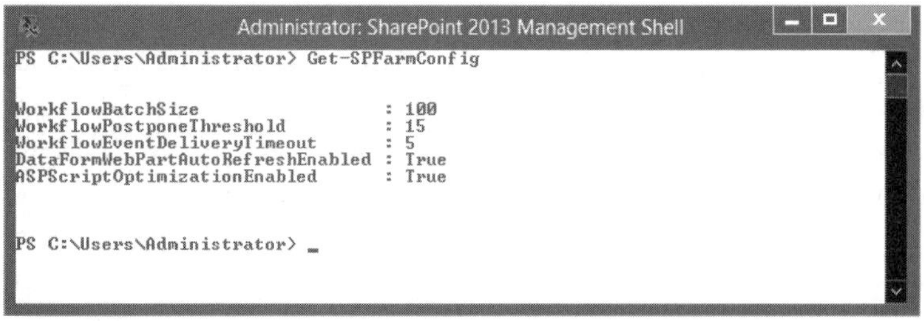

FIGURE 7-13

You can use the corresponding Set-SPFarmConfig command to modify the values. It is a little bit more involved than a single command. You need to get the FarmConfig into a variable, change the value of the property, and then pipe the modified FarmConfig variable to the Set-SPFarmConfig command. Figure 7-14 shows example output.

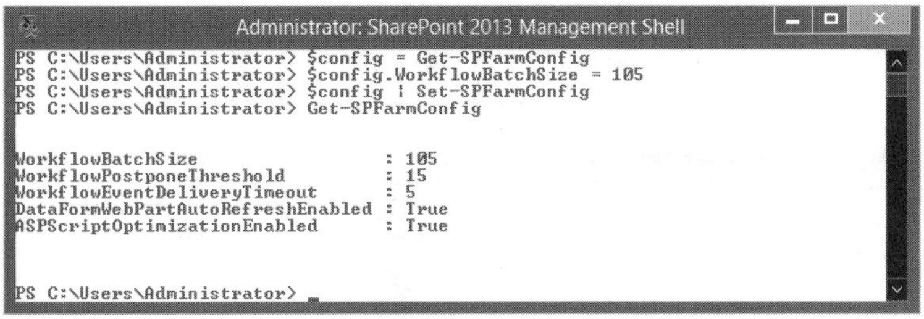

FIGURE 7-14

The commands in Figure 7-14 modify the farm's `WorkFlowBatchSize` property, which determines how many workflows can be processed at one time by the farm. The default value is 100. In this case, the setting is changed to 105 and the value is written back to the farm.

Web Applications

Each site collection in SharePoint is associated with a single web application represented by the `SPWebApplication` object. The `SPWebApplication` object contains many properties that an administrator might want to look at, such as those associated with the Recycle Bin, list throttling, and status of the web application. Using the SharePoint PowerShell commands, you can list all web applications, including the Central Administration web application; create new web applications; remove web applications; and modify web application properties.

To begin, suppose you want to see all the web applications on the farm. As shown previously, by default, the `Get-SPWebApplication` command returns all the web applications on the farm except for the Central Administration web application. To get all web applications on a farm, including the Central Administration web application, use the `Get-SPWebApplication` command with the `IncludeCentralAdministration` switch parameter.

Getting all the web applications might not be exactly what you need. Sometimes you need a single web application. To do that, you use the `-Identity` parameter. This parameter is smart enough to accept the name, URL, or ID of the web application. You rarely see the `-Identity` parameter actually named. As shown earlier with the `Format-Table` command, you can omit the name of the parameter, and name only the URL or ID as shown in Figure 7-15.

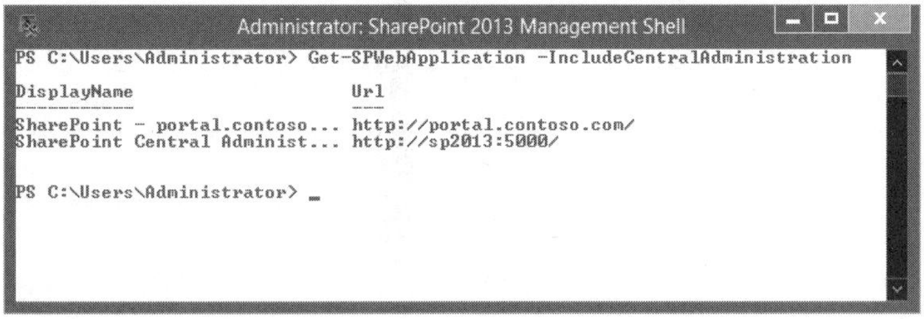

FIGURE 7-15

The `SPWebApplication` has a lot of properties and methods. To see the properties of this specific web application, you can pipe it to `Format-List`, as shown in Figure 7-16.

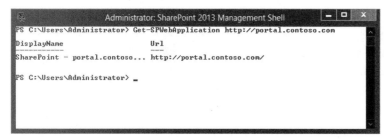

FIGURE 7-16

As you can see, the web application object has a lot of properties. To be honest, all the SharePoint objects have a lot of properties. How are you supposed to discover all these properties and keep track of them? Fortunately, there is a command for that. `Get-Member` will return the members of the object passed into it via the pipeline. To determine what properties and methods are available on the `SPWebApplication` object, use the following command (the output is shown in Figure 7-17):

```
Get-SPWebApplication http://portal.contoso.com | Get-Member
```

```
PS C:\Users\Administrator> Get-SPWebApplication http://portal.contoso.com | Get-Member

    TypeName: Microsoft.SharePoint.Administration.SPWebApplication

Name                                        MemberType      Definition
----                                        ----------      ----------
AddBackupObjects                            Method          void Add...
AddMigrateUserToClaimsPolicy                Method          void Add...
Clone                                       Method          System.O...
CurrentUserIgnoreThrottle                   Method          bool Cur...
Delete                                      Method          void Del...
EnsureDefaultJobs                           Method          void Ens...
Equals                                      Method          bool Equ...
GetChild                                    Method          T GetChi...
GetDeletedSites                             Method          Microsof...
GetHashCode                                 Method          int GetH...
GetIisSettingsWithFallback                  Method          Microsof...
GetListItemLastModifiedDates                Method          Microsof...
GetMappedPage                               Method          string G...
GetObjectData                               Method          void Get...
GetResponseUri                              Method          uri GetR...
GetSecurityTokenServiceEndPointAddress      Method          uri GetS...
GetSelfServiceCreationPageUrl               Method          string G...
GetType                                      Method          type Get...
GrantAccessToProcessIdentity                Method          void Gra...
Invalidate                                  Method          void Inv...
IsUnthrottledPrivilegedOperationsAllowed    Method          bool IsU...
IsUserLicensedForEntity                     Method          bool IsU...
Migrate                                     Method          void Mig...
MigrateUsers                                Method          void Mig...
MigrateUsersToClaims                        Method          bool Mig...
OnAbort                                     Method          bool OnA...
OnBackup                                    Method          bool OnB...
OnBackupComplete                            Method          bool OnB...
OnPostRestore                               Method          bool OnP...
OnPrepareBackup                             Method          bool OnP...
OnPreRestore                                Method          bool OnP...
OnRestore                                   Method          bool OnR...
Provision                                   Method          void Pro...
ProvisionGlobally                           Method          void Pro...
QueryFeatures                               Method          Microsof...
RenameApplicationPool                       Method          void Ren...
RequireDynamicCanary                        Method          bool Req...
SelfServiceCreate                           Method          Microsof...
SetDailyUnthrottledPrivilegedOperationWindow Method         void Set...
SetRequireDynamicCanary                     Method          void Set...
ToString                                    Method          string T...
```

FIGURE 7-17

If piping the output through `Get-Member` returns more information than one screen can handle, you can additionally pipe it to the `Out-Host -paging` cmdlet:

```
Get-SPWebApplication http://portal.contoso.com | Get-Member | out-host -paging
```

This command returns one page of output at a time. Press the spacebar to see the next screen. You can also scroll one line at a time by pressing the Enter key.

To access a specific property on the `SPWebApplication` object, use the dot notation described earlier. To access the ID of the http://portal.contoso.com web application, use the following command:

```
(Get-SPWebApplication http://portal.contoso.com).Id
```

In addition to being able to access the web applications, you can also use PowerShell to create or remove a web application. It's clear why you might want to remove a web application, but why would you want to create a new one using PowerShell? Using PowerShell to create new web applications can be useful for repeatedly building out development or demo environments. The following `New-SPWebApplication` cmdlet creates a new web application, which contains many parameters — some required and some optional. To see all the parameters, use `Get-Help New-SPWebApplication`.

```
New-SPWebApplication -Name "Portal" -Port 80 -HostHeader portal.contoso.com
-Url
http://portal.contoso.com -ApplicationPool "Default SharePoint Web App Pool"

-ApplicationPoolAccount (Get -SPManagedAccount contoso\SP_webeapps)
```

> **NOTE** *When running the preceding code, you may get an error indicating that you need "machine privileges." This happens if your SharePoint 2013 Management Shell was not started with the Run as Administrator option. Without elevated permissions, SharePoint can't always access what it needs. If you get an error like this, ensure that your Management Shell window has "Administrator:" at the beginning of the title bar.*

After creating your new web application, you can use the `Get-SPWebApplication` command to verify that it was created properly. However, you may have noticed that the `New-SPWebApplication` cmdlet output the web application's information upon completion. You could capture that object directly in a variable or pass the object onto another command via the pipeline. If you do capture the object in a variable, be sure you read the section "Disposing of SharePoint Variables" at the end of this chapter. Notice that you are calling the `Get-SPManagedAccount` command to retrieve an `SPManagedAccount` object, which is required for the AppPool account. You can see what managed accounts you have by using the `Get-SPManagedAccount` command with no parameter, as shown in Figure 7-18.

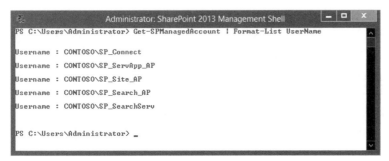

FIGURE 7-18

Of course, creating a web application through PowerShell wouldn't be very useful if you couldn't similarly remove it. The `Remove-SPWebApplication` command follows the same verb-noun convention discussed previously, and as you might expect it is used to remove the specified web application from the farm. This command requires you to select a specific web application, which prevents the deletion of multiple applications at once. Figure 7-19 shows how to remove the web application you just created.

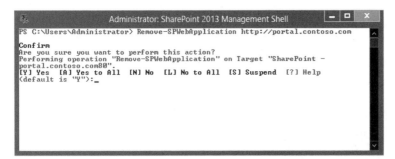

FIGURE 7-19

Notice how PowerShell prompts you before permanently destroying your data. The cmdlet offers a way to "override" this prompt, but we leave that as a future exercise once you are comfortable enough with PowerShell that you won't accidentally destroy production data.

Working with Site Collections

The site collection level is the level at which all your webs and data live. It can seem a little odd when you first encounter how webs and site collections are referenced in SharePoint Central Administration versus the object model in PowerShell. In PowerShell, a site collection is referred to as an *SPSite*. In the browser, a web is often referred to as a site, while it is referred to as an *SPWeb* in PowerShell. These are important distinctions when you are looking for that verb-noun pair for the cmdlets you need. Note also that the objects you will be working with in this section require proper disposal. If you don't dispose of your objects, you can wind up with what developers call a *memory leak* — essentially, memory that has been used up by your script but never released back to the system. If you look in Task Manager and notice the Windows PowerShell process holding on to too much memory (over 1GB if it's not doing anything), then you're probably suffering from a disposal issue. To get the memory back to the server, close the SharePoint Management Shell and open it again.

You have looked at site collections in various chapters of this book already. The site collection belongs to one and only one web application. The site collection is generally defined as a boundary for items such as content types and permissions. Like other objects in SharePoint 2013, you can list, create, modify, and remove a site collection, or SPSite, using the SharePoint PowerShell commands. You can also back up and restore a site collection using PowerShell.

> **NOTE** *The* SPSiteAdministration *commands* Get-SPSiteAdministration *and* Set-SPSiteAdministration *allow administrators who do not have access to the site collection to manage certain elements of it. Use of the* SPSite-*based commands assumes some degree of access to the site collection.*

Let's start by listing all site collections on the farm. There are two common methods to do this. If you do not need to list the Central Administration site collection (see the section "Working with Web Applications"), you can use the Get-SPSite command as described earlier in this chapter. As usual, the default formatting for the SPSite object provides only a few items for display. Figure 7-20 shows the Get-SPSite command in action.

FIGURE 7-20

The Get-SPSite command, as well as other Get commands in SharePoint 2013, will return only 20 items before providing a warning that the list was limited. These commands limit the number of objects returned for performance reasons. You will greatly appreciate the limit functionality of the Get commands the first time someone tries to return hundreds of sites and webs. The Get-SPSite command has an optional -Limit parameter that can be set to a number or to All if you wish to return all items. You will see how to use the -Limit parameter in the following section.

As covered previously, if you want to include site collections associated with Central Administration, you need to start with the Get-SPWebApplication command along with the IncludeCentralAdministration parameter. You then need to pipe the results to the Get-SPSite command, as shown in Figure 7-21.

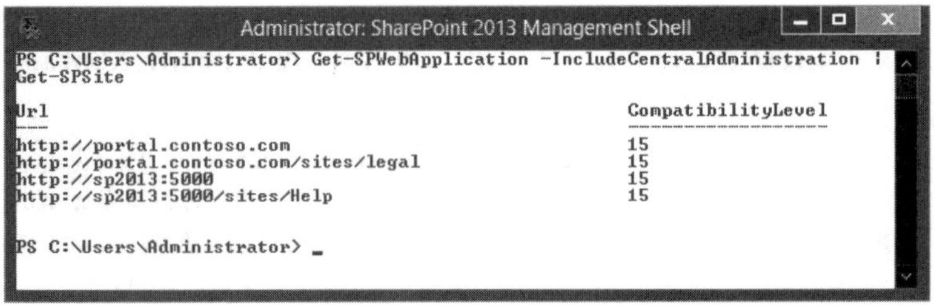

FIGURE 7-21

Using SharePoint 2013, along with some basic PowerShell commands, you have the flexibility to get just a single site collection or define parameters for getting a subset of the site collections.

As with many of the cmdlets described so far, you can get a single site collection by using the -Identity parameter, which accepts a few different types of values. In this case, the -Identity parameter can use wildcards as well as regular expressions (when used in conjunction with the RegEx switch parameter). To get a single site collection, simply pass in the URL as a parameter to the Get-SPSite command, which is piped to the Format-List command, as demonstrated in Figure 7-22. You can use an asterisk as a wildcard to limit your results to just the site collections that match your string.

FIGURE 7-22

WHAT'S THIS $_ BUSINESS?

When you start working with looping, you'll notice a weird $_ character working its way into your PowerShell. Earlier in this chapter we mentioned that in PowerShell, variables always start with a $, so you know it's a variable of some sort. In fact, $_ is a special variable used when a collection of objects is being looped through by something such as ForEach-Object or Where-Object. $_ means "the current object," but you can think of it as a "fill in the blank" variable. As ForEach-Object or Where-Object works through the collection, it fills in the $_ variable with the current object.

Don't forget about using the pipeline to filter your site collections. You can reach for the Where-Object command. The Where-Object command is a PowerShell command that uses a script block to filter objects. You commonly use the $_ reference to the current pipeline object to check a property and decide whether to keep the object or ignore it. Use Get-Help Where-Object to learn more about the Where-Object command. The following example reaches out a little further and retrieves only those site collections that have a single SPWeb object, which is the root web:

```
Get-SPSite –Limit All | Where-Object {$_.allwebs.Count -eq 1}
```

Before removing any site collections, let's look at the backup and restore options. It's a good practice to back up a site in case you realize you really needed it after removing it.

By now you should be able to guess that the command to back up a site is Backup-SPSite. The site collection backup requires that you identify the site to back up and the path, including the filename, to save the backup image. This command by itself will back up only a single site collection. For example, to back up the portal.contoso.com/teams/IT site collection, you would use the following command:

```
Backup-SPSite http://portal.contoso.com/teams/IT -path c:\backups\contoso\it\it.bak
```

While that's handy, it doesn't scale very well. Part of the "power" of PowerShell is its ability to loop through objects. Earlier in this chapter you saw how easy it is to get a list of all of your site collections. You also know how to back one up. Therefore, you may be thinking that you should be able to combine those two tasks in order to back up all of your site collections. If so, you've been paying attention in this chapter. PowerShell provides exactly that capability. Behold, the "back up all your site collections in a single script" script:

```
Get-SPSite | ForEach-Object{$FilePath = "c:\backups\" +
$_.Url.Replace
("http://","").Replace(https://,"").Replace("-","--").
Replace("/","-").Replace
(";","-") + ".bak";
Backup-SPSite -Identity $_.Url -Path $FilePath}
```

There's a lot going on there, but when it's broken down it's easy to understand. The first cmdlet, Get-SPSite, gets all the site collections in the farm. The next part walks through the list of site collections and for each one creates a variable named $FilePath that consists of C:\ backups\ plus the name of the site collection, with the protocol (http:// or https://) removed and any slashes in the URL replaced with dashes. Because the URL might legitimately have dashes in it, first you replace them with two dashes so you can tell them apart. Next you strip out any colon (:) in case the web app is not on a standard port. Finally, you use your old friend `Backup-SPSite` to back up the current site collection to the location you just built with `$FilePath`. So simple, yet so powerful.

You've probably already figured out that you would use the `Restore-SPSite` command to restore the backup. The `Restore-SPSite` command requires the usual standard `-Identity` and `-Path` parameters. For example, to restore the `it.bak` file, use the following command:

```
Restore-SPSite http://portal.contoso.com/teams/IT

-path c:\backups\contoso\it\it.bak
```

Now that you have a backup and know how to restore the site collection, it is time to finally remove it. To do that, you use the `Remove-SPSite` command. Like other destructive commands, you will be prompted to confirm the deletion of each site collection you specify. Although the `Remove-SPSite` command will remove only one site collection, you are free to pass the `SPSite` object into the `Remove-SPSite` command using the PowerShell pipeline. You can now appreciate the fact that PowerShell prompts you to allow the deletion of each and every site collection.

Now is also a good time to talk about PowerShell's wonderful `-WhatIf` parameter. Well-behaved cmdlets that are potentially destructive in nature support the optional `-WhatIf` switch parameter, and the `Remove-SPSite` cmdlet is indeed one of those cmdlets. If you add the `-WhatIf` parameter to the `Remove-SPSite` command, the command will not actually remove the site but instead indicate what will happen if you remove the `-WhatIf` parameter. Nice touch, isn't it? It might not make sense if you are working with a single site, but imagine if you ran this command:

```
$WebApps = Get-SPWebApplication -IncludeCentralAdministration
```

Now you have a variable that contains all web applications. Suppose you later decide to remove all site collections. That is easy enough:

```
$WebApps | Get-SPSite | Remove-SPSite
```

That's fine until you realize, too late, that you just deleted the Central Administration site collection. With the `-WhatIf` parameter, you are forewarned about the pain you are about to inflict on yourself. Figure 7-23 demonstrates how smart administrators can leave work on time and without being escorted out by security with all their belongings in a box.

Consider using the `-WhatIf` parameter whenever you use a command that might destroy your data. It will help avert those frantic late-night restores and a fair amount of swearing.

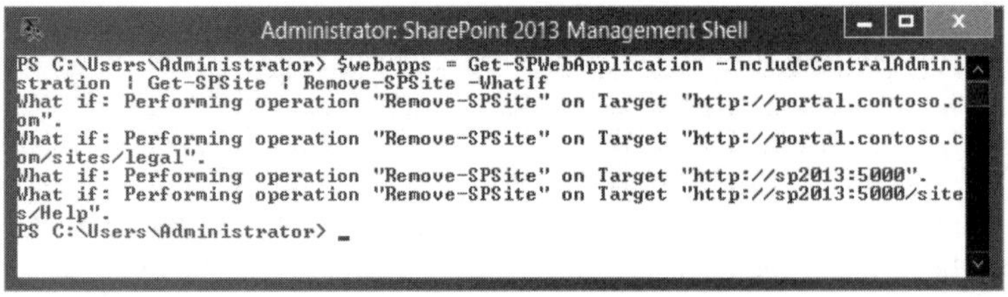

FIGURE 7-23

Working with Webs

Site collections contain webs, or SPWebs if you are speaking about SharePoint PowerShell commands. Like the other main objects in the SharePoint hierarchy, you can list, add, modify, and remove webs. Administrators tend to spend a lot of time working with webs because they are so numerous and this is where end users actually do their work. The SPWeb object contains many items that end users work with, such as lists and libraries. Now is probably a good time to let you know that there are no cmdlets to access objects below the SPWeb object. This means that there are no commands for lists, libraries, or files, to name a few objects, below the SPWeb object. However, that does not mean you cannot access them via PowerShell — just that you will not find cmdlets specific to these objects. You are free to access these objects via the object model.

Listing all the webs of the farm is slightly different from listing SPWebApplications or SPSites. The Get-SPWeb cmdlet requires at least one parameter. It will not list all SPWebs on the farm if you omit the parameters; there's just too many SPWebs in a farm for that to make sense. On the plus side, you are allowed wildcards, regular expressions (with the use of the -RegEx switch parameter), and filters (with a script block), similar to Get-SPSite. The -Identity parameter will also accept a relative path if the -Site parameter is used.

Let's look at a few ways to list SPWebs, starting with a single web. To access a single SPWeb object, use the -Identity parameter, passing in the URL, as demonstrated in Figure 7-24.

FIGURE 7-24

The next example returns all the SPWebs in the farm, including any Central Administration webs, sorted by URL and displaying only the Title and URL:

```
Get-SPWebApplication -IncludeCentralAdministration | Get-SPSite |
Get-SPWeb |
Sort-Object Url | Format-Table Title, Url
```

Figure 7-25 displays the results of the attempt to display all the SPWebs on the farm. As discussed earlier, the cmdlet will limit the number of objects returned to 20 for performance reasons. If the number of objects is greater than 20, a warning will be displayed. To display all the SPWebs, you need to add the -Limit property set to All for both Get-SPSite and Get-SPWeb:

```
Get-SPWebApplication -IncludeCentralAdministration | Get-SPSite -Limit All |
Get-SPWeb -Limit All | Sort-Object Url| Format-List Title, Url
```

```
Administrator: SharePoint 2013 Management Shell                          [ - ] [ □ ] [ X ]
PS C:\Users\Administrator> Get-SPWebApplication -IncludeCentralAdministration ¦
Get-SPSite ¦ Get-SPWeb ¦ Sort-Object Url ¦ Format-Table Title, Url
WARNING: More results were found in Get-SPWeb but were not returned.  Use
'-Limit ALL' to return all possible results.

Title                                  Url
-----                                  ---
Portal                                 http://portal.contoso.com
Human Resources                        http://portal.contoso.com/hr
Blog                                   http://portal.contoso.com/hr/blog
Meetings                               http://portal.contoso.com/hr/meetings
Manager's Forum                        http://portal.contoso.com/hr/mgrforum
Portal                                 http://portal.contoso.com/hr/portal
Team                                   http://portal.contoso.com/hr/team
Marketing                              http://portal.contoso.com/marketing
Blog                                   http://portal.contoso.com/marketing/...
Discussions                            http://portal.contoso.com/marketing/...
Managers Forum                         http://portal.contoso.com/marketing/...
Portal                                 http://portal.contoso.com/marketing/...
Team                                   http://portal.contoso.com/marketing/...
Nursing                                http://portal.contoso.com/nursing
discussions                            http://portal.contoso.com/nursing/di...
team                                   http://portal.contoso.com/nursing/team
Legal                                  http://portal.contoso.com/sites/legal
Blog                                   http://portal.contoso.com/sites/lega...
Discussions                            http://portal.contoso.com/sites/lega...
Meetings                               http://portal.contoso.com/sites/lega...


PS C:\Users\Administrator> _
```

FIGURE 7-25

Creating a new web is similar to creating new site collections. You use the `New-SPWeb` command and a host of parameters to define the new SPWeb. One of these parameters, `-Url`, is required, but the rest are optional, such as `-Name` and `-Template`. The following command creates a new SPWeb based on the Team Site template. Once the web has been created, the SPWeb object is returned and displayed on the screen:

```
New-SPSWeb -Url http://portal.contoso.com/teams/IT/SP2013, -Template "STS#1"
-Name "SP 2013 Implementation"
```

You cannot back up or restore an individual web; that is reserved for the site collection and farm. You can work around this limitation, however. SharePoint has content deployment functionality that enables you to automate the process of copying content from one farm to another. It does this at the SPWeb level. PowerShell has two cmdlets, `Export-SPWeb` and `Import-SPWeb`, that are built on that framework. While you can't back up and restore webs, we can export them and import them. Be careful — these exports are not full fidelity, as their focus is on content. They won't contain non-content pieces such as alerts, workflows, or permissions.

You just created a new web, so go ahead and export it. Use the `Export-SPWeb` command, passing in the `-Identity` and `-Path` parameters. The `-Path` parameter indicates where the exported web file will be placed, and it must include both a filename and the path:

```
Export-SPWeb http://portal.contoso.com/ops -Path c:\ExportWeb\opsExport.cmp
```

You can import the web into an existing or new web. The `Import-SPWeb` command requires the identity of the web to import to and the path to the exported web file. The command to import your exported site to a new web is as follows:

```
Import-SPWeb http://portal.contoso.com/DemoImport -Path c:\ExportWeb\opsExport.cmp
```

Finally, you can remove your web by using the `Remove-SPWeb` command. This command is similar to the `Remove-SPSite` command. It removes one web at a time, prompting users for confirmation along the way. You can pipe an unlimited number of SPWebs into the `remove` command. Don't forget the earlier discussion of the `-WhatIf` parameter. As shown in Figure 7-26, use the `-WhatIf` parameter to see what would happen if you ran this command:

```
Get-SPSite | Get-SPWeb -Limit All | Remove-SPWeb -WhatIf
```

FIGURE 7-26

As you can see, the pipeline is very powerful. Be careful when you pipe objects into destructive commands. The `-WhatIf` parameter and PowerShell's confirm message will help to keep you out of trouble — that is, if you pay attention.

Working with Objects Below the Web Level

As mentioned earlier, SharePoint PowerShell commands generally work from the `SPWeb` object and above. That means you will not find commands such as `Get-SPList` or `New-SPLibrary` in the out-of-the-box commands. However, with a little digging, and liberal usage of the `Get-Member` cmdlet, you can use PowerShell and the object model to list a web's lists and libraries, as well as add and then remove a SharePoint list. That provides you with the foundation to move beyond the commands supplied by SharePoint 2013.

Lists and libraries are child objects of the `SPWeb` object you just looked at. The `SPWeb` object contains a single property, `Lists`, which is a collection of all its lists and libraries. To retrieve all the lists and libraries of a specific web, you can use the following command, as shown in Figure 7-27, within the Management Shell or a host with the SharePoint commands registered:

```
(Get-SPWeb http://portal.contoso.com/team/blog).Lists
```

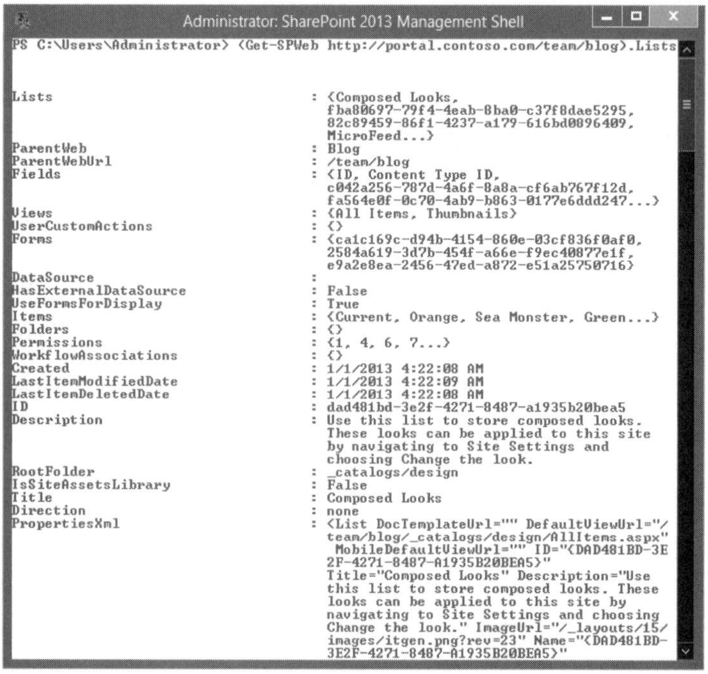

FIGURE 7-27

In all likelihood, a lot of text is flying across your screen now as all the properties of all the lists and libraries are displayed. Unlike the previous SharePoint objects you have worked with, the SPList list object that is returned from the preceding command does not have a defined default format; therefore, PowerShell dumps all the properties.

> **NOTE** *Ctrl+C will exit the current processing and return you to your prompt.*

None of us can read that fast. Fortunately, you can control how each list is formatted and slow down some of that flying text. Run the same command, but this time send the lists and libraries out to Format-Table, another PowerShell formatting command, shown in Figure 7-28:

```
(Get-SPWeb http://portal.contoso.com/team/blog).lists | Sort-Object Title |
Format-Table Title, Id, ItemCount, hasUniqueRoleAssignments,
EnabledAttachments, EnableThrottling
```

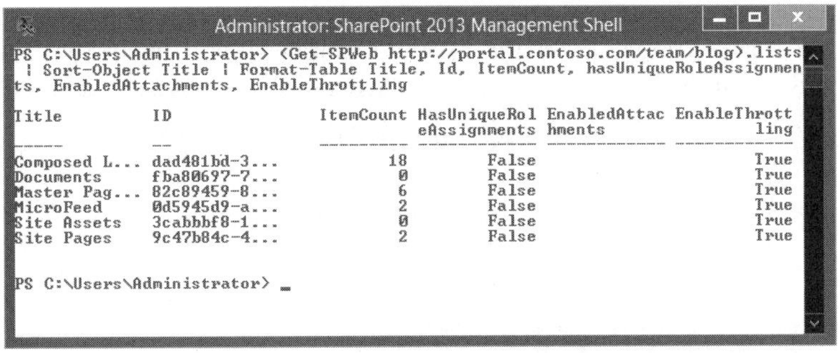

FIGURE 7-28

> **NOTE** *Many of the lower-level objects such as* `SPList` *and* `SPListItem` *do not save their changes to the content database until the* `Update` *method is called on the object.*

Now that you know how to retrieve all the lists and libraries contained within a SharePoint web, the following example demonstrates how to get just one specific list. The `Lists` property on the `SPWeb` object returns a collection of lists, like many of the properties associated with SharePoint objects. You can retrieve any list by using the index, ID, or title. For example, to get the third item in the lists collection, use the following:

```
(Get-SPWeb http://portal.contoso.com/team/blog).lists[2] |
Format-Table Title, Id,
ItemCount, hasUniqueRoleAssignments,
EnabledAttachments, EnableThrottling
```

In the preceding example, note that the value 2 is used, rather than 3, because developers like to start counting at 0. Therefore, the first item in a collection is number 0, so the third item is 2.

As mentioned previously, you can also get a list by using the ID or list title. Simply replace the number 2 with the ID or Title:

```
(Get-SPWeb http://portal.contoso.com/team/blog).lists["Posts"] |
Format-Table Title, Id, ItemCount, hasUniqueRoleAssignments,
EnabledAttachments, EnableThrottling
```

At this point, you know how to get down to the list level and enumerate all of your lists and libraries. Creating a new list is a little tricky. First, you need to decide what type of list you will create. To keep it simple, the next example creates a Links list. The Links list template has an ID of 103, which is information you can find by looking in the SharePoint documentation. You can also get this information by running the following command:

```
(Get-SPWeb http://portal.contoso.com/team/blog).ListTemplates |
Where-Object {$_.Name -eq "Links"}
```

To create the Links list, you need to call the `Add` method of the List collection you have already been working with. The `Add` method requires three parameters for this example: `Title`, `Description`, and `ListTemplateId`. Armed with all this information, add that list using the following command:

```
(Get-SPWeb http://portal.contoso.com/team/blog).Lists.Add("Demo Links List",
"This is the description", 103)
```

Figure 7-29 shows the new, improved list of lists — now sporting a new Links list.

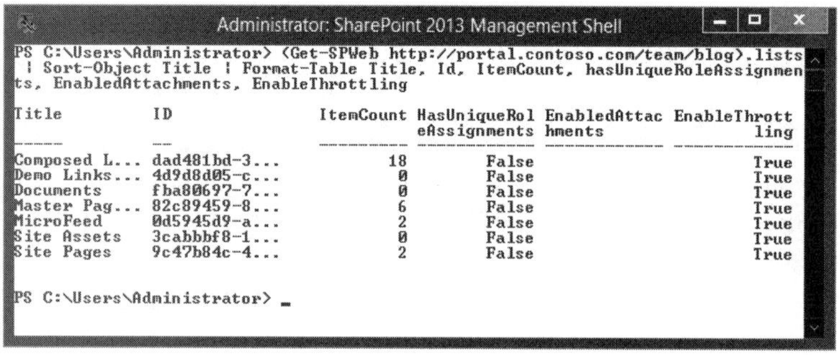

FIGURE 7-29

Finally, to close out this section you will delete your list. Yes, delete; not remove. The `Delete` method is a method of the `SPListCollection` object (the `Lists` property), not a command in PowerShell, which is why you can use it. The `Delete` method of the List collection requires the list ID, so you are going to use a variable this time to grab the list ID in one line and use it in the `Delete` on the next line. Following are the two lines needed to delete the list you just created (Figure 7-30 shows what it looks like):

```
$listId = (Get-SPWeb http://portal.contoso.com/team/blog).
lists["Demo Links List"].Id

(Get-SPWeb http://portal.contoso.com/team/blog).lists.Delete($listId)
```

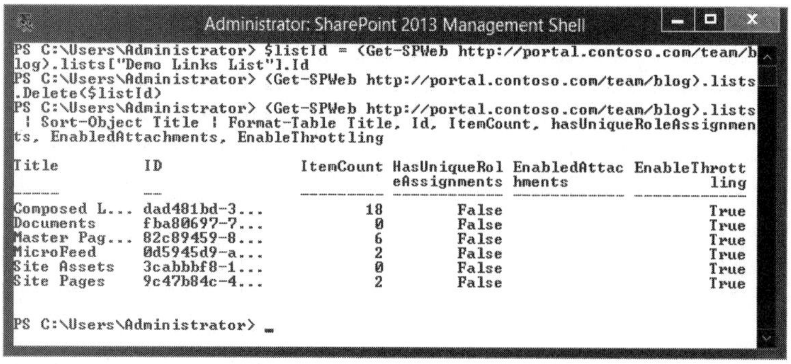

FIGURE 7-30

Again, you can verify that you did indeed remove the list by using the following command to list all your lists.

```
(Get-SPWeb http://portal.contoso.com/team/blog).lists | Sort-Object Title |
Format-Table Title, Id, ItemCount, hasUniqueRoleAssignments,
EnabledAttachments, EnableThrottling
```

A USEFUL RESOURCE

This section can't close without at least pointing new admin developers to the key documentation that will help you with these more interesting creations: the SharePoint 2013 developer reference site, currently located at `http://msdn` `.microsoft.com/en-us/library/jj193038.aspx`. This set of web pages provides documentation on the various objects in SharePoint. PowerShell uses the SharePoint 2013 object model, so any references about it, regardless of the target language, will be helpful.

Disposing of SharePoint Variables

As covered earlier, certain objects need to be disposed of properly in order to protect your server from dreaded memory leaks. This section discusses a couple of different methods for proper disposal of your objects.

Although a few variables slipped into the examples, this chapter specifically avoided scenarios that required their use. It instead focused on single-line commands, which includes commands that are chained using the pipeline, because single-line commands properly handle the disposal of SharePoint objects. The more you stick to one-liners, the less chance you have of forgetting to properly clean up after yourself.

The disposal issue becomes a problem as soon as you start to capture certain SharePoint objects, such as SPSite, SPSiteAdministration, and SPWeb, and hold on to them. They cannot be disposed of at the end of the pipeline because you are still using the object.

Luckily, there are two commands to help you work with situations in which you might run into disposal issues: Start-SPAssignment and Stop-SPAssignment. These commands help you to both track objects and then dispose of them when they are no longer needed.

This section describes two ways to use these commands. The first method is the simple assignment method, which uses the -Global switch parameter. Basically, before you start to use objects that might need to be disposed of, you call Start-SPAssignment using the -Global switch parameter. This starts the tracking of all resources being used, which, quite frankly, can be a lot. Once you are done working with your variables and objects, you need to call Stop-SPAssignment with the same -Global switch parameter. At this point, all the objects that were tracked will be released and properly disposed of. Once you call Stop-SPAssignment you should not use the resources for that block of commands, as the contents of the variables will have been disposed of and may lead to unexpected behavior in your script.

Figure 7-31 demonstrates the use of Start-SPAssignment and Stop-SPAssignment with the -Global switch parameter.

While using the simple assignment method is easy, it does have some drawbacks. Any trackable SharePoint object between the Start-SPAssignment and Stop-SPAssignment will be managed by the commands. Therefore, if you run many one-liners that do not necessarily need to be tracked, they will be tracked anyway, which means more memory that is waiting to be released.

If you know when you need to track a SharePoint object, you can manually assign your resources to be tracked. This enables you to be selective regarding the objects that are assigned for tracking and disposal. You can do this with the same Start-SPAssignment and Stop-SPAssignment commands. With this technique, you create a new SPAssignmentCollection using Start-SPAssignment — for example, $spAssign = Start-SPAssignment.

```
Administrator: SharePoint 2013 Management Shell
PS C:\Users\Administrator> Start-SPAssignment -Global
PS C:\Users\Administrator> $webs = (Get-SPSite)[0] | Get-SPWeb
PS C:\Users\Administrator> $webs | Format-Table Title, URL

Title                           Url
-----                           ---
Portal                          http://portal.contoso.com
Human Resources                 http://portal.contoso.com/hr
Blog                            http://portal.contoso.com/hr/blog
Meetings                        http://portal.contoso.com/hr/meetings
Manager's Forum                 http://portal.contoso.com/hr/mgrforum
Portal                          http://portal.contoso.com/hr/portal
Team                            http://portal.contoso.com/hr/team
Marketing                       http://portal.contoso.com/marketing
Blog                            http://portal.contoso.com/marketing/...
Discussions                     http://portal.contoso.com/marketing/...
Managers Forum                  http://portal.contoso.com/marketing/...
Portal                          http://portal.contoso.com/marketing/...
Team                            http://portal.contoso.com/marketing/...
Nursing                         http://portal.contoso.com/nursing
discussions                     http://portal.contoso.com/nursing/di...
team                            http://portal.contoso.com/nursing/team
Team                            http://portal.contoso.com/team
Blog                            http://portal.contoso.com/team/blog

PS C:\Users\Administrator> Stop-SPAssignment -Global
PS C:\Users\Administrator> _
```

FIGURE 7-31

When you need to track objects, you can use $spAssign in the pipeline. For example, you can assign all webs from a particular site collection for tracking and disposal:

```
$Webs = $spAssign | Get-SPSite http://portal.contoso.com | get-SPWeb
```

You can also throw in a few one-liners as you have been doing up until now. These do not need to be tracked, as they will be disposed of properly. Because these objects will not be assigned to the SPAssignmentCollection object, they will be disposed of at the end of their lifetime and will not hold on to extra memory. Once you are done with your block of commands, you can clean up using the Stop-SPAssignment command, passing in the $spAssign variable. Like the simple assignment, once you call Stop-SPAssignment you should not use the variables that were assigned to the SPAssignmentCollection. Figure 7-32 demonstrates the assignment of a collection of web objects and their proper disposal with the call to Stop-SPAssignment.

FIGURE 7-32

Note in Figure 7-32 that you do not assign the `SPWeb` object you used to display the `SPList` objects. This `SPWeb` object is in a one-liner and will be disposed of correctly without the need for any tracking.

SOME SAMPLE POWERSHELL SCRIPTS

So far in this chapter we've covered some PowerShell basics and some SharePoint basics. What you haven't seen yet are some real-world examples of PowerShell scripts you can use. First, a word of warning: There are some really terrible PowerShell scripts out there. Some PowerShell scripts do bad things like run your servers out of memory, delete things they shouldn't, shave your cat, all kinds of unsavory things. Before you run any script you didn't write yourself, including the scripts in this chapter, be sure you read through it and understand what it's doing. It's also a good idea to run an unknown script on a test environment until you're sure you can trust it.

Creating Your SharePoint 2013 Farm with PowerShell

In Chapter 3, "Installing and Configuring SharePoint 2013," you used a little PowerShell to get things installed and configured, but you can also use PowerShell to build your farm. The following script completely replaces using the Configuration Wizard to build your SharePoint 2013 farm:

```
# This script can be used to build a SharePoint 2010 or 2013 farm
# Written by Todd Klindt v1.0
# http://www.toddklindt.com/createfarm

# Add the SharePoint Snapin, in case PowerShell wasn't started with the Management
Shell
Add-PSSnapin microsoft.sharepoint.powershell -ErrorAction SilentlyContinue

# Verify that PowerShell is running as an Admin
```

```
if ( -not ([Security.Principal.WindowsPrincipal] [Security.Principal.
WindowsIdentity]::GetCurrent()).IsInRole([Security.Principal.WindowsBuiltInRole]
"Administrator"))
{
    Write-Output "This PowerShell prompt is not elevated"
    write-output "Please start PowerShell with the Admin token and try again"
    return
}

# Everything looks good. Let's build us a SharePoint farm

$domain = (Get-ChildItem env:userdomain).value
$tempfarmaccount = $domain.ToString() + '\sp_farm'
$tempsqlserver = (Get-ChildItem env:computername).value

$farmaccountname = Read-Host -Prompt "Enter Farm Account Name. Press Enter for
$tempfarmaccount"
If ($farmaccountname -eq "") {$farmaccountname = $tempfarmaccount}
$farmaccountpassword = Read-Host -Prompt "Enter Farm Account Password. Press Enter
for pass@word1"
If ($farmaccountpassword -eq "") {$farmaccountpassword = 'pass@word1'}
$farmpassphrase = Read-Host -Prompt "Enter Farm Passphrase. Press Enter for
 pass@word1"
If ($farmpassphrase -eq "") {$farmpassphrase = 'pass@word1'}
$sqlserver = Read-Host -Prompt "Enter SQL Instance name. Press Enter for
$tempsqlserver"
If ($sqlserver -eq "") {$sqlserver = $tempsqlserver}

$password = ConvertTo-SecureString  $farmaccountpassword -AsPlainText -Force
$farmaccount = New-Object system.management.automation.pscredential
$farmaccountname, $password

Write-Host "Using that information to build your SharePoint Farm"

New-SPConfigurationDatabase -DatabaseName SharePoint_Config -DatabaseServer
$sqlserver -AdministrationContentDatabaseName SharePoint_Admin_Content
-Passphrase (convertto-securestring $farmpassphrase -AsPlainText -Force)
-FarmCredentials $farmaccount

Write-Host "Config database built, now configuring local machine."

Install-SPHelpCollection -All
Initialize-SPResourceSecurity
Install-SPService
Install-SPFeature -AllExistingFeatures

Write-host "Creating Central Admin on port 10260"

New-SPCentralAdministration -Port 10260 -WindowsAuthProvider "NTLM"
Install-SPApplicationContent
```

As indicated by the comments, this script will work with SharePoint 2010 or SharePoint 2013. It employs not only several SharePoint cmdlets we have covered (those for which the noun starts with "SP"), but also many new PowerShell techniques such as asking for input, error control, and flow control. Once the script has completed successfully, your farm will be created, including Central Administration.

Creating Managed Accounts and Service Application Pools

When you're configuring your farm, one of the first things you need to do is create the managed accounts and service app application pools your farm will use. The following PowerShell lines will do that:

```
# Create Managed Accounts
$password = ConvertTo-SecureString 'pass@word1' -AsPlainText -Force

# create sp_webapps
$account = New-Object system.management.automation.pscredential
'contoso\sp_webapps', $password
New-SPManagedAccount $account

# create sp_serviceapps
$account = New-Object system.management.automation.pscredential
'contoso\sp_serviceapps', $password
New-SPManagedAccount $account

# Create the Service App Pool
New-SPServiceApplicationPool -Name "Default SharePoint Service App Pool"
-Account contoso\sp_serviceapps
$apppool = Get-SPServiceApplicationPool "Default SharePoint Service App Pool"
```

Of course, you need to ensure that the usernames and passwords match those in your actual farm. The chances are pretty slim that your domain is Contoso.

Creating the Search Service Application in SharePoint 2013 Server

While you can create your Search service application in Central Admin, doing so will create all your Search databases with GUIDs at the end. No one likes GUIDs. They were always picked last for kickball in grade school, every, single, time. If you instead create the Search service with PowerShell, you can specify the database names SharePoint should use. The following script will do that for you (note that it assumes that the service application pool from the previous section exists):

```
# Based on scripts at http://www.harbar.net/articles/sp2013mt.aspx
# Thanks Spence!

# Get App Pool
$saAppPoolName = "Default SharePoint Service App Pool"

# Search Specifics, we are single server farm
$searchServerName = (Get-ChildItem env:computername).value
$serviceAppName = "Search Service Application"
$searchDBName = "SearchService_DB"


# Grab the Appplication Pool for Service Application Endpoint
```

```
$saAppPool = Get-SPServiceApplicationPool $saAppPoolName

# Start Search Service Instances
Write-Host "Starting Search Service Instances..."
Start-SPEnterpriseSearchServiceInstance $searchServerName
Start-SPEnterpriseSearchQueryAndSiteSettingsServiceInstance $searchServerName

# Create the Search Service Application and Proxy
Write-Host "Creating Search Service Application and Proxy..."
$searchServiceApp = New-SPEnterpriseSearchServiceApplication -Name $serviceAppName
-ApplicationPool $saAppPoolName -DatabaseName $searchDBName
$searchProxy = New-SPEnterpriseSearchServiceApplicationProxy -Name "$serviceAppName
  Proxy" -SearchApplication $searchServiceApp

# Clone the default Topology (which is empty) and create a new one and then
activate it
Write-Host "Configuring Search Component Topology..."
$clone = $searchServiceApp.ActiveTopology.Clone()
$searchServiceInstance = Get-SPEnterpriseSearchServiceInstance
New-SPEnterpriseSearchAdminComponent -SearchTopology $clone -SearchServiceInstance
  $searchServiceInstance
New-SPEnterpriseSearchContentProcessingComponent -SearchTopology $clone
-SearchServiceInstance $searchServiceInstance
New-SPEnterpriseSearchAnalyticsProcessingComponent -SearchTopology $clone
  -SearchServiceInstance $searchServiceInstance
New-SPEnterpriseSearchCrawlComponent -SearchTopology $clone
-SearchServiceInstance $searchServiceInstance
New-SPEnterpriseSearchIndexComponent -SearchTopology $clone
-SearchServiceInstance $searchServiceInstance
New-SPEnterpriseSearchQueryProcessingComponent -SearchTopology $clone
-SearchServiceInstance $searchServiceInstance
$clone.Activate()


Write-Host "Search Done!"
```

After running this script, head over to Central Admin and enjoy the fruits of your labor.

Creating a Claims Web Application

You looked at some web application cmdlets earlier in this chapter. The following little beauty will create a new web application and use claims-based authentication:

```
$ap = New-SPAuthenticationProvider -UseWindowsIntegratedAuthentication
-DisableKerberos

New-SPWebApplication -Name "Contoso Portal"
-ApplicationPool "Default SharePoint Web Apps"
-HostHeader portal.contoso.com -Port 80 -Url http://portal.contoso.com
-AuthenticationMethod NTLM -AuthenticationProvider $ap
-DatabaseName "WSS_Content_Portal"
```

Getting Site Collection Size

You can use this one-liner to list all the site collections in your farm, sorted by size:

```
Get-SPSite | select url, @{label="Size in MB";Expression={$_.usage.storage/1MB}} |
Sort-Object -Descending -Property "Size in MB" | Format-Table –AutoSize
Getting Database Size
```

The following will list all the databases in your farm, sorted by size:

```
Get-SPDatabase | select name, @{label="Size in MB";Expression=
{$_.disksizerequired/1MB}} | Sort-Object -Descending -Property "Size in MB"
```

Hopefully you'll be able to grab some useful nuggets from these scripts and write some amazing scripts of your own.

SUMMARY

PowerShell, as the name implies, is a powerful tool for SharePoint and general system administration. The chapter discussed basic topics such as common SharePoint cmdlets, variables, objects, and their disposal, and even touched on some basic scripting concepts. Additionally, it walked through some more advanced topics to include building a working SharePoint Farm, and creating many of the Service Applications your end-users will be clamoring to use. In essence, this chapter has taken you from being a PowerShell newbie to using advanced techniques on your SharePoint farm.

As a SharePoint Administrator you could probably skate by without much use for PowerShell. However, understanding the concepts put forth in this chapter will help you respond to the needs of your farm and your users. You'll also be able to tell amusing anecdotes about SPSites and SPWebs to your developer "friends" around the water cooler, and they'll laugh along. Oh, and you'll be able to better administer your SharePoint 2013 farm, too.

8

Configuring SharePoint for Business Intelligence

A quick glance at the preceding list of topics covered in this chapter explains why this chapter is so long. Business intelligence (BI), which refers to an enterprise's approach to working with, analyzing, and storing large amounts of data, is often a challenge for administrators both new and experienced. One of the main reasons is because the guides and documentation aren't usually very practical. They are typically written by fellow administrators who understand the nuts and bolts but have no clue about the data. Not that it really matters, as such guides rarely include a walk-through of the technology because sample data is difficult to find and deploy. Of course, the opposite approach is equally insufficient, because a guide written purely by a data specialist enables an administrator to get things working but without any real understanding of the process.

This chapter takes a different approach. It was written by two SharePoint administrators and one BI expert, together working out all the kinks and then documenting it. Every section first describes how to install and configure the given item, and then walks you through the process of actually deploying the resulting report or other BI output so you can see it working.

FIND BONUS INFORMATION

Since the BI guy was feeling generous he has included in each section a screenshot of a more complex BI solution using the tool from that section. He couldn't include building that complex solution in the chapter so he did the next best thing. If you go to `http://www.rackspace.com/sharepoint-bi/` you will find a recording of him building the more complex solution. What a nice guy.

In order to get the most from this integrated approach, you begin by deploying SQL Server Analysis Services, and then add the AdventureWorks database. The reasoning is quite simple: you need real data to do the real examples that follow throughout the chapter.

One more thing to keep in mind is the version of SQL Server matters. Throughout the chapter the various tools will identify the minimum version of SQL Server you need for a given toolset. If you want to just have one ready to go, SQL Server 2012 Enterprise with Service Pack 1 can do everything in this chapter. When you are building test environments and licensing is not an issue that may be the best way to go. But the Enterprise edition costs a small fortune so for production you may want to think a little harder and roll with the cheapest license you can. Remember service packs are free so no matter what you do the latest, greatest service pack is always recommended.

INSTALLING SQL SERVER ANALYSIS SERVICES

In order to test some of the service applications you will configure later in the chapter, you need a working instance of SQL Server Analysis Services (henceforth referred to as SSAS). The following sections step you through the process of installing SSAS and deploying the AdventureWorks sample database and cube to your environment.

NOTE *A cube is an object, created in an Analysis Services database, that is used to analyze related data. Cubes pre-aggregate data allowing them to handle very large sets of data while maintaining fast query response times. Some front-end tools such as the PerformancePoint Analytic Chart require the use of a cube as its data source.*

Installing SSAS and Data Tools

In a production environment, your instance of SSAS would most likely live on a separate server, but for the example you're going to install SSAS on your existing SQL box. SSAS is installed using the SQL Server 2012 installation disc, so you need to have that handy in order to complete the following steps:

1. Log onto your SQL server as an account that has the system administrator SQL role. In this example, the server is sql and the account is contoso\administrator.

2. Navigate to your SQL Server 2012 installation disc and double-click setup.exe to open the SQL Server Installation Center window.

3. Select Installation from the left pane.

4. Select "New SQL Server stand-alone installation or add features to an existing installation," as shown in Figure 8-1.

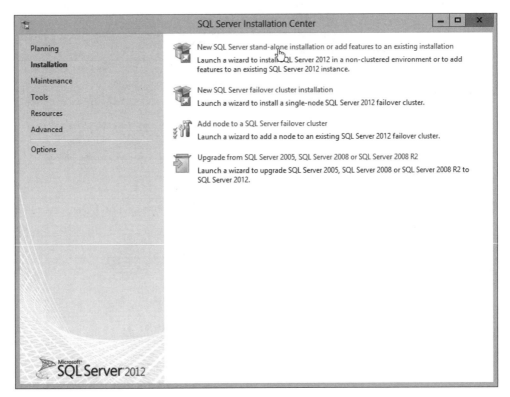

FIGURE 8-1

5. Click OK on the Setup Support Rules dialog.

6. Click Next on the Product Updates dialog.

7. Click Next on the Setup Support Rules dialog.

8. On the Installation Type dialog, select "Add features to an existing instance of SQL Server 2012" and ensure that the default instance of MSSQLSERVER is selected in the drop-down as seen in Figure 8-2. Click Next.

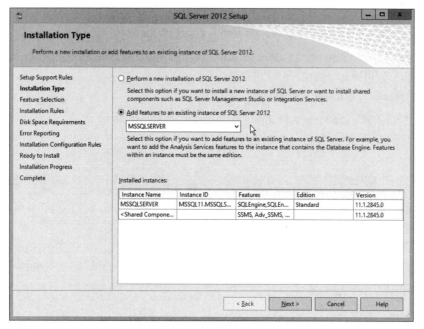

FIGURE 8-2

9. In the Feature Selection dialog, select both Analysis Services and SQL Server Data Tools from the list of options, as shown in Figure 8-3.

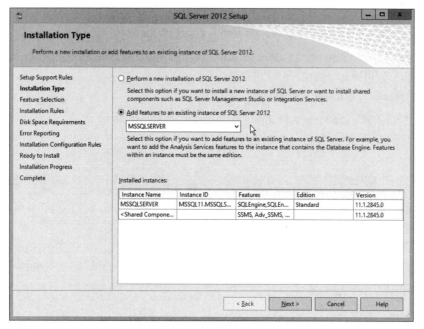

FIGURE 8-3

10. Click Next on the Installation Rules dialog.

11. Click Next on the Disk Space Requirements dialog.

12. On the Server Configuration dialog, change the account name under which the SQL Server Analysis Services service runs. This account just needs to be domain user. In this example, use **contoso\sql_ssas** as shown in Figure 8-4.

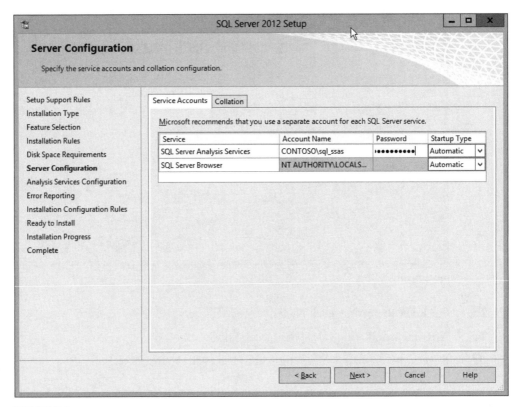

FIGURE 8-4

13. On the Analysis Services Configuration dialog, ensure that Multidimensional and Data Mining Mode is selected as the Server Mode.

14. Grant the logged-in account administrator permissions for the SSAS instance by clicking the Add Current User button. When complete, the dialog should look like Figure 8-5. Click Next.

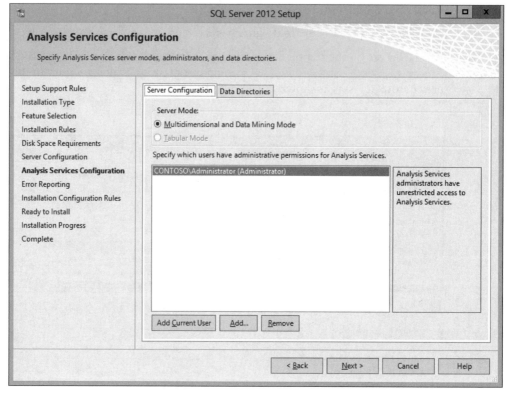

FIGURE 8-5

15. For Error Reporting, click Next.

16. After the installation rules pass successfully, click Next.

17. Review the summary information and then click the Install button.

Once installation completes, you can verify the SSAS installation by opening SQL Server Management Studio and connecting to the SSAS instance. To do so, follow these steps:

1. From the Start menu, open SQL Management Studio.

2. Select Analysis Server from the Server type, type in your SQL server's name, and click Connect. In this example it would be **sql**.

3. Confirm that the SSAS instance is displayed in the Object Explorer window.

Deploying AdventureWorks

Now that SSAS is installed, it's time to obtain and deploy some sample data you can use. The easiest way to do that is to use the AdventureWorks sample database and SSAS project. The files can be downloaded from CodePlex at `http://msftdbprodsamples.codeplex.com/releases/view/55330`. Download the following files from that site:

➤   `AdventureWorksDW2012_Data.mdf` — You will attach this to the SQL Server instance so you have a source from which your cube can pull data. Listed on the site as "AdventureWorksDW2012 Data File". Make sure you get the one with DW in the name.

➤   `AdventureWorks Multidimensional Models SQL Server 2012.zip` — You will use this to deploy an SSAS cube. Listed on the site as "AdventureWorks Multidimensional Models SQL Server 2012."

Deploying AdventureWorks2012_Data.mdf

In order for the newly downloaded .mdf file to be of any use, you need to attach it to the SQL Server instance. To do so, follow these steps:

1.   Copy the `AdventureWorksDW2012_Data.mdf` file to your SQL server data directory. By default, this should be `C:\Program Files\Microsoft SQL Server\MSSQL11 .MSSQLSERVER\MSSQL\DATA`. If you are unsure, you can find the location by connecting to SQL Server using SQL Server Management Studio, right-clicking on your instance, and selecting Properties. The location where SQL Server keeps the data files should be listed on the Database Settings page under Database default locations.

2.   Open SQL Server Management Studio and connect to the default SQL instance.

3.   In the Object Explorer window, right-click on the Databases folder.

4.   From the drop-down select Attach...

5.   From the Attach Databases dialog, click the Add... button.

6.   Navigate to the location where you copied your MDF file. Once there, select the file and click OK.

7.   Note that there is no log file that goes along with the MDF file you are attaching. You need to remove the log file from the AdventureWorksDW2012 Database details section of the dialog by selecting it and then clicking the Remove button. When completed, your screen should look similar to Figure 8-6.

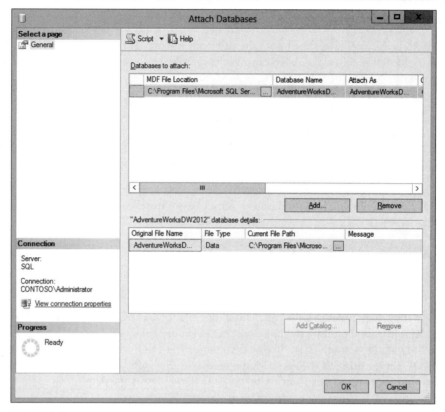

FIGURE 8-6

8. Click OK to finish attaching the MDF file.

Confirm that the database was successfully added by locating it in the Object Explorer window. The new database should be called AdventureWorksDW2012 and will most likely appear at the bottom of the list until the Databases folder is refreshed.

Configuring a Service Account for Reporting

Now that the AdventureWorksDW2012 database is up and running, you can set up a service account that has read-only privileges on it. This account will be used to connect to the database in the Reporting Services and Visio Services configuration sections later in this chapter. Doing it now saves a little time, as SQL Server Management Studio is already open and you know where the database is located:

1. In the Object Explorer window, expand the Security folder.

2. Right-click the Logins folder, and select New Login....

3. In the Login name text box, enter an account you want to use for read-only access to the database. For this example, use an AD user named **contoso\sql_read**. The account only needs to be a domain user.

4. Under Select a page, click the User Mapping link.

5. Place a check next to AdventureWorksDW2012. Then, under Database role membership for AdventureWorksDW2012, confirm `db_datareader` is automatically selected, as shown in Figure 8-7. Click OK.

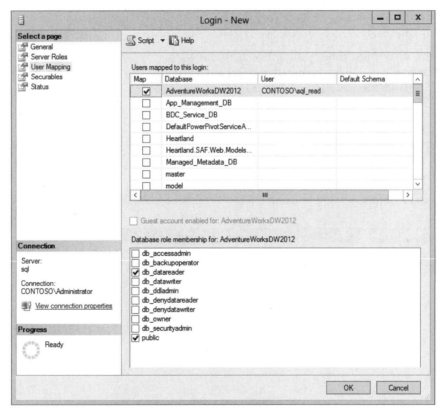

FIGURE 8-7

6. Repeat the previous steps for your SSAS service account you used when installed SSAS. For this example, the account is **contoso\sql_ssas**.

Deploying the AdventureWorks Multidimensional Model

Now that you have the source data for the cube attached to SQL, it's time to deploy the SSAS cube. In order to do that you need the `AdventureWorks Multidimensional Models SQL Server 2012.zip` file mentioned earlier. If you have not yet downloaded this file, do so now, and then follow these steps:

1. Log into the SQL server as an account that has the systemadministrator SQL role. In this example the server is sql and the account is contoso\administrator.

2. Copy the `AdventureWorks Multidimensional Models SQL Server 2012.zip` file to the desktop.

3. Double-click the zip file, locate the Standard folder, and extract it from the zip file. Failure to extract this folder before opening the solution inside of it will cause errors during cube processing.

4. Find and double-click on the `AdventureWorksDW2012Multidimensional-SE.sln` file inside the extracted Standard folder. The path will be <extracted location>\AdventureWorks Multidimensional Models SQL Server 2012\Standard.

5. If this is your first time opening Visual Studio on this computer, you will be prompted to select a template for Visual Studio to use. Select Business Intelligence.

6. When the solution finishes opening, locate the `Adventure Works DW.ds` file in the Data Sources folder of the Solution Explorer window in Visual Studio as shown in Figure 8-8. Double-click the file to open the Data Source Designer window.

7. Click the Impersonation Information tab (see Figure 8-9).

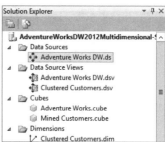

FIGURE 8-8

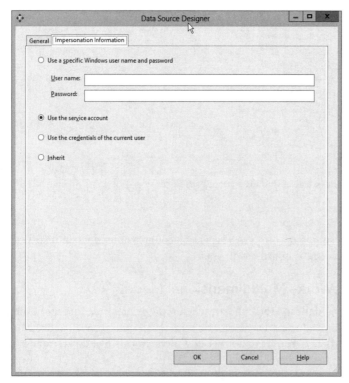

FIGURE 8-9

8. This is where you specify the account that will be used to pull data from your AdventureWorksDW2012 SQL database. Select the "Use the service account" option, which will use the service account you defined for SSAS. If you want to use another account, you can select the "Use a specific Windows user name and password" option, specifying the account you want to use. Click OK.

9. In the Visual Studio Solution Explorer window, right-click on the AdventureWorksDW2012Multidimensional-SE project.

10. Select Process….

11. Click Yes for the pop-up asking "Would you like to build and deploy the project first?"

12. Once the project has been deployed, Visual Studio will display the Process Database dialog. Click Run…. Processing of the cube may take a few minutes to complete.

13. When the process progress status reads "Process succeeded" you can click Close on all the remaining open dialogs and then exit Visual Studio.

Now that the cube is deployed, you need to connect to the SSAS instance and confirm that everything went OK by browsing through some of the data:

1. Open SQL Server Management Studio.

2. Select Analysis Services as the server type.

3. Enter your server name (in this example it is **sql**), and then click Connect.

4. Expand the Databases folder.

5. Expand AdventureWorksDW2012Multidimensional-SE.

6. Expand Cubes.

7. Under the Cubes folder, right-click on AdventureWorks as shown in Figure 8-10.

8. From the menu, select Browse. Doing so should open a new AdventureWorks cube browser.

9. In the left pane of the cube browser, expand Measures, and then expand Internet Customers.

10. Drag the Customer Count measure into the center pane of the cube browser window. You should see a displayed customer count value of 18484.

11. In the left pane of the cube browser, expand the Product dimension.

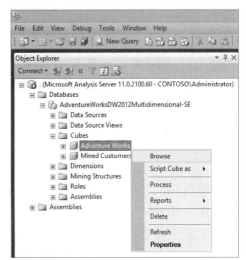

FIGURE 8-10

12. Drag the Product Categories hierarchy into the center pane of the cube browser window. This displays customer count broken out by category, subcategory, and product, as shown in Figure 8-11.

FIGURE 8-11

If data appears in your cube's browser, you have met your objective for this section. You now have more than enough test data in both SQL Server and Analysis Services to test all the BI functionality in SharePoint.

A Quick Word About Firewalls

Note that in order to be able to connect to the sample cube and database from other computers; you must ensure that the ports over which they communicate are not blocked. Assuming you are using the default SQL ports, make sure exceptions have been set up for the following:

➤ SSAS — TCP port 2383

➤ SQL Server — TCP port 1433

CREATING A BUSINESS INTELLIGENCE CENTER

Assuming you have already read Chapter 3, "Installing and Configuring SharePoint 2013," creating a site collection using the Business Intelligence Center template should be child's play; but just to ensure that everyone is on the same page and working from the same location for the examples remaining in this chapter, here are the quick steps:

1. Open Central Administration. Under Application Management, click Create site collections.

2. For Web Application, ensure that you have the correct web application listed. For this example, it should be http://portal.contoso.com. If it isn't listed, then click the drop-down beside the listed web application and click Change Web Application. From the pop-up window, choose the proper web application.

3. For Title, enter **Business Intelligence is fun!** For Description, enter **something creative**. For URL, enter **bi**. Figure 8-12 shows the resulting dialog.

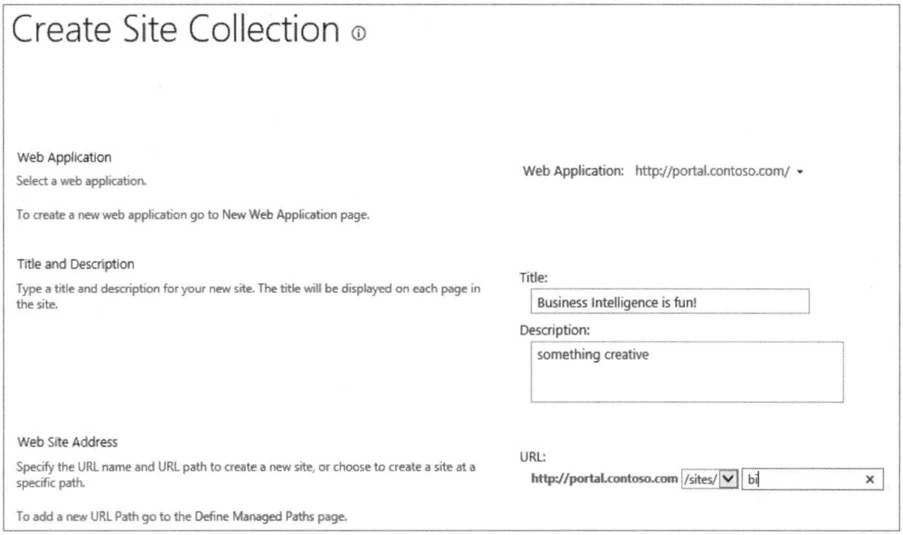

Create Site Collection ⓘ

Web Application
Select a web application.

To create a new web application go to New Web Application page.

Web Application: http://portal.contoso.com/ ▾

Title and Description
Type a title and description for your new site. The title will be displayed on each page in the site.

Title:

> Business Intelligence is fun!

Description:

> something creative

Web Site Address
Specify the URL name and URL path to create a new site, or choose to create a site at a specific path.

To add a new URL Path go to the Define Managed Paths page.

URL:

http://portal.contoso.com /sites/ ▾ bi ✕

FIGURE 8-12

4. Leave the Select experience version setting at 2013.

5. For Select a template, click the Enterprise tab.

6. On the Enterprise tab, select Business Intelligence Center.

7. Set a user for the Primary Site Collection Administrator. In this example, use **contoso\administrator**.

8. Set a user for the Secondary Site Collection Administrator. In this example, use **contoso\sp_install**.

9. For Quota Template, accept the default of No Quota.

10. Click OK at the bottom of the page to create the site collection.

11. When the snarky Working on it... page finishes, you will get a page indicating success. You can either click the blue link to go to the site collection or click OK to return to Central Administration.

That's all that is required to set up a home base site collection you can use for kicking the tires on some of this business intelligence stuff as you walk through the different service applications.

CONFIGURING EXCEL SERVICES

Excel Services is a good first step into the world of BI for many organizations simply because almost everyone is familiar with Excel at some level. Chances are good that someone in your organization is already creating reports in Excel, and Excel Services makes SharePoint the perfect place to store and share those Excel workbooks. Excel Services enables SharePoint users to view workbooks that have been published to SharePoint from right inside of their browser, so they don't even need to have Microsoft Office or Excel installed on their machine in order to view them.

This section walks you through configuring Excel Services, and then you can validate that the configuration was successful by creating a simple Excel report that is connected to the AdventureWorks cube you deployed earlier. Finally, you will upload your new Excel workbook to SharePoint so it can be viewed by others.

Configuring the Excel Services Service Application

The following steps describe how to create the Excel Services service application. If you followed along with Chapter 3 to install your farm, then you have already successfully completed these steps:

1. Log onto your SharePoint box as the install account. In this example use contoso\sp_install.

2. Open SharePoint Central Administration, and then select Manage service applications under the Application Management heading.

3. From the Manage service applications screen, click the New button in the Ribbon.

4. From the menu, select Excel Services Application.

5. For Name, enter **Excel Services**.

6. Scroll down to Application Pool and select "Use existing application pool."

7. From the drop-down, select Default SharePoint Service App Pool.

8. Leave the default of "Add this service application's proxy to the farm's default proxy list." Click OK at the bottom of the page.

To start the service application:

1. From the left-hand menu, click Application Management.

2. Under the Service Applications section, click "Manage services on server."

3. Find Excel Calculation Services and click Start to the right of it.

The Excel Services service application is now up and running, configured for SharePoint. Users should now be able to upload basic workbooks and view them inside of SharePoint.

If you navigate to the BI site collection created in the previous section, you can confirm Excel Services is working by doing the following:

1. Log onto your SharePoint box as the install account. In this example use contoso\sp_install.

2. Navigate to your BI site collection in your browser. In this example it is http://portal .contoso.com/sites/bi.

3. Click Libraries from the site navigation menu on the left.

4. Click Documents.

5. Click the Excel Services Sample Workbook to open it.

CONSIDERATIONS FOR OFFICE WEB APPLICATIONS

If you have already configured Office Web Applications in your SharePoint environment, you need to run the following PowerShell command in order to allow Excel documents to be rendered via Excel Services, rather than the Excel Web App:

```
New-SPWOPISuppressionSetting -Extension "XLSX" -Action "view"
```

If all has gone well, you should be looking at a nice example of a dashboard made in Excel. This also confirms that the Excel Services configuration has been successful.

Configuring Excel Services to Use the Secure Store

Although the Excel example that's included with the BI site is nice, to truly test things out you will create an Excel workbook that connects directly to the SSAS cube. To make that work you need to do a few additional configurations, such as setting up an unattended service account in the Secure Store for Excel Services to use. The unattended service account will be what Excel Services uses when refreshing data in the workbook.

This section assumes you've already performed the necessary steps to create the Secure Store service application in SharePoint, and generate a key for it. If you haven't yet performed those actions, please see the "Configuring the Secure Store" section in Chapter 3 for more information:

1. Log onto your SharePoint box as the install account. In this example use contoso\ sp_install.

2. Open SharePoint Central Administration, and select Manage service applications, under the Application Management heading.

3. Click the Excel Services service application.

4. Click Global Settings on the Manage Excel Services Application page.

5. Scroll down to the very bottom of the Excel Services Application Settings page. In the External Data section, configure a new unattended Service Account by entering a username. This will be the account that is used to access the data in the SSAS cube. The account needs to be only a domain user. In this example use contoso\sp_excel.

6. Enter the password and click OK.

Now that the unattended service account has been set up in the Secure Store, you have to tell SharePoint which users are allowed to use the account. For this example, you will configure all users to have this access:

1. Log onto your SharePoint box as the install account. In this example use contoso\ sp_install.

2. Open SharePoint Central Administration, and select Manage service applications, under the Application Management heading.

3. Click the Secure Store service application.

4. Click the Excel Services Application Unattended Service Account Target application.

5. Add an e-mail address for the contact e-mail. In this example use **todd@hesmellsrealbad .com**. It doesn't matter whether the e-mail address works or not. Click Next.

6. Click Next on the Edit Secure Store Target Application screen, which displays the field name and field type of the service account being used.

7. Note the Target Application Administrators and Members sections. The Members section contains the list of users and groups allowed to use the unattended service account. To configure this application so everyone can use it, add your domain users group here. In this example enter **contoso\domain users**.

8. Click OK to update the Secure Store.

Now that the unattended service account is ready to go, you need to give that account access to the SSAS cube. To do so, you create a role inside of SSAS. Once that role is created, you add the unattended account to the role:

1. Log onto your SQL server as the administrator account. In this example use **contoso\ administrator**.

2. Open SQL Server Management Studio and connect to SSAS by selecting Analysis Services as the server type.

3. For the server name, enter your SQL server's name (in this example it is **sql**), and click Connect.

4. In the Object Explorer window of SQL Management Studio, expand the Databases folder.

5. Expand the AdventureWorksDW2012Multidimensional-SE database.

6. Right-click the Roles folder, and from the drop-down menu select New Role.

7. In the Role name text box, type **Excel Services** as shown in Figure 8-13.

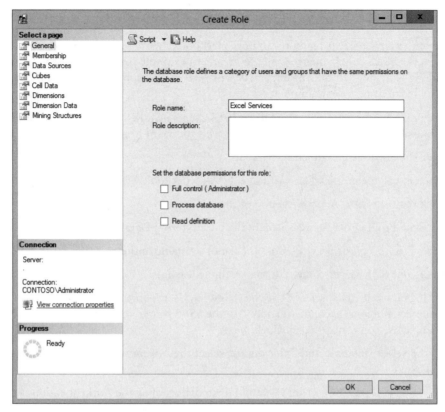

FIGURE 8-13

8. Click Membership on the left side of the Create Role window.

9. Click the Add... button on the Membership page.

10. Under Enter the object names to select type **contoso\sp_excel** and click OK.

11. Click Cubes on the left side of the Create Role window.

12. On the Cubes page, change the Access for the AdventureWorks cube to Read. Click OK.

Excel Services should now be able to refresh data in any workbook connected to the AdventureWorks cube. At this point the only thing left to do is confirm that everything is working properly by creating an Excel workbook, connecting it to the cube, and uploading it to SharePoint. As you probably guessed, that is exactly what you'll do in the next section.

Testing the Excel Services Unattended Service Account

Now that your environment is ready to support workbooks with a data connection to the AdventureWorks SSAS cube, you are going to create an example in Excel 2013 to confirm that everything is up and running as expected. The goal here is simply to test Excel Services functionality by creating a very simple workbook:

1. Log into a machine that has the Office 2013 clients installed with an account that has permissions to add data in the SharePoint web you want to use.

2. From the Start menu, launch Excel 2013.

3. When Excel opens, click "Create a new blank workbook."

4. Click the Excel DATA tab at the top of the window.

5. Click the From Other Sources icon in the Get External Data section.

6. Select From Analysis Services from the list of available options.

7. Enter your SQL server name. For this example use `sql`.

8. For log on credentials, select "Use the following User Name and Password" and enter the information for the account you added to the SSAS role in the previous section. In this example use contoso\sp_excel. Click Next.

9. On the Select Database and Table dialog, select the AdventureWorks cube and then click Next.

10. On the Save Data Connection File and Finish dialog, click the Authentication Settings... button.

11. Select "Use a stored account."

12. For the Application ID, enter **Excel Services Application Unattended Service Account**.

13. Click OK, and then click Finish.

14. Select PivotTable Report from the Import Data screen.

You should now have a pivot table on sheet 1 of your Excel workbook that is connected to the AdventureWorks SSAS cube. Next, you need to add a measure and a slicer to the pivot table so that you can confirm everything is working correctly once the workbook is published to SharePoint:

1. Click on the pivot table area in your workbook. This is cell A1 in your workbook unless you specified somewhere else.

2. Once you click on the pivot table area, a list of available fields from the cube should appear on the right-hand side. Place a check next to Customer Count under Internet Customers. You should now see a customer count number in your pivot table.

3. With your pivot table still selected, click the ANALYZE tab from the ribbon.

4. Click the Insert Slicer button in the Filter section.

5. Expand Customer and Customer Geography on the list of available fields.

6. Place a check next to Country in the list of Customer Geography fields, as shown in Figure 8-14.

7. Click OK to close the window.

8. Save the workbook as **CustomerCount.xslx** to your desktop or another location you can easily access.

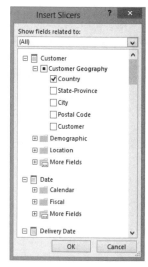

FIGURE 8-14

Voilà! Your masterpiece is complete. While you probably won't receive any accolades for the report you just created, except maybe from Mom, it's sufficient for testing Excel Services and the unattended service account in SharePoint.

Use the following steps to upload it to a document library on the BI SharePoint site and refresh the data:

1. Open your BI Portal site collection. In this example it is http://portal.contoso.com/sites/bi.

2. From the left-hand menu, click Site Contents.

3. Click the icon for the Documents app.

4. Click new document.

5. Browse to and select the CustomerCount.xlsx file you just saved. Click OK.

6. If you get a SharePoint pop-up message to Save the document, click Save.

7. Click on the CustomerCount workbook in the document library once it is uploaded to open it in Excel Services.

8. Confirm that the Excel slicer works by clicking United States.

9. When prompted to allow the refresh, click Yes.

10. Confirm that the Customer Count number changes when you select other countries. Figure 8-15 shows what you should be seeing.

FIGURE 8-15

Hopefully, all went well and your data is refreshing as expected. If you got an error when you tried to refresh your data, there's a good chance you are using the wrong account somewhere in the steps. Confirm that the account you're using in your unattended service account has access to the SSAS cube, and that the Excel connection in your workbook is using the correct application ID to reference that same account.

The example shown in Figure 8-16 demonstrates the power of Excel Services.

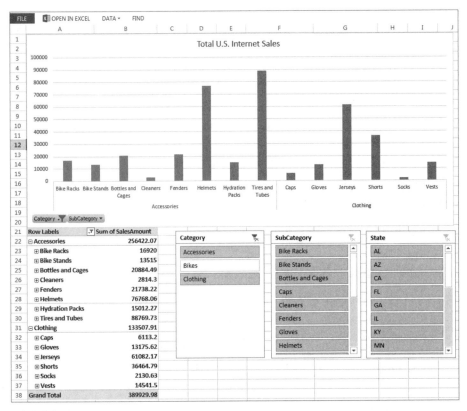

FIGURE 8-16

POWERPIVOT 2012

PowerPivot at first glance looks like Excel Services, and it actually runs on top of and requires Excel Services to run. The difference is what lies under the hood. PowerPivot allows for the creation and usage of an actual data model, which can pull together data from many different systems and enables you to define the relationships between those systems. With this data model in place, building and working on reports is a breeze. Even cooler is the fact that another major feature of PowerPivot is its ability to scale. It can easily handle millions of rows of data without breaking a sweat.

PowerPivot for SharePoint is provided by SQL Server. To use it, SharePoint 2013 must be the Enterprise license and SQL Server must be either the Enterprise or the BI edition. For help choosing the version of SQL Server that best suits your needs, see `http://www.microsoft.com/sqlserver/en/us/editions.aspx`.

Once you pick your edition of SQL Server 2012, note that it must be Service Pack 1 or later. Prior to SP1 the BI features didn't integrate properly with SharePoint 2013. If you don't have SQL Server 2012, you can find a free 180-day trial available at `http://www.microsoft.com/sqlserver/en/us/get-sql-server/try-it.aspx`.

Like SQL Server Reporting Services, SharePoint Server and SQL Server 2012 must be installed on the same machine to use PowerPivot. You will actually run the SQL Setup media on one of the SharePoint servers in your farm — typically one of the application servers but that is up to you. This requires another SQL Server license, so keep that in mind when planning your farm topology.

In a lot of ways, PowerPivot serves as a special instance of SQL Server Analysis Services (SSAS). In fact, when you run setup, you will see that SSAS is the type of instance that is installed. This could be important if you ever found yourself needing to punch a hole in the firewall or were just wondering why you keep seeing references to SSAS when you just have PowerPivot.

Installing PowerPivot

The following install example assumes you have used Chapter 3 to install and configure your SharePoint farm. The install will be on the server named Server. In Chapter 3 this was the server on which SharePoint Server 2013 Enterprise was installed. For storing the associated databases, you will point to the SQL server named Sql. Remember that PowerPivot and SharePoint have to be installed on the same server in your environment.

> ### IS SQL SERVER CRAZY?
>
> Just a friendly warning. If you have previously run the SQL Server installer on the computer on which you are about to run the following steps, you might notice some weird behavior in the first few steps. All of the steps related to installing and configuring PowerPivot will be the same, but things such as when the installer prompts you for a product key or whether it checks for updates will vary. Don't be alarmed; for all of these screens the answer is usually Next. When you get to the hard parts everything will fall back in line.

Follow these steps to install PowerPivot:

1. Log onto the SharePoint server as your install account. This account needs to be a local administrator on the SharePoint server and have the SQL Server roles of dbcreator, public, and securityadmin. In this example use Contoso\sp_install and log onto the server named Server.

2. Run SQL Server `setup.exe`. Remember that the edition must be SP1 or later and be either the BI or Enterprise edition.

3. When the SQL Server Installation Center opens, click the Installation link on the right side of the window.

4. From the Installation window, click "New SQL Server stand-alone installation or add features to an existing installation."

5. The Setup Support Rules dialog will check to ensure you won't have any of the common issues associated with installation. If any issues are identified here, be sure to address them. When everything has passed the checks, click OK.

6. On the Product Key dialog, enter your product key and click Next.

7. On the License Terms dialog, read everything very carefully and then if you agree, select "I accept the license terms" and click Next.

8. Wait a minute for the Install Setup Files dialog to process. When it finishes, you will be taken to Setup Support Rules. Make sure you have no failures and click Next. A common warning on this screen is Windows Firewall. If you have the firewall enabled you may need to open one or more ports. For PowerPivot you are not required to open in ports, as SharePoint calls the farm locally. You can continue through warnings, but if you have any failures you must correct those issues before moving on.

9. On the Setup Role dialog, choose SQL Server PowerPivot for SharePoint.

10. Deselect "Add SQL Server Database Relational Engine Services to this installation."

11. Check your settings against Figure 8-17 to confirm you have everything configured properly and click Next.

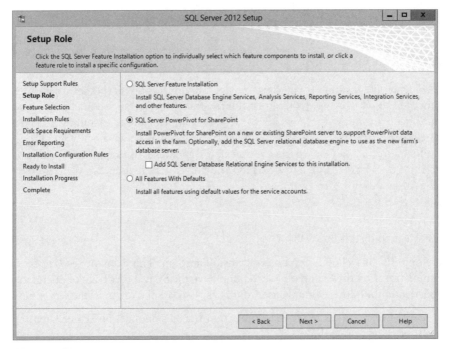

FIGURE 8-17

12. From the Feature Selection dialog, click Next.

13. After the Installation Rules dialog says you passed everything, click Next.

14. For the Instance Configuration option, accept the default Instance ID: of POWERPIVOT and click Next.

15. At the Disk Space Requirements dialog, click Next.

16. For Server Configuration, you need to specify an Account Name for the SQL Server Analysis Services to run as. This should be a dedicated domain user account just for this purpose. In this example use Contoso\SQL_SSAS, as shown in Figure 8-18.

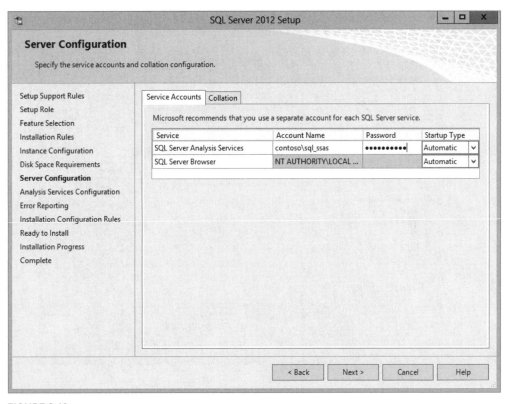

FIGURE 8-18

17. For the SQL Server Browser service, accept the default and click Next to continue.

18. On the Analysis Services Configuration screen, click the Add Current User button.

19. Now you must also add the app pool account for your service application, the farm account, and your Excel and PerformancePoint unattended accounts. Click the Add... button.

20. Type the following names if you are using the book examples: **contoso\sp_farm**; **contoso\sp_serviceapp**; **contoso\sp_excel**; and **contoso\sp_pps**, as shown in

Figure 8-19, and press OK. If you haven't created the sp_excel or sp_pps account yet, those are the unattended accounts used for the Excel and PerformancePoint service applications, respectively. You can create them now if you wish or you can add them to the permissions later. These accounts just need to be domain user accounts; they don't require any other special permissions right now.

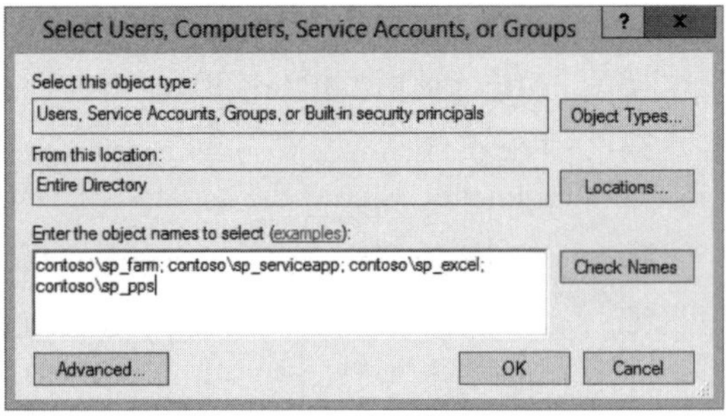

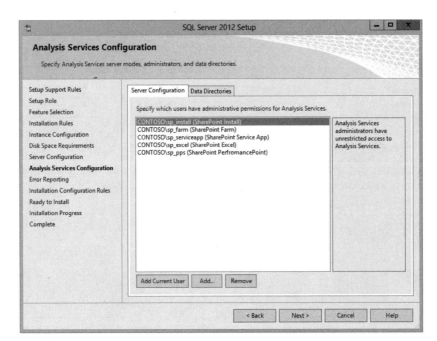

FIGURE 8-19

21. Double-check your settings against Figure 8-20 and then click Next.

FIGURE 8-20

22. From the Error Reporting screen, click Next.

23. When the Installation Configuration Rules appear, ensure that everything passed and then click Next.

24. From the Ready to Install screen, click Install.

25. If you get a pop-up about rebooting, click OK.

26. When the Complete screen appears, click Close.

27. Now that the install is complete, you should reboot. Most likely you got a pop-up message instructing you to do that.

Now that you have PowerPivot installed on your SharePoint server, you need to configure the SharePoint and PowerPivot integration.

Configuring PowerPivot Integration

To configure the integration between SharePoint and PowerPivot, the SQL team was kind of enough to provide a handy little tool with a very helpful name of PowerPivot Configuration Tool. It works perfectly to do the configuration, you just have to be extra careful when you run it. The tool is just that — a tool — and not really a wizard, so it skips prompting you for information that is important. Be careful, be thorough:

1. Make sure you are still logged into the SharePoint server as your install account. In this example the server is Server and the account is Contoso\sp_install.

2. From the Start menu, right-click on PowerPivot for SharePoint 2013 Configuration, and run as administrator. Look at Figure 8-21 to ensure you have the proper link because there are two very similar wizards.

FIGURE 8-21

3. When the PowerPivot for SharePoint 2013 Configuration tool opens, click OK to Configure or Repair PowerPivot for SharePoint.

4. The first screen that appears prompts you for several pieces of configuration information. For the Default Account Username, enter your install account. In this example that is **Contoso\sp_install**.

5. Enter the Default Account Password. In this example that is **pass@word1**.

6. For Database Server, enter the name of the SQL server that is running the database engine to host the database. In this example that is **sql**.

7. For Passphrase and Confirm Passphrase, enter a passphrase to allow servers to join or leave this farm. In this example use **pass@word1**.

8. For PowerPivot Server for Excel Services, enter *your severname*\POWERPIVOT. In this example, enter **server\POWERPIVOT**. Confirm all your settings against Figure 8-22.

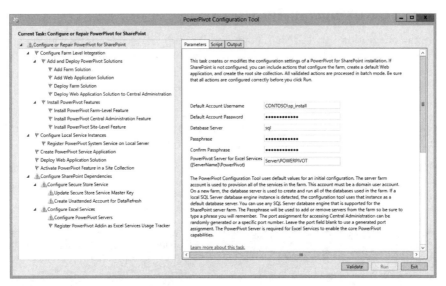

FIGURE 8-22

9. In the left-hand pane, click Deploy Web Application Solution.

10. From the drop-down, select the URL of the web application to which you want to deploy the PowerPivot solution. In this example it is http://portal.contoso.com, as shown in Figure 8-23.

FIGURE 8-23

11. In the left-hand pane, click Create PowerPivot Service Application.

12. Change the Service Application Name setting to **PowerPivot Service Application**.

13. For Database Name, they are trying to sneak in a GUID. Yuck! Change the name to **PowerPivot_Service_DB**. Confirm your settings against Figure 8-24.

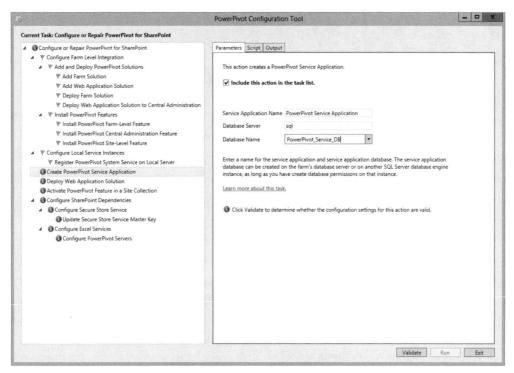

FIGURE 8-24

14. In the left-hand pane, click Activate PowerPivot Feature in a Site Collection.

15. From the drop-down, choose your BI site collection. In this example use http://portal.contoso.com/sites/bi.

16. Poke around the pages and check out the other options available. It never hurts to at least know what buttons you could press. When you are done looking around, click Validate at the bottom of the screen.

17. If everything has green flags, then you click Run. If not, you need to resolve any errors. A common error is your install account doesn't have access to the web application or site collection you chose. If that is the case, you need to give the account the SQL Server user mapping of SPDataAccess. You do this from SQL Server Management Studio on your SQL server. Figure 8-25 shows this setting.

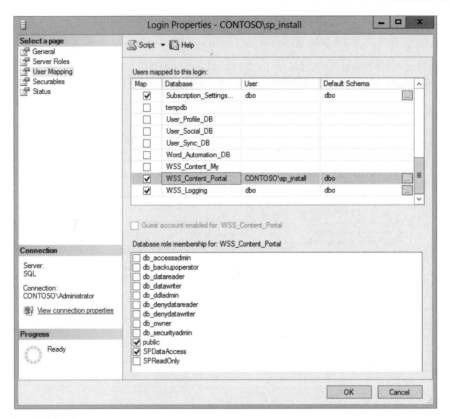

FIGURE 8-25

18. At the pop-up Warning, click Yes.

19. After all the processing is finished, a completed pop-up will appear. Click OK.

20. Click Exit to close the PowerPivot Configuration Tool.

Congratulations; you have PowerPivot integrated into your SharePoint farm. You still have a few more things to do, but if you have made it this far you are doing great.

Adding Permissions to Central Administration

If you were to navigate to central admin now and try to open the PowerPivot Service service application, you would just see a lot of errors. This is because the service account doesn't have access to the central admin content database to query for data. To correct this, you need to set the User Mapping for your app pool account (Contoso\sp_serviceapp) to have the Database role membership for the SharePoint_Admin_Content database of SPDataAccess. Before you do this, the log contains the following error the first time you try to access the service application's homepage:

```
System.Data.SqlClient.SqlException (0x80131904): The EXECUTE permission was
denied on the object 'proc_ReturnWebFeatures', database
SharePoint_Admin_Content', schema 'dbo'...
```

Creating and Configuring a PowerPivot Workbook

Now it is time for the fun stuff — building a PowerPivot workbook and playing with a slicer. To do this, you need to open Excel and add the PowerPivot add-in. Then you connect to the AdventureWorks data you deployed earlier.

Back to the Excel client:

1. Log in to a client machine with Excel 2013 installed. If you don't have one handy, you can always install Office on one of your test VMs. This isn't recommended for production but it works fine for learning.

2. Open Excel 2013.

3. From the available templates, choose Blank Workbook.

4. Click the File tab and select Options from the menu.

5. From the left-hand pane, click Add-Ins.

6. At the bottom of the window, click Manage and choose COM Add-ins, as shown in Figure 8-26.

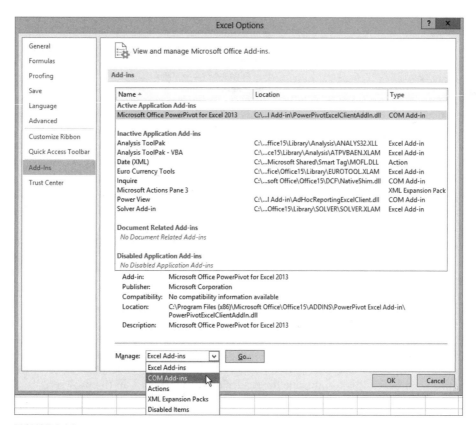

FIGURE 8-26

7. Click Go....

8. Under Add-Ins available, select Microsoft Office PowerPivot for Excel 2013. Click OK.

Now that you have the add-in configured, you are ready to create a data connection:

1. From the Ribbon, click the DATA tab.

2. From the Get External Data section, click From Other Sources.

3. With the fly-out menu displayed, click From Analysis Services.

WHICH SQL SERVER ANALYSIS SERVICES (SSAS) SERVER?

If you were paying attention earlier, you know that when you install PowerPivot on the SharePoint server, that is technically a special instance of SSAS. However, that instance doesn't house any real data. You installed SSAS on your SQL server and then deployed the AdventureWorks data warehouse and cube. This is your SSAS instance with actual data. Don't let that PowerPivot instance confuse you.

---

4. For Server name:, enter the SQL server that is running SQL Server Analysis Services. In this example that is the server named **sql**. Click Next.

5. From the Select Database and Table dialog, choose AdventureWorks as shown in Figure 8-27, and click Next.

6. In the Save Data Connection File and Finish dialog, all the defaults will work; but before you finish, click Authentication Settings... at the bottom.

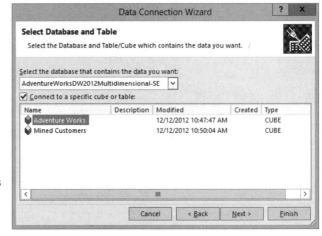

FIGURE 8-27

After performing step 6 in the preceding list, the dialog shown in Figure 8-28 appears, which contains three options. Before selecting one, it is very important to understand that PowerPivot just enhances Excel Services. Therefore, when you take this workbook in a moment and publish it to SharePoint, PowerPivot is actually doing the heavy lifting on the data side, while Excel Services is responsible for rendering the workbook in the browser.

FIGURE 8-28

WHAT IS EFFECTIVEUSERNAME?

`EffectiveUserName` is a new option in SharePoint Server 2013 that allows you to implement user specific security when connecting to SQL Server Analysis Services in "double hop" scenarios. This is a nice option for environments where Kerberos is not configured, but you want to leverage the use of SSAS Roles to limit the data to which the user has access, based on who they are. The `EffectiveUserName` property is configurable in both the PerformacePoint and Excel Services service applications. More information on setting up the EffectiveUserName property can be found at `http://technet.microsoft.com/en-us/library/jj219741.aspx`.

If you choose the first option, Use the authenticated user's account, the behavior is dependent on Excel Services. If Excel Services is configured to use the `EffectiveUserName` property, then that is how this data connection will be made and no Kerberos is required. Otherwise, using this setting requires you to configure Kerberos authentication.

If you choose the second option, Use a stored account, then you must enter the Application ID of a Secure Store application that you have previously configured to store and map credentials for this data source's authentication.

Finally, if you choose None then you would either rely on the PowerPivot unattended account that you configured or you would hard-code the authentication information in your connection string.

As you can see, it is crucial to properly configure this information for your environment before you try to get this workbook to render through SharePoint. Remember that while you are connected in the Excel client, it is using the credentials of the user running Excel, not any of the SharePoint server accounts or processes.

1. For this example select "Use a stored account" and then for Application ID: enter **Excel Services Application Unattended Service Account.**

2. Click OK, and then click Finish.

3. At the Import Data pop-up, select PivotChart.

4. Leave the existing worksheet selected, double-check your settings against Figure 8-29, and click OK.

5. From the PivotChart Fields pane on the right, look under Internet Sales and check Internet Sales Amount, as shown in Figure 8-30.

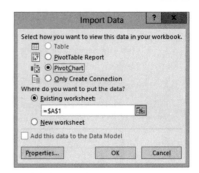

FIGURE 8-29

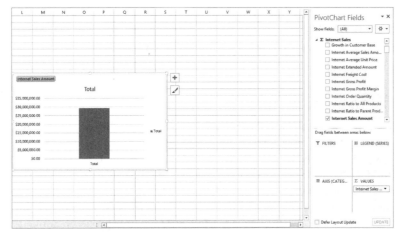

FIGURE 8-30

6. From the ANALYZE tab of the Ribbon, click Insert Slicer.

7. From the Insert Slicers window that appears, select Country (under Customer ⇨ Customer Geography) as shown in Figure 8-31. Click OK.

8. Drag the Country window to the left so it isn't covering your beautiful chart (see Figure 8-32).

9. Save your workbook as **InternetSales.xlsx** to your desktop, and close Excel.

FIGURE 8-31

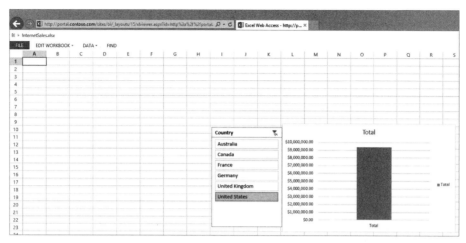

FIGURE 8-32

Now that you have a working workbook you need to upload it to SharePoint so you can play with it in the browser:

1. Open a browser to your BI site collection, logged in as a user who has permissions to create a list. In this example that is http://portal.contoso.com/sites/bi, logged in as contoso\ sp_install.

2. From the left-hand navigation, click Site Contents.

3. Click the icon to add an app.

4. Under Apps, select PowerPivot Gallery.

5. In the pop-up window for Name:, enter **PowerPivot Gallery**, and click Create.

6. Click the icon for the PowerPivot Gallery to open it.

7. From the Ribbon, click the FILES tab. Then, from the FILES Ribbon, click Upload Document.

8. From the pop-up window for Add a document, click Browse..., navigate to the location where you saved the file `InternetSales.xlsx`., and click on the file and select Open.

9. Back on Add a document, click OK to upload the file.

10. From the library, click on the file `InternetSales.xlsx` to open it in the browser.

11. The file should open in the browser using Excel Services. Click on the United States slicer.

After a moment the bar graph should update to reflect the total sales amount for the United States only, as shown in Figure 8-33. If it does, then you have successfully deployed PowerPivot.

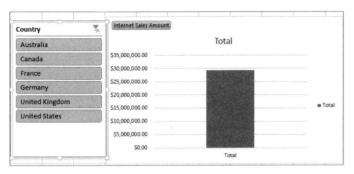

FIGURE 8-33

There are literally hundreds of other options and features you can play with using PowerPivot now. You will have to dig into those on your own, however; from an administrator's point of view, the war is won. Figure 8-34 shows an example of what the BI guy built to show off PowerPivot. Isn't it pretty?

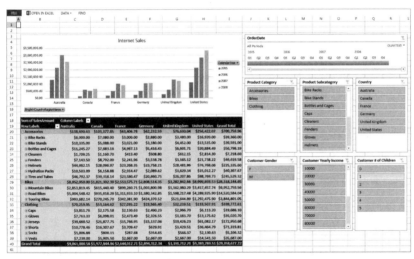

FIGURE 8-34

SQL SERVER REPORTING SERVICES FOR SHAREPOINT 2013

These days, SQL Server Reporting Services (SSRS) is considered the old man of the BI tools. Introduced in 2003 as a component of SQL Server 2000, it is generally used to create static or operational reports that focus on providing data you need. To provide these reports, SQL Server has its own web engine, which looks like it was made in the technological stone age using Paint and Notepad, but in terms of functionality it works well.

Fortunately, the SQL Server team got the memo that SharePoint has become the center of the BI universe, and added a few years ago was the capability to run SSRS in SharePoint integrated mode. In this mode, SSRS retains all its awesome reporting power; but instead of using a website similar to what the cavemen used to sell the wheel, the reports are integrated directly into SharePoint document libraries. This makes SSRS ready to go mainstream, enabling users to work with and access their reports in the same way they do their collaboration documents — in a pretty browser.

Even cooler is the automatic inclusion of Report Builder, a click-once application that enables users to build their own reports.

In order to install SSRS in SharePoint integrated mode, you must install both SharePoint and SSRS on the same server. Typically this means inserting your SQL Server disk in one of the application servers in your SharePoint farm. Then you can install just the SSRS components onto that machine. You configure SSRS to store its databases on the same SQL server that SharePoint uses. Remember that means you need a SQL license for your SharePoint server.

SQL Server 2012 Standard Edition provides everything you need to roll out SSRS for most farms, unless you want to use PowerView or you require high availability for SSRS. In that case, you have to use SQL Server 2012 Enterprise. The following example assumes you have SQL Server 2012 Enterprise. If you don't, then the PowerView material will not be applicable to you.

Follow these steps to install SSRS:

1. Log onto the SharePoint server as your install account. This account needs to be a local administrator on the SharePoint server and have the SQL Server roles of dbcreator, public, and securityadmin. In this example use contoso\sp_install and log onto the server named Server.

2. Run SQL Server `setup.exe`. Though not required, SP1 or later is recommended.

3. When the SQL Server Installation Center opens, click the Installation link on the left.

4. From the Installation dialog that appears, select the first option, "New SQL Server stand-alone installation or add features to an existing installation."

5. The Setup Support Rules will run a check to identify any potential problems with your installation. If any issues appear here, make sure you address them. When everything has passed the checks, click OK.

6. Another Setup Support Rules dialog will appear. Ensure you have no failures and click Next. A common warning on this screen is Windows Firewall. If the firewall is enabled you may need to open one or more ports. For SSRS you are not required to open any ports because SharePoint calls the farm locally. Note that you can continue through warnings, but any failures must be corrected before moving on.

7. At the Installation Type screen, click "Perform a new installation of SQL Server 2012."

8. On the Product Key dialog, enter your product key and click Next.

9. On the License Terms screen, read everything carefully and then if you agree click "I accept the license terms" and click Next.

10. In the Setup Role dialog, choose SQL Server Feature Installation. Click Next.

11. In the Feature Selection dialog, under Shared Features, select the following three options:

   ➤ Reporting Services — SharePoint

   ➤ Reporting Services Addin for SharePoint Products

   ➤ SQL Server Data Tools

   Confirm your settings against Figure 8-35.

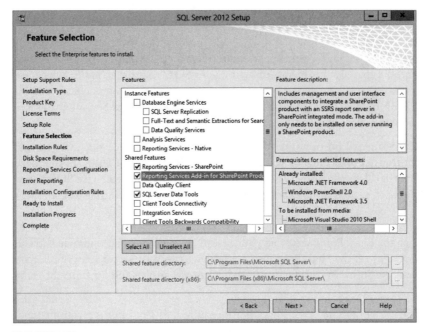

FIGURE 8-35

12. Under Shared Features, select Management Tools - Complete, as shown in Figure 8-36, and click Next.

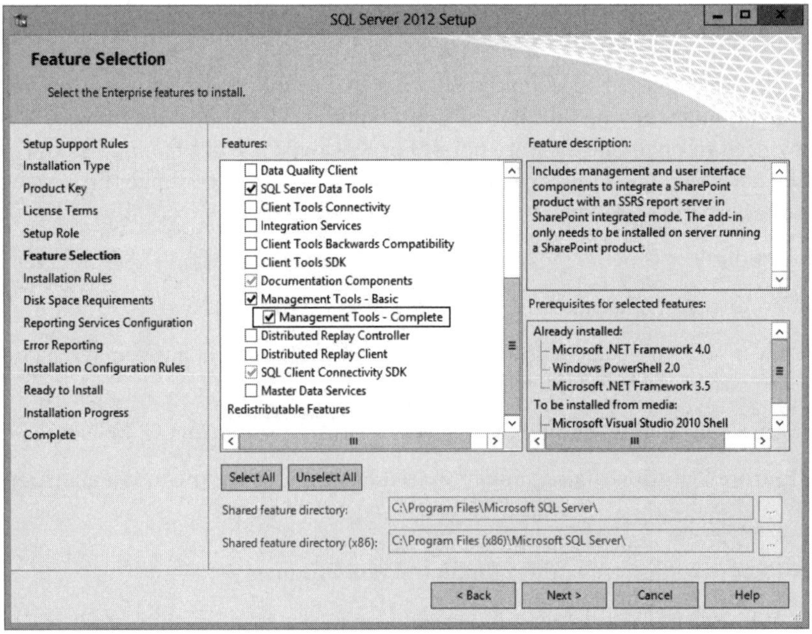

FIGURE 8-36

13. On the Installation Configuration Rules dialog, click Next if everything passes.

14. On the Disk Space Requirements dialog, click Next.

15. On the Reporting Services Configuration dialog, enable the Install only radio button under the heading Reporting Services SharePoint Integration Mode, as shown in Figure 8-37. This should be the only option available, with everything else grayed out. If not, double-check your work to this point.

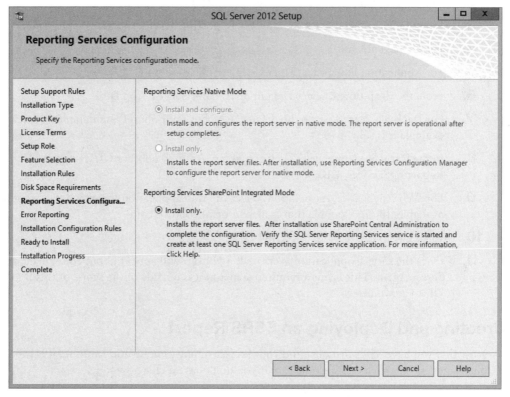

FIGURE 8-37

16. On the Error Reporting screen, click Next.

17. From the Installation Configuration Rules screen, click Next when everything passes.

18. From the Ready to Install screen, click Install.

19. When the Complete screen appears, click Close.

That completes the installation of SSRS, which you can now configure for SharePoint integration. If you still have the SQL Server Installer open, you can close it.

Creating the Service Application

In SharePoint 2013 with SQL Server 2012, Reporting Services manifests itself as a separate service application, unlike its predecessors, which were integrated in a less streamlined way.

To create the service application, perform the following steps, which assume you have followed the farm installation procedures described in Chapter 3:

1. From the homepage of Central Administration, click Manage service applications.

2. In the SharePoint Ribbon, click the New button.

3. From the New menu, click SQL Server Reporting Services Service Application.

4. For Name, enter **SSRS**.

5. For Application Pool, select Use existing application pool.

6. From the drop-down, select Default SharePoint Service App Pool.

7. For Database server:, leave the default, which is your SharePoint default SQL server. In this example it is sql.

8. In the Database name: field, they are trying to slip in another GUID on you. Change it to **ReportingServices_DB**.

9. For Web Application Association, select the web application for which you want SSRS available. In this example that is http://portal.contoso.com.

10. Click OK to create the service application.

11. Once the service application is created, a pop-up will appear about configuring the SQL Server Agent. This is not a required step and it is outside of the scope of this book. Click OK to continue.

Creating and Deploying an SSRS Report

Now that you have SSRS installed and your service application up and running, it is time to try it out. What good is such an awesome tool if you don't have a clue how to use it?

Create your report with the following steps:

1. Navigate to your BI site collection as a site collection administrator. In this example it is http://portal.contoso.com/sites/bi.

2. Click the gear icon at the top of the page.

3. From the drop-down, select Site settings.

4. Under the Site Collection Administration section, click the link for Site collection features.

5. Scroll down the list and click Activate for the Report Server Integration Feature.

6. On the left, click Site Contents.

7. Click the icon to add an app.

8. Under Apps you can add, click Report Library.

9. From the pop-up window for Name:, enter **SSRS Reports**.

10. Click Create.

11. Back on the Site Contents page, click SSRS Reports to open the library.

12. From the Ribbon, click the drop-down for New Document.

13. In the fly-out menu, click Report Builder Report, as shown in Figure 8-38. If Report Builder Report doesn't show up, then go to `http://msdn` `.microsoft.com/en-us/library/bb326289.aspx`.

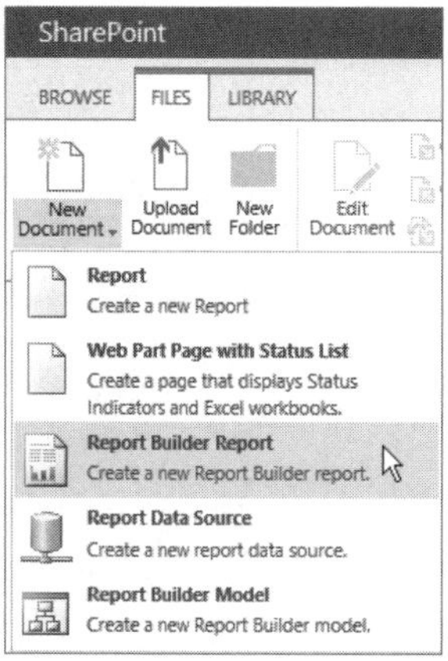

14. A ClickOnce application will try to launch. At the pop-up window, click Run, as shown in Figure 8-39.

FIGURE 8-38

FIGURE 8-39

15. A window will appear while the tool downloads and processes. This installer is being downloaded from your SharePoint server, not the Internet. When it is complete, the Getting Started window for Report Builder will open, as shown in Figure 8-40. Click the top option, Table or Matrix Wizard.

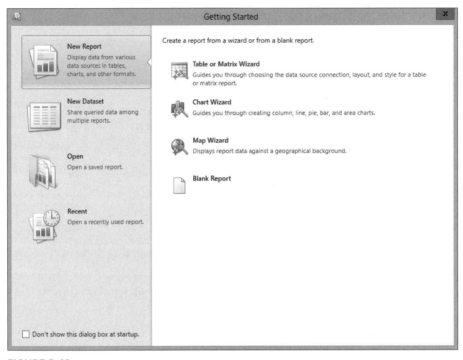

FIGURE 8-40

REPORT BUILDER

Report Builder is an application that is used to build SSRS reports. You can download it free from Microsoft.com and manually install it, but that isn't necessary when SSRS is integrated with SharePoint, as a content type called Report Builder Report is created. Clicking that link launches a special kind of application called a ClickOnce application. The first time you click the link, Report Builder is downloaded from the SharePoint server directly, after which it will just be launched automatically. It's a great way to avoid having to roll out more software through your IT department.

16. From the Choose a dataset screen, accept the default of Create a dataset and click Next.

17. On the Choose a connection to a data source screen, click New....

18. From the Data Source Properties screen, click the Build... button.

19. For Server name:, enter your SQL server name. In this example use **sql**.

20. Under Select or enter a database name:, click the drop-down and select AdventureWorksDW2012. Click OK.

21. Back in the Data Source Properties window, click Credentials.

22. Select "Use this user name and password."

23. For User name:, enter an account that has access to the selected database. In this example use **Contoso\sql_read**.

24. For Password:, enter the password. In this example it is **pass@word1**.

25. Check the box for "Use as Windows credentials" and then click OK.

26. In the "Choose a connection to a data source" window that appears, your new connection is highlighted. Click Next to use that data source.

27. The New Table or Matrix window will open. Expand out Tables, select the following from the list, and click Next:

- ➤ DimCustomer
- ➤ DimGeography
- ➤ FactInternetSales

28. From the Available fields, drag SalesAmount under Values.

29. From the Available fields, drag EnglishCountryRegionName under Row groups. Click Next.

30. For Choose the layout, click Next.

31. For Choose a style, click Finish.

THE MAGIC OF REPORT BUILDER

If you were paying attention, you likely noticed in step 27 that you selected three different tables; but when you created the report you used only two items. That is the magic that is Report Builder. SalesAmount and EnglishCountryRegionName don't have a direct relationship but they both share a key with DimCustomer that establishes the necessary relationship. Report Builder handles such relationships for you.

Before you publish the report you might want to make it slightly prettier. If the following steps seem too complicated or hard to follow, you can skip them. Your previous experience with this type of editor will likely determine whether this makes sense or not.

1. From the design pane, click the column head for English Cou. Edit the text to say **Country**.

2. At the top of the screen, click the heading of "Click to add title" and change it to say **Internet Sales by Country**.

3. Click the white box that says [Sum(SalesAmo.

4. From the Ribbon, click the $ button to format that column as currency.

5. Click the blue box below it that says [Sum(SalesAm.

6. From the Ribbon, click the $ button to format that column as currency.

7. Resize the first column by dragging it out to the 1.5-inch mark in the ruler.

8. Resize the second column by dragging it out to the 3-inch mark in the ruler.

9. Figure 8-41 shows the result of the previous steps. After verifying that everything looks good (or good enough), click the Save icon in the top-right corner of the window.

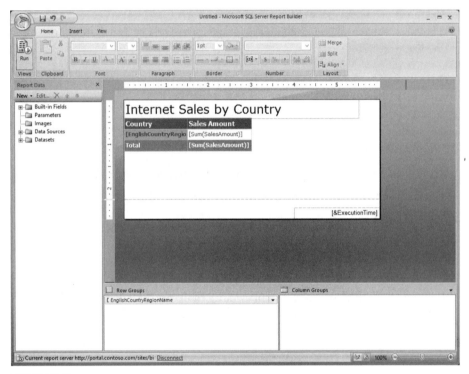

FIGURE 8-41

10. In the Save As Report window, navigate to your SSRS Reports library. In this example the URL would be http://portal.contoso.com/sites/bi/ssrs reports.

11. For Name:, enter **Internet Sales by Country**. Click Save.

12. Open your browser to the SSRS library. In this example the URL would be http://portal .contoso.com/sites/bi/ssrs reports. If the browser is already in the library, then you need to refresh the page.

13. Click on the report Internet Sales by Country to open it. After a moment to load, you should see something similar to Figure 8-42.

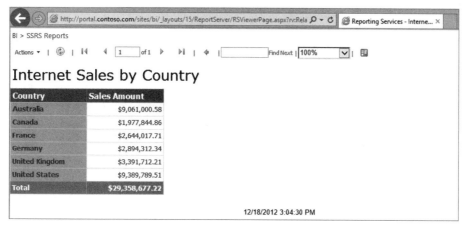

FIGURE 8-42

That will do it, folks. You have successfully built and deployed an SSRS report. While it might not win any awards, it gets the job done; and you have seen how you can easily customize it with simple changes such as formatting numbers as currency and updating the headings to be more meaningful. Unfortunately, all that fun stuff is beyond the scope of this book, but Figure 8-43 shows an example of a rather awesome report that was built by a trained BI ninja against that same AdventureWorks data set.

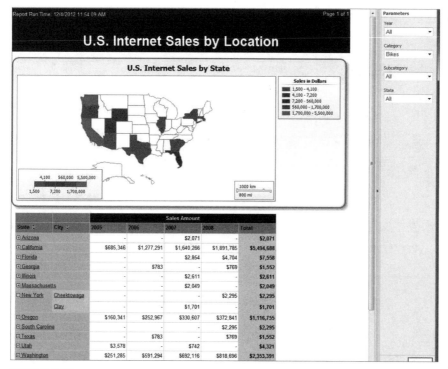

FIGURE 8-43

PowerView

PowerView is installed as part of SQL Server 2012 Reporting Services. It enables end users to easily and intuitively create ad-hoc reports from within their browser using either PowerPivot or SSAS tabular data models as the data source. PowerView has an impressive assortment of visualization options, and even animations, that can be used to make your reports a highly interactive experience for the user. Because PowerView is dependent on either a PowerPivot or an SSAS tabular model, you need to have the Enterprise version of SharePoint, and either an Enterprise or Business Intelligence version of SQL Server in order to use it.

Follow these steps to enable PowerView in your farm:

1. As a site collection administrator, navigate to your BI site collection. In this example it is http://portal.contoso.com/sites/bi.

2. Click the gear icon at the top of the page.

3. From the drop-down, select Site settings.

4. Under the Site Collection Administration section, click the link for Site collection features.

5. Scroll down the list and click "Activate for the PowerView Integration Feature."

That's all you need to do have the PowerView functionality available within your site collection. One way to confirm you were successful is by navigating to a PowerPivot Gallery, where you should now see an icon for PowerView to the right of your workbook, as shown in Figure 8-44.

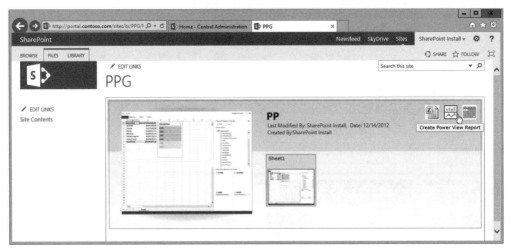

FIGURE 8-44

If you're wondering what you can do with PowerView, Figure 8-45 shows what that crazy BI guy came up with this time. It has so much going on it looks more like a fancy cartoon than a real report; but it is a real report. Wow!

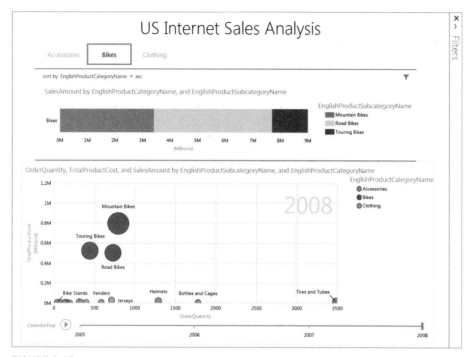

FIGURE 8-45

CONFIGURING PERFORMANCEPOINT SERVICES

PerformancePoint is all about putting together dashboards. Within PerformancePoint you can create KPIs, scorecards, filters, and several different types of reports and charts. Those components can then be used to construct dashboards that are relevant to the end user. PerformancePoint can also incorporate into its dashboards reports you've created in other tools such as Excel Services and Reporting Services, so you can leverage those technologies as well.

PerformancePoint also has some very powerful analytic tools such as the analytic chart and the decomposition tree. These tools enable users to navigate through data dynamically by drilling up, down, or even across different areas of their data. PerformancePoint is both flexible and customizable, empowering end users to explore and analyze data in the way that best suits their decision making.

In this section you will configure the PerformancePoint Services application, create an unattended service account for PerformancePoint, and then construct and deploy a simple dashboard to confirm that the service is up and running.

The following steps walk you through the process of creating a PerformancePoint service application. If you followed Chapter 3 step by step, then you have already done this exercise.

With this service application, in order to properly connect to Analysis Services you must also install ADOMD.NET v11, which is interesting because the SharePoint prerequisite installer already installed v9 for you. You also might find some situations require v10. Oh, the mysteries of BI. Keeping with the script, install v11 before continuing. No reboot is usually required, so it should be pretty easy:

1. Download the 64-bit version from `http://go.microsoft.com/fwlink/?LinkID=239662&clcid=0x409` and run the MSI.

2. At the Welcome dialog, click Next.

3. Read the license, select "I accept the terms in the license agreement," and click Next.

4. At the Ready to Install dialog, click Install.

5. At the setup completion screen, click Finish.

To create the service application, follow these now familiar steps:

1. Log onto your SharePoint box as the install account. In this example use contoso\sp_install.

2. Open SharePoint Central Administration.

3. Under the Application Management heading, click Manage service applications.

4. From the Manage service applications screen, click the New button in the Ribbon.

5. From the menu, select PerformancePoint Service Application.

6. For Name, enter **PerformancePoint Service**.

7. Check the box for "Add this service application's proxy to the farm's default proxy list."

8. For Database Name, enter **PerformancePoint_Service_DB**. This time you are removing the spaces and the GUID from the name. Spaces are even worse than GUIDs.

9. Scroll down to Application Pool and select Use existing application pool.

10. From the drop-down, select Default SharePoint Service App Pool.

11. At the bottom of the page, click Create.

12. After a minute a pop-up window will appear, indicating that the service application was created successfully and specifying the additional steps you need to perform. Click OK.

Now that the service application is created, you need to start the service:

1. From the left-hand menu of Central Administration, click Application Management.

2. Under the Service Applications section, click Manage services on server.

3. Find PerformancePoint Service and click Start to the right of it.

Next, grant the application pool service account access to the SharePoint Content database by following these steps:

1. Log onto your SharePoint box as the install account (CONTOSO\sp_install in this case).

2. Open the SharePoint 2013 Management Shell as administrator by right-clicking on it and then clicking Run as administrator.

3. At the prompt, type the following PowerShell command and press Enter:

```
$w = Get-SPWebApplication -identity http://portal.contoso.com
```

4. At the prompt, type the following PowerShell command and press Enter. Use Figure 8-46 to confirm your work.

```
$w.GrantAccessToProcessIdentity("contoso\sp_serviceapp")
```

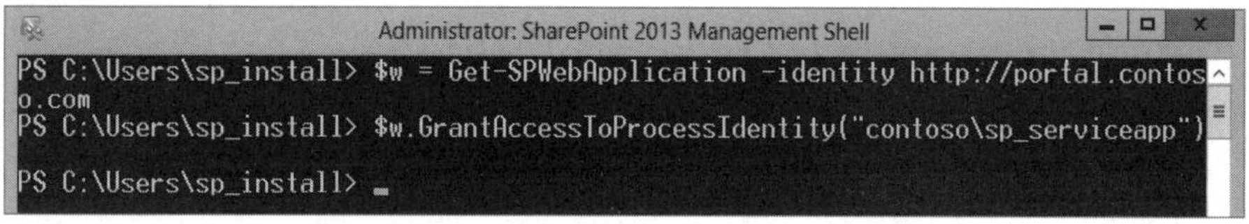

FIGURE 8-46

Now that the PerformancePoint Services service application is up and running, you need to create a new unattended service account for it to use when accessing data from outside sources.

Configuring PerformancePoint Services to Use the Secure Store

The PerformancePoint dashboards need to be capable of accessing data located in the AdventureWorks SSAS cube. In order to get that working, you need to make a few additional configurations, such as setting up an unattended service account in the Secure Store for PerformancePoint Services to use. The unattended service account will tell PerformancePoint Services what account to use when you attempt to refresh data in the dashboards.

This section assumes you have already performed the necessary steps to create the Secure Store service application in SharePoint and generate a key for it. If not, please see the section, "Configuring the Secure Store," in Chapter 3 for details.

1. Log onto your SharePoint box as the install account. In this example use contoso\sp_install.

2. Open SharePoint Central Administration.

3. Under the Application Management heading, click Manage service applications.

4. Click the PerformancePoint Services service application, and then click PerformancePoint Service Application Settings.

5. Select the Unattended Service Account radio button if it is not already selected.

6. Enter the User Name. In this example it would be **contoso\sp_pps**. This account just needs to be a regular domain user and have access to your SSAS cube.

7. Enter the password. For this example use **pass@word1**.

8. Click OK to close the PerformancePoint Service Application Settings screen.

Now that the unattended service account has been set up in the Secure Store, you need to tell SharePoint which users are allowed to use it. In this case, all domain users should be able to use the account. Configure access to the unattended service account as follows:

1. Log onto your SharePoint box as the install account. In this example use contoso\sp_install.

2. Open SharePoint Central Administration.

3. Under the Application Management heading, click Manage service applications.

4. Click on the Secure Store service application.

5. Look for a Target Application ending with "PPSUnattendedAccount" and click on it.

6. Add an e-mail address for the contact e-mail, and then click Next. In this example use **scuba@ineedtwochains.com**. Fake e-mail addresses can be fun.

7. Click Next on the Edit Secure Store Target Application screen, which displays the field name and field type of the service account being used.

8. The Edit Secure Store Target Application page contains two sections: Target Application Administrators and Members. The Members section shows the list of users and groups that are allowed to use the unattended service account. To configure this application so everyone can use it, add your domain users group here. In this example enter **contoso\domain users**.

9. Click OK to update the Secure Store.

Now that your unattended service account is ready to go, you need to give that account access to the SSAS cube by creating a role inside of SSAS. After that role is created, you add the unattended service account to it:

1. Log onto your SQL server as the administrator account. In this example use contoso\administrator.

2. Open SQL Server Management Studio and connect to SSAS by selecting Analysis Services as the server type.

3. For the server name, enter your SQL server's name. In this example it is sql. Click Connect.

4. In the Object Explorer window of SQL Management Studio, expand the Databases folder.

5. Expand the AdventureWorksDW2012Multidimensional-SE database, and right-click on the Roles folder.

6. From the drop-down menu, select New Role.

7. In the Role name text box, type **PPS Services**.

8. Click Membership on the left-hand side of the Create Role dialog.

9. Click the Add button on the Membership dialog.

10. Add **contoso\sp_pps** to the role.

11. Click Cubes on the left-hand side of the Create Role dialog. When the Cubes dialog appears, change the Access column for the AdventureWorks cube to Read. Click OK.

PerformancePoint services should now be ready to connect to the AdventureWorks SSAS cube. At this point the only thing left to do is confirm that everything is working by creating and deploying a dashboard, which is exactly what the next section covers.

Testing the PerformancePoint Services Unattended Service Account

Now that the environment is ready to support PerformancePoint dashboards with external data connections to the AdventureWorks SSAS cube, you are going to create an example using SharePoint Dashboard Designer to confirm that everything is up and running as expected. The goal here is simply to test PerformancePoint functionality, so keep the dashboard as simple as possible:

1. Log onto your SharePoint box as the install account. For this example use contoso\sp_install.

2. Navigate to `http://portal.contoso.com/sites/bi` in Internet Explorer.

3. Click the Site Contents link on the left-hand side of the screen.

4. Click the PerformancePoint Content library to open it.

5. Click New item at the top of the screen.

6. If this is your first time opening Dashboard Designer, you will be prompted to download and install the application. Approve the download and install. Figure 8-47 shows Dashboard Designer in all of its glory.

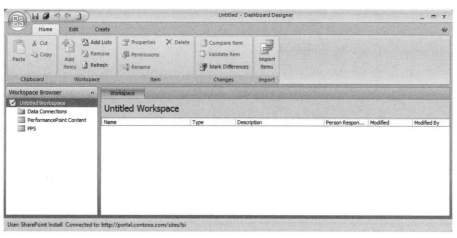

FIGURE 8-47

Once Dashboard Designer has been installed, it should open the application automatically. You will need to create a few different objects, including a data source, an analytic chart, and then finally a dashboard. The next few sections walk you through creating each of these items.

Creating a Data Source in Dashboard Designer

1. With Dashboard Designer open, click the Create tab at the top-left corner of the window.

2. Click the Data Source icon from the Dashboard Items section.

3. Select Analysis Services as the template, as shown in Figure 8-48, and then click OK.

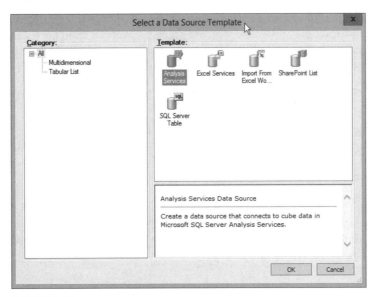

FIGURE 8-48

4. Ensure that Use Standard Connection is selected.

5. In the text box labeled Server, enter your SQL server's name. In this example use **sql**.

6. In the Database drop-down, select AdventureWorksDW2012Multidimensional as the database. If you don't see any databases available, please see the tip.

WHY ISN'T MY DATABASE DISPLAYED IN THE DROP-DOWN?

At the time of writing, we had to install ADOMD.NET 10 on our SharePoint server in order for our available SSAS database to be displayed in the Database drop-down. If this hasn't been resolved by the time you read this, you can download `ASADOMD10.msi` as part of the Microsoft SQL Server 2008 R2 SP1 Feature Pack at the following URL (be sure to get the correct version x64/IA64 for your server):

`http://www.microsoft.com/en-us/download/details.aspx?id=26728`

1. In the Cube drop-down, select AdventureWorks as the cube. Leave the Authentication set to Unattended Service Account.

2. Click the Test Data Source button to ensure you are able to connect to the cube.

3. Click the Properties tab of the New Data Source window.

4. In the Name text box, type **PPSTest** to rename the data source. You need to click out of the Name text box before the data source name will change in the Workspace Browser window on the left.

5. Right-click on the PPSTest data source in the Workspace Browser on the left, and then select Save. It's important that you save the data source before moving on to create the analytic chart, as not doing so can prevent the data source from being available to your chart.

Creating an Analytic Chart in Dashboard Designer

Now that the data source is set up, the next thing to do is create a chart that will ultimately reside on the example dashboard. Follow these steps to create an analytic chart:

1. With Dashboard Designer open, click PerformancePoint Content in the Workspace Browser.

2. Click the Create tab at the top-left corner of the dialog.

3. Click Analytic Chart in the Reports section of the Create tab. The menu on the Create tab is context sensitive, so make sure you have PerformancePoint Content highlighted in the Workspace Browser if you don't see Analytic Chart as an available option.

4. Choose PPSTest as the data source as shown in Figure 8-49 and then click Finish.

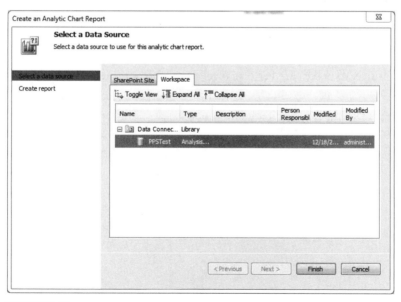

FIGURE 8-49

5. While the report item is being created you may be prompted for your credentials. If so, use the account you are logged in with. In this example that is contoso\sp_install.

6. On the Design tab of the new analytic chart, in the Details pane on the far right side of the screen, expand Measures.

7. Under Measures, locate Average Sales Amount, right-click it, and select Move To Bottom Axis.

8. Collapse Measures.

9. Expand Dimensions in the Details pane.

10. Under Dimensions, expand Date. Under Date, expand Calendar, and then right-click Calendar Year.

11. From the drop-down menu, select Move To Series.

12. Click the Properties tab near the top of the report.

13. In the Name field, type **Avg Sales by Year**.

14. Click out of the Name field so that the name change takes effect.

15. In the Workspace Browser of Dashboard Designer, right-click the report and then click Save.

Creating and Deploying a Dashboard in Dashboard Designer

Now that you have created the report, follow these steps to place the new report into a dashboard and deploy it to SharePoint:

1. With Dashboard Designer open, click PerformancePoint Content in the Workspace Browser.

2. Click the Create tab at the top-left corner of the dialog.

3. Click Dashboard in the Reports section of the Create tab. The menu on the Create tab is context sensitive, so make sure PerformancePoint Content is highlighted in the Workspace Browser if you don't see it as an available option.

4. In the Select a Dashboard Page Template window, select 1 Zone for the template type, as shown in Figure 8-50. Click OK.

5. With your new dashboard open, locate the Details window on the right and expand Reports.

6. Under Reports, expand PerformancePoint Content.

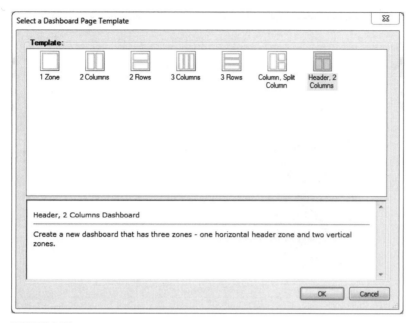

FIGURE 8-50

7. Add the Avg Sales by Year report to the dashboard by clicking and dragging it from the Details pane into the Dashboard Content window in the middle of the screen.

8. Click the Properties tab near the top of the dashboard.

9. In the Name field, type **Test Dashboard**.

10. Click out of the Name field so that the name change takes effect.

11. In the Workspace Browser of Dashboard Designer, right-click the dashboard.

12. From the drop-down menu, click Deploy to SharePoint.

13. In the Deploy To window, click OK.

After clicking OK, you should be presented with a progress window informing you that your dashboard is being deployed. When it's finished, your browser will automatically open to the URL to which your dashboard was deployed, where you can bask in the greatness of your own BI dashboard. Figure 8-51 shows an example of what you just built. Rejoice! You have successfully configured and tested PerformancePoint.

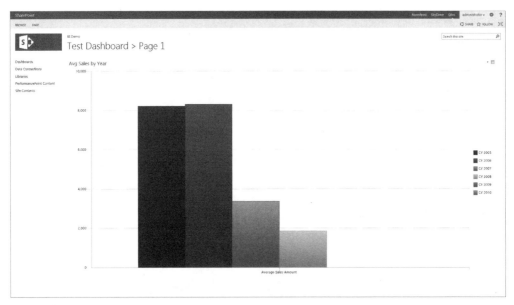

FIGURE 8-51

Of course, just to make sure you don't feel too awesome, Figure 8-52 shows you what the BI ninja built to show off. It is OK if you are starting to not like him.

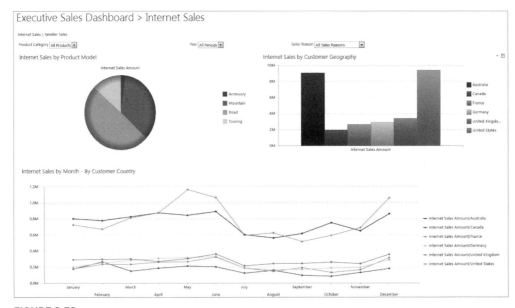

FIGURE 8-52

CONFIGURING VISIO SERVICES

Visio Services enables you to tie data to visualizations created in Visio. Once uploaded to SharePoint, users don't need to have Visio installed on their computer to view the Visio workbook. This is a great option if you have diagrams of processes or workflows, and supporting data available to show status, progress, and so on. This section steps through configuring the Visio Services service application in SharePoint and creating an unattended service account for the service to use when it refreshes data. Once that's done, you will test the configuration by creating a simple Visio diagram that pulls data from the AdventureWorks database.

MORE TOMATO OR "TAMAHTO"

You may notice sometimes this service application is called Visio Services and sometimes it is called Visio Graphics Service. Technically both are correct. Generally speaking people will use the name Visio Services and most of TechNet is written that way but in the Central Administration site you will see Visio Graphics Services when you create a new service application. Don't let it confuse you. The two terms are interchangeable.

Configuring the Visio Unattended Service Account

Unlike some of the other service applications that you have configured, you need to manually create the unattended service account for Visio in the Secure Store service application. Once the unattended account is created, you associate it with Visio Services during the configuration process. The first step is to create the unattended service account:

1. Log onto your SharePoint box as the install account. In this example use contoso\sp_install.

2. Open SharePoint Central Administration, and click Manage service applications under the Application Management heading.

3. Click the Secure Store service application.

4. Click New at the top of the screen in the Manage Target Applications section.

5. In the Target Application ID text box, enter **Visio**.

6. In the Display Name text box, enter **Visio**.

7. In the Contact E-mail text box, enter an e-mail address. In this example use **nothingcreative@tiredauthor.com**.

8. For Target Application Type, select Group from the drop-down menu. Click Next.

9. Accept the default Field Names and Field Types by simply clicking Next.

10. In the Target Application Administrators text box, enter your account. In this example use **contoso\sp_install**.

11. In the Members text box, enter **contoso\domain users**. Click OK.

After clicking OK, you are taken back to the main window of the Secure Store service application, where you should now see a Target Application ID of Visio in the list.

Follow these steps to set the credentials of the account that will be used to refresh data:

1. Select the Visio Target Application ID by checking the box to the left of Visio.

2. Click the Set icon in the Credentials area of the Edit Ribbon at the top of the page.

3. In the Windows User Name text box, type the name of your SQL read account. In this example, you previously configured **contoso\sql_read**.

4. Enter the password and confirm it. In this example it is **pass@word1**. When you are done, your page should look like Figure 8-53. Click OK.

```
Set Credentials for Secure Store Target Application (Group)          ✕

Warning: this page is not encrypted for secure communication. User names, passwords, and any other
information will be sent in clear text. For more information, contact your administrator.

Target Application Name:   Visio
Target Application ID:     Visio
Credential Owners:         ┌──────────────────────────────────────────┐
                           │ CONTOSO\domain users                       │
                           │                                            │
                           │                                            │
                           └──────────────────────────────────────────┘

Name                       Value
Windows User Name          ┌──────────────────────────────────────────┐
                           │ CONTOSO\sql_read                           │
                           └──────────────────────────────────────────┘
Windows Password           ┌──────────────────────────────────────────┐
                           │ ●●●●●●●●●●                                  │
                           └──────────────────────────────────────────┘
Confirm Windows Password   ┌──────────────────────────────────────────┐
                           │ ●●●●●●●●●●                                  │
                           └──────────────────────────────────────────┘

Note: Once the credentials are set, they cannot be retrieved by the administrator. Any existing credentials
for this credential owner will be overwritten.

                                                      ┌──────┐  ┌────────┐
                                                      │  OK  │  │ Cancel │
                                                      └──────┘  └────────┘
```

FIGURE 8-53

Configuring the Visio Graphics Service Application

Now that the unattended service account is ready to roll, you will create and configure the Visio Graphics Services service application. If you followed all of Chapter 3, you have already done these steps:

1. Log onto your SharePoint box as the install account. In this example use contoso\sp_install.

2. Open SharePoint Central Administration, and under the Application Management heading, click Manage service applications.

3. From the Manage service applications screen, click the New button in the Ribbon.

4. From the menu, select Visio Graphics Service.

5. For Name, enter **Visio Services**.

6. Scroll down to Application Pool and select Use existing application pool.

7. From the drop-down menu, select Default SharePoint Service App Pool.

8. Leave the "Create a Visio Graphics Service Application Proxy and add it to the default proxy group" option checked and click OK.

Now that you have created the service application you need to start the service:

1. From Central Administration, click Application Management on the left, and then click Application Management.

2. Under the Service Applications section, click Manage services on server.

3. Find Visio Graphics Service and click Start to the right of it.

Now that the Visio Graphics Services application is created, you need to configure the unattended account:

1. Log onto your SharePoint box as the install account. In this example use contoso\sp_install.

2. Open SharePoint Central Administration, and under the Application Management heading, click Manage service applications.

3. Click on the Visio Services service application.

4. Click Global Settings on the Manage the Visio Graphics Service page.

5. In the External Data section of the Visio Graphics Service Settings page, type **Visio** in the Application ID text box. Click OK.

That was pretty easy. All that's left to do now is create a sample drawing and try it out.

Creating and Deploying a Visio Web Drawing

Time to show off some of your skills with Visio 2013. With SharePoint 2013, you need to use Visio Professional 2013 to perform the following steps. You are going to create a Visio web drawing that pulls in a little data from the AdventureWorks database. This will enable you to test the configuration for Visio Services and the unattended service account:

1. Log in to a client machine with Visio 2013 Professional installed. The account you log in with must have a SQL login with the public role at minimum.

2. From the Start menu, open Visio 2013.

3. Click Basic Diagram to create a new drawing.

4. When the pop-up appears, choose your units of measure and click Create.

5. In the Ribbon, click the DATA tab.

6. In the External Data section, click the Link Data to Shapes icon.

7. From the Data Selector, select Microsoft SQL Server database as the type of data source you want to use. Click Next.

8. For Server name:, enter your SQL server's name. In this example use **sql**.

9. For Log on credentials, select Use Windows Authentication. If you wanted to use the other option, you would need to specify a SQL login, which you don't have, not a Windows account. Click Next.

10. From the drop-down for Select the database that contains the data you want:, select AdventureWorksDW2012.

11. In the list of tables, highlight FactInternetSales by clicking on it, as shown in Figure 8-54. Click Next.

12. On the bottom of the Save Data Connection File and Finish screen, click Authentication Settings.

13. The pop-up window that appears contains the same options that were available with Excel: Use the authenticated user's account, Use a stored account, or None. For now, select None. Click OK and then click Finish.

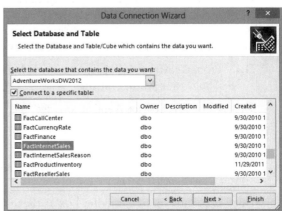

FIGURE 8-54

After clicking Finish on the Data Connection Wizard screen, the Data Selector screen should automatically open. In the following section you will tell Visio what data to show in the diagram:

1. Ensure that the data connection you just created is listed as the data connection you want to use, and then click Next.

2. Under the Columns to include: area, click the Select Columns... button.

3. Click the Uncheck all button on the Select Columns window.

4. Locate SalesAmount near the bottom of the list and check the box next to it. Click OK.

5. Under the Rows to include: area, click the 'Select Rows... button.

6. Click the drop-down menu for ProductKey.

7. From the lengthy drop-down menu, select 310 as shown in Figure 8-55.

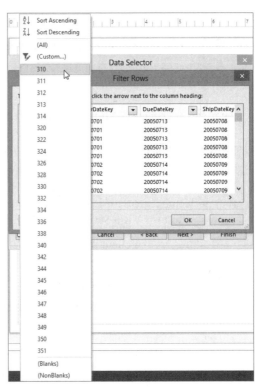

FIGURE 8-55

8. Click the drop-down menu next to OrderDateKey and select the value 20050701.

9. With these filters applied, you should have only one row of data now visible. If you have more than one, that's fine; but in the event you don't have any, adjust the filters so that at least one row of data is available. Click OK in the Filter Rows window.

10. With the filters applied, your Data Selector window should now look like Figure 8-56. Click Next.

11. On the Configure Refresh Unique Identifier, select the option "Rows in my data do not have a unique identifier. Use the order of the rows to identify changes." Click Next, and then click Finish on the final dialog.

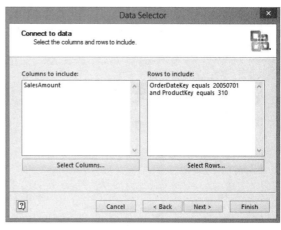

FIGURE 8-56

Now that Visio knows what data you need, you should see a new External Data window at the bottom of the drawing. All you need to do now is add a data element to the drawing, and then save and upload your document to SharePoint.

Note that the following steps save your Visio drawing as a web drawing with an extension of .vdw. This is important, as your Visio diagram will not be viewable in SharePoint if you save it as a diagram with the extension .vsd:

1. Drag the SalesAmount in your External Data window onto the Visio main canvas. Once complete you should see a shape with the sales amount listed next to it.

2. Click the File tab at the top of your Visio document.

3. Click Save As ➪ Computer ➪ Browse, and navigate to your BI Site collection. In this example, that's http://portal.contoso.com/sites/bi.

4. Choose the Documents library.

5. For File name, enter **Sales Amount**. Click Save.

Follow these steps to check it out in the browser:

1. Open your BI site collection in the browser. In this example use http://portal.contoso.com/sites/bi.

2. From the left-hand navigation, click Site Contents.

3. Click the icon for Documents.

4. In the list of Documents, click Sales Amount.

5. Click All Refresh from the ugly yellow bar at the top of the screen. Note that you can go into the Visio Services service application settings and disable the refresh warning.

If all goes well, you shouldn't see anything but a quick blink of your screen as the data refreshes. Figure 8-57 shows an example of all your hard work. Congratulations! Visio Services is now configured and tested.

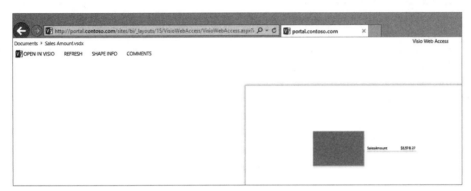

FIGURE 8-57

Once again the BI guy had to be fancy. Check it out in Figure 8-58.

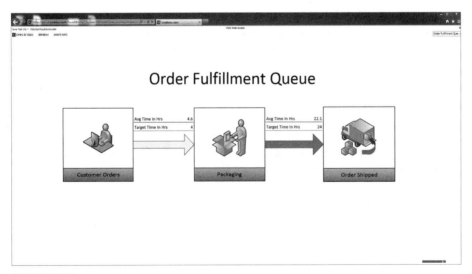

FIGURE 8-58

INTRODUCTION TO ACCESS 2013

Access Services 2013 is a new service application for users of SharePoint 2013 Enterprise. Unlike the previous version of the service application, Access data is now stored outside of SharePoint content databases, and instead stored inside databases specifically created for Access web applications. Due to these changes, a number of items need to be carefully considered before configuring Access Services 2013.

Prerequisites

The following are prerequisites for using Access Services 2013 with an in-house deployment of SharePoint 2013:

➤   SharePoint Server 2013 Enterprise

➤   An isolated app domain

➤   A configured Secure Store service application in your farm

➤   Microsoft SQL Server 2012

➤   Microsoft Access 2013 client

Although this section covers everything you need to get Access Services up and running, there are plenty of additional nuisances you may encounter over time. See the following TechNet article for further information if needed: `http://technet.microsoft.com/en-us/library/jj714714.aspx`.

Items to Consider for Access 2013

You really, really, really want a separate dedicated database environment for storing the Access Services databases. If a separate dedicated SQL Server 2012 environment is just not an option, the next best solution would be to set up an additional instance of SQL Server 2012 completely dedicated to those databases generated by Access 2013. Both SQL Server 2012 Standard and Enterprise Editions are supported for use.

A separate database is preferable because of the numerous configuration changes that would need to be made to SQL Server in order to use Access Services. First of all, the `Contained Databases` property has to be set to `TRUE`. Microsoft has identified a number of unique threats with this mode, most of which relate to the USER WITH PASSWORD authentication process. Microsoft provides an overview document of these threats at `http://msdn.microsoft.com/en-us/library/ff929055.aspx`.

The SQL Server security mode also has to be set to SQL Server and Windows Authentication mode. The DBA in your organization may not want to do this for security reasons, especially in situations where the SQL Server hosts other non-SharePoint databases.

Another reason for a dedicated resource is to control database growth and resource utilization. Access Services 2013 generates a new database for each new Access web app created in the farm. The number of databases can quickly spiral out of control, and you wouldn't want that to affect your production environment.

Having a dedicated resource also enables you to specifically write maintenance plans geared toward the Access Services databases.

Configuring an Isolated App Domain

An isolated app domain is required because Access Services 2013 makes use of the new app model. Setting up the app model is not a trivial task. Fortunately, Chapter 11, "Managing and Configuring

Apps," has an entire section devoted to correctly configuring the app model. If you haven't walked through those steps yet you will need to complete them before deploying Access Service 2013.

During setup, you create an App Management and Subscription Settings Service Application inside of SharePoint. Once the setup is complete, you need to ensure that the App Management Service and the Microsoft SharePoint Foundation Subscription Settings Service are both started in Central Administration's Services on Server section. All of this is covered in Chapter 11.

Microsoft SQL Server 2012 Required Features for Access Services 2013

Several features have to be installed in SQL Server 2012 prior to configuring Access Services 2013 inside of SharePoint:

➤ Database Engine Services

➤ Full-Text and Semantic Extractions for Search

➤ Client Tools Connectivity

➤ Management Tools – Complete

If your organization already has an installation of SQL Server 2012, some of these features may be activated. Check with your database administrator to ensure that they are configured. If not, you need to set them up by running SQL Server's built-in setup utility. All of the preceding items are available under the Feature Selection section of the SQL installer. If you don't have the features, you can simply rerun SQL Server setup and then choose "Add features to an existing instance of SQL Server 2012."

After configuring all your SQL features, you also need to confirm that the following ports are open on your SQL server if you are using any type of firewall:

➤ TCP 1433

➤ TCP 1434

➤ UDP 1434

Microsoft SQL Server 2012 Options Required for Use with Access Services 2013

As mentioned previously, integrating an existing SQL Server 2012 installation with Access Services 2013 is probably the most challenging scenario. The following two items require changes to the SQL Server operating mode. Consulting with a DBA or other stakeholders in the business is paramount before making any of these changes. Again, the ideal setup is a dedicated SQL installation or at least a dedicated instance of SQL Server.

Enabling Contained Databases

Contained databases were introduced in SQL Server 2012. When this mode is enabled, databases are isolated from each other and from the instance that contains the database. This means that the metadata that was typically stored inside the master database is now completely stored inside each independent database. Enabling this mode on a SQL instance that hosts databases for other applications, especially other non-SharePoint databases, may be problematic. Microsoft has a great article describing all the changes at `http://msdn.microsoft.com/en-us/library/ff929071.aspx`.

To enable contained databases:

1. Log into the SQL server as a SQL administrator. In this example, the server name is sql and the account you would use is contoso\administrator.

2. Open SQL Server Management Studio and connect to the local SQL server.

3. Right-click the server node and choose Properties, as shown in Figure 8-59.

4. Under Select a page, click Advanced.

5. Under Containment, click False next to Enable Contained Databases and switch it to True (see Figure 8-60). Click OK.

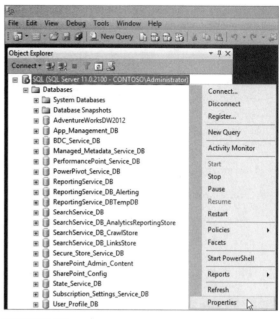

FIGURE 8-59

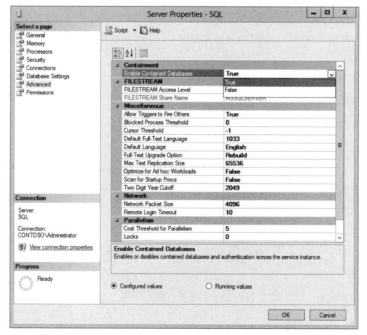

FIGURE 8-60

Note that this same page contains an option for Allow Triggers to Fire Others. This must also be set to True, which is its default setting. If this is set to False, you should ask the owner of the SQL server why it was changed. This is yet another reason why you should have a dedicated instance of SQL Server for Access Services databases.

SQL Server needs to be restarted for the change to take effect, which causes all programs that use SQL Server databases to lose connection. Therefore, be sure to save any work and stop any software using SQL prior to restarting. The next two sections also require a restart of SQL Server, so if you will be making all the changes, you could skip this for now and just do one restart later.

To restart SQL Server:

1. From the Start menu, open SQL Server Configuration Manager.

2. Select SQL Server Services.

3. Right-click on the instance of SQL Server and select Restart.

That does it. Hopefully, you ensured that no one was using SQL Server before you restarted it.

SQL Server Authentication

The SQL Server security mode also needs to be changed. For policy and security reasons, some organizations specifically only allow Windows Authentication mode. Changing this setting enables SQL Server to create and grant user accounts and permissions that fall outside of an Active Directory structure. This is one of those things that make security professionals and DBAs cringe (and, again, why a dedicated environment or a separate instance is recommended).

To change or check SQL's authentication mode:

1. From the Start menu, open SQL Server Management Studio and connect to the SQL server.

2. Right-click the server node and choose Properties.

3. Under Select a page, click Security.

4. Under Server authentication, select SQL Server and Windows Authentication mode. Click OK.

SQL Server must be restarted for the change to take effect, which causes any programs that use SQL Server databases to lose connection. Be sure to save any work and stop any software using SQL prior to restarting.

To restart SQL Server:

1. From the Start menu, open SQL Server Configuration Manager.

2. Select SQL Server Services.

3. Right-click on the instance of SQL Server and select Restart.

That does it. Hopefully, you ensured that no one was using SQL Server before you restarted it.

SQL Server Protocols

Ensure that the TCP/IP and Named Pipes features are enabled. Named pipes are also required for an AlwaysOn availability group for SharePoint 2013. Availability groups are covered in Chapter 9, "Configuring SharePoint 2013 for High Availability Backups," if you need more information.

To check whether these options are enabled:

1. From the Start menu, open SQL Server Configuration Manager.

2. Select SQL Server Network Configuration.

3. Double-click the Protocols item for your instance of SQL Server, as shown in Figure 8-61. MSSQLSERVER is the default instance.

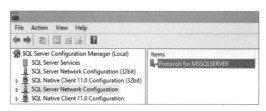

FIGURE 8-61

4. Under Protocol Name, ensure that TCP/IP and Named Pipes are set to Enabled, as shown in Figure 8-62.

If a protocol is not enabled, you can enable it by right-clicking on it and selecting Enable. You will likely need to do this for Named Pipes.

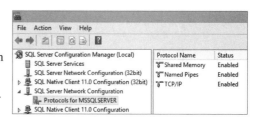

FIGURE 8-62

SQL Server must be restarted for the change to take effect, which causes all programs that use SQL Server databases to lose connection. Be sure to save any work and stop any software using SQL prior to restarting. If you need help restarting the SQL Server service see the previous section for step-by-step instructions.

Service Account Permissions

It's highly recommended that you create a dedicated service account inside Active Directory specifically for use with Access Services. This account will be used to create all Access databases inside SQL, and as the service account running the application pool for the service application. You should grant this account db_owner, public, and securityadmin roles inside of SQL.

The AD account just needs to be a regular domain user. If you are following the examples in the book, you would use the naming convention of contoso\sp_accsvc.

To grant the service account permissions in SQL:

1. Log into the SQL server as a SQL administrator. In this example the server name is sql and the account you would use is contoso\administrator.

2. Open SQL Server Management Studio and connect to the local SQL server.

3. Expand the Security node, and then expand the Logins node.

4. Right-click Logins and select New Login, as shown in Figure 8-63.

FIGURE 8-63

5. For Login name:, enter your Access Services account. In this example that is contoso\sp_accsvc.

6. Under Select a page, click Server Roles.

7. Check dbcreator and securityadmin.

8. Confirm that public is still selected, verify your work against Figure 8-64, and click OK.

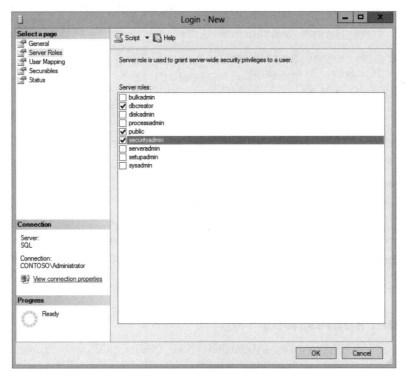

FIGURE 8-64

Remember this account. You will need it in the next section.

At this point, you can close up anything you still have running on the SQL server and log out.

Creating the Access Services 2013 Service Application

Now you are headed back to SharePoint Central Administration for a common set of tasks. You need to make your new Access Services AD account a managed account and then create a new service application. It isn't difficult, just don't skip any steps.

To register a managed account:

1. On the SharePoint server, open Central Administration and click Security ➪ Configure managed accounts.

2. Click Register Managed Account.

3. For User name, enter your Access Services AD account. In this example that is **contoso\ sp_accsvc**.

4. Enter the account's password. In this example use **pass@word1**. Click OK.

To create the service application:

1. From the left-hand navigation, click Application Management.

2. Under Service Applications, click Manage service applications.

3. From the Ribbon, click New.

4. From the drop-down, select Access Services.

> **NOTE** *For this example you are working with Access Services, also known as Access Services 2013. For an overview of Access Services 2010 and the differences between the two, please see Chapter 3, "Installing and Configuring SharePoint 2013."*

5. For Name, enter **Access Services 2013**.

6. For Application Database Server, choose the SQL server you made all the wild changes to in the previous section.

7. Leave the check box enabled for "Validate the application database server (recommended)." This way, when you click OK it will confirm that all those SQL changes were made.

8. For Application Pool, use Create new application pool.

9. For Application pool name, enter **Access Services 2013 App Pool**.

10. From the drop-down below Configurable, select your Access Services AD account. In this example it is contoso\sp_accsvc. You can double-check yourself using Figure 8-65.

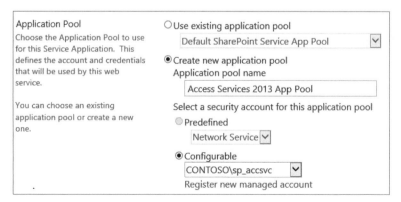

FIGURE 8-65

11. Click OK to create the service application.

To start the service:

1. Switch to your IE tab for Services on Server.

2. Find Access Services and click Start to the right of it.

That will do it. If you did have any errors during validation of your SQL server, you will need to fix those before trying again. Fortunately, SQL Server is checked before creating any other pieces. Therefore, when you return to create the service application again, the steps are identical; either your service app or app pool were not created.

Setting SQL Permissions for Your Service Account

Now that you have configured your service application to use a dedicated account, you need to ensure that account has all the necessary SQL permissions to get things working. To do this, you need to give that account the SPDataAccess database role on the Access Services database, and to all the content databases for web applications for which you want to use Access Services.

To grant the necessary SQL permissions:

1. Log into the SQL server as a SQL administrator. In this example the server name is sql and the account you would use is contoso\administrator.

2. Open SQL Server Management Studio and connect to the local SQL server.

3. Expand the Security node, and then expand the Logins node.

4. Find your account in the list and double-click it. In this example that is contoso\sp_accsvc.

5. Under Select a page, click User Mapping.

6. In the list of databases, click App_Management_DB. If you configured your Access Services service app to host the database on another SQL instance, then this database will not be listed. In that case you will need to log into that SQL instance and do this step and the next step there.

7. In the Database role membership for: APP_Management_DB section, check SPDataAccess as shown in Figure 8-66.

8. In the list of databases, click on your web application content database. In this example it is WSS_Content_Portal.

9. In the Database role membership for: WSS_Content_Portal section, check SPDataAccess.

10. At the bottom of the window click OK.

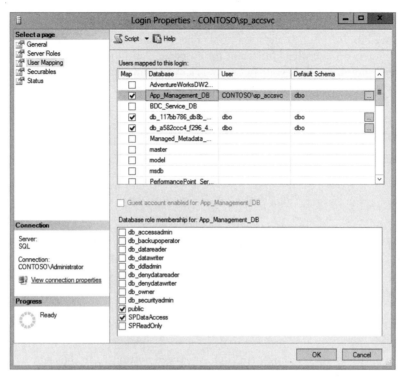

FIGURE 8-66

Now your service account has permissions to the necessary databases. Remember that if you add more SharePoint content databases later or want to use Access Services with other web applications, you need to repeat these steps.

Configuring IIS

Because Access Services is an equal opportunity offender, you have to make one change to IIS. Please avoid rolling your eyes while you make this necessary change.

To update IIS:

1. Log into the SharePoint server as a local administrator. In this example the server is named server and the account to use is contoso\sp_install.

2. From the Start menu, open Internet Information Services (IIS) Manager, and expand the Server node.

3. Under Server, click Application Pools.

4. Now you need to find your application pool. The trick here is to skip the name, which is a bunch of letters and numbers (different for everyone), and locate the application pool in the Identity column, which is your Access Services account. In this example that would be contoso\sp_accsvc. Click on the application pool, as shown in Figure 8-67.

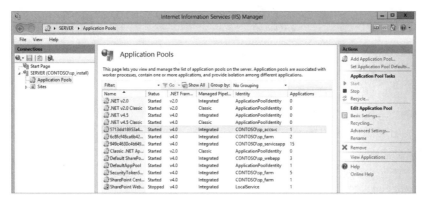

FIGURE 8-67

5. With the application pool highlighted, click Advanced Settings... in the right-hand menu.

6. Under Process Model, change Load User Profile from False to True. Click OK.

7. Close IIS Manager.

Hooray! You have now completed all the wacky prerequisites to get Access Services working. In the next section you can try out this new toy of yours.

CREATING A CUSTOM WEB APP USING ACCESS 2013 CLIENT

Finally, after all that hard work you are ready to create an Access web app. To get started, you need to have a machine running the Access 2013 client that is part of the normal Office suite.

To create an Access web app:

1. Log into a machine that has the Office 2013 clients installed with an account that has permissions to create lists in the SharePoint web you want to use.

2. From the Start menu, launch Access 2013.

3. When Access opens, click Custom web app. The Custom web app window will appear.

4. For App Name, enter Customer Tracking.

5. For Web Location, enter a SharePoint site collection. In this example you can use **http://portal.contos.com/sites/bi.**

6. Click the Create button.

Now that the app is created, you need to build something:

1. Still in Access 2013, you should now be on the screen for Add Tables. In the search box, type **People** and press Enter (see Figure 8-68).

FIGURE 8-68

2. From the list of options that appears, click Customers. This will create a Customers table with some default fields in the app.

3. On the left, click Customers (with the little star beside the name).

4. This brings up the table and list that were created. Click Edit in the center of the screen to make some quick changes. A new Customer List tab opens. Here you will see a lot of different options and actions for customizing your app. You are welcome to put your Access skills to use at this point and customize away.

To take a look at your work in the browser:

1. Navigate to the site collection to which you just published your app. In this example that is http://portal.contoso.com/sites/bi.

2. From the left-hand menu, click Site Contents.

3. Click the pretty, red Custom Tracking icon to open it.

There is your app in all its glory. An example is shown in Figure 8-69. You can now add customers and start to play with the data. On the far right you will see a second gear icon. You can click that gear icon to open your app again in Access 2013 if you wanted to edit it.

FIGURE 8-69

You might also notice that your URL is something crazy now. That's because you are running a true app, so it is being hosted by the app management service you set up in Chapter 3. It's pretty cool to see all these pieces working together.

The one sad part of this success is that if you go look at your SQL server now, you will see that it created a database for your app with a hideous name. Just another reminder why hosting these databases in their own SQL instance is a good idea.

Looking for the usual BI ninja example? It turns out he doesn't have anything awesome to demo here. Maybe he needs to brush up on his Access Services skills.

SUMMARY

Are you exhausted? If you worked through all the examples and demos in this chapter you deserve a gold star. The road was tough but hopefully worth the journey. You have seen that a lot of the service applications do very similar things but with a different feel or specialization; and to get the most benefit you sometimes need to install one in order to use another. For example, PowerPivot is exciting but it doesn't work until Excel Services is deployed. Keep these close associations in mind as you plan your deployment.

The order the service applications in this chapter appear is done for a reason. Hopefully, its emphasis on the data specialist and the administrator working together in harmony has been effective in that not only do you feel empowered to deploy the given functionality but you have a better feel for how it is used.

Configuring SharePoint for High-Availability Backups

WHAT'S IN THIS CHAPTER?

➤ Identifying business needs for disaster recovery

➤ Backing up and restoring SharePoint content and configuration

➤ Ensuring SharePoint's resiliency against the unexpected

In the day-to-day business of IT, the unexpected can and does happen. To whatever extent possible, we need to anticipate the unexpected. Hardware will fail. Users will make mistakes. As an administrator, your job is to minimize the impact of these failures on your users, as well as yourself and your business. Planning is key to ensuring that when disaster strikes, your business can recover with an acceptable amount of service interruption.

Understanding what options are available out of the box is the first step to devising a plan and determining what is acceptable to your business. Every business situation is different, with different requirements and acceptable costs. For example, an internal SharePoint intranet farm for a small business doesn't have quite the same uptime demands as a public-facing e-commerce SharePoint site selling decorative spoons with pictures of cats on them. This chapter covers the most common failure scenarios an enterprise is likely to face, along with the different out-of-the-box options available in SharePoint 2013 for proactively devising a strategy and recovering from them.

DETERMINING YOUR BUSINESS REQUIREMENTS

As a business, your first duty is to your customers. In an IT shop, your customers are typically your end users. In order to effectively meet the needs of your customers, the following agreements are put into place to define the level of service that is expected from a service provider:

➤ **Service-level agreement (SLA)** — This is an agreement between the service provider and the consumer of services. In this case, that's the party responsible for the keeping the SharePoint lights on and the end users. Having a good SLA in place protects both parties. It gives customers an accurate expectation of services that will be provided and offers IT protection from customers who might demand more than the SLA defines. Some common requirements for an SLA are outlined below:

➤ **Service availability** — This defines the availability requirements for services such as networking and server infrastructures, not accounting for planned maintenance times. This is normally expressed as a guaranteed percentage of uptime, i.e., 99.999% or 99.95%.

➤ **Performance** — This defines the expected performance thresholds of the service, beyond which must be considered out of threshold and must be resolved.

➤ **Reliability** — This generally defines the amount of times business impacting service interruption can be tolerated.

➤ **Operational-level agreement (OLA)** — This agreement defines the roles and responsibilities between different operational groups. In the case of a complex ecosystem such as a SharePoint farm, it could be shared between Active Directory support, SQL Server Database support, and SharePoint support teams. Additionally, as other Microsoft products become more tightly integrated with SharePoint, such as Lync and Exchange, it may also be necessary to involve these support teams in the OLA.

At the forefront of any examination of business needs vs. acceptable loss will be business continuity planning (BCP). BCP is a defined process for building a road map that maintains operations in the event of a service-interrupting catastrophe.

The first step in the process is the *analysis phase*, which as its name suggests is used to analyze the threats, and potential impact of these threats, on the business. The threats could be fire, earthquake, hacking, loss of power, locust invasion, or anything else that can result in data loss or downtime. The impact of these threats must also be analyzed and guarded against. The following objectives help to define the tolerance of the business against these threats, and later help to identify the technical implementations required to meet these tolerances:

➤ **Recovery-point objective (RPO)** — This objective identifies the maximum amount of data loss that is tolerable. For example, a business might define that no more than one hour of data can be lost at any given time. It might also be defined as something more specific, such as "recovering files that existed at midnight when the backups run." The shorter the RPO, the more expensive the solution.

➤ **Recovery-time objective (RTO)** — The RTO defines the maximum amount of time allowed to restore service. For example, it might be defined that data must be restored within three hours of an outage. When combined with the preceding RPO, only one hour of data may be lost but it may require up to three hours to restore it according to the RTO. As with the RPO, the shorter the RTO, the more expensive the solution.

➤ **Recovery-level objective (RLO)** — The RLO defines the granularity level at which you must be able to recover (i.e., entire farm, web application, site collection, site, list or library, or item).

As noted for each objective, the more granular the level of recovery, the more expensive the solution generally becomes. Of course, ideally your users want no data loss (short RPO), immediate availability (short RTO), and recovery down to the item level (short RLO). Unfortunately, you cannot completely eliminate the possibility of downtime or data loss, and the closer you get to that unobtainable goal the more exponentially expensive the solution gets. Unless your company has a collection of solid gold coins that fills a swimming pool, like Scrooge McDuck, you need to find a compromise that balances customer needs with the IT department's budget and manpower.

The second step in the process is the *solution design phase*. This phase is intended to identify the most cost-effective implementations for meeting the preceding objectives regarding tolerable data loss and downtime. For this phase it is essential to understand what out-of-the-box capabilities and features are available in not only SharePoint 2013, but also SQL Server, Windows Server, and IIS so that you can identify and recommend the most effective solutions based on the analysis of business impact and the identified objectives for mitigating it. It is also important to understand that different types of data require different levels of impact mitigation. However, the chosen solution, typically based on the most critical data, usually ends up applying to all the data. In addition, it is during this phase that documentation is created detailing the implementation and testing of the recommended solutions.

The *implementation phase* technically implements the selected solutions and tests them for intended functionality. Once the implementation phase is complete, it is time to move on to *organizational testing*. During this phase, the solutions are tested under real workloads to validate projected workloads, adjusting as necessary, to ensure stability and reliability of the recovery objectives, and to drive acceptance within the organization.

After testing is successfully completed, the final phase is *maintenance*. During this phase, data accuracy is verified, documentation is handed off, and further testing is conducted at regular intervals to ensure that the solutions remain functional as the business and its requirements change.

The rest of this chapter discusses the methods available for content recovery, disaster recovery, and high availability using SharePoint 2013. These features play a significant role in designing solutions to meet the needs of your business continuity plan.

CONTENT RECOVERY

The most accessible, and most frequently used, method of data recovery in SharePoint is at the content level. Several options are available for content recovery depending on the retention policies in place and the nature of the deletion or corruption from which you need to recover:

➤ Version history

➤ Recycle Bin

➤ Export and import of subwebs

➤ Site collection backup and restore

➤ SQL Server snapshots

Some of the preceding recovery methods provide more than one way to accomplish the task, including PowerShell, Central Administration, and even SQL Server Management Studio, all three of which is covered in detail in this section.

Content Storage Overview

Before we get into the methods for recovering data, it is important to understand how the data itself is stored in SharePoint. Each content database is created with a common table structure, with tables for Site Collections, Users, Web Parts, Lists and Libraries, and the documents themselves. Each item in these tables is relationally linked to the items in other tables via ID columns. For example, in order for SharePoint to know that item.docx belongs to a specific library, there is an entry for the document in the dbo.AllDocs table in the content database with a Document ID column for the document itself, as well as a reference List ID column pointing to the library it belongs to in the dbo .AllLists table.

The document itself is stored in another table called dbo.DocStreams as what is called a binary large object, or BLOB, with a reference Document ID column pointing to the document in the dbo.AllDocs table. In other words, the way data is represented to an end user does not translate directly to how the data is stored and interacted with in the content databases. A document does not physically reside in a SharePoint list as displayed in the browser. Instead, it is associated with it in the manner just described.

As long as you have a good content database backup, you will have a way to recover all content — even if a site or list is corrupted and no longer viewable via the browser. It may require some creative thinking to access it, but it is there. A good database backup means you can probably save both your users' content and your job. And of course, always keep a backup of your resume on a USB thumb drive at home. You know, just in case that database backup isn't as good as you think it is.

Version History

While version history is not a disaster recovery technique in the classic sense, it is your first line of defense against users making potentially unwanted changes to files, or even corruption. The version history provides users with a self-service means to quickly revert to an earlier version of any documents or list items.

Versioning is not enabled by default on user-created document library apps when they are created. However, some system-created apps, such as those that are created by activating the Publishing Infrastructure feature, do enable version history by default. To enable versioning, a user must have at least Manage List permissions to the desired app. The version history configuration dialog consists of four sections:

➤ **Content Approval** – This section specifies whether the Content Approval workflows for the current library are required when submitting changes. Whether or not content approval should be enforced depends on business processes and how much control users should have over changes.

➤ **Document Version History** – This section offers options for version history retention such as No Versions, Create Major Versions (1.0, 2.0, 3.0, etc.), and Create Major and Minor (also known as Draft) Versions (1.0, 1.1, 1.2, 2.0, 2.1, etc.). Note that only the major versions option is available for lists, while both major and minor versions are available for libraries.

➤ **Draft Item Security** – In a list this section is grayed out unless Content Approval is enabled, while for a library the setting is activated when minor versioning is enabled. It controls who can see Draft items once they are submitted. Options are Any User, Users with Edit permissions, or Approvers.

➤ **Require Check Out** – This section specifies whether an item must be checked out prior to being edited. Enabling this option for a library prevents multiple users from editing the same document concurrently, potentially overwriting each other's changes. It also enables users to submit check-in comments when they upload their changes.

In previous releases of SharePoint, storing multiple versions had the potential to significantly increase the size of your content databases because each uploaded version of a file was stored as an entire file. For example, suppose you had a 100MB PowerPoint file in your content database explaining why cats are better pets than dogs. If someone opened that document and simply replaced the word "cat" with "kitties" on the first slide, the new version would occupy another 100MB of space in the content database. Before you know it, your content database is as big as a house.

SharePoint 2013 introduces a new technology called *Shredded Storage.* This technology enables SharePoint to store only the changes made to a document, instead of the entire file each time. Of course, despite the magic of Shredded Storage, all your site collections should have size quotas in place to ensure they don't grow out of control.

Enabling Versioning

The following steps describe how to configure versioning for libraries:

1. Browse to the library for which you want to enable versioning.

2. Click the Library tab in the upper-left corner to display the Library Ribbon and then select Library Settings (see Figure 9-1).

FIGURE 9-1

3. On the Library Settings page, under General Settings, click Versioning settings.

4. If you want to enable Content Approval select the Yes radio button. This will also enable the Draft Item Security section for further configuration, giving you more control over who can view and interact with the submitted documents before they are approved.

5. The Document Version History section, shown in Figure 9-2, enables you to choose the level of version history retention you want. When you enable version history, you can also select the maximum number of major and minor versions to keep. Teaching your users to set reasonable limits here can save cleanup time later and keep database sizes to a minimum.

6. The next configuration option is Draft Item Security. If you chose to enable Content Approval for a list, or minor versions for a library, then this section is available for further configuration; otherwise, it remains grayed out. The settings here enable you to control who can see draft items before they've made it through the approval process. By default, if Content Approval is enabled, the last option is selected, preventing draft items from being visible to anyone except the approvers and the original author. This helps to minimize confusion, as users won't see draft versions that are not considered finalized. If Content Approval is not enabled, then the default gives all users read-access.

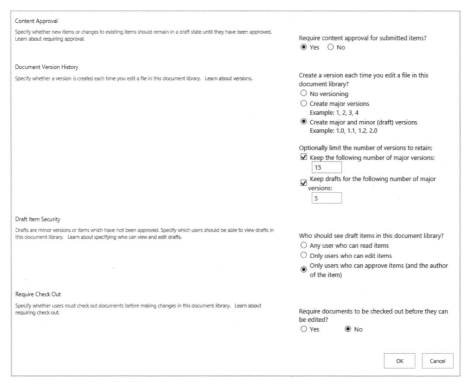

FIGURE 9-2

7. The last option specifies whether check out is required before editing.

   Enabling version history for a list is virtually identical to libraries, but with a few minor differences:

1. Browse to the list for which you want to enable versioning.

2. Click the List tab in the upper-left corner to display the List Ribbon and then select List Settings (see Figure 9-3).

FIGURE 9-3

3. On the List Settings page, under General Settings, click Versioning settings.

4. If you want to enable Content Approval, select the Yes radio button. As with document libraries, this also enables the Draft Item Security section.

5. The Item Version History section, shown in Figure 9-4, enables you to choose the level of version history retention you want for list items. Note the lack of major and minor versions here. However, you still have the option to control the number of versions to keep, along with the option to specify how many drafts of approved versions should be saved.

6. The last configuration option is Draft Item Security. If you chose to enable Content Approval, then this section is available for further configuration; otherwise, it remains grayed out. As with the document library, the settings here enable you to control who can see draft items before they've made it through the approval process. The default is also approvers and authors only.

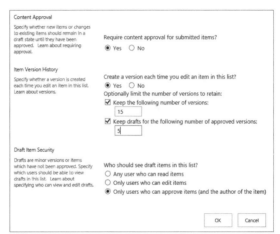

FIGURE 9-4

Reverting to a Previous Version

To restore a previous version, perform the following steps:

1. Browse to the library for which you want to revert to an earlier version document.

2. Select the Files tab in the upper-left corner to access the Files Ribbon.

3. Select the document in the library for which you want to view the versions. This will enable the Version History link in the Manage section of the Ribbon (see Figure 9-5).

FIGURE 9-5

4. Click the Version History link to open the Version History dialog, where you can interact with current and past versions of the document. (see Figure 9-6).

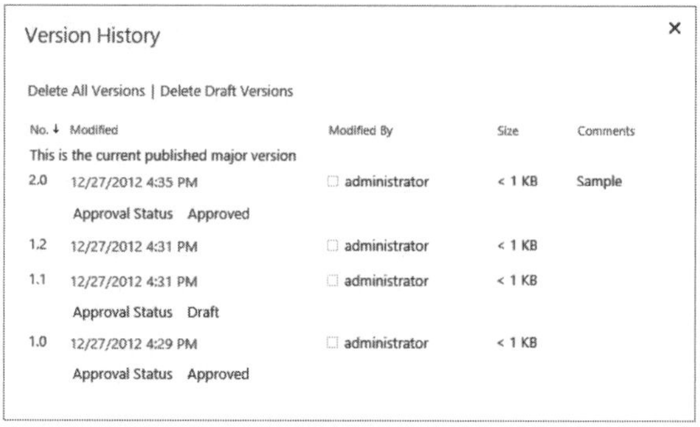

5. To restore to a previous version, move your mouse over the desired version, click the drop-down arrow, and select Restore. You will see a new incremental version added to the top of the list of versions. The previously live version is still there, but it is now a historical version, while the restored version has become the new live version.

FIGURE 9-6

Although versioning isn't technically a disaster recovery technique, it can be quickly used by a user to bring back an old version of a document if the current version is corrupt or unacceptable for some reason.

The Recycle Bin

The Recycle Bin has been around since Windows SharePoint Services (WSS) 3.0 and has seen many enhancements over the last couple of versions. The Recycle Bin offers a self-service capability for users to recover deleted content — whether it be documents, lists, or list items. SharePoint 2010 Service Pack 1 added the Site and Site Collection Recycle Bins, which are covered in more detail here.

The Recycle Bin is enabled by default and can be configured at the web application level through Central Administration. The Recycle Bins themselves are divided into the following stages:

➤ **Stage 1** — The first-stage Recycle Bin is the highest level. It is available directly to end users for self-service recovery. The minimum permissions necessary to use the stage 1 Recycle Bin is Contribute or higher. The files in this Recycle Bin have not been removed from the content database and are therefore included in the overall site quota until the configured number of retention policy days has been reached. The default retention policy is 30 days, but farm administrators can change this setting for the web application through Central Administration.

➤ **Stage 2** — The stage 2 Recycle Bin is found at the site collection level and is accessible only to site collection administrators. When a user deletes a file from the stage 1 Recycle Bin, it is moved here. Items are then retained in the stage 2 Recycle Bin for the configured number of days, which has the same default 30-day retention policy as stage 1, unless it is configured otherwise.

Farm administrators can configure the maximum size limit to specify when the oldest files in the Recycle Bin should be deleted automatically. SharePoint determines the age of the file according to when it was first deleted, not when it was moved to the stage 2 Recycle Bin.

Files in the stage 2 Recycle Bin do not count toward the site collection quota. Instead, the size of the Recycle Bin is calculated at a percentage (default is 50%) of the size of the site collection quota. This means that in addition to the size quota for each site collection, you must also factor in an additional 50% overhead on the content database size for stage 2 Recycle Bin growth. If no quota is assigned to the site collection, then there is no limit to the size of the stage 2 Recycle Bin. Be sure your site collections have quotas.

Configuring the Recycle Bin

The Recycle Bin is enabled by default and configured at the web application level in Central Administration. To configure each web application's Recycle Bin policies, use the following steps:

1. Open SharePoint 2013 Central Administration.

2. Under Application Management, click Manage web applications.

3. Select the web application you want to modify and click the General Settings link in the Ribbon.

4. In the dialog that appears, scroll down to the Recycle Bin section.

5. As shown in Figure 9-7, the default retention policy is set to 30 days. This affects both the stage 1 and stage 2 Recycle Bins. Note that if you disable the Recycle Bin completely here, it will immediately flush any deleted content out of all stage 1 and stage 2 Recycle Bins throughout the entire web application.

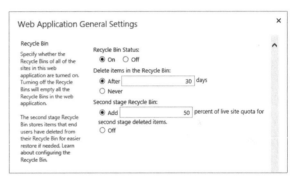

FIGURE 9-7

Recovering Items from the Stage 1 Recycle Bin

For readers who keep accidentally deleting their content, this Recycle Bin is for you. To get your content back, follow these steps:

1. Browse to the site in which you deleted the item.

2. On the Site Actions Cog, click the Site Contents link.

3. On the far right of the page you will now see a link for the Recycle Bin, with the number of deleted items in parentheses. Click that link.

4. If fewer than 30 days have passed since you deleted the item and the Recycle Bin hasn't been emptied, you should see your item listed here. Select it and click Restore Selection, which restores the item to its original location.

Recovering Items from the Stage 2 Recycle Bin

If you can't find your document in the stage 1 Recycle Bin, the next place to look is the Site Collection Recycle Bin. To get to the Site Collection Recycle Bin, you need to take a slightly different route:

1. Click the Settings icon (the cog) in the upper-right section of the page.

2. Select Site Settings.

3. Under Site Collection Administration, click Recycle Bin.

4. Now the default view will be of the stage 1 Recycle Bin contents, which if it has already been emptied will not show anything. Click the link labeled "Deleted from end user Recycle Bin."

5. You should now see your deleted file. Select it and click Restore Selection to recover the file to its original location. Note that if you have deleted any sites in your site collection, they will also be displayed in the stage 2 Recycle Bin. Figure 9-8 shows the difference between a deleted site and a deleted document.

FIGURE 9-8

Recovering a Site Collection from the Site Collection Recycle Bin

Site Collection recovery is handled a little differently. Obviously, you can't restore a site collection from within the stage 2 Recycle Bin, as it would be contained within the site collection you are trying to recover! Instead, site collections must be recovered through the PowerShell cmdlet, `Get-SPDeletedSite`. This recovery method is unchanged from SharePoint 2010 Service Pack 1, where it was first introduced. To recover a deleted site collection, do the following:

1. Open the SharePoint 2013 Management Shell.

2. Get a list of deleted site collections by using the following cmdlet:

   ```
   Get-SPDeletedSite
   ```

3. Find the site collection and path you are looking for and copy the SiteId (see Figure 9-9).

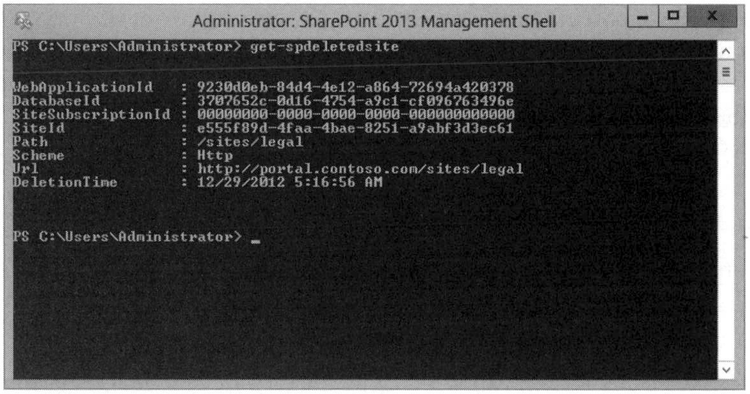

```
Administrator: SharePoint 2013 Management Shell                    _ □ X

PS C:\Users\Administrator> get-spdeletedsite

WebApplicationId    : 9230d0eb-84d4-4e12-a864-72694a420378
DatabaseId          : 3707652c-0d16-4754-a9c1-cf096763496e
SiteSubscriptionId  : 00000000-0000-0000-0000-000000000000
SiteId              : e555f89d-4faa-4bae-8251-a9abf3d3ec61
Path                : /sites/legal
Scheme              : Http
Url                 : http://portal.contoso.com/sites/legal
DeletionTime        : 12/29/2012 5:16:56 AM


PS C:\Users\Administrator> _
```

FIGURE 9-9

4. Run the following command to restore the site collection, replacing "SiteId" with the ID you copied from step 3:

```
Get-SPDeletedSite -Identity "SiteId" | Restore-SPDeletedSite
```

5. After this command completes, you should be able to see the site collection listed in Central Administration under View All Site Collections, and you can browse it again.

If at this point you are thinking that recovering a deleted site collection is the best thing since sliced bread, there are some shortcomings to keep in mind. First, only site collections that are deleted from the browser can be recovered. If a site collection is deleted from PowerShell, or from code, it can't be recovered. Second, in order to recover a site collection, the user running PowerShell must be in the ShellAdmins group of that content's database.

Exporting and Importing Sites, Lists, and Libraries

SharePoint 2013 maintains much of the Content Deployment feature set that provides the functionality for the Export and Import process from SharePoint 2010. Using either Central Administration or PowerShell, it is possible to export and import lists, libraries, or even whole webs, with a number of options for maintaining security settings and version history. The exported content is compressed into Microsoft standard CAB files with an extension of .cmp (which is an acronym for content migration package), and it may span one or more files.

The Content Deployment application programming interface (API) in SharePoint is primarily intended, as its name suggests, for deploying content between site collections, web applications, and even farms. However, a side benefit is that it can also be used to deploy that content out to the filesystem (considered exporting) to be later imported to the same location as a data recovery tool, or to an alternate path. This flexibility makes it a useful tool not only as a backup strategy, but also in your development and migration from testing to production strategies.

Before using the import and export cmdlets, ensure that you are a member of the WSS_ADMIN_WPG local group on the server you are logged into. If you have a lot of servers in the farm and need to add this privilege to all of them at once, you can use the following command in the SharePoint 2013 Management Shell to add a user to the WSS_ADMIN_WPG group on all servers, and add the user to the SharePoint_Shell_Access role in the farm configuration database and any content databases where data is being either exported or imported:

```
Add-SPShellAdmin contoso\administrator
```

This is covered in more detail in Chapter 7, which focuses on PowerShell.

Exporting Sites, Lists, and Libraries with PowerShell

Windows PowerShell cmdlets provide a great deal of functionality and automation to the arsenal of SharePoint 2013 features. The `Export-SPWeb` cmdlet provides the capability to export not only webs, as the name suggests, but even lists and libraries, which can be imported back to the same farm or other SharePoint 2013 farms.

When using the `Export-SPWeb` cmdlet, the following options are available:

➤ `Identity` — This parameter specifies the URL or GUID of the web you want to export.

➤ `Path` — This parameter specifies where you want to save the .cmp files to the filesystem.

➤ `Force` —This switch lets you overwrite existing .cmp files from previous export attempts.

➤ `IncludeUserSecurity` — This specifies that you wish to maintain site- and item-level permissions, along with time stamps, in the exported content.

➤ `IncludeVersions` — Use this parameter to set the version level of history files to export. The following values can be specified for this parameter:

   ➤ Last major version for files and list items (default)

   ➤ The current version, either the last major version or the last minor version

   ➤ Last major and last minor version for files and list items

   ➤ All versions for files and list items

➤ `ItemUrl` — This parameter specifies the URL or GUID of the object you want to export. It is used for granular backups of lists and libraries within the site specified in the `Identity` parameter.

➤ `NoFileCompression` — Use this switch to disable compression of the exported content. This can be useful in situations where processing and memory resources are limited or you just want to increase the performance of the export. If your exports are failing due to time outs or other errors, this may be able to resolve them. Instead of writing out a .cmp file, the export is written to a directory.

➤ `NoLogFile` — This switch suppresses the creation of a log file during the export, which by default is generated in the same location as the export package.

➤ `UseSQLSnapshot` — If SharePoint is using an edition of SQL Server that supports snapshots, you can use this switch to specify whether the export should be executed against an SQL snapshot. To export a site using Windows PowerShell, use the following command in the SharePoint Management Shell:

```
Export-SPWeb -identity http://portal.contoso.com -path C:\backups\site.cmp
```

To export a list or library, use the following command syntax, (all on one line) adding the `ItemUrl` parameter:

```
Export-SPWeb -identity http://portal.contoso.com
-path C:\backups\list.cmp -ItemUrl
  "/Shared Documents"
```

To see all the parameters for this or any other PowerShell cmdlet, use the following syntax from the SharePoint 2013 Management Shell:

```
Get-Help Export-SPWeb -full
```

Importing Sites, Lists, and Libraries with PowerShell

Similar to the export functionality, the `Import-SPWeb` cmdlet provides the capability to import sites, lists, and libraries via the SharePoint 2013 Management Shell with the following options:

➤ `Identity` and `Path` — These parameters are used as you would use them with the `Export-SPWeb` cmdlet.

➤ `ActivateSolutions` — Use this switch if you want to automatically activate User Solutions during import.

➤ `Force` — As its name implies, this forces the import to continue, which is useful for overwriting existing content at the destination URL.

➤ `HaltOnError` and `HaltOnWarning` — These cause the import process to stop for failures, letting you know something went awry and enabling you to view the logs to determine what went wrong without having to wait for the entire import process to complete.

➤ `IncludeUserCustomAction` — This parameter specifies whether or not to import user custom actions during import.

➤ `IncludeUserSecurity` — This specifies whether or not to import the site and item-level security. This option is useful only if you specified the `IncludeUserSecurity` switch during export.

➤ `NoFileCompression` — Use this switch if the export was done using the same switch. Mixing compression switches between export and import packages results in failed imports.

➤ `NoLogFile` — As with the `Export-SPWeb` cmdlet, this suppresses the creation of a log file during import.

➤ `UpdateVersions` — This parameter, specifies the overwrite policy you want to use during import. You don't need to know what values were used for `IncludeVersions` in `Export-SPWeb`. All versions will be imported based on the following values:

   ➤ `Append` — Adds new versions to the current file (this is the default if nothing is specified)

   ➤ `Overwrite` — Deletes the existing file, then inserts the imported file and all of its versions

   ➤ `Ignore` — Skips the file if it exists on the destination

To import a site, list, or library, use the following syntax: (enter this all on one line)

```
Import-SPWeb http://portal.contoso.com
-Path C:\backups\list.cmp -UpdateVersions
Overwrite
```

When importing a site, the URL into which you are importing must be using the same template as the exported content. For example, if an exported site was created using the Team Site template (STS#0), the destination site must also use the STS#0 template.

Exporting Sites, Lists, and Libraries with Central Administration

As you can see, PowerShell provides a lot of flexibility when you are performing exports and imports, but sometimes you just need a quick and easy way to export some desired content. Central Administration also provides a way to export sites, lists, and libraries easily.

As we go through this section you will notice that the Backup and Restore page in Central Administration doesn't offer any means for importing your newly exported package. You will still need to use the PowerShell cmdlets covered earlier to perform an import.

To export a site, list, or library using Central Administration, do the following:

1. From the SharePoint 2013 Central Administration HomePage, click the Backup and Restore link in the Quick Launch.

2. On the Backup and Restore page, click the Export a site or list link under Granular Backups.

3. On the Site or List Export page (see Figure 9-10), select the drop-down for the site collection and choose your desired site collection in the pop-up window. You can switch the web application at this point as well.

4. Make similar selections for the Site and List drop-downs. If you don't want to get as granular as a list, just leave it unselected.

5. Once you have made your selections, enter the UNC path for the destination location and specify whether or not to overwrite the files at the destination.

6. The next check box specifies whether user security should be included with the export.

7. The last option is Export Versions. This option is set to All Versions by default. Other options, similar to the PowerShell options, are: Last Major, Current Version, and Last Major and Minor.

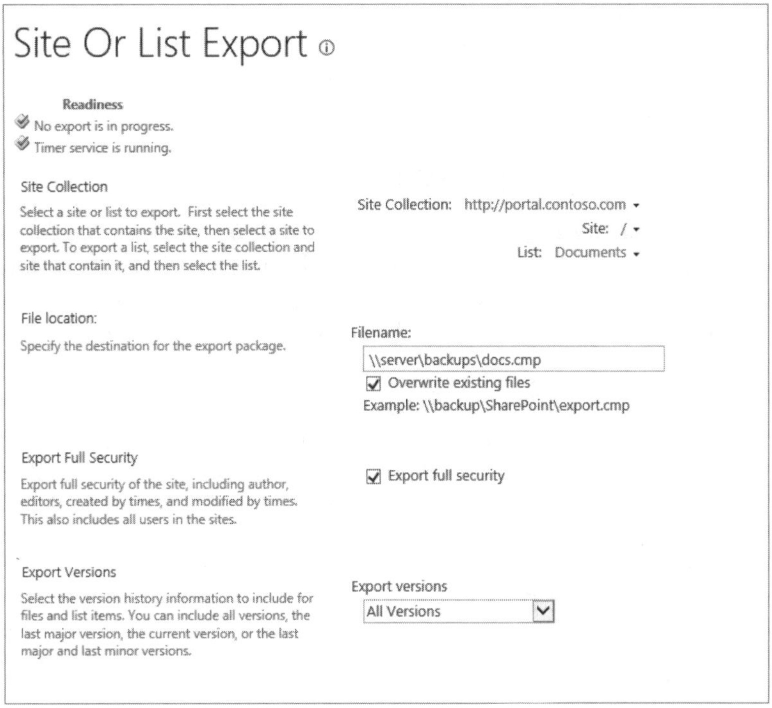

FIGURE 9-10

Why is there a UNC path, and not just a normal drive path? If you've set your farm up correctly (Least Privilege), your SharePoint Timer service is running as a user who has no privileges to the local filesystem on the Central Administration server. Requiring a UNC path forces you to configure a new file share (don't use the default admin file shares!) on any one of your servers, and give both the Timer Service and the SQL Service accounts Read/Write permissions to it. This little bit of up-front work offers greater flexibility and greatly reduces the likelihood of a failed export due to unknown permissions requirements, which could make your server less secure.

The reason this is not a requirement when exporting with PowerShell is because, as you've seen, the PowerShell code executes directly as the logged-in user, not the Timer Service. If the user is logged in directly to the server, it stands to reason that the user has permissions to the destination folder. If the user doesn't, PowerShell is kind enough to point that fact out.

Note that nondeclarative workflows and alerts are not exported with the content. Declarative workflows (workflows created with SharePoint Designer) will get exported, however they will not automatically be re-associated with their targeted lists or libraries. This is because the export and import tools are primarily focused on content deployment, so functionality that is not content is not always brought over. This is also true for many third-party add-ons that may have been used through the sites.

Also of note is that exports and imports, in addition to being part of a backup strategy, are also intended to be used to duplicate subsites, sometimes in the same farm. When exporting and importing a subsite, web and list IDs do not get retained. This can have a significant impact on web parts, or other processes, that refer to specific list IDs, and these will need to be reconfigured to point to the new list IDs once the import is completed. Be sure to test content exports and imports to verify that they cover all the pieces you think you are covering before you consider your disaster recovery mission accomplished.

Backing Up and Restoring Site Collections

Up to this point you have seen that sites, lists, and libraries can be backed up using PowerShell or Central Administration, but only PowerShell can restore them. The same holds true for site collection backups and restores with the exception of restoring from an unattached content database, which can only be done through Central Administration, not PowerShell.

Site collection backups can be a very useful tool in any backup strategy, but its usage should be limited to very important site collections under 100GB in size. That's because the site collection backup and restore can be very resource-intensive for the SQL server, which can affect performance or even fail if the site collection coexists with other active site collections in the same database. In any case, for site collections over 100GB, it is recommended that you backup and restore the content database itself, as covered later in this chapter.

Backing Up Site Collections with PowerShell

Like exports and imports, PowerShell is a very effective tool for performing site collection backups, whether you want to automate the task or just have more flexibility and control over it.

The `Backup-SPSite` cmdlet produces a single-file backup of a site collection with a .bak extension. Unlike the exports you performed earlier, these backups are full fidelity, meaning workflows, alerts, and everything else within the site collection is backed up. Site collection backups are portable, but with some restrictions. If you want to restore the site collection to the same farm from which it was backed up, you have to do some fancy footwork. A content database can contain only one copy of a given site collection. If you want to restore your backup to the same web application from which it was backed up, you need to either delete the original site collection or create a new content database into which the backup can be stored. Aside from that, the site collection backup may be restored to either the same farm or a different farm, as long as the destination farm is the same build or later as the source farm.

The `Backup-SPSite` cmdlet for performing a site collection backup offers some familiar and some not-so-familiar parameters for control:

➤ `Identity` and `Path` — These parameters, and the `Force` switch, should be familiar to you now. They work the same here as they do with other commands in this chapter.

➤ `NoSiteLock` — This switch specifies that the site collection should remain read/write during the backup operation.

➤ `UseSQLSnapshot` — If SharePoint is using an edition of SQL Server that supports snapshots, this switch specifies that an SQL Database Snapshot will be created when the backup begins, and all site collection data will be retrieved directly from the database snapshot, which is then deleted automatically when the backup completes. This parameter ensures that a valid backup occurs while enabling users to continue reading and writing to the site collection during the backup. It is not necessary to specify the `NoSiteLock` parameter when specifying this parameter.

The syntax for performing a single site collection backup is as follows (enter it all on a single line):

```
Backup-SPSite -Identity http://portal.contoso.com/sites/legal
-Path C:\backups\legal.bak
[-Force] [-NoSiteLock] [-UseSQLSnapshot] [-Verbose]
```

The beauty of PowerShell is the ability to get more done with less administrative effort. For example, if you needed to back up 30 site collections across 10 web applications, it would be a huge hassle to run the preceding command so many times. Instead, you can use the following syntax to loop through each web application in the farm, then each site collection, and back each one up (again, enter this all on a single line in PowerShell):

```
Get-SPWebApplication | Get-SPSite -Limit All | ForEach-Object{$FilePath =
"C:\backups\" +

$_.Url.Replace("http://","").Replace("/","-") +

".bak"; Backup-SPSite -Identity $_.Url -Path $FilePath}
```

Before you go off to conquer the world of site collection backups, check the size of any site collections you will be backing up to ensure that you won't exceed your server's drive space and risk corruption. The following command will print out the size of all of your site collections, in megabytes:

```
Start-SPAssignment -Global; Get-SPWebApplication | Get-SPSite |
ForEach-Object{
(Get-SPSiteAdministration -Identity $_)} |
ForEach-Object{Write-Host $_.Url "size in megabytes: ";

 [math]::truncate($_.DiskUsed / 1MB)}; Stop-SPAssignment -Global
```

Restoring Site Collections with PowerShell

Site Collection backups are not much good unless you can restore them. As you likely assume, just as there is a `Backup-SPSite` cmdlet, there is a complementary `Restore-SPSite` cmdlet. As always, using the `Get-Help` cmdlet will provide all the gory details about the `Restore-SPSite` cmdlet.

Along with the regulars such as `Identity`, `Path` and `Force`, the `Restore-SPsite` cmdlet has some additional parameters that provide flexibility in terms of how your site collections are restored:

➤   `DatabaseName` and `DatabaseServer` — These parameters enable you to direct the restore to not only a specific content database, but even to an alternate SQL server than your default.

➤   `HostHeaderWebApplication` — This parameter restores the site collection as a host-named site collection (i.e., the site collection is named `site.domain.com` instead of `/sites/sitename`). When this parameter is used, the `Identity` parameter becomes the URL of the host-named site collection, while the `HostHeaderWebApplication` parameter is the URL of the web application that will host the site collection.

➤   `Force` — If you are using the `Force` switch to overwrite an existing site collection that is very large, it is recommended to use the `GradualDelete` switch. This switch specifies that the existing site collection should be deleted slowly over time to minimize the resource impact on the SQL server during the restore.

To restore a site collection using PowerShell, use the following syntax (you guessed it, all on a single line in PowerShell):

```
Restore-SPSite -Identity http://portal.contoso.com/sites/legal
-Path
C:\backups\legal.bak [-DatabaseServer <Database Server Name>]
[-DatabaseName
<Content Database Name>] [-Force] [-GradualDelete]
[-Verbose]
```

Backing Up Site Collections with Central Administration

Similar to the export functionality, Central Administration provides functionality for performing site collection backups. Unfortunately, the same limitations apply — namely there is no functionality for restoring a site collection through Central Administration. You must use PowerShell, as discussed earlier in this chapter, to restore any backed up site collections to your farm.

To perform a site collection backup using Central Administration, follow these steps:

1. From the Central Administration homepage, click the Backup and Restore link in the Quick Launch.

2. Under Granular Backup, click Perform a Site Collection backup.

3. On the Site Collection Backup page (see Figure 9-11), select the drop-down for the site collection and choose your desired site collection in the pop-up window. You can switch the web application at this point as well.

4. The only other setting you need to set on this page is the UNC path to the file location, as explained earlier in the section, "Exporting Sites, Libraries, and Lists with Central Administration."

5. Click Start Backup to begin the backup process.

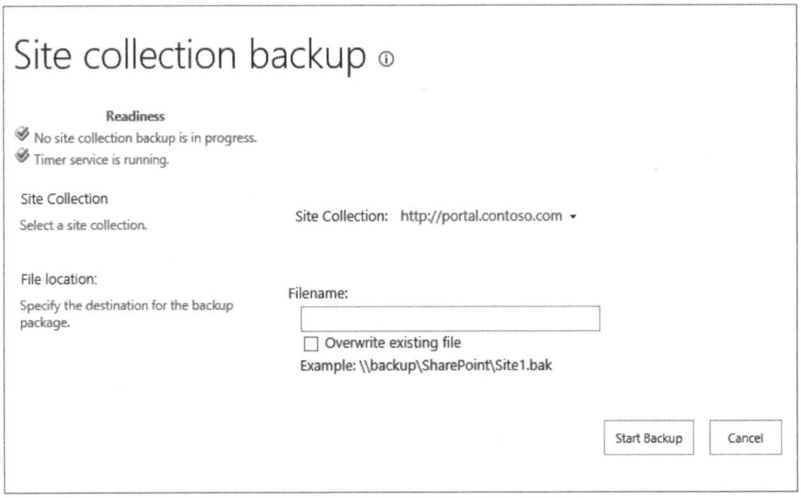

FIGURE 9-11

Whether you back up your site collections with PowerShell or Central Admin, you need to practice restoring them *before* a disaster strikes. Those practice runs let you test the process in peace without your phone ringing constantly, your IM client blinking incessantly, and your boss tapping his foot impatiently while you figure out how to restore a site collection. It's much easier to figure it out without all those distractions. A couple of practice runs will also help you build your confidence, so in the unlikely event of a SharePoint disaster you'll know you can restore that important content, and maybe you'll be able to avoid that painful knot in the pit of your stomach.

Restoring from an Unattached Content Database

Imagine a situation in which a deleted document has expired or was emptied out of the stage 1 and stage 2 Recycle Bins. It wouldn't make sense to restore an entire content database, site collection, site, or even a whole library just to retrieve this one document. Any of these method's actions would result in a lot of collateral damage, as all the other documents are restored along with these containers.

Recall from earlier in the chapter that as long as you have a content database, you can always recover data. This is your first line of defense for the preceding situation. The capability to restore a content database to SQL Server and then recover data from it without ever attaching it to a web application is a feature that was added in SharePoint 2010, and it remains a lifesaving option in SharePoint 2013.

In order to restore content from an unattached content database, do the following:

1. Make sure that you have already restored a content database to your farm SQL server, or any other SQL server with which your SharePoint servers can communicate, and given your farm account DBO permission to it.

2. On the SharePoint 2013 homepage, select the Backup and Restore link in the Quick Launch.

3. Under the Granular Backup section on the Backup and Restore page, click the link "Recover data from an unattached content database."

4. On the Unattached Content Database Data Recovery page:

   a. Specify the database server to which the database has been restored, and the name of the restored database.

   b. Choose whether to use Windows Integrated or SQL authentication. The default is Windows and will be the one most often used.

   c. Choose from the three operations: Browse content, Backup Site Collection, or Export site or list. These three options reflect the different methods discussed for getting data at each container level. Figure 9-12 shows an example.

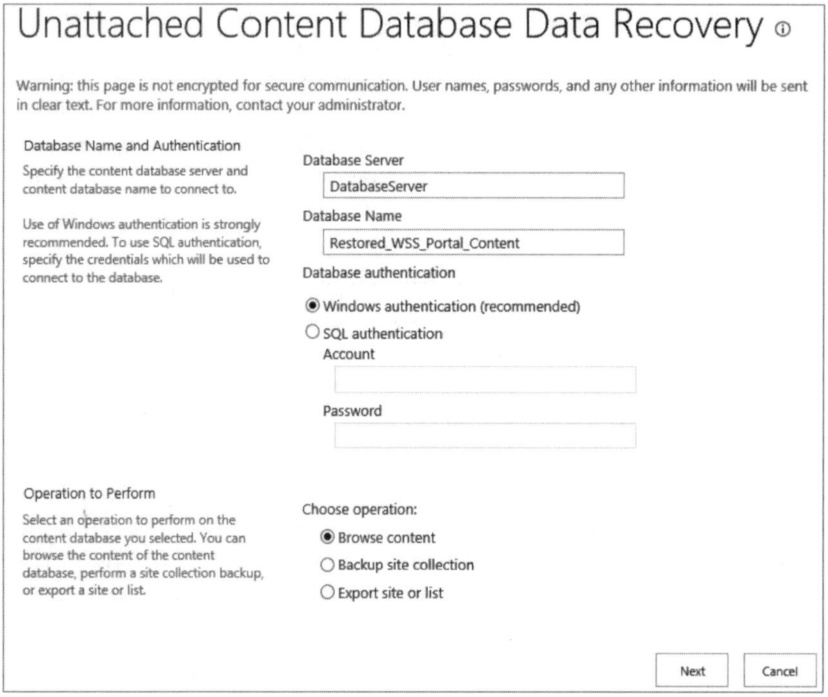

FIGURE 9-12

5. Click Next on the Unattached Content Database Data Recovery page.

6. If you chose the browse content operation, a dialog similar to the one shown in Figure 9-13 will appear:

  a. Select the site collection, site, or list (if desired) in the Site Collection section.

  b. Select either the Backup Site Collection or the Export site or list operation to perform.

FIGURE 9-13

7. If you chose to back up a site collection, the Site Collection backup page shown in Figure 9-14 will appear:

  a. Select the site collection from the drop-down in the Site Collection section.

  b. Specify the destination UNC path in the Filename field.

  c. Click Start Backup to begin the site collection backup process.

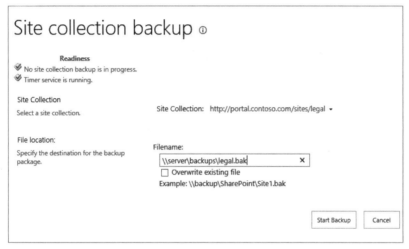

Site collection backup ⓘ

Readiness
✔ No site collection backup is in progress.
✔ Timer service is running.

Site Collection
Select a site collection.

Site Collection: http://portal.contoso.com/sites/legal ▾

File location:
Specify the destination for the backup package.

Filename:

\\server\backups\legal.bak   ✕
☐ Overwrite existing file
Example: \\backup\SharePoint\Site1.bak

[Start Backup]   [Cancel]

FIGURE 9-14

8. If you choose Export site or list, the Site or List Export page shown in Figure 9-15 will appear:

  a. Select the site collection, site, or list in the Site Collection section.

  b. Specify the destination UNC file path in the Filename field.

  c. In the Export Full Security section, choose whether or not to export with full security, which includes authors, editors, time stamps, and users.

  d. Click Start Export to begin the export process.

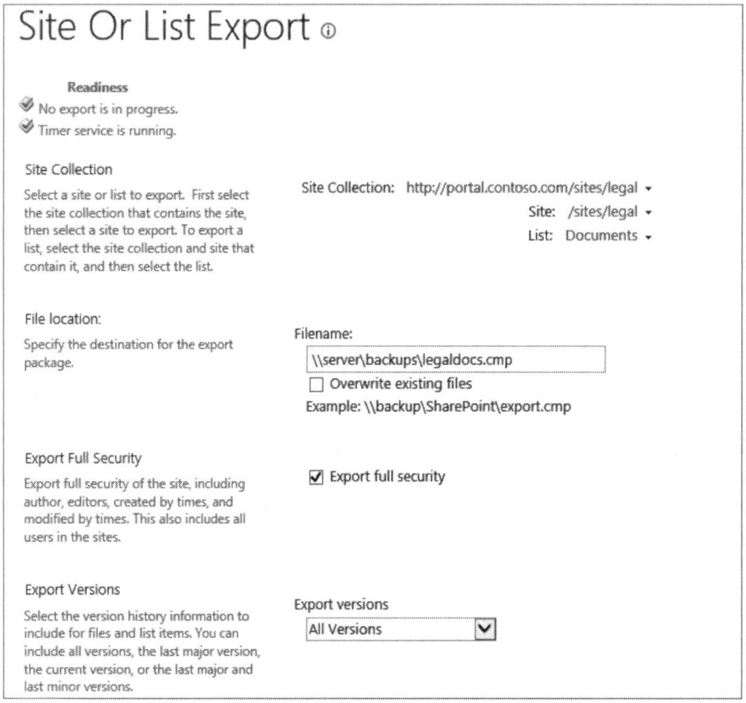

FIGURE 9-15

Recovering from SQL Server Snapshots

SQL Server snapshots are a feature of SQL Server Enterprise Editions only. This feature enables you to create a read-only view of the source database that is transactionally consistent with the source database at the time the snapshot is created. Restoring a snapshot to a live site overwrites previous values, bringing the content in the database back to the point in time at which the snapshot was created.

Although snapshots are useful for both reporting and recovery, they can have an adverse effect on the performance of an SQL server. This is due to the overhead of writing previous values to the snapshot because they are overwritten in the source, as well as the disk space required for an ever-growing snapshot. For this reason, the snapshot functionality is best used in development scenarios or as a method of rollback during a content push that may have undesirable effects.

Support for database snapshots was introduced in SharePoint 2010 and continues in SharePoint 2013. The only means for creating a snapshot is by using T-SQL statements through supported APIs, or via SQL Server Management Studio as shown in Figure 9-16. The method for creating the snapshot in SQL Server 2012 is virtually identical to its predecessors.

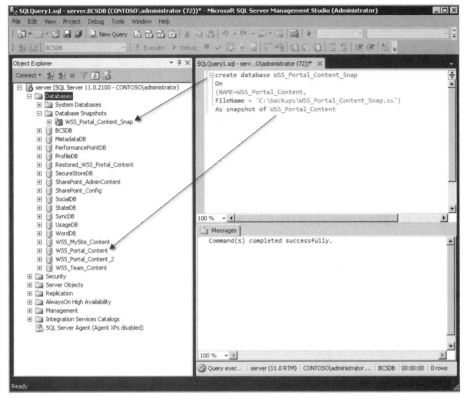

FIGURE 9-16

Some SharePoint operations, such as `Backup-SPSite`, automatically manage the creation of the SQL Server snapshot if you use the appropriate parameters.

BACKING UP AND RECOVERING FROM DISASTER

The preceding sections have covered many out-of-the-box features provided by SharePoint 2013 for recovering deleted or corrupted content. While these features should be an integral part of any business continuity plan for quickly recovering lost content, none of these features are truly sufficient for disaster recovery scenarios.

If your SQL server crashes, or the entire farm is wiped out due to a natural disaster and has to be rebuilt, recovering the data through individual site collection restores would be an arduous task, and it really only covers the content. You also need to get the rest of the farm services and service applications back up and running as quickly as possible. You would also need rebuild all the web applications and configure them. This section covers your available options for meeting the disaster recovery needs of your business continuity plan.

SharePoint 2013 provides tools and features to help you protect the following aspects of your farm and recover quickly from disaster:

- ➤ Full farm backup and restore
- ➤ Configuration databases
- ➤ Web applications
- ➤ Service applications
- ➤ Services

As with all content backup and restore functionality, all of the preceding disaster recovery backups can be performed through Central Administration and Windows PowerShell.

Backing Up and Restoring Content Databases

So far this chapter has focused on backing up and restoring different content within a content database. However, in a disaster or migration scenario, you are going to need a way to back up and restore entire content databases using either full or differential (any changes since the last full backup) methods.

Backing Up Content Databases with PowerShell

To back up a content database using Windows PowerShell, use the following syntax (on a single line):

```
Backup-SPFarm -Directory <Backup Folder> -BackupMethod (Full | Differential)
-Item
 <Content Database Name> [-Verbose]
```

Restoring Content Databases with PowerShell

Restoring a content database via Windows PowerShell is very similar in syntax to the backup command (on one line):

```
Restore-SPFarm -Directory <Backup Folder> -RestoreMethod Overwrite
-Item
 <Content Database Name> [-BackupId <GUID>] [-Verbose]
```

Backing Up Content Databases with Central Administration

To back up a content database using Central Administration, follow these steps:

1. Open the SharePoint 2013 Central Administration homepage and click the link for Backup and Restore on the Quick Launch.

2. Under Farm Backup and Restore, click Perform a backup.

3. In the first dialog that appears, "Perform a Backup - Step 1 of 2: Select Component to Backup", expand the web application node for the database you want to back up, and select the content database or web applications you want to backup. Unfortunately, in order to

back up multiple content databases in a single backup job, you have to back up an entire web application. Nor can you back up content databases across multiple web applications in a single backup job without backing up the entire farm. The check boxes lead you to assume that you can select several, but only the last content database you selected will be displayed on the next page. Be sure to double-check that what you think is being restored is what SharePoint thinks is being restored.

4. In the next dialog that appears, "Perform a Backup - Step 2 of 2: Select Backup Options", select Full in the Backup Type section, as shown in Figure 9-17.

5. Enter a UNC file path in the Filename field.

6. Click Start Backup.

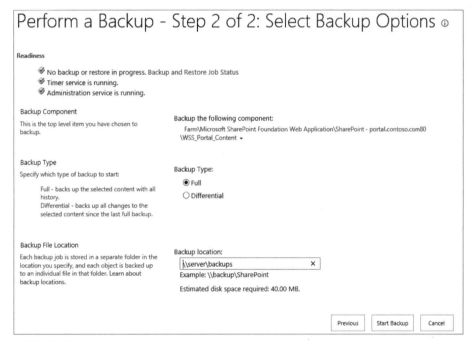

FIGURE 9-17

After the backup starts you can view the status of the job on the Backup and Restore Job Status page, shown in Figure 9-18. Selecting the View History link on the page will show you the status of previous jobs that have been run. If you have already browsed away from the page, you can get back to it by returning to Backup and Restore and clicking Check Backup and Restore Status under the Farm Backup and Restore section.

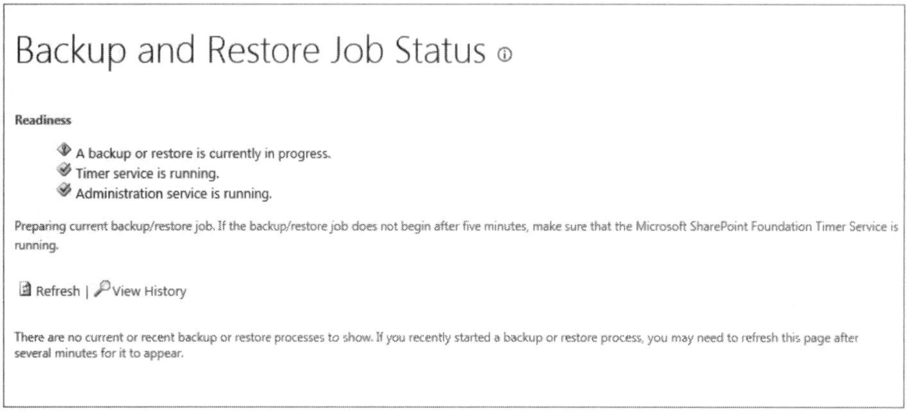

Backup and Restore Job Status ⓘ

Readiness

◆ A backup or restore is currently in progress.
◈ Timer service is running.
◈ Administration service is running.

Preparing current backup/restore job. If the backup/restore job does not begin after five minutes, make sure that the Microsoft SharePoint Foundation Timer Service is running.

🔲 Refresh | 🔎 View History

There are no current or recent backup or restore processes to show. If you recently started a backup or restore process, you may need to refresh this page after several minutes for it to appear.

FIGURE 9-18

Restoring Content Databases with Central Administration

Unlike previous examples, in which you could only back up certain content through Central Administration, but not restore it, you can restore content databases directly through Central Administration:

1. Open Central Administration and select Backup and Restore from the Quick Launch.

2. Under the Farm Backup and Restore section, click Restore from a backup.

3. On the Backup and Restore History page that appears, the Backup Directory field should already be filled in. If not, add the UNC path to the backup location. Once it loads you should be able to select from the previous backups in the bottom of the page.

4. Select the radio button for the backup from which you want to restore.

5. On the "Restore from Backup - Step 2 of 3: Select Component to Restore" page, expand down to the level you want to restore — in this case, the content database you just backed up. Click Next.

6. On the "Restore from Backup - Step 3 of 3: Select Restore Options" page, you are presented with the following restore options:

    ➤ **New Configuration** — This option allows you to perform a restore using alternative configurations such as different server names, web applications, and a different database server. Selecting this option enables the fields for these three parameters, enabling you to change their configuration. This is useful in a migration scenario, or perhaps to restore to a recovery farm so you can recover content without impacting a live farm.

    ➤ **Same Configuration** — This option restores the data directly back to its original location, overwriting as it goes. This is most useful if you just have missing content that you need to put back, but it overwrites any existing content.

Backing Up Content Databases with SQL Server

In addition to the core SharePoint backup and restore functionality, SQL Server provides several options for backing up and restoring content databases. Full and Simple recovery models enable you to specify whether you just want database backups at regular intervals (Simple), or whether you will need point-in-time recovery (Full).

If you have a third-party backup utility, you will probably use the Simple recovery model. Otherwise, you are likely to run into disk space issues as your SQL transaction logs grow very large without any maintenance. If you will be doing your backups via SQL maintenance plans, you may want to use the Full recovery model, which provides greater flexibility at the cost of more frequent backups. Maintenance plans can be configured to automatically truncate and shrink the transaction log files every time they are backed up, preventing the unmanaged growth mentioned earlier. It is not uncommon to see hourly transaction log backups to greatly reduce the risk of data loss in the event of a disaster and to keep the transaction log sizes small. For the greatest safety, you should never store the backup files on the same storage location as the original data files, but be aware that frequent transfers of large backup files across the network is not without its own impact on available resources.

In addition to the recovery models there are backup types, including Full, Differential, and Incremental. Depending on your specific recovery point and recovery time objectives, you will most likely combine these options to meet business needs. The Full database backup is the simplest form of backup, providing a complete copy of the content database. This works well for smaller databases for which the backup can be accomplished in a minimal amount of time. For larger databases it is common to move to a less frequent Full backup, weekly in some cases, with daily Differential or Incremental backups to pick up any changes since the Full backup.

Differentials capture any changes since the last full backup, so they tend to get bigger as the period between the last Full backup and the next Differential backup grows. When restoring via a Full/Differential combination, you only need to restore the Full database and then the last Differential right before the point-in-time you need restored. This can greatly speed up recovery time and is less likely to succumb to a bad backup due to data corruption in the backup files.

Incremental backups capture changes since the last Incremental backup was taken. This results in very fast and very compact backup files. However, when restoring, it is necessary to first restore the Full backup and then restore every Incremental up to the point in time you need restored. The other downside is that if any of the Incremental backup files in the chain are lost or corrupted, you won't be able to recover anything past that recovery point.

Follow these steps to perform a Full backup of an individual SharePoint 2013 content database using SQL Server Management Studio:

1. Open Microsoft SQL Server Management Studio and connect to the instance of SQL Server that hosts the SharePoint content database you want to back up.

2. In the Object Browser, click the server name to expand the server tree.

3. Expand the database and right-click the content database you want to back up.

4. Select Tasks ⇨ Back Up.

5. In the Back Up Database dialog (see Figure 9-19), verify the database name in the Database list box.

6. In the Backup type list box, select Full.

7. For Backup component, select Database.

8. For the Backup set name, you can either use the default name that is given or provide your own descriptive name. You may also add a description of the backup set in the Description field to help identify the backup set more easily in larger, more complex environments.

9. Choose Disk for the Backup destination type.

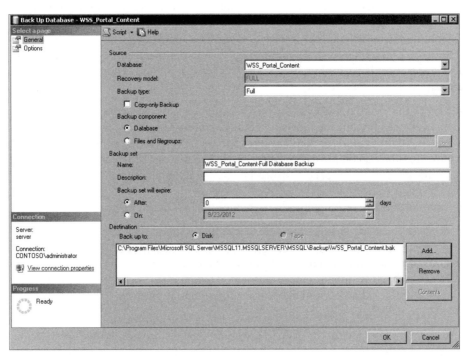

FIGURE 9-19

Restoring Content Databases with SQL Server

To perform a restore of an individual SharePoint 2013 content database using SQL Server Management Studio, do the following:

1. Open Microsoft SQL Server Management Studio and connect to the instance of SQL that hosts the SharePoint content database you want to back up.

2. In the Object Browser, click the server name to expand the server tree.

3. For production databases it is most common to restore the database to an alternate database and then use the built-in SharePoint tools to recover content from an unattached database. To do this, right-click Databases and select Restore Database.

4. In the Restore Database dialog (see Figure 9-20), verify the database name in the Database list box.

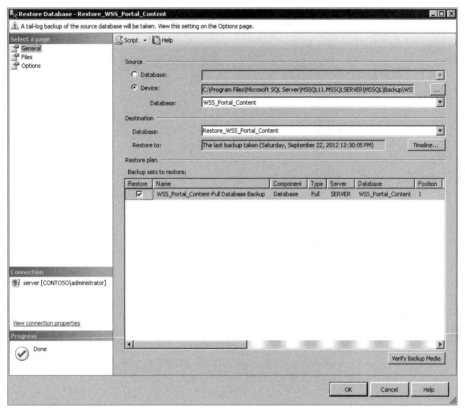

FIGURE 9-20

5. Under the Source section, select Device: and click the ellipsis (...) button.

6. Click the Add button and select the database backup file you created in the previous section, and then click OK twice to return to the Restore Database dialog.

7. Under Destination, change the Database: field to a database name other than the original name.

8. To ensure that the database also restores to a new set of .mdf and .ldf files, click the Files link in the left-hand menu.

9. In the Restore As section, ensure that you rename both files to match your new database name. Failure to do this step will result in SQL Server trying to restore over the existing filesystem files even though you gave it a new database name (see Figure 9-21).

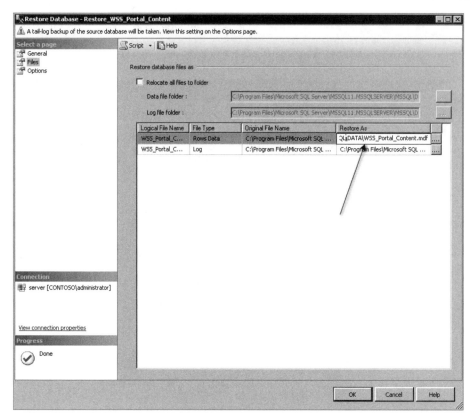

FIGURE 9-21

10 The default setting when restoring a database in SQL Server 2012 is to take a tail-log backup of the source database prior to restoring and leave it in the restoring state (using the WITH NORECOVERY option). A *tail-log backup* captures any log transactions that have not been backed up yet. Before you can perform a point-in-time recovery of an SQL Server database, you must back up the tail of its transaction log. Because you are restoring to a new database and not over the original, you need to remove this setting; otherwise, the restore will fail because SQL Server cannot gain exclusive access to the in-use content database in order to change its restore state, which you wouldn't want it to do in this case anyway.

11. Click the link on the left named Options.

12. Under Tail-Log backup, un-check the box labeled "Take tail-log backup before restore."

13. Click General to return to the main settings page.

14. Ensure that the backup set is checked and click OK to begin restoring the database to a new name.

Backing Up and Restoring Service Applications

The service application architecture of SharePoint 2013 expands upon the service applications provided in the previous version. Several new service applications, with associated databases, have been added, while others have been updated or removed. The methods for backing up and restoring service applications remain much the same as they were before.

As with many of the other backup and restore scenarios covered previously, the two options available are Windows PowerShell cmdlets and Central Administration. Using these tools you have the option to back up entire service applications, including data, or just each service application's unique configuration.

Backing Up Service Applications with PowerShell

To back up a service application using Windows PowerShell, you first need to get the path and name of the service application you want to back up using the following command:

```
Backup-SPFarm -ShowTree
```

This command outputs a tree structure of the farm layout. You need to know the full path of the service application through this tree in order to use to the Backup-SPFarm command. It looks something like the following:

```
Farm\Shared Services\Shared Services Applications\

Business Data Connectivity Services\
```

To perform the backup of the service application, use the following syntax in the SharePoint Management Shell, replacing the example -Item path with the correct path to your service application:

```
Backup-SPFarm -Directory C:\backups -BackupMethod (Full | Differential)
-Item
"Farm\Shared Services\Shared Services Applications\
Business Data Connectivity Services\" [-Verbose]
```

Restoring Service Applications with PowerShell

To perform a restore of a service application, first look up the Operation ID of the backup you want to restore from using the following command:

```
Get-SPBackupHistory -Directory C:\backups -ShowBackup
```

To perform the actual restore, use the following syntax:

```
Restore-SPFarm -Directory C:\backups -Item "Farm\Shared Services\
Shared Services
Applications\Business Data Connectivity Services\"
-RestoreMethod Overwrite [ -BackupId <OperationID>] [-Verbose]
```

Backing Up Service Applications with Central Administration

Backing up and restoring a service application in Central Administration is nearly identical to the content database backup. To perform a service application backup, do the following:

1. Browse to the Central Administration homepage, and under Backup and Restore click the Perform a Backup link.

2. On the Perform a Backup page, expand down to the Shared Services ⇨ Shared Services Applications node, select the service application you want to back up, and then click Next.

3. For step 2 you can choose either the Full or Differential backup type. If you are unsure or this is the first backup, just leave it at the default selection, which is Full.

4. Enter a UNC path for the backup location and click Start Backup to begin the backup process.

Restoring Service Applications with Central Administration

To restore a service application through Central Administration, do the following:

1. Browse to the Central Administration homepage, and under Backup and Restore click the Restore from a backup link.

2. Ensure that the backup location path is correct, select the desired backup to restore from, and click Next.

3. On the "Restore from Backup: Step 2" page, you will see a breakdown of what can be restored from this backup. Expand down to Shared Services ⇨ Shared Services Applications, and select the service application you want to restore from this backup.

4. At Step 3 you are presented with the option of either restoring to a new service application, which is the default, or overwriting the existing service application. If you choose to restore to a new service application, you will have the following fields to fill out:

   ➤ **Login Names and Passwords** — This is the login and password for the application pool under which the service application runs. The default is the service application account name that was backed up. To continue with this account you just need to provide the password for that account.

   ➤ **New Name** — This is the display name of the service application. You should specify a different name here to avoid conflicts.

   ➤ The following three database configuration options will be repeated for each database associated with the service application being restored:

      ➤ **New Directory Name** — This is the location where you want the SQL Server database files to be stored when they are restored to SQL Server.

      ➤ **New Database Name** — This is the database name. Choose a new name to avoid naming conflicts.

      ➤ **New Database Server Name** — The database server name enables you to either use the original database server or specify a different one.

5. Click Start Restore.

Backing Up Service Applications with SQL Server

Many service applications have databases; and when they do, the contents of the database are what you really care about — the configuration of the service application itself is pretty trivial. In most cases you can back up the service application's database in SQL Server and restore it to a new instance of that service application. You'll still need to configure it, but you won't lose any data.

For instance, if you back up your Managed Metadata service application database, you've backed up all your term sets. To recover that data you could create a new Managed Metadata service application, in either the original farm or a new one. When you're asked to provide a database name for the service application, give it the name to which you restored the database. When the Managed Metadata service application comes online, it will have all the terms that were in the database. You may still need to configure the service application's permissions, or whether it's the default Managed Metadata service application, but that's small potatoes compared to re-creating the terms themselves. The following service applications support being created with restored databases:

➤ Managed Metadata

➤ Business Connectivity Services

➤ Search (Admin database only)

➤ User Profile Service (Social and Profile databases only)

➤ Secure Store

Backing Up the Farm

The capability to perform a Full farm backup is useful in situations for which an entire farm topology needs to be recovered to existing hardware or to a standby configuration. However, the usefulness of this type of backup depends on your RPOs and RTOs, as this sort of farm restore results in prolonged downtime in order to bring a new standby farm online. Organizations with large, complex topologies will be better served using more efficient methodologies such as a warm standby solution using SQL Server log-shipping to maintain up-to-date copies of the farm databases between live and standby SQL servers.

In addition to Full farm backups is the capability to back up just the farm configuration. This feature makes hardware migration scenarios, and duplicating farm configurations between development and production, a breeze. The farm configuration backup backs up only the elements of the configuration that are not tied to the unique properties of the farm being backed up, such as server names, web applications, service applications, and so on. This enables you to duplicate the root configuration of your farm, such as InfoPath Forms Service configuration, sandbox solutions, farm solution configuration, and so on, without having to worry about differences in topology.

Backing Up the Farm with PowerShell

To perform a farm backup using Windows PowerShell, enter the following command in the Microsoft SharePoint 2013 Management Shell:

```
Backup-SPFarm -Directory <Backup folder> -BackupMethod {Full | Differential}

[ -Verbose]
```

If an error occurs during the backup, you can view the `spbackup.log` file created in the backup directory. As a best practice, you should always use the `-Verbose` switch to monitor the operation and its status. For farms that have not been previously backed up, you must use the `-Full` switch. If you only want to capture the farm configuration, add the `-ConfigurationOnly` switch to the preceding command.

> **BACKUP-SPCONFIGURATIONDATABASE**
>
> If you're the curious type and you've done some spelunking in PowerShell, you might be familiar with a similarly named cmdlet called `Backup-SPConfigurationDatabase`. These would seem to do the same thing. Microsoft didn't do this just to confuse you, but there is a slight, but significant difference. You use `Backup-SPFarm` to back up your live farm, the way you're accustomed to using PowerShell. `Backup-SPConfigurationDatabase` backs up the configuration from a ConfigDB that is not attached to your current SharePoint farm. You would use this to back up the configuration from a ConfigDB you've restored in SQL Server but are not actually using in the current SharePoint farm. The use for this cmdlet is extremely limited, but it's there if you need it.

Restoring the Farm with PowerShell

To restore from a full farm backup, use the following syntax:

```
Restore-SPFarm -Directory C:\backups -RestoreMethod {New | Overwrite} [ -Verbose]
```

As with a farm backup, if an error occurs during the restore, you can view the `spbackup.log` file created in the backup directory. As a best practice, always use the `-Verbose` switch to monitor the operation and its status. Similarly, use the `-ConfigurationOnly` switch to restore only the farm configuration.

Backing Up the Farm with Central Administration

By now a pattern should be emerging. Backing up various elements of a farm is done using the same Perform a Backup link in Central Administration. The primary difference is the selections you make. To perform a backup of the entire farm, do the following:

1. Browse to the Central Administration homepage. Under Backup and Restore, click the Perform a Backup link.

2. On the "Perform a Backup – Step 1 of 2: Select a Component to Back Up" page, select Farm under the Components section, and then click Next.

3. On the "Perform a Backup – Step 2 of 2: Select Backup Options" page you can choose either the Full or Differential backup type. Select "Full" unless you have already performed a Full backup and just want the changes.

4. You can also specify whether to back up content and configuration, or just the farm configuration.

5. Enter a UNC path for the backup location and click Start Backup to begin the backup process.

Restoring the Farm with Central Administration

To restore a farm through Central Administration, do the following:

1. Browse to the Central Administration homepage. Under Backup and Restore, click the Restore from a backup link.

2. Ensure that the backup location path is correct, select the desired backup to restore from, and click Next.

3. On the "Restore from Backup: Step 2" page, you will see a breakdown of what can be restored from this backup. Select the farm.

4. At Step 3 you are presented with the option of restoring either content and configuration, which is the default, or just the configuration. If you choose to restore the content and configuration, you will be presented with the following groups of options to configure:

   ➤ **Restore Options** — Select from New Configuration or Same Configuration. New configuration enables you to specify new server names, web application names, or database servers. Same Configuration assumes that all the pieces of the farm are the same as when the backup was taken.

   ➤ **Login Names and Passwords** — This specifies the login and password for the application pools under which the service applications and web applications will run. The default is the account names that were backed up. To continue with these accounts you just need to provide the passwords for each account.

   ➤ **New Names** — This specifies the display name of the service applications and web applications. You should specify a different name here to avoid naming conflicts. Also, many of the service application and web application configurations have additional modifiable fields where you can customize their restored configuration.

5. Click Start Restore.

Backing Up IIS

Another area that you should address in your backup strategy is the IIS configuration of your SharePoint farm. While not recommended as a restore source due to SharePoint's control of the site configuration, the backups should be performed as a documentation strategy to keep track of nonstandard changes to the web.config file or the folder structure of the sites in case they ever need to be rebuilt.

IIS includes a command-line utility for performing backups and restores of the \windows\system32\inetsrv\config directory. This is the location where all IIS configuration settings are stored.

In order to back up your IIS configuration, run the following command:

```
%windir%\system32\inetsrv\appcmd.exe add backup "First IIS Backup"
```

Use this to restore:

```
%windir%\system32\inetsrv\appcmd.exe add restore "First IIS Backup"
```

In addition to the capability to perform the preceding on-demand IIS backup, IIS 7 has an out-of-the-box feature that automatically captures the configuration history as changes take place. This feature takes snapshots of the `ApplicationHost.config` file anytime a change is detected, enabling you to restore up to 10 previous versions. IIS checks every 120 seconds for a new version of the `ApplicationHost.config` file, and then stores the versions in the `%systemdrive%\inetpub\history` folder. You can find and change the settings that specify how often IIS checks and where the versions are stored in the `<system.applicationHost/configHistory>` section of the `ApplicationHost.config` file itself.

Backing Up Customizations

Although all your content will be backed up with the content databases, if you have made any sort of customizations you should be sure to back up every piece of supporting material to ensure a smooth recovery. Some of the possible customizations include the following:

➤ Registry modifications in support of third-party add-ons such as an iFilter

➤ Custom assemblies deployed to the global assembly cache (GAC)

➤ `Web.config` changes made manually, outside of the object model

Customizations that are typically contained within the content database, but could have elements found elsewhere in the filesystem, such as new SharePoint Features which are the primary type of customizations deployed in on-premises configurations, include the following:

➤ Master pages, cascading style sheets (CSS), or custom page layouts (though these should really be stored in SharePoint)

➤ Web Parts, site and list definitions, content types, custom actions, and so on (these should be installed via Solutions)

➤ Third-party solutions

The preferred method for backing up customizations deployed by a development team is to use the built-in features of the development environment, such as Visual Studio Team Foundation, through which the development team can maintain version histories of the codebase along with any related documentation. The benefit of this development method is that it makes it much easier to redeploy any solutions in the event of a disaster.

In addition to the preceding examples, there could also be customizations that fall outside the scope of the development environment's control. Other places that you might find additional customizations include the SharePoint 15 root, located at `%commonfiles%\Microsoft Shared\Web Server Extensions\15`, the website root folder, at `%systemdrive%\inetpub`, and the GAC, at `%windir%Assembly`. It is important to ensure that any customizations deployed to these locations are well documented and captured in the standard filesystem backups.

HIGH-AVAILABILITY CONFIGURATIONS

Up to this point the chapter has discussed what to back up and what to do in the case of an outage, or worse. However, as stated by Ben Franklin, "An ounce of prevention is worth a pound of cure." This is just as true when it comes to technology, if not more so. This section covers several things you can do to both avert and weather a bad storm caused by hardware failures, natural disaster, and anything else known to keep administrators from sleeping well at night.

SharePoint 2013 offers several configurations to support scalability, redundancy, and efficient mitigation of downtime. The configurations discussed in this section cover load-balancing, SQL Server 2012 AlwaysOn Failover Clustering and Availability Groups, request-throttling, and site collection gradual deletion. Each of these configurations has a price tag that must be weighed against any service-level agreements in place in your organization.

Load-Balancing

SharePoint 2013 supports several options for load-balancing the environment, some of which can be configured within SharePoint itself, and others that will likely require additional hardware and resources. The most common configuration is to load balance through either a hardware or a software load balancer to ensure that requests going to the SharePoint sites are divided equally among the web front ends. Whether you choose a hardware or a software, load balancer will mostly depend on the capabilities and scale required to meet your objectives.

New to SharePoint 2013 is the Request Manager service. This new service works in concert with a hardware or software load balancer. It enables a SharePoint administrator to define rules that control what traffic goes to which web front-end server. One of the many rules you can create is based on server health, which helps you balance the load and relieve your farm's busiest servers. You can read more about the Request Manager service in Chapter 2, "Architecture and Capacity Planning."

SharePoint's service application architecture enables you to create multiple service endpoints throughout your farm to help with load-balancing and failover redundancy of service application requests. You can accomplish this by doing the following:

1. Browse to the Central Administration homepage.

2. Select System Settings ➪ Manage services.

3. Change to the server to which you want to add a service application endpoint and find the service for that service application.

4. Click Start next to the service.

Once you have a service running across multiple servers, SharePoint will manage the service application requests in a round-robin fashion. A service application proxy will request an endpoint for a connected service application from SharePoint's internal load balancer, which is a software component that executes in the same process as the proxy itself. The load balancer keeps a cache of each of the service application endpoints, and returns the next available endpoint.

SQL AlwaysOn Failover-Clustering

Introduced in SQL Server 2005, failover-clustering remains one of the most valuable means for averting SharePoint disasters, as the majority of SharePoint configuration and content is stored within the databases themselves.

Clustering enables the use of a local online spare, referred to as a *passive node*. If the first, or *active node*, reboots, has a service crash, or dies altogether, the passive node becomes active and picks up where the previous server left off. Because the active and passive nodes share the same storage, this can shave hours, and in some cases days, off of a hardware or software failure recovery. The clustered servers are directly connected by a network connection through which a "heartbeat" signal is bounced between the servers. Anytime the active node does not respond to a heartbeat, the passive node assumes all clustering responsibilities.

The clustering itself is accomplished through the use of software such as Microsoft Clustering Services. You can find more information on configuring a cluster at `http://technet.microsoft .com/en-us/library/cc731844(v=ws.10).aspx`.

SQL Server AlwaysOn Availability Groups

SQL Server clustering is great for protection against local hardware or software failures, but it is not going to be much help if your server room is flooded, or in the case of a power outage. Although SQL Server mirroring has been deprecated as of SQL Server 2012, SharePoint 2013 also offers support for the new SQL Server 2012 Availability Groups (AG) in order to provide the capability to replicate your configuration and data to different geographic locations in either a hot or warm spare configuration. Some of the enhancements in SQL Server 2012 Availability Groups over mirroring include the following:

➤ You can configure up to four additional copies of your databases across different SQL server nodes.

➤ You can configure the copies to be a mix of synchronous and asynchronous, to meet the communicative limitations between the nodes.

➤ AGs enable a separate SharePoint recovery farm to have read-only access to the mirrored databases on a remote SQL Server node. This is useful in DR scenarios for which you need immediate access to recover up-to-the-minute data.

The two configuration types for Availability Groups allow for both high availability and disaster recovery at the same time, which is in stark contrast to SQL Server mirroring:

➤ **Synchronous** — This configuration provides a hot standby solution for rapid failover with minimal (in-flight transactions at the moment of network disruption) data loss. It is accomplished by requiring that the mirror acknowledge each transaction before it can be committed to the principal database. This configuration provides the quickest failover and data resiliency, but it has inherent inefficiencies when long distances separate the servers, such as network problems or issues with the mirror database, which can have a detrimental impact on the principal. This configuration should be used when the network link between nodes is greater than 1Gb with less than 10ms of latency.

➤ **Asynchronous** — This configuration is better suited to disaster recovery scenarios, as it operates in high-performance mode, rather than high availability. This provides greater efficiency and has less impact on the principal if there are minor errors with the mirror. This configuration is ideally suited to slower network links between SQL Server nodes, such as with WAN links.

Availability Groups are included only with the Enterprise Edition of SQL Server 2012. For those still using Standard Edition of SQL Server 2012, or earlier versions of SQL Server, mirroring is still an option supported by both SharePoint 2013 and SQL Server 2012, but it is scheduled to be phased out of the product line in future releases.

HTTP Request Throttling

As with any website, there may come a time when the user load overtakes your server resources in the farm. This can lead to lost farm data if a user clicks Submit and gets an error. The obvious solution is to add more servers or give your existing servers more resources; but despite how my Dell loves this option to vendors, it can sometimes involve lengthy order and delivery processes, not to mention the red tape associated with justifying new expenses.

In the meantime, you don't want your users to experience extremely long page load times and latency when trying to access their content — or worse yet, dropped sessions altogether. A feature added in SharePoint 2010 and continued in SharePoint 2013 is HTTP Request Monitoring and Throttling. Servers use the settings of this feature to determine how to handle resource load on each of the SharePoint servers in the farm. Each server checks resources every five seconds to determine load, comparing the data against the defined acceptable thresholds. If a server exceeds the acceptable thresholds three times in a row, it goes into throttled mode. Web applications that have the HTTP Throttling enabled stop accepting new session requests, opting to instead deliver an HTTP 503 error, "The server is busy now. Try again later." Meanwhile, existing sessions continue to function, ensuring that the impact of server load is as minimally disruptive as possible.

Additionally, no new timer jobs will start on that server, and any running jobs will be paused if possible. The server continues to check itself every five minutes, and remains throttled until the server resources fall back below the defined thresholds. All the throttling activity is logged to the System log in the Event Viewer. By default in SharePoint 2013, HTTP Request Monitoring and Throttling is enabled for any new web applications that are created. However, you can disable it through either PowerShell or Central Administration (covered in the following sections).

Enabling HTTP Request Monitoring and Throttling with PowerShell

To get the current values associated with HTTP Request Monitoring and Throttling via PowerShell, use the following syntax:

```
Get-SPWebApplicationHttpThrottlingMonitor -identity http://portal.contoso.com
```

To change the current settings for HTTP Request Monitoring and Throttling, use this syntax:

```
Set-SPWebApplicationHttpThrottlingMonitor -identity http://portal.contoso.com
```

Enabling HTTP Request Monitoring and Throttling with Central Administration

To configure HTTP Request Monitoring and Throttling from Central Administration, follow these steps:

1. On the SharePoint 2013 Central Administration homepage, select Application Management ➪ Manage web applications.

2. On the Manage Web Applications page, select a web application from the list of available web applications and click the General Settings drop-down menu on the Ribbon.

3. From the General Settings menu options, select Resource Throttling.

4. In the Resource Throttling dialog, select On or Off in the HTTP Request Monitoring and Throttling section.

5. Click OK.

List-Throttling

In addition to overall server resource monitoring and throttling functionality, SharePoint 2013 helps administrators proactively limit resource consumption caused by large SharePoint list views. This is accomplished through settings that can be used to restrict queries executed against large lists. These settings are configured per web application, which provides the flexibility to choose behavior rules based on need or importance.

To configure list-throttling from Central Administration, follow these steps:

1. On the SharePoint 2013 Central Administration homepage, select Application Management ➪ Manage web applications.

2. On the Manage Web Applications page, select a web application from the list of available web applications and click the General Settings drop-down menu on the Ribbon.

3. From the General Settings menu options, select Resource Throttling.

4. In the Resource Throttling dialog, specify a value for each setting you wish to configure:

➤ **List View Threshold** — Specifies the maximum number of items that can be retrieved in a single request. The default value is 5,000; the minimum value is 2,000.

➤ **Object Model Override** — Users to whom you give appropriate permissions can override the list view threshold programmatically. The default is yes, leaving it up to the administrator to determine who has this access.

➤ **List View Threshold for Auditors and Administrators** — This setting enables a greater number of items to be queried by auditors and administrators when using the object model. Default setting is 20,000 items.

➤ **List View Lookup Threshold** — This setting specifies the maximum number of Lookup, Person/Group, or Workflow status fields that are returned in a single request. Default setting is 8.

➤ **Daily Time Window for Large Queries** — This setting specifies a time and duration during which users can execute large queries without triggering the configured thresholds. This setting is disabled by default.

➤ **List Unique Permissions Threshold** —When querying a list view, items are security trimmed to ensure that users see only what their permissions allow. When a large list also has an excessive amount of individual permissions, it takes longer to trim and return relevant results. This setting specifies the maximum number of unique permissions that an individual list can support. The default value is 50,000.

5. Click OK.

Gradual Site Deletion

In the good old days, sodas cost a dime, the talky movies cost a quarter, and you could take SharePoint down simply by deleting a web or site collection. In some rare, though not nearly rare enough, circumstances, if a web containing a lot of documents was deleted, SQL Server would lock the AllDocs table as it deleted them all. As you surely know, a locked AllDocs table makes for very sad SharePoint. As soon as that table locked, all the site collections in that content database were unavailable. As SharePoint's adoption grew, this scenario became more and more common. Microsoft put their best and brightest minds to finding a solution. Gradual Site Delete was the silver bullet they came up with, and it's a pretty good one.

Gradual Site Delete operates via a timer job to efficiently dispose of deleted sites with minimal impact to the server's resources.

The Gradual Site Delete timer job, which is scoped at the Web Application level, breaks up the site deletion into smaller chunks, which are less likely to cause resource contention. The first piece that is removed is the pointer to the Site Collection from the configuration database and from the Sites table in the content database. The timer job deletes 1,000 rows at a time until the site has been completely removed. Although there isn't any configuration that a farm administrator can change to affect how this job executes, it warrants a mention in this section to round out our discussion of making a farm more highly available.

> **NOTE** *When using PowerShell cmdlets, such as* `Remove-SPSite` *or* `Remove-SPDeletedSite`, *the Gradual Site Delete Timer jobs are not executed by default.*

SUMMARY

As you can tell from the size of this chapter, you have many methods for protecting SharePoint data and configuration. The types of business problems you are protecting against and the budget you have to work with will largely determine which of these techniques you make use of in your business continuity planning.

Content recovery tends to be the first and most important aspect of any backup strategy. The more end users can do for themselves in regard to using the Recycle Bin and versioning functionality, the better. In addition to entire content backups, you also looked at methods for backing up or exporting specific pieces of content such as lists, sites, and site collections.

The second area of attention for mitigating catastrophe is to make use of the high-availability support in SharePoint 2013, and related products such as SQL Server Failover Clustering and AlwaysOn Availability Groups. The scope of your high-availability solution will be largely determined by your service-level agreements and budget constraints.

Disaster recovery is something that everyone needs and hopes never to use. When all else fails, a good disaster recovery solution can save the day. Although numerous technologies and methods were discussed in this chapter, no one solution will fit every scenario. This introduction to what SharePoint 2013 has to offer should help you get started building a solid business continuity plan. Remember, the three most important parts of any business continuity plan is test, test, and test. Test restoring your backups. Test failing over your databases. Test it all. That's the best way to build confidence in your plan, and hone your skills. The best way to get better at anything is to do it a lot.

10

Managing SharePoint Developer Solutions and Features

WHAT'S IN THIS CHAPTER?

➤ Understanding and managing farm solutions

➤ Understanding and managing sandbox solutions

➤ Working with Features

WROX.COM CODE DOWNLOADS FOR THIS CHAPTER

The wrox.com code downloads for this chapter are found at www.wrox.com/remtitle .cgi?isbn=1118495810 on the Download Code tab. The code for this chapter includes the following major examples:

➤ ManageSolutionsSampleProject.wsp

DEFINING SOLUTIONS AND FEATURES

All SharePoint administrators need to have an understanding of both SharePoint solutions and SharePoint Features, as administrators are ultimately responsible for installing and deploying these components to the farm. A *SharePoint solution* is a set of one or more components that have been created to customize and/or add functionality to the SharePoint environment. Solutions are delivered as a *solution package*, and this package is what is installed and deployed to the farm. A solution package contains one or more Features. A *Feature* is the smallest unit of functionality within a SharePoint farm, and it is the supported mechanism for adding capabilities and functionality. Although solutions and Features are typically created by a developer, administrators need to understand their main components in order to manage and support them, as well as to understand how they impact the farm. This section provides a little more detail about each of these terms before discussing them in depth later in the chapter.

The SharePoint solution infrastructure provides a consistent, manageable interface for SharePoint customizations. This infrastructure enables you to have a single deployment point for all the servers in your farm, and to schedule deployments and updates to all the servers in the farm. The deployment process is simplified because the solution infrastructure alleviates the need to copy files to every server in the farm, or to make web.config changes to all servers in the farm. After initial deployment by the administrator, installation of the solution package is handled by the infrastructure.

A solution package is a .cab file whose extension is changed to .wsp (Web Solution Package). This solution package, or solution, contains features (and their associated elements), .NET assemblies, and a manifest file (XML file) that instructs SharePoint how the solution's components should be deployed. When a solution is deployed or activated, SharePoint inspects the manifest and unpacks the package based on the instructions in the manifest. Therefore, the solution represents a self-contained set of code and instructions for the automated deployment of custom functionality.

A *Feature* is a collection of elements that are grouped together. Usually they are logically related elements, although this is not required because a Feature can include functionality that spans more than one customization, and these customizations can be independent of each other. An element can be almost anything in SharePoint: a Web Part, a workflow, a content type definition, an event receiver, and so on. In fact, native SharePoint functionality (e.g., lists, libraries, Web Parts, ribbon buttons, etc.) is deployed using Features. Once Features are installed, they can be activated and subsequently deactivated so that their functionality can be enabled and disabled. Feature activation is said to "light up" the functionality, making it available for use. In previous chapters, you are sometimes asked to either activate a Feature or ensure that a specific Feature was already activated. Thus, Feature deployment involves both installation and activation, the latter of which you can perform later.

SharePoint 2013 continues to support both *full trust* and *partial trust* for both farm and sandboxed solutions, just as they were supported in SharePoint 2010. Administrators will continue to manage these solutions in SharePoint 2013 as companies upgrade their SharePoint 2010 environments and redeploy their SharePoint 2010 solutions. Developers familiar with these approaches may choose to continue to leverage their skills and expertise, but they are strongly encouraged to utilize the new application solution methodology discussed in Chapter 11, "Managing and Configuring Apps." Management of these solutions is discussed in detail in this chapter, beginning with full-trust solutions, followed by sandbox solution management and understanding and managing Features. If you're an administrator who is very familiar with solution management in SharePoint 2010, you may choose to skip this chapter and proceed to the next chapter, which introduces the new *SharePoint App Model,* which is also referred to as the *Cloud App Model.*

UNDERSTANDING FARM SOLUTIONS

The most common type of solution package is the *farm solution.* The SharePoint farm administrator is responsible for installing farm solutions, and the solution infrastructure provides a straightforward and consistent manner for installing and managing solutions across all the servers in the farm. Solution package installation is done using the familiar `SP-AddSolution` cmdlet. Once the solution has been installed, the administrator can use the Solution Management web page in Central Administration to view the status of the solution and to deploy the solution to the entire farm. The administrator can also use PowerShell cmdlets to manage the solution. For those interested, the SharePoint 2013 PowerShell cmdlet reference is found here: `http://technet.microsoft.com/en-us/library/ee890108(v=office.15).aspx`. This section looks at the contents of a solution before reviewing the process for installing the package.

You can view a solution package by renaming the file extension from .wsp to .cab, and opening the .cab file using Windows Explorer. For example, Figure 10-1 shows the contents of a solution named `ManagingSolutionsSampleProject.wsp`. In this case, the solution is designed to deploy a custom Web Part. As you can see, the solution contains multiple files, but note in particular the manifest file.

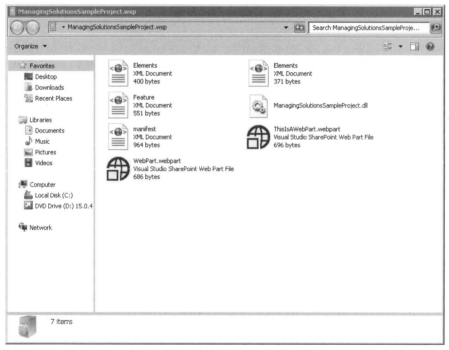

FIGURE 10-1

A solution is required to have a manifest file (`manifest.xml`), which defines the list of constituent Features, site definitions, resource files, Web Part files, and assemblies that will be processed. This specific solution manifest (whose XML contents are shown in the following code snippet) deploys a Feature and adds a *SafeControl* entry to the `web.config` file. The internal details of this manifest file are not pertinent to our discussion, but the interested reader is directed to `http://msdn.microsoft.com/library/ms442108(office.14).aspx` for a complete description of the solution manifest and the XML schema.

```xml
<?xml version="1.0" encoding="utf-8"?>
<Solution xmlns="http://schemas.microsoft.com/sharepoint/" SolutionId="39b2b22b-
    9ddb-4078-af78-5e62031c9bed" SharePointProductVersion="15.0">
  <Assemblies>
    <Assembly Location="ManagingSolutionsSampleProject.dll"
        DeploymentTarget="GlobalAssemblyCache">
      <SafeControls>
        <SafeControl Assembly="ManagingSolutionsSampleProject, Version=1.0.0.0,
            Culture=neutral, PublicKeyToken=454f5f085eabc506"
            Namespace="ManagingSolutionsSampleProject.ThisIsAWebPart.WebPart"
            TypeName="*" />
      </SafeControls>
    </Assembly>
  </Assemblies>
  <FeatureManifests>
    <FeatureManifest Location="ManagingSolutionsSampleProject_This Is A Web Part
        Feature\Feature.xml" />
  </FeatureManifests>
</Solution>
```

When a farm solution is installed, SharePoint reads the manifest, unpacks the assets from the archive, and copies the contents to the appropriate locations on the SharePoint server. SharePoint will also make any changes to the `web.config` file that the solution may require. These files and configuration changes are then replicated across all SharePoint servers. The following sections describe how the solution is installed and managed.

> **NOTE** *SafeControl entries provide the necessary registration information for custom code that allows it to be executed in the SharePoint farm. For example, these types of entries are necessary for any new Web Parts that are created.*

MANAGING FARM SOLUTIONS

Making the contents of a solution available to the SharePoint farm is a two-step process for an administrator. First, the solution package itself must be installed, or added, to the *solution store*. You add the solution package to the store using the `Add-SPSolution` PowerShell cmdlet as shown below.

```
Add-SPSolution -LiteralPath "c:\ManagingSolutionsSampleProject.wsp"
```

In the preceding example, ManagingSolutionsSampleProject.wsp is the name of the solution package. For a review of how to execute PowerShell commands, you should refer to Chapter 7, "Administering SharePoint with Windows PowerShell." Once the solution package is in the store, it can be deployed, retracted, and removed through the Central Administration website. PowerShell cmdlets are also available for all the administrative tasks.

> **NOTE** *The details of the* Add-SPSolution *cmdlet are provided here* http://
> technet.microsoft.com/en-us/library/ff607552(v=office.15).aspx.

Managing Farm Solutions via the User Interface

As mentioned previously, you can manage solutions in SharePoint using Central Administration
and PowerShell. Most functionality is available through the web browser user interface, except you
cannot add or update solutions as discussed previously. When managing a solution through the
web browser, navigate to the Farm Management web page using the following sequence: Central
Administration ⇨ System Settings ⇨ Farm Management, as shown in Figure 10-2.

FIGURE 10-2

Deploying Solutions

The first step in deploying a solution using the user interface is to navigate to the Solution
Management page (select the Manage farm solutions hyperlink on the Farm Management page). The
Solution Management page, shown in Figure 10-3, gives you an overview of all the solutions in the
farm, along with their deployment status and location once the solution is deployed.

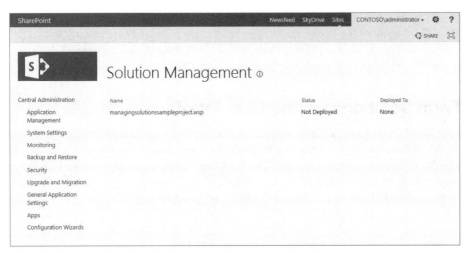

FIGURE 10-3

From the Status column in Figure 10-3, the administrator can see that the `ManagingSolutionsSampleProject.wsp` solution is not deployed. To deploy this solution, click the solution name. This will take you to the Solution Properties page shown in Figure 10-4. The Properties page provides some basic information about the solution, such as whether it contains web application resources, assemblies to be deployed in the global assembly cache (GAC), or a custom code access security policy, as well as previous operations, deployment status, and deployment locations (if any).

FIGURE 10-4

This page also contains a link labeled Deploy Solution. Clicking this link navigates the administrator to the Deploy Solution page (see Figure 10-5). From here, you can specify when the solution should be deployed and to which web application(s) it should be deployed. By default, solutions are set to deploy immediately and to all content web applications, or globally if no web application resources are present. Whether the solution is set to deploy immediately or at a scheduled time, the actual deployment is performed by a timer job scheduled with the Timer Service. The job uses the SharePoint Foundation Administrative web service to deploy solution files, so administrators should ensure that both services are running on each server in the farm. Note that deployments may occur close to the time specified; they are not necessarily exact.

> **NOTE** *The administrator can verify that the SharePoint Timer Service and SharePoint Administration Service are both started using the Services Management Console, or refer to this article for starting the services*: `http://technet.microsoft.com/en-us/library/ee513051.aspx`.

In addition to specifying when a solution is deployed, administrators may also need to specify where a solution should be deployed. In cases for which no web application resources are part of the solution, globally deploying the solution is the only option available. That's because any solution that does not have a web application resource is considered to be a global solution. Examples of web application resources might be *SafeControl* entries destined for the `web.config` file or a .NET assembly that will be stored inside a specific web application's bin folder. After specifying the deployment time and location (if applicable), the deployment can be scheduled and processed.

FIGURE 10-5

Removing a Solution

Solutions that may have been replaced or may have simply outlived their usefulness can be removed from the farm to eliminate any risk of them being accidentally utilized. Removing a solution deletes it from the solution store. Solutions that have not been deployed, or that have been retracted (solution retraction is covered in the next section) from all web applications, can be removed from the solution store. When you click the Remove Solution link on the Solution Properties page (refer to Figure 10-4), you are prompted for confirmation, as shown in Figure 10-6. Once confirmed, the solution is removed. Remember that solutions cannot be added to the solution store through the user interface; therefore, before removing a solution, ensure that you have or can get access to SharePoint via PowerShell.

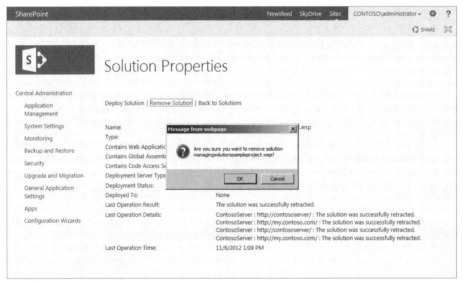

FIGURE 10-6

Retracting a Solution

Solution packages can be retracted if the functionality they provide is no longer desired. You should be aware that solutions currently in use should not be retracted due to the potential loss of data and the general confusion it may cause. The administrator should ensure that company employees have been notified of the discontinuation of the solution, and that all steps have been taken to minimize any issues caused by retracting the solution. After a solution has been deployed, the Solution Properties page provides a Retract Solution link next to the Deploy Solution link, as shown in Figure 10-7. (Note that before a solution is deployed, the link next to Deploy Solution is Remove Solution, as described in the previous section and shown in Figure 10-4.)

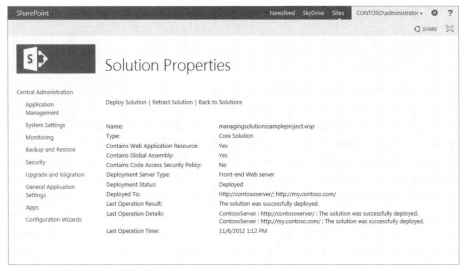

FIGURE 10-7

Clicking the Retract Solution link takes you to the Retract Solution page, which is very similar to the Deploy Solution page. Similar to deploying solutions, you can specify when the retraction should occur and which web application(s) the operation will affect. After specifying and submitting this information, the job is scheduled for retraction.

Managing Farm Solutions via the Command Line

The command line provides all the administrative functions needed to manage solutions. From here, you can view information about currently installed solutions; add, remove, and update solutions; and deploy/retract solutions either globally or to/from specific web applications.

Viewing Solution Information

Using the PowerShell cmdlet `Get-SPSolution`, you can view basic information about a solution. The `Get-SPSolution` cmdlet returns the following results when executed without parameters:

```
Get-SPSolution
Name                        SolutionId                       Deployed
----                        ----------                       --------
samplewebpart.wsp           177004f5-c0ba-4f54-80d0-e2afb78d4865 False
```

The cmdlet returns nothing if no solutions are in the solution store.

You can retrieve the properties of a specific solution by specifying a name, as in the following example:

```
Get-SPSolution samplewebpart.wsp
Name                        SolutionId                       Deployed
----                        ----------                       --------
samplewebpart.wsp           177004f5-c0ba-4f54-80d0-e2afb78d4865 False
```

> **NOTE** *For full documentation on the* Get-SPSolution *cmdlet, see* http://technet.microsoft.com/en-us/library/ff607754(v=office.15).aspx.

Adding, Updating, and Removing Solutions

The capability to add and update solutions is limited to the command line. There is no out-of-the-box functionality that allows an administrator to accomplish these tasks through a user interface. Conversely, solutions can be retracted and removed using either the command line or the user interface. The commands used to add, update, and remove solutions are Add-SPSolution, Update-SPSolution, and Remove-SPSolution, respectively.

The following Add-SPSolution cmdlet is straightforward. It takes a single parameter that indicates the path to the .wsp file:

```
Add-SPSolution C:\SampleWebPart.wsp
Name                        SolutionId                             Deployed
----                        ----------                             --------
samplewebpart.wsp           177004f5-c0ba-4f54-80d0-e2afb78d4865   False
```

Note that when adding a solution parameter, the path to the .wsp file must be a fully qualified, absolute path (e.g., C:\folder1\folder2\thewspfile.wsp).

Updating a solution is a little more involved, as it can require knowledge of the solution package. The Update-SPSolution cmdlet has several parameters, some of which may be required depending on the contents of the solution. In addition to the required attributes indicating the name of the solution (-Identity) and the file path to the updated .wsp file (-LiteralPath), you may be required to specify one or more of the following:

- ➤ -CASPolicies — If the solution contains a custom code access security policy
- ➤ -GACDeployment — If the solution contains assemblies that have a target deployment location of the GAC (global assembly cache)
- ➤ -Time — If the update should be scheduled for a future time (the default is immediately)
- ➤ -Force — If the safety checks that SharePoint uses need to be bypassed

The Update-SPSolution cmdlet returns no output when executed:

```
Update-SPSolution SampleWebPart.wsp -LiteralPath C:\SampleWebPart.wsp
```

Like the Add-SPSolution cmdlet, the -LiteralPath parameter requires a fully qualified, absolute path to the solution's .wsp file.

> **NOTE** *Full documentation about the* Add-SPSolution *cmdlet can be found on MSDN at* http://technet.microsoft.com/en-us/library/ff607552(v=office.15).aspx, *and documentation for the* Update-SPSolution *cmdlet is at* http://technet.microsoft.com/en-us/library/ff607724(v=office.15).aspx.

To remove a solution, execute the `Remove-SPSolution` cmdlet, including the name of the solution. A solution being removed cannot be deployed globally or to a web application unless you use the `-Force` parameter. Removing solutions with the `-Force` parameter is never recommended because it can create unpredictable results. Instead, you should fix any issues that are preventing the solution from being removed gracefully. The `Remove-SPSolution` cmdlet returns no output:

```
Remove-SPSolution SampleWebPart.wsp
```

An easy way to determine the name of the solution file is to leverage the `Get-SPSolution` cmdlet, which returns the names of all solution packages installed in the solution store.

> **NOTE** *Full documentation on the* `Remove-SPSolution` *cmdlet can be found on MSDN at* `http://technet.microsoft.com/en-us/library/ff607748(v=office.15).aspx`.

Deploying and Retracting Solutions

The commands used to deploy and retract solutions are named using a different nomenclature compared to the web browser management capability: `Install-SPSolution` and `Uninstall-SPSolution`, respectively. The `Install-SPSolution` cmdlet has some of the same optional parameters as the `Update-SPSolution` cmdlet (`-GACDeployment`, `-CASPolicies`, `-Time`), and they serve the same purposes. The required parameters for the cmdlet are the name/identity of the solution and the web application to which it should be deployed. The web application parameter takes one of two forms. The `-AllWebApplications` parameter instructs SharePoint to deploy the solution to all content web applications, whereas the `-WebApplication` parameter deploys the solution to a specific web application. The `Install-SPSolution` cmdlet returns no output:

```
Install-SPSolution SampleWebPart.wsp -WebApplication http://sharepoint
```

To retract the solution, use the following cmdlet:

```
Uninstall-SPSolution SampleWebPart.wsp -WebApplication http://sharepoint
```

UNDERSTANDING SANDBOX SOLUTIONS

SharePoint 2007 introduced the solution infrastructure for customizing and extending the SharePoint platform. These advancements made SharePoint a true application platform upon which a wide variety of business problems could be solved. Unfortunately, the introduction of solutions also created the possibility that custom-developed code deployed to the farm could cause unpredictable results and negatively impact performance. *Sandbox solutions,* introduced in SharePoint 2010, enable developers to customize their SharePoint websites while minimizing the chance of negative effects.

Sandbox solutions execute in a restricted environment that isolates the program from other applications and websites in the server environment. These types of solutions differ greatly from farm solutions, with some of the key points summarized in the following list (for a more in-depth summary of sandbox solutions and their capabilities, see `http://msdn.microsoft.com/en-us/library/ee536577.aspx`):

➤ In general, the sandbox solution architecture gives administrative control to the site collection owner, but this enhanced freedom is offset by what functionality is available, what resources can be accessed, and the amount of resources that can be consumed. Administrators interested in the details of the overall architecture of sandbox solutions should refer to `http://msdn.microsoft.com/en-us/library/ee539417.aspx`.

➤ The restricted execution environment enables programs to access only a subset of the SharePoint server object model, and a subset of the .NET Framework assemblies. Any problems that occur will not affect the rest of the server environment. Readers interested in more details about what can and cannot be done using sandbox solutions should refer to `http://msdn.microsoft.com/library/gg615464.aspx`.

➤ Sandbox solutions are typically deployed at the site collection level by a site collection administrator or by a user who has the Full Control permission. Solutions are deployed to the site collection solution gallery.

➤ Sandbox solutions are governed by setting resource usage limits (throttling) and monitoring the usage. This protects the farm from potentially dangerous or inefficient code. Administrators can have SharePoint automatically shut down any solutions that run excessive database queries, throw a lot of unhandled exceptions, or otherwise perform poorly. Only a farm administrator can configure the usage settings.

➤ Sandbox solutions can be promoted to farm solutions but only by a farm administrator.

Overall, sandbox solutions have been less widely adopted relative to farm solutions due to the performance overhead introduced by monitoring and isolating the code, combined with the reduced functionality that is available. With the availability of SharePoint 2013, developers are encouraged to use the new App Model discussed in Chapter 11, "Managing and Configuring Apps." The following section discusses sandbox solution management.

> **WARNING** *As of SharePoint 2013, sandbox solutions have been deprecated, meaning future versions of SharePoint may not support them. Therefore, administrators and the developers with whom they collaborate should start looking for replacement components for any functionality provided by sandbox solutions. More information on the deprecation of sandbox solutions can be found on MSDN at* `http://msdn.microsoft.com/en-us/library/jj163114`.

MANAGING SANDBOX SOLUTIONS

Like farm solutions, sandbox solutions are installed in two steps, but sandbox solutions are installed by the site collection administrator. The first step is uploading the solution to the site collection solution gallery and the second step is activating the solution after it has been uploaded. Solutions can be uploaded, activated, deactivated , and upgraded using the browser as shown in Figure 10-8. These functions can also be performed using the SharePoint 2013 Management Shell with PowerShell, just like farm solutions. The specific steps and commands for installing solutions are provided at `http://msdn.microsoft.com/library/gg615450.aspx`.

FIGURE 10-8

The farm administrator is responsible for governing a sandbox solution's resource consumption. This governance is achieved by setting resource quotas using Central Administration from the Site Quotas and Locks page, which is accessed from the Configure quotas and locks link in the Site Collections management section (see Figure 10-9).

FIGURE 10-9

The bottom section of the Quotas and Locks page, which is shown in Figure 10-10, provides the Sandboxed Solutions Resource Quota option, which administrators can use to restrict the resources that solutions can consume by configuring the "Limit maximum usage per day" option. This is accomplished by defining the maximum number of points that are available for all solutions in a given site collection, and this number represents the quota for the entire site collection. Quotas can also be configured using PowerShell, as described in the documentation at `http://technet .microsoft.com/en-us/library/hh230318.aspx`.

Points are used to measure the resources consumed by a solution, and sandbox solutions are subject to three different kinds of resource usage restrictions. For a complete list of the individual resources, usage restrictions, and resources per point for each resource, see `http://msdn.microsoft.com/ en-us/library/gg615462.aspx`.

The resources consumed by all solutions in the site collection are aggregated and compared to the quota that has been set for the whole site collection. If the aggregated resource total exceeds the quota set for the site collection, all sandbox solutions in the site collection are stopped.

Farm administrators can also prevent any sandbox solution from executing by *blocking* the solution. A solution that is blocked does not run. The steps for blocking and unblocking a solution are covered at `http://technet.microsoft.com/en-us/library/ff535782.aspx`.

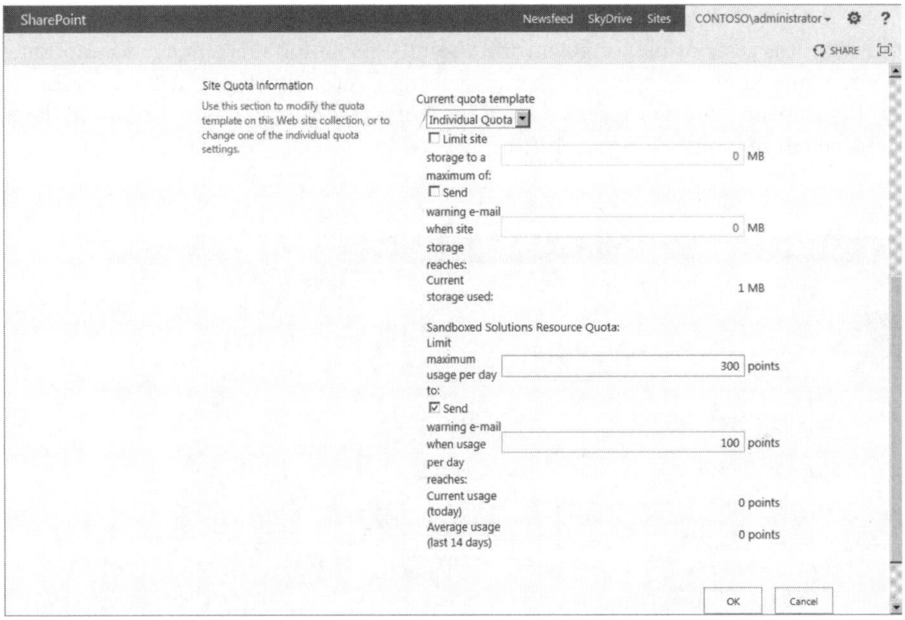

FIGURE 10-10

UNDERSTANDING FEATURES

SharePoint Features are a deployment mechanism that enables administrators to "light up" functionality across the farm. Features can deploy files, event handlers, lists, content types, and just about any other type of SharePoint asset.

Features are located in the TEMPLATE\FEATURES subdirectory of the SharePoint root folder located at C:\Program Files\Common Files\Microsoft Shared\Web Server Extensions\15\TEMPLATE\ FEATURES. Within the FEATURES directory, each Feature has its own subdirectory; and at a minimum, that subdirectory contains a Feature manifest file called feature.xml. It is in this file that the Feature is actually defined. A Feature definition is comprised of a series of *elements* called element manifests, dependencies, upgrade actions, and/or properties, and it is used to register functionality at a given *scope* within SharePoint. Feature directories often have additional files and/or subdirectories that contain supporting files where the elements and other parts of the Feature are defined. For most Features, it is the elements that you care about, not so much the Feature definition itself. The elements are what define the Web Parts, workflows, menus, content types, lists, and so on that you or your users will use. Let's take a closer look at the Feature manifest.

Feature Manifest

Features, like solutions, have manifest files that provide instructions to SharePoint whenever the Feature is activated. The contents of an example Feature manifest file (feature.xml) look similar to the following:

```xml
<?xml version="1.0" encoding="utf-8"?>
<Feature xmlns="http://schemas.microsoft.com/sharepoint/"
    Title="ManagingSolutionsSampleProject Feature1"
    Description="My Visual Web Part Feature"
    Id="cbfab278-2cfa-49b3-9b88-f45d86fe8f81" Scope="Site">
  <ElementManifests>
    <ElementManifest Location="ThisIsAWebPart\Elements.xml" />
    <ElementFile Location="ThisIsAWebPart\ThisIsAWebPart.webpart" />
    <ElementManifest Location="WebPart\Elements.xml" />
    <ElementFile Location="WebPart\WebPart.webpart" />
  </ElementManifests>
</Feature>
```

The feature.xml file contains several different types of XML tags that are based on the Feature and element schema. By adding tags to the manifest, you declare different types of functionality. When the Feature is activated, SharePoint interrogates the element designations to determine what type of assets it needs to create in the associated SharePoint site, site collection, web application, or farm. These assets could include lists, list templates, Web Parts, CSS files, master pages, and many other components. One of the ElementManifest tags in the preceding XML references another file called Elements.xml, instructing SharePoint to open and read the contents of this file. The contents of an example Element.xml file are shown in the following example. The Module element designates functionality that deploys a .webpart file to the Web Part gallery (Url="_catalogs/wp").

```xml
<?xml version="1.0" encoding="utf-8"?>
<Elements xmlns="http://schemas.microsoft.com/sharepoint/" >
  <Module Name="WebPart" List="113" Url="_catalogs/wp">
    <File Path="WebPart\WebPart.webpart"
        Url="ManagingSolutionsSampleProject_WebPart.webpart"
        Type="GhostableInLibrary">
      <Property Name="Group" Value="Custom" />
    </File>
  </Module>
</Elements>
```

The XML also specifies that the associated Web Part, which is described in the `Webpart.webpart` file, be added to a web page. Deploying SharePoint components in this way, through Feature and element XML instructions, is known as a *declarative* implementation. Essentially, developers deploy components by having SharePoint interpret the declared XML instructions instead of actually writing the .NET code themselves to complete the task.

> **NOTE** *The full SharePoint Feature and Element schema is documented on MSDN at* `http://msdn.microsoft.com/en-us/library/ms414322.aspx`.

Defining Scope

Features are activated for a single scope — at the farm, web application, site collection, and site level. The scope determines how broadly the functionality is available, where the Feature needs to be activated, and whether and how Feature dependencies will work. Feature scope is determined by the value of the `Scope` attribute in the `Feature` element of the manifest file. In the `Feature.xml` file shown above in the previous section, the `Scope="Site"` designation indicates that the Feature is scoped to the site collection level.

> ### SHAREPOINT SCOPE NAMES
>
> The nomenclature for scopes in SharePoint has changed over time but some of the legacy terms remain for compatibility purposes. In the online table viewable at the previously referred link, you will see the current term used to describe SharePoint's scopes and another term in parentheses — for example, Site (site collection). The term in parentheses is the term SharePoint uses internally to refer to the scope, and the one that it expects to see in the `Scope` attribute of the Feature element in the `feature.xml` file. For example, for Features that have site collection scope, you need to specify `Site` as the scope; and for Features that will have a site scope, you need to specify a scope of `Web`. This can be a little confusing at first, and it is worth a review if you are having scoping issues with a Feature.

Feature Receivers

Features can include an element known as a *Feature Receiver*. A Feature Receiver enables SharePoint developers to execute .NET code whenever a Feature is activated or deactivated. For example, a Feature scoped to the web application level may have a Feature Receiver that adds database connection strings to the web application's `web.config` file. In general, the Feature activation and deactivation process can be supplemented by an application that adds or removes functionality. For example, when a document library is provisioned by Feature activation, the library could be populated with training documents pertinent to all users of the library.

MANAGING FEATURES

SharePoint's flexibility enables you to manage things in a number of different ways, and Features are no different. You can manage Features through the user interface or via the command line using PowerShell. Like solutions, Features can be installed/uninstalled, activated/deactivated, and viewed.

Managing Features via the User Interface

The user interface provides a limited amount of functionality for managing Features. It allows users with the Manage Web permission to see the visible Features for the current site or site collection. In order to manage Features scoped for the farm or web application, you must be a farm administrator. Site collection Features and site Features are managed from different locations.

> **NOTE** *The Manage Web permission must be given on the root site of a site collection in order for the user to be able to manage Features at the site collection level.*

Sites and Site Collections

To manage Features scoped to the site and the site collection, go to the Site Actions menu and choose Site Settings, as shown in Figure 10-11.

FIGURE 10-11

Once you choose the Site Settings link you will be taken to the Site Settings web page as shown in Figure 10-12. If you have used the Site Settings web page before then you know that if you are at the root of the site collection you will see both site functionality and site collection functionality. This is sometimes confusing to the first time administrator. To manage Features for the site, choose the Manage site features link under the Site Actions section on the Site Settings page. To manage Features for the site collection, choose Site collection features link under the Site Collection Administration section.

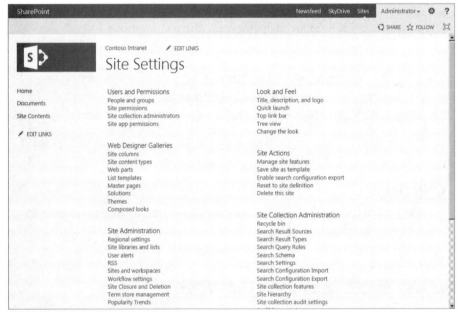

FIGURE 10-12

Farm

To manage Features scoped to the web application and farm level through the user interface, administrators must access Central Administration. The simplest way is to use the Manage farm features link on the Central Administration home page under the System Settings section, as shown in Figure 10-13.

FIGURE 10-13

Web Applications

Web application Features are accessed a little differently than the other scopes because they are accessed via the Ribbon. To access web application Features, click the Manage web applications link that is available on the Central Administration home page in the Application Management section, as shown in Figure 10-14.

FIGURE 10-14

Initially when you navigate to the Web Applications Management page the ribbon will be visible but many of the buttons will be disabled. After you select a specific web application, the buttons on the ribbon will become enabled as shown in Figure 10-15. Once you click on the Manage Features button you are taken to the Manage Web Application Features page where you are able to activate and deactivate the appropriate Features.

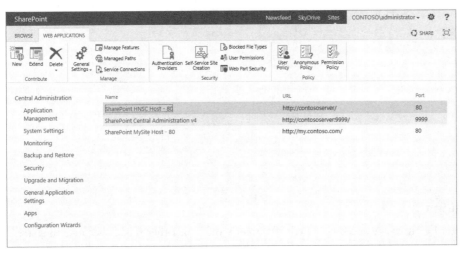

FIGURE 10-15

Feature Management Pages

Each Feature management page allows Feature activation and deactivation for its given scope. These pages show only the visible Features for the given scope. For each Feature, the page includes an activation/deactivation button, whose status appears immediately to the right of the Feature (see Figure 10-16). A status is shown only if the Feature is active. Users can toggle the status of a Feature by using this button. The action performed on the Feature after clicking the button is determined by the current state of the Feature, with the action to be taken labeled on the button.

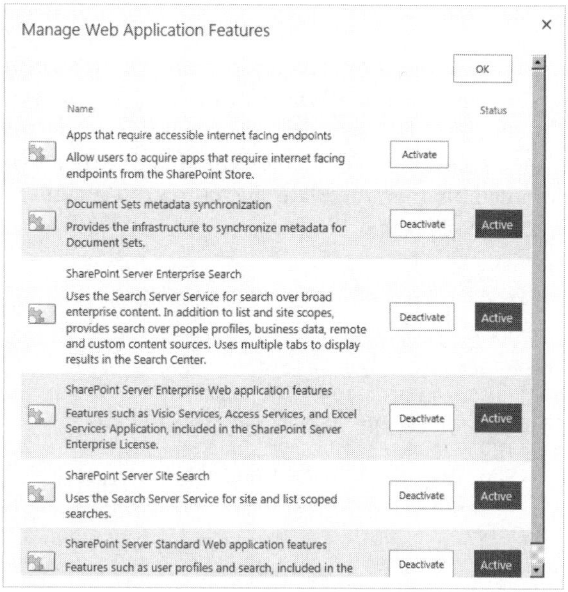

FIGURE 10-16

> **NOTE** *The user interface will not necessarily show all the Features for a given scope because a Feature can be hidden. A Feature is hidden when its* `hidden` *attribute is set to* `true` *(this attribute is found on the Feature element in the* `feature.xml` *file). For Features that are marked as hidden, your only option for managing them is the command line, using PowerShell cmdlets.*
>
> *Why hide a Feature? You may not want to allow users to activate or deactivate it. For instance, you may not want users to deactivate a Feature that has an event receiver that enforces data validation when an item is added or updated in a list, or you may not want them to activate a Feature that is not intended for all sites in the farm. In addition, keep in mind that SharePoint displays all the visible Features in the farm for the given scope. Therefore, if you have a lot of Features deployed on a farm, the user interface can quickly become cluttered. For these types of environments, it is preferable to mark the Feature hidden unless it is necessary for a user to be able to control its status.*

Managing Features via the Command Line

The command line provides you with all the administrative functions needed to manage Features, such as viewing information, installing/uninstalling, and activating/deactivating. All these functions are available from PowerShell. PowerShell cmdlets for Features include `Get-SPFeature`, `Enable-SPFeature`, `Disable-SPFeature`, `Install-SPFeature`, and `Uninstall-SPFeature`.

Viewing Feature Information

The PowerShell cmdlet `Get-SPFeature` enables administrators to view information about Features from the command line. Using this cmdlet, you can view a list of all the Features in the entire farm or for a given scope. Executing the cmdlet `Get-SPFeature` by itself yields a list of all Features for all scopes. If you need a review of PowerShell and the execution of PowerShell commands then revisit Chapter 7. The following PowerShell examples show how to manipulate the output to view all Features in the farm that are scoped to the site collection level:

```
Get-SPFeature
DisplayName                       Id                                       Scope
-----------                       --                                       -----
PublishingStapling                001f4bd7-746d-403b-aa09-a6cc43de7942     Farm
BasicWebParts                     00bfea71-1c5e-4a24-b310-ba51c3eb7a57     Site
XmlFormLibrary                    00bfea71-1e1d-4562-b56a-f05371bb0115     Web
LinksList                         00bfea71-2062-426c-90bf-714c59600103     Web
workflowProcessList               00bfea71-2d77-4a75-9fca-76516689e21a     Web
GridList                          00bfea71-3a1d-41d3-a0ee-651d11570120     Web
...

Get-SPFeature | Where-Object {$_.Scope -Eq "Site"} | Sort DisplayName
DisplayName                       Id                                       Scope
-----------                       --                                       -----
AccSrvSolutionGallery             744b5fd3-3b09-4da6-9bd1-de18315b045d     Site
AdminReportCore                   b8f36433-367d-49f3-ae11-f7d76b51d251     Site
AssetLibrary                      4bcccd62-dcaf-46dc-a7d4-e38277ef33f4     Site
BaseSite                          b21b090c-c796-4b0f-ac0f-7ef1659c20ae     Site
BasicWebParts                     00bfea71-1c5e-4a24-b310-ba51c3eb7a57     Site
...

Get-SPFeature -Site http://<Server>/<SiteCollectionPath> | Sort DisplayName
DisplayName                       Id                                       Scope
-----------                       --                                       -----
AccSrvSolutionGallery             744b5fd3-3b09-4da6-9bd1-de18315b045d     Site
AdminReportCore                   b8f36433-367d-49f3-ae11-f7d76b51d251     Site
AssetLibrary                      4bcccd62-dcaf-46dc-a7d4-e38277ef33f4     Site
BaseSite                          b21b090c-c796-4b0f-ac0f-7ef1659c20ae     Site
BasicWebParts                     00bfea71-1c5e-4a24-b310-ba51c3eb7a57     Site
...
```

Installing and Uninstalling Features

Generally, Features should not be uninstalled or installed outside of the solution infrastructure, but in some cases it may be necessary. For example, several different Features could be installed as part of a solution, but one may need to be modified. A single Feature could be uninstalled and rein-stalled once its functionality is repaired. To install and uninstall individual Features, you can use the `Install-SPFeature` and `Uninstall-SPFeature` cmdlets, respectively. The following examples show how to use these to install and uninstall a Feature named HelloWorldWebPart.

Both the install and uninstall cmdlets accept a `-Force` parameter. When this parameter is specified, SharePoint bypasses some of the checks that it normally performs when the command is executed. For example, the `Install-SPFeature` with the `-Force` parameter will ensure that the target Feature gets installed even if a Feature of the same name has already been installed. Without the `-Force` parameter, the target Feature would not be installed. This can be helpful when you are trying to troubleshoot or fix issues with a Feature.

The following PowerShell cmdlet will install the Feature:

```
Install-SPFeature HelloWorldWebPart
DisplayName                    Id                                    Scope
-----------                    --                                    -----
HelloWorldWebPart              d157638b-0fbd-4196-8683-155e24330314  Site
...
```

Conversely, this PowerShell cmdlet will uninstall the Feature:

```
Uninstall-SPFeature HelloWorldWebPart
```

Activating and Deactivating Features

As shown in the preceding section, you can activate and deactivate a visible Feature through the user interface. Those same tasks can also be accomplished through the PowerShell `Enable-SPFeature` and `Disable-SPFeature` cmdlets, respectively. The cmdlet names use a different nomenclature than the user interface: `Enable-SPFeature` performs the activation of a Feature, and `Disable-SPFeature` performs the deactivation.

The `-URL` parameter for the enable and disable cmdlets is used to identify the web application, site collection, or site on which the cmdlet will take action.

Like the install and uninstall cmdlets, the enable and disable cmdlets support a `-Force` parameter. This parameter can also be useful when troubleshooting issues with a Feature. In the case of `Enable-SPFeature`, it allows you to issue the enable cmdlet for an already activated Feature. This can be useful if you want to update a Feature definition without first having to deactivate it. You should always proceed with caution when disabling (deactivating) Features, because the functionality that is enabled could be associated with very important data or critical capability that might be lost once the Feature is deactivated.

The following PowerShell cmdlet enables the Feature (no output is returned):

```
Enable-SPFeature HelloWorldWebPart -URL http://sharepoint
```

The following PowerShell cmdlet disables the Feature:

```
Disable-SPFeature HelloWorldWebPart -URL http://sharepoint
```

> **WARNING** *The* `-Force` *parameter is a useful option with Features but you should exercise caution when using it. Not all Features are built to handle being installed/uninstalled or activated/deactivated repeatedly without first having the inverse command executed. For these Features, you can end up with issues that manifest themselves in many ways, such as Feature elements appearing in the system multiple times, errors being generated during the execution process that may leave things in an inconsistent state, Feature or content corruption, and so on. The possible issues that can result from using the* `-Force` *parameter are usually limited to complex Features but they can occur in simple ones as well.*

SUMMARY

As demonstrated in this chapter, Features and solutions provide essential ways to add and manage SharePoint functionality. Although there are other ways you can add functionality to SharePoint, it is recommended that you make use of the many helpful options, tools, and commands described in this chapter, as they were designed to make your life as an administrator easier.

11

Managing and Configuring Apps

WHAT'S IN THIS CHAPTER?

➤ Understanding the SharePoint 2013 App Model

➤ Setting up a SharePoint environment for working with apps

➤ Managing and Monitoring SharePoint 2013 apps

CODE DOWNLOADS FOR THIS CHAPTER

The wrox.com code downloads for this chapter are found at `www.wrox.com/remtitle .cgi?isbn=1118495810` on the Download Code tab. The code for this chapter is divided into the following major examples:

➤ SampleHighTrustApp.zip

➤ HelloWorldApp.zip

SharePoint 2013 introduces the *Cloud App Model*, a new development model for adding and extending SharePoint capability. This chapter refers to this new model as the *App Model* or just *apps*.

> **NOTE** *Previous versions of SharePoint introduced the Full Trust Solution and sandbox solution models, which were covered in Chapter 10, "Managing SharePoint Developer Solutions and Features."*

Developers are encouraged to build their solutions using this new model for a few key reasons. First, more companies are utilizing cloud functionality, creating the need for a robust model designed to handle the challenges of both on-premises SharePoint deployments and those in

SharePoint Online. Sandbox solutions were an attempt to provide this capability but they are not robust enough, as discussed in Chapter 10. Second, we need a model that does not require installing and running code from the SharePoint server, which can negatively affect performance and upgradability. Finally, we need a model that is flexible enough to enable developers to write their applications in any language they choose, not just .NET. Let's take a deeper look at each of these reasons.

Companies are utilizing capabilities and resources that reside in the public cloud or the private cloud. The authors work with many companies that have implemented SharePoint as a private cloud, and many more have begun to utilize SharePoint Online to host their SharePoint intranets. The cloud's locked-down environment makes deploying code more difficult, as developers don't have access to Central Administration, and it limits the type of customizations that can be deployed because the cloud environment may be a shared, or multi-tenant, environment. A more robust app model is needed to support these very different environments.

Developing and deploying custom solutions to SharePoint enhances the functionality and adoption of the collaboration platform, but it can affect overall performance and the ease of upgrading to a new version. SharePoint has matured as an application development platform with each new release. The SharePoint 2003 application development platform was somewhat limited: Developers could build and install Web Parts to the Web Part Gallery, and deploy web applications into SharePoint's layouts folder. SharePoint 2007 was significantly more robust with the introduction of solution packages, Features, control delegates, and a strongly supported developer infrastructure. This development capability was largely designed with on-premises implementations of SharePoint Server in mind. SharePoint 2010 built upon these capabilities but also added capabilities for less pervasive solutions through client technologies such as REST APIs and client-side object models. SharePoint 2010 also introduced sandbox solutions, a new development model designed for a multi-tenant, hosted infrastructure such as the one used in Office 365 and SharePoint Online. With each new release, the SharePoint platform has made it easier and more developer-friendly to create and deliver custom solutions. Unfortunately, each solution adds complexity and requires testing when upgrading to the next version is considered. Clearly, we need a model that doesn't impact performance and upgradability.

Developers want the flexibility to write their customizations in the language they know and understand, which is fundamentally based on web standards. Historically, SharePoint development was done using .NET, and .NET developers needed to learn new APIs and the SharePoint development process, which differed from their usual .NET development process. Because SharePoint is a web application, composed of multiple websites, the language preference for a large part of the developer community would be HTML and JavaScript.

The new SharePoint 2013 App Model is designed to overcome each of these challenges and limitations. It provides an architecture that enables customizations to run in isolation so that they don't affect other apps or applications. SharePoint apps effectively have a zero deployment footprint on a SharePoint farm. Yes, you read that right; developer code is not deployed to the SharePoint server. Apps can leverage SharePoint application components such as lists, libraries, and workflows. The apps themselves can be hosted within the SharePoint farm (as long as there's no server code), or they can be cloud hosted in Windows Azure or privately hosted elsewhere in the cloud. Because apps don't physically deploy any assets to the SharePoint servers, they eliminate a significant challenge to adding new customizations to multi-tenant cloud environments such as Office 365. Apps can be written using the standards of the Web, HTML, and JavaScript, or developers can choose PHP, Java, or .NET. For the first time, this new model unifies the development process for on-premise or cloud-hosted applications.

This chapter introduces the SharePoint 2013 administrator to the configuration and management of apps. Because apps will typically not be created by administrators, details about writing them are not included. Instead, this chapter covers the app architecture in detail, including the different hosting options for apps and app permissions. You will also walk through an example that demonstrates how to set up an app-enabled SharePoint environment. Finally, you will learn about managing and monitoring apps in SharePoint 2013.

UNDERSTANDING THE SHAREPOINT 2013 APP

A brief review of the three different development models illustrates the significant differences of the new App Model. Application code built using the new App Model runs predominantly on the client's browser, on application servers, or in a company's data center. This is very different from the full-trust farm solution and sandbox solution covered in Chapter 10.

The farm solution has the longest tenure. This model's code is usually hosted by the SharePoint farm, runs predominantly in the SharePoint host process with full farm privileges, and may access resources anywhere in the farm. This solution also requires farm administrator permissions to deploy. Because these applications run in a highly privileged security context across the farm, this model does not lend itself to multi-tenant scenarios such as SharePoint Online. The sandbox solution is designed for multi-tenant hosts.

The sandbox solution runs in a less-privileged process on the SharePoint server and only accesses resources in the site collection where it is installed, and deployment requires only site collection administrator privileges. While sandbox solutions allowed server-side code to execute, the reduced set of APIs limited functionality, and the sandbox architecture reduced performance versus full trust code. In many cases, developers would use sandbox solutions to deploy HTML/Javascript applications rather than to deploy server-side code. Unfortunately, in SharePoint 2010, there were few tools for governance, security, and management of these types of solutions.

With SharePoint apps, logic is not deployed to the SharePoint server, and instead lives predominantly on hosted application servers or on the client devices connecting to SharePoint. The following sections discuss the App Model architecture, the App Marketplace and Catalog, hosting options, and app security in more detail.

ARCHITECTURE

SharePoint apps are available from two locations. First, Microsoft hosts and governs a public Office Store, where any developer is able to publish and sell his or her app for general use by any SharePoint user. Publishing an app is as simple as uploading a file to a SharePoint library. Second, a private corporate app catalog can be hosted on SharePoint 2013 on-premises or online, and owned by the company hosting on-premises SharePoint 2013 or the online tenant. Company personnel or licensed tenants will be able to acquire and install these apps for personal or corporate use.

The App Model enables end users to install apps into their SharePoint sites. As part of the installation process and prior to being installed, the app will request certain permissions from the site on which it is being installed; this site is known as the *host site* or *host web*. If the user has the permissions requested by the app, it can be successfully installed. Note that the functional components of the app, whether they are SharePoint components or externally hosted components, are not deployed to the host web. External components and functionality are deployed to external servers, although the host web does contain a limited set of UI elements that give users access to the app's other components.

Once installed, the app is created in its own isolated SharePoint website known as the *app site* or *app web*. The app web is created in the same site collection as the host web unless it is installed with *tenant scope*. In that scenario, the app web is in the site collection of the corporate app catalog.

The app web can contain all kinds of different SharePoint components as long as they don't require that code be run on the SharePoint server itself. Lists, libraries, workflows, and web pages can all be created within the app web. Combined with the JavaScript client-side object model and the SharePoint REST data APIs, a large variety of applications can be built. The following section provides more details about the app marketplaces, the different app hosting options, and app security.

> **NOTE** *SharePoint apps can be assigned either a* web scope *or a* tenant scope, *and it is the tenant administrator in a multi-tenant environment who defines this property. Tenant administrators can choose to make certain apps available to only certain websites within a tenancy. In this scenario, only one app web is created and it is shared by all the host websites on which the app is installed. The app web is located in the site collection of the corporate app catalog. For a more in-depth discussion of tenancy, refer to* http://msdn.microsoft.com/en-US/library/fp179896(v=office.15).

SharePoint 2013 App Marketplaces

SharePoint apps can be obtained from the public Office Store or from the private corporate app catalog. This chapter refers to these locations collectively as the App Marketplace. Much like an app store for a mobile phone or tablet operating system, all marketplace apps are reviewed prior to being approved for sale and download. Publishing an app to the Office Store makes the app publically available; therefore, it can be obtained by any SharePoint user. To publish an app to the Office Store, the developer must first register with the Microsoft Seller Dashboard, as described at http://msdn.microsoft.com/en-us/library/jj220034(v=office.15).aspx.

Apps published to an organization's private app catalog are available for company-only use, and accessible to corporate users with appropriate permissions. As mentioned in the preceding section, a private app catalog is a dedicated site collection in a SharePoint 2013 web application, which makes it easier for the web application administrator or tenant administrator to control permissions to the catalog. Apps are uploaded to the catalog just like uploading a file, and the app is expected to pass a series of validation checks before being admitted to the catalog. Users with permission to access the app catalog (granted through standard SharePoint permissions) can then browse and install apps to their sites.

Apps can be installed and deployed by any user who has Manage Web Site and Create Subsite permissions. These permissions are available to site owners by default, and are typically granted to others by providing the specific user with the Full Control permission level or placing them in the Site Owners group.

SharePoint 2013 provides a full licensing platform for apps. The licensing model enables administrators to govern how and where apps are installed on their platform. Developers can also benefit from the licensing model, as they are permitted to provide evaluation and trial apps to the marketplace and determine who has installed them. Details about configuring web application app catalogs and managing app licenses are provided later in the "Managing SharePoint 2013 Apps" section.

> **NOTE** *The public SharePoint App Store is part of the public Office Store, which is currently located at* `http://office.microsoft.com/en-us/store/apps-for-sharepoint-FX102804987.aspx`*.*

SharePoint 2013 App Hosting Options

The goal of the SharePoint 2013 App Model is to enable the developer ecosystem to extend SharePoint's capabilities and functionality, and provide a single development model for both on-premise and cloud deployments without adversely affecting farm performance and future upgrades. To achieve this goal, different hosting models are available to provide developers and software vendors with the flexibility to choose where the components of their app would be hosted and how they would execute. Developers can now build their solutions using the tools and platforms they are most comfortable working with, and engage with the SharePoint platform using standard web tools and protocols such as JavaScript and REST.

The App Model utilizes two broad approaches to hosting apps: SharePoint-hosted and cloud-hosted. SharePoint-hosted apps include only SharePoint components, and they are installed in the corporate-owned SharePoint Online tenant or the on-premises SharePoint farm. Cloud-hosted apps include at least one remote component and may also include SharePoint-hosted components. The cloud-hosted model is further divided into two categories, ultimately resulting in three different approaches and three different types of apps that can be deployed to a SharePoint site: *SharePoint-hosted apps*, *provider-hosted apps*, and *auto-hosted apps*. All of these apps have the same options available to them in terms of how they interact with the SharePoint platform. They differ in how they're deployed, what web server services the web page requests, and how the apps authenticate to the host site. The following sections discuss each of the models in more detail.

SharePoint-Hosted Apps

These apps are installed on a SharePoint 2013 website called the host web. The app resources are hosted on the app web, a website typically in the same site collection as that of the host web. This approach enables you to reuse common SharePoint artifacts, such as lists and Web Parts. For example, Figure 11-1 shows a website's Site Contents page, which indicates that a new SharePoint-hosted app called Customer Billing and Time Tracking has just been installed. The resources for the app, such as lists, content types, workflows, and pages, are deployed to the app web, which resides in a special isolated domain. The app web may also have links and connections to a remote website or application, as in the provider-hosted model discussed next.

The app cannot directly provision any files or SharePoint-related artifacts such as lists and libraries to the host web. However, apps can provide a special type of Web Part, known as an *app part*, to the host web. An app part exists as an HTML iframe, and the app part could host a web page for the app. In addition, SharePoint apps can deliver tools known as *custom actions*, which typically manifest themselves as buttons on the Ribbon.

> **NOTE** *Although an app cannot provision files or SharePoint-related artifacts to the host web when it is installed, that doesn't mean the app cannot make changes to the host web. When an app is installed, it may request permissions to create lists or upload files. If these permissions are granted, then the app could use the client-side object model or REST APIs to manipulate data or even create lists or websites from within the host web.*

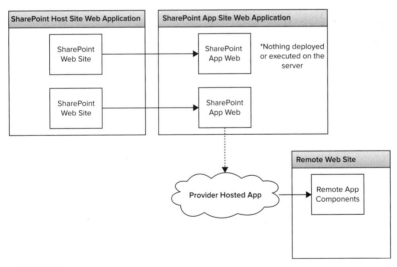

FIGURE 11-1

When the app is provisioned, SharePoint creates a unique domain name for it. This unique DNS domain name is created by combining a static prefix that is defined by the farm administrator with a randomly generated ID. SharePoint then deploys the app web to this unique domain where all of the resources associated with a SharePoint-hosted app will be deployed and requested. To better illustrate this unique domain name, consider the Customer Billing and Time Tracking app that is deployed to the Contoso Sales website with the following URL:

```
https://www.contoso.com/sites/Sales
```

The Customer Billing app will be deployed to the newly created website with this URL:

```
https://app-4523a34b45def.contoso-apps.com/sites/Sales/CustomerBilling
```

Fortunately, users will access the app through links in the host site, so they won't need to worry about remembering this URL. In general, the dynamically created URL has the format:

```
https:// AppPrefix - AppID . AppDomain / HostWeb / AppName
```

where each of the parameters in the URL is defined as follows:

➤ `AppPrefix` — This prefix is any string set by the farm administrator in central administration. The default string is `"default"`. It is set to `app` in the example.

➤ `AppID` — This represents a hexadecimal number generated internally when the app is installed. It is set to `c4523a34b45def` in the example.

➤ `AppDomain` — This string is configured by the farm administrator in Central Administration. The recommendation is to have a separate domain compared to the SharePoint web application. It is set to `contoso-apps.com` in the example.

➤ `HostWeb` — This is the relative URL of the parent host web, which in this case is `sites/Sales`.

➤ `AppName` — This is the value of the `Name` attribute assigned to the app when it is registered.

This is just an overview of how this unique name is created. The actual steps for configuring the app domain are discussed in the section "Setting Up an App Enabled SharePoint Environment."

One benefit of SharePoint-hosted apps not available to the other hosting options is the capability for a developer to leverage SharePoint application components from within the app web. That is, developers can provision lists, workflows, and other SharePoint components within their app and leverage them as part of the app's solution.

Provider-Hosted Apps

Provider-hosted apps are very similar to SharePoint-hosted apps. The key difference is that some app components reside outside of the SharePoint farm. When a provider-hosted app is provisioned, a trust is set up between the external components on a remote host and the SharePoint farm. This allows the external components to communicate and leverage the SharePoint components, as well as utilize resources and services that reside on the remote site.

A key advantage of this model is that the app's components can live on any platform and hardware, which provides the flexibility to use any hosting service. For example, the app can be hosted on Windows Azure or any remote web platform, including non-Microsoft platforms. This model can be deployed using cloud-based remote components or on-premise remote components. The remote components interact with SharePoint via the client-side object model or through web services. The app and its remote components must be authenticated and authorized just like any SharePoint user.

The app model can use different authentication and authorization approaches, but developers are encouraged to use the Open Authentication (OAuth) standard. Typically, provider-hosted apps use OAuth to access SharePoint components, inside both the host web and the app web. For on-premise implementations, there is an option to bypass OAuth and set up what is known as a *high-trust app* using the *Server-to-Server* protocol. The security mechanism for permission requests, OAuth, and Server-to-Server authentication are topics covered in more detail in the "App Model Security" section.

> **NOTE** *The details of OAuth are not pertinent to our discussion, but readers interested in a more in-depth discussion can refer to* `http://oauth.net/`.

Provider-hosted apps can also be considered *hybrid apps*, as they can technically leverage everything that SharePoint-hosted apps deliver, plus their own custom remote-platform capabilities.

Auto-Hosted Apps

Auto-hosted apps are essentially provider-hosted apps that are hosted in Windows Azure. Developers who construct an auto-hosted app can define what type of remote platform resources the app will require, such as SQL Server databases, Azure websites, and Azure app webs. When site users install an auto-hosted app to their SharePoint site, the required components are automatically created within their Windows Azure account.

App Model Security

App permissions are broken down into permission requests and request scopes. Additionally, SharePoint 2013 has a set of app authorization policies that determine whether the app should be authorized to act on behalf of the user, the app and the user, or just the app.

When developers create an app in Visual Studio 2012, one file in particular provides all the details relevant to the app; this file is known as the *app manifest*. The app manifest includes a section, denoted by the `AppPermissionRequest` element, dedicated to the types of permissions the app requires of the host web.

Each `AppPermissionRequest` denotes a permission that the app needs to have on the host web. This element contains a permission request scope, which provides a URI describing what object(s) the app requires permission to in the SharePoint object hierarchy. For SharePoint content, four permission request scopes are supported, as described in Table 11-1.

TABLE 11-1 SharePoint App Permission Request Scopes

SCOPE URI	DESCRIPTION
Site Collection `http://sharepoint/content/sitecollection`	Includes all objects in the site collection to which the app is being installed, including subsites, lists, and files within each site.
Website `http://sharepoint/content/sitecollection/web`	Includes all the objects in the website to which the app is being installed, including subsites, lists, and files within the site.
List `http://sharepoint/content/sitecollection/web/list`	Includes all the lists in the current SharePoint website to which the app is being installed. It includes all items within the lists.
Tenancy `http://sharepoint/content/tenant`	Includes all the objects in the tenant to which the app is being installed.

In addition to the permission request scope, an `AppPermissionRequest` needs to specify what rights the app requires for the given scope. For the preceding permission request scopes, SharePoint supports the following rights:

➤ Read

➤ Write

➤ Manage

➤ FullControl

These rights are equivalent to the similarly named SharePoint permission levels. When users install a SharePoint app into their site, SharePoint interrogates the app manifest and asks the user to grant the app the appropriate permissions. Provided the user installing the app has the required permissions, the app will be provisioned.

High-Trust Apps

SharePoint 2013 uses OAuth to authorize remote provider-hosted applications to access SharePoint 2013 data on behalf of a user from a provider-hosted app. In order to authorize cloud apps to connect to data, SharePoint must receive what is referred to as an *OAuth token* from Windows Azure Access Control Services (ACS). This token is used as an app identity provider. As of this writing, this use case only applies to apps in an Office 365 environment, which is not pertinent to SharePoint administrators with on-premise deployments.

For on-premises scenarios, it is possible for apps to authenticate to SharePoint without using OAuth. This can be accomplished by setting up a server-to-server trust and creating a high-trust app environment. High-trust apps should not be confused with full trust permission or any other permission set used within the SharePoint environment. High-trust apps simply refer to apps that are responsible for creating the user portion of the access token. This effectively means that a high-trust app can assert any user identity it chooses, and instead of using OAuth the app authenticates to SharePoint just like any user.

This is a useful scenario for organizations that want to position the app model as the primary solution for SharePoint customizations. Enterprise developers can build and construct apps for SharePoint with platform and technology independence. High-trust on-premises apps provide a framework for flexible extensions to the SharePoint platform while maintaining farm and process isolation between the customizations and the core SharePoint environment.

The steps for configuring a high-trust app environment are dependent upon SharePoint being configured to support the App Model. Both of these configurations are covered in the very next section.

SETTING UP AN APP-ENABLED SHAREPOINT ENVIRONMENT

Many of the exercises remaining in this chapter require a SharePoint 2013 app file. You can read through the process without actually installing and managing an app, or the administrator can download the file from the book's collateral website.

This section provides a detailed, step-by-step walk-through demonstrating how to set up a SharePoint 2013 farm to support apps. These steps assume that SharePoint 2013 is already installed and configured as discussed in Chapter 3, "Installing and Configuring SharePoint."

The steps require the following:

➤ The user account performing the configuration must be a member of the Farm Administrators group.

➤ The SharePoint Timer Service and SharePoint Administrator Services must be running.

➤ The web application must be configured for claims-based authentication.

> **NOTE** *While it is possible to make the SharePoint app domain a subdomain of another SharePoint host site domain (i.e.,* apps.contoso.com*), this is considered less secure, as it exposes the host site domain to cross-site scripting attacks. This section implements the best practice of setting the app domain up as its own root DNS domain.*

A high-level summary of the steps is as follows:

1. Create and configure a DNS name to host all apps.

2. (Optionally) Add/install an SSL certificate for the DNS name.

3. Configure the service applications.

4. Configure app URLs.

Configuring a Forward Lookup Zone in DNS

The first step in configuring an app is to configure the app's isolation, which essentially involves creating a unique DNS hostname. All apps must be created in the default intranet zone. Keep in mind that the app domain must have the same private and public DNS accessibility as the SharePoint web application hosting the app. If the app domain is only accessible from the intranet but the web application can be accessed from the Internet, any attempt to access the app from the Internet will return a 404 Page Not Found error.

In the following steps, DNS Manager is used to create a forward lookup zone and enable app isolation:

1. Log in to the domain controller as a local administrator.

2. Select Start ➪ Administrator Tools ➪ DNS Manager.

3. Right-click Forward Lookup Zones... and then click New Zone.

4. The New Zone Wizard, shown in Figure 11-2, opens. Click Next.

FIGURE 11-2

5. In the Zone Type page, accept the default of Primary zone and click Next.

6. In the Active Directory Zone Replication Scope dialog that appears (see Figure 11-3), choose the appropriate replication setting for the environment and click Next.

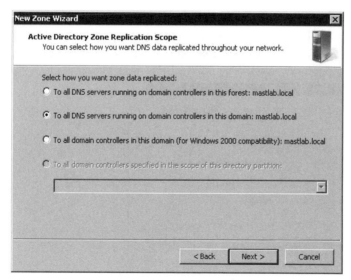

FIGURE 11-3

7. The Zone Name dialog shown in Figure 11-4 will appear. This should be the host name for the app domain (i.e., contosoapps.com). Click Next.

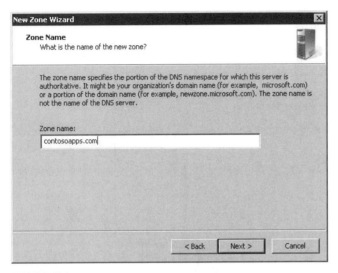

FIGURE 11-4

8. If the New Resource Record dialog appears, the Alias name field should always be: *
(wildcard). This instructs DNS to route all requests that match the host name to this
zone, regardless of subdomain. As previously described in "SharePoint 2013 App Hosting
Options" section, because each app will receive a random subdomain within the host name
as it is installed from a host web. Any request for the host name should always be forwarded
to the app domain, regardless of subdomain.

9. In the Dynamic Update dialog (not shown here), select "do not allow dynamic updates." Since
there shouldn't be any client computers registered in the DNS zone, this feature is unnecessary
and can be disabled. Finally, click Finish to complete the wizard (see Figure 11-5).

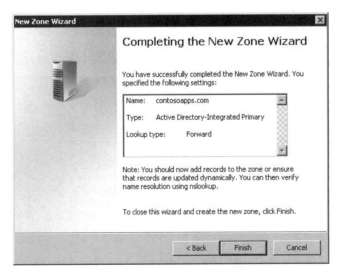

FIGURE 11-5

The forward lookup zone (and domain name) has now been configured. You can use the ping command to confirm that requests are being appropriately routed.

Configuring SSL for the App Domain (Optional)

Once the domain host name is set up and configured in DNS, SSL should also be set up. In this scenario, the app domain is a unique root domain separate from other SharePoint site domains. Therefore, a new wildcard SSL certificate should be created to support HTTPS (i.e., *.contosoapps .com). Because each installed app will have its own subdomain, the wildcard certificate is required. Without a wildcard certificate, individual certificates for every app that was installed would be required. This is very difficult to manage for an environment with many apps, and it would be expensive if the organization requires commercial server certificates.

> **NOTE** *While HTTPS is not required to support apps, it is a good idea, especially for app domains that are Internet-facing or apps that connect to systems external to SharePoint. For more information on configuring a wildcard certificate, see the following MSDN article:* http://technet.microsoft.com/en-us/ library/cc757451(WS-10).aspx.

Configuring the Service Applications

Prior to configuring the specific app settings, additional configuration is necessary on the service applications that the apps will utilize. The Subscription Settings service establishes subdomains for apps. The App Management service predominantly serves the role of providing app permissions. Both of these service applications need to be configured and started. Additionally, because SharePoint 2013 leverages some of the multi-tenancy features to create subdomains for apps, you must configure the default tenant name.

These steps are all executed using the SharePoint Windows PowerShell Administrator Console. The user executing these steps should have the following memberships:

➤ securityadmin inside the SQL Server instance that will contain the databases for the security applications

➤ If the databases have been pre-created, the db_owner fixed database role on the App Management and Subscription Service databases

➤ The Administrators group on the SharePoint server from which the Windows PowerShell cmdlets are being executed

Configuring and Starting the Service Applications

The following PowerShell command gets and starts the two necessary service instances:

```
Get-SPServiceInstance | where{$_.GetType().Name -eq "AppManagementServiceInstance"
   -or $_.GetType().Name -eq "SPSubscriptionSettingsServiceInstance"}
   | Start-SPServiceInstance
```

Creating Application Pools for the Service Applications

Once the services are started, the service applications need to be configured to use an application pool in IIS. For security reasons, these app pools need to run as the farm account. The following steps configure the application pool.

1. First, get and store the farm account in a variable:

```
$account = Get-SPManagedAccount "domain\farm_account"
```

2. Next, create application pools for each service app, and store them in appropriate variables:

```
$apSub = New-SPServiceApplicationPool -Name SettingsServiceAppPool -Account
$account
$apApp = New-SPServiceApplicationPool -Name AppServiceAppPool -Account
$account
```

Notice the use of the `$account` variable. The two application pools are stored in variables so they can be passed into cmdlets in the next step.

3. Now create the service applications and proxies; the database names are passed to the cmdlets by the administrator executing the commands:

```
$subSvc = New-SPSubscriptionSettingsServiceApplication
  -ApplicationPool $apSub -Name SettingsServiceApp
  -DatabaseName <SettingsServiceDB>
$subSvcProxy = New-SPSubscriptionSettingsServiceApplicationProxy
  -ServiceApplication $subSvc
$appSvc = New-SPAppManagementServiceApplication -ApplicationPool $apApp
  -Name AppServiceApp -DatabaseName <AppServiceDB>
$appSvcProxy = New-SPAppManagementServiceApplicationProxy -ServiceApplication
$appSvc
```

In the preceding code, `$apSub` and `$appSvc` are variables from previous steps in the configuration. `SettingsServiceDB` and `AppServiceDB` should be either the names of pre-created service application databases, or appropriate names for databases that will be created by SharePoint. The service applications are now created and running.

Configuring App URLs

This section outlines the steps for setting up a single tenant configuration for apps. The instructions are outlined for doing this through both Central Administration and the PowerShell Administrator Console.

Via Central Administration

1. From the Central Administration home page, click Apps (see Figure 11-6).

2. On the Apps page, click Configure App URLs, as shown in Figure 11-7.

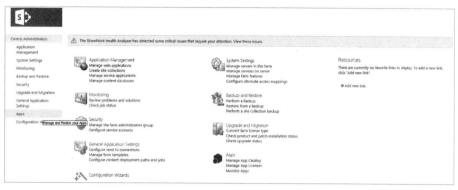

FIGURE 11-6

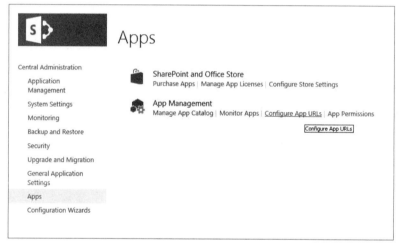

FIGURE 11-7

3. The Configure App URLs dialog, shown in Figure 11-8, will appear. In the App Domain text box, provide the DNS host name for the isolated app domain.

FIGURE 11-8

4. In the App Prefix text box, provide a prefix for the URL of the apps.

> **NOTE** *The app prefix, plus a randomized string and the isolated app domain, comprise the URL of every app web. For example, if the app prefix is configured to be "app" and the DNS host name is "contosoapps.com," an app URL may be* `app-appname-12345-abcd.contosoapps.com`.

5. Click OK.

Via the SharePoint PowerShell Administrative Console

Execute the PowerShell cmdlets:

```
Set-SPAppDomain <isolated app domain>
Set-SPAppSiteSubscriptionName -Name "app prefix" -Confirm:$false
```

where `<isolated app domain>` is the DNS host name configured for the isolated app domain, and `"app prefix"` is the app prefix for provisioned app URLs.

> **NOTE** *The user executing these PowerShell cmdlets is required to be a member of the SQL Server securityadmin group on the associated SQL Server instance, as well as a member of the local administrator group on the SharePoint server from which the cmdlets are being executed.*

The SharePoint farm is now configured to support apps.

Setting Up a High-Trust App Environment

> **NOTE** *The process for setting up a High-Trust App typically involves the developer of the app. There are certain app artifacts, such as the app certificate and issuer ID, that would be provided along with the app to the administrator. For this section, feel free to download the SampleHighTrustApp.zip file from the book's website. This file contains a provider-hosted app that is ready to be configured as a High-Trust App, and it can be used as part of this configuration exercise.*

High-trust apps are provider-hosted apps that utilize server-to-server authentication rather than OAuth. In this deployment model, the app and SharePoint create a trust using a shared certificate rather than using OAuth tokens. This model is not compatible with Office 365 deployments at the time of this writing. Office 365 would require a SharePoint-Hosted or Auto-Hosted deployment model.

The current process for setting up a High-Trust App environment is as follows:

1. Configure dependent SharePoint 2013 services.

2. Configure SharePoint 2013 to trust the provider hosted app.

3. Ensure the provider hosted app is configured properly.

The following sections describe these steps in detail.

Configuring Dependent SharePoint 2013 Services

High-trust apps require that both the App Management and User Profile Services are set up and configured. Configuring the App Management Service was detailed previously in the section "Setting Up an App-Enabled SharePoint Environment." Configuring the User Profile Service is detailed in Chapter 14, "Configuring User Profiles and Social Computing." In the following steps, you verify that these services have been started and are properly configured.

1. Verify that these services are started by navigating to Central Administration ➪ Application Management ➪ Manage Service Applications, as shown in Figure 11-9.

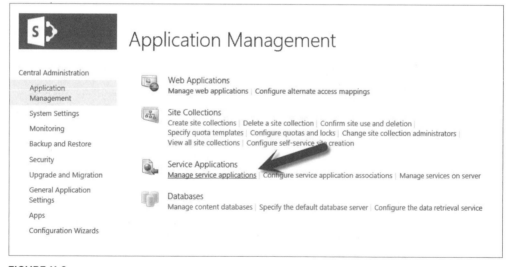

FIGURE 11-9

2. Verify that the following service applications are started (see Figure 11-10):

   ➤ User Profile Service Application

   ➤ App Management Service

FIGURE 11-10

3. Under Application Management, select Manage Services on Server.

4. Ensure that the User Profile Service is started, as shown in Figure 11-11.

FIGURE 11-11

5. To ensure that at least one user profile has been created, select Application Management ➪ Manage Service Applications. Then select User Profile Service Application ➪ People ➪ Manage User Profiles. Verify that Total Number of Profiles is greater than zero.

The dependent SharePoint service applications are now configured.

Configuring SharePoint 2013 to Trust the Provider-Hosted App

SharePoint needs to establish a trust with the Provider-Hosted App. This involves generating or obtaining an issuer ID for the app, getting a certificate file from the app developer, and then performing several configuration scripts using the SharePoint Windows PowerShell Management Shell. These steps are required for each Provider-Hosted App installed into a SharePoint environment.

Every High-Trust App must be installed and associated with an "issuer." An issuer is defined by the combination of an issuer ID (a GUID) and a public certificate. The certificate is generally purchased from a commercial security vendor, and it is provided along with the app by the developer. This certificate and the issuer ID are tightly coupled, meaning that if you create another certificate you must also create a new issuer ID. For the sake of demonstration, these steps are provided below, but typically they will be provided to the administrator by the app developer.

First, you will create a locally signed certificate.

1. Start IIS Manager and open the Server Certificates console by clicking on the Server Certificates icon, as shown in Figure 11-12.

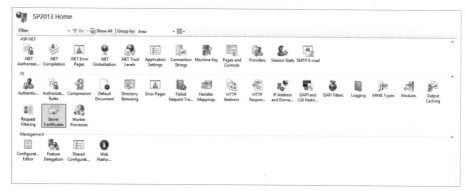

FIGURE 11-12

2. In the right-hand pane, select Create Self-Signed Certificate, as shown in Figure 11-13.

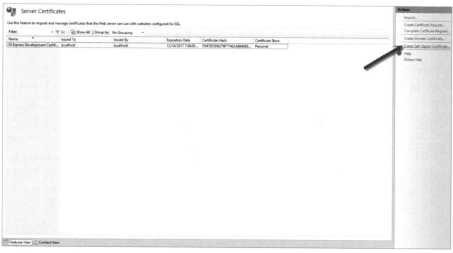

FIGURE 11-13

3. In the Windows Server 2012 Create Signed Certificate dialog, enter **HighTrustCert** for the name and leave Personal as the option chosen for the certificate store, as shown in Figure 11-14. Then click the OK button. You should see the HighTrustCert certificate listed in the Server Certificates window of IIS Manager. Next, copy this certificate to a file.

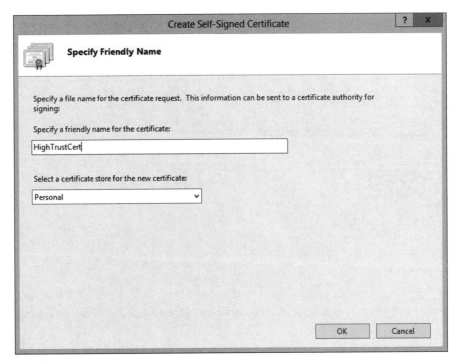

FIGURE 11-14

4. From the Server Certificates window, double-click the HighTrustCert certificate entry. In the Certificates dialog on the Details tab, click the Copy to File button, as shown in Figure 11-15.

5. In the Certificate Export Wizard, choose "No, do not export the private key," and "DER encoded binary X.509 (.CER)," which are both the default values. Next, enter **c:\HighTrustCert** for the file name. The wizard summary screen should resemble that shown in Figure 11-16. Click Finish and the certificate file is created and stored at the

FIGURE 11-15

FIGURE 11-16

specified location. The certificate file will be used as part of a PowerShell script to establish a trust between SharePoint and the Provider-Hosted App. Next, export the certificate to a .pfx file.

6. In the Server Certificates window of IIS Manager, right-click the HighTrustCert certificate entry, and select Export. Enter **c:\HighTrustCert.pfx** as the filename, and a password, as shown in Figure 11-17.

FIGURE 11-17

> **NOTE** *It may seem redundant to export the certificate twice, but it was done because both SharePoint and the app require a version of the certificate. The certificate represents a "shared secret" as part of the trust relationship. The .cer file will go to SharePoint, and the .pfx file will go to the app.*

7. Finally, SharePoint 2013 needs to be configured to use and trust the app. This is accomplished by executing the following script.

```
$appCertPath = "c:\HighTrustCert.cer"
$issuerId = [System.Guid]::New Guid().ToString().ToLower()
$spurl ="https://<host site URL>"
```

```
$spweb = Get-SPWeb $spurl
$realm = Get-SPAuthenticationRealm -ServiceContext $spweb.Site
$certificate = Get-PfxCertificate $appCertPath
$fullAppIdentifier = $issuerId + '@' + $realm
New-SPTrustedSecurityTokenIssuer -Name "<unique name>" -Certificate $certificate
    -RegisteredIssuerName $fullAppIdentifier
$appPrincipal = Register-SPAppPrincipal -NameIdentifier $fullAppIdentifier
    -Site $spweb -DisplayName "<unique display name>"
```

The script in the preceding code listing does the following things:

1. Sets up variables that contain: a path to the previously created security certificate, an issuer ID created earlier in the configuration steps, and the URL to the SharePoint site that will host the app ($appCertPath, $issuerId, $spurl).

2. Gets the SPWeb object for the host web ($spweb).

3. Gets the authentication realm for the host web's site collection ($realm).

4. Creates a certificate object for the given certificate path ($certificate).

5. Creates an app identifier based on the app's issuer ID and the authentication realm.

6. Creates and configures a new token issuer for SharePoint 2013 using the New-SPTrustedSecurityTokenIssuer cmdlet. The -Name parameter must be unique relative to any other apps in the farm as this issuer is specific to the current app.

7. Creates a new app principal using the Register-SPAppPrincipal cmdlet. The -DisplayName parameter must be unique relative to any other apps in the farm as it is specific to the current app being configured.

Apps require HTTPS to be configured for successful OAuth negotiation. For development environments, you can allow the OAuth process to occur using HTTP. This can be enabled using the following PowerShell scripts.

```
$serviceConfig = Get-SPSecurityTokenServiceConfig
$serviceConfig.AllowOAuthOverHTTP = $true
$serviceConfig.Update()
```

Ensuring the Provider-Hosted App Is Correctly Configured

The Provider-Hosted App must also be configured to be a part of the server-to-server trust, which requires changes to the app's web.config and appmanifest files. This is accomplished in the steps that follow.

> **NOTE** *In general, the steps outlined here will be performed by the app developer, but they are included here for completeness and because they may be helpful in troubleshooting any problems if the app is not working properly. The following steps assume you have downloaded and are configuring the HighTrustSampleApp.zip from the book's website.*

1. The following nodes must exist and have correct values in the app's web.config appSettings node (configuration/appSettings):

    ➤ **IssuerId** — the issuer ID was created when the app was registered. This can be determined using the `GetSPTrustedSecurityTokenIssuer` cmdlet, and locating the NameId property in the results. The issuer ID will be a string of characters in front of the "@" symbol.

    ➤ **ClientSigningCertificatePath** — represents the location of the .pfx file that is used to create the trust between the app and SharePoint.

    ➤ **ClientSigningCertificatePassword** — the password used to sign the .pfx certificate.

The appSettings node in the app's web.config file should resemble the following:

```
<appSettings>
    <add key="ClientId" value="4a7dcab1-308e-409c-a84c-4fb027e4e73f" />
    <add key="ClientSecret" value="GGO+5/JqzFsNgK+CKrpj+cRXTkeSPRFQR9/DXVylbOA=" />
    <add key="ClientSigningCertificatePath" value="C:\HighTrustCert.pfx" />
    <add key="ClientSigningCertificatePassword" value="p@ssw0rd1" />
    <add key="IssuerId" value="d26f0f19-bf88-4e68-9d0f-7e3509536e1a" />
</appSettings>
```

Inside the `appmanifest.xml` file, update the `ClientId` to be a wildcard value *. This provides an additional level of security for app developers in the other app deployment models.

Lastly, deploy the Provider-Hosted App files to an IIS website that is configured with Windows Authentication enabled, and anonymous authentication disabled, as shown in Figure 11-18.

The high-trust app configuration is now complete.

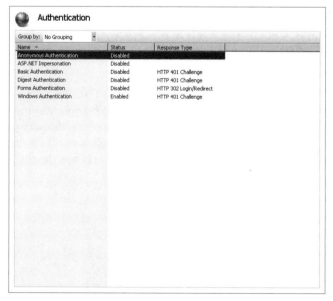

FIGURE 11-18

MANAGING SHAREPOINT 2013 APPS

SharePoint 2013 delivers a great deal of functionality and flexibility through the new app model. Many administrators will view these new capabilities as a double-edged sword: while it will be great for their users to take advantage of and extend their SharePoint investment, it could easily become an administrative nightmare for the administrators.

Fortunately, SharePoint includes a number of capabilities directly geared toward the management and governance of apps. These tools include corporate App Catalogs, specific app licensing management capabilities, and multiple methods for adding and removing apps to SharePoint sites.

This section describes the methods and location for interacting with these tools. Specifically, this section covers:

➤ App Catalogs

➤ Adding and Removing Apps from SharePoint Sites

➤ Monitoring SharePoint App Usage

➤ Monitoring and Managing SharePoint App Licenses

Configuring an App Catalog

SharePoint 2013 provides an App Catalog that stores an organization's apps for internal use. Administrators can license apps from the online marketplace and directly from third-party developers. Once purchased, the app is installed directly into their farm and made available in the App Catalog. The App Catalog is scoped to a web application and resides in its own site collection within the web application. Because each web application can have an App Catalog website, a farm can have more than one App Catalog. Administrators can control which users have access to which apps through standard permissions, and can control which apps are available. An App Catalog is created from Central Administration by a person who is a member of the Farm Administrators group.

The following steps explain how to configure an App Catalog:

1. From Central Administration, click Apps.

2. Under App Management, click Manage App Catalog. The Manage App Catalog dialog appears. Each web application can have only one App Catalog. If the web application was already configured with an App Catalog, SharePoint provides the name of the Primary Administrator as well as a link to the App Catalog and the App Catalog's SharePoint site settings (see Figure 11-19). For this exercise, select a web application that is not already associated with an App Catalog.

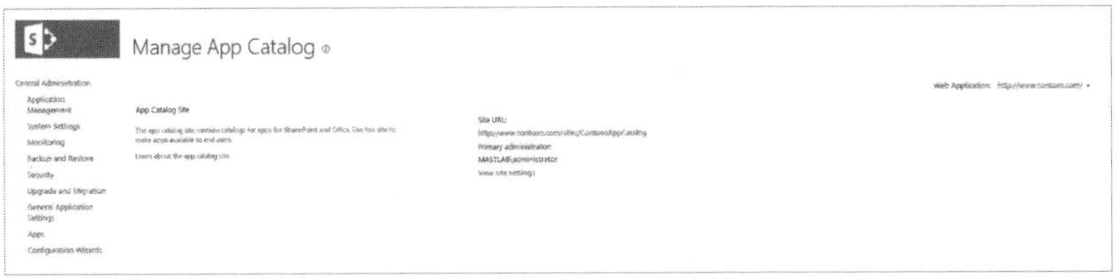

FIGURE 11-19

3. Select "Create a new app catalog site." Click OK.

4. On the "Create App Catalog" screen, populate the appropriate fields. From here you can specify the URL of the catalog, the site collection administrator, and which users will be able to install apps (see Figure 11-20). Click OK when you are done.

FIGURE 11-20

5. You just created the Contoso App Catalog shown in Figure 11-21, or the equivalent App Catalog with a different name.

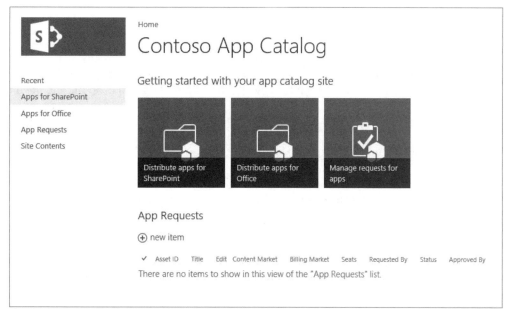

FIGURE 11-21

Managing Apps in the App Catalog

> **NOTE** *The book's website contains a basic "HelloWorldApp.zip" that can be used in the following exercises.*

Once an App Catalog has been created, apps can be added and removed from the catalog. This allows users that have access to the App Catalog to install a specific or limited set of apps into their SharePoint sites.

To add an app to an App Catalog:

1. Navigate to the App Catalog site collection that was created in the previous section, the Contoso App Catalog. The App Catalog contains a series of lists that provide the feature's functionality.

2. On the left-hand side, click the Apps for SharePoint link, which will take you to the Apps for SharePoint page shown in Figure 11-22. This list is the SharePoint App Catalog.

FIGURE 11-22

3. Items in this list can be added, edited, and removed the same as any SharePoint list content is managed. In order to add an app to this SharePoint App Catalog, click the Add Item button on the Ribbon, click the new app button, or drag and drop the app file onto the list.

Adding an App to a SharePoint Site

There are several ways to add apps to SharePoint sites:

➤ Using the list of SharePoint apps available to the current site

➤ Using the App Catalog associated with the SharePoint farm

➤ Downloading from the SharePoint Store (App Marketplace)

➤ Using Windows PowerShell

In all cases, the user installing the app must be a member of the Site Owners group prior to installing an app.

Adding an App from the Site's Available App List

1. Click the Settings icon, and click Add an App. This takes you to the Your Apps page shown in see Figure 11-23.

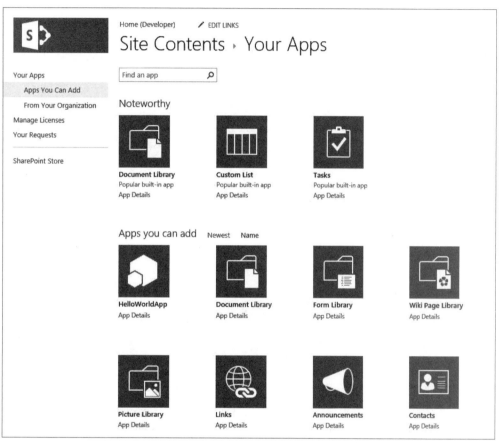

FIGURE 11-23

2. In the Your Apps list, click the HelloWorldApp.

3. If necessary, accept the request to trust the app (see Figure 11-24).

The app is now available in the Apps section of the Site Content list.

FIGURE 11-24

Adding an App from the App Catalog

1. Return to the Site Contents: Your Apps page shown previously in Figure 11-23.

2. Under the section Your Apps, click the link From Your Organization.

3. Click the app to be added.

4. If necessary, accept the request to trust the app.

The app is now available in the Apps section of the Site Content list.

Adding an App from the SharePoint Store

1. Return to the Site Contents: Your Apps page shown previously in Figure 11-23.

2. From the options on the left, click the SharePoint Store link. This will take you to the public SharePoint Store so you will need to have Internet access. The SharePoint Store website is shown in Figure 11-25.

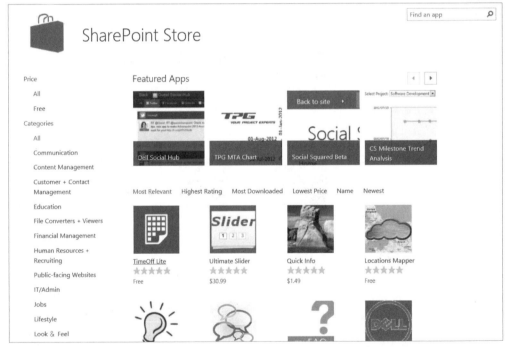

FIGURE 11-25

3. Browse the Featured Apps catalog and enter the text **Facebook** into the Find an app search box. A results page showing the Facebook Integration App is shown in Figure 11-26.

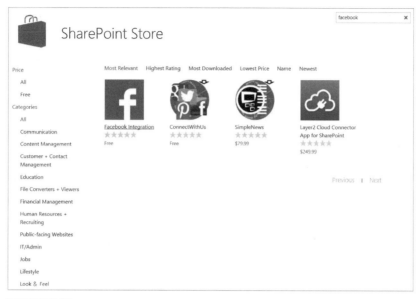

FIGURE 11-26

4. Click the Facebook Integration App icon and it will take you to the app page shown in Figure 11-27.

FIGURE 11-27

5. Free apps will show an Add It button on this page, while paid apps will display a Buy It button. Click the Add It button, and you'll see a trust dialog similar to what is shown in Figure 11-28. This dialog should look familiar because it is similar to what you have seen previously when adding an app from the App Catalog. Click the Trust It button.

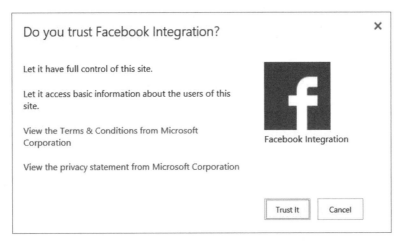

FIGURE 11-28

6. The app is now available in the Apps section of the Site Content list, as shown in Figure 11-29.

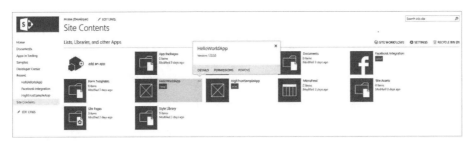

FIGURE 11-29

Adding an App via Windows PowerShell

To use the following steps, in addition to being a site owner on the site to which the app should be added, the user must have permission to execute SharePoint PowerShell cmdlets:

1. Open the SharePoint 2013 Management Shell.

2. Use the `Import-SPAppPackage` to import the app from the file system and store it in a variable.

```
$spapp = Import-SPAppPackage -Path Path to app -Site URL -Source Source
```

where:

➤ -Path provides the fully qualified path to the app file on the file system

➤ -Site provides the URL of the site collection to which the app should be imported

➤ -Source is one of the following: SharePoint Store, App Catalog, or SharePointService.

When asked to confirm the action, type Y.

3. Install the app to the appropriate site with the Install-SPApp cmdlet

```
Install-SPApp -Web URL -Identity $spapp
```

where:

➤ -Web provides the URL of the SharePoint website where the app should be installed

➤ -Identity is the variable in which the imported app was stored

Removing an App from a SharePoint Site

One of the great parts of the App Model is that users can deploy apps to their site, try them out, and, if they aren't what they are looking for, simply remove them from their site. Apps can be removed from a SharePoint website via the SharePoint user interface or Windows PowerShell. This section describes the steps for both of these approaches. A user must have the Manage Web Site permissions in order to uninstall an app.

Via the SharePoint Interface

1. Verify that the user account performing this procedure is a member of the Site Owners group.

2. Navigate to the specific site, click the Settings icon, and select View Site Contents.

3. In the Apps section, choose the app to remove, click the ellipses (...), and then click Remove.

4. Click OK to confirm the app's removal.

Via Windows PowerShell

In addition to having Manage Web Site permissions on the site from which the app should be removed, the user account must also have permissions to execute SharePoint PowerShell cmdlets:

1. Open the SharePoint 2013 Management Shell.

2. Execute the following PowerShell command:

```
$appToRemove = Get-SPAppInstance -Web <URL> | where {$_.Title -eq '<APP_TITLE>'}
Uninstall-SPAppInstance -Identity $appToRemove
```

The preceding code retrieves the app to remove at the URL provided in `<URL>` and the `Title` given in `<APP_TITLE>`. When found, a reference to the app is stored in the `$appToRemove` variable, and the app is uninstalled using the `Uninstall-SPAppInstance` cmdlet. SharePoint lists the available apps that have been installed to a SharePoint site on the Site Contents page. Installed apps can be found alongside lists and libraries; clicking on the app tile or link will launch the app, and clicking on the ellipsis (...) provides management options.

Monitoring SharePoint Apps

SharePoint provides facilities through Central Administration that enable you to discover and monitor important details about app usage inside their environment. You can monitor app details such as status, licenses in use, licenses purchased, install locations, and runtime errors.

The following sections demonstrate how to perform common tasks related to monitoring SharePoint 2013 apps.

> **NOTE** *Administrators must be granted Farm Administrator access in order to perform these actions. In addition, you must properly configure and start the Search Service Application for the monitoring data that is collected.*

Adding an App to the Monitor List

1. In Central Administration, click Apps.

2. Under the Apps section, click Monitor Apps.

3. In the Manage group of the Ribbon, select Add App, as shown in Figure 11-30.

FIGURE 11-30

4. On the Add an app to monitor page shown in Figure 11-31, choose the the Facebook app that we added previously.

5. Once chosen, click Add to include it in the monitor list.

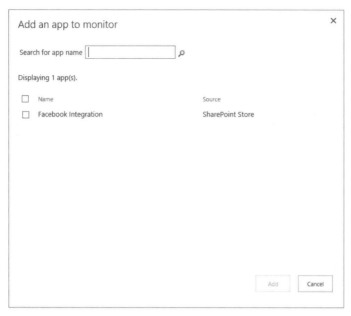

FIGURE 11-31

Removing an App from the Monitor List

1. In Central Administration, click Apps.

2. Under the Apps section, click Monitor Apps.

3. Select the check box of the app to be removed.

4. In the Manage group of the Ribbon, select Remove App.

Monitoring App Usage from Central Administration

After apps have been added to the Monitor Apps page, you can view error and usage details associated with that app in multiple ways. The following steps describe how to view the app details via Central Administration:

1. In Central Administration, click Apps.

2. Under App Management, click Monitor Apps.

3. On the Monitor Apps page, select the appropriate app.

4. The App Details page, shown in Figure 11-32, is launched.

5. You can manipulate the usage chart time frame by selecting Days, Months, or Years.

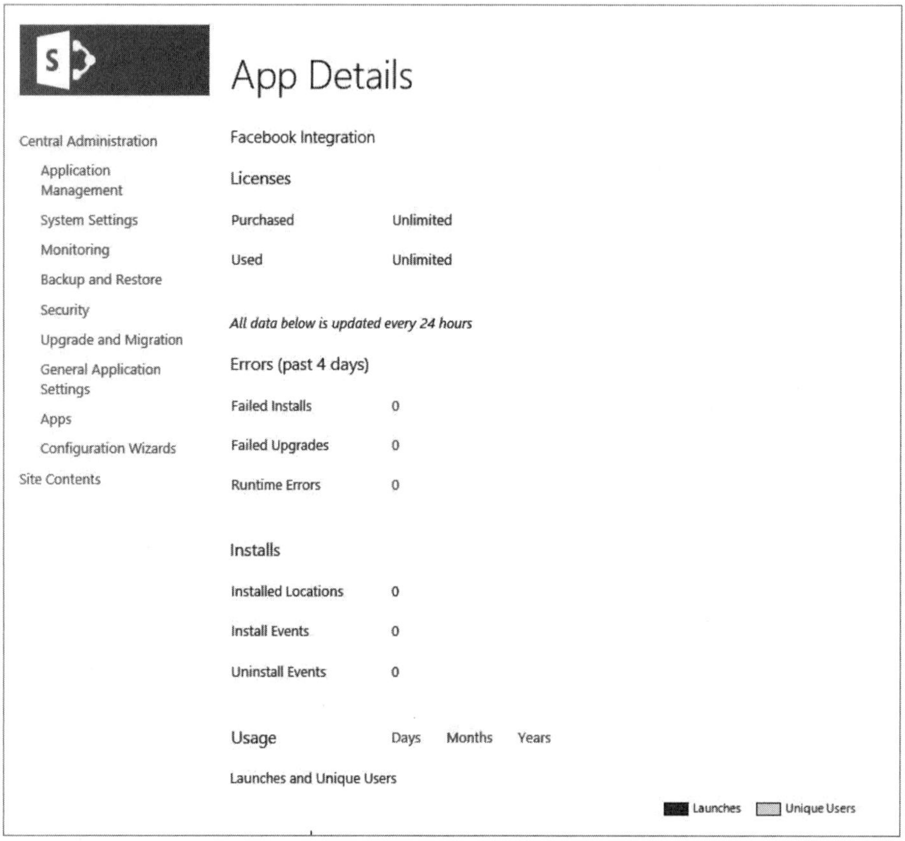

FIGURE 11-32

Monitoring App Errors from Central Administration

App runtime errors are also reported on the Monitor Apps page in Central Administration. Use the following steps to discover them:

1. In Central Administration, click Apps.

2. Under App Management, click Monitor Apps.

3. You can launch the Runtime Errors dialog by clicking on the number in the Runtime Errors column for the appropriate app or by selecting the app's check box and choosing View Errors in the App Details group of the Ribbon.

4. Additional details for individual errors can be discovered by clicking the URL in the Location column.

Monitoring App Usage in a SharePoint Site

Apps are automatically monitored at the site level in SharePoint 2013. This means that it is possible to view the App Monitoring Details of an individual app within an individual site. These details can be viewed with the following steps:

1. Click the Site Actions icon and select Site Contents. This will launch a page that shows all the installed apps.

2. To discover the error details of a specific app, click on the app's ellipsis. You may need to drill into multiple additional details, as shown in Figure 11-33, and select the Details option.

FIGURE 11-33

3. A page very similar to the details screen in Central Administration provides monitoring data for a given app. To discover more specific error details, click the number next to Install, Runtime, or Upgrade errors.

4. Usage details can be organized by Day, Month, and Year. This is the exact same behavior available from Central Administration.

Monitoring and Managing App Licenses

Of course, SharePoint 2013 apps support a licensing model. Developers of apps are responsible for supporting and delivering the licensing model through their own code, although administrators can manage and monitor these licenses. SharePoint 2013 is not responsible for enforcing licensing. Licenses can be transferred up to three times between SharePoint farms.

SharePoint administrators can track the number of users for each license through Central Administration's Manage App Licenses page. They can also add and remove user licenses as well as add additional users to manage licenses.

Viewing App License Details

1. Verify that the user account performing this procedure is a member of the Farm Administrators group or a license manager.

2. In Central Administration, click Apps.

3. On the Apps page in the SharePoint and Office Store section, click Manage App Licenses, as shown in Figure 11-34.

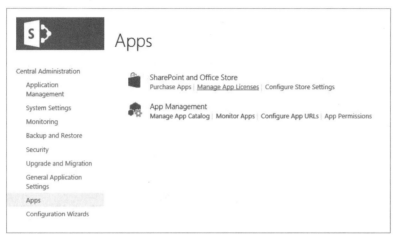

FIGURE 11-34

4. On the App Licenses page, click an app for SharePoint in the list to view the license details, as shown in Figure 11-35.

FIGURE 11-35

> **NOTE** *The Manage App License page shows detailed licensing information, including the name of the app, the developer, and current license details.*

5. In the top section of the Manage App License page shown in Figure 11-36, click the drop-down arrow to see purchase details for the selected app.

FIGURE 11-36

The app details include the following information:

➤   Number of licenses available for users

➤   License type

➤   App purchaser name

> **NOTE** *Click Actions ⇨ View in the SharePoint Store to see the app details.*

In the People with a License section, the number of available licenses and a list of the people who currently have licenses for this app are shown. In the License Managers section, all app managers are listed.

Adding Users to an App License

1.   Verify that the user account performing this procedure is a member of the Farm Administrators group.

2.   On the Manage App Licenses page, click an app for SharePoint for which users should be added.

3.   In the People with a License section, click Assign People.

4.   In the dialog that appears, enter the user name to add and then click Add User.

The list of user names at the bottom of the page, as well as the number of licenses, should be updated.

Purchasing More Licenses for an App

1. Verify that the user account performing this procedure is a member of the Farm Administrators group.

2. On the Manage App Licenses page, click the app for which additional licenses need to be purchased.

3. In the People with a License section, click Buy more licenses.

4. The SharePoint Store will open, displaying the specific app and details with links to purchase additional licenses. Choose the number of app licenses to purchase and click OK.

Adding a License Manager

1. Verify that the user account performing this procedure is a member of the Farm Administrators group.

2. On the Manage App License page, in the License Managers section, click Add Manager.

3. Below the License Managers section, confirm that the new license manager appears in the list.

SUMMARY

As you have seen in this chapter, the new SharePoint 2013 App Model enables users to embrace customizations and extensions to the SharePoint platform. It provides this capability to extend SharePoint functionality while reducing any potential negative impact of these customizations to the farm's health and operations. Administrators who familiarize themselves with the terms and concepts of the new model, and the various hosting options, will be able to configure and manage a farm effectively. Although full-trust farm solutions and sandbox solutions may still be used, the new App Model is the recommended approach for creating and delivering custom solutions.

12

Branding SharePoint

In this chapter, you'll learn what it takes to brand a SharePoint 2013 site, including some of the various components you'll likely encounter when dealing with branding, and what changes have been introduced with SharePoint 2013 and how they relate to your job as an administrator. By the end of this chapter, you will be able to achieve the nirvana that is known as "making SharePoint not look like SharePoint."

WHAT IS BRANDING?

Branding is a familiar term whose meaning varies depending on the context in which it is used. If you're in the supermarket, maybe you're trying to decide whether to get the known name brand of a bag of chips, or if you should save a little money and go with the store brand instead. If you are a ranch hand, maybe you're thinking of marking cattle with red-hot branding irons. If you are in marketing, you understand how a company's product or service can be represented through its logo, colors, slogan, website, and advertisements. With these variations in mind, it might be useful to spend a bit of time considering what branding means to you, the SharePoint administrator, and why you should care about it.

When you think of well-known products or companies with good reputations, what comes to mind? Maybe it is a familiar logo or a set of colors or images that remind you of that product or company. Companies that offer products or services with strong brand recognition among consumers nearly always have a marketing and branding strategy that applies the same set of colors, logos, and images across all forms of media: television, print ads, billboards, and websites. Indeed, this recognition can be so strong that companies that want to change their branding, even in small ways, often meet with fierce customer resistance. This close association of a design with a company or product can be translated to a SharePoint site as well. In this sense, the definition of branding a SharePoint site aligns closely with a marketer's view of branding.

To "brand" a SharePoint site, you apply custom master pages, page layouts, CSS, XML, images, and Web Parts to it to make it unique. This means it will look (and in some cases behave) much different than it does out of the box. In other words, you are branding a SharePoint site to make it look, well, not like SharePoint. You can think of branding as being synonymous with "user interface design," but with the added purpose of applying a unique and consistent appearance. You are essentially applying a brand to a website that represents your company, department, or team.

Microsoft put a lot of effort into making SharePoint look a certain way out of the box. The visual style of SharePoint 2013 is very much in line with the visual style of Office 2013 and the Windows 8 UI. Changes have also been made to make the interface easier to use for end users. However, Microsoft has also ensured that the interface of SharePoint 2013 is fully customizable, enabling designers and nondesigners alike to make SharePoint look and respond in whatever way works best for them. Later in this chapter we'll spend some time covering the various methods that allow you to change the look of a SharePoint site, from the simple to the complex. Figure 12-1 shows the SharePoint team site as it looks out of the box.

FIGURE 12-1

BRANDING CONSIDERATIONS

Just as you can't create the content in your SharePoint site without some prior planning and organization, you need to spend some time analyzing your branding requirements. What kind of site are you building? Is it going to be a public-facing Internet site or a company intranet? What information are you going to be presenting? How important is the look and feel of the site in relation to the overall company branding? Does the site need to be branded at all?

These are just a few of the questions that should be given some thought before beginning a branding project. Another important consideration is the level of effort that you are willing to put into changing the look of SharePoint. You can roughly divide these levels of effort into three basic categories:

➤ **Low Effort | High Impact** — Changing the look and feel of the site using an out-of-the-box composed look.

➤ **Medium Effort | Medium to High Impact** — Changing the look and feel of the site by applying alternate CSS to the site.

➤ **High Effort | High Impact** — Changing the look and feel of the site through a completely custom branding effort.

Low-effort branding is achieved by using a composed look that you can select from a gallery included with SharePoint. Medium-effort branding involves creating an alternate CSS file and applying it to the site in order to modify some of the site's look and feel while keeping much of the overall structure the same. Finally, high-effort branding involves creating a custom design, custom master pages, page layouts, CSS, and more. You'll be looking at more of the various components of these different levels of effort later in the chapter. With the many changes and enhancements made to SharePoint 2013 branding, you can certainly find an option that will fit your needs. In addition, you don't need to worry about choosing the "wrong" level at first. If you're not sure where to start, start with the low-effort option and see how it goes. If you decide you need more flexibility, or just hate the idea of having free time, then move up to the medium-effort option. If that is too limiting, you can break out the big guns and move up to the high-effort option. Everything you've learned in earlier methods will help as you move up the branding ladder.

Another important factor that comes into play is the type of site you are working with. Generally speaking, an internal collaborative site such as an intranet has a different set of branding requirements than a public-facing Internet site. The type of branding and level of effort needed varies according to how the site is going to be used and what options are available in the various site templates included with SharePoint 2013. Table 12-1 outlines key differences between the two most common types of sites, an Internet-facing site and an internal, intranet site.

TABLE 12-1: Internet Sites vs. Intranet Sites

INTERNET	INTRANET
Public facing	Internal facing
Usually anonymous users	Usually authenticated users
Driving information to the public	Communicating among a smaller group
Many visitors, fewer authors	More authors, contributors, and visitors
Content more tightly controlled	Some freely created content
Slower connection to server	Fast connection to server

SHAREPOINT AND PUBLISHING

Like SharePoint 2010 and SharePoint 2007 before it, SharePoint 2013 also includes a Publishing feature. If you have used the Standard or Enterprise versions of either of the previous editions of SharePoint, you likely know what publishing is. If you have only used Windows SharePoint Services (WSS) 3.0 or SharePoint Foundation 2010, or are using SharePoint Foundation 2013, you may not be familiar with the concept of publishing. Publishing is important from a SharePoint branding perspective because it opens up more options for controlling the look of your site, such as being able to easily change the master page, navigation, and using custom page layouts.

In SharePoint terms, publishing is a feature that enables content authors to make pages available when they are ready to be shared with the rest of the team, the company, or the world. Essentially, its main purpose is to give authors more control over when their content is consumed on the web. However, the SharePoint Publishing feature also gives designers much more flexibility when creating their sites. It enables the creation of custom page layouts (you'll learn more about these in the section "Page Layouts and Wiki Pages"), which are basically templates for displaying content on a page. It also provides much more flexibility in terms of how navigation is structured, and enables you to choose whether you want to build your navigation from a managed meta data term set (called *managed navigation*) or use the traditional SharePoint navigation structure (called *structured navigation*). Finally, with a Publishing Site template, you can more easily change master pages within the browser. Without publishing it is still possible to change a master page, but doing so requires SharePoint Designer 2013. Using composed looks (which are covered in the "Composed Looks" section later in this chapter), it is possible to change master pages in the browser; but without some sweating, and maybe even some swearing, you won't be able to select any custom master pages until a composed look has been built around it.

If you plan to do a good deal of custom branding for your website, whether it is for an intranet or Internet site, you should consider enabling the publishing features to take full advantage of what it has to offer. The publishing features are available only on SharePoint Server 2013, Standard and Enterprise editions. They are not available for SharePoint Foundation 2013. This isn't to say that you can't brand a SharePoint Foundation 2013 site, but you have fewer options and features available for creating a custom-branded site than you do with the full server versions.

Even if a site is going to be an internal collaboration site, you might want to consider using a publishing site template as the root site when creating your site collection. You can still build team sites underneath it, but with the added benefit of being able to take advantage of some of the publishing features that allow management of the master page throughout the site collection.

Here's how you can create a publishing site collection from Central Administration (note that you'll need to have administrative access to Central Administration in order to perform these steps):

1. Open the Central Administration site.

2. Under the Application Management header on the Central Administration home page, click Create site collections.

3. In the Web Application section, click the drop-down next to the Web Application URL and select the Web Application in which you'd like to create the site collection.

4. Enter a Title and optionally a description for the site collection.

5. In the Web Site Address section, type the URL that will be used to access the site collection.

6. In the Template Selection section, make sure the Select experience version drop-down is set to 2013. Then click the Publishing tab, and make sure Publishing Portal is selected.

7. In the Primary Site Collection Administrator section, enter a user name in the field. Optionally type a user name in the Secondary Site Collection Administrator field.

8. Click OK to create your new site collection. When the process has finished, you'll be presented with a link to open the newly created site in a new browser tab.

You can also enable publishing features for a non-publishing site with a few button clicks (note that in order to perform these steps, you need to be logged in as a site collection administrator):

1. At the root of the site collection, click the Site Actions menu and select Site Settings.

2. Under the Site Collection Administration heading, click Site Collection Features.

3. Scroll down to SharePoint Server Publishing Infrastructure and click the Activate button next to it, as shown in Figure 12-2. After a few seconds, the page will refresh and the Activate button will now say Deactivate, as shown in Figure 12-3. A note next to the button will show that the feature is active.

4. Click the Site Actions button again and select Site Settings.

5. Under the Site Actions heading (not the drop-down menu in the Ribbon), click Manage Site Features.

6. Scroll down to the SharePoint Server Publishing feature and click the Activate button. Presto chango! The Team Site template has been essentially turned into a publishing site.

FIGURE 12-2

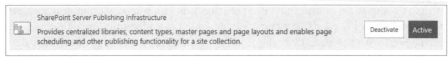

FIGURE 12-3

When the SharePoint Server Publishing feature is activated, any new pages created will automatically be created in the Pages library (which was provisioned by the Publishing feature) instead of the Site Pages library, which team sites use by default for storing wiki pages.

One final thing you may need to do, depending on your requirements, is set a publishing page as the site's home page:

1. Click Site Actions ⇨ View Site Contents.

2. Click the Pages library icon.

3. In the Ribbon, click the Files tab.

4. Click the New Document drop-down and select Welcome Page.

5. Give the page a title. Optionally, enter a description.

6. The URL Name field auto-populates with whatever value you added to the Title field. You can change this if you wish.

7. Select a page layout (for example, select "(Welcome Page) Splash").

8. When the Pages library is displayed, click your new page to open it.

9. In the Ribbon, click the Page tab and then click the Make Homepage button.

10. In the pop-up dialog, click OK to confirm that you want to set this page as the home page.

11. Test your new home page by typing the root of your site collection into the browser's address bar (e.g., `http://portal.contoso.com`). The new page should load instead of the old default team site page.

12. Pat yourself on the back. You have turned your boring old team site into a fancy new publishing site.

COMPONENTS OF SHAREPOINT BRANDING

Early websites were usually built with all the HTML and styles needed to attain the site's look on every single page. This approach quickly fell out of favor, however, because if an update was wanted to the overall look of the site, generally every single page in the site needed to be changed. Later techniques alleviated some of the pain of maintaining a sizeable HTML website (Cascading Style Sheets, for example), but it wasn't until other technologies such as ASP.NET 2.0 emerged that maintaining websites became much less tedious. With ASP.NET, a web designer could define the common elements of a site in a centralized location, called a *master page*. This approach had two main benefits.

First, it enabled mass changes to the site's look by changing one or two central files, which was very convenient. Second, it also decoupled the responsibility of creating the site's content from the site's look. This enabled people to create content without needing to concern themselves with making a site look pretty. It also created opportunities for people to just brand websites without having to contribute content.

A custom branded SharePoint site isn't all that much different from a traditional website in many ways. It relies on HTML, Cascading Style Sheets (CSS), and images to achieve the desired look you're seeking. The major difference is that SharePoint, being built on the .NET platform, utilizes master pages and page layouts to control where the various site elements are positioned.

Master Pages

Master pages can be thought of as the skeleton of the site; it is what the rest of the site is built upon. Generally speaking, the master page contains the major, common elements that are found on every page of a site, such as the site's header, search box, navigation, and footer, among other common elements. It contains a place where each individual page's content will be injected as the browser renders the page. A master page is used to control the overall look and structure of the site.

A major change to the way that SharePoint 2013 uses master pages compared to previous versions is that each master page is tied to a corresponding .html file. When the HTML file is edited, the changes are reflected in the master page file. This approach is designed to provide more flexibility to the process of editing and maintaining a master page. You'll learn about this topic later in the chapter in the "Using the Design Manager" section.

In a publishing site, the master page can be changed in the browser. Out of the box, SharePoint 2013 comes with several master pages:

➤ **v15.master** — The default master page used throughout SharePoint 2013, particularly on team sites.

➤ **overlay.master** — A centered design that overlays the main content on a transparent container so some of the background image is visible.

➤ **belltown.master** — No left navigation, this focuses more on content. This combines elements of v15.master and overlay.master. It is partially full width with some centered content.

Changing the master page uses the same process used in previous versions of SharePoint. The only difference this time is that with device channels (discussed in the "Device Channels" section of this chapter), you can apply a different master page for displaying in different browsers or devices that access the site.

The following steps will show you how to change the master page for your publishing site:

1. Click the Site Actions menu.

2. Under the Look and Feel header, click Master page.

3. Select the master page you want to use for the site master page. The site master page is the page that is applied to content pages.

4. Select the master page you want to use for the system master page. System master pages are pages such as the Site Settings page that are served from the /_layouts directory. Also, team sites built under a publishing site that have the SharePoint publishing feature activated will inherit the system master page setting.

5. Click OK to set the master pages (see Figure 12-4).

FIGURE 12-4

Traditionally, team sites didn't have an interface for choosing the master page from within the browser. Without enabling publishing, the only way to set a custom master page previously was to manually set it using SharePoint Designer. This hasn't changed much in SharePoint 2013, but the interface for setting composed looks (also discussed later in this chapter) enables you to choose out-of-the-box master pages along with the rest of the composed look settings.

Page Layouts and Wiki Pages

Content on each page in a SharePoint site is stored in a page layout or text layout.

Page layouts in SharePoint can be thought of as templates for content layout on a page. In the master page/page layout relationship, a page layout fits in the main content placeholder of the master page (see Figure 12-5). Page layouts, which are found only on sites with the Publishing features enabled, offer the most flexibility to designers and content managers alike, as designers can create custom page layouts to display content on a page. If none of the numerous out-of-the-box layouts are suitable, a custom page layout can be easily created in the site, with custom fields to capture more content and custom zones to add Web Parts to the page.

FIGURE 12-5

Page layouts rely on field controls on the page to display text and/or images. A *Web Part zone* is an area on the page where you can add one or more Web Parts to enhance the page's functionality, such as adding additional text areas or rolling up content.

Out of the box, SharePoint 2013 contains many text areas. You can find them in the master page gallery by clicking Site Actions ⇨ Site Settings ⇨ Master Pages and Page Layouts. Generally speaking, any file that ends in .aspx is a page layout. Much like master pages, page layouts in SharePoint 2013 are tied to a corresponding HTML file that can be edited in an editor of your choice. What that means is discussed in more detail later in the "Using the Design Manager" section.

If you want to see how page layouts can affect the appearance of your page, simply select a new layout by following these steps:

1. On a Publishing site, click Site Actions ⇨ New Page.

2. Type a name for your page. Note that SharePoint provides the URL for your page as you type in the page name.

3. Click OK.

4. Your new page will open in edit mode. Click the Page tab in the Ribbon.

5. Click the Page Layout drop-down and select one of the available layouts. Note how additional fields are displayed or hidden depending on the layout you select. (Changing a page layout is allowed only when the page is in edit mode.)

Page Layout Content Types

Page layouts are based on content types, which help define what fields are available on a page. The basic definition of a *content type* is a grouping of site columns that help define a category of content in SharePoint. You can also think of them simply as templates for new objects, whether pages or documents. In other words, the type of meta data collected in a list's or library's columns determines whether an object in SharePoint is a document, a link, or a web page, for example. When creating custom page layouts, you select an existing content type that serves as the parent of the page. This parent content type determines the fields that are available when creating your page.

Content types live at the site-collection level and are composed of site columns, a large set of which is used repeatedly throughout SharePoint. Content types are simply groupings of these columns that hold information about an object in a site. For the purpose of page layouts, some site columns are designed to store content, and these are the fields that are available to be displayed on a page layout. For instance, an Article page content type consists of a title field, a byline field, a date field, an image picker field, an image caption field, and a page content field.

Wiki Pages and Text Layouts

Wiki pages are similar to page layouts, but they are found primarily on team sites. Their function is to help content authors add information to a page quickly and without much hassle. Much like the page content area of a page layout, wiki pages enable click-and-type functionality. Both Web Parts and rich content can be added to a page using the familiar Ribbon interface. So how do wiki pages differ from page layouts? Wiki pages use what are called *text layouts*, which also act as templates for storing content on individual pages within a SharePoint site; however, text layouts offer less flexibility than a page layout. For example, site designers can't edit the zones of a text layout or add additional text layouts. The eight text layouts included with SharePoint are the only eight you can use. If you need additional layouts or customized layouts for your site, then a wiki page will not be adequate; you need to look to page layouts to meet your requirements.

To change the text layout of a wiki page, put the page in edit mode and click the Format Text tab in the Ribbon. Click the Text Layout drop-down button and choose one of the styles. The location to set a text layout in SharePoint 2013 is different from SharePoint 2010, where the Text Layout button was found under the Page tab in the Ribbon. Figure 12-6 shows the available text layouts from which you can choose.

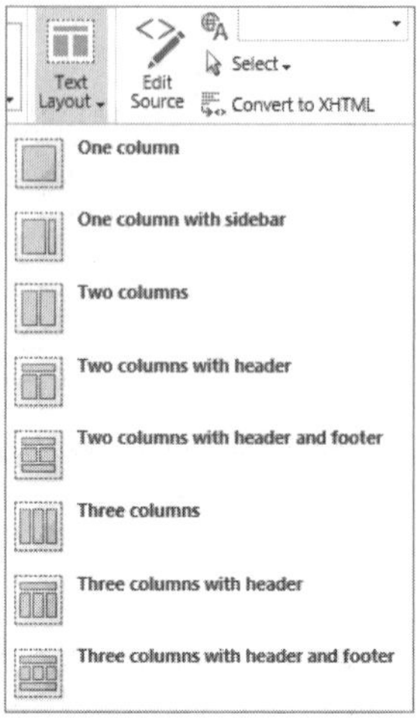

HTML, Cascading Style Sheets, and More

FIGURE 12-6

Another important component of a complete SharePoint brand includes straight HTML, CSS, images, and scripts. Together, these will determine the overall look of the site. HTML tells the browser what to render and provides structure to the page; CSS tells the browser how to style the HTML; images add to the overall design of the page; and scripts add functionality.

In previous incarnations of SharePoint, the main location for storing images, scripts, and CSS was in the Style Library, a special document library to which all users had access. The Style Library still exists in SharePoint 2013, but the recommended place for storing branding assets for a custom design is now in a folder within the master page gallery. That's because you can now map a drive directly to the master page gallery to upload your design assets, making it a convenient place to access everything for editing later.

WHAT'S NEW IN BRANDING FOR SHAREPOINT 2013

When you buy a new version of an existing product, chances are you will get some new or enhanced features. For example, when you buy a newer model of a car, you can expect it has some worthwhile upgrades, like that back up camera that lets you watch your kid's bike when you run over it. When you upgrade your phone, you take advantage of the latest technology. From a branding perspective, SharePoint 2013 is no different. It includes a lot of the technology you have become familiar with over the years, but with some nice new features that make the upgrade compelling. This section covers some of the bells and whistles that SharePoint 2013 includes to make your site branding experience easy and fun.

Composed Looks

In SharePoint 2003, the concept of *themes* was introduced. Themes were intended to enable you to change the basic look and feel of a site with some CSS and images, but they were somewhat tricky to make and required knowledge of CSS and direct access to the SharePoint server. They weren't much better in SharePoint 2007.

SharePoint 2010 changed the underlying model of themes quite a bit with the theming engine, which simplified their creation, but some users argued that they were not as flexible and customizable as in SharePoint 2003 or 2007. Applying themes essentially recolored the site and in some cases swapped out the fonts used on a site, but that was basically the extent of what they offered. Some customization of themes was possible within the browser, or theme files could be created in the Office client and uploaded to a SharePoint site.

SharePoint 2013 combines the best parts of these two theming approaches into what are called *composed looks*. You can think of composed looks as the next evolution of theming a site: You get to choose images, fonts, and a color scheme, and you can build the composed look easily within in the browser.

Composed looks consist of a background image or color, an overall color scheme, a master page selection, and fonts. Out of the box, 14 composed looks are available. Each composed look can be customized, enabling you to give your site a unique look with minimal effort.

Creating a composed look in the browser is simple. Just execute the following steps to create a composed look:

1. If you are starting out with a freshly created team site template, you can click the What's your style? tile, shown in Figure 12-7. If you have an established site and have removed the Getting Started Web Part, you can access composed looks from the Site Settings page by clicking the Site Settings gear icon at the top right of the Ribbon and selecting Site Settings. Under the Look and Feel header, click the link that says "Change the look."

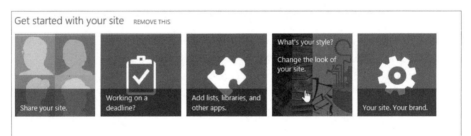

FIGURE 12-7

2. On the Change the Look page, shown in Figure 12-8, browse through the options to find a custom look that you want to start with.

   a. When you select it, you'll get a small preview of what the site will look like when it is applied. You can substitute the background image with another if you like.

   b. Then you can select your color scheme.

   c. Next, you can select from the two out-of-the-box master pages, v15 and Belltown. The preview window shows the difference between the two as you hover over the master page options.

   d. Finally, you can select the set of fonts you want for the site. Figure 12-9 shows the Change the Look page that you use to build a composed look.

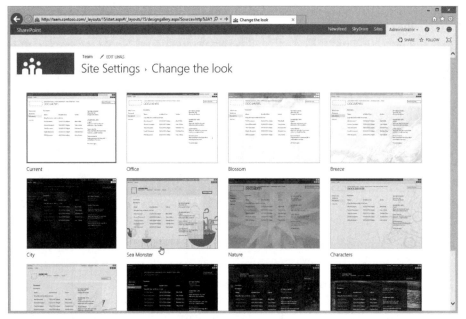

FIGURE 12-8

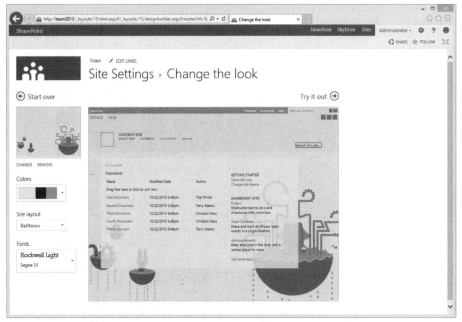

FIGURE 12-9

3. When you have made your selections, simply click the Try it out link above the preview for a larger preview image.

    a. If you like what you see, you can click the "Yes, keep it" link.

    b. If you want to make some adjustments, just click "No, not quite there yet."

When you apply the theme, your site will have the new look. Figure 12-10 shows a site with a composed look applied.

FIGURE 12-10

If you want to use composed looks with custom master pages, you need to put some effort into the master page in order to integrate it with the various changes that result from composed looks. Generally speaking, most projects that need custom master pages will probably have a unique look already and therefore won't gain anything from the composed looks. Composed looks are useful when you want a quick, easy way to change SharePoint's appearance without getting your hands too dirty.

Device Channels

The rapid adoption of mobile devices, including smartphones and tablets, to browse the Internet has been unprecedented. As this mobile device technology continues to explode, many website owners have started creating customized versions of their site to give visitors using a mobile device a better experience. For instance, a smartphone browser can benefit from a condensed version of the same site displayed on a desktop browser. Although the phone's browser may be capable of handling the full version of a site, it may not be practical to navigate a traditional website on a phone or tablet for a variety of reasons, such as the touch interface, screen size, or hardware limitations. In order to offer mobile device users the best experience, many websites default mobile traffic to an optimized version of the site. This practice isn't limited to phones or desktop PCs, of course. For years now sites have been offering different optimized versions for various browsers, which vary according to the browser's capabilities. Typically, older browsers see a version of the site with fewer bells and whistles than a modern browser, which are optimized for the latest technologies.

SharePoint 2013 offers a similar approach to this practice. Through the use of device channels, administrators and designers can assign different master pages to the SharePoint site depending on the browser used to access it. Note that the use of device channels is limited to publishing sites. Team and other collaboration sites can still use a URL query string to access the built-in mobile version of a site. For example, `http://sharepointsite/?Mobile=1` will render the site as a mobile version. The mobile version of the site is similar to the SharePoint 2010 mobile site, though in SharePoint 2013 the mobile version has some minimal styling and is optimized for touch devices.

When setting up a device channel, you are essentially telling the SharePoint server to look at the browser's user agent string (which is a string of text that all browsers send to a server when a page is requested), and match up keywords that you specify with the user agent string. For instance, you can be very specific and add the following browser user string for Firefox 14.0.1:

```
Mozilla/5.0 (Windows; U; Windows NT 6.1; WOW64; en-US; rv:2.0.4) Gecko/20120718
AskTbAVR-IDW/3.12.5.17700 Firefox/14.0.1
```

Alternately, you can simply add the keyword "Firefox" to your device channel, and SharePoint will pick "Firefox" out of the long user string name that the browser sends. You can add multiple keywords or full user agent strings to a particular channel. SharePoint 2013 has a limit of 10 device channels, and you can define a maximum of 150 different keywords or user agents per channel. That should be enough to satisfy just about every scenario! Once you have your device channel set up, you can open the Master Page settings page and apply a different master page to each channel you created.

For example, say you want to set up a specific channel for mobile phones and display a simplified master page when these devices access the site. You could create a device channel called "Mobile Phones" and insert keywords such as "Android," "iPhone," and "Windows Phone." Or, if you wanted to target every mobile device, you could use the string `$FALLBACKMOBILEUSERAGENTS;` in the Device Inclusion Rules field.

After creating your device channel, you would go to the master page settings screen, where you could apply a mobile-optimized master page to your Mobile Phones channel. When a user visits the site on a mobile device, the site will be displayed with the custom mobile master page loaded.

Although device channels are intended mainly for mobile devices, you can test the functionality using desktop browsers and the out-of-the-box master pages to see how it works:

1. Using Internet Explorer, click the Site Actions menu on the home page of your site.

2. Click Site Settings.

3. On the Site Settings page, under the Look and Feel header, click Device Channels.

4. In the Ribbon, click the New Item button (or click the New Item link on the page).

5. In the Name field, type **Firefox**.

6. In the Alias field, type **Firefox**.

7. In the Description field, type **Testing Device Channel for Firefox**.

8. In the Device Inclusion Rules field, type **Firefox**.

9. Check the Active box and then click Save. Figure 12-11 shows the completed dialog for the device channel.

FIGURE 12-11

10. Click the Site Actions menu and choose Site Settings.

11. Under the Look and Feel header, click Master Page.

12. Note that you now have two drop-downs to set the Site Master Page. In the Firefox drop-down, select Belltown as the master page.

13. In the Default drop-down, select v15.master for the master page (see Figure 12-12). Click OK.

14. Navigate back to the home page of the site.

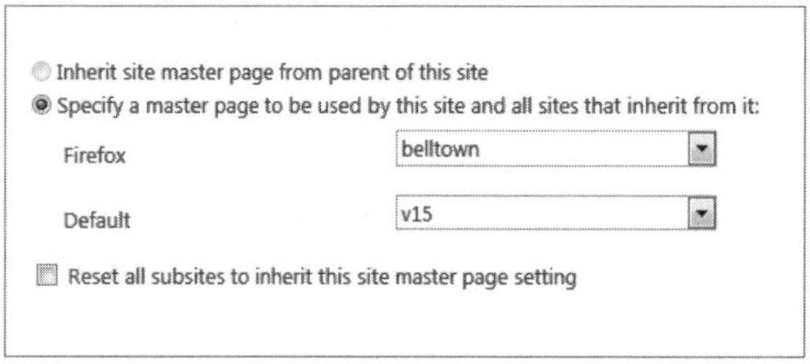

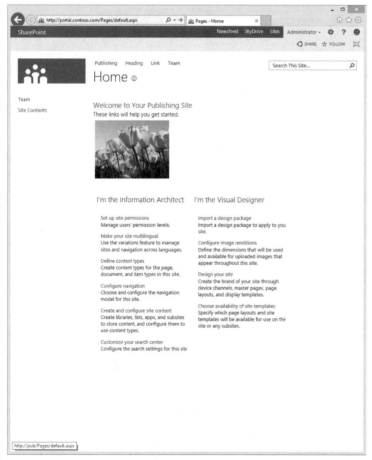

> ○ Inherit site master page from parent of this site
> ● Specify a master page to be used by this site and all sites that inherit from it:
>
> Firefox   belltown ▾
>
> Default   v15 ▾
>
> ☐ Reset all subsites to inherit this site master page setting

FIGURE 12-12

15. Open the site using the Firefox browser. Although the master pages look similar, you should be able to tell that the two browsers are loading different master pages.

Figure 12-13 shows the site loaded in Internet Explorer, and Figure 12-14 shows the same site loaded in Firefox, with a different master page applied thanks to the device channel. Notice that the Firefox version does not have a left navigation pane, which is a feature of the Belltown master page.

FIGURE 12-13

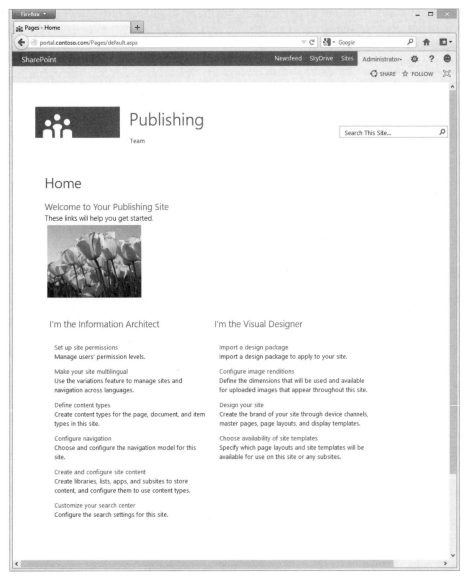

FIGURE 12-14

Device Channel Testing

You can also test your different device channels regardless of what browser you are using by appending ?DeviceChannel=AliasOfDeviceChannel to the URL of the site (replacing AliasOfDeviceChannel with the name you provided for the device channel's alias. For example, you could test the device channel we created for Firefox within Internet Explorer by adding ?DeviceChannel=Firefox to the end of the URL and pressing Enter. This loads the specified device channel's master page. This would be a good way to preview a mobile version of your master page without needing various mobile devices to test with, or having to download the various mobile SDKs from each manufacturer's website.

Device Channel Panel

Page layouts in SharePoint 2013 should display no matter what master page is being called in using device channels, but should you want to display or hide certain content on a page layout, you can use what is called a *device channel panel* in your master page code. You can add a device channel panel to a page layout and define its specific channel or channels. Device channel panels could be used in conjunction with a custom master page in order to hide certain elements on a page layout, such as images or entire sections of your page. You could also show elements within a device channel panel.

When you add a device channel panel to your page, a large yellow block of text appears as a placeholder to help you determine where to put your specific content, such as HTML or CSS that should be rendered when browsing the site with a device that has a channel specified.

Image Renditions

A problem familiar to many SharePoint site administrators is users uploading gigantic (3MB or more) photo files to an image library and displaying them on a page. Even with the fastest current bandwidth capabilities, downloading such large images is going to slow things down, especially when there is considerable distance between the SharePoint server and the user viewing the page.

SharePoint 2013 introduces a new way to manage images intended to solve this issue. This method uses what SharePoint calls *image renditions*, a group of "profiles" that administrators can create for rendering images on the site. It uses the BLOB cache storage and a set of templates that define the width and height of the image. Therefore, when John uploads a 3MB photo of his cat to the site, or Mary uploads a 4MB photo of her new car, they can choose one of the preconfigured templates to display the image in a much smaller format. This isn't simply resizing the image on the page; image renditions are actually pulling a physically smaller file from the BLOB cache to serve to the end user.

Before you can take advantage of image renditions, you'll need to enable BLOB caching for the web application you are working in. This requires making a change to the web.config file, so be sure to make a backup of the original before you start making changes. Follow these instructions to enable BLOB caching:

1. Log on to your SharePoint server with an administrator account

2. Navigate to C:\inetpub\wwwroot\wss\VirtualDirectories\

3. Find the folder for the web app for which you want to enable BLOB caching and open it (For example, if your web application is portal.contoso.com, you would open the folder "portal.contoso.com80")

4. Make a backup copy of the web.config file

5. Open web.config

6. Perform a find for **<BlobCache** and hit Enter to find this line:

```
<BlobCache location="C:\BlobCache\14" path="\.(gif|jpg|jpeg|jpe|jfif|bmp|di
b|tif|tiff|ico|png|wdp|hdp|css|js|asf|avi|flv|m4v|mov|mp3|mp4|mpeg|mpg|rm|r
mvb|wma|wmv|ogg|ogv|oga|webm|xap)$" maxSize="10" enabled="false" />
```

7. Change the property `enabled="false"` to **`enabled="true"`**

8. Optionally change the `location` property if you want to change the location of the cache

9. Save the web.config file

Now that the BLOB cache is enabled, you can take full advantage of SharePoint 2013's image renditions.

Out of the box, SharePoint 2013 includes four predefined image renditions, which you can use, modify, or delete depending on your needs. To create your own image rendition, follow these steps (this section assumes you have uploaded images to your site already and that BLOB cache has been enabled on the web application):

1. Click the Site Actions menu and select Site Settings.

2. Under the Look and Feel header, click Image Renditions.

3. Click the Add New Item link.

4. In the Name field, type **My Custom Image Rendition**.

5. Specify a width for the rendition (note that the dimensions are measured in pixels).

6. Specify a height for the rendition. If you specify only one dimension, the image will retain its proportion as it is scaled down. Click Save.

7. Navigate to a page in your site. Click Site Actions ⇨ Edit Page.

8. Click in the Page Content area to place the cursor.

9. In the Ribbon, click the Insert tab.

10. Click the drop-down under the Picture button.

11. Select an image from your site and click the Insert button.

12. With the image selected, click the Pick Rendition button in the Ribbon and select My Custom Image Rendition (see Figure 12-15). The image will be resized to the dimensions you selected.

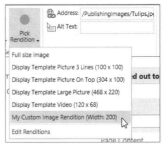

FIGURE 12-15

13. Click Save & Close in the Ribbon to exit edit mode.

Remember that this isn't simply displaying the original image on the page with new dimensions: SharePoint has created new image files in the BLOB cache folder from the original image and is pulling them from the server's hard drive. You can verify for yourself that the image's dimensions and file sizes are smaller by examining the image's properties: Open your page in edit mode again and select the image. In the Ribbon, click the Image tab, then click the Pick Rendition button and select "Full size image." Click Save & Close, then right-click on the image and select Properties (or View Image Info, depending on the browser you are using). Note the image file size. Apply your new image rendition to the image and right-click the smaller image and view its properties to see its smaller file size.

If you don't like the way your image has been cropped in your custom image rendition (or any of the out-of-the-box image renditions), you can edit the display area of an image rendition for a specific image. There are several ways to access the editing screen for an image. You can edit the image that you are using on your page by clicking the Pick Rendition button in the Ribbon and selecting Edit Renditions; or you can open your image library, click the ... (ellipses) on the bottom-right corner of the image thumbnail to open the menu, and select Edit Renditions (see Figure 12-16).

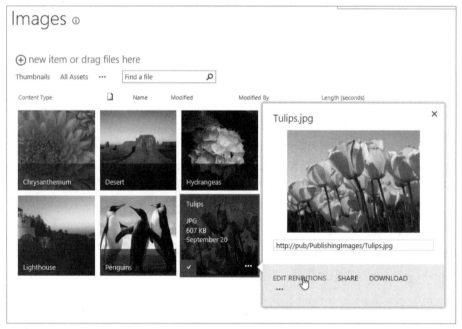

FIGURE 12-16

Now find the rendition that you want to change and click the Click to Change link under the preview image (see Figure 12-17). Here you can select the display area of the image and see a preview below the selection area. Click the Save button to save your new selection, but be aware that changing the display area for a particular image rendition will update all instances of the image rendition that are referenced throughout the site.

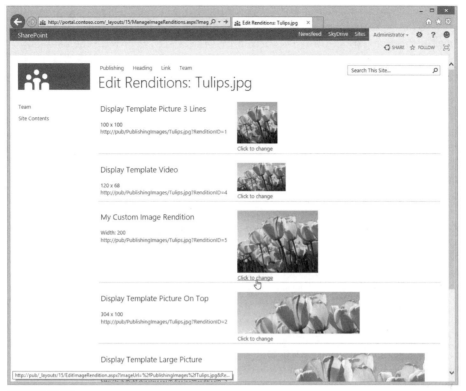

FIGURE 12-17

You can see how reducing image size will drastically reduce the page load for SharePoint. That means reducing the amount of time it will take to download all those photos from the last company Christmas party — at least the ones that can be shared.

Display Templates

In past iterations of SharePoint, search result pages were driven by XSLT, which many developers and designers agree is not the friendliest language to work with for creating good-looking results. Most users have resigned themselves to the look and feel of out-of-the-box search results.

Display templates, new to SharePoint 2013, will make it much easier to customize search results and search-driven Web Parts such as the new Content By Search Web Part. A display template offers additional options for customizing the display of search-driven content. When search results match a set of predefined templates, known as *result types*, search will display those results according to the selected display template. For example, if PDF results appear in search, a PDF display template will be loaded and displayed in the results.

The new search-driven Content By Search (CBS) Web Part also takes advantage of display templates. Previous versions of SharePoint used the Content Query Web Part for rolling up content. The look and feel of the web part's results was driven by `itemstyle.xsl`. With the new CBS Web Part, the look and feel is controlled by display templates. Essentially, the CBS Web Part is the new version of the Content Query Web Part. Its styling will be much easier than writing XSL to achieve the same results, and its performance will be better because it is leveraging the search index.

Display templates consist of an HTML file and a corresponding JavaScript file. All display templates can be found in the master page gallery in the Display Templates folder. Because search results are no longer driven by XML and XSLT, creating a custom display template is much easier. The recommended method is to copy a display template that is close to the look you want to achieve and modify it to meet your needs.

Improving Speed with Minimal Download Strategy

Because no one has ever accused SharePoint of being too fast, a new concept in SharePoint 2013 is the *Minimal Download Strategy (MDS)*. Generally speaking, as you browse around in a SharePoint site, every element on each page is reloaded each time a page is opened. Between the CSS files, JavaScript files, images, and HTML that are repeatedly reloaded, a SharePoint site is pretty bulky. The idea behind the MDS is to reload only those elements on a page that differ from the previously loaded page. This means that anything that stays the same on a page — such as the header area, the navigation, and the search box — are cached. By reloading only the new content on a page, the amount of content that needs to be sent from the server to the client machine each time a page is loaded is drastically reduced.

The Minimal Download Strategy is a SharePoint feature found at the web level. You can enable or disable it, but in general there is no reason not to use it in collaboration scenarios, as it will greatly improve the overall performance of SharePoint on the client side.

> **NOTE** *Unfortunately, the MDS is not compatible with sites that use the Publishing features. If it is enabled on a publishing site, SharePoint will actually end up loading the page twice: Once to check what has changed from the previous page, and again, without the MDS feature, when it realizes that it is a publishing site.*

The MDS is made possible by `<SharePoint:AjaxDelta>` controls wrapped around SharePoint content on the master page. Nearly every content placeholder in an out-of-the-box SharePoint 2013 master page is wrapped in the `AjaxDelta` tag. When the MDS feature is enabled, SharePoint looks at the content in this tag to determine whether the content has changed. If not, no new information is sent from the server to fill those areas. Instead, cached information is used. When the MDS feature is disabled, SharePoint simply ignores the `AjaxDelta` tags and serves up the entire page regardless of whether anything has changed from the previous page.

Design Manager

The approach to creating branding in SharePoint 2013 is quite different from previous versions, and one of the biggest reasons is the new Design Manager, which is found in SharePoint publishing sites. Although a new version of SharePoint Designer has been released to coincide with SharePoint 2013, and it's still freely available from Microsoft for working with SharePoint sites, it is deprecated as a tool to use for creating branding. As mentioned elsewhere, the Design View has been removed from SharePoint Designer. Although it seems counterintuitive to remove a Design View from an application with "Designer" in its name, designers are now encouraged to use whatever web design tools they are accustomed to working with in order to create and maintain the branding for their site.

Once an HTML version of a design has been created, it can be imported into SharePoint and converted to a master page file, which you can accomplish using the new *Design Manager*. The Design Manager is a new component of a SharePoint 2013 Publishing site. It is more or less a wizard that walks you through the process of mapping a network location from the SharePoint server to your local computer, uploading your HTML files and site assets, and converting the plain HTML version of your branding into SharePoint master pages and page layouts. The wizard also provides some guidance in the form of steps, such as creating custom design templates if necessary, publishing and applying your custom design, and creating a design package for saving your custom branding. Figure 12-18 shows the Design Manager interface.

FIGURE 12-18

SharePoint 2013 automatically converts your HTML page to a master page and adds several placeholders. You can preview your master page to see how it functions before you actually apply it to the site. After your master page has been converted, you use what's known as the *Snippet Gallery* to add SharePoint-specific controls such as the search box, navigation elements, site logo, breadcrumb trails, and even Web Parts. The Snippet Gallery enables you to customize a control's properties, including the capability to apply a custom CSS class if you wish or changing other properties. You can select your control, make changes to its properties if you wish, and SharePoint provides a code snippet that you can copy and paste in the correct location of your original HTML file. SharePoint will make the same update automatically in the corresponding .master file.

After configuring your master page and page layouts, the Design Manager provides links for publishing and applying your custom master page to the site. Finally, you can save your work as a design package for reuse in another site if needed.

UNDERSTANDING THE SHAREPOINT 2013 BRANDING PROCESS

As mentioned earlier, one of the biggest changes to SharePoint 2013's approach to branding is that designers are no longer restricted to using only SharePoint Designer for creating and maintaining a custom look and feel for a site. Indeed, they are discouraged from doing so. Thanks to the new Design Manager in SharePoint 2013, designers can use just about any common web design tool, including Dreamweaver, Microsoft Expression Web, Notepad, or any plain text editor. Even vi! This flexibility removes some of the obstacles to creating SharePoint branding by enabling designers to use tools they are already familiar with and prefer.

Most major branding projects start out with a creative mockup, usually done in a photo-editing program such as Photoshop or GIMP. A designer can then slice up the mockup into image components and begin turning the static image into a working HTML page. Many web design tools are available for this purpose, the most popular choices being Adobe Dreamweaver and Microsoft Expression Web. Of course, some web designers prefer to use text-based programs such as Notepad++ (a free alternative to the standard Windows Notepad that has nice features such as code highlighting).

Other useful tools you'll likely need as you brand your site are the IE Developer Toolbar (included with Internet Explorer since IE 8), and the useful Firebug plug-in for Firefox. These tools will assist you in identifying what CSS class(es) are being applied to a particular element on the page, which is very helpful when you are trying to override an out-of-the-box SharePoint style with your custom styles.

Because this book is primarily focused on SharePoint administration, not the full web design process, this chapter assumes you have a basic HTML design ready to go at this point and skips right ahead to the fun stuff: importing your file into SharePoint to let the magic begin!

Using the Design Manager

You spent some time earlier going over the basic idea of the Design Manager. In this section you can dive in and see how it actually works. When you first load a publishing site, you'll see two columns of links. On the left is a set of links for information architects to start setting up permissions, content types, and navigation. On the right are links specifically for designers. These links are shortcuts to some common locations that designers need to access to start branding their site. One of these links, "Design your site," opens the Design Manager, where you can start converting your HTML. There is also a link in the Site Actions menu that takes you directly to the Design Manager.

Converting an HTML File to a SharePoint Master Page

The following steps describe how to convert an HTML file to a SharePoint master page. Figure 12-19 shows an example of a full HTML mockup of a site that will be converted to a SharePoint master page and page layout.

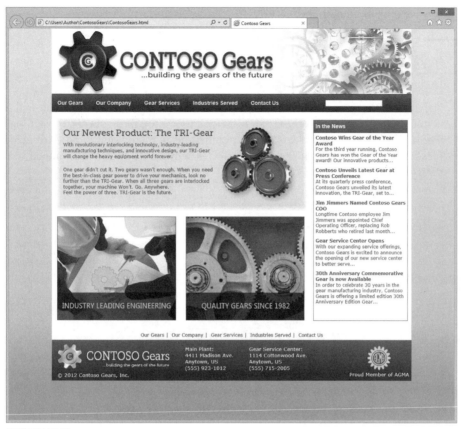

FIGURE 12-19

1.   Open the Design Manager by clicking "Design your site" from the home page of a newly created Publishing site, or click the Site Actions menu and select Design Manager.

2.   The Welcome screen of the Design Manager gives you the option to either import an already created design package (essentially a WSP file created through the Design Manager) or pick a preinstalled look, which will take you to the composed look gallery. For this example, neither option is wanted, so click to the next step, Manage Device Channels.

3.   As you learned earlier in this chapter, device channels enable you to specify particular master pages for different types of browsers (i.e., mobile browsers). For this example, you won't create any extra device channels, so continue on to the next step, Upload Design Files.

4.   This step provides instructions on mapping a drive to your master page gallery to upload your branding files. There are two ways to map the master page gallery to your computer: You can map a drive through your computer or create a new network location. Either option works just as well as the other, but the process of mapping the location is slightly different depending on your preference.

To map a drive to your computer:

a. Click Start ⇨ Computer ⇨ Map Network Drive.

b. In the dialog that appears, select a drive letter.

c. In the Folder field, type **\\portal.contoso.com_catalogs\masterpage**.

d. Specify whether you want the drive reconnected at logon, and whether you will connect with credentials other than those you use to log into your local machine. The account must have at least design permissions in SharePoint in order to upload files to the master page gallery. Click Finish. Figure 12-20 shows the mapped network drive settings.

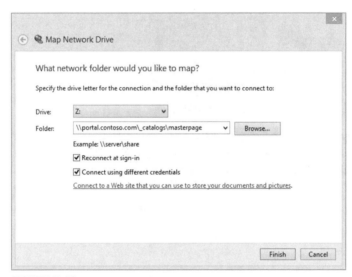

FIGURE 12-20

e. Provide your alternate credentials if necessary.

To map a network location:

a. Right-click on Computer and select Map Network Location.

b. Select Choose a custom network location and click Next.

c. Copy and paste the URL from the Design Manager (in this case, `http://portal.contoso.com/_catalogs/masterpage/`) into the Internet or Network Address field and click Next.

    d.   If prompted, enter your credentials.

    e.   Give the location a name, click Next, and then click Finish.

5.   After mapping your network drive or location, open it and copy your HTML file and any folders containing your custom CSS, scripts, and images into the master page gallery. This is the new recommended approach for SharePoint 2013, which differs from previous versions, in which all images and styles were normally deployed to the Style Library or the /_lay-outs/ directory on the SharePoint server. You can still deploy files to these locations if you wish, however. As a best practice, try to name your folder and HTML file something similar to keep everything organized.

6.   When your files are uploaded, proceed to the next step of the design manager, Edit Master Pages.

7.   In the Edit Master Pages dialog that appears, shown in Figure 12-21, you have the option to either convert an HTML file to a SharePoint master page or create a minimal master page to start from scratch. The latter option is useful for upgrading an existing master page, whereby you could copy the HTML of an existing master page into a new 2013 master page. For this example, select "Convert an HTML file to a SharePoint master page."

8.   In the "Select An Asset" window, browse the master page gallery for the HTML file you just uploaded, select it, and click Insert.

9.   After a few seconds, the file will appear in the list of converted master pages (refer to Figure 12-21). (Note: If the status of your conversion is "Warnings and Errors," click the link and SharePoint will try to point you to the line in your HTML that is causing problems. HTML files imported into SharePoint 2013 must be XML compliant.)

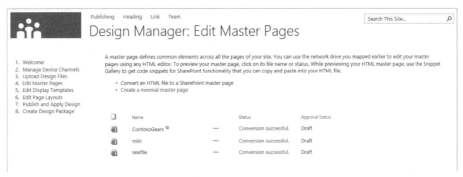

FIGURE 12-21

10.   To preview your master page, click its name.

11.   When the preview window opens, you'll see a representation of your converted master page (see Figure 12-22).

FIGURE 12-22

If anything doesn't look right or you are missing images, you may need to check the paths in your HTML. Try right-clicking on an empty image placeholder and selecting Properties to see the location from which the site is trying to load the image. If it's not trying to pull from the correct location, you may need to adjust the style sheet and/or the image paths in your HTML. You'll see how to make changes to the HTML file in a bit.

On your master page, usually near the bottom, is a yellow bar that says, "This div, which you should delete, represents the content area that your Page Layouts and pages will fill. Design your Master Page around this content placeholder."

12. Open the mapped folder and find your original HTML file. Note that there is also a .master file with the same name as the HTML file. You only need to work with the HTML file, as SharePoint makes the same updates in the .master file automatically.

13. Open the HTML file in your editor of choice.

14. The first thing you'll notice is that during the conversion process, SharePoint destroyed your finely tuned HTML and inserted all sorts of placeholders, comments, and code. This may be a shock at first; but if you look through the newly added code and comment blocks, you'll see your original HTML layout. If you need to make adjustments to the image paths, do so now. If you have a separate style sheet, you can open it as well from the mapped folder and make changes there, too. When you save your changes, refresh the preview window in the browser to ensure that everything is displayed correctly.

15. Find the bright yellow `<div>` tag that SharePoint inserted. In the code, look a few lines above the yellow `<div>` and find a tag that looks like this: `<div class="customMainContent">`.

16. Select that `<div>` tag to its closing `</div>` (approximately 14 lines down).

17. Cut that tag and then paste it in your HTML, in the main content area of your site. If your HTML file has content that would normally be created as a page layout, rather than be included with the master page, you can cut and paste that content into a separate file for the time being. In the next section, "Creating Page Layouts using the Design Manager," you'll go through the process of creating a custom page layout.

18. Save your page, return to the browser, and refresh the preview to confirm that the main content placeholder has been positioned correctly (see Figure 12-23).

FIGURE 12-23

19. Return to the HTML editor, find the `<div>` tag that begins with `<div class="DefaultContentBlock"`, and delete it. Save your file and refresh the preview window.

20. Still in the preview window, click the Snippets link in the top-right corner. This opens the Snippet Gallery in a new tab or window. The Snippet Gallery enables you to select SharePoint-specific placeholders for various page elements, such as navigation, bread-crumbs, site titles, and logos (see Figure 12-24).

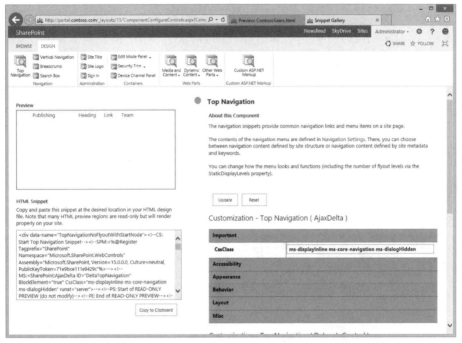

FIGURE 12-24

21. In the Ribbon, click the Search Box button.

22. The Preview section shows what your search box will look like when it is inserted into your site. Below that, the HTML Snippet section shows the code you will copy and paste to add a SharePoint search box to your site.

23. In the Customization section, click the various section headers to see the different attri-butes you can change and customize. For this example, leave the default settings; but if you decided to make changes to the control, you would click the Update button to update the code in the HTML Snippet window. If you don't like the changes you made, you can click the Reset button to return the control to its default look.

24. Below the HTML Snippet window, click the Copy to Clipboard button (if you are prompted by a pop-up dialog to allow access, click the Allow Access button).

25. Return to your HTML editor, determine where you would like to place your search box, and paste in the SharePoint code you copied from the Snippet Gallery. If you are using a program that has a preview window of your site, you might notice that the SharePoint controls you add don't display well. That's because most programs won't understand SharePoint-specific placeholders and markup, but the control should render just fine in the browser.

26. Save your HTML page.

27. Return to the browser and refresh the page. You should now see your SharePoint search box (see Figure 12-25).

FIGURE 12-25

28. Continue clicking through the Snippet Gallery and adding the necessary controls to your master page, checking your progress in the preview screen in the browser.

You will likely need to make some adjustments and do some additional styling in order for some of the SharePoint controls to match your initial HTML mockup. As mentioned earlier, some useful tools for helping with this process are the IE Developer Toolbar and Firebug for Firefox. In the browser, each of these components can be opened with the F12 key, enabling you to select an element and click through the HTML to see what classes are being applied. Figure 12-26 shows an example of using Firebug in Firefox to check the styles of the various page elements.

FIGURE 12-26

Another potential "gotcha" when converting your HTML page is that all the extra code added by SharePoint may make it difficult to find locations for some of the elements from the Snippet Gallery. Therefore, when the design is in its HTML form, it might be helpful to spend some time adding beginning and ending comments around elements that you know will be replaced with a snippet, such as a top navigation control, a search box, and breadcrumbs. That way, when you are ready to insert your snippets, you will know exactly where to paste them.

Creating Page Layouts with the Design Manager

When you are previewing your page and working with the Snippet Gallery, you may accidentally lose the window containing the Design Manager. The easiest way to return to the Design Manager is to click the Site Actions menu in the Snippet Gallery and select Design Manager.

You'll recall from earlier in the chapter that page layouts fill in the main content area of a publishing site. When you converted your HTML file to a master page and moved the yellow block of content around on it, you were setting the area of the master page in which page layouts are rendered.

Page layouts also live in the master page gallery alongside master pages, so everything is neatly organized in one location. With your mapped drive, you have access to all the master pages, page layouts, and site assets for your branding.

In this example, you'll create a custom page layout:

1. Now that you have converted your master page and added all the SharePoint components you need, you can click Edit Display Templates to continue where you left off.

2. For this example, you won't create a custom display template, so you can click to the next step, Edit Page Layouts.

3. From this dialog, you can modify an existing page layout or create a new one. For this example, you'll be creating a new page layout, so click the "Create new page layout" link.

4. In the Create a Page Layout dialog that appears (see Figure 12-27), type **CustomHomePageLayout** in the Name field.

5. In the Master Page drop-down, select your custom master page.

6. In the Content Type drop-down, select Welcome Page (refer to Figure 12-27).

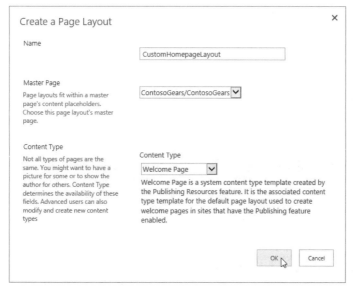

FIGURE 12-27

7. Click OK. Note that by default SharePoint creates your page layout in the root of the master page gallery. If you want to keep all your custom files together in one folder, you can drag the newly created `CustomHomePageLayout.html` file into your custom folder. The corresponding .aspx page will automatically move.

8. Click CustomHomePageLayout to open it in preview mode. You'll see a preview of your page within your master page. Depending on the content type selected, different types of fields will be displayed.

9. In your mapped folder, open the `CustomHomePageLayout.html` file in your HTML editing program (not the .aspx version). You'll see the blocks of SharePoint code in the page layout file.

10. Open the Snippet Gallery from the preview window in the browser.

11. Adding content placeholders for a page layout is exactly the same process as it is for the master page. For this example, click the Page Fields button in the Ribbon and select Document Modified By (see Figure 12-28).

12. Click the Copy to Clipboard button below the HTML Snippet window.

13. Switch to your HTML editor with the `CustomHomePageLayout.html` file opened. Near the end of the code, find the `</div>` tag above the line `<!-- ME:</asp:ContentPlaceHolder>-->`.

14. Place the cursor after the closing `>` of the `</div>` tag and press Return to go to the next line.

15. Paste in the code you copied from the Snippet Gallery and save your page layout.

16. Switch back to the preview in the browser and refresh the page. You will see a couple of lines near the bottom of the page indicating which user last modified the document (see Figure 12-29).

FIGURE 12-28

FIGURE 12-29

This was a basic example of creating a page layout from scratch. If you are working from an existing HTML design, you could paste the main content from your HTML file into the page layout and add any additional controls from the Snippet Gallery. If you do this, you will want to find the tag `<!--MS:<asp:ContentPlaceHolder ID="PlaceHolderMain" runat="server">-->` and place your content between that tag and the corresponding closing tag `<!--ME:</asp:ContentPlaceHolder>-->` near the bottom of the page. This is the placeholder SharePoint uses to display content on page layouts. Figure 12-30 shows the example site fully branded and working within SharePoint.

FIGURE 12-30

Publishing and Applying Your Design

When you have added all the content to your master page and page layouts and are satisfied with the results, you need to publish all the contents of the design, including the master page(s), page layout(s), all images, CSS, and script files. Then you need to actually apply the master page to the site (and to any Device Channels that you plan to use). Fortunately, the Design Manager provides convenient links for accomplishing both these tasks:

1. In step 7 of the Design Manager, click the link "Go to the Master Page Gallery." The master page gallery will open in a new browser tab.

2. Find the HTML version of your custom master page (the file with the .html extension, not .master). You may have to page through the master page gallery to find it.

3. Check the box that appears to the left of the filename when you hover over it with the cursor.

4. In the Ribbon, click the Page tab, and then click the Publish button (see Figure 12-31).

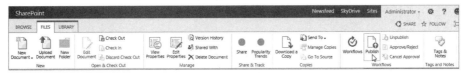

FIGURE 12-31

5. Optionally, type a comment in the Comments field and click OK. The corresponding .master file will be automatically published as well.

6. Repeat this process for your custom page layouts.

7. Open the folder that contains all your design assets and check the box to the left of the Type column to select all items. Notice that there is no option to publish all items. Instead of publishing all the items one by one, you'll use the Content and Structure tool to publish all the files at once.

8. Click the Site Actions menu and select Site Settings.

9. Under the Site Administration header, click Content and Structure.

10. In the left pane of the Site Content and Structure page (which remains basically unchanged since SharePoint 2007), click the + next to Master Page Gallery. Figure 12-32 shows the Site Content and Structure page.

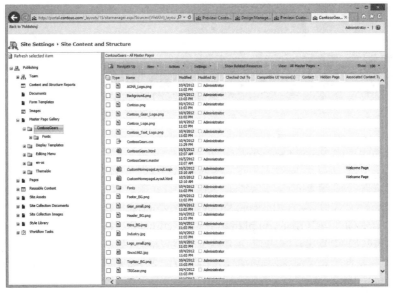

FIGURE 12-32

11. Click on the folder that contains your design assets. The content of that folder will open in the right pane of the page. Click the check box just to the left of the Type column to select all items in the folder.

12. In the toolbar above the files, click the Actions menu and select Publish, as shown in Figure 12-33.

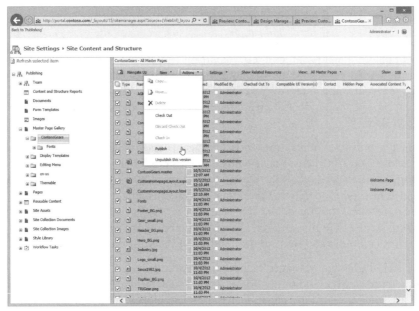

FIGURE 12-33

13. In the pop-up dialog, optionally type a comment and click OK to publish all the items at once.

14. Switch back to the browser tab with the Design Manager still open.

15. Click the link "Assign master pages to your site…"

16. The Site Master Page Settings open in a dialog over the Design Manager (you can also access this page by selecting Site Actions ➪ Site Settings ➪ Master Page). In the Site Master Page section, select your custom master page in the Default drop-down. This controls the master page that will display for all content pages. If you have any device channels set up, you can apply additional master pages to those now, too.

17. In the System Master Page section, make the same selection as the Site Master Page. The System master page is what displays for pages that are stored in the / _layouts/ directory on the server.

18. Click OK to apply the master page. The dialog will close. You may need to refresh the page to see your design applied to the site if you are in the Design Manager. (If you access the Master Page Settings directly from Site Actions ➪ Site Settings, you won't need a refresh when you click OK after setting the master page.)

Note that in SharePoint 2013, it isn't necessary to approve files in the master page gallery after they have been published, which was the default in previous versions. You can still enable approval for items in the master page gallery if you prefer, and the process is unchanged from SharePoint 2007 and 2010: In the Ribbon, select the Library tab. Click the Library Settings button, and then click Versioning settings. Select Yes for "Require content approval for submitted items?", and then click OK.

Deploying Branding Assets

You have a couple of options for deploying your SharePoint branding. Ideally, branding is created in a development environment (or at least a development site) before being deployed to the production environment. The simplest method for deploying your custom branding is to simply copy your master page, page layouts, and assets over to the production environment. However, this is a labor-intensive manual process, and it doesn't create reference versions of the files on the server, as creating a branding WSP does.

A WSP file (which stands for Windows Solution Package) is essentially a .cab file with a different extension. It packages up all the custom elements of your branding and, following a set of instructions included in the package, deploys the files to their correct locations. WSP files are the preferred and recommended method for deploying branding files (and usually any other type of custom code as well) to the SharePoint farm. Inside the WSP are instructions for a SharePoint feature (or set of features) that activate the branding on a site. The only real downside to this method is that creating a WSP requires Visual Studio and some understanding of the process.

In SharePoint 2013, the Design Manager includes the capability to package up your customizations into a WSP, which previously could only be done using Visual Studio. While this sounds like an easy solution, there are some caveats for using it. Generally speaking, creating a WSP file in Visual Studio is still going to be the recommended and preferred method, but in some instances the WSP Design Manager will work fine. First and foremost, when the Design Manager creates a WSP it creates it as a sandbox solution. Depending on how you have your site set up, this may not be an ideal way to deploy the branding, as sandbox solutions have some limitations, such as having to deploy the WSP to every site. Second, the Design Manager grabs everything that you customized and then some. If you started with only a handful of files that you added to SharePoint in addition to your master page and page layouts, you might end up with a barrel full of files in your WSP. The Design Manager grabs just about everything it can get its hands on and adds it to the WSP. Fortunately, the WSP shouldn't overwrite any existing files that it finds when the design package is imported into SharePoint.

If you are importing a design into an Office 365 site, creating the WSP file using the Design Manager would probably be a good way to go, but for many other cases, you're better off creating a WSP in Visual Studio to take advantage of some of the extra features that you get there, such as being able to use event receivers to automatically swap out the master page and set subsites and team sites to use the custom master page without any effort.

Customizing SharePoint Files

Once your files have been deployed to the SharePoint farm through a WSP, they are in what is known as an *uncustomized state*. (You may also hear these files referred to as "ghosted" but according to many surveys that have been done, users find this term too scary.) When a file is uncustomized, it means that a reference file on the drive of the server is provisioned to the database server when a site is created. When a user visits a page, SharePoint checks the database, sees that a reference file exists on it, and serves that file up when rendering the page. Many pages can reference the same page layout and master page; even CSS and image files can be in an uncustomized state.

When an uncustomized file is edited, either through an editing program such as Dreamweaver or SharePoint Designer, a file is said to be customized, or unghosted. The file's reference remains unchanged on the server drive, but its pointer file in the database has been changed from the reference file. The file is then in a customized state. This can start to cause issues when updates need to be made to the WSP file and deployed to the server. A customized file won't be automatically updated with the latest version. For instance, if a page layout on a subsite is edited to include an extra zone, and the WSP is updated with a newer version of that page layout that includes two extra zones, the customized page layout won't get the changes. While this might not seem like such a big deal, consider this scenario: You make a small change to your CSS file after it was deployed, and now have several more updates to make. You want to redeploy an updated WSP, but your style sheet won't update with the new WSP. This is because of the change you made to it earlier. Now, although the WSP has been updated and deployed, none of the new styles are showing.

It's possible to reset a customized file back to its uncustomized state using SharePoint Designer. You can identify your customized files by the "i" in the blue circle next to a filename in the SharePoint Designer interface. When you see this, you can right-click on the file and select Reset to Site Definition. This reverts the customized file back to match the contents of the reference file on the server, and it can pick up any updates that have been made to the files deployed via WSP.

UPGRADING BRANDING TO SHAREPOINT 2013

When SharePoint 2007 was released, designers jumped for joy at the news that SharePoint would be much easier to customize because it was rewritten on the .NET platform. This meant that custom master pages and page layout could be created. No longer would they be constrained by FrontPage 2003 and hacking their way through customizing a SharePoint 2003 site. While not too many brave souls attempted to customize SharePoint 2003, the ones who did likely still have nightmares about the experience. The product simply didn't lend itself to easy customization. SharePoint 2007, with its flexibility, surely seemed like a breath of fresh air.

Some of the changes that arrived with SharePoint 2010 took some time getting used to, most notably the Ribbon. Close behind was the implementation of the new theming engine, which was completely different from how SharePoint 2003 and 2007 used themes. This meant that any custom themes created in SharePoint 2007 needed to be recreated as master pages if they contained extensive customization.

SharePoint 2013 looks a lot like SharePoint 2010 from a user-interface perspective, aside from a more minimal, modernized appearance. Most of the familiar features from SharePoint 2010 are still around, and in some cases pages and settings are laid out almost identically. The Ribbon is present with a slightly new look. The Site Actions menu has been moved back to the right side from its new home on the left in SharePoint 2010. It is now a gear icon instead of an actual menu button, which is sure to give some users pause, as it sits beneath the Internet Explorer gear icon.

This brings us to our main point here: How do you take your 2010 branding and upgrade it to work in 2013? Fortunately, the answer is that branding upgrades should be much less painful going from 2010 to 2013. While SharePoint 2010 featured the Visual Upgrade mode, whereby a site's branding could exist in a pseudo-2007 environment until branding could be fully upgraded, SharePoint 2013 offers a full 2010 experience right in the product. In fact, when creating a new site collection you can choose whether to use the 2010 interface or the 2013 interface.

When upgrading a SharePoint 2010 site, a full preview mode is offered. This is different from the visual upgrade in SharePoint 2010. A full copy of the site is created and rendered in SharePoint 2013, and actions taken on the preview site won't affect the original. This enables you to see how your custom branding behaves and gives you a chance to make changes to the controls and CSS if necessary. SharePoint 2013 uses some new controls and some new CSS classes. If you were overriding some of the out-of-the-box styles from SharePoint 2010, many of those classes began with `.s4-` to designate that the class was from SharePoint version 4. In SharePoint 2013, many out-of-the-box classes have been renamed to begin with `.ms-` instead, which is what many classes in SharePoint 2007 used. For example, in SharePoint 2010, you could use the class `.s4-notdlg` to hide an element from appearing in the modal dialogs. In SharePoint 2013, that class has been renamed to `.ms-dialogHidden`. Another big-ticket item to switch out is replacing the SharePoint 2010 Ribbon control with the SharePoint 2013 Ribbon control.

Depending on your desired level of customization and how the site renders in SharePoint 2013, you can either make the changes to your existing master page or create a minimal master page from the Design Manager and transfer the HTML from your existing page to the new master page, adding in control snippets and placeholders from the Snippet Gallery as you go.

Many organizations view the switch to a new product version as a good opportunity to evaluate the site's branding and potentially create a new upgraded look to go with the upgraded functionality of the product. If your company decides to go that route, then you don't have to worry about upgrading your existing branding to look exactly the same in SharePoint 2013, which is nice, but that means starting from scratch and designing a whole new look and feel. Another upside to creating a new design for your site is that when you redesign your site for SharePoint 2013, you're more likely to work with some of the new SharePoint 2013 design ideas and functionality. If you simply upgrade your look from SharePoint 2010 to SharePoint 2013, then you might not incorporate some of the elements of the fancy new interface (formerly known as Metro). Even worse, if you upgraded your branding from SharePoint 2007 to SharePoint 2010, you might be two generations behind. That's just embarrassing.

CONTROLLING ACCESS TO SHAREPOINT BRANDING

With SharePoint 2007, Microsoft initially released SharePoint Designer 2007 as a paid-for program. About halfway through the product's life cycle, the decision was made to make SharePoint Designer a free download. Unfortunately for many site administrators, there wasn't a way to lock down the SharePoint site and protect it from inexperienced SharePoint Designer users. As SharePoint 2007 administrators soon discovered, a user with SharePoint Designer and some spare time could make a pretty good-size mess of a defenseless SharePoint 2007 site.

In SharePoint 2010, site administrators breathed a collective sigh of relief when access to Share Point Designer 2010 could be controlled granularly. The story is largely the same with SharePoint Designer 2013; however, because it is not the preferred method for creating branded SharePoint sites, this issue doesn't come into play as much from a branding perspective.

The most effective way to control access to SharePoint's branding is through the Design and Administrators groups. Administrators, of course, have access to all components of the SharePoint site, including the branding files in the master page gallery. Users in the Design group also have access to edit files and map a drive to the master page gallery.

If a user with permissions lower than Design attempts to map a drive to the master page gallery to upload an image gallery of his cat's birthday party, he won't be allowed. The Design Manager is also off limits, so he's out of luck there too. If you end up feeling sorry for him and he proves to have some design skill, you can add him to the Designers group to create his cat gallery. For more information, see Chapter 6, "Claims and Security" for instructions on adding and removing users from groups.

SUMMARY

From a branding perspective, SharePoint 2013 brings a lot to the branding party. Although a lot has remained the same, from master pages and page layouts to SharePoint's publishing features, there are also lot of changes in SharePoint 2013's approach to branding. No matter what your branding requirements may be, there are several tools at your disposal for achieving the look you're after. Composed looks, which can be thought of as the next evolution of SharePoint 2010 themes, offer a lot of possibility for adding a high impact design to your site with minimal effort. Or, you can create a highly customized look and feel by using the new Design Manager to convert HTML files to master pages and page layouts in order to meet your design goals for your SharePoint site. Perhaps one of the biggest changes to the branding approach in SharePoint 2013 is that designers now have the ability, and are encouraged, to use just about any web editing tool they'd like in order create and maintain the branding of the site.

Although composed looks, the Design Manager, and the ability to use any web design tool to create branding are some of the most noticeable changes, there are also a lot of other smaller changes that Microsoft has incorporated into SharePoint 2013 that are sure to make administrators' and designers' lives easier. For example, image renditions will greatly improve page load times for SharePoint sites by taking advantage of BLOB storage and creating smaller versions of images uploaded to the site. Another significant addition to SharePoint 2013 is the idea of device channels, which allow administrators to display an alternate master page depending on the type of browser or device accessing the site. Other additions to SharePoint 2013's branding arsenal are the minimal download strategy, which significantly reduces page loading times on team sites by only delivering the content that has changed from the previously loaded page, and display templates, which make styling search results and Content By Search Web Parts much easier than styling Content Query Web Parts was in SharePoint 2010.

Upgrading your SharePoint 2010 site's branding to SharePoint 2013 is going to be a much easier task this time around. SharePoint 2013 includes a SharePoint 2010 mode where sites can exist as

2010 versions and previewed as a SharePoint 2013 site independent of the original. This gives you a chance to test out your custom 2010 branding and make any adjustments as needed before fully committing to upgrading the branding.

Now that we've covered the many aspects of branding a 2013 site, don't you feel inspired to go create a beautiful site? Sure, SharePoint 2013 looks nice on the surface, but get those creative juices flowing and create a site your mom (or your boss) will be proud of! Or, at the very least, you can tear this chapter out of this book and hand it to your web designers. You'll be glad to know that they are on the same page as you when it comes to developing and deploying SharePoint branding.

13

Configuring and Managing Enterprise Search

WHAT'S IN THIS CHAPTER?

➤ What's new in enterprise search

➤ Understanding the search architecture

➤ Configuring enterprise search

➤ Managing the search UI

SharePoint 2013 search is a great addition to a fully featured product. It has been re-architected to take full advantage of the new SharePoint functionality, the best of FAST search, and new search technology features previously not commercialized. Although SharePoint search can be used in the typical bread-and-butter user scenario, by typing queries into a box and filtering through the results, that only scratches the surface of its integration and capabilities across the platform. It introduces many new features to improve the display and relevancy of the traditional search experience, but it can also be used to process usage patterns such as user clicks and other user behavior to make recommendations. All of these capabilities of SharePoint 2013 search are covered in this chapter.

WHAT'S NEW IN ENTERPRISE SEARCH

SharePoint 2013 offers numerous improvements to existing features of search and introduces new features. It is hands down the best enterprise search capability in SharePoint's history. The following sections, while not exhaustive, highlight the key changes. For a more detailed summary, refer to, "What's new in search in SharePoint Server 2013," at http://technet .microsoft.com/en-us/library/ee667266.aspx.

Single Search Architecture

SharePoint 2013 is based on a single search architecture, which includes a single Search Service application. FAST search and FAST technology is now native to the product, not a separate product. The search architecture scales to support greater content and increased query loads, and search administration is now fault tolerant. This is not a mere merging of SharePoint 2010 search and FAST search; this is a complete re-architecture, and many of the components are brand-new or revised.

The search topology is readily scalable. There are separate crawling and indexing processes, and the entire index is now stored in a set of folders on disk; the properties database is no longer used to store index information. A new crawl, the continuous crawl, joins the incremental and full crawl to better meet the index freshness requirements of the new search system. A new analytics processing engine provides search analytics and usage analytics, which are used to make recommendations. There is a new distributed system processing engine called NodeRunner, which hosts a process instance for every search component except the crawler. Our old friend MSSearch.exe is still around, except it is limited to the crawl component. Last but not least is the Host Controller, which monitors the NodeRunner processes, detects failures, and restarts processes.

Search Center and Search UI

The new look for SharePoint 2013 is also displayed in the Search Center. The Search Center includes deep refiners with exact counts, and document previews with the new "take a look inside" functionality available in the new hover panel using the new Office Web Applications. *Search verticals* is the new name for what used to be the tabbed interface, with People search still occupying its place in the interface. There are four new Web Parts, each of which provides new features, including the capability to customize the look and feel of the results using display templates and result types. Query rules provide tremendous flexibility for making the results more meaningful, with result boosting and result blocks to highlight the most relevant results. Refiners can be added to the page using visual tools, rather than hacking configuration files and modifying XSLT.

Relevancy Improvements

SharePoint 2013 improves relevance in areas such as freshness of search results, linguistics, and document parsing. Relevance is improved using new ranking models. A ranking model determines which items are displayed and the order in which they are displayed in the search results. You can also create custom models.

The search engine works with the new analytics component to better determine relevance based on how often an item appears in search results, and the click-through patterns of users. It also uses this information to generate operational reports for the administrator. Because most of this information is constantly changing, the relevance is continuously and dynamically improved. The search engine is also responsible for issuing recommendations to users for what sites, people, and documents they might find useful.

Result sources specify the location from which to pull information, and the protocol to use so that you can limit searches to a certain set of content or subset of search results. You can use the FAST technology query transform to restrict queries to a subset of content.

Query rules make query results more relevant, without any custom code. In a query rule, you specify conditions and subsequent actions. When a query meets the conditions in a query rule, the search system performs the specified actions to improve the relevance of the search results. These actions include promoting key results just like Best Bets used to do, and changing the ranking of the results.

SEARCH ARCHITECTURE

SharePoint 2013 search has been re-architected, and the goal of achieving a single enterprise search platform has introduced a number of changes. You can consider SharePoint 2013 search to be a combination of SharePoint 2010 search, FAST Search for SharePoint 2010, and FAST technology.

Microsoft acquired FAST search in mid-2008, and introduced the FAST Search Server for SharePoint 2010 alongside SharePoint Server 2010 when the 2010 products were released. The original FAST ESP product was also available. For SharePoint 2013, the goal was to integrate the best of the current products, along with new components not yet introduced, into a single enterprise search architecture. The result is a search platform that combines the crawler and connector framework from SharePoint Search, updated content processing and query processing from FAST technology, and a search core based on FAST Search. This architecture also includes the new analytics engine, which is used for ranking and recommendations. The FAST Search product, and the brand name FAST are gone, and SharePoint 2013 search is the current incarnation. This single architecture is most obvious during the install process, where you will notice the single Search Service application.

> **NOTE** *In addition to eliminating the separate FAST search products, including FAST for SharePoint, FAST ESP, and FAST Search for Internet Sites, the standalone Microsoft Search Server product does not have a 2013 version. There is some search functionality in the free download, SharePoint Foundation Services 2013, but this chapter discusses SharePoint Server 2013 search functionality only.*

The search topology has several key improvements:

➤ Separate crawl and indexing processes.

➤ A new analytics process that provides search and usage analyses, including link analysis and recommendations.

➤ The entire index is stored locally on disk, and it no longer uses the property database.

➤ Search is scalable in two dimensions, content and query load.

➤ The administration component can be made fault tolerant.

➤ Native support for repartitioning the index as part of scaling out the topology.

Topology

The topology can be broken down into search components and databases that work together to provide search capability, as shown in Figure 13-1. In a multi-server farm, these components reside on application servers, and the databases exist on SQL Server database servers. When designing the search topology to support your requirements, you should take into account whether you are providing search for a public website or an internal intranet. Additionally, you should consider high availability and fault tolerance requirements, the amount of content, and the estimated page views and queries per second. The search components can be categorized into five groups or processes:

> ➤ **Crawl and content** — Includes the crawl and content processing components and the crawl database

> ➤ **Analytics** — Includes the analytics processing component, and the links and analytics reporting databases

> ➤ **Index** — Includes the index component, index partition, and index replica

> ➤ **Query** — Includes the query processing component

> ➤ **Administration** — Includes the administration component and the administration database

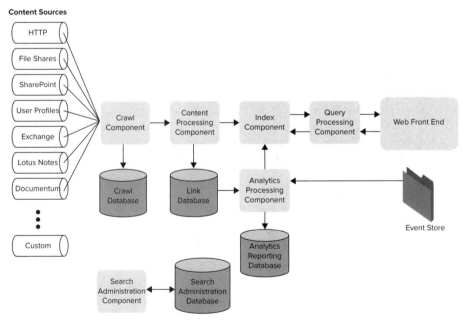

FIGURE 13-1

You must define and scale the topology to accommodate your requirements. SharePoint 2013 uses Central Administration to show the current status of the search topology. Unlike SharePoint 2010, which used Central Administration to change and scale the search topology, the SharePoint 2013 search topology is created and managed using PowerShell. SharePoint 2013 has a more complex and flexible search topology, which you can manage more efficiently using PowerShell. You'll learn how to do this in the section, "Configuring Enterprise Search." The following sections take a detailed look at these five main search components.

Managing the Crawl Process and Crawled Properties

Search effectiveness requires that the necessary content be indexed and accessible to end users. The whole process begins with the crawl component, which is also referred to as the *crawler*. This component crawls *content sources*, and it delivers the crawled content and associated metadata to the content processing component. The crawl process interacts and retrieves data using connectors and protocol handlers. SharePoint 2013 includes more out-of-the-box connectors than SharePoint 2010, as well as Business Connectivity Services (BCS) extensibility.

> **NOTE** *The list of SharePoint 2013 connectors is summarized by the article,* "Default connectors in SharePoint Server 2013," *which is found at* http://technet.microsoft.com/en-us/library/jj219746(v=office.15); *the* "Search connector framework in SharePoint 2013" *is discussed at* http://msdn.microsoft.com/en-us/library/sharepoint/ee556429.aspx.

Content sources that you create in the Search service application specify the repositories to be crawled. The content source represents a group of crawl settings, which includes the host to crawl, the type of content, the crawl schedule, and how deep to crawl. By default, you have the Local SharePoint Sites content source upon installation, but you can create new sources, similar to how you did with SharePoint 2010.

To manage crawl volume and performance, you can simultaneously crawl content using multiple crawl components. As the crawler processes data, it caches the content locally in preparation for sending content to the content processing component. The crawl component also uses one or more crawl databases to temporarily store information about crawled items and to track crawl history. There is no longer a one-to-one mapping of the crawl database to crawler as in SharePoint 2010; each crawl database can be associated with one or more crawlers, so you can scale them independently.

To support the need for a "fresher" index, SharePoint 2013 includes a new crawl type, the continuous crawl. The continuous crawl is applicable only to SharePoint content sources, and is a new option you can choose when you create a new content source. You can think of the continuous crawl as being similar to the incremental crawl but without the need to be scheduled. With continuous crawl, changed content is crawled every 15 minutes by default, but the frequency is configurable. If a full crawl has started, the new system allows the latest changes to appear in results before the full crawl completes. As in SharePoint 2010, all crawler configurations are stored in the administration database.

The content and metadata that has been crawled and extracted from a document or URL are represented as *crawled properties*. They are grouped into categories based on the iFilter or protocol handler used to retrieve the property. Examples of properties are Author and Title. New crawled properties are created after each new crawl, as new content is added to the enterprise. Crawled properties are passed to the content-processing component for further analysis.

Content Processing

This is a very specialized node in the search architecture, whose purpose is to analyze and process the data and metadata that will be included in the index. The processing node transforms the crawled items and crawled properties using language detection, document parsing, dictionaries, property mapping, and entity extraction. This component is also responsible for mapping crawled properties to *managed properties.*

> **NOTE** *The content processing component parses the crawled content from numerous file types. A list of the filename extensions and file formats that are processed by default is provided at* `http://technet.microsoft.com/en-us/library/jj219530.aspx.`

Content processing also extracts the links and anchor text from web pages and documents, because this type of information helps influence the relevancy of the document. This raw data is stored in the link database. When a user performs a search and clicks a result, the click-through information is also stored unprocessed in the link database. All this raw data is subsequently analyzed by the analytics processing component, which updates the index with relevancy information.

Once completed, the transformed data is then sent to the index component. Content processing configurations are stored in the search administration database. This includes new crawled properties, so administrators can manually create a mapping of crawled properties to managed properties. The content-processing component is also highly extensible, by using web services that would provide information about how content should be processed.

Managed Properties

Crawled properties are mapped to managed properties to include the content and metadata in the search index. Only managed properties are included in the index; therefore, users can search only on managed properties. Managed properties have attributes, which determine how the contents are shown in search results. For an extensive list of the default SharePoint 2013 managed properties, and the associated mapped crawled properties, see `http://technet.microsoft.com/en-us/library/jj219630.` As the Managed Properties Overview table displayed in the reference indicates, managed properties also have associated attributes, also referred to as properties; yes, the managed properties have properties. The list of default managed properties, also referred to as the *search schema* or *index schema,* contains the managed properties, their associated properties, and the mapping between crawled properties and managed properties. You can edit the search schema yourself, by manually mapping crawled properties to managed properties, and configuring property settings. The content-processing component utilizes this schema to perform any necessary mapping.

A single managed property can be mapped to more than one crawled property, as shown in the preceding reference. In this case, the order in which the crawled properties are mapped determines the content of the managed property that is stored in the index when a crawled document contains values for more than one of the mapped crawled properties. You can also map a single crawled property to multiple managed properties.

Site columns in SharePoint libraries automatically generate a new managed property after crawling, and a mapping between the new crawled property and the new managed property. By editing the search schema, you can change the default mapping, create new mappings, or create new managed properties. A full crawl must be completed after the creation of a new managed property to ensure that its value is included in the search index.

Search Schema

The search schema is stored in the search administration database, and the schema web page, which is called Search Service Application: Managed Properties, is shown in Figure 13-2. This page is available from the Search Service Application: Search Administration page in Central Administration, using the Search Schema link in the Queries and Results section. Note that this page is similar to the page referenced in the preceding section, except that this page reflects the current state rather than the default state. This is the page you use when making changes to the schema. You will use it later in the chapter when you create new managed properties. Key points to remember about the search schema include the following:

➤   It contains the mapping between crawled properties and managed properties, including the order of mapping for those cases that have mapped multiple crawled properties.

➤   It maintains the settings for which index stores the managed property.

➤   It contains the settings or properties for each of the different managed properties.

➤   Site collection administrators can change the search schema for a particular site collection using the Site Settings page, and customize the search experience for that specific site collection. This is a new capability in SharePoint 2013; SharePoint 2010 only allowed schema changes in Central Administration. Site owners can view the schema, but they are not allowed to make changes.

➤   It is possible to have multiple search schemas.

> **NOTE** *You can create more than one search schema by creating additional Search Service applications, each of which has its own.*

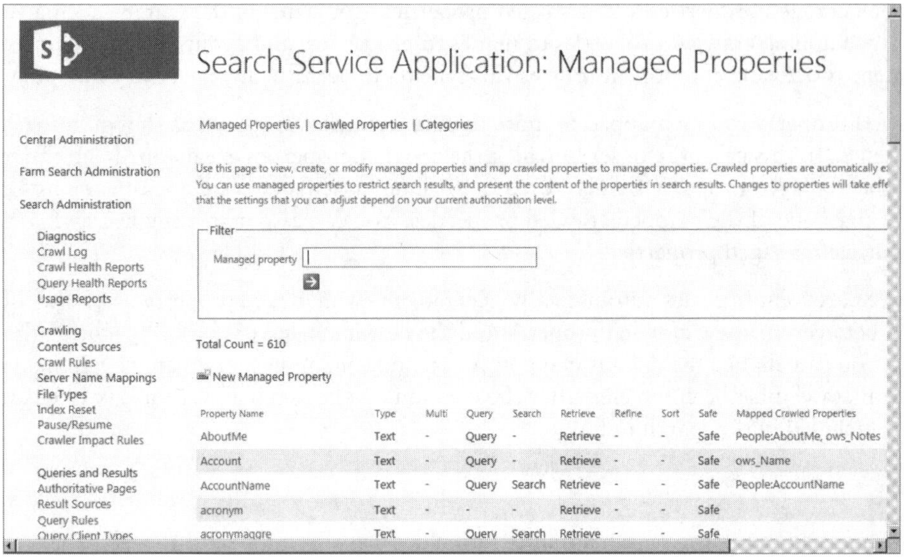

FIGURE 13-2

Analytics Processing

This is a brand-new component for the search architecture. Its purpose is to analyze the content and how users interact with the content to improve search relevance, create search reports and recommendations, and create deep links. The analytics component analyzes two different types of information: information from crawled items that is stored in the index (search analytics), and information about how users interact with the search results, such as how many times an item is viewed (usage analytics). The results from the analyses of the search analytics, the link database, and user actions (usage events) such as page views and liking a document, are used to update the search index with relevancy information. This helps to ensure that search relevance improves automatically over time. These user events are what drive recommendations.

> **NOTE** *The Web Analytics capability in SharePoint 2010 has been discontinued, replaced by the analytics processing component in SharePoint 2013. This change was necessary to increase performance and scalability. The analytics component provides additional capabilities such as a report of top items, recommendations, and dynamic improvement of search result relevancy.*

Search Analytics

The search analytics component involves several different types of analyses, which are summarized in Table 13-1. Administrators should review each of the analyses to ensure an understanding of how the index is updated and made more relevant.

TABLE 13-1: Search Analytics Analysis

TYPE OF ANALYSIS	DESCRIPTION
Link and Anchor text	This analysis determines how items in the index are associated with each other. The results improve relevancy by adding ranking points to the items in the search index.
Search Clicks	Search result relevancy is increased (boosted) or decreased (demoted) based on which items users click the search results. This dynamically alters the ranking of index content in the search results.
Deep Links	This analysis also uses search click results to calculate the most important site pages. These pages are displayed in the search results to provide easy access during the user's search requests.
Click Distance	This calculates the number of clicks between an important site or page, called an *authoritative page*, and the items in the search index. The index is updated to ensure that authoritative pages are more relevant. An authoritative page is defined by an administrator in Central Administration.
Social Distance	This analysis is based on the assumption that information from people you follow is more relevant to you, a metric called *social distance*. Social distance is used to sort people search results: information from people whom you follow is most relevant, information from people followed by those whom you follow is the next most relevant, and so on.
Social Tags	This analysis uses words or phrases supplied by users to categorize information. By default, this information is not used in relevancy determination, but it can be applied to custom search experiences like query rules.
Search Reports	The Search Service application stores search reports based on the aggregation of data in the analytics reporting database, which originated from the analytics component analyses. These reports include Number of queries, Top queries, Abandoned queries, No result queries, and Query rule usage. The search reports are viewable from the View Usage Results page in Search Administration, shown in Figure 13-3.

FIGURE 13-3

Usage Analytics

Usage analytics involves analyzing user actions, such as clicks or viewed items. This analysis combines the data from user actions, also called usage events, and crawled content information. Once complete, recommendations and usage event data is added to the search index, which dynamically improves relevancy, and statistical data is written to the analytics reporting database. The default usage events are described in Table 13-2, but SharePoint also allows up to 12 custom events, based on the following criteria:

➤ Viewed or clicked items

➤ Recommendations displayed and clicked

For example, you can add a custom event that tracks how often an item is liked, and then use this information to customize a recommendation. This information is used to calculate two usage reports: Popularity Trends and Most Popular Items.

TABLE 13-2: Usage Analytics Analysis

TYPE OF ANALYSIS	DESCRIPTION
Usage Event Counts	This analysis counts how many times an item is opened or clicked, which includes search clicks and when a document is opened. The data is aggregated at the site and site collection levels. Usage events are temporarily stored on the WFE for processing, and once processed the results are stored in the Search Service application. Events are defined as *recent* and *all time*, with the former being configurable between 1 and 14 days (the default). This enables sorting the Most Popular Items report by Recent or Ever.

Recommendations	A recommendation between items is created based on analyzing the usage patterns contained in the Usage Event Counts analysis. This pattern analysis creates a graph that describes the relationships between items, and this graph is stored in the analytics reporting database, and added to the index to be used for user personalization. For example, you could create a recommendation that says "People who viewed this also viewed."
Activity Ranking	This analysis is used to enhance search relevance by tracking rates and trends in usage events. It considers both recent and longer term activity to define the appropriate ranking.

Index Processing

The index is the key to providing the best search experience, as its content determines what users find when executing search queries. SharePoint 2013 Search, however, is more than just users typing into the search box and getting results. SharePoint 2013 Search is a *data access technology*, because it provides access to information beyond just the search box query. The index component receives crawled and processed content and this information is added to the search index. This component also handles incoming queries, retrieves information from the search index, and sends back the result set to the query processing component. The index processing architecture can be divided into the *index partition*, the *index replica*, and the *index component*. Unlike SharePoint 2010, which stored part of the index information on disk and part in the property database, SharePoint 2013 stores all of the index on disk. Search capability is scaled using index partitions and index replicas; the "rows and columns" terminology from SharePoint 2010 is gone.

Index Partition

The index can be partitioned or divided into discrete portions called *index partitions*, with each partition containing a separate part of the index. The search index, which is stored in a set of files on disk, is an aggregation of all the index partitions. This enables scaling of the index in two ways: to handle crawl volume and to handle query volume. First, index partitions are added to handle the crawl load associated with greater content volume. The primary partition receives the processed information from content processing, and it is sent to the other partitions via *journal shipping*. Second, the index can be scaled for query volume using index replicas.

Index Replica

Each index partition contains one or more index replicas, with each replica containing the same index information. You add the necessary number of replicas based on your query volume and fault tolerance requirements. Search queries are sent to the index replicas by the *query processing component*. SharePoint automatically load balances the incoming queries to the index replicas. Fault tolerance and redundancy are achieved by creating additional replicas for each index partition, and distributing the index replicas over multiple application servers. You should maintain the same number of replicas for each partition created.

Index Component

You need to provision one index component for each index replica. The index component does the work in the indexing process, and during the query process. This component receives processed items from the content processing component, writing those items to an index file. The index component also receives incoming queries from the query processing component, retrieves information from the search index, and returns the query results to the query processing component.

> **NOTE** *You can choose the location that will be used to store the index files. Your first option is during the SharePoint 2013 install. The second option is during creation of the index component using the* -RootDirectory *switch for the* New-SPEnterpriseSearchIndexComponent *cmdlet. This switch specifies the root directory that will be used for the index associated with the new index component. Specifying the root directory can be helpful if you wish to isolate the index on dedicated disks, or separate disks from the OS. The root directory can be configured for each index component. In general, you should separate the index from the disk that contains the ULS logs.*

Query Processing, Query Rules, and Result Sources

The query-processing component analyzes incoming queries, which are sent to the index component, which returns a set of results. This component performs linguistic analysis of the query, including word-breaking, which determines the boundaries of the words in the query (these vary by language), and stemming, which defines the base or root form of the words in the query. Once the query is processed, the query is submitted to the index component, which returns results from the index. The results are returned to the query component, where they are further processed before returning the results to the search front end.

Query rules and result sources are new features in SharePoint 2013. Query rules can be used to conditionally promote certain results, display the results in blocks, and tune relevancy. Result sources are used to scope the search results. SharePoint 2010 search scopes have been deprecated, replaced by result sources.

Administration

This component is responsible for running processes that are essential to search, including new component provisioning. The search administration database stores search configuration data, such as the topology, crawl rules, query rules, and the mappings between crawled and managed properties. Each Search Service application can have only one search administration component. The current search configuration is accessible through Central Administration, but modifying the search topology requires PowerShell.

This completes the architecture overview. As you have seen, several enhancements have been made to the search architecture, and these changes have resulted in a very powerful search capability. In the next section, you will learn how to configure and manage this capability.

CONFIGURING ENTERPRISE SEARCH

Your search topology is created and configured from the point when you install SharePoint 2013, and then scaled out to improve performance and fault tolerance. You can think about the topology being created and modified in four distinct steps:

➤ Install initial farm — Your default topology is created when you install SharePoint and create the Search Service application. This topology may be good enough, but you will likely need to scale it out at some point.

➤ Create a new topology — This is accomplished with the new PowerShell cmdlet `New-SPEnterpriseSearchTopology`. You never modify the active topology. When you want to create a new topology, you create a *clone* of the active topology using `New-SPEnterpriseSearchTopology -Clone`, and then make changes to the clone.

➤ Add search components and assign servers — The search components discussed previously are created and assigned to servers in the clone topology. The following cmdlets are used to create the search components:

 ➤ `New-SPEnterpriseSearchAdminComponent`

 ➤ `New-SPEnterpriseSearchAnalyticsProcessingComponent`

 ➤ `New-SPEnterpriseSearchContentProcessingComponent`

 ➤ `New-SPEnterpriseSearchCrawlComponent`

 ➤ `New-SPEnterpriseSearchQueryProcessingComponent`

➤ Activate the topology — The new topology is made the active topology by activating the clone using the following cmdlet:

```
Set-SPEnterpriseSearchTopology
```

Scaling Out Topology

SharePoint 2013 administration of the search topology is accomplished using PowerShell. The Central Administration web interface used in SharePoint 2010 has been deprecated. This section walks through the process of changing the default search topology. As a starting point, the discussion assumes the following:

➤ SharePoint Server 2013 is installed on a single server, and a Search Service application with a default search topology has been created according to the installation instructions in Chapter 3.

➤ You are using an account with farm administrator permissions for the Search Service application.

➤ Use the Small Search Farm as your target topology. This topology includes full search functionality with fault tolerance for up to 10 million items. The target topology is described in the document "Enterprise Search Architectures for SharePoint Server 2013," available for download from `http://go.microsoft.com/fwlink/p/?LinkId=258448`.

> **NOTE** *The white paper, "Enterprise Search Architectures for SharePoint Server 2013," also includes the topology for a medium and large search farm. The process we are going to use to create a small search farm can be applied to creating the larger farms. If you are creating a search farm to support a public Internet website, you should review the white paper, "Internet Sites Search Architectures for SharePoint Server 2013," available for download from* `http://go.microsoft.com/fwlink/?LinkId=263989&clcid=0x409.`

➤ SharePoint 2013 is installed on all the application servers that will be hosting the search components, and they have been added to the farm according to the instructions in Chapter 3.

The default search topology delivered by the install procedure in Chapter 3 is good for a development environment, and this is the topology discussed here. Because of the demands the search processes place on CPU and memory, administrators should familiarize themselves with the recommended hardware requirements necessary to support search, and the search topology limits and boundaries. These topics are discussed in detail in the references shown in Table 13-3. Some of this information is discussed throughout the section.

TABLE 13-3: Search Topology Limits and Boundaries

INFORMATION	DESCRIPTION	REFERENCE
Search boundaries and limits	Search topology guidelines for the number of crawl databases, crawl components, index components, partitions and replicas, etc.	`http://technet.microsoft.com/en-US/library/6a13cd9f-4b44-40d6-85aa-c70a8e5c34fe.aspx#Search`
Scaling search for performance and availability	A summary of the hardware requirements for search topologies, and the corresponding scaling and redundancy considerations	`http://technet.microsoft.com/en-US/library/jj219628.aspx`

Creating and Managing the Search Topology

The following steps will create a small enterprise search topology on multiple SharePoint 2013 application servers. You should download the document, "Enterprise Search Architectures for SharePoint Server 2013," referenced earlier, and become familiar with the topology. The portion of the topology pertaining to the search components is shown in Table 13-4.

TABLE 13-4: Small Farm Search Topology

SERVER1	SERVER2	SERVER3	SERVER4
Administration	Query	Administration	Query
Crawl	Index	Crawl	Index
Content		Content	
Analytics		Analytics	

This topology uses virtual machines on physical application servers, but the use of virtual machines is not required. As you can see, the topology includes fault tolerance, which means that all search components and index partitions on Server1 and Server2 are duplicated to Server3 and Server4, with the latter servers deployed across a different physical host. This topology includes one index partition, and one index replica on Server2 and Server4. Each replica contains the same search index, and they are hosted on different physical servers to achieve fault tolerance. Note the following guidelines when assigning search components to the same server:

➤ Content processing and analytics should be together.

➤ Administration and crawl should be together.

➤ Index and query processing should be together.

The following steps will change the default search topology (with an empty search index) created in Chapter 3 to what is referred to as a small search farm. You may recognize many of the PowerShell commands as the same commands used previously in Chapter 3, but applied across multiple servers:

1. Open a SharePoint 2013 Management Shell with the Run as administrator option.

2. Start a new Search Service instance on the target servers, using the following PowerShell cmdlets. This must be completed before you can add any search components to the server, because this instance starts all the necessary Windows services:

```
$host1 = Get-SPEnterpriseSearchServiceInstance -Identity "server1"
$host2 = Get-SPEnterpriseSearchServiceInstance -Identity "server2"
$host3 = Get-SPEnterpriseSearchServiceInstance -Identity "server3"
$host4 = Get-SPEnterpriseSearchServiceInstance -Identity "server4"
Start-SPEnterpriseSearchServiceInstance -Identity $host1
Start-SPEnterpriseSearchServiceInstance -Identity $host2
Start-SPEnterpriseSearchServiceInstance -Identity $host3
Start-SPEnterpriseSearchServiceInstance -Identity $host4
```

3. Before adding the search components, you need to ensure that each of the instances is running. To do so, execute the following command for each server, and you should receive output similar to the following, with status "Online" once the instances are running:

```
Get-SPEnterpriseSearchServiceInstance -Identity $host1

TypeName    : SharePoint Server Search
Description : Index content and serve search queries
```

```
Id          : 82ce8815-ecbd-4cf3-a98e-33f20bd86039
Server      : SPServer Name=Server1
Service     : SearchService Name=OSearch15
Role        : None
Status      : Online
```

4. Create a new search topology that is associated with the Search Service application:

```
$ssa = Get-SPEnterpriseSearchServiceApplication
$newSearchTopology = New-SPEnterpriseSearchTopology -SearchApplication $ssa
```

5. View the active search topology of the Search Service application using the following cmdlets, and you should receive similar output to that shown:

```
$ssa = Get-SPEnterpriseSearchServiceApplication
$activeTopology = Get-SPEnterpriseSearchTopology -Active -SearchApplication
$ssa
$activeTopology

TopologyId      : fc35e4ad-df07-4c1e-8c03-46e0bb91180c
CreationDate    : 12/20/2012 6:10:00 AM
State           : Active
ComponentCount  : 6
```

6. Create the search components and add them to the appropriate servers as specified in Table 13-4:

```
New-SPEnterpriseSearchAdminComponent -SearchTopology $newSearchTopology
    -SearchServiceInstance $host1
New-SPEnterpriseSearchCrawlComponent -SearchTopology $newSearchTopology
    -SearchServiceInstance $host1
New-SPEnterpriseSearchContentProcessingComponent -SearchTopology
$newSearchTopology
    -SearchServiceInstance $host1
New-SPEnterpriseSearchAnalyticsProcessingComponent -SearchTopology
$newSearchTopology
    -SearchServiceInstance $host1
New-SPEnterpriseSearchQueryProcessingComponent -SearchTopology
$newSearchTopology
    -SearchServiceInstance $host2
New-SPEnterpriseSearchIndexComponent -SearchTopology $newSearchTopology
    -SearchServiceInstance $host2 -IndexPartition 0
New-SPEnterpriseSearchAdminComponent -SearchTopology $newSearchTopology
    -SearchServiceInstance $host3
New-SPEnterpriseSearchCrawlComponent -SearchTopology $newSearchTopology
    -SearchServiceInstance $host3
New-SPEnterpriseSearchContentProcessingComponent -SearchTopology
$newSearchTopology
    -SearchServiceInstance $host3
New-SPEnterpriseSearchAnalyticsProcessingComponent -SearchTopology
$newSearchTopology
    -SearchServiceInstance $host3
New-SPEnterpriseSearchQueryProcessingComponent -SearchTopology
$newSearchTopology
    -SearchServiceInstance $host4
```

```
New-SPEnterpriseSearchIndexComponent -SearchTopology $newSearchTopology
    -SearchServiceInstance $host4 -IndexPartition 0
```

7. The search components for each of the servers can be viewed using the following cmdlets. The output is sent to a text file, so that you have easy access to the ComponentId of the search components. You use this in step 11 when you remove a search component:

```
$file = "c:\componentinfo.txt
$ssa = Get-SPEnterpriseSearchServiceApplication
$activeTopology = Get-SPEnterpriseSearchTopology -SearchApplication $ssa -Active
Get-SPEnterpriseSearchComponent -SearchTopology $activeTopology | Out-File $file
```

8. Activate the search topology as follows:

```
Set-SPEnterpriseSearchTopology -Identity $newSearchTopology
```

9. The following cmdlet verifies that the topology is active, an example output is shown beneath the cmdlet. The default topology should be listed first in the output, but with the State Inactive, and the new topology listed next, with ComponentCount 12. This completes the creation of the small search topology. If you needed to make changes to a topology, such as delete, add, or move a component, the steps for these operations start with step 10:

```
Get-SPEnterpriseSearchTopology -SearchApplication $ssa

TopologyId       : fc35e4ad-df07-4c1e-8c03-46e0bb91180c
CreationDate     : 12/20/2012 6:10:00 AM
State            : Inactive
ComponentCount   : 6

TopologyId       : b68d64b2-df38-42be-b7f3-9ababc483832
CreationDate     : 12/20/2012 7:02:00 AM
State            : Active
ComponentCount   : 12
```

10. To remove a search component, you must first create a clone of the topology, because you cannot change the active topology. This process also applies to making changes to a search topology that already has items in the search index:

```
$ssa = Get-SPEnterpriseSearchServiceApplication
$activeTopology = Get-SPEnterpriseSearchTopology -SearchApplication $ssa -Active
$clone = New-SPEnterpriseSearchTopology -SearchApplication $ssa -Clone
    -SearchTopology $activeTopology
```

11. Use the following cmdlet to remove the search component from the server of interest. You need the ID of the search component you wish to remove, called the ComponentId, which is part of the output from step 7:

```
Remove-SPEnterpriseSearchComponent -Identity <ComponentId>
    -SearchTopology $clone
```

12. You can also add any of the search components using the first set of cmdlets that follows. Recall that these cmdlets were used previously in step 6. The single cmdlet shown beneath

the top five cmdlets adds the crawl component to Server2, but using the clone topology. You can also verify that the process was successful, just as you did in step 7.

```
# Cmdlets for creating new search components
New-SPEnterpriseSearchAdminComponent
New-SPEnterpriseSearchAnalyticsProcessingComponent
New-SPEnterpriseSearchContentProcessingComponent
New-SPEnterpriseSearchCrawlComponent
New-SPEnterpriseSearchQueryProcessingComponent

# Cmdlet to add the crawl component to Server2 in the clone topology
New-SPEnterpriseSearchCrawlComponent -SearchTopology $clone
    -SearchServiceInstance $host2

# Verify component was added successfully
Get-SPEnterpriseSearchComponent -SearchTopology $clone
```

13. To move a search component to a different server, you create a clone topology, create the component on the server of interest using the clone, and then delete the desired component from the clone.

14. After you have made changes to the clone topology, you need to make the clone the active topology, as follows:

```
Set-SPEnterpriseSearchTopology -Identity $clone
```

That completes this section on managing search topology. The next section focuses specifically on the index component of the search topology. Managing the index component is similar, and you will reuse much of what you have already learned from the discussion in this section.

Managing the Index Topology

The following discussion applies to adding a replica to an existing partition, adding a new partition, and deleting (also called removing) and moving an index component. The PowerShell cmdlet `New-SPEnterpriseSearchIndexComponent` is used to manage both index partitions and index replicas. An index component represents an index replica. As mentioned previously, the index is divided into discrete portions called partitions, with each partition stored as a set of files on a local disk. You manage more content by adding a new partition for each 10 million items. Replicas help manage query volume, and provide fault tolerance.

Removing an Index Component

This is accomplished using the same process described in step 7 of the previous section. To remove a search component, in this case the index replica on Server4, you would first create a clone of the topology, and remove the replica from the clone topology by using the ConponentId of the index component on Server4. You would then need to make the clone topology the active topology, just as you did before. This process works as long as you have more than one active index replica for an index partition. To remove all replicas for a partition, you need to remove and re-create the Search Service application, and then create the new topology.

Adding an Index Component

Just as you can remove a replica, as described in the previous section for the replica on Server4, now you can add it back, using the same process: Create a clone topology, add the index component, and finally activate the clone topology. The following cmdlets create an index replica on Server4 for the index partition on Server2, and monitor the status of updating the new index replica. During the update process, all components will have a State of Degraded until the process is complete, then the State will be Active. This takes only a few minutes in your development farm, but on a production farm this could take hours depending on the size of the index:

```
# Add the new index replica to existing partition
New-SPEnterpriseSearchIndexComponent -SearchTopology $clone
    -SearchServiceInstance $host4 -IndexPartition 0
# Monitor status of updating new replica
Get-SPEnterpriseSearchStatus -SearchApplication $ssa -Text
```

Moving an Index Component

To move the component, you need to add a new index component to the search topology, and then remove the old index component. The previous two sections explain how to add and remove an index component, and you can reuse the same logic in this section:

1. Clone the search topology and add a new index replica. After the index has replicated to the new index replica, activate the search topology.

2. Use the Get-EnterpriseSearchStatus cmdlet to determine when the new replica is Active, and clone the search topology once again.

3. Remove the unwanted index component, and activate the topology. Going through the process of making two clones helps to ensure fault tolerance while you are moving the index.

Adding a New Partition

You scale the search topology by adding a new index partition for each additional 10 million items. The new index component is added to the search topology and associated with a new partition number. For example, the small search farm scenario uses IndexPartition 0, so we would now be adding IndexPartition 1 to the topology. A new partition requires the search index to be repartitioned, as there is now more than one partition. Because there are two replicas for IndexPartition 0, you should also add two replicas for IndexPartition 1 to maintain fault tolerance. Before beginning the process, there are a few points you should consider:

➤ The repartitioning process can take several hours, and during this time the Search Service application is paused — and therefore unavailable for crawling, indexing, and responding to queries. You should not initiate other search topology changes during the repartitioning process.

➤ It is recommended that you make a backup of the Search Service application and the current index. This may sound a little paranoid, but the repartitioning process is a significant change to the index. If you are not sure how to create a backup, see http://technet .microsoft.com/en-us/library/ee748635.

> ➤ Ensure that you have sufficient disk space on the server that will host the new partition. For guidance on capacity planning, refer to http://technet.microsoft.com/en-us/library/jj219628, which is also referenced in Table 13-3.

Follow these steps to begin the process of adding a new partition to the small search farm scenario. You will add a second index partition, IndexPartition 1, to Server2 and Server4:

1. Check the status of the current search topology. The status can be viewed in the Search Administration page in Central Administration or run the PowerShell cmdlet Get-EnterpriseSearchStatus as you have done previously.

2. As before, create a clone of the topology prior to making changes:

```
$ssa = Get-SPEnterpriseSearchServiceApplication
$activeTopology = Get-SPEnterpriseSearchTopology -SearchApplication $ssa -Active
$clone = New-SPEnterpriseSearchTopology -SearchApplication $ssa -Clone
    -SearchTopology $activeTopology
```

3. Add a new index partition by adding an index component to Server2 and Server4, and associate them with the new index partition, IndexPartition 1:

```
New-SPEnterpriseSearchIndexComponent -SearchTopology $clone
    -SearchServiceInstance $host2 -IndexPartition 1
New-SPEnterpriseSearchIndexComponent -SearchTopology $clone
    -SearchServiceInstance $host4 -IndexPartition 1
```

4. Before you make the clone topology the active topology, it is a good practice to check the state of the Search Service application. To do so, execute the following cmdlets. If the service is paused, check the ULS logs and the SharePoint Health Analyzer alerts for a possible explanation. Fix any errors, and restart the service, which can be done using a forced resume if necessary using the cmdlet shown. As part of the repartitioning process, you will pause the service, so this check is to ensure that no other process has kick-started, such as backup, and paused the service before you enter repartitioning:

```
# If IsPaused() returns False, the service is running
# If True, the service is paused
$ssa = Get-SPEnterpriseSearchServiceApplication
$ssa.IsPaused() -ne 0

# Force the service to resume
$ssa.ForceResume($ssa.IsPaused())
```

5. To start the repartitioning, make the clone topology the active topology, which as you know by now commits the changes to the search topology:

```
$ssa.PauseForIndexRepartitioning()
Set-SPEnterpriseSearchTopology -Identity $clone
```

The repartitioning process typically takes hours, but in your development environment with minimal content, this process should take less than 10 minutes, so grab a refill on the coffee and by the time you come back it should be complete.

6. You can monitor the progress of updating the index replicas just as you did before using the following cmdlet. Make sure you open a second instance of the PowerShell window when you run this cmdlet:

```
# The newly added index replicas will show state Degraded
# until the process is complete
Get-SPEnterpriseSearchStatus -SearchApplication $ssa
```

Continuous Crawl and Content Sources

Content sources specify the repositories to be crawled, and a group of crawl settings that includes the host to crawl, the type of content, the crawl schedule, and how deep to crawl. When you created the Search Service application in Chapter 3, a content source named Local SharePoint sites was created, and it was configured to crawl all SharePoint sites in your farm. SharePoint has historically had two different types of crawls: a full crawl, which crawls all content, and an incremental crawl, which crawls content that has been modified since the last crawl. These crawls can be scheduled and are configurable on the content source from Central Administration.

A key disadvantage of both these types of crawls is index freshness. You want the index as fresh as possible. When a new document is added, or when an existing document is changed, the new version will not be available for search until it has been crawled and incorporated into the index. For example, if an incremental crawl is initiated at 12:00 P.M., and it takes one hour, then any content added during this crawl will automatically be at least one hour old. This is because once a crawl has been initiated on a content source, you cannot initiate a second crawl on the same content source. Therefore, index latency is inherent in the crawling process. If an incremental crawl is configured every hour and it takes longer than one hour to complete the crawl, the next scheduled crawl will be skipped. One solution is to provide for simultaneous crawl processes, which is what the continuous crawl delivers.

Crawling Content Sources

The continuous crawl process maintains a fresher index. It is configured on the content source, and once enabled it will automatically crawl at regular intervals:

➤ Continuous crawl can run in parallel with the incremental crawl.

➤ It is only available on SharePoint Sites content sources.

➤ The continuous crawl cannot be paused or stopped, but it can be disabled.

➤ The continuous crawl runs every 15 minutes by default, but this interval is configurable using the PowerShell cmdlet Set-SPEnterpriseSearchCrawlContentSource.

Use the following steps to enable continuous crawl and create a new content source:

1. From the Search Service Application: Search Administration page in Central Administration, click the Content Sources link, which will take you to the Manage Content Sources page shown in Figure 13-4. You should have at least one content source, named Local SharePoint sites. This page looks very similar to SharePoint 2010. You could create another SharePoint sites content source if you wish, or you can use the Local SharePoint sites source for the following steps.

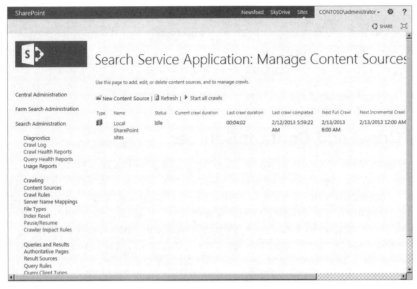

FIGURE 13-4

2. Using the Local SharePoint sites content source, place your cursor over the name to reveal the drop-down menu arrow. After noting the menu options, click Edit to open the Edit Content Source page.

3. From there, enable the option Enable Continuous Crawls, and create an incremental and full crawl schedule, as shown in Figure 13-5. You can configure the schedules however you like, but for now you want to generate some crawl data so you can view the example reports in the next section. You also need to ensure that the sites being crawled have content. Click the OK button when you are finished. The Status column on the Local SharePoint sites content source should report Crawling Continuous after a short time. You can also monitor the continuous crawl using the following cmdlets:

```
$ssa = "Search Service Application"
Get-SPEnterpriseSearchCrawlContentSource -SearchApplication $ssa | select *
```

Crawl Schedules

Select the crawl schedules for this content source.

Continuous Crawl is a special type of crawl that eliminates the need to create incremental crawl schedules and will seamlessly work with the content source to provide maximum freshness. Please Note: Once enabled, you will not be able to pause or stop continuous crawl. You will only have the option of disabling continuous crawl.

◉ Enable Continuous Crawls
○ Enable Incremental Crawls

Incremental Crawl
Every 5 minute(s) from 12:00 AM for 24 hour(s) every day, starting 2/14/2013 ▾
Edit schedule

Full Crawl
Every 15 minute(s) from 12:00 AM for 24 hour(s) every day, starting 2/14/2013 ▾
Edit schedule

OK   Cancel

FIGURE 13-5

4. After Crawling Continuous is displayed in the Status column, click the drop-down menu on the content source and you should see a new option, Disable Continuous Crawl, as shown in Figure 13-6. You can also disable continuous crawling by editing the content source and enabling incremental crawl. If you do this, you will receive the notification shown in Figure 13-7.

5. You could also create a new SharePoint sites content source, or a content source of another type. The process for creating a new content source remains unchanged from SharePoint 2010, but with the new option of the continuous crawl. From the Manage Content Sources page, click the New Content Source button. Briefly browse the Add Content Source page, noting the different types of content sources supported, and the continuous crawl option, which is not enabled by default.

FIGURE 13-6

6. Select the Web Sites option under Content Source Type, or any other option, and you will see that the option Enable Continuous Crawls is not available for anything but SharePoint sites.

7. If you wish, create a new SharePoint sites content source with continuous crawl enabled. If you choose a site whose Start Address already exists in another content source, you will receive an error.

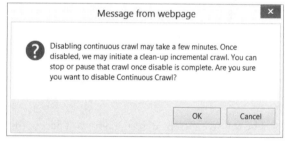

FIGURE 13-7

New Crawl Reports

Several new reports are available to the administrator for viewing the status and history of crawls. You need to be an administrator of the Search Service application to view the reports, or the farm administrator can assign Read permissions to users to give them access to the Search Service application status page, the crawl log, and the health reports.

The status of crawled content is shown in the crawl log. The log summarizes crawl information: crawled content successfully added to the index, content excluded because of a crawl rule, indexing errors, the time of the last successful crawl, and any crawl rules that were applied. The crawl log page provides the following different views:

➤ **Content Source** — This shows the status of items that have already been crawled and included in the index, the content source size, as well as a crawl history.

➤ **Host Name** — This gives a breakdown of the items crawled per host, such as the items already indexed for intranet.contoso.com, www.contoso.com, etc.

➤ **Crawl History** — This provides a summary of crawl transactions for each of the crawl types: full, incremental, delete, and continuous. The results are filterable by content source.

➤ **Error Breakdown** — This is a summary of crawl errors filterable by content source and host name.

➤ **Databases** — This view provides the document count for each of the crawl databases used by the Search Service application.

➤ **URL View** — You can search the crawl logs for all items in the index. This view is filterable by content source, status, message, start time, and end time.

SharePoint 2013 provides the following reports about crawl health:

➤ **Crawl Rate** — Number of content items crawled per minute

➤ **Crawl Latency** — Two graphs display content load distribution between crawler queue, submission to content processing, and waiting to commit to SQL; and time in each of these stages, respectively:

➤ **Crawl Freshness** — Summarizes how recently the items in the index have been indexed

➤ **CPU and Memory Load** — Shows resource utilization (%CPU and memory) for the key search system processes

➤ **Content Processing Activity** — Indicates the time spent in the various functions of the content processing component

➤ **Crawl Queue** — Number of items in the queue to be crawled, and the items crawled that are queued for processing

➤ **Continuous Crawl** — Time spent in the various subprocesses associated with the continuous crawl

The following steps describe how you access these reports in Central Administration and provide example reports for illustration:

1. Place the cursor over one of the content sources, and select View Crawl Log from the drop-down menu. The Crawl Log page shown in Figure 13-8 is a set of new reports that provide administrators with some very good information. Across the top of the page is a navigation menu, with options for selecting the different crawl log views: Content Source, Host Name, Crawl History, Error Breakdown, Databases, and URL View. You should review each of these options to familiarize yourself with the type of information available. The Crawl Log page is also accessible from the Crawl Log link in the Diagnostics section on the main Search Service application page.

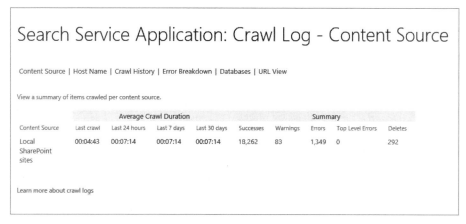

FIGURE 13-8

2. Another set of new crawl reports called the Crawl Health Reports is also accessible from the Diagnostics section. An example of this report is shown in Figure 13-9. You should view each of the crawl reports, and in particular the Crawl Freshness and Continuous Crawl reports. The information in these reports becomes more valuable as more crawling is initiated, and they are excellent diagnostic tools for the administrator.

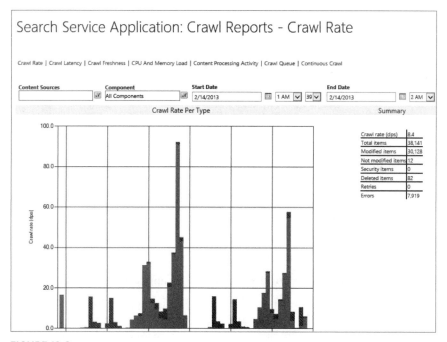

FIGURE 13-9

Result Sources

Result sources, new in SharePoint 2013, provide a way to limit search queries to specific content, whether that content is inside or outside of SharePoint (e.g., Exchange Server). In SharePoint 2010, search scopes and federated locations limited search queries to certain content. Result sources replace scopes, which have been deprecated. The old search scopes such as People and All Sites are still viewable but they cannot be edited. SharePoint 2013 provides 16 predefined result sources, as shown in Figure 13-10.

Provided by SharePoint (16)			
Conversations	10/28/2012 4:40:57 PM		Active
Documents	10/28/2012 4:40:57 PM		Active
Items matching a content type	10/28/2012 4:40:57 PM		Active
Items matching a tag	10/28/2012 4:40:57 PM		Active
Items related to current user	10/28/2012 4:40:57 PM		Active
Items with same keyword as this item	10/28/2012 4:40:57 PM		Active
Local People Results	10/28/2012 4:40:57 PM		Active
Local Reports And Data Results	10/28/2012 4:40:57 PM		Active
Local SharePoint Results	10/28/2012 4:40:57 PM	✓	Active
Local Video Results	10/28/2012 4:40:57 PM		Active
Pages	10/28/2012 4:40:57 PM		Active
Pictures	10/28/2012 4:40:57 PM		Active
Popular	10/28/2012 4:40:57 PM		Active
Recently changed items	10/28/2012 4:40:57 PM		Active
Recommended Items	10/28/2012 4:40:57 PM		Active
Wiki	10/28/2012 4:40:57 PM		Active

FIGURE 13-10

These result sources are viewable from the Manage Result Sources page in Central Administration using the Result Sources link on the main service application page. The following summarizes a few key points about result source creation and management:

➤ The default result source is Local SharePoint Results. Any result source can be configured as the default.

➤ You can create new result sources.

➤ You can create result sources for the Search Service application, a site collection, or a site:

    ➤ Result sources created using the Search Service application require farm administrator or service application administrator permissions, and these result sources will be available to any site that is part of a web application that consumes this service application. Result sources are managed using the Result Sources link in the Queries and Results section of the search administration page in Central Administration.

➤ For site collection configuration, you need to be a site collection administrator, and the result source can be used by any site in the collection. Result sources at this level are configured from the Site Settings page using the Search Result Sources link.

➤ Site owner permissions are necessary to configure result sources at the site level using the Result Sources link in the Search section of the Site Settings page, and these sources can only be consumed within the site.

➤ You can use result sources to restrict search queries to a subset of content using a *query transform*. For example, the out-of-the-box Documents result source returns all file types that match the following file types: .doc, .docx, .xls, .xlsx, .ppt, .pptx, and .pdf.

The following exercise steps you through the process of creating a new result source and demonstrates how to use the query transform. You can create the new result source at any scope you wish. You will be making a copy of the Documents results source, and using this as your starting point. To prepare the environment, six documents were added to it, each with the same name, Extranet Search, but they are different file types: .docx, .pdf, .png, .pptx, .vsd, and .xslx. Continuous crawl is enabled on the content source, so the content was crawled and the index updated in a very short time:

1. To create a new result source, click the Documents results source drop-down menu and choose Copy.

2. On the Add Result Source page, enter a unique name for the result source, because two result sources at one level cannot have the same name. Call this **Word Docs**, and for the Description enter **Word documents only**. The description is optional, but it is displayed as a tooltip, so go for it and add one.

3. Select Local SharePoint as the Protocol. This will provide results from the local index of the Search Service application. The Remote SharePoint option uses the index of another SharePoint farm. OpenSearch returns results from any search engine that supports the OpenSearch 1.0/1.1 standard, and results from Exchange 2013 is the other option. Unfortunately, the Exchange option is available only via the eDiscovery Center in SharePoint 2013.

4. Choose SharePoint Search Results because you want results from the whole index, not just from the user profiles.

5. Click the Launch Query Builder button, and you should see the Build Your Query dialog shown in Figure 13-11. Note the Query text, and the Search Result Preview. Of the six documents added, the query is not returning the .png and .vsd files, which it shouldn't, based on the file extensions defined in the query. Modify the query so that .doc and .docx are the only file extensions being queried, and click the Test query button. Only one result is returned, as shown in Figure 13-12. Applying the query transformation defines a subset of the result source. On a search results page, you can expose query results using a result source in several ways, such as in a *result block* or in a dedicated Web Part. This provides a very powerful way to display a preferential set of results. This essentially makes the results more relevant. You'll learn more about this in the next section.

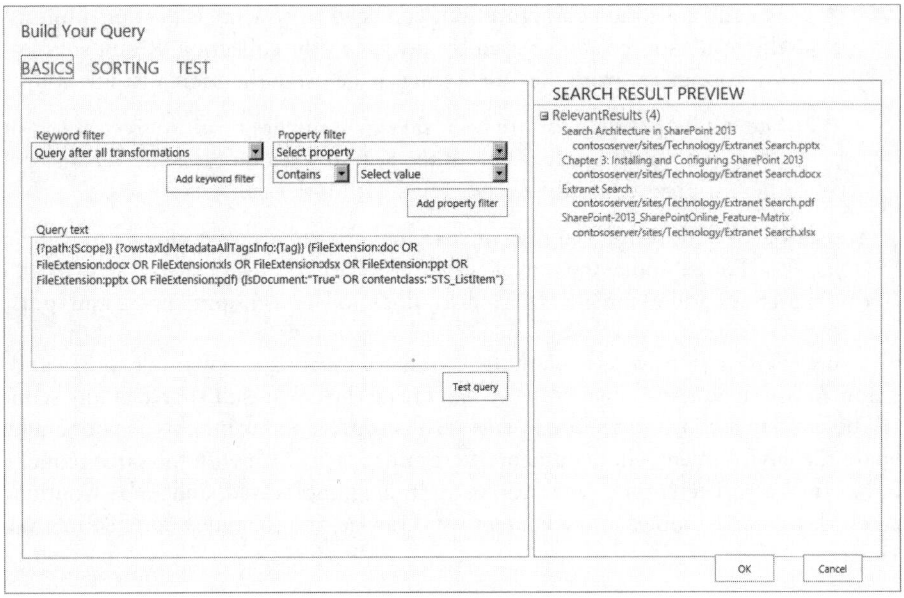

FIGURE 13-11

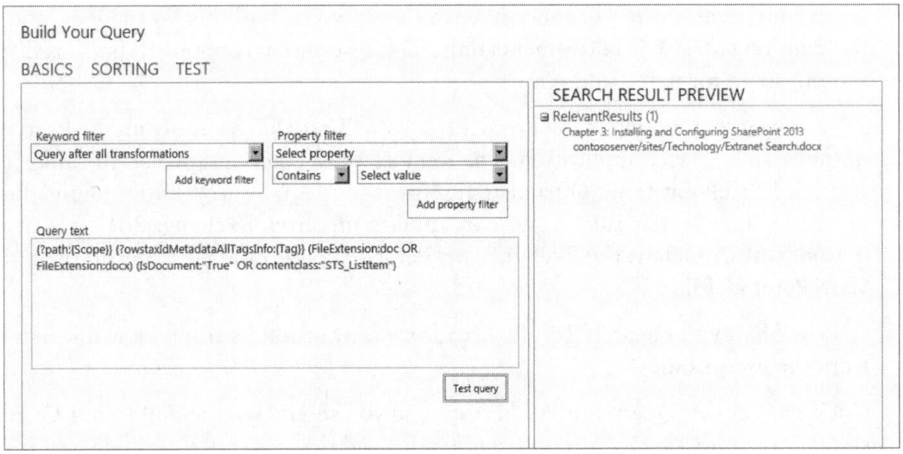

FIGURE 13-12

6. Click the Sorting option at the top of the dialog and review all the different options you have for sorting your results.

7. Click the Test option at the top of the dialog and review all the different testing options you have, and then click Show more.

8. Return to the Basics view and click the OK button.

9. Click the Save button on the Add Result Source page.

10. You also have the option to make a result source the default. This is accomplished using the Set as Default option in the drop-down menu of the result source, as shown in Figure 13-13. One of the benefits of this is that a search Web Part will automatically use the default result source.

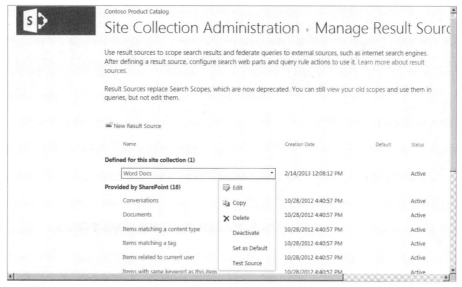

FIGURE 13-13

MANAGING THE SEARCH UI

The search UI consists of the enterprise search center, where users enter their queries and review their results. This interface is key to a successful user search experience, and therefore a successful enterprise search deployment. There are several new major enhancements to the user interface, as well as to improving the relevancy of the result, which also affects the user's experience. These enhancements include several new Web Parts, display templates and result types, and query rules, to mention just a few. The following sections discuss all these features.

Search Center

SharePoint 2013 provides an enterprise search center, and an enterprise search center template, just as it did in SharePoint 2010. The enterprise search center is the user interface for submitting search queries and viewing the results. The search center is created using one of two different site collection templates: Enterprise Search Center or Basic Search Center. A search center was not created during the installation described in Chapter 3, so you will create it now. The Search Service application also has an option for creating the Global Search Center URL, which is pretty descriptive of its purpose. You will create both of these in the following section. You need farm administrator permissions to configure the search center and the global URL.

Creating the Search Center

In the following steps, you create a new search center site collection, and configure the global URL in Central Administration:

1. Create a new search center using the Enterprise Search Center site collection template. Open the Create Site Collection page in Central Administration. Change the web application if necessary.

2. In the Template Selection section, choose the Enterprise Search Center template on the Enterprise tab, as shown in Figure 13-14. Review the description of this template versus the description of the Basic Search Center template, and you will see that the Enterprise Search Center template is more full featured, and as such is the recommended template.

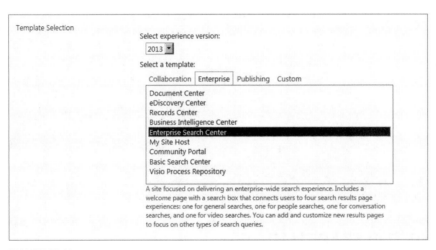

FIGURE 13-14

3. Because you have created multiple site collections by now, that is not covered again here. This site collection doesn't contain data, so you do not need to configure a quota. Fill out the remainder of the information, and click the OK button when you are done.

4. On the Top-Level Site Successfully Created page, click the link to the Search Center that was just created.

5. The search center consists of a default search homepage and a default search results page. You will learn more about the search center in the next section.

6. Configure any necessary permissions for users accessing the site. Keep in mind that this is the search center for the enterprise, so typically (but not always) this would include all users. If someone else is going to configure permissions, make sure they have been granted site collection administrator permissions. Copy the URL for use in step 7.

7. Go to the Search Administration page in Central Administration. At the top of the page is a gray banner asking "Where should users' searches go? Provide the location of the global Search Center," as shown in Figure 13-15. As the name implies, this is where users will be redirected to run the queries if not specified elsewhere. Note that the Global Search Center URL value in the System Status section needs updating. Click the word "location" in the banner, which is hyperlinked and will display the Search Center Settings dialog.

> ⓘ **"Where should users' searches go?"** Provide the location of the global Search Center

FIGURE 13-15

8. Paste into the Search Center URL box the search center URL you copied in step 5, and click OK. Under System Status, the value of the Global Search Center URL should be populated with your search center URL.

Now that you have the search center configured, it's time to look at some of the new and improved features of the search UI.

Search Center Overview

The search center is the UI for performing search queries. Upon provisioning, it consists of a default search homepage, a default search results page, and several pages referred to as *search verticals*. Search verticals are customized for searching specific content, such as People, Conversations, and Videos. The search verticals display search results that are filtered and formatted for specific content. All of these pages, described in the following list, are physically located in the Pages library:

- ➤ `default.aspx` — Search center homepage where users enter their queries
- ➤ `results.aspx` — Default results page for the search center, and the Everything search vertical
- ➤ `peopleresults.aspx` — People search vertical results page
- ➤ `conversationresults.aspx` — Search results page for the Conversations search vertical
- ➤ `videoresults.aspx` — Search results page for the Videos search vertical
- ➤ `advanced.aspx` — Advanced search page

The search center is not a new SharePoint concept, but SharePoint 2013 introduces several new features, which are best explored by executing a query. Figure 13-16 shows the results for the search center query "Extranet Search."

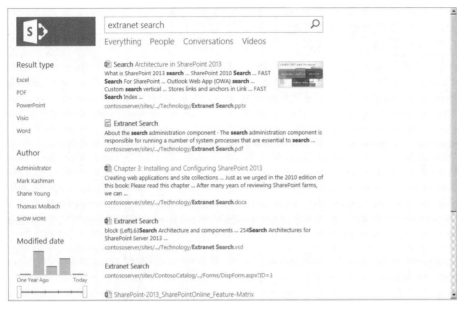

FIGURE 13-16

The search results page shows the deep refiners on the left-hand side, including the new modified date visual refiner. Note that refiner counts are not displayed because they are not enabled by default. True, they would only show one count for each, but that's beside the point. You will see how to enable refiner counts in the Display Templates section later in the chapter. The search verticals are hyperlinked across the top of the page, with the Everything vertical selected by default. The results show the six documents previously added during the Result Sources section, including the .pdf document. Note that .pdf files are indexed natively without any additional configuration. If you have the Office Web Application server installed per the instructions in Chapter 15, you will see the PowerPoint thumbnail, and the PowerPoint web app preview as you "hover over" the result, as shown at the top of Figure 13-17.

The document preview capability of the Office Web Applications is an excellent way to determine whether a specific document is what you need, without having to download and open the document; the preview is accomplished directly on the search result page. It is also possible to edit the document for the options listed at the bottom of the preview window. Note also the "Take a look inside" section just below the preview on the right. This provides a synopsis of the document, and links that take you to relevant locations in the document.

The following sections take a deeper look at the four new Web Parts delivering the search center results.

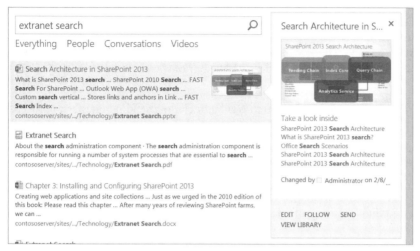

FIGURE 13-17

Search Center Web Parts

There are four new Web Parts in the search center: Search Box, Search Navigation, Refinement Panel, and Search Core Results. By placing the results page in edit mode, you can see the individual Web Parts and their names, as shown in Figure 13-18. Once in edit mode, you can click the Add a Web Part link to see the additional Web Parts available. Two search categories appear in the Web Part dialog: Search and Search-Driven Content, each containing several Web Parts you should review for familiarity. In the Content Rollup category, note the Content Query and Content Search Web Parts. These two Web Parts are discussed in Chapter 21, "Configuring and Managing Web Content Management and Internet Sites," so they are not covered here. The following sections describe each of the four new Web Parts and how their settings affect the displayed results. By default, the Web Parts on the search vertical pages are the same, but the Search Results Web Part is configured differently.

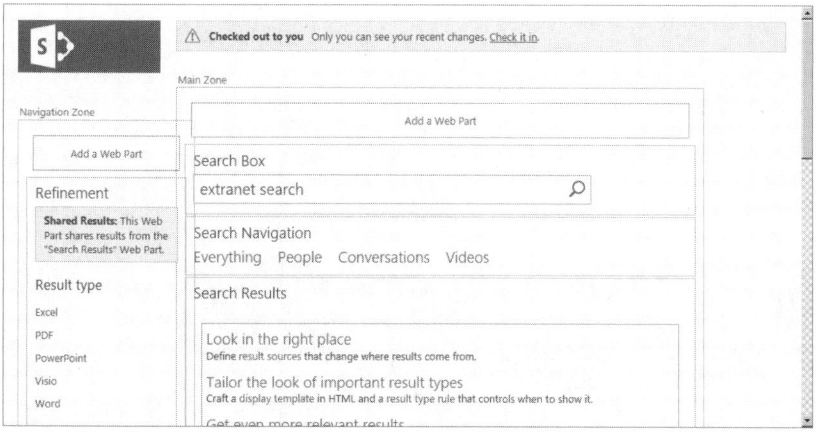

FIGURE 13-18

Search Box Web Part

This Web Part is used on the homepage and all search results pages for each of the verticals. To take a look at the configuration settings, choose Edit Web Part from the Search Box Web Part drop-down menu. The following summarizes what you can do with the options in the Properties for Search Box panel:

➤ Change the page that will display the search results, including sending queries to other Web Parts on the page, and enabling a drop-down menu in the search box.

➤ Enable query suggestions and people suggestions. Query suggestions or search suggestions are words or phrases that users have already queried; they appear below the search box as users type their query. This helps users return to important sites and documents by tracking what they have previously searched and clicked. Suggestions can be entered manually by the administrator, and they are also automatically defined by the search engine based on previous user analytics.

➤ Enable the display of links to a search preference page, and an advanced search page. The display template applied to the Web Part can be changed, and the search box can be configured to have focus when the page is loaded.

➤ There are Appearance, Layout, and Advanced properties, which are the same properties you have seen before.

Search Navigation Web Part

This Web Part displays links to the four different search verticals displayed by default. When users click a search vertical, the corresponding page is displayed with the filtered set of results using the Search Result Web Part. By default, the search vertical pages (`results.aspx`, `peopleresults.aspx`, `conversationresults.aspx`, `videoresults.aspx`, `advanced.aspx`) contain the same Web Parts, but the query in the Search Results Web Part is configured differently. The search vertical properties are configured on the Search Settings page for the corresponding site, as shown in Figure 13-19.

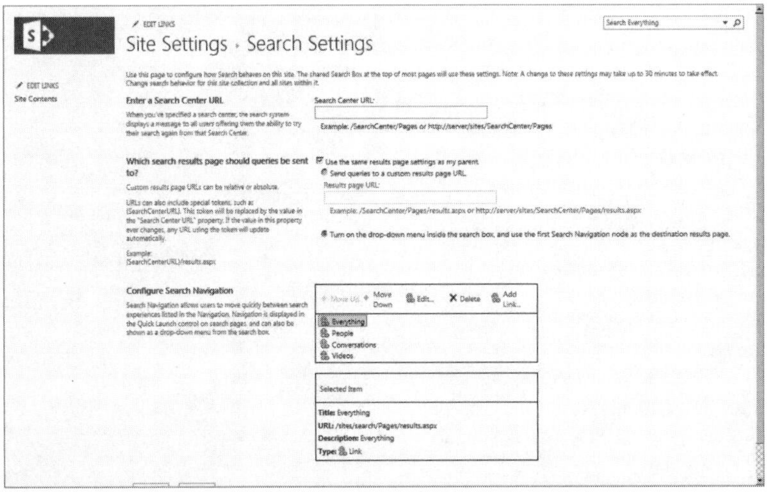

FIGURE 13-19

The Search Navigation Web Part can be configured in the following ways:

➤ Change the properties of the search vertical using the Edit hyperlink in the Configure Search Navigation section (refer to Figure 13-19). You can also add a new search vertical using the Add Link hyperlink, as well as change the order of the verticals.

➤ Use the results from a Web Part other than the Search Results Web Part, which is the default.

➤ Specify the number of search vertical links to display; five is the default.

Search Results Web Part

This Web Part displays the search results from a query entered into the Search Box Web Part. It is used on all search vertical pages by default. In addition to displaying the search results, it also passes the search results to the Refinement Web Part and the Search Navigation Web Part on the same page.

It utilizes several new features for filtering and displaying results, and these features are highlighted and described directly on the edit page without even opening the properties pane, as shown in Figure 13-20. The four hyperlinks provide the following options:

➤ **Result Sources** — Specify where the results come from; these were discussed earlier in the chapter. Clicking this hyperlink takes you to the Manage Result Sources page in the Site Settings of the site.

➤ **Display Template** — Control the appearance of the results. This link takes you to the Edit Display Templates page within Design Manager.

➤ **Result Type Rule** — Control when to use the display template. Clicking this link takes you to the Manage Result Types page that is part of Site Settings.

➤ **Query Rules** — These are used to promote specific results, show result blocks, and help control ranking. The Manage Query Rules page is available directly from the link.

Note that result sources, display templates, result types, and query rules are all highlighted directly on the page for the user, along with links to their corresponding pages for creating new items. This should tell you that someone thinks these are pretty cool. These features are all new to SharePoint 2013, and they provide tremendous power and flexibility for controlling and displaying the results. You have already looked at result

FIGURE 13-20

sources; the other options are covered later in the chapter. The Search Results Web Part can be configured in the following ways:

➤ Use results from the Results Web Part or from another Web Part. For each search vertical page, the Results Web Part query is directed to a specific result source by default. For example, for the Everything vertical it is scoped to the Local SharePoint Results result source, while for People and Video it is the Local People Results and Local Video Results sources, respectively. These can be changed to any result source for the default verticals or any custom search vertical.

➤ Control what is being searched, and how the query is defined using the Query Builder tool. The Query Builder tool enables you to create and test query transforms — transforming the query into a very specific set of instructions that enable you to customize the search results.

You looked at this tool previously (refer to Figure 13-11), but here you have a slightly different tool, with more bells and whistles. The tool has two modes. Advanced Mode, which is the default mode, is shown in Figure 13-21; Quick Mode is shown in Figure 13-22. One difference you notice immediately is the new Refiners tab, which enables you to specify which refiners to display. Specifically, you can accomplish the following with the Query Builder tool:

➤ Define the result source using any of the native sources for the default search verticals, or any of the other result sources available.

➤ Scope the results to a specific site, library, list, or URL, and limit results to content tagged with specific terms.

➤ Filter your search results using keyword filters. Keyword filters add query variables to the query, and they are automatically replaced with the actual value when the query is executed. For example, the query variable {SearchBoxQuery} will be replaced with the value entered into the search box when the user executes a query. The following describes additional capabilities for specifying the query.

> **NOTE** *A list of the available query variables is provided in "Query Variables in SharePoint Server 2013," at* `http://technet.microsoft.com/en-us/library/jj683123.aspx`*. In general, you can learn about constructing queries using the Keyword Query Language (KQL) from "Keyword Query Language (KQL) Syntax Reference," at* `http://msdn.microsoft.com/en-us/library/ee558911(v=office.15).aspx`*.*

➤ Use property filters to query the content of managed properties.

➤ Choose the type and number of refiners to use as part of the query. The Refiners tab lists the managed properties that are enabled in the search schema.

➤ Sort results based on a number of different attributes, including rank, author, and click distance, for example, and sort based on different ranking models. You can also promote and demote results dynamically based on specific rules.

➤ Specify whether query rules are used or not.

➤ Preview the final query that will be sent to the Search Results Web Part, along with the corresponding results.

➤ Control how results are displayed by selecting the display template and the result type. You can also specify which properties in the results are hit-highlighted.

➤ Specify the number of results per page, and various other settings.

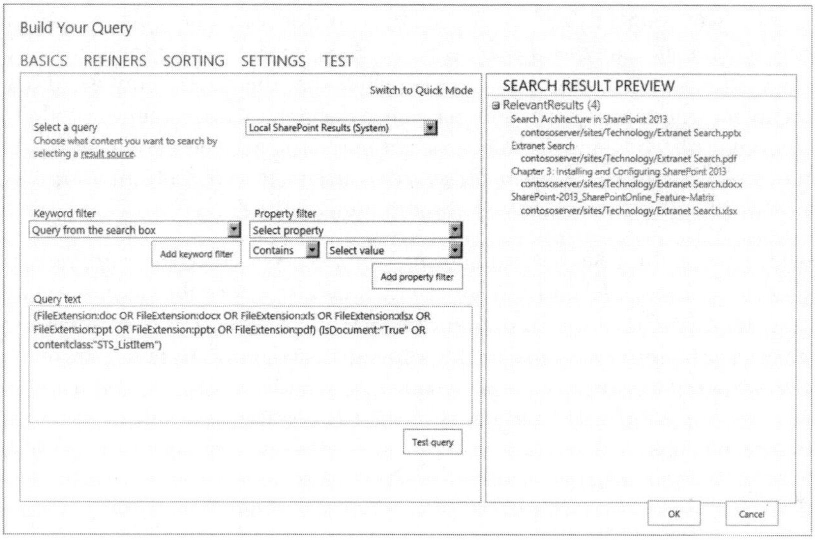

FIGURE 13-21

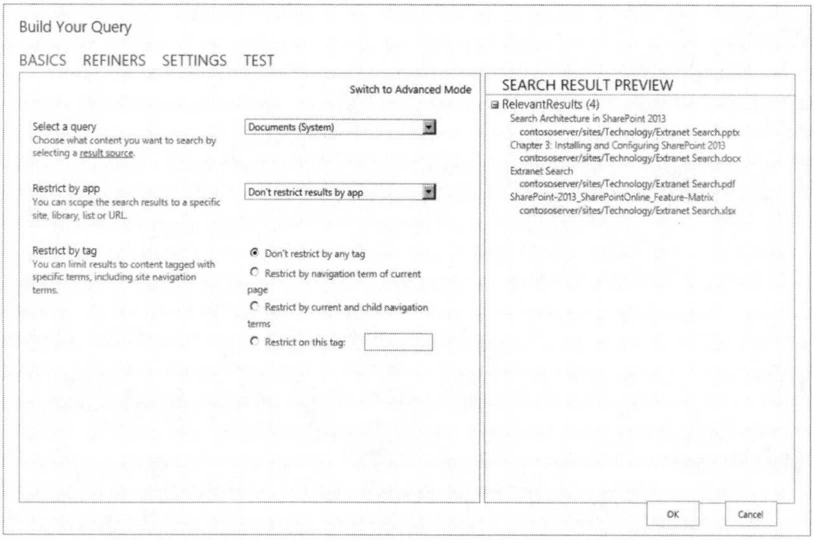

FIGURE 13-22

Refinement Web Part

Last but not least is this key Web Part. It's present on all search vertical pages by default, and it filters results into categories to help users "refine" their results. Search refiners have been around since SharePoint 2010 and FAST Search for SharePoint 2010, but there was a big difference between the two.

SharePoint 2010 and FAST provided shallow and deep refiners with item counts, respectively. Shallow refiners are based on the first 50 search results, whereas deep refinement includes all the search results, which is why item counts can be included. This may not seem like a big deal, but it can drastically affect the number and type of refiners that are surfaced. For example, if a word document doesn't appear in the refiner results, then you can conclude that there aren't any Word documents if you have deep refinement. Otherwise, shallow refinement says the Word document didn't exist in the top 50 results. It could still exist in the results, just not in the top 50. SharePoint 2013 includes deep refinement only! However, be aware that item counts are disabled by default for all text refiners. You learn how to enable item counts in the "Display Templates" section.

If you open the Properties of the Search Refinement Web Part, you'll see there are essentially two different modes: *search results* and *faceted navigation* (also referred to as *contextual navigation*). These modes reflect the two options labeled "Choose refiners in this web part," and "Use the refinement configuration defined in the Managed Navigation term set," respectively. Search result refinement in SharePoint 2013 uses the new display templates, and faceted navigation for refiners is also new in SharePoint 2013. If you click the Choose Refiners button, the Refinement configuration for 'Refinement' dialog shown in Figure 13-23 appears. Specifically, this Web Part can be configured in the following ways:

➤ Refine results using the Search Results Web Part or another Web Part.

➤ Faceted navigation is used in conjunction with term sets that are used for navigation. With each term, you can select the managed properties that will be used as refiners.

➤ Specify which refiners to display, their order, and the display template that is applied to each refiner using the Refinement configuration dialog.

➤ Control the display of the Web Part, and how the refiners are organized within it.

FIGURE 13-23

Customizing the UI

Search is about finding information, but great search is about finding the information you need easily. Most of us have experienced the endless loop of clicking a search result, browsing the answer, and then starting the process again to find the right result. The user interface can help with that, and refiners are a good approach to making search easier. SharePoint 2013 improves the search experience beyond the use of refiners, through display templates and result types. When displaying the search results, each different result type has a display template, including the hover panel, and the refinement controls, and each is customizable. Display templates and result types are discussed in the next two sections.

Display Templates

You can say goodbye (happily) to the need for using XSLT to modify the search results UI, and say hello to display templates, which control how an item is displayed. A display template consists of two files: an HTML file and a JavaScript file. The specific display pattern is contained in the HTML, and the JavaScript is generated automatically when you upload the HTML file. SharePoint 2013 provides several display templates, which you can copy and customize. They are located in the Display Templates folder of the Master Page Gallery in the site collection. Recall from Figure 13-16 that refiner counts, the number of items for each refiner, are not enabled by default. Therefore, the following example walks through the process of modifying a display template so that refiner counts are displayed. The user modifying the template requires at least Designer permissions:

1. Browse to the Master Page Gallery of your search center site collection.

2. Click the folder labeled Display Templates. Note the different categories of templates.

3. On the Display Templates page, click the folder called Filters. Browse the names of the different templates, and open a few of them to see what each does.

4. Locate and download a copy of the `Filter_Default.html` file.

5. Using your favorite text editor, locate the variable called `ShowCounts`, using the following code as guide, or perform a search within the file. `ShowCounts` should be set to `false`; change the value to `true` as shown in Figure 13-24 and the following code:

```
this.Options = {
ShowClientPeoplePicker: false,
ShowCounts: true
};
```

6. After changing the value, save the file.

7. Upload the file to the Display Templates: Filters library, replacing the previous file.

8. Browse to the search center and create a query. Using the "Extranet Search" query used earlier, you will see that refiner counts have been added to the refiners on the results page, as shown in Figure 13-25.

9. The other option is to create a new display template by making a copy of the `Filter_Default.html` file, modify the `<title>` element and `ShowCounts` variable, and update the Refinement Web Part. To do that, rename the downloaded file `Filter_Default_wItem_Counts.html`, and make the necessary changes:

```
<title>Refinement Item with Item Counts Displayed</title>
ShowCounts: true
```

```
<head>
<title>Refinement Item</title>

<!--[if gte mso 9]><xml>
<mso:CustomDocumentProperties>
<mso:CompatibleManagedProperties msdt:dt="string"></mso:CompatibleManagedProperties>
<mso:TemplateHidden msdt:dt="string">0</mso:TemplateHidden>
<mso:CompatibleSearchDataTypes msdt:dt="string"></mso:CompatibleSearchDataTypes>
<mso:MasterPageDescription msdt:dt="string"></mso:MasterPageDescription>
<mso:ContentTypeId msdt:dt="string">0x0101002039C03B61C64EC4A04F5361F385106604</mso:ContentTypeId>
<mso:TargetControlType msdt:dt="string">;#Refinement;#</mso:TargetControlType>
<mso:HtmlDesignAssociated msdt:dt="string">1</mso:HtmlDesignAssociated>
<mso:HtmlDesignConversionSucceeded msdt:dt="string">True</mso:HtmlDesignConversionSucceeded>
<mso:HtmlDesignStatusAndPreview
msdt:dt="string">https://microsoft.sharepoint.com/teams/CaravajalSite/_catalogs/masterpage/Display
Templates/Filters/Filter_Default.html, Conversion successful.</mso:HtmlDesignStatusAndPreview>
<mso:CrawlerXSLFile msdt:dt="string"></mso:CrawlerXSLFile>
<mso:HtmlDesignPreviewUrl msdt:dt="string"></mso:HtmlDesignPreviewUrl>
</mso:CustomDocumentProperties></xml><![endif]-->
</head>
<body>
    <div id="4">

<!--#_

    this.Options = {
        ShowClientPeoplePicker: false,
        ShowCounts: true
    };
```

FIGURE 13-24

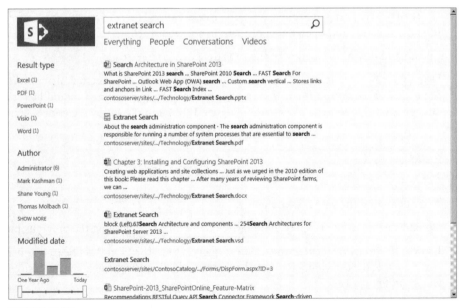

FIGURE 13-25

10. When you are done, upload the `Filter_Default_wItem_Counts.html` file, and the JavaScript file will be automatically generated.

11. Modify the display template values for each of the refiners, as shown in the configuration panel in Figure 13-26. Note that the Refinement Item with Item Counts Displayed template is highlighted for selection. Once the template has been associated with each of the refiners, the search results will display item counts just as before. Creating a new template is a better approach, because now you have an easy way to disable item counts from the UI.

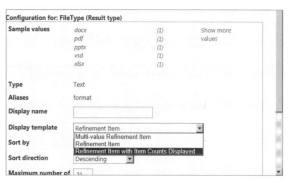

FIGURE 13-26

Result Types

A result type is a set of one or more rules that identify a type of result, such as a Word document, for example. When a search result satisfies the rules, the result type specifies how the result should be displayed on the search page. When a query is executed, the search results are evaluated against the rules. Result types work hand-in-hand with display templates, which are covered next. Result types enable administrators and site owners to customize how results are displayed. Result types can be summarized as follows:

➤ They are configurable using the Search Result Types link and the Result Types link, at the site collection and site level, respectively.

➤ They are reusable, and they apply to Search Results and Content-based Web Parts.

➤ They are bound to a given result source.

➤ They are defined by one or more conditions or rules. Rules determine when a result type should be applied. You can consider this a rules engine — and when a result matches the rules, it triggers a response, in this case how the result should be displayed.

➤ There is a property list that associates the rule to a document type, content type, or other managed property. Managed properties are added to the list and used in the display template. When the rules are satisfied, you can specify which managed properties to return in the results.

➤ They are associated with a display template that determines how the result is displayed.

The following example uses the Excel result type to demonstrate how the out-of-the-box result type is configured:

1. Browse to the Site Collection Administration: Manage Result Types page in the search center site collection as shown in Figure 13-27. Note that a priority is associated with result types, with those higher in priority taking precedence. Therefore, you could have more than one result type, each with different rules or conditions, for a given result. You can also see that result types are based on result conditions and result actions.

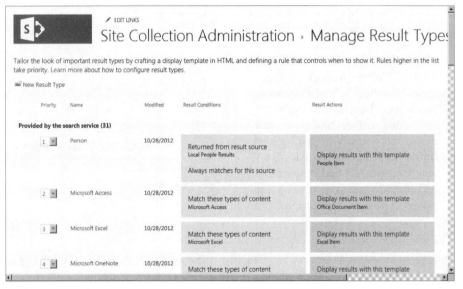

FIGURE 13-27

2. Hover over the Excel result type, and choose Copy from the drop-down menu. The Add Result Type page, shown in Figure 13-28, will appear. Review the options for the various conditions, noting the different possible result sources, the types of content that can be matched, and the possibility of using more than one condition. The values in the result type have been updated to reflect a new type, still based on Excel but that will display results using the Best Bet Item display template.

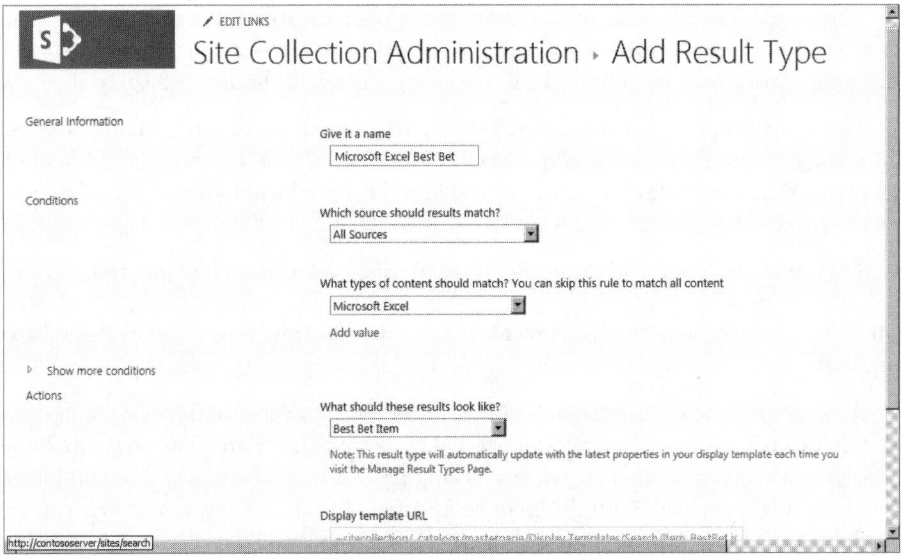

FIGURE 13-28

3. When you are done, click Save. Notice that the new result type is added with priority 1, and a new category for just the site collection is created. Result types of a given priority take precedence over those from the search service. Figure 13-29 displays the new search results, and you can see that the Best Bet display has been applied to the Excel document, but it has not been altered in rank in the results.

FIGURE 13-29

Query Rules

The query rule determines whether a search result meets a set of predefined conditions, and if it does it will perform actions to improve the relevance of the search results. The focus here is improving relevance, in contrast to the result type, whose purpose is to enhance the display of the results. You can see how they can be used together. The following summarizes the key points for query rules:

➤ They are applied to a given result source.

➤ You can create a query rule for a Search Service application, a site collection, or a site:

➤ Query rules created at the Search Service application require farm administrator or service application administrator permissions, and these rules will be available to any site that is part of a web application that consumes this service application. Query rules are managed using the Query Rules link in the Queries and Result section of the search administration page in Central Administration.

➤ For site collection configuration, you need to be a site collection administrator, and the query rule can be used by any site in the collection. Rules created at this level are configured from the Site Settings page using the Search Query Rules link.

➤ Site owner permission is necessary to configure query rules at the site level using the Query Rules link in the Search section of the Site Settings page, and these sources can only be consumed within the site.

➤ The query rule fires when a search result matches the query rule conditions.

➤ Query rule actions are executed when the query rule fires and the relevancy of the result is changed. You can promote individual results or a group of results, or change the ranking of the results.

➤ Query rules can be published, which means they go live on a certain date and subsequently become inactive on a certain date. They can also be scheduled for review on a certain date.

➤ Query rules are inherited. Rules created at the service application level are inherited by all site collections and sites in web applications that consume the service application. Likewise, sites inherit rules created at the site collection level. You can disable a query rule by making it inactive if you don't want it to apply to a site collection or site.

Creating a Query Rule

The following steps create a query rule that boosts the Excel document result to the top of the page:

1. Navigate to the Site Settings page from the search center site collection homepage.

2. On the Site Settings page in the Search section, click the Query Rules link. You will also see the Search Query Rules link in the Site Collection Administration section if you are a site collection administrator. You want the query rule to apply to this site only, not all sites in the site collection, so you won't use the site collection link.

3. Review the different options available on the Manage Query Rules page before you get started creating your new rule.

4. Because query rules are configured for a specific context, this is the first option to specify. As shown in Figure 13-30, beneath the question "For what context do you want to configure rules?" are three drop-down menus in the first row of options. Open the drop-down menu for the Select a Result Source option as shown in the figure. As you consider which result source to select, consider the user's context and the search verticals: everything or enterprise search, people search, conversations or videos. Each experience can have its own query rules. After selecting a source, you will see a list of all the rules that fire for queries on that source at the bottom of the page. Select the Local SharePoint Results source. Recall that each search query sends the request to a result source, and the result source responds with results that satisfy specific conditions. You want your query rule to fire for all search requests across the enterprise, or the Everything vertical. Therefore, your queries will be sent to the Local SharePoint Results result source, which includes everything SharePoint crawls except people. If you wanted only people results, you would choose the Local People Results source.

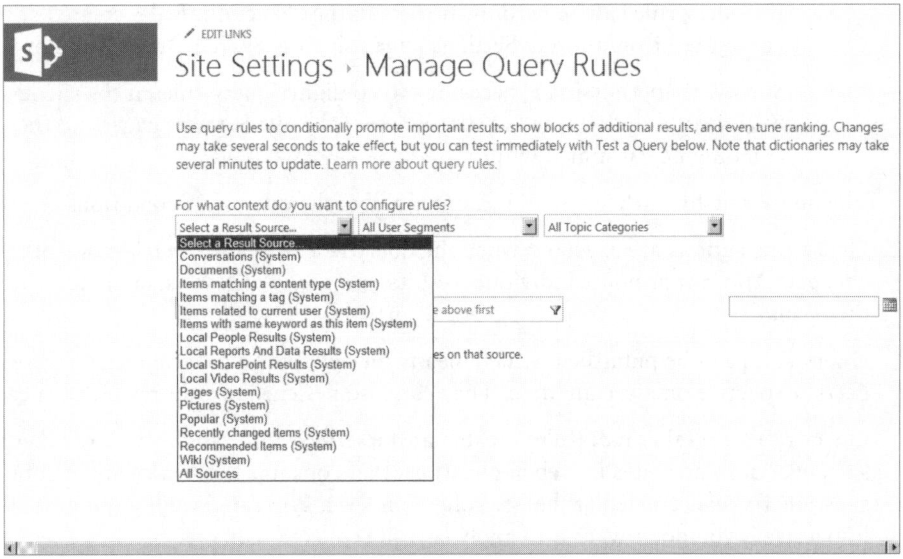

FIGURE 13-30

5. Click the New Query Rule link.

6. On the Add Query Rule page, add the name **Boost Excel to the Top**. You want your rule to fire every time, boosting the Excel documents to the top of the results.

7. Take a moment to review the Context section before making your selection. Ensure that the Context section is expanded, displaying the three radio button options. You can select the All sources option to apply the query rule to all result sources, or you can apply the rule to one source. By default, the result source you previously selected is chosen. You can also restrict the query to categories, which will fire your rule when a term from the managed navigation term set is included in the query. To configure this option, click Add Category. The Import from term store dialog will appear, where you can choose a term. You can also restrict the query to a user segment, which is also based on a term from a managed term set. Leave the three options at their default values and minimize the section.

8. Look at the options in the Query Conditions section. You need to create one or more conditions or remove all conditions. In order for the rule to be applied, "fire" in geek speak, the query must meet a rule condition. If met, query actions are triggered. Open the drop-down menu, which contains the following options:

➤ **Query Matches Keyword Exactly** — Search keyword exactly matches a specific word or phrase.

➤ **Query Contains Action Term** — An action term is a word or words that occur at the beginning or end of the query, and they can be chosen from a dictionary, which can be imported from a managed term set in the term store.

➤ **Query Matches Dictionary Exactly** — You need to select a term set dictionary, and the query must match exactly one of the terms.

➤ **Query More Common in Source** — This condition checks whether the query is one of the top queries in the result source you specify. For example, a user might query for "SharePoint 2013 Ignite Training" in the Local SharePoint Results source, but this query is actually more popular and more common in the Videos result source. Therefore, your query will fire if it is more common in the selected result source.

➤ **Result Type Commonly Clicked** — Similar in some ways to the previous condition, this condition is also applied based on user behavior. For example, if users commonly click video search results every time "SharePoint 2013 Ignite Training" is queried, then you might want to select Video in the result type drop-down menu. This will cause your query condition to fire.

➤ **Advanced Query Text Match** — Use this condition for complex query matching requirements, such as a regular expression, a phrase, or a dictionary entry.

> **NOTE** *Your query rule will fire when any of the conditions are true.*

The first question to ask yourself is whether you want your query to fire every time. If yes, then delete the default condition that was added when the new rule was created, and your rule will fire every time because there aren't any conditions. This is done using the Remove Condition link. In general, however, you may want to have conditions, and you can add one or more conditions. When a condition is met, the rule fires and the actions are executed. To complete this step, click the Remove Condition link so your rule fires every time.

9. In the Actions, you specify the action that should occur when the query rule fires. The actions will alter the search results in one of three ways:

   ➤ **Promoted Results** — This promotes individual results above ranked results. In SharePoint 2010, promoted results were called Best Bets, and Visual Best Bets in FAST for SharePoint 2010. The promoted result is represented by a hyperlink.

   ➤ **Result Blocks** — This promotes a result or group of results above ranked results. These results are managed as a block, and they are represented as a fully formatted HTML block of information. Items are added to a results block by the execution of an additional query, created using the Query Designer. The results block can be placed ahead of the core results, or interleaved based on ranking. You can apply a display template to a results block.

   ➤ **Change Ranked Results** — This promotes or demotes search items based on a specific query created in the Query Builder. This approach, based on xRank, a FAST search technology, enables you to boost the relevancy of items at query time.

10. In the Actions section, click Add Result Block.

11. In the Edit Result Block dialog, click the Launch Query Builder button.

12. In the Query Builder, select FileType in the Property filter option, and choose Equals and Manual in the two drop-downs beneath that. Enter **xls** and click the Add property button, and repeat the process for **xlsx**. Your Query text should be as follows:

```
{sujectTerms} FileType=xls FileType=xlsx
```

13. Click the OK button once for the Query Builder dialog, and again for the Edit Result Block dialog.

14. On the Edit Query Rule page, review the options in the Publishing section, which control when a rule is active. There are options to configure the start date, end date, or always active, which is the default. You can also assign a review date, which triggers an e-mail to an assigned reviewer. Click the Save button when you are done reviewing the Publishing section options.

15. Return to the search center and test the "Extranet Search" query. You should see the Excel spreadsheet promoted to the top of the page, while still showing all the results in the same order, as shown in Figure 13-31.

FIGURE 13-31

16. You can also make any query rule inactive, which disables the query rule but doesn't delete it. Go to the Manage Query Rules page and hover over the Boost Excel to the Top rule, click the drop-down menu, and choose Make Inactive.

17. Test the search results to confirm that the original ranking is returned.

Multiple query rules will typically be firing for every query that is executed, as you will have more than one rule for a given level. By default, the rules do not fire in any prescribed order, but you can specify the order for query rules by creating query groups. You can only group rules created for a specific level at that level. For example, you cannot group inherited rules, you must navigate to the level at which they were created and group them at that level. The grouping will be inherited just like the rules are inherited.

To group a set of rules, you first select the different rules and then click the Order Selected Rules button on the Manage Query Rules page. This opens the Order Selected Rules dialog shown in Figure 13-32. Here you can move the rules to a group with a specific name, such as My Rules.

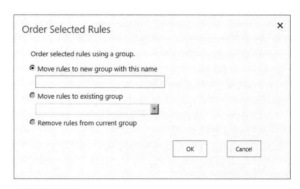

FIGURE 13-32

Once the rules are in a group, you can specify the order in which they fire when triggered, as shown in Figure 13-33. You can even prevent a query rule that ranks lowest in a group from firing. To do so, choose the Stop option in the drop-down menu in the Actions column associated with the rule on the Manage Query Rules page. This drop-down menu is also displayed in Figure 13-33; the options are Continue and Stop.

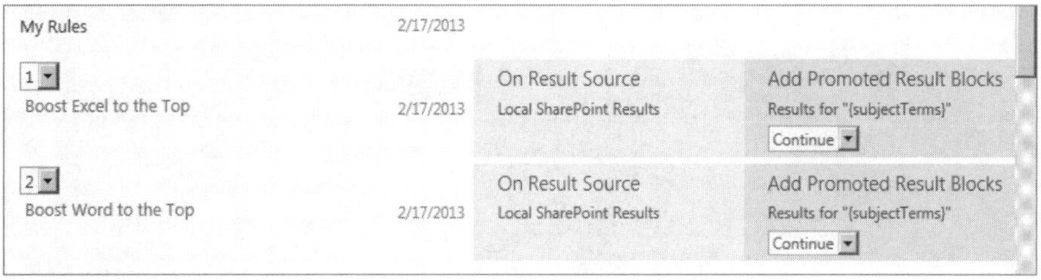

FIGURE 13-33

You can remove the rules placed into a group just as easily. Select the rules, click the Order Selected Rules button, and choose the "Remove rules from current group" option.

As you can see, query rules are very powerful and flexible, not to mention very fun and cool.

Managed Properties

Managed properties were covered briefly earlier in the "Content Processing" section, but this section demonstrates their new capabilities in SharePoint 2013, some of their attributes, and how they are configured. Recall that managed properties are very important to a successful search experience because many of the features discussed so far apply to managed properties. For example, refiners can only be created from managed properties.

Managed properties are created from crawled properties. In general, crawled properties represent content and metadata extracted from a document or URL during crawls. Metadata can be structured content, such as the Title or Author from a Word document, or unstructured content, which could be a language attribute or extracted keywords.

The purpose of the crawl is to retrieve this content and metadata, and transform it using mapped properties so that this information can be included in the index. You can map multiple crawled properties to a single managed property, or map a single crawled property to multiple managed properties. Only managed properties, not crawled properties, are included in the index. Therefore, the quantity and quality of your managed properties exert tremendous influence on the effectiveness of the search experience. Managed properties play a key role in the search experience, and as such they have a large number of settings, or attributes, that determine how content is saved in the index. These settings are summarized in Table 13-5, which includes the property, a brief description, and whether it is configurable in Central Administration only or also available at the site collection.

TABLE 13-5: Managed Property Settings

MANAGED PROPERTY SETTING	DESCRIPTION	CONFIGURABLE IN CENTRAL ADMIN	CONFIGURABLE IN SITE COLLECTION
Searchable	Managed property included in the index; its contents can be queried.	X	X
Advanced Searchable Settings	Property can be viewed, and changed. Its relevance can also be changed.	X	X
Queryable	Property can be queried but the name must be included in the query, either directly or programmatically.	X	X
Retrievable	The property's values can be returned in search results.	X	X
Allow multiple values	Allows multiple values of the same data type.	X	
Refinable	Yes - Active: Property can be used as a refiner after a full crawl. Manual configuration of the refiner in the Web Part is required. Yes - Latent: Enables switching Refinable to Active without requiring an additional full crawl. The property Queryable must also be enabled for either Active or Latent.	X	
Sortable	Yes – Active: Result set can be sorted before it is returned. Yes – Latent: Enables switching to Active without having to do a full re-crawl. Both options require a full crawl to take effect.	X	
Alias	Defines an alias for a managed property. Alias can be used instead of the managed property. Use the original managed property and not the alias to map to a crawled property. This could be helpful if you don't want to or don't have permission to create a new managed property.	X	X

continues

TABLE 13-5 *(continued)*

MANAGED PROPERTY SETTING	DESCRIPTION	CONFIGURABLE IN CENTRAL ADMIN	CONFIGURABLE IN SITE COLLECTION
Token normalization	Results are returned independent of letter casing and diacritics used in the query.	x	x
Complete matching	Queries will only be matched against the exact content of the property.	x	x
Mappings to crawled properties	List of crawled properties mapped to this managed property. The managed property can get its content from one or more crawled properties.	x	x
Company name extraction	Company name entities can be extracted and later be used to set up refiners. There is one pre-populated, editable dictionary for company name extraction in the term store.	x	x
Custom entity extraction	Enables one or more custom entity extractors, which can be used to extract entities and to set up refiners.	x	x

SharePoint 2010 had a couple of limitations related to how managed properties were created that made them difficult to use:

➤ They could only be created at the Search Service Application level.

➤ The process first required a full crawl of all your content to create a crawled property, and then a second full crawl of all your content to create a managed property. Depending on the size of the corpus, this could be a very lengthy undertaking.

SharePoint 2013 addresses these limitations, making managed properties more accessible, which will facilitate implementation and adoption. The following summarizes key benefits:

➤ Managed properties can still be created at the service application level in Central Administration. Only certain managed property attributes are configurable in Central Administration, as specified in Table 13-5.

➤ You can create managed properties at the site collection level, as listed in Table 13-5.

➤ A managed property is automatically configured as a crawled property without performing any crawl.

The following section demonstrates how to create and configure managed properties at the site collection level. Not covered is this process using Central Administration, because it is very similar to the SharePoint 2010 process, and several very good, thorough references already document the process, such as "Manage the search schema in SharePoint Server 2013," at `http://technet.microsoft.com/en-us/library/jj219667`.

Creating Managed Properties for the Site Collection

Site collection administrators can create new managed properties for a site collection and map crawled properties to them. Alternatively, you can reuse existing, unused managed properties that do not have crawled properties mapped to them, and rename them using an alias. Then you must map the crawled properties to the renamed managed property with the defined alias. When you create a new managed property in the tenant or site collection administration, there are some limitations:

➤ They can only be of data type Text or Yes/No.

➤ They cannot be sortable.

➤ They cannot be refinable.

Follow these steps to create a new managed property:

1. Using the Search Schema link in the Site Collection Administration section of the Site Settings page, go to the Managed Properties page for the site collection, shown in Figure 13-34. Compare it to its equivalent in Central Administration.

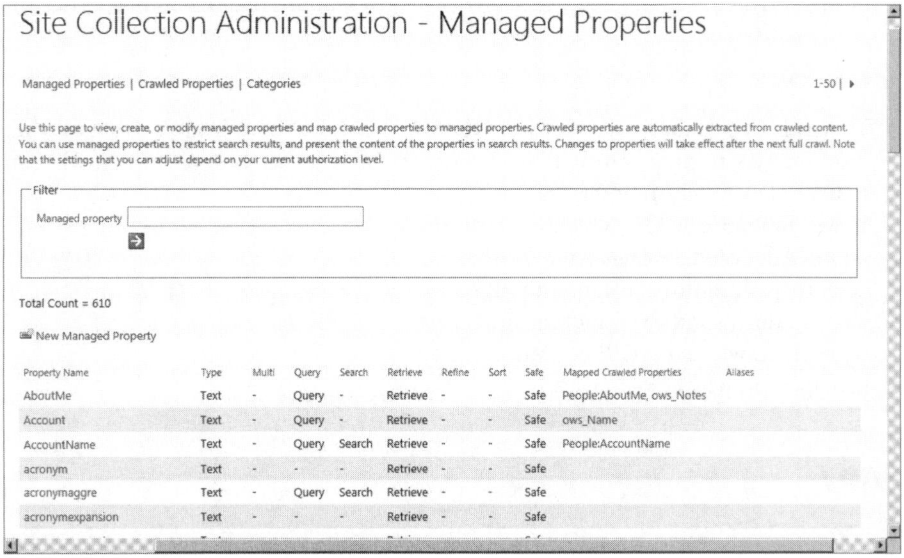

FIGURE 13-34

2. Click the New Managed Property button, which takes you to the New Managed Property page. Review the options on the page, and compare it to the Central Administration page. Under Type, note that only Text and Yes/No data types are available, all others are grayed out as previously mentioned. Also note that the attributes Refinable and Sortable are not available.

3. You can also use this page to map the managed property to crawled properties using the Add a Mapping button. Click the button and review the options, and complete the desired mapping.

4. Unfortunately, the limitations discussed earlier can affect the process, but you have another option if you need a managed property without these limitations. You can create a managed property by renaming an existing managed property, one that does not have the aforementioned limitations.

5. On the Managed Properties page, locate the managed properties beginning with Refinable00. You will need to browse to the 250–300 item pages, so it takes several page clicks. These managed properties are unused, meaning they are not mapped to a crawled property. Find the property that is the correct data type and you can use it as your own.

6. After choosing an unused managed property, edit the property by clicking the Edit/Map Property option in the drop-down menu.

7. Add the name of your managed property to the Alias field.

8. In the Mappings to crawled properties section, click the Add a Mapping button.

9. On the Crawled property selection page, select a crawled property to map to the managed property and then click OK. Repeat this step to map more crawled properties to this managed property.

10. Click OK.

11. You still need to do a full crawl, but there's something new. You can request that the list or library containing your managed property be scheduled for a "full crawl" using the Reindex Document Library option, shown in Figure 13-35, which is located on the Advanced Settings page for the list or library. Actually, the content will be indexed during either an incremental crawl or a full crawl, and it will be available as a managed property.

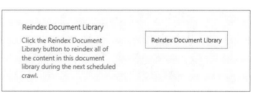

FIGURE 13-35

SUMMARY

The new search capability in SharePoint 2013 is awesome! This chapter focused on most of the key new features associated with the architecture, and demonstrated how to configure search so that you have a good understanding of how things have changed and how you can get the most out of it. Search just keeps getting better with each new SharePoint release. Its capabilities in SharePoint

2013 mark a dramatic evolution from the search text box and user query interaction of the past. These early capabilities are still present, but search has become an integral part of the platform's operation, and users can personalize and customize it in ways that have not been possible previously. Search has become a data access technology that is used by multiple features in the SharePoint platform. Gone are the days when an enterprise deploys SharePoint without also implementing the search capability.

14

Configuring User Profiles and Social Computing

WHAT'S IN THIS CHAPTER?

➤ What's new in Enterprise Social?

➤ Managing and configuring user profile synchronization

➤ Managing and configuring My Sites

➤ Managing and configuring communities

Several computing megatrends are occurring in the enterprise today: cloud computing, the proliferation of mobile devices, big data, and the introduction and proliferation of enterprise social applications. As part of the "consumerization of IT," social applications such as Facebook and Twitter, and many others, are moving from the consumer world to the enterprise. In this chapter, we use the term *enterprise social* to refer to the adoption of social capability applications and tools within the corporation. These enterprise social applications are increasing employee engagement, improving team collaboration, and helping solve real business challenges. Because SharePoint is a collaboration platform, it has historically provided a limited set of enterprise social features, but it's fair to say that the feature set was incomplete relative to other applications. With the introduction of SharePoint 2013, enterprise social capability has dramatically increased, and it is now a key part of the platform. SharePoint 2013 implements features that make enterprise social computing and collaboration easier. These enterprise social features are built upon user profiles, and a database of user properties or attributes that integrate information from many kinds of directory services and business applications.

This chapter covers the new enterprise social capability, as well as the existing features that have been improved since their introduction in SharePoint 2010. Using step-by-step examples, you will also learn how to configure and administer the services that are required to support enterprise social capability.

WHAT'S NEW IN ENTERPRISE SOCIAL?

Enterprise social includes the social networking features and the infrastructure to support that capability. By now, most of us are familiar with social networking features such as microblogging, posting to an activity feed, liking posts, communities, and targeting users. SharePoint 2013 has all these capabilities, as well as several additional features that make it very attractive to enterprises that want to implement some sort of enterprise social capability. This section provides the administrator with a brief overview of some of these new features, many of which are discussed in more detail later in the chapter.

My Sites

My Sites included social capability in SharePoint 2010, but in general the scope and breadth of the functionality was considered insufficient versus other social applications. In SharePoint 2013, My Sites have a new look, some improved capability for the activity feed, new functionality in the form of SkyDrive Pro, and some significant infrastructure changes. Overall, My Sites include three different sets of components:

➤ A web application, content databases, and services

➤ A My Sites host site collection

➤ A personal site collection

My Sites are discussed in more detail later in the chapter but the following subsections provide a brief description of these changes.

Activity Feed

Those of you familiar with SharePoint 2010 know that it included a rudimentary activity feed ("My Newsfeed") on the My Site host page. This displayed microblog posts and profile changes related to the user's colleagues, such as when a user gets a new manager. This information was stored in a social database. While this was a good first step, it lacked the interactive nature that a true social feed such as Facebook provides, which is what users have come to expect. With SharePoint 2013, the new activity feed finally supports two-way conversations; therefore, it is a more fully functional microblogging environment. The My Site host site collection and web pages contain the activity feed or newsfeed page, and the About Me page of the user. A user can post activities, ask questions, comment on other posts, and "like" content in their feed. In addition, users see the activities from all their community memberships, and can follow people, documents, websites, and tags. A big change from SharePoint 2010 is that all activity feed content is stored in the user's personal site, and this content is stored in one or more content databases. This means every user needs to have a personal site in order to use this capability.

> **NOTE** *Activity feed information, documents in the new personal document library called SkyDrive Pro, and information about sites and documents being followed are stored in content databases, which differs from SharePoint 2010, which stored social information in the social database. User profile data is still stored in the profile database in SharePoint 2013, just like it was in SharePoint 2010. Information about following people and tags is also stored in the profile database, just as it was in SharePoint 2010.*

Hashtags

People who have never used Twitter may be wondering what a hashtag is. A *hashtag* is simply a keyword or topic that can be added to a microblog entry to enable other users to consume and filter content from their activity feed. For example, if you create a microblog entry that contains content about SharePoint 2013, you could add the hashtag "#sharepoint2013." This simple action enables some very powerful behavior. In SharePoint 2013, hashtags can be followed as well as searched. Although in SharePoint 2010, the Managed Metadata service enabled you to tag documents and pages within your site, in SharePoint 2013 the tagging capability has been enhanced with this new hashtag capability in the activity feed.

Personal Site

The personal site is also a site collection, just like the My Site host site collection. This site contains two different SharePoint lists that contain the activity feed information, the SkyDrive Pro page and content, a page displaying the documents being followed, and a page displaying the sites being followed.

SkyDrive Pro

Personal file storage services have become very popular over the last few years. Numerous different applications, such as Box.net, Dropbox, and even Microsoft's own SkyDrive, enable users to save, share, and synchronize personal files from any computer in the world. Typically, an application runs locally on the device, and the content is stored in data centers in the cloud. This may work well for personal information, but many corporations consider cloud storage a security risk and don't allow employees to store company information in the cloud.

It is a private, personal file storage for the enterprise; therefore, SkyDrive Pro (SDP) differs from the public SkyDrive capability mentioned earlier. SDP provides a central location for storing all of a user's documents, and sharing them with other employees. In addition to the SharePoint library, there is also a desktop application called SkyDrive Pro that is installed when Office 2013 is installed on the user's desktop. The library and desktop application work together to deliver the following functionality:

- ➤ An improved user interface and easier process for sharing documents with other people in the organization
- ➤ Synchronization of the SkyDrive Pro library to your computer or mobile device

Distributed Cache

New to SharePoint 2013, the Distributed Cache service provides caching to various features in SharePoint 2013. This service is built on top of Windows Server AppFabric, which is installed as one of the SharePoint 2013 prerequisites. If you plan to use activity feeds, your farm must have the Distributed Cache service enabled. This cache temporarily stores the microblog entries so that they are immediately available to others in the environment.

Communities

SharePoint 2013 introduces a new site template called *Community Site*. This template builds upon the standard site template by adding a specifically tailored, moderated discussion board that helps to facilitate conversations between members of the community. In addition to creating and participating in discussions, community owners can also assign badges and set up a reputation system in their community. Another new template associated with communities is the *Community Portal* template. This enterprise site template provides results for any sites that use the Community Site template in the SharePoint farm.

In order to give users more incentive to participate in communities, SharePoint has included another new feature in their social toolbox, Reputation. *Reputation* enables users to find and engage experts, and encourages enterprise-wide social media adoption. After it is enabled on a community site, site owners can assign point values to various activities such as creating a new post or replying to a post. They can also define achievement levels that users can reach by accruing the defined number of points for that level. A user's achievement level is displayed near his or her name throughout the site. An important part of the reputation system is *badging*, whereby a site owner can configure automatically assigning a badge to users when they reach an achievement level, or users can manually assign badges to other users.

User Profile Synchronization

User profile synchronization configuration in SharePoint 2010 was one of the more difficult, if not the most difficult, challenges administrators faced when deploying a new farm. Fortunately, SharePoint 2013 introduces a new option for synchronizing user profiles from Active Directory. Called *Active Directory Import*, this capability is similar to the SharePoint 2007 import process. There are many benefits to using this new import process, such as faster performance, easier setup, and the ability to use LDAP filters to limit the objects being imported. Unfortunately, there are also some drawbacks, the biggest of which is that the process is import only, which means there's no capability to write back to Active Directory.

User profile synchronization using Forefront Identity Manager (FIM) is still available in SharePoint 2013. The FIM process is similar in configuration, but the full and incremental synchronization performance has been improved. Also available is support for custom synchronization using the User Profile Service web service and object models.

User Profile Replication Engine

The only real change to the User Profile Replication Engine is that it has been absorbed by the SharePoint team. This means that it is included with the other SharePoint 2013 components and therefore doesn't require a separate download. Presumably, this also means that it will be given a little more attention in the future if updates or changes are needed.

MANAGING AND CONFIGURING PROFILE SYNCHRONIZATION

The User Profile service in SharePoint 2013 is a shared service just as it was in SharePoint 2010, and it enables administrators to create and edit user profiles. In Chapter 3, "Installing and Configuring SharePoint 2013," you learned how to provision the User Profile Service Application (UPSA) and configure your My Site host web application and site collection.

> **NOTE** *For a review of the installation, configuration, and prerequisite information for creating the UPSA, administrators can also refer to the TechNet article at* http://technet.microsoft.com/en-us/library/ee721052.aspx. *This article also discusses the PowerShell cmdlets for completing the process.*

To navigate to the UPSA web page in Central Administration, click the Manage Service Applications link on the homepage, and then click the User Profile Service Application link in the list of installed service applications. Figure 14-1 shows the User Profile Service Application home page. For those familiar with the SharePoint 2010 version, you will see that there aren't many differences between the SharePoint 2010 UPSA and the SharePoint 2013 UPSA. The following sections discuss key aspects of the People and Synchronization settings of user profiles.

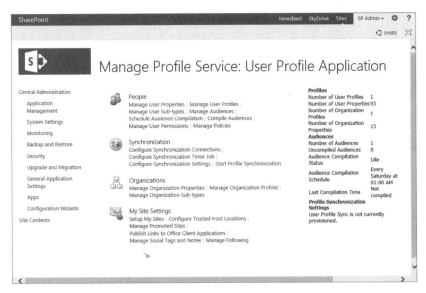

FIGURE 14-1

Profile Synchronization

SharePoint 2013 relies on user profiles to a much greater extent than SharePoint 2010. Because the user profile information represents a collection of properties or attributes of the user, My Sites, search, Azure Workflow, and the new server-to-server authentication all rely on user profiles. In order for this information to be available, the user profile data must be imported into SharePoint.

Synchronization, or syncing, is the process that SharePoint uses to import user profile data from other data sources, such as Active Directory, LDAP, or by using Business Connectivity Services (BCS) to pull data from line-of-business applications. In addition to syncing user profiles, you can also sync groups. As mentioned earlier, there are now two Central Administration options for profile synchronization in SharePoint 2013: SharePoint Profile Synchronization using FIM, and the new Active Directory Import method.

Choosing a Synchronization Method

Before you can configure profile synchronization, you first need to decide which synchronization option you are going to use. Note that you can switch between sync modes, so you can start with one and later switch to the other. Table 14-1 summarizes the different sync options available to the administrator. Use the following steps to choose your sync option:

1. In the Synchronization section of the Manage Profile Service page, click Configure Synchronization Settings.

2. On the Configure Synchronization Settings page, shown in Figure 14-2, select the option to synchronize Users and Groups or Users Only.

3. If you chose SharePoint Profile Synchronization and want to include BCS connections in the process, check the appropriate box.

4. Choose the Synchronization Option that you want to use and then click OK. This completes the synchronization type selection process.

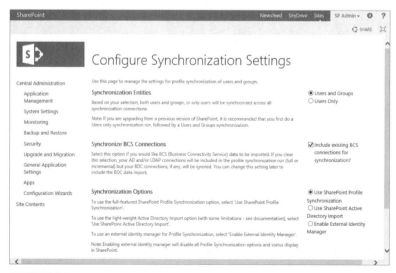

FIGURE 14-2

TABLE 14-1: SharePoint 2013 Synchronization Options

OPTION	DESCRIPTION
SharePoint Profile Synchronization	Full-featured option using FIM. This option allows two-way synchronization, and the use of BCS to augment property import. This approach is more difficult to set up and slower than Active Directory Import.
Active Directory Import	This approach is easy to set up and very fast compared to other options. Only one-way Active Directory import is supported, and you can use LDAP filters for users and groups. This approach allows one connection per domain, and custom property mapping for simple data types. Mapping to SharePoint system properties and BCS import is not supported.
External Identity Manager	This approach disables profile synchronization features from SharePoint. You must use a custom solution that utilizes the SharePoint API to create user profiles.

Active Directory Import

The Active Directory Import (ADI) synchronization method provides administrators with a new option for syncing profiles. One of the benefits of choosing this method is that you don't have to provision the User Profile Synchronization Service. No, this is not a joke. Recall reading that ADI is much easier to configure. This synchronization process runs entirely in the context of the User Profile Service Application. In general, ADI is configured in three steps: selecting ADI as the sync option, as covered in the previous section; creating a connection; and mapping user profile properties. The following steps provide the details for creating a connection:

1. In the Synchronization section of the Manage Profile Service page, click Configure Synchronization Connections.

2. Click Create New Connection.

3. Enter a name in the Connection Name box.

4. Enter the fully qualified domain name of the domain you wish to sync.

5. Select the Authentication Provider type. Most administrators will use Windows Authentication. Click the Authentication Provider Type drop-down menu to familiarize yourself with the options available.

6. Enter the account name and password of the Active Directory account you configured to do the import. Figure 14-3 shows an example of a completed connection.

7. Make sure the default port is correct and check whether your domain uses SSL.

8. Optionally, check the box to filter disabled users from the import.

9. Add any LDAP filters that you want to use to filter users from the synchronization process. Here's a common filter that includes accounts that are not disabled:

```
(&(objectCategory=person)(objectClass=user)
    ( !(userAccountControl:1.2.840.113556.1.4.803:=2))).
```

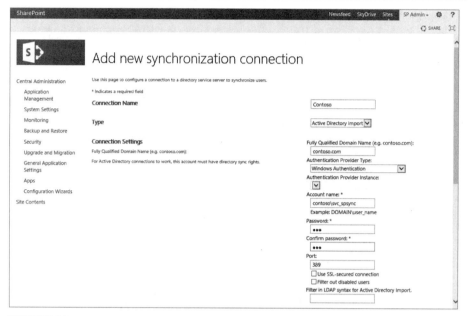

FIGURE 14-3

> **NOTE** *The LDAP filters used here are* inclusion *filters; they tell the sync process what to include, not what to exclude. This is different from the User Profile Synchronization process, where the filters are* exclusion *filters. Also, since there is a check box for excluding disabled users, you could use the following filter as another example for users with an e-mail address:* `(&(objectCategory=Person)` `(objectClass=User)(!(userAccountControl:1.2.840.113556.1.4.803:=2))` `(mail=*))`.

10. Click Populate Containers to load the tree view.

11. Select the objects that you want included in the import.

12. Click OK. The connection information is stored in the profile database.

As you can see, this is much easier and faster to configure compared to configuring the SharePoint Profile Synchronization process. However, administrators need to be aware of the limitations:

➤ This is a single Active Directory forest sync.

➤ Mapping to SharePoint system properties that begin with "SPS-" is not allowed.

➤ Mapping multi-value data types to single-value data types and vice versa is not supported.

➤ Mapping two different attributes to the same property is not supported.

➤ Augmenting profile information using the BCS is not supported.

By default, the import process runs every five minutes. Either you can wait for the job to run or you can manually start a full synchronization from the Manage Profile Service page. To change the schedule of the job, click Configure Synchronization Timer Job under the Synchronization heading on the Manage Profile Service page. Note that a full import is required whenever a configuration change occurs. A configuration change includes one of the following:

➤ Adding or removing organizational units (OUs)

➤ Changing the filter properties

➤ Adding or changing property mappings

It's a good idea to purge the profile database after a full import has been completed. You can do that using the following PowerShell cmdlet, which is discussed in more detail at `http://technet` `.microsoft.com/en-us/library/ff608004(v=office.14).aspx`:

```
Set-SPProfileServiceApplication - Identity $UPS_to_Update
   -PurgeNonImportedObjects $true
```

The final configuration step involves mapping user properties in the user directory to SharePoint properties. This is discussed in the next section, but keep in mind that it also applies here. To summarize the preceding, the ADI process requires selecting the ADI option, creating a new connection, and mapping user attributes. Once completed, the farm administrator can initiate an incremental or full sync from the Start Profile Synchronization page. This page is accessed using the Start Profile Synchronization link in the Synchronization section of the Manage Profile Service page. The sync is initiated by choosing one of the following:

➤ **Start Full Synchronization** — Use this if syncing for the first time or if connections have been added or modified since the last sync.

➤ **Start Incremental Synchronization** — Use this to synchronize only information that has changed since the last sync.

For a more detailed discussion of the ADI steps, see the article at `http://technet.microsoft.com/` `en-us/library/jj219646.aspx`. The next section covers how to use the second sync option.

SharePoint Profile Synchronization

This sync option relies on configuring the User Profile Synchronization service. Readers familiar with SharePoint 2010 will recognize this more involved process, described in the following sections.

Configuring the User Profile Synchronization Service

The User Profile Synchronization service is responsible for creating and provisioning the necessary tools that enable synchronization. The following steps describe the process. This example assumes you already have the User Profile Service Application created; therefore, only one additional account is required. The first step in the process requires configuring an Active Directory user account that will be used to perform the sync. This account needs to be granted "Replicating Directory Changes" permissions on the domain. Here are the steps to do that:

1. Open the Active Directory Users and Computers snap-in.

2. Right-click the domain name in which the account resides, and select Delegate Control. Click Next, and then click the Add button.

3. Enter the account you want to use for the synchronization process and click OK.

4. Click Next, and then select Create a custom task to delegate.

5. Click Next again. Then, in the Permissions box, select the Replicating Directory Changes option.

6. Click Next, and then click Finish to close the dialog.

You need to perform two other tasks to ensure that the User Profile Synchronization Service starts correctly:

➤ Ensure that the farm account is a member of the Local Administrators group on the server that hosts the synchronization service.

➤ Ensure that the farm account has been granted "Allow log on locally" right in the Local Security Policy on the server that hosts the synchronization service.

At this point, you should reboot the machine that is hosting the User Profile Synchronization service. After the server reboots, navigate to Central Administration so you can begin the process of starting the User Profile Synchronization service:

1. From the Central Administration home page, click Systems Settings.

2. Under the Servers section, click Manage services on server.

3. Using the Server drop-down at the top of the page, select the server that hosts the User Profile Synchronization service.

4. Find the User Profile Synchronization service and click Start. Figure 14-4 shows the resulting dialog. If the User Profile Synchronization Service page has a red banner at the top stating "This can only be used if SharePoint Profile Synchronization is enabled in the Configure Synchronization Settings for this User Profile Application," then return to the section "Choosing a Synchronization Method," and ensure that you selected the SharePoint Profile Synchronization option.

FIGURE 14-4

5. Select the User Profile Service Application that will be associated with this sync service instance.

6. Enter the password for the farm account in both the Password and Confirm Password boxes, and then click OK.

At this point you'll be redirected back to the Services on Server page, where you will see that the status of the User Profile Synchronization service is Starting. The service can take up to 10 minutes to start, so now would be a good time to take a break, grab a beverage, or just catch your breath. If after 10 minutes you notice that the status is still Starting or is now Stopped, don't panic. Check the ULS logs and the Event Log on the server for any relevant entries. In general, if the process wasn't successful, you will find one or more entries in the logs that need to be addressed. After resolving any errors, start the process again.

Configuring the Synchronization Connection

The process for creating a synchronization connection for SharePoint Profile Synchronization is very similar to the process for Active Directory Import. The only significant difference is how you configure the connection filters, which is described in the next set of steps. First, create the connection:

1. Under the Synchronization section of the Manage User Profile Service page, click Configure Synchronization Connections.

2. Click Create New Connection. At this point you may get an error indicating that the sync service is not running; if so, you need to ensure that the service has started or you won't be able to create a connection.

3. Enter a name in the Connection Name box.

4. Enter the fully qualified domain name for the synchronization.

5. You can let SharePoint auto-discover your domain controller or you can specify one.

6. Select the Authentication Provider type. Most administrators will use Windows Authentication.

7. Enter the account name and password of the Active Directory account you configured to do the import. Figure 14-5 shows the resultant dialog.

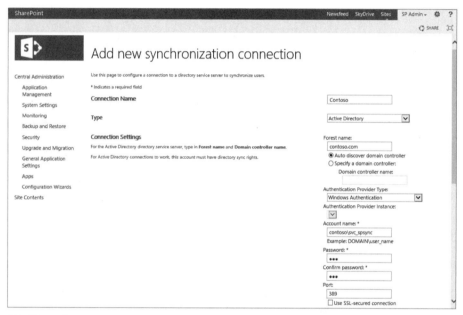

FIGURE 14-5

8. Make sure the default port is correct, and enable the check box if your domain uses SSL.

9. Click Populate Containers to load the tree view.

10. Select the objects to be included in the import, and click OK.

Editing Connection Filters

At this point, you could proceed with a full profile synchronization, but it is a good practice to add connection filters before you start the process. It will make the synchronization execute faster, and it will keep your user profile database more compact. You can filter on numerous Active Directory attributes, but Table 14-2 lists some common filters that should be used in most environments.

TABLE 14-2: Common Exclusion Filters

ATTRIBUTE	OPERATOR	FILTER	DESCRIPTION
userAccountControl	Bit on equals	2	Excludes accounts that have been marked as disabled
userAccountControl	Bit on equals	17	Excludes accounts whose passwords never expire
Mail	Is not present		Excludes accounts that do not have an e-mail address

Follow these steps to configure exclusion filters for users:

1. Under the Synchronization section of the Manage User Profile Service page, click Configure Synchronization Connections.

2. Hover over the connection you want to configure, click to reveal the drop-down menu, and then click Edit Connection Filters, which takes you to the Edit Connection Filters dialog shown in Figure 14-6.

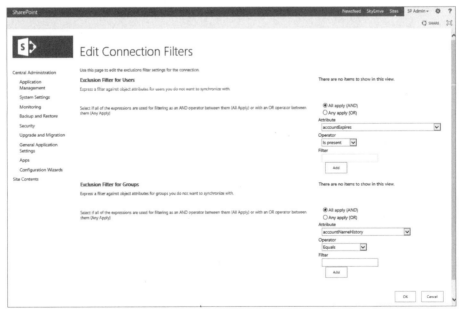

FIGURE 14-6

3. From here you can create filters that apply to users and to groups. You can also create multiple filters, and then decide whether all the filters need to be applied together to filter the user, or if each of the filters is applied individually to filter users. This difference is determined by which option is enabled: All apply (AND) or Any apply (OR). Select the option you desire. If you're unsure, select the OR option.

4. In the Attribute drop-down menu, choose the attribute that should be used for filtering.

5. In the drop-down menu of the Operator field, select the operator that you want applied.

6. Enter the value of the attribute that will be used to determine whether a user account is excluded.

7. Click Add. Figure 14-7 shows an example of an exclusion filter. Notice that the filter can be removed after it has been added.

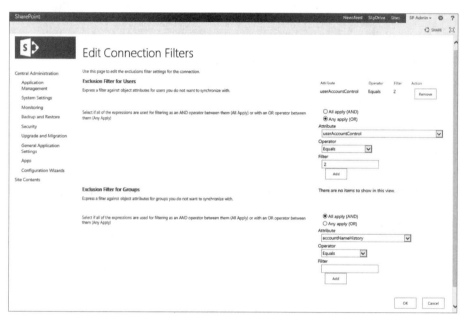

FIGURE 14-7

You can create additional filters using the same process, and you can add exclusion filters for groups. When you are finished adding filters, click the OK button at the bottom of the dialog to save your changes.

Configuring the User Profile Image Export

The following steps illustrate how to utilize the SharePoint Profile Synchronization method to export a user's image to the directory store, such as Active Directory, for example. This is a common request, because seeing a user's face helps facilitate collaboration, especially when the people who are interacting have not been introduced. Once exported from SharePoint, the user's picture can then be used by other applications such as Outlook. Exporting these images from one source provides consistency throughout your organization as users interact with people through e-mail, chat, and in SharePoint. Here are the steps to export the user's picture:

1. Ensure that you are using SharePoint Profile Synchronization to import your profile data, and that the import is coming from Active Directory or another LDAP-compliant data source. These steps assume you're using Active Directory.

2. The Active Directory account that is doing the synchronization requires additional permissions. Follow the same steps outlined at the beginning of the section, "SharePoint Profile Synchronization," but this time grant the Create All Child Objects permission to the account.

3. In Manage User Properties, find the Picture property, hover over the name, and then click Edit.

4. In the Add new mapping section, pick the source data connection that you wish to use.

5. Select thumbnailPhoto as the Attribute that will receive the exported picture.

6. Set the Direction of the mapping to export, and click OK.

7. Run a full synchronization.

When the synchronization has completed, the Active Directory attribute should contain data for those users who have uploaded their picture in SharePoint.

> **NOTE** *The image might not appear right away in the various Office clients until you close and reopen them.*

Managing User Properties

Property mapping is one of the steps involved in the profile import or sync process. User properties are mapped to SharePoint properties, and this constitutes the SharePoint user profile. User properties are comprised of the attributes or fields associated with the database of users in the organization. This information is stored in a directory service, such as Active Directory. A long list of properties is included and already configured by default. They are separated into sections for easier viewing and organization. You can view the properties that are part of the SharePoint user profile by viewing the Manage User Properties page. This page, shown in Figure 14-8, is accessed from the Manage Profile Service page by clicking the link in the People section. The Add User Profile Property page is shown in Figure 14-9. This page is very similar to the Edit User Profile Property page, which is accessed by choosing Edit from the drop-down menu of a specific property.

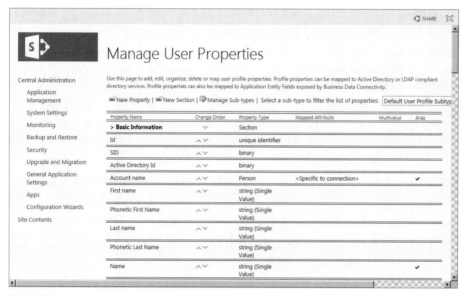

FIGURE 14-8

FIGURE 14-9

It is these properties that are mapped to properties in the user directory, and upon synchronization the directory property values are assigned to the mapped SharePoint properties. You can set properties to automatically pull or push data to the directory service, or you can configure them to be editable by end users from within their SharePoint My Site. As you configure property mappings, edit properties, and create new properties, you will encounter several terms associated with properties. Therefore, as you view Figure 14-9, and hopefully in keeping with your own farm setup, it would be useful to review the terminology:

➤ **Property Settings** — The property name is used by the User Profile service to access the specific property, and it cannot contain any spaces. The display name is the name of the property that users see. The property type is a field type, such as a string, a date, or an integer. The different property types available are shown by selecting the drop-down menu of the Type input box. Properties can be single or multi-valued, configured to use a metadata term set, and support multiple languages.

➤ **Sub-Type** — These can be used to more granularly categorize people, such as by a company's major divisions or a company's location. Each profile property can be selectively added or removed from these subtypes. To create a new subtype, click the Manage Sub-types button on the Manage User Properties page. This will take you to the Manage User Sub-type dialog shown in Figure 14-10. After you create a new subtype, it will appear on the Add User Profile Property page (as Company Location is shown previously in Figure 14-9).

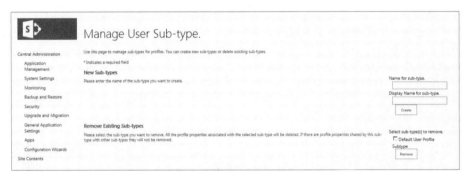

FIGURE 14-10

➤ **Policy Settings** — Use this section to configure whether fields are required optional or disabled, and who should be able to see them. The privacy setting determines who can view the property. For example, a property such as Home Phone will most likely be set up with a default privacy setting of Only Me or My Manager. If the organization's policy is to allow end users to modify the privacy setting, check the box next to "User can override." When the default privacy setting is set to Everyone, the property may also be set as Replicable, which means the property will be propagated to each site's user information list. You will learn how to configure policies for the entire profile service application in the section, "Managing Policies." Once configured, these policies are then applicable to user profile properties.

➤ **Edit Settings** — Use this section to specify whether users should be allowed to edit the value of this property. For properties that are automatically populated from the directory service, it is a best practice to choose "Do not allow users to edit values for this property," because the value will be overwritten during the next synchronization.

➤ **Display Settings** — If a property is set as visible to everyone in the policy settings, there will be an option to Show in the profile properties section of the user's profile page. This means that when a user's My Site profile is being viewed, this property will be displayed. When Show on the Edit Details page is enabled, it is available as an editable property when a user clicks Edit my profile, which is a link located under the user photo on the My Site. If the Edit Settings section is set to not allow users to edit the property value, then selecting to Show on the Edit Details page will not have any effect.

➤ **Search Settings** — The Alias setting is used only for the unique fields associated with each user, such as Account name, Name, User name, and Work e-mail. Configuring a property as indexed allows the data to be searched when people search is utilized.

➤ **Mapped Data** — Each property in the list can be mapped to a specific attribute in another line-of-business directory service, such as Active Directory. To create a mapping, a Source Data Connection must be chosen. Then, from within that source, pick an attribute, which is a field in the user database. Finally, choose whether to either import this attribute into SharePoint or export it from SharePoint.

This completes the review of the different configuration options associated with profile properties. Property mapping is an important step in the sync configuration process, and typically the last step prior to the profile sync. The profile sync can be initiated manually as described previously, but the administrator should create a sync schedule to ensure that profile sync is occurring automatically. A sync schedule is created by editing the timer job responsible for profile sync. This timer job is configured on the Edit Timer Job page, which is accessed using the Configure Synchronization Time Job hyperlink on the Manage Profile Service web page.

ACTIVE DIRECTORY ATTRIBUTE NAMES

When mapping attributes from Active Directory to the profile properties in SharePoint, sometimes it is a little difficult to discern the correct attribute, simply because the names don't necessarily match up. For example, if you were creating a new profile property called `zip` to map to the ZIP Code attribute in Active Directory, it might take you a minute to figure out that `zip` is actually called `postalCode` in the list of SharePoint properties, and there isn't a need to create a new property called `zip`.

You can use ADSI Edit to take a look at the real attribute names:

1. From a server with the Active Directory domain services role installed, click Administrative Tools in the Start menu and choose ADSI Edit.

2. Click Action ⇨ Connect to, and type your domain.

3. Navigate through the Active Directory structure to where the user objects reside. Right-click a user's name and choose Properties. Scroll through the Attribute Editor tab to see the names of the attributes and the data in them.

Managing User Profiles

Once user profiles have been synchronized, they are available in the Manage User Profiles web page. Scroll through the list of users, or use the Find Profiles box to search for specific users by name. To modify a profile, click an account name and choose Edit. You can also use the New Profile button to create a new user profile, but this is typically not necessary if you are using profile sync.

> **NOTE** *When editing an individual user profile, note that the icons next to profile properties provide a quick indication as to which ones are required, and which properties were imported through a data connection.*

Managing Policies

These policies apply to the User Profile Service Application, and they are used to determine how personal information is shared, along with who can view this information about users. Use these policies to configure privacy settings and access for My Site personalization features and user profile properties. Administrators can configure policies for each specific feature or user profile property, which enables them to be aligned with the organization's existing privacy and sharing policies. SharePoint 2013 has added a significant number of new policies in order to facilitate management of the new social capabilities that have been introduced. These new policies include the following:

- ➤ Following a document or site on My Site
- ➤ Tagging an item on My Site
- ➤ Liking or rating something
- ➤ Participation in communities
- ➤ Following a person on My Site

Administrators should review the Manage Policies page for a complete list of all the available policies. Use the following steps to change the settings of a profile service policy:

1. In the People section of the User Profile Service Application home page, click Manage Policies.

2. Click the drop-down box on a policy, and select Edit Policy.

3. The policy setting can be enabled or disabled. The default privacy setting determines who is allowed to see the information in this property. There is also an option that allows users to override the default policy setting.

4. Specify whether the end user is allowed to override the privacy setting, and click OK.

Managing User Subtypes

Earlier in the chapter, in the "Managing User Properties" section, you looked at the use of subtypes. From the Manage Profile Page, you can easily access the Sub-types page by clicking the Manage

User Sub-types link. You can create new user subtypes or remove existing ones from this page. Use subtypes for classification of user properties, which means that if desired, user properties can be associated with only specific subtypes. For example, suppose a large company has many vendor user accounts with whom it does business. A user subtype called Vendors could be created, along with a new property called Vendor Company. This property could be associated with only those users who are categorized in the Vendors subtype.

Organization Profiles

The concept of organization profiles in the User Profile Service Application is similar to the user profiles, with the difference that organization properties are related to entire organizations. Organization subtypes can be used to more granularly categorize multiple organizations, such as a company's major divisions or subsidiaries. This capability is still supported in SharePoint 2013, but only for backward compatibility; companies are encouraged to focus on user profiles.

> **NOTE** *The Organization Profiles feature is deprecated in SharePoint Server 2013, and future versions of SharePoint will not support this capability, as summarized at* `http://office.microsoft.com/en-us/sharepoint-help/discontinued-features-and-modified-functionality-in-microsoft-sharepoint-2013-HA102892827.aspx#_Toc339867828.`

Audiences

SharePoint audiences are used to target content to specific sets of users. Audiences are not a security setting, but a filtering mechanism used to display pertinent information to specific people. Audiences can only be used to their full advantage when the user data is accurate in the user profiles. Whether this information comes from Active Directory or another line-of-business directory service such as PeopleSoft, accurate and up-to-date profile data is imperative. The following is a list of places in SharePoint 2013 where audiences are applicable:

➤ Personalization site links

➤ Publish links to Office client applications

➤ Web Parts

➤ Web Part pages

➤ Navigation links

Configuring Audiences

Use the following steps to configure audiences in the User Profile Service Application:

1. In the People section, click Manage Audiences.

2. Click the New Audience button. The Create Audience web page shown in Figure 14-11 will appear.

FIGURE 14-11

3. Give the audience a Name and Description.

4. Define the audience owner.

5. Multiple rules can be defined, so specify whether all or any of the rules need to be satisfied in order for a user to be included in the audience. Click OK.

6. Using the Add Audience Rules dialog shown in Figure 14-12, set up a rule based on a user or a profile property that defines the audience. By selecting a user, a rule can be created based on membership in a Windows security group, membership in a distribution list, or location in an organization hierarchy. A property is a public, user profile property. The administrator should review the Operator and Value sections when a user is selected as the Operand, and review the options when the Operand is a property.

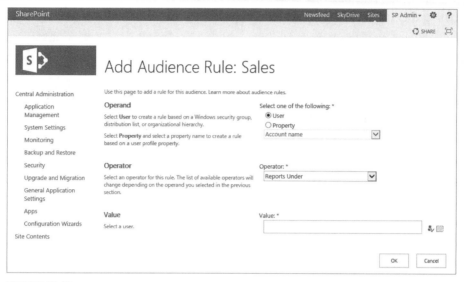

FIGURE 14-12

7. Create a rule based on either the User or Property Operand, and click OK.

Audience Targeting Rules and Logic

This section illustrates how rules are created, and the logic behind the rule, using a couple of examples.

For the first example, suppose you want to ensure that new employees receive relevant content such as on-boarding information. You could create an audience called New Hires, using the following rule:

Property of Hire Date >= 1/1/2010

This rule could be changed once per year to include everyone hired in the past year. The second example uses an audience called Marketing, with three possible ways to define this group of people:

1. Define an audience according to a group of people who report to the same manager. This option is useful as long as the Manager property is accurate in the user profiles. The downside to this option is handling employee attrition and organizational changes. Because this rule is based on an individual person, when that person leaves the company or changes assignments, this audience must be redefined to include the new marketing manager's name. The rules for this example would be as follows:

➤ **Operand** = User

➤ **Operator** = Reports under

➤ **Value** = Select the name of the manager of the marketing department

2. Define an audience based on group membership. Any security-based distribution list in Active Directory can be selected as the basis for an audience. In this example, we have already created a group called Marketing, which contains all the members of the marketing department. The rules for this example would be as follows:

   ➤ **Operand** = User

   ➤ **Operator** = Member of

   ➤ **Value** = Marketing

3. Define an audience based on information in the user profile. In this example, the `Department` property contains the word "Marketing." The rules for this example would be as follows:

   ➤ **Operand** = Property

   ➤ **Operator** = Contains

   ➤ **Value** = Marketing

Given the different rules that might define the marketing department in the company, consider how you can maximize the effectiveness of the rule or rules. For example, you could include users who satisfy all the rules: each person must report to the specific marketing manager, *and* have membership in the Marketing group in Active Directory, *and* have the word "marketing" as part of their department name. Alternately, you could choose to include users who satisfy any of these rules. If any one of the rules is satisfied, that user will be a member of the audience. The second approach is obviously more inclusive, allowing a larger number of users to be included in the audience.

Audience Compilation

Once created, the audience needs to be compiled; compiling the audience populates the audience with users that satisfy the audience rules. This compilation process can automatically occur on a schedule. The audience compilation process scans the user property values, compares the values to the rules for membership, and adds users accordingly. For example, if a user currently in the marketing department was not in the marketing department during the last compilation, then the new compilation will recognize the change to the user's profile and add the individual as a member of the audience.

Follow these steps to set up an audience compilation schedule in the User Profile Service Application:

1. In the People section, click Schedule Audience Compilation.

2. Check the box to Enable Scheduling.

3. Configure settings for daily, weekly, or monthly compilation, and click OK.

At any time, you can start a manual compilation of all audiences by clicking Compile Audiences in the People section. Any individual audience can be manually compiled from that audience's properties screen by clicking Compile Audience.

Targeting Content to Audiences

This section describes several targeting options, along with instructions for implementation:

➤ **Personalization Site Links and Publish Links to Office Client Applications** — In the My Site Settings section of the User Profile Service Application, the Personalization Site Links and the Publish Links to Office Client application options both allow content to be audience targeted. Read more about these features in the "Managing and Configuring My Sites" section of this chapter.

➤ **Web Parts** — Any Web Part can be targeted to an audience. In the Web Part's properties tool pane, the Advanced section contains a Target Audiences field at the bottom. You can choose from audiences, distribution lists, and SharePoint groups for content targeting. This means that if an audience for a Web Part simply needs to be an Active Directory or SharePoint group, then it is not necessary to define this audience in the User Profile Service Application.

➤ **Web Part Pages** — SharePoint publishing sites contain a library called Pages. By editing the properties of any individual page in the library, you will see a field called Target Audiences. Pages that have been targeted to an audience are displayed only to that audience. You can choose from audiences, distribution lists, or SharePoint groups. This means that if an audience for a Web Part page simply needs to be an Active Directory or SharePoint group, then it is not necessary to define this audience in the User Profile Service Application.

➤ **Navigation Links** — Within the navigational structure of the site, individual links may be audience targeted. In the Look and Feel section of the Site Settings page, click the Navigation hyperlink. You can choose a link in the navigation, and then click the Edit button. (Some items are not editable because they are part of the built-in site structure.) The Navigation Heading dialog is displayed in Figure 14-13. Type an audience name and click OK. You can choose from audiences, distribution lists, or SharePoint groups for targeting. Audiences based on an Active Directory or SharePoint group do not need to be defined in the User Profile Service Application.

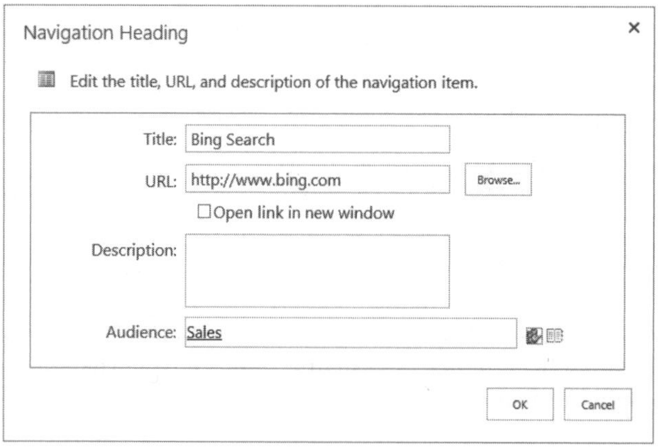

FIGURE 14-13

➤ **Trusted My Site Hosted Locations** — In larger SharePoint deployments with geographically distributed User Profile Service Applications, administrators manage a list of Trusted My Site host locations, which can be targeted to audiences. This setting is found in the My Sites section of the application.

> **NOTE** *Audiences are not a method for controlling security. Navigation links are automatically security trimmed, which means that users without permission to access a list, library, or website will not see the corresponding link. In terms of navigation, audience-targeting is most useful with links that have been manually added, such as links to external websites, or links to other site collections.*

MANAGING AND CONFIGURING MY SITES

SharePoint 2013 reorganizes how users access their newsfeeds and other social networking capabilities. SharePoint 2010 provided users with a personal site called My Site, which combined social networking, document sharing tools, and other tools. SharePoint 2013 divides the My Site into two sites, a personal site that includes SkyDrive Pro for document sharing, and a newsfeed site for social networking, task management, and other functions. This new organization simplifies the user interface to social networking functions and provides more room for the expanded newsfeed. The following sections discuss the features and functionality that are configured using the My Site Settings on the Manage Profile Service page in Central Administration.

Configuring My Sites

A user's My Site is a site collection, and each user is the site collection owner of his or her My Site. The My Sites architecture includes a web application that hosts My Sites, a My Site host site collection, the user's personal site collections, and several required service applications.

In Chapter 3, you already created the My Site host when you provisioned the User Profile Service Application. As a reminder, the following prerequisites need to be in place before you configure your My Sites:

➤ Distributed Cache

➤ Managed Metadata Service Application

➤ Search Service Application

➤ User Profile Service Application

➤ A web application host

Once these prerequisites are in place, My Sites are configured using the following six steps. For a detailed step-by-step configuration, administrators should refer to these references: `http://technet` `.microsoft.com/en-us/library/cc262500%28v=office.15%29` and `http://technet.microsoft` `.com/en-us/library/ee624362`.

1. Create a new web application.

2. Create a My Site host site collection.

3. Add a wildcard inclusion managed path to the web application.

4. Enable self-service site creation for the web application.

5. Set up My Sites.

6. Enable the User Profile Service Application - Activity Feed Job.

The following sections highlight key information that applies to configuring My Sites.

Dedicated Web Application

You have the option to configure My Sites in any existing web application, but we recommend that you create a web application that is dedicated to hosting My Sites. This approach provides optimal performance, helps to ensure proper security, and simplifies management. You also need to ensure that Self-service Site Creation has been enabled, so that each user's My Site site collection is automatically provisioned the first time they view their My Site. The data for the host site collection and individual site collections is maintained in one or more content databases that are associated with the host web application.

My Site Host Site Collection

The host site collection contains the newsfeed and profile pages of all users. This site collection is provisioned using the My Site Host site template, which is available from the Enterprise tab of the Create Site Collection page. A host can only be provisioned once, for each User Profile service application. Once the host has been provisioned, you need to define a managed path to the web application. A wildcard inclusion managed path is the path used to specify the namespace for each of the user's site collections. A user's site collection is created the first time the user navigates to the My Site URL. Because each user will have his or her own site collection, you need to consider the following regarding the My Site host:

➤ **Storage requirements** — Each My Site host is a site collection in which each My Site owner can create multiple libraries and lists, and subsequently upload many files to these libraries. My Site storage can grow very rapidly. Host contents include user photos, About Me information, and newsfeed attachments. You should consider setting up a relatively small site quota as a default, such as 100MB. Keep in mind that as more storage is needed, the quota can be changed. If the quota is exceeded, users won't be able to add a profile picture, post pictures in newsfeeds, or provision a personal site.

➤ **URL planning** — What URL will be used for My Sites? It is a best practice to create a new web application for this purpose. Some commonly used URLs for the My Site web application are "my" or "mysite." For example, if your company were called Contoso, and the main SharePoint site were `http://intranet.contoso.com`, then the My Sites web application would be `http://my.contoso.com`.

➤ **User Permissions** — You are able to configure whether or not certain users or groups can create personal sites, follow other people, and edit their profile, and whether they can use the tags and notes. Figure 14-14 illustrates how the settings are configured when the User Profile Service Application is first provisioned. We recommend that you allow users to create personal sites if you want to utilize the new social features.

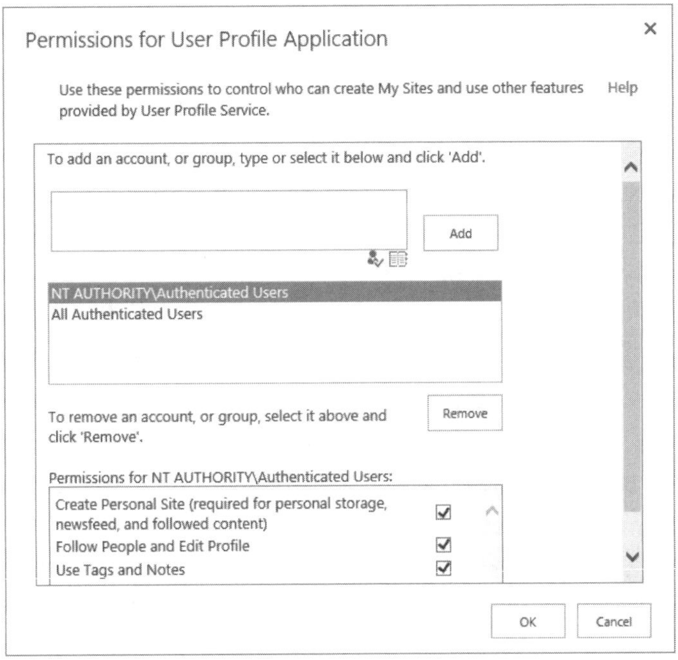

FIGURE 14-14

> **NOTE** *Because SharePoint 2013 now stores user social activity in lists in their personal site, users must be able to create their own personal site if they want to use any of the social features. By default, this permission is enabled for all authenticated users. If users are not given permission to create personal sites, they will be able to have what is referred to as a "profile-only" experience. This means they are allowed to view and edit their profile, visit other user's profiles, be @mentioned by others, follow people, and, using their People page, see and reply to other microblog posts. Unfortunately, they will not have a newsfeed, so they will not be able to create any microblog posts. Nor can they follow content or tags, or aggregate tasks, and they will not have a SkyDrive Pro site.*

Setting Up My Sites

Once the host site collection has been created, and the wildcard inclusion managed path has been configured, you will likely need to update the My Sites settings in the User Profile Service Application. This is accomplished using the Setup My Sites link. These settings may have already been configured during initial installation and configuration, but you should review and modify them appropriately. Table 14-3 summarizes the My Site Settings page fields that you need to configure.

TABLE 14-3: My Site Settings

FIELD	DESCRIPTION
Preferred Search Center	This is the URL to the Search Center you want the sites in the My Site host to use when they perform a search. You can also change the default scopes for both people and document search.
My Site Host Location	This is the URL to the My Site web application, with "/my" at the end. This will be the beginning of the URL for each user's public profile — for example, `http://my.contoso.com/my`. The profile page of a user with the login name of "mollyc" on the contoso domain will have a URL of `http://my.contoso.com/my/Person.aspx?accountname=CONTOSO%5Cmollyc`.
My Site Host URL in Active Directory	This is the URL of the My Site host site collection that is returned to applications that use Exchange Auto Discovery to find a user My Site URL. This is an optional setting.
Personal Site Location	This is the beginning of the URL for each user's content area, which is different from the user's profile page URL. This is the personal site collection for each user, where they can store their data in lists and libraries. An example URL is `http://my.contoso.com/personal`.
Site Naming Format	This is the suffix of the personal site location URL. For single-domain environments, the first option, called "User Name," is a good choice. Because there are no duplicate usernames in a single domain, there will be no conflicts. In multiple-domain environments, pick one of the other two options. In a single-domain environment, a user with the login name of "mollyc" will have a personal site collection URL of `http://my.contoso.com/personal/mollyc`.
Read Permission Level	By default, all authenticated users are given Read permissions to new personal sites as they are created, which is a best practice for My Sites.
Security Trimming Options	This setting determines how system-generated posts (such as document upload activities) are checked for permissions before being displayed in the activity feed. It is recommended that you use the default setting of "Check all links for permission."

Newsfeed	This setting controls whether system-generated activities appear on the My Site newsfeeds.
Email Notifications	Enter the e-mail address that will be used as the sender when system-generated e-mail messages are sent to users.
My Site Cleanup	This setting provides access to a user's My Site if the user leaves the company or for any other reason the user's profile is deleted.
Privacy Settings	By default, user My Sites are private. Enable this setting if you want them to be public. Many organizations enable this setting because it helps facilitate social adoption. You should consider what option is the best choice for your company. If you don't enable this setting, no system activities will be posted to the newsfeed.

Enabling the Activity Feed Job

The User Profile Service Application - Activity Feed Job creates and sends system-generated updates to the user's newsfeed based on different user activities. When a user performs a specific action, an event is generated that subsequently produces an update in the newsfeed. A few examples of events that generate newsfeed updates include the following:

➤ Following a tag

➤ Tagging an item

➤ Changing a job title

➤ Updating Ask Me About

➤ Posting on a note board

This timer job is enabled from the Monitoring section in Central Administration. You need to browse to the Edit Timer Job page for the User Profile Service Application - Activity Feed Job, and configure the job to run on the schedule most appropriate for your environment. The default is every 10 minutes.

This completes the configuration of My Sites, except for the scenario that utilizes multiple User Profile Service Applications, which is discussed in the section, "Trusted My Site Host Locations." Assuming users have permission to create a personal site, and self-service site creation is enabled, Figure 14-15 shows the newsfeed site landing page when users navigate to their My Site at `http://my.contoso.com/default.aspx`.

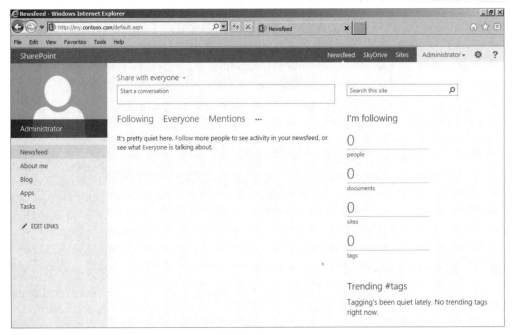

FIGURE 14-15

You can see several navigation links on the left-hand side of the page, the newsfeed in the center of the page, and a summary of the objects being followed on the right-hand side. The following steps provide a brief walk-through of the features, highlighting a few key points:

1. Click the About Me link on the left-hand side. This is the page that other users see when they navigate to someone's My Site. Investigate the other links, and note that you can add your own links to the navigation.

2. The newsfeed should be empty because you are not following any objects yet, and you are not a part of any communities. You can view posts from only those objects you are Following, or posts from Everyone, or posts that specifically mention your name. Create a microblog post, and review the menu options for the post, shown in Figure 14-16. Click the Follow Up option in the menu. You should receive a notification in the upper-right corner that a task has been created. My Tasks aggregates all the user's tasks from Outlook 2013 and SharePoint 2013, and you can see the task you just created by clicking the Tasks link on the left-hand navigation. Note that #tags are contained in a new term set, so you may want to pre-populate that term set with important #tags. In order for @mentions to be included in the microblog post, the person being mentioned must be included in the profile database.

FIGURE 14-16

3. To view the Web Parts on the page, enable editing by clicking Edit Page from the drop-down menu. Explore the various Web Parts and zones on the page.

4. These Web Parts are new, so browse their properties by clicking Edit Web Part. When you are done, click the Newsfeed link and return to the newsfeed page.

5. Click each object link underneath I'm Following, and notice the changes in the URL, as well as the pages that are revealed.

6. The My Site also includes two other sites, SkyDrive Pro, and the Sites website, which are shown in Figures 14-17 and 14-18, respectively. You should browse to these sites and note the changes in the URL. These sites are collectively referred to as the user's personal site, and they are discussed later in the chapter.

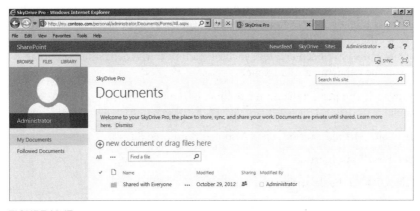

FIGURE 14-17

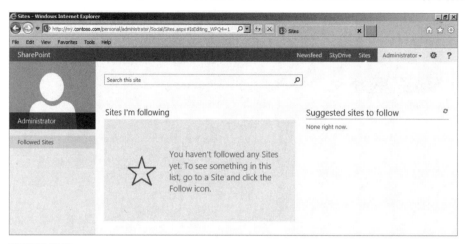

FIGURE 14-18

Trusted My Site Host Locations

SharePoint deployments with geographically distributed farms can have multiple User Profile Service Applications, and subsequently multiple My Site host locations. Recall from earlier that only a single My Site host can be configured per User Profile Service Application. Also, you need to prevent a user from creating more than one My Site when multiple User Profile Service Applications exist, which they can do by default. Trusted My Site host locations provide this capability, and their configuration is optional. Administrators manage a list of trusted My Site host locations, and then target each location to the appropriate users.

Promoted Sites

Promoted sites are links that will appear on the Sites page in a user's My Site. Each link that is added can be targeted to a specific audience or to the default audience of All Site Users. This enables end users to quickly navigate from their My Site to other locations that are relevant to them.

The following example demonstrates how promoted sites can be used to target departmental home pages to users in each company department. The company, called Contoso, has five major departments, each with its own SharePoint departmental home page that is used for team collaboration. Five different audiences have been created, one for each department; and five personalization site links have been created, each one a link to the departmental home page, and targeted to users in the departmental audience.

Follow these steps to set up personalization site links in the User Profile Service Application, per the preceding example:

1. In the My Site Settings section, click Manage Promoted Sites.

2. Click the New Link button.

3. Fill in the URL to the departmental team site.

4. The Description will be the text that is displayed.

5. Add a URL to a image you want displayed, which will be hyperlinked to the promoted site.

6. The owner is a required field, and represents the person responsible for maintaining this link.

7. The Target Audience in this example is called Marketing, which is comprised of all users in an Active Directory group called Marketing.

8. Click OK to save the new link. The image and link are added to the Sites website, shown in Figure 14-18. Follow the preceding steps for each company department.

Publishing Links to Office Client Applications

The configuration to publish links to Microsoft Office client applications is conceptually similar to the personalization site links. The Publish Links to Office Client Applications setting enables SharePoint links to be pushed out, so that they are available to end users within the Office applications, such as Word and Excel. When users have such quick and easy access to open and save files to common SharePoint locations, their daily work processes can be even more efficient.

In the My Sites section, click Publish Links to Office Client Applications. The steps to create a new link are identical to the personalization site link steps in the previous section, except for an additional drop-down box to select what type of item is being published, such as a document library or a team site.

Where does the end user see the published links? In any Office 2013 application, click the File tab at the top left, choose the Share tab, and click Save to SharePoint. This section lists the published links on the right side, which the file can then be saved to as long as the user has Contribute rights to the library selected.

Managing Social Tags and Notes

Within the My Site Settings section of the User Profile Service Application is a setting called Manage Social Tags and Notes. This feature is provided primarily for SharePoint 2010 sites that have been upgraded, as this functionality has been deprecated. As shown in Figure 14-19, SharePoint 2013 includes a management console for administrators that enables them to search existing tags and notes, as well as delete specific ones as needed.

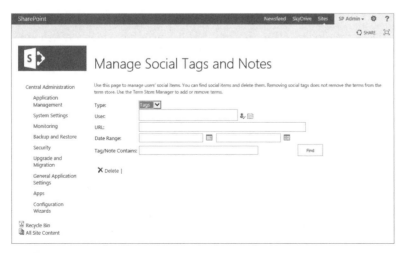

FIGURE 14-19

To perform a search for either tags or notes, the username or URL must be specified. You can narrow down the search results by specifying a date range or a keyword or both. Click the Find button to see the results of the query. When the list of results is displayed, the only action that can be taken is to delete the item. Only the user who created a note is allowed to edit it.

Manage Following

This page enables you to change the thresholds for the content and people that a user can follow. Figure 14-20 shows the three options that you can configure.

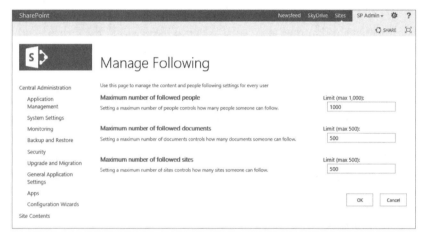

FIGURE 14-20

It's a good idea to leave these values at their default setting unless you have a good reason to change them. Decreasing the limits to a very low number may prevent users from using the social features effectively.

SkyDrive Pro

A user's personal site includes the SkyDrive Pro site and the Sites website, which were shown previously in Figure 14-17 and Figure 14-18, respectively. SDP is different from the SkyDrive functionality available from `http://skydrive.live.com`, the consumer file storage and sharing repository:

1. Users can utilize both SkyDrive and SDP, but they should check their organization's corporate policy for the SkyDrive utilization because that information is stored in the cloud.

2. SDP is a private file repository for the user's documents. You could consider SDP to reflect the evolution and consolidation of the old "Personal Documents" and "Shared Documents" libraries in SharePoint 2010. A single folder appears in the library upon provisioning, which is called Shared With Everyone (the people icon indicates that it is shared). All documents placed in this folder will be available to any authenticated users.

3. SDP has 100MB storage quota by default, but this is configurable by the administrator.

4. Documents can be uploaded to the SDP library, and the library supports drag-and-drop from the desktop. The following browsers support drag-and-drop. In order for IE8 and IE9 to work, Office 2013 has to be installed on the desktop. This list may be modified and updated over time:

> ➤ Internet Explorer 10

> ➤ Internet Explorer 9 with Office 2013 installed

> ➤ Internet Explorer 8 with Office 2013 installed

> ➤ Firefox latest version

> ➤ Chrome latest version

5. Document viewing has been dramatically simplified. Figure 14-21 shows the preview window of a private Word document. To preview any document in the SDP library, just click the ellipsis (...) next to the name and it will open the preview window. If you have the Office Web App server installed and configured you will see a preview of the Word document. This preview capability is available with any SharePoint document library, not just the SDP library. Note that you can edit the document, share the document with others, and follow the document from the preview window.

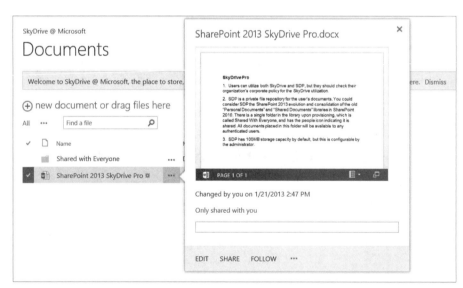

FIGURE 14-21

6. Document sharing, shown in Figure 14-22, has also been simplified. In the sharing dialog window, type the name of a colleague in your organization and specify whether you want the person to view or edit the document; when you are finished, the person will receive an e-mail message by default, indicating that you have shared a document with them.

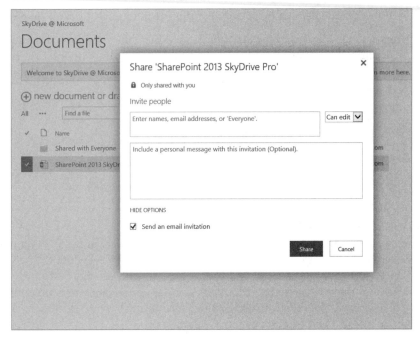

FIGURE 14-22

7. Documents can be taken offline and synchronized with the copy inside the SDP library. This is accomplished by clicking the SYNC button in the upper-right corner, and the dialog shown in Figure 14-23 will be displayed. Note that you can change the location where documents will be stored on the desktop. After clicking the Sync Now button, you should receive an acknowledgment that the documents are syncing, as shown in Figure 14-24. Figure 14-25 shows the new SDP folder added to your favorites in Windows Explorer.

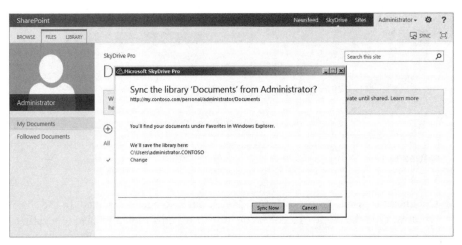

FIGURE 14-23

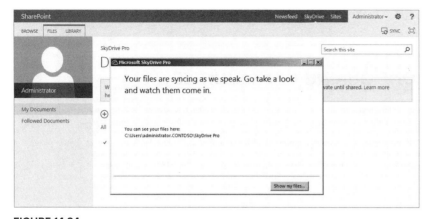

FIGURE 14-24

FIGURE 14-25

> **NOTE** *At the time of writing, the SkyDrive Pro desktop client requires that Office 2013 Standard or Professional Plus be installed on the computer prior to synchronizing SDP library content.*

8. The maximum number of documents you can synchronize is 20,000 and 5,000 for SDP and team site libraries, respectively.

9. One more thing to note. Click the Site Contents link to display the page shown in Figure 14-26. Note that two different lists support the social features, the Social list and the MicroFeed list.

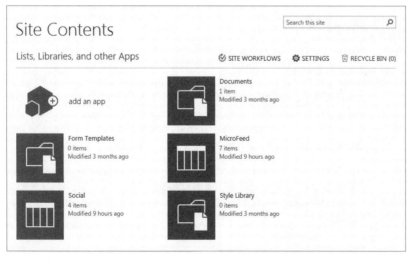

FIGURE 14-26

That completes our brief tour of SDP, which is an important addition to the SharePoint 2013 toolset.

MANAGING AND CONFIGURING COMMUNITIES

Communities provide an environment that encourages open communication between people who want to share their expertise and get help from others who share their common interests. Many different types of communities can be created, such as the following examples:

➤ **Communities of practice** — A group of people who share a hobby, craft, or profession

➤ **Communities of purpose** — A group of people with a common goal, need, or mission

➤ **Communities of interest** — A group of people who share a common interest or passion for a topic

➤ **Communities of social interaction** — A group of people who enjoy interacting with each other for any number of reasons, such as creating relationships, networking, and so on

The following sections describe the two community templates available with SharePoint 2013, and discuss some key aspects and configuration options for community websites.

Community Templates

SharePoint 2013 includes two different templates: the Community Portal template and the Community Site template. Each template is briefly described in Table 14-4.

TABLE 14-4: SharePoint 2013 Community Templates

TYPE	DESCRIPTION
Community Portal	This is an enterprise website template. The purpose of this site is to provide information about any community sites that exist in the farm. This is accomplished using two different Web Parts: a Search Web Part to search for communities, and a Popular Communities Web Part to display communities. Popularity is determined by the number of posts, replies, and members. You can have only one community portal per farm. An example of a Community Portal is shown in Figure 14-27.
Community Site	This is a collaboration website template. The features and capabilities are very similar to that of a team site, as the Community Site template is based on the Team Site template, but the Community Site template includes many additional features.

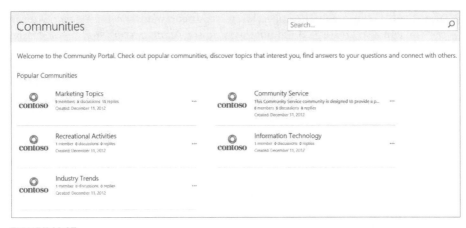

FIGURE 14-27

Creating and Using Community Sites

One of the first things to consider before creating a new community is how public you want your community. With a goal of corporate participation, you want your communities to be "Open with explicit action required to join." This enables everyone to view the conversations, and they can decide if they wish to be a community member. However, some communities require greater privacy, so that is also an option. You could also choose to make your community "Open but with no explicit requirement to join." Unfortunately, this option precludes users from having their communities automatically added to their followed sites list. The following summarizes the four options available:

➤ **Private** — Available only to invited users. Each person has Member permissions. The owner adds new members.

➤ **Closed** — Everyone can view conversations, but only approved members can contribute. The owner gets an action request when someone wants to join, or auto-approval can be enabled. You need to enable access requests in Central Administration under System Settings, and configure the option "Configure outgoing e-mail settings," so that requests can be sent.

➤ **Open with explicit action required to join** — When nonmembers browse to the site, the "Join this community" button is displayed on the page. You need to configure the "Enable auto-approval" option on the Community Settings page. This page can be accessed from the Site Settings page or from inside the community using the Community Settings option in the Community Tools Web Part.

➤ **Open with no explicit requirement to join** — Anyone can participate without joining. Without joining, however, there is no automatic following of sites.

So it's time to create your first community. You create a community site by choosing the Community Site template on the Collaboration tab when you are creating a new website. Do so by executing the following steps:

1. You should create a new site collection for your community using Central Administration, but you can also create a community as a subsite of an existing site. If you create a community as a subsite, ensure that you select the "Use unique permissions" option. This is very important, and it will help avoid any confusion associated with the fact that there is a difference between community members and the SharePoint security group Members. When you create a community site with unique permissions, SharePoint automatically provisions default security groups: Owners, Members, Visitors, and Moderators. These groups have Full Control, Contribute, Read, and Moderator permissions, respectively. When you create a SharePoint Team site, the Members group has Edit permission by default. Users with Edit permission can edit pages, which allows them to delete Web Parts, for example. You do *not* want any community members to have Edit permission. A community member is someone who has explicitly joined the community. After they join, they are listed as a member on the home page, and the site is automatically added to their list of followed sites. To invite others to your community, you can use the Share button in the upper-right corner of the site. An example of a community is shown in Figure 14-28.

> **NOTE** *You need to activate the SharePoint Server Standard Site Collection feature if the Community Site template is not shown on the Collaboration tab. This can occur when you are creating a community as a subsite.*

FIGURE 14-28

2. Now that your community site has been created, briefly review some of the features. There are four basic pages to the community site: Home, Categories, Members, and About. Links to these pages are shown on the left-hand side of the home page. Home is the landing page for the community, as shown in Figure 14-28. Click on the Categories link, and it will take you to the Categories page.

An example Categories page is shown in Figure 14-29. The Categories page provides a more organized view of all the community conversations. As you can see from Figure 14-29, the Categories page displays an alphabetical listing of the different categories as well as a What's Hot link to show the most popular conversations. When you first create your community, you will only have one category called General. Right after the community is created, and before it is opened to the organization, the owner should create a set of categories that users can assign to their conversations when they are created. New categories are created using the Create Categories link in the Community Tools section in the upper-right corner of the Categories page.

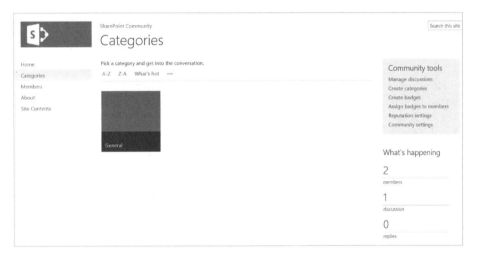

FIGURE 14-29

3. The administrator should review the Members page and the About page by clicking the links on the left-hand side of the Home page. The purpose of these pages is self-evident and won't be reviewed here.

4. Click the Edit link in the upper-right corner, and then review the number and type of Web Parts on the page. You should become familiar with the different Web Parts by reviewing their individual properties. The Community Tools Web Part is displayed only to owners of the community. The Join Web Part is displayed only to visitors, who can click the Join button if they wish to join the community.

5. Next, browse to the Site Contents page, and review the different community lists: Community Members, Discussions, and Categories. Because community membership is maintained in a list within the site, membership is specific to only the community site. These lists contain information specific to the members and conversations in the community.

6. You should also assign one or more individuals as community moderators. The moderator's job is to monitor, facilitate, and manage the community. Moderators have permission to manage categories and manage conversations, including editing and deleting content.

Moderators are assigned by adding users to the Site Moderators group. The Site Moderators group is automatically created when the community is provisioned. To add users to this group, click the Site Permissions link on the Site Settings page, and then click the Site Moderators link, which takes you to the Site Moderators security page where you will add new members. This is the same process you have used to add users to any SharePoint group.

If you plan to use a community portal, be sure to execute an incremental search crawl after community sites are created. You should factor this in as you configure the crawl schedule.

Administrators should familiarize themselves with all the other links and features on the community site. Communities will be used as the organization adopts the social capability in SharePoint 2013.

SUMMARY

In this chapter, you learned that social computing has truly become a first-class citizen in SharePoint 2013. Microsoft added and improved many features that enable users to communicate with each other in ways that weren't possible in previous versions. They've also made life easier for administrators with the addition of Active Directory Direct Import, which is both fast and easy to configure. Understanding these new features is critical for both the architecture and maintenance of your SharePoint 2013 farm.

15

The Office Web Applications for SharePoint

WHAT'S IN THIS CHAPTER

➤ Introduction to Office Web Apps

➤ New and improved features

➤ Compatibility with Lync and Exchange

➤ Desktop and mobile features

➤ Installing and configuring Office Web Apps

➤ Working with Office Web Apps

Office Web Apps (OWA) is a browser-based add-on to the SharePoint 2013 farm, delivering Office desktop functionality at the server level. With Office Web Apps, users can open and edit Microsoft's desktop Office products by using Word Web App, Excel Web App, PowerPoint Web App, and OneNote Web App. The Office Web Apps add-on delivers the same rich Microsoft Office environment that exists in the SkyDrive environment to your private SharePoint farms, with on-premises security and control. The user experience has also been enhanced for desktop computers, mobile phones, tablets, and any device supporting browser functionality.

First released with Office 2010, the Web Apps are so cool this time around that they are no longer only for SharePoint. They actually install on their own server(s); and while the focus of this chapter is how they work with SharePoint, they can be used in conjunction with Exchange 2013 and Lync 2013 to provide the same Office document viewing and collaboration capabilities as SharePoint. Even better, they use a new API called WOPI (Web application Open Platform Interface) that enables developers to utilize Office Web Apps directly through their own code, which opens the door to some great solutions.

As with the previous version of Office Web Apps, features are delivered through SharePoint Foundation 2013 or SharePoint Server 2013 products. This chapter focuses on using Office Web Apps in a SharePoint context. It begins by describing new features offered by Office Web Apps 2013 to SharePoint 2013 but also covers new functionality with Exchange 2013, Lync 2013, and Windows file shares. It then takes a look at the architecture of the new Office Web Apps, including prerequisites, and continues with a guided installation. Finally, the chapter wraps up with a discussion of how you can integrate Office Web Apps functionality with the SharePoint 2013 platform.

FUNCTIONALITY OVERVIEW

Before looking at the topology and installation of the Office Web Apps, this section first takes a look at its improved feature set, underlying technology, and expanded functionality. As mentioned earlier, OWA is now a standalone product that, unlike other SharePoint 2013 features, sits outside of the SharePoint 2013 farm. With other SharePoint features, the normal progressions model has been to integrate deeper into the SharePoint architecture. An example of this is the Project Server progression between SharePoint 2007 and SharePoint 2010. In the SharePoint 2007 farm you were able to leverage Project functionality, but only when specific interface programs were in place to make SharePoint 2007 aware of Project 2007. In SharePoint 2010 the entire Project product was based in SharePoint 2010, and it cannot be separated from that SharePoint 2010 farm because it is installed as a service application in the farm. Now, the Office Web Apps product stands outside of the SharePoint 2013 farm but still provides the same, and some greatly improved, features to it.

NEW FEATURES IN SHAREPOINT OWA 2013

Office Web Apps 2013 offers users a whole new set of features, greatly increasing its value in a SharePoint 2013 farm. Among these are the following:

➤ **Change tracking** — Enables a true collaborative experience, showing tracked changes akin to the desktop Word product in the Word Web App

➤ **Comments** — Enables users to view, add, and even reply to comments in the Word Web App and the PowerPoint Web App

➤ **Co-authoring** — Enables concurrent editing across Word, Excel, PowerPoint, and OneNote documents

➤ **Embedding** — Supports native embedding of Word, PowerPoint, Excel, and OneNote documents

➤ **Ink support** — New Ink support for Word and OneNote documents within SharePoint 2013

➤ **Quick preview** — Enables fast previewing of search results, a feature previously available only in FAST search results

➤ **Share by link** — Enables users to send a link of a document so that the recipient can use Office Web Apps outside of SharePoint

➤ **Shorter URLs** — Unlike OWA in SharePoint 2010, which created massive URLs if you linked to a document, now you get friendly URLs.

This is a rather brief subset of the new features of the Office Web Apps. Further details for each of these improvements are provided later in the chapter.

ADDITIONAL FUNCTIONALITY FOR MULTIPLE SHAREPOINT FARMS, LYNC, EXCHANGE 2013, AND FILE SHARES (VIA OPEN-FORM URL)

New Office Web Apps functionality is not limited to a single instance of SharePoint 2013; it now supports multiple SharePoint 2013 farms, Lync 2013, Exchange 2013, and even the capability to open files from a URL. This represents a drastic shift in how the Office Web Apps functions to provide its service to multiple applications.

Integrating OWA with Exchange 2013

Exchange Server 2013 leverages Office Web Apps 2013 to preview e-mail Office file attachments. Using Word Web App, Excel Web App, and PowerPoint Web App, the Exchange 2013 server can deliver a full-fidelity preview. Moving the Office Web Apps service to the server level makes the clients less dependent on desktop-installed software to provide this functionality. Office Web Apps also lends this functionality to the Exchange 2013 Outlook Web Application.

Using Office Web Apps, you can work with the following file types in Exchange:

➤ Word documents

➤ Excel documents

➤ PowerPoint documents

Integrating OWA with Lync 2013

Office Web Apps 2013 has also been extended to Lync 2013. This enables the standard file types in SharePoint 2013 to have the same functionality in Lync 2013. PowerPoint Broadcast has been removed from SharePoint 2013 and added to Lync 2013. Deployed in Lync 2013, PowerPoint Broadcast addresses some previous limitations regarding the use of dynamic content. Lync 2013 leverages Office Web Apps 2013 to deliver presentations via the PowerPoint Web App. Note that Lync 2013 is now the engine behind the PowerPoint Broadcast server while the Office Web Apps provides the viewer. The PowerPoint Web App uses standardized DHTML and JavaScript to provide PowerPoint Broadcast's improved features, which include the following:

➤ Better mechanism to support native PowerPoint animations, slide transitions, and embedded video

➤ Better support for a wider range of tablet and mobile devices

➤ The capability for users to interactively scroll through slides without affecting the actual presentation

LICENSING AND VERSIONS

Office Web Apps offers some significant changes from the previous version in the licensing arena. There are two licenses in Office Web Apps this time around. The default Office Web Apps mode is view-only, and it is provided free. The other mode enables both viewing and editing, and this mode must be licensed. Users must have the appropriate license, known as WacEdit, before they can edit in the browser. To enable this mode in Office Web Apps, you must set the -EditingEnabled parameter to $true either when creating a new farm with the New-OfficeWebAppsFarm cmdlet or when updating an existing farm with Set-OfficeWebAppsFarm:

➤ New-OfficeWebAppsFarm — This is used when you are creating a new Office Web Apps farm on the server. The following example creates a new Office Web Apps farm as an internal resource with a certificate whose friendly name is server.internal.contoso.com:

```
New-OfficeWebAppsFarm -InternalUrl https://server.internal.contoso.com
-EditingEnabled:$true -CertificateName server.internal.contoso.com
```

➤ Set-OfficeWebAppsFarm — This is used when you are configuring settings on an existing Office Web Apps farm. The following command enables view-and-edit mode for an existing Office Web Apps farm:

```
Set-OfficeWebAppsFarm -EditingEnabled:$true
```

In the "Preparing the Server and Installing OWA via the GUI" section of this chapter is a step-by-step guide to creating a new farm, so don't worry if you are not familiar with that command right now.

You can even divide the licensing into separate groups. As with SharePoint 2013, you can leverage different licensing levels to achieve the appropriate functionality. For example, it wouldn't make much sense to license your entire company for enterprise functionality if you only have a small group of power users who need the SharePoint Server Enterprise advanced feature set. By default, when you enable editing capabilities via the New-OfficeWebAppsFarm or Set-OfficeWebAppsFarm cmdlets, all users in SharePoint are granted editing rights and therefore must be licensed appropriately.

Because Office Web Apps uses SharePoint 2013 licensing capabilities, the associated SharePoint farm must already be configured to leverage individual SKUs. Using the New-SPUserLicenseMapping cmdlet, you can isolate specific Active Directory security groups, forms-based roles, or SharePoint user licenses to a particular Office Web Apps licensing model. After you create the groups to your satisfaction, you can use the Add-SPUserLicensingMapping cmdlet to add them to the Office Web Apps farm. Finally, you enable the group using the Enable-SPUserLicensing cmdlet. To review your licensing groups, you can use the Get-SPUserLicenseMapping cmdlet. In addition to the preceding cmdlets, also available are the following cmdlets, which should be self-explanatory:

➤ Disable-SPUserLicensing

➤ Get-SPUserLicense

➤ Get-SPUserLicensing

➤ Remove-SPUserLicenseMapping

A final note about controlling farm behavior is necessary. On the SharePoint 2013 farm, an administrator can use the PowerShell cmdlets `New-SPWOPIBinding` on a new farm or `Set-SPWOPIBinding` on an existing farm to set the file open behavior on a per-file-type basis for the farm. At the site collection or document library level, site collection administrators and SharePoint 2013 users with appropriate permissions can set the default file behavior for Office Web Apps files. This is covered in greater detail in the Default Open Behavior for Documents section later in this chapter.

DESKTOP ENHANCEMENTS

A primary concern for Microsoft following the release of Office Web Apps 2010 was the varying user experience between different operating systems. For example, users of Office Web Apps on a Mac had only some functions available. For the new version, Microsoft wanted to provide a consistent user experience, regardless of what desktop operating systems were used. With Office Web Apps 2013, Mac users can work from a personal laptop or the corporate workstation and enjoy the same features and capabilities, enabling a smooth, unified experience — one that is associated with the browser's capability to use HTML5, not the machine. In this section you will take a look at some of the new capabilities that will really help to extend user productivity.

User Experience Improvements

To achieve the improved user experience that Microsoft sought for Office Web Apps, the focus was placed on eliminating the dependence on the desktop in order to create a consistent, browser-based UI. For example, when editing a document within the Office suite, users can expect to find screen elements in the same position, and the mostly commonly used features are available from within the browser. Similarly, users of the Word Web App have more control over their documents, including the ability to view documents in a print layout and even perform a simple word count. Another more prominent example of added features to make the Office Web Apps feature set more enticing is the capability to create PowerPoint presentations with animations. By enhancing and unifying these features across applications, Microsoft has brought the full desktop experience closer to the user via any modern browser.

PowerPoint Broadcasting

With the previous Office Web Apps you could, in conjunction with SharePoint, set up a PowerPoint Broadcast site and then publish your PowerPoint presentation to a URL where others could watch in their browser as you presented thanks to Attendee View. That feature has now gone the way of the dodo bird — if the dodo bird now lives on Mars, that is. The broadcasting functionality is no longer part of SharePoint in any way and is instead integrated with Lync Server 2013. As part of the Lync platform they have introduced enhancements, including display capabilities and support, for a greater number of mobile devices. Unfortunately, all of this is dependent on Lync Server 2013. Equating Lync to Mars seems appropriate in a SharePoint book.

Excel Web App vs. Excel Services

SharePoint Excel Services is often confused with the Excel Web App provided by OWA, in terms of both functionality and use. While both applications enable the end user to view and interact with Excel workbooks, there are some critical differences. The chief difference is that the SharePoint-specific Excel Services offers business-level intelligence to use PowerPivot and slicers. Using the Excel Web App provided by the Office Web Apps does not offer these advanced business intelligence tools, but it does enable users to create and edit new workbooks in the browser. Before deciding which functionality to use in your SharePoint 2013 farm, it is important that you identify which parts of Excel functionality are critical to your business needs. Keep in mind it is common to use them both. Each one just scratches a different itch.

If, after comparing functionality, you decide you would prefer to default to Excel Services you can use the `New-SPWOPISupressionSetting` cmdlet. For example, the following command will stop XLSX files from opening using OWA so you can open them with Excel Services instead:

```
New-SPWOPISuppressionSetting -Extension "XLSX" -Action "view"
```

Table 15-1 provides a summary of how common functionality differs between Excel Services and Excel Web App.

TABLE 15-1: Excel Services vs. Excel Web App

FUNCTIONALITY	EXCEL SERVICES	EXCEL WEB APP
Create or edit workbook in browser	No	Yes
Publish workbooks using external data	Yes	Yes, with limitations
Publish a single item via a Web Part	Yes	Yes
Refresh workbook data	Limited functionality dependent on data source	Limited functionality dependent on data source

Change Tracking

New to Office Web Apps 2013 is the capability to open a document that has Track Changes enabled. Not only can you open the document, but you can also edit the document and your changes will be tracked. Unfortunately, you still have to go back to the client if you wish to do things like Accept and Reject changes or look at various markup styles, but this is still a great step forward compared to the previous OWA, which would not open these documents at all.

Comments

The Comments feature, available in both Word and PowerPoint, enables users to work collaboratively, annotating a document without actually changing the text, by adding comments or queries to a separate section of the original document. Using either the Word Web App or the PowerPoint Web app, users can view, add, edit, and reply to comments in either of these file types. Look at Figure 15-1 for an example of both viewing and adding a comment to a Word document from the browser.

FIGURE 15-1

Co-Authoring

Co-authoring in Office Web Apps is a handy feature that enables multiple authors to work in a single document simultaneously. This prevents people from getting locked out of the most current document or working on an outdated file version. In addition, the co-authoring functionality enables a single document to track all intended changes, preventing a loss of the last known changes. Co-authoring has been greatly expanded in Office Web Apps 2013, with its functionality extended beyond the Excel Web App and OneNote Web App into the Word Web App and the PowerPoint Web App.

Embedding

Embedding is a new feature to Office Web Apps. Previously, when you wanted to open or edit a document in SharePoint, you only had that control from a SharePoint document library. Now, with embedding, you can incorporate the Word Web App, the Excel Web App, and the OneNote Web App directly into the page. For example, this functionality enables you to embed a PowerPoint presentation on the page. You can even flip through the presentation without having to open a link. Figure 15-2 shows an example of a classic SharePoint presentation on the home page of a team site.

FIGURE 15-2

EMBEDDING A DOCUMENT

This is apparently one of those super-secret features. If you would like to embed a document on your SharePoint page, it is a two-step process. First, open the document in the browser and then click File. From that menu, choose Share; and then from the fly-out click Embed. Now you can copy the source code you will need. With the source code in hand, edit the SharePoint page in which you want to embed the document. From the Insert tab on the Ribbon, click the Embed link and insert the code. There it is. <sarcasm> Not sure why everyone cannot just figure that out? </sarcasm>

Ink Support

Ink support, a feature that enables users to write and draw in documents using a finger, mouse, or stylus, has long been a part of the Microsoft Office suite. The latest version of Office Web Apps enables Ink elements to be viewed, created, and edited reliably in Microsoft Office Word and OneNote documents via the web browser. Combined with enhanced support for web browsers on phones, tablets, and other devices lacking a native version of Microsoft Office, this creates the opportunity for a wider range of people and devices to participate more easily in document collaboration.

Quick Preview

New to Office Web Apps 2013 is the capability to preview supported documents in a preview window directly from SharePoint 2013 search results. This enables users to quickly determine whether they have found the correct file. Figure 15-3 shows an example of what a user might see while previewing a document.

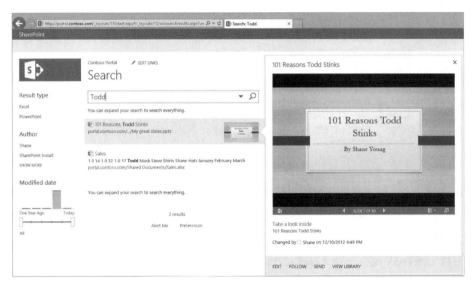

FIGURE 15-3

SEARCH PREVIEWS NOT WORKING?

If you are having problems getting search previews to work after you install and configure OWA, blame search. You have to do a full crawl after your install the OWA to get the search previews to kick in.

Sharing a Document

An example of how Office Web Apps 2013 has expanded beyond just SharePoint 2013 is clearly evident with the new Share feature. Now a SharePoint user can send a link for a document to another user, enabling the recipient to leverage Office Web Apps and preview that document. When sharing documents, you also have the option to specify whether the recipient has permission to edit the document, rather than just view it.

> **NOTE** *When sending documents using the share-by-link feature, ensure that the proper configuration is set for recipients. Documents sent by share by link can be edited via Office Web Apps regardless of licensing status or whether editing is disabled on the Office Web Apps.*

Office Web Apps URLs

Another improvement to Office Web Apps 2013 is how URLs are generated for user consumption. If you have ever seen a URL produced from Office Web Apps 2010, then you know how long it can be, as shown in the following example:

```
http://portal.contoso.com/sites/IT/_layouts/PowerPoint.aspx?PowerPointView=Reading
View&PresentationId=/sites/IT/Docs/wac.pptx&Source=http%3A%2F%2Fportal.contoso
.com%2Fsites%2IT%2Fdocs%2FTraining%2520Module%2Fdocsethomepage%2
Easpx%3FID%3D96%26FolderCTID%3D0x0120D52000DC71A13124DA52
49ACA958C4DFD092C90037E1F59EB3515B4F940A3806D9B183F0%26List%3Dc910e954%2D68ca%2D42a
e%2Dbb0f%2D1c6908c73e77%26RootFolder%3D%252Fsites%252FIT%252
Fwac%252015&DefaultItemOpen=1
```

Fortunately, users no longer need to work with such unwieldy URLs, as the new Office Web Apps 2013 URL format is greatly condensed. This enables users to easily share a URL directly from the browser, as the following revamped URL demonstrates:

```
http://portal.contoso.com/sites/IT/Docs/wac.pptx?Web=1
```

Default Open Behavior for Documents

Office Web Apps 2013 offers farm and site collection administrator control over how a document is opened at the farm or site-collection level. By default, when OWA 2013 is made available to SharePoint 2013, it opens all Word, PowerPoint, Excel, and OneNote files in the browser, as opposed to the desktop client application.

Farm-Level Document Control

To control the document opening behavior at the farm level on a per-file-type basis, a farm administrator can run the following Office Web Apps cmdlets to modify an existing Office Web Apps farm:

```
Get-SPWOPIBinding -Action "edit" -Application "Excel"| Set-SPWOPIBinding
-DefaultAction:$true
```

Site Collections and Document Libraries

At the site-collection level and lower, site collection administrators and users with appropriate permissions can determine file behavior. Users with appropriate permissions can change the setting of a document library via the properties of that particular library. A site collection administrator can change file behavior for the entire site collection by activating the site collection option Open Documents in Client Applications by Default.

MOBILE DEVICE SUPPORT

Just as the nature of how SharePoint information is accessed has evolved, so has its delivery method. The previous model, which offered a rather static view that lacked graphics suited for small, low-resolution displays, has been radically updated for use as an appropriate communications platform. Office Web Apps 2013 has been developed around the premise that today's mobile workforce needs the same robust collaborative experience enjoyed by desktop users.

Office Web Apps allows a mobile user on a Windows Phone, iOS, or Android device to view and interact with documents. This functionality is automatically made available by the default install of OWA. It adds things such as touch support and some smarts such as extra zooms and handling of content that would exceed the screen's real estate. For a deeper look at the features available, take a look at `http://office.microsoft.com/en-us/web-apps-help/use-office-web-apps-on-your-android-iphone-or-windows-phone-HA010389583.aspx`. Also worth noting as an administrator, you can remove this binding from your farm if you do not want to enable mobile support.

PowerPoint Changes

As noted earlier in the chapter, PowerPoint Broadcast has been removed from SharePoint and moved over to Lync 2013. This is good news for mobile device users who can take advantage of its enhanced functionality. Previously, although the Broadcast Service could be used by mobile users, it was designed from a desktop browser perspective. This left mobile users at a distinct disadvantage in terms of both engagement and quality. Because Broadcast Services are integrated with Lync 2013, mobile users can issue status updates that include wait times, broadcast connection information, and follow broadcasts tuned for mobile devices.

Enhanced User Experience

Mobile users of Office Web Apps 2013 can now benefit from Microsoft's focus on creating an expanded, unified user experience. As previously noted, browsing to the Office Web Apps was primarily designed for desktop viewers. Office Web Apps 2013 automatically configures itself to the platform on which it is being used. For example, a typical tablet browser may not want to see a Word document that uses a lot of images, as it takes longer to load and can cause formatting issues depending on the user's specific mobile browser. Therefore, rather than display the entire image, now it is displayed as a thumbnail, which the user can select if desired. This may seem like a minor difference, but it greatly improves the daily life of the tablet user.

Technologies Used

As mentioned elsewhere in this chapter, Microsoft aimed to increase the interoperability of Office Web Apps 2013, ensuring that its users have the same experience regardless of operating system or browser. To achieve this, Office Web Apps 2013 were developed to deliver services using HTML5. At the onset of the Internet, HTML was developed as a means to communicate and format information for users. Of course, it wasn't created to deliver the rich multimedia experience we currently expect from our browsers, so it has evolved over the years in an attempt to meet the demands of rapidly changing technology, and it is still under development. During the so-called *browser war* of the late 1990s, companies began to develop their own technologies, such as ActiveX, Flash, and Silverlight. Unfortunately, this led to a variety of end-user experiences depending on what operating system and browser was being used, not to mention any third-party plug-ins installed.

Web 2.0 technologies, which refer to second-generation web technologies intended for online collaboration, have been designed to deliver a seamless data-rich experience. One of those latest and greatest technologies is HTML5, which Office Web Apps 2013 has embraced to provide a consistent, cross-platform user experience.

Platform and Browser Compatibility

Microsoft has realized now more than ever people are accessing information from any number of devices. Office Web Apps makes this possible so that we don't have to be tied to a desk when opening or editing using an Office Web Apps service. User experience and functionality may slightly vary from platform to platform, but you will see it has been greatly expanded to accommodate all of your various needs. Platform compatibility can be divided into two areas: *Viewing and Editing* or *Viewing Only*.

Viewing and Editing

➤ PC

➤ Mac

➤ Windows Tablet, such as the Surface*

➤ Apple iOS, such as the iPad*

Viewing Only

➤ Windows Phone*

➤ iOS iPhones*

➤ Android phones*

➤ Any other phones with browser capability

   * *Specific devices utilizing touch capabilities with Office Web Apps 2013*

Office Web Apps 2013 now supports a greater variety of web browsers. The current official list of supported browsers is the latest release of the following:

➤ Internet Explorer

➤ Firefox

➤ Chrome

➤ Safari

For example, the Office Web Apps leveraging HTML5 uses the WebKit layout engine, which powers a great number of modern browsers.

TOPOLOGY

As discussed at the beginning of this chapter, Office Web Apps has moved from an exclusive SharePoint service onto its own standalone server. This change is critical to how you configure and architect Office Web Apps to service the SharePoint 2013 farm. The primary benefit of this topology change is that Office Web Apps can offer its services not only to SharePoint 2013, but also to Lync 2013, Exchange 2013, and anything else that can be connected through its WOPI interfaces.

Because it is separate, Office Web Apps are served up from their own farm, much like SharePoint. This enables you to build and scale your OWA infrastructure to meet your needs. Much like a SharePoint farm, your OWA farm can be configured with everything on one server or separated onto multiple servers. If you have multiple servers in a farm, they must leverage a hardware or software load-balancing solution, however, as OWA does not include that capability with the product. Each server within the Office Web Apps farm contains a copy of the farm settings, but only one server can act as the authoritative Master Machine for the Office Web Apps farm. A copy of the farm settings from the Master Machine is made available to other subordinate Office Web Apps servers within the farm on a regular basis.

Office Web Apps Logical Configuration

Now that Office Web Apps 2013 has been moved from the SharePoint farm to its own standalone farm, a separate logical container is required. This logical container concept is based in the Web application Open Platform Interface (WOPI). It enables the Office Web Apps farm to act as a WOPI app, and other server programs such as a SharePoint 2013 farm act as a WOPI host. While this may be contrary to what you typically conceptualize as a host and app relationship, it actually reflects the scheme quite accurately. Consider that the users of SharePoint never directly interact with Office Web Apps servers, which need the SharePoint 2013 farm to act as host, which in turn consumes the WOPI app from the Office Web Apps farm. This logical configuration enables the integration with not only SharePoint 2013, but also Exchange 2013, Lync 2013, Windows files shares, and even custom third-party applications.

Office Web Apps Farm Guidelines

Whether you have one server farm or multiple farms, it is important to keep the following guidelines in mind:

➤ Keep the Office Web Apps farm close to its servicing applications. If separated by any distance, such as separate data centers, you will see a degradation of performance when opening and editing documents.

➤ Servers within the Office Web Apps farm must be within the same geographical area. Typically, one farm will be able to accommodate most configurations, but security might require an isolated configuration with its own Office Web Apps farm.

➤ All servers in an Office Web Apps farm must be able to communicate with each other. This is addressed in greater detail in the section "Firewall Considerations for Office Web Apps."

➤ All servers in an Office Web Apps farm must be in the same Active Directory organization unit (OU).

➤ Servers in an Office Web Apps farm may be virtualized. The following section provides greater detail.

Roles for Office Web Apps Servers

In large and highly customized Office Web Apps farms, consider giving each Office Web Apps server a specific role. By default, every Office Web Apps server has all roles installed and ready for use. However, you can limit, or specialize, a specific Office Web Apps server to a specific role. This should only be done if your farm has a particular performance requirement. For example, maybe your SharePoint 2013 farm has a high demand for Excel Web App services because Excel is used extensively throughout the farm.

In general, it is recommended that you allocate Office Web Apps servers to specific roles only when your farm exceeds 10 Office Web Apps servers and you have noticed performance degradation. As you might expect, an Office Web Apps server can be specialized into the following roles:

➤ Front End

➤ Excel Back End

➤ Word Back End

➤ PowerPoint Back End

These role names are self-explanatory. For example, an OWA server dedicated to the Word Back End role would process requests only for the Word Web App. The specific role of the Office Web Apps Front End server is to control the communications of the Farm State traffic between the servers within the farm.

Security Considerations

The Office Web Apps can leverage either the HTTP or the HTTPS protocols. Using the HTTP protocol may be appropriate for test configuration farms, but for live production data it is recommended that you use the secure HTTPS protocol. If HTTPS is chosen as the primary communications mechanism, then each Office Web Apps server must contain the appropriate valid SSL certificate, or it must be offloaded via a properly configured load balancer. The Office Web Apps farm can communicate with SharePoint 2013, Lync 2013, and Exchange 2013 over HTTPS. Whereas SharePoint 2013 and Exchange 2013 will work on the HTTP protocol, Lync 2013 only allows HTTPS.

> **NOTE** *Remember that the following examples are using Office Web Apps cmdlets and that are only available on Office Web Apps servers.*

You can further control your Office Web Apps farm, preventing exposure of sensitive documents. The first step is to set your Office Web Apps farm's allow list. Using the New-OfficeWebAppHost cmdlet, you can add entries to the allow list as shown here:

```
New-OfficeWebAppsHost -domain "contoso.com"
```

Once this Office Web Apps PowerShell command is executed, only requests from the contoso.com domain will be honored. Conversely, using the Remove-OfficeWebAppHost cmdlet removes entries in the allow list. If the Office Web Apps' allow list is left empty, it will respond to any request regardless of originating domain. This is an important consideration if the Office Web Apps farm is exposed to the Internet.

Next, you can leverage a specific Active Directory organization unit (OU) for your Office Web Apps servers. Once implemented you can prevent a rogue Office Web Apps server from joining the farm by using the `FarmOU` parameter with either the `New-OfficeWebApps` cmdlet when building the farm or the `Set-OfficeWebAppsFarm` cmdlet of an existing farm, as shown in the following example:

```
New-OfficeWebAppsFarm -InternalURL https://server.contoso.com -EditingEnabled:$true
    -FarmOU "OU=OWA Servers,DC=Contoso,DC=com"
```

The preceding example builds a new Office Web Apps farm for internal use only using a secure URL protocol, `https://server.contoso.com`. It also enables editing, and limits access to Office Web Apps servers that are specifically in the "OWA Servers" OU.

The next example assumes you already have an existing Office Web Apps farm in place. In this case, you are specifying that all Office Web Apps servers must be part of the "OWA Servers" OU:

```
Set-OfficeWebAppsFarm -FarmOU "OU=OWA Servers,DC=Contoso,DC=com"
```

Virtualizing Office Web Apps Servers

Virtualization is commonplace in many data centers, and Office Web Apps 2013 has no problems running in this type of configuration. While not requirements, the following recommendations should be followed:

➤ No other server software should be installed on the Office Web Apps server. This includes SharePoint, Exchange, or even the workflow engine. The server should be dedicated to OWA.

➤ You can, as needed, install Office Web Apps server as a guest on the same physical server (host) that has a SharePoint guest.

➤ When redundancy is a concern, each virtual instance of the Office Web Apps server should be hosted on different physical servers (hosts).

Firewall Considerations for Office Web Apps

Firewalls that block traffic are often the source of communications issues that prevent Office Web Apps from offering its services. Keep the following guidelines in mind when setting up an Office Web Apps farm:

➤ If unsecure communications exist between the SharePoint farm and Office Web Apps server, keep port 80 open for HTTP communications.

➤ If secured communications exist between the SharePoint farm and Office Web Apps server, keep port 443 open for HTTPS communications.

➤ If there are multiple servers in an Office Web Apps farm, ensure that port 809 is open between Office Web Apps servers to allow for proper operation.

Load Balancing an Office Web Apps Farm

If you have multiple servers within an Office Web Apps farm, it is important to provide a mechanism for load balancing. Whether your load balancing solution is software of hardware, it should include the following features:

➤   Layer 7 routing

➤   Client affinity, or so-called sticky session

➤   SSL off-loading

DNS Requirements

As you might expect, proper DNS can be critical for Office Web Apps services. When setting up an Office Web Apps farm using HTTPS, the DNS must be configured to a fully qualified domain name (FQDN) — either the single Office Web Apps server or the virtual IP of the load balancer servicing the Office Web Apps farm. When using nonsecure communication, the same DNS routing applies, but a FQDN is not required.

AUTHENTICATION REQUIREMENTS

As you move into the latest iteration of SharePoint — that is, SharePoint 2013 — Office Web Apps 2013 has very specific requirements regarding authentication. Office Web Apps 2013 will work with SharePoint 2013 web applications only when they are configured with claims-based authentication. Any SharePoint 2013 web application built using classic-mode authentication will not have the capability to communicate with the Office Web Apps service and will be unable to open or edit documents.

Migrating from Classic-Mode to Claims-Based Authentication

If you are unsure if your web application is using Claims or Classic authentication, PowerShell can quickly help you find out. Open a SharePoint 2013 Management Shell window, type the following, and press Enter:

```
Get-SPWebApplication | Select URL, UseClaimsAuthentication
```

If the `UseClaimsAuthentication` parameter is set to `False`, then your SharePoint 2013 web application is using classic-mode authentication. In order to ensure proper communications between the SharePoint 2013 web application and Office Web Apps service, you can use the following SharePoint 2013 cmdlet to set it to use claims-based authentication:

```
Convert-SPWebApplication -Identity "http://<yourURL>:port" -To Claims
-RetainPermissions [-Force]
```

The *<yourURL>* portion of the preceding command is the default zone URL of the SharePoint 2013 web application. After the conversion is complete, take a minute to ensure that everything is working correctly.

> **WARNING** *Converting a SharePoint web application to claims-based authentication is a one-way conversion; it cannot be undone. This is a significant and permanent change that should not be made without proper due diligence. Ensure that any other functionality associated with this action will work properly after the conversion.*

PREPARING THE SERVER AND INSTALLING OWA VIA THE GUI

As noted earlier, the evolution and expansion of OWA has changed the installation procedures greatly from the previous version. The first step to any OWA install is to prepare and configure the server. OWA has very strict requirements about how and where it should be installed. You cannot have any other Microsoft server-level software installed on the same machine. That includes the following:

➤ Exchange Server

➤ SharePoint Server

➤ Lync Server

➤ SQL Server

➤ No version of the desktop Office suite may be installed on the OWA server(s).

As you might suspect, because each Office Web Apps server has so many great services to offer, it requires its own Windows server with the proper hardware requirements:

Operating System Requirements

➤ Windows Server 2008 R2 SP1 or later

➤ Windows Server 2012 RTM or later

Hardware Requirements

➤ 8GB RAM

➤ 4-core processor

➤ 80GB hard disk space

Installing Prerequisites for Windows Server 2012

If you are installing on Windows Server 2012, then you need to configure the following specific roles and services:

1. Your install account must be a local administrator on the Office Web Apps server. In this example, set `contoso\sp_install` as a local administrator of the server and then remote desktop to the server as that account.

2. Open your Windows 2012 Server Manager Dashboard and from the left-hand menu select Local Server.

3. Select Manage on the top-right menu bar, and select Add Roles and Features from the drop-down menu. The Add Roles and Features Wizard will appear. Click Next.

4. Select "Role-based or feature-based installation" in the second screen of the Add Roles and Features Wizard and click Next.

5. Select the local server onto which you will be installing the new roles and features. In this example it is owa.contoso.com. Click Next.

6. Check the Web Server (IIS) role, which will invoke the window shown in Figure 15-4.

7. From the window select the Add Features button. This will install the necessary IIS role and IIS management console. Back on the screen, select Web Server (IIS) and click Next.

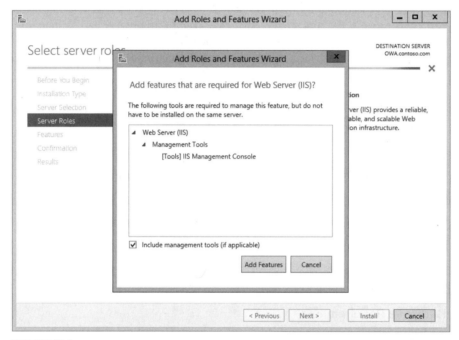

FIGURE 15-4

8. From the list of Features select the Ink and Handwriting Services and click Next.

9. On the Web Server Role (IIS) screen with lots of boring text click Next.

10. In the Web Server Role (IIS) role services dialog, ensure that the proper settings are selected:

    ➤ In the Common HTTP Features section, both Default Document and Static Content options should be checked by default.

    ➤ Select Dynamic Content Compression under the Performance section. In that same section also confirm that the default Static Content Compression is selected.

    ➤ Scroll down to the Security section and select Windows Authentication. In that same section also confirm that the default Request Filtering is selected.

11. Expand the Application Development section. Check the box for .NET extensibility 4.5, which will invoke the window shown in Figure 15-5. From the window click Add Features.

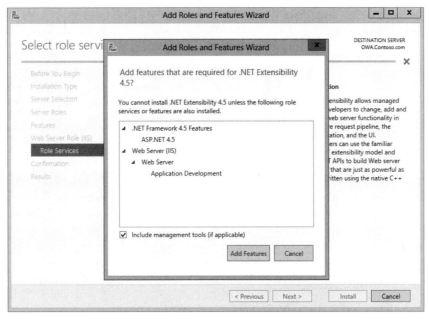

FIGURE 15-5

12. Check ASP.NET 4.5, which will invoke the window shown in Figure 15-6. From the window, click Add Features.

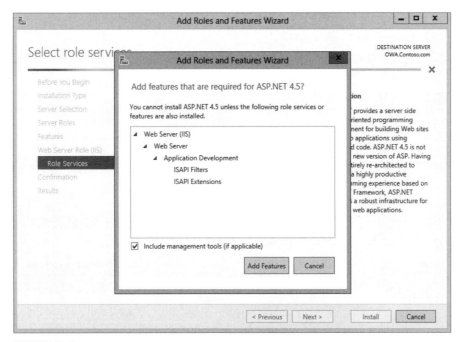

FIGURE 15-6

13. Scroll down a little and check Server Side Includes. That will do it. To continue, click Next at the bottom of the window.

14. Click Install to confirm adding the roles and features.

When the installation completes you may or may not be prompted to reboot depending on the mood of the server. If it asks you to reboot, please do so before continuing. With all of this done you have the prerequisites in place and you are ready to install the Office Web Apps.

Installing Prerequisites for Windows 2008 R2

Installing on Windows 2008 R2 is possible if that is your only option. To install on old faithful, keep a few things in mind. Windows Server 2008 R2 must be patched to Service Pack 1 or later, plus all Windows updates. You also need to manually download and install .NET Framework 4.5, Windows PowerShell 3.0, and KB259525. Once you have all those pieces, you then need to add similar roles and features as you would for Windows Server 2012. To avoid clicking through multiple pages, you can do it with PowerShell:

1. Open Windows PowerShell.

2. Type the following at the command prompt and press Enter:

```
Import-Module ServerManager
```

3. Type the following at the command prompt and press Enter:

```
Add-WindowsFeature Web-Server,Web-WebServer,Web-Common-Http,Web-Static-Content,
Web-App-Dev,Web-Asp-Net,Web-Net-Ext,Web-ISAPI-Ext,Web-ISAPI-Filter,
Web-Includes,Web-Security,Web-Windows-Auth,Web-Filtering,Web-Stat-Compression,
Web-Dyn-Compression,Web-Mgmt-Console,Ink-Handwriting,IH-Ink-Support
```

4. If prompted, reboot the server.

That covers the prerequisites for Windows Server 2008 R2.

Installing Office Web Apps

After completing the requisite configuration on the server and rebooting if you were prompted, you can install the OWA software:

1. Make sure you are still logged into the OWA server with your install account. In this example, it is Contoso\sp_install.

2. Download Office Web Apps to the server and run setup.exe.

3. When the license screen appears, read everything very carefully, check the box for "I accept the terms of this agreement" if you do, and then click Continue.

4. In the Choose a file location dialog, click Install Now to install into the default file location.

5. When the install is completed, you will see the confirmation dialog, and click Close.

This completes the install of the Office Web Apps software to a single server. The following sections outline configuring this server using either the HTTP or HTTPS protocols. If you ever need to add additional Office Web Apps servers to the farm, just follow the preceding steps to prepare it for configuration.

OFFICE WEB APPS CONFIGURATION OPTIONS

At this point you now have options regarding how you want to configure the protocol that enables Office Web Apps 2013 to talk to SharePoint 2013. The first section outlines the steps needed to install a nonsecure, or HTTP, farm. After that you will walk through the steps to create an Office Web Apps farm using HTTPS communications. As you might expect, the HTTP farm is easier to configure and is suitable for development, for small or highly isolated farms. The standard is to use HTTPS communications, which involves an extra layer of complexity related to the use of SSL certificates. Using a certificate purchased from an external vendor requires that it is resolvable on the Internet. Using a certificate that can be validated internally requires extra services on different servers to act as a certificate authority. Weigh your requirements against the complexity and security each of these options brings to the table.

Creating Your Own Certificate for Testing

If after reading the preceding section you think it might be a great idea to use HTTPS but the only thing holding you back is lack of an SSL certificate, you are in luck. IIS supports creating a self-signed certificate, and this section will walk you through the steps to take advantage of this capability. Keep in mind that self-signed certificates are not trusted by browsers by default, and most modern browsers will issue warnings if you try to access a site that has an untrusted certificate. That means this section is not suitable for production. However, because you need your servers to trust this certificate to hook everything up, this section describes the process. Just keep in mind that it is not a production solution!

Use the following steps to create your own certificate. They assume you are running on Windows Server 2012 but are similar on Windows 2008 R2.

1. Log into the Office Web Apps server as an administrator.

2. Open Internet Information Services (IIS) Manager from the Start menu.

3. From the menu on the left, click on the server name. In this example the server's name is OWA.

4. On the right this will open *<servername>* Home. Look at Figure 15-7 to verify you're in the right spot. Under the IIS section, double-click Server Certificates.

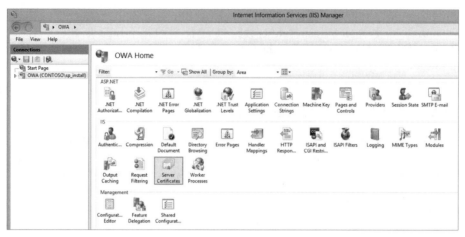

FIGURE 15-7

5. From the far right side of the window, under Actions, click Create Self-Signed Certificate....

6. Under Specify a friendly name for the certificate:, enter the fully qualified domain name (FQDN) of your server. In this example, that's owa.contoso.com.

7. Leave the certificate store at the default of Personal and click OK.

You now have an SSL certificate you can use when configuring your OWA farm to use HTTPS.

Before you can use the certificate, you need to manually add it to the Trusted Root Certification Authorities for the computer account on any machine you would like to actually trust the certificate. In this example you should do to that, at a minimum, on the OWA and SharePoint server. If you have a client machine from which you want to test the Office Web Apps, you also need to do it there. These steps shouldn't be done arbitrarily with random certificates. Remember that this process is ultimately saying you completely trust this certificate, which is OK because you created it. The evil hackers of the world would love for you to do this with one of their certificates, so always tread lightly when adding certificates.

The first step is to export the certificate from the OWA Personal store:

1. Still on the OWA server, open the MMC by using the Search charm (Windows key+F), typing **mmc**, and pressing Enter.

2. Click File. From the drop-down, click Add/Remove Snap-in....

3. Under Available snap-ins, select Certificates and click Add.

4. From the pop-up window, select Computer account and click Next.

5. Accept the default of Local computer on the next screen and click Finish.

6. Back at the Add or Remove Snap-ins screen, double-check yourself against Figure 15-8 and then click OK.

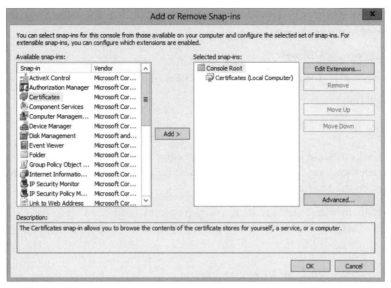

FIGURE 15-8

7. Expand Certificates (Local Computer).

8. Expand Personal. Under Personal, click Certificates.

9. When your newly created certificate appears, right-click on it and choose Export.... Figure 15-9 shows an example.

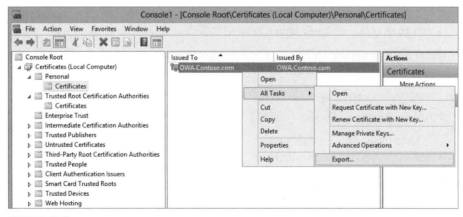

FIGURE 15-9

10. At the Welcome screen, click Next.

11. Select Yes, export the private key, and click Next.

12. For Export File Format, accept the defaults and click Next.

13. Select the box for Password:. Type the Password: and Confirm Password:. In this example use **pass@word1**, and click Next.

14. For File to Export click Browse....

15. Navigate to your Desktop, set the filename to **OWA.pfx**, and click Save; then click Next.

16. At the Completing screen, click Finish.

17. At the Successful screen, click OK.

Now that you have the certificate exported to a file, you can import it to the Trusted Root Certification Authorities store on the necessary machines. Perform these steps on an OWA server and then repeat them on the SharePoint server:

1. Open the MMC by using the Search charm, typing **mmc** and pressing Enter. (You might still have the MMC open from the previous steps.)

2. Click File.

3. From the drop-down, click Add/Remove Snap-in....

4. Under Available snap-ins:, select Certificates, and then click Add.

5. From the pop-up window, select Computer account.

6. Click Next.

7. Accept the default of Local computer on the next screen and click Finish.

8. Back at the Add or Remove Snap-ins screen, click OK.

9. Expand Certificates (Local Computer).

10. Expand Trusted Root Certification Authorities.

11. Right-click on Certificates under Trusted Root Certification Authorities.

12. From the menu, select All Tasks > Import..., as shown in Figure 15-10.

13. From the Welcome screen click Next.

14. Click the Browse... button.

15. Navigate to the OWA.pfx file you saved in the previous steps. From the File type section, you need to specify PFX files or all files. If you are now on the SharePoint server, you probably need to copy the file to the SharePoint server. Hopefully, in this age, you can do so without using sneakernet.

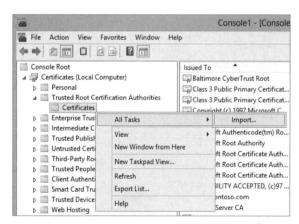

FIGURE 15-10

WHAT IS SNEAKERNET?

Darn kids these days. When writing this chapter, I casually mentioned sneakernet and kept on going, but then I realized there are probably just as many admins today who have no clue what sneakernet is as those who do. So there is no confusion, sneakernet is how people used to move things from one computer to another. You popped in a floppy disk (hope you at least have an idea what those are) and copied the file to the floppy. Then you ejected it and walked it over to the other computer to copy it to that computer. Since us IT folks like to wear casual shoes (aka sneakers) and that was the way the file was flying across the room we adopted the name sneakernet. It was very similar to the way your parents walked to school in the snow, uphill both ways. Don't you feel smarter now?

16. Back on the File to Import screen, click Next.

17. When prompted, enter the password. In this example, use **pass@word1**.

18. Leave all the other check boxes at the their default values and click Next.

19. At the Certificate Store screen, confirm that your defaults match Figure 15-11. You have to import into the Trusted Root Certification Authorities store or all this work was for naught.

20. Click Next.

21. At the Completing screen, click Finish.

22. Click OK at the Successful message.

23. Close the MMC console. At the pop-up asking if you want to save your settings, click No.

FIGURE 15-11

That does it; now the server trusts that self-signed certificate. The easiest way to confirm you did all of this correctly is in the section "Using the HTTPS Protocol;" when you are asked to navigate to https://owa.contoso.com/hosting/discovery, you should not receive any type of SSL error. Keep in mind that the URL will not work until you go through those steps. If you do get an error, come back and try these steps again. Remember to also confirm that the URL works without certificate errors from the SharePoint server.

Configuring the Security Token Service

In the next two sections you choose whether you want to access the OWA farm from SharePoint over HTTP or HTTPS. In most cases you will choose HTTPS because this is a more secure solution, but there is one other consideration. You need to know if your SharePoint content web applications will use HTTP or HTTPS. If there is any chance your web app will use HTTP, then you need to change the Security Token Service to allow OAuth to pass over HTTP. What happens, in a simplified nutshell, is that SharePoint passes the request over to the OWA server using HTTPS but then the OWA server accesses SharePoint over the calling web application's URL. If that URL is `http://portal.contoso.com`, the communication will fail, with some cryptic errors in the ULS logs of the OWA server.

In order for HTTP to work properly, you must make the following change on the SharePoint farm:

1. From the SharePoint server, open the SharePoint Management Shell as an administrator.

2. Type the following PowerShell command and press Enter:

   ```
   $config = (Get-SPSecurityTokenServiceConfig)
   ```

3. Type the following PowerShell command and press Enter:

   ```
   $config.AllowOAuthOverHttp = $true
   ```

4. Type the following PowerShell command and press Enter:

   ```
   $config.Update()
   ```

Refer to Figure 15-12 to confirm what you typed. Once these commands are run your farm will allow OAuth to happen over the HTTP protocol, which is a security risk in itself. The only way to avoid making this change is to have everything in your environment run over SSL. This means you will make this change if you are using the HTTP method described in the next section, but also even when using the HTTPS method you would have to make this change if your SharePoint content is accessible using HTTP.

FIGURE 15-12

Using the HTTP Protocol

After the Office Web Apps program is installed on your target server you can begin the actual configuration of that server. As you walk through the configuration process, note that you are using HTTP communications for intra-farm communications. As mentioned previously, it is recommended that any production-level farm use the HTTPS protocol. This section outlines a single Office Web Apps server, which will be configured with the farm.

The first step is to access the OWA server and create the OWA farm:

1. Remote desktop into the OWA server as the account with which you performed the install. In this example, that is Contoso\sp_install.

2. Open Windows PowerShell by right-clicking on it and choose Run as Administrator.

3. Type the following line and press Enter to load the Office Web Apps PowerShell cmdlets:

   ```
   Import-Module OfficeWebApps
   ```

4. To create the farm, type the following PowerShell command and press Enter:

   ```
   New-OfficeWebAppsFarm -InternalURL http://OWA.contoso.com -AllowHttp
   -EditingEnabled:$true
   ```

5. Acknowledge yes, that you are enabling this specific functionality, by pressing Enter when prompted.

6. When completed, you will receive the OWA summary farm confirmation shown in Figure 15-13.

FIGURE 15-13

7. Confirm your farm is operational by using a web browser. To do so open the following URL: http://owa.contoso.com/hosting/discovery. You should see the web app Open Platform Interface (WOPI)-discovery XML file, as shown in Figure 15-14.

FIGURE 15-14

That completes the installation and configuration of the Office Web Apps farm. From here you need to bind that farm to whichever host you choose. In this case, the next section steps you through binding the Office Web Apps farm with the SharePoint 2013 farm. You will bind to the SharePoint farm using HTTP.

The final step is the connection of SharePoint and OWA using HTTP. Skip this section if you want to use HTTPS and proceed directly to the next section.

1. Remote desktop to the SharePoint server using `Contoso\sp_install`.

2. Open the SharePoint Management Shell by right-clicking on the icon and run it as an administrator. If you followed Chapter 3, "Installing and Configuring SharePoint 2013," the icon should still be pinned to your taskbar.

3. To create a binding between the SharePoint 2013 farm and the new OWA 2013 farm, run the following command and press Enter:

   ```
   New-SPWOPIBinding -ServerName owa.contoso.com -AllowHTTP
   ```

4. Set up a zone that instructs SharePoint to communicate with OWA 2013:

   ```
   Set-SPWopiZone -zone "internal-http"
   ```

Now SharePoint is ready to take advantage of the Office Web Apps.

Using the HTTPS Protocol

The previous section outlines the basic steps for binding a SharePoint 2013 farm to an Office Web Apps farm, but only using the HTTP protocol. The following steps create a farm using the HTTPS protocol:

1. Remote desktop into the OWA server as the account with which you performed the install. In this example, it is `Contoso\sp_install`.

2. Open Windows PowerShell by right-clicking on it and choose Run as Administrator.

3. Type the following line and press Enter to load the Office Web Apps PowerShell cmdlets:

    ```
    Import-Module OfficeWebApps
    ```

4. To create the farm, type the following PowerShell command and press Enter:

    ```
    New-OfficeWebAppsFarm -InternalURL https://owa.contoso.com -EditingEnabled:$true
    -CertificateName "owa.contoso.com"
    ```

5. Acknowledge yes, that you are enabling this specific functionality, by pressing Enter when prompted.

6. When completed, you will receive the OWA summary farm confirmation shown in Figure 15-15.

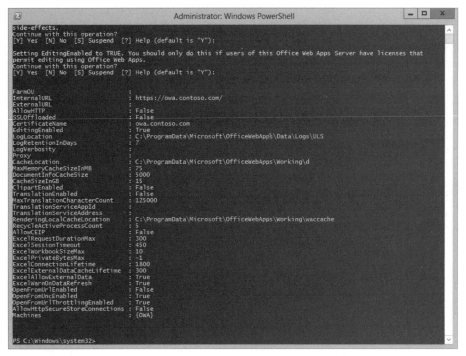

FIGURE 15-15

7. Confirm your farm is operational by using a web browser. To do so, open the following URL: `https://owa.contoso.com/hosting/discovery`. You should see the Web app Open Platform Interface (WOPI)-discovery XML file shown in Figure 15-16.

FIGURE 15-16

That completes the installation and configuration of the Office Web Apps farm. From here you need to bind that farm to whichever host you choose. In this case, the next section steps you through binding the Office Web Apps farm with the SharePoint 2013 farm using HTTPS.

The preceding steps are almost identical to those outlined in the "Single-Server Installation (HTTP)" configuration section. The critical difference here to note is that this Office Web Apps farm will be using HTTPS communications. By default, whenever you use the `New-OfficeWebAppsFarm` cmdlet, it defaults to using the HTTPS protocol.

Binding to a SharePoint Farm Using HTTPS

Now that you have completed building an Office Web Apps farm using the HTTPS protocol, you must bind it to the SharePoint 2013 farm. Creating the binding is relatively straightforward; just keep in mind the previously mentioned SSL complexity included with this configuration. An important consideration in step four is to note the zone you will be setting up is a secure configuration.

1. Remote desktop to the SharePoint server using `Contoso\sp_install`.

2. Open the SharePoint Management Shell by right-clicking on the icon and run it as an administrator.

3. To create a binding between the SharePoint 2013 farm and the new OWA 2013 farm, enter the following command and press Enter:

   ```
   New-SPWOPIBinding –ServerName owa.contoso.com
   ```

4. Set up a zone that instructs SharePoint to communicate with OWA 2013:

   ```
   Set-SPWopiZone -Zone "internal-https"
   ```

Now that you have completed building an Office Web Application farm using the HTTPS protocol, you must bind it to the SharePoint 2013 farm. Creating the binding is relatively straightforward; just keep in mind the previously mentioned SSL complexity included with this configuration. In this example, you will bind SharePoint to the Office Web Apps farm internally using the `Set-New-SPWOPIBinding` PowerShell cmdlet. Then the zone for that binding connection is declared using the `Set-SPWOPIZone` cmdlet. There are four possible zones for `Set-SPWOPIZone`: `internal-http`, `internal-https`, `external-http`, and `external-https`. HTTP zones should be reserved for testing, strictly trusted, or fully encrypted internal networks. In production, HTTPS zones are almost always the best choice. For this exercise `internal-https` was chosen because all the communication is happening internally on the same network. If the communication between the SharePoint farm and the Office Web Applications farm travels over the Internet or any public network, `external-https` would be more appropriate.

Removing a Binding

Sometimes as a good administrator you like to "tinker" with your SharePoint server. Of course, you always use a lot of VM snapshots and would never "tinker" with a production farm, especially when trying to deploy Office Web Apps, but in case you ever find yourself in a pickle while playing with the two, there is a way to undo most of the damage. You can run the following command from the SharePoint Management Shell to remove the binding:

```
Remove-SPWOPIBinding -ALL
```

After running that, you can go back to tinkering with the `New-SPWOPIBinding` cmdlets from the previous sections.

Scaling Office Web Apps

The Office Web Apps service is a now run as a farm configuration. In the previous examples you created an Office Web Apps farm, but that farm only contained a single Office Web Apps server. This is adequate for most small SharePoint 2013 farms, but it would not be enough for larger, more complex configurations that place a premium on uptime and quick responses. To add scale and provide fault tolerance, you need to leverage a load balancer and multiple Office Web Apps servers. The load balancer addresses the fault tolerance requirement using those same multiple servers. Once you have established an existing Office Web Apps farm, you can use the Office Web Apps PowerShell cmdlets to add additional servers. After installing the Office Web Apps software on the server, you can attach it to the farm by using the following command:

```
New-OfficeWebAppsMachine -MachineToJoin OWAServer2.contoso.com
```

Office Web Apps Patching

Another primary advantage of moving Office Web Apps to a standalone farm is evident during the patching process. Because the previous version of Office Web Apps was fully integrated into SharePoint, there was no feasible way to patch the Office Web Apps without causing a major interruption to the SharePoint farm, meaning taking all of SharePoint offline while you patched. It is now possible to patch the Office Web Apps farm with only minimal interruption to any of the applications to which it provides services, such as SharePoint or Exchange. As with everything in OWA patching, it is not performed via a GUI but rather via the Office Web Apps PowerShell cmdlets.

The unique thing about the patching process is that you actually remove a server from the farm, patch it, and then add it back to the farm. Rinse and repeat for all the servers in your farm. So if you build your OWA farm with more than one server, you should be able to avoid any downtime. To patch the master server, you need to use the `Set-OfficeWebAppsMachine -Master` PowerShell cmdlet.

NEW POWERSHELL OWA CMDLETS

Table 15-2 describes the cmdlets used on the SharePoint farm when connecting to the OWA farm.

TABLE 15-2: SharePoint Cmdlets for Working with OWA

CMDLET	DESCRIPTION
`Get-SPWOPIBinding`	Returns a list of bindings that were created by using `New-SPWOPIBinding` on the current SharePoint farm where this cmdlet is run
`Get-SPWOPISuppressionSetting`	Returns the suppression settings on the current SharePoint farm where this cmdlet is run
`Get-SPWOPIZone`	Returns the zone that is configured on the current SharePoint farm for the WOPI application to use
`New-SPWOPIBinding`	Creates a new binding to associate filename extensions or applications with actions on the current SharePoint farm where this cmdlet is run
`New-SPWOPISuppressionSetting`	Turns off Office Web Apps Preview for the action and document type or binding you've specified on the current SharePoint farm
`Remove-SPWOPIBinding`	Removes bindings for applications, filename extensions, and their associated actions on the current SharePoint farm where this cmdlet is run
`Remove-SPWOPISuppressionSetting`	Removes the suppression settings for a file type or program ID (ProgID) on the current SharePoint farm where this cmdlet is run
`Set-SPWOPIBinding`	Updates the default click action for an application or filename extension binding

`Set-SPWOPIZone`	Configures the zone that the current SharePoint farm will use to navigate the browser to the WOPI application
`Update-SPWOPIProofKey`	Updates the public key that is used to connect to the WOPI application on the current SharePoint farm where this cmdlet is run

SUMMARY

After digging into this chapter you now are up to speed on everything Office Web Apps 2013. Compared to its predecessor, it gets double thumbs up for improvements. The decoupling from SharePoint is great for ease of management, and its ability to now support additional applications such as Exchange 2013 increase its value in the data center. Enhancements such as being able to participate in co-authoring of a document and work on documents that have tracked changes further increase productivity. Finally, speaking of increased productivity, added functionality supporting mobile clients rounds out a great product. Take what you have learned here and conquer the world . . . or at least make your SharePoint farm more awesome.

16

Installing and Configuring Azure Workflow Server

WHAT'S IN THIS CHAPTER?

➤ What's new with workflow?

➤ Installing and configuring Windows Azure Workflow Server

➤ Creating workflows in SharePoint 2013

There are very big changes to the workflow architecture and functionality in SharePoint 2013. This version of SharePoint introduces its new workflow partner, Windows Azure Workflow Server. Workflow functionality is now part of a workflow farm, and this farm can be part of the SharePoint farm or installed on separate servers. This change reflects two of the key challenges users faced with SharePoint workflow in the past: performance and scalability. The new workflow architecture addresses these issues head on.

In this chapter you will learn about the new workflow features in SharePoint 2013, and how to install and configure Azure Workflow Server. We also describe some of the capability for creating custom workflows in order to illustrate how business processes are modeled.

ENHANCEMENTS IN WORKFLOW

For many enterprises, the ability to model and automate business processes, and to include these automated processes as part of SharePoint collaboration, is an important goal. To meet this need, Microsoft introduced workflow capability into SharePoint 2007 using the then new Workflow Foundation (WF). WF was introduced with the release of .NET 3.0, and its capability was updated in WF 3.5 and WF 3.5 SP1. As one of the first Microsoft products to utilize WF, SharePoint 2007 provided native workflows, but custom workflows could also be created using SharePoint Designer and Visual Studio. Many users, however, judged this capability to be lacking in ease of use, capability, and performance. The following sections provide a brief history of how the workflow capability has evolved between SharePoint 2010 and SharePoint 2013. First, let's briefly review the workflow capability in SharePoint 2010 for those who may not be familiar, and to provide a reference for the improvements in SharePoint 2013.

Workflow in SharePoint 2010

While workflow in SharePoint 2010 was similar architecturally to SharePoint 2007, it did introduce several significant, new capabilities, including the following:

- ➤ Creating site-based workflows that did not need to be associated with a list or document library
- ➤ A new workflow event model that enabled developers to override events
- ➤ Modifying the out-of-the-box workflow templates by importing them into SharePoint Designer 2010
- ➤ Modeling workflows in Visio 2010 and then importing the design into SharePoint Designer 2010
- ➤ Creating reusable workflows, and using Visio Services to visualize the status of the workflow
- ➤ Importing SharePoint Designer workflows into Visual Studio 2010

Although these features were a great step forward from SharePoint 2007, users still encountered challenges during the SharePoint 2010 workflow life cycle:

- ➤ Workflows weren't scalable because they were stored inside content databases; therefore, they were tightly coupled with SharePoint 2010.
- ➤ Workflows were designed primarily for on-premise deployments.
- ➤ Workflows could not call external systems, such as web services.
- ➤ Advanced features such as looping were not supported out of the box (although many partner solutions provided this capability). Nor could you call external web services unless you used Visual Studio 2010 to create your workflow.
- ➤ State machine workflows could only be created using Visual Studio 2010.
- ➤ Extending workflows usually required deploying customizations as a farm administrator via Central Administration.

Although most users agreed that SharePoint 2010 introduced huge improvements versus the workflow capability in SharePoint 2007, performance and scalability remained key challenges. To address these, Microsoft made numerous architectural changes, which were introduced in WF 4.0 and WF 4.5, which serve as the foundation for SharePoint 2013.

Workflow in SharePoint 2013

SharePoint 2013 workflow has a major architectural change, and introduces a new kind of workflow engine. These workflows, which are built using WF 4.5, run out of process from SharePoint 2013; therefore, they are not governed by constraints SharePoint might introduce. The fact that workflow is no longer a part of the SharePoint core infrastructure, but instead a separate server product, is a huge change from previous versions! This separate product is called *Windows Azure Workflow*. Even though the name includes Azure, this capability runs on-premises.

SharePoint 2013 workflows execute in an Azure service called *Workflow Manager 1.0*. The Workflow Manager server application should be installed on a separate set of servers, which can be part of the SharePoint 2013 farm or separate. The SharePoint web front end (WFE) includes *Workflow Client* software that handles the integration between the manager and the SharePoint farm. Communication between the manager and the client occurs using the REST API, and it is secured using OAuth. The net result is a workflow platform with improved performance and scalability. There are also improvements to custom workflow development using SharePoint Designer 2013 and Visual Studio 2012.

> **NOTE** *The SharePoint 2013 workflow platform is available only to SharePoint Server 2013; it is not supported on SharePoint Foundation 2013.*

New Workflow Architecture in SharePoint 2013

Workflow now executes within Windows Azure Workflow, which is the new workflow host that exists outside of SharePoint 2013. Windows Azure Workflow 1.0 is a new service that introduces new capabilities for authoring, hosting, and managing workflows. The service builds on the successful programming model, runtime, and activity library that was introduced with WF 4.0.

SharePoint 2013 workflows are also now fully declarative — another big change from previous versions. This means that workflows are no longer compiled into .NET assemblies; instead, XAML files define your workflows and their execution. Azure Workflow capability is also multi-tenant, which means it is available in SharePoint online as part of Office 365. Figures 16-1 and 16-2 illustrate the high-level architectural differences between SharePoint 2010 workflow and SharePoint 2013 workflow.

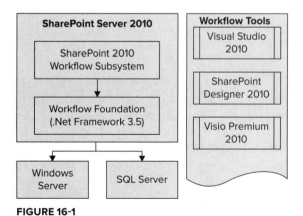

FIGURE 16-1

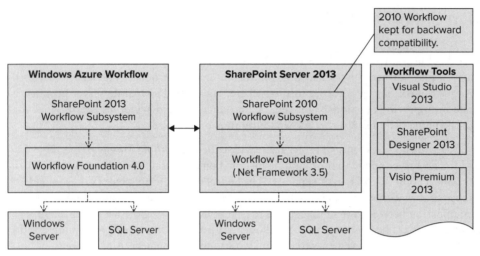

FIGURE 16-2

Windows Azure Workflow brings a new class of workflow to SharePoint Server 2013. Workflows built by using Windows Azure Workflow can take advantage of several new capabilities:

➤ Multi-tenancy

➤ Elastic scaling

➤ Activity/workflow artifact management

➤ Tracking and monitoring

➤ Instance management

➤ Fully declarative authoring

➤ REST and service bus messaging

➤ Managed service reliability

> **NOTE** *The SharePoint 2010 workflow platform has been carried forward to SharePoint Server 2013 for backward compatibility. This means that all your workflows built using SharePoint 2010 will continue to work in SharePoint 2013; but because SharePoint 2010 workflows are very different from SharePoint 2013 workflows, the 2010 workflows will not be upgraded to 2013, so you need to do the manual upgrade yourself, which means rewriting them on the new platform.*

Windows Azure Workflow is available in two flavors:

➤ **Windows Azure Workflow Server** — Provides a scalable, robust, workflow capability for on-premises deployments

➤ **Windows Azure Workflow Services** —Provides a scalable, robust workflow platform in Office 365 and cloud-based solutions

SharePoint Designer Enhancements

SharePoint Designer 2013 is now a first-class tool for creating workflows. It includes new functionality designed specifically for Windows Azure Workflow:

➤ A visual workflow development experience that uses a Visio 2013 add-in

➤ A new action that enables no-code web service calls from within a workflow

➤ New actions for creating a task and starting a task

➤ New coordination actions that enable you to start a workflow built on the SharePoint 2010 Workflow platform from a workflow built on the SharePoint 2013 Workflow platform

➤ A new Dictionary data type for working with complex data types

➤ New workflow building blocks such as Stage, Loop, and App Step

Improved Workflow Design Features

Although previous versions of SharePoint Designer gave workflow authors a lot of power, the design tools still lacked ease of use. SharePoint Designer 2013 includes several design features to make workflow authors even more productive:

➤ **Visual Workflow Designer** — With SharePoint 2010 workflows, you could use the Visual Designer included with Visio 2010 to visually create workflows. SharePoint Designer 2013 now includes both a text-based designer and a visual designer, and switching between design views is accomplished with a mouse click.

➤ **Copy and paste** — SharePoint 2013 enables users to copy and paste logic and actions within the text designer. This feature will definitely save workflow designers a lot of time.

➤ **Better packaging** — In previous editions of SharePoint, you had to create a reusable workflow if you wanted to package and use that workflow in another site. Unfortunately, list workflows did not support this feature, which made it very difficult to share and reuse list workflows across sites. In SharePoint Designer 2013, you can now save your list workflow as a template and reuse it in other sites.

Improved Workflow Logic and Control

Previously, workflow designers had to rely on custom actions or Visual Studio to achieve complex logic and flow. SharePoint Designer 2013 contains several improvements that provide greater flexibility and control:

➤ **Stages** — Previous versions of SharePoint workflow required using Visual Studio to create state machine workflows. A state machine workflow enables you to structure your workflow logic in a nonlinear manner, providing movement in and out of logical stages. For example, a document could move in and out of *Draft*, *Approved*, and *Rejected* states, with conditions dictating the flow. This is accomplished by using the new Stage shape in SharePoint Designer 2013.

➤ **Loops** — Loops enable you to repeat one or more actions a specified number of times. In prior versions of SharePoint workflow, you had to rely on hacks or third-party extensions to achieve looping.

➤ **SharePoint 2010 Workflow Re-use** — SharePoint Designer 2013 now enables starting an existing SharePoint 2010 workflow, including passing workflow initiation parameters. This enables you to assemble and reuse workflows built on SharePoint 2010. In addition, you can still create and modify SharePoint 2010 workflows using SharePoint Designer 2013.

New and Improved Workflow Actions

SharePoint 2013 includes several key improvements to workflow actions available in SharePoint 2010, including the following:

➤ **Web Services** — SharePoint 2013 now includes the capability to call web services. This capability results primarily from the new scalable workflow architecture of Azure Workflow Server.

➤ **Dictionary Data Type** — The `Dictionary` data type enables the creation and use of complex data structures, which is important for web service input and output. SharePoint 2013 workflow contains new actions for working with these complex types.

➤ **Project Server** — SharePoint Designer 2013 enables you to create workflows that integrate with Project Server 2013.

➤ **Task Actions** — In previous versions of SharePoint, workflow tasks could be a bit difficult to utilize. Simple behavior such as determining the outcome (Approved, Rejected, etc.) of a task was confusing. This has been dramatically improved, as discussed later in this chapter.

➤ **Document Translation** — SharePoint Designer 2013 includes a new action for translating documents via the Machine Translation Service, a new service application.

INSTALLING AND CONFIGURING WINDOWS AZURE WORKFLOW SERVER

Installing Azure Workflow Server is very much like installing SharePoint:

1. Install the Windows Azure Workflow Server software.

2. Configure a workflow farm.

3. Join the SharePoint farm to the workflow farm, which enables the new workflow capability for SharePoint 2013.

The following sections describe how to use the Web Platform Installer (Web PI) to install the necessary software requirements, how to use the configuration wizard to configure the farm, and how to use PowerShell to configure SharePoint to use the Workflow Server.

Hardware and Software Requirements

SharePoint 2013 installation and configuration is described in detail in Chapter 3, "Installing and Configuring SharePoint," but it does not cover workflow installation. To install the Workflow Server, you should meet the same requirements specified for SharePoint 2013, also covered in Chapter 3 and published on TechNet (see "Hardware and software requirements for SharePoint

2013" at `http://technet.microsoft.com/en-us/library/cc262485.aspx`. System requirements for Workflow Manager are also specifically articulated at `http://msdn.microsoft.com/en-us/library/jj193451(v=azure.10)`, but many of these requirements are already included in the previous reference. Administrators should check these references, as they will likely be updated as experience with SharePoint 2013 increases.

Supported Operating Systems

The following operating systems are supported:

➤ Windows Server 2008 R2 SP1 x64

➤ Windows Server 2012 x64

> **WARNING** *Windows 7 SP1 ×64 and Windows 8 ×64 are not supported for production environments, but you can install Workflow 1.0 on them for development purposes.*

The following editions for these operating systems are supported:

➤ Standard

➤ Enterprise

➤ Core

➤ Datacenter

SQL Server Requirements

The following SQL Server releases are recommended:

➤ SQL Server 2012

➤ SQL Server 2008 R2 SP1

> **NOTE** *SQL Server can be installed on the same physical machine with Workflow 1.0 and Service Bus, or on a different one. The Service Bus databases can reside on multiple machines as well. This flexibility is most valuable for your development environment, minimizing the number of servers or virtual machines you need.*

Following are the requirements for SQL Server, which serves as the repository for workflow configuration and runtime information:

➤ TCP/IP, shared memory, and named pipes must be enabled.

➤ Ports 1443, 12290, and 12291 on the firewall must be open to inbound and outbound communications.

➤ The name of the machine on which the SQL Server instance is running should have a name with no more than 16 characters.

➤ Named pipes use NetBIOS names, which also carry the 16-character restriction.

➤ The SQL Server Browser service should be running on the SQL Server.

➤ Your workflow service account, domain\sp_workflow, is a registered login for your SQL Server instance.

Service Account Requirements

This account needs to be part of the local domain, but only as a standard user, and it does not require special domain privileges (such as a domain administrator). The service account is used for the following Windows services:

➤ Service Bus Gateway

➤ Service Bus Message Broker

➤ Windows Fabric Host Service

➤ Workflow Service Backend

> **WARNING** *It is permissible to run Azure Workflow Server under a SharePoint farm account in development environments, but this isn't considered a best practice. For production environments, to abide by the principle of least privilege, it is recommended that you run Azure Workflow Server under a dedicated service account.*

Workflow Manager Install

You can install Workflow Manager using the Web Platform Installer (Web PI). The Web PI automatically checks for prerequisites before it installs workflow manager, and it will automatically download and install any prerequisites that it does not find as long as you have Internet access on the installation server. You do not need to install any prerequisites separately. You should download the Workflow Manager Installer, which includes the Web PI, from the following URL:

```
http://go.microsoft.com/fwlink/?LinkID=252092
```

The installer requires Internet access, and it will download and install the necessary prerequisite components, which include the following:

➤ .NET Framework 4 Platform Update 3 or .NET Framework 4.5

➤ Service Bus 1.0 — `http://www.microsoft.com/en-us/download/details.aspx?id=35374`

➤ Workflow Client 1.0 — `http://www.microsoft.com/en-us/download/details.aspx?id=35375`

➤ Microsoft Windows Fabric — `http://go.microsoft.com/fwlink/?LinkID=247564&CLCID=0x409`

After installation is complete, the Configuration Wizard will be launched. You can choose to perform the configuration later by opening the Configuration Wizard from the Start menu (select Start ⇨ All Programs ⇨ Workflow Manager 1.0 ⇨ Workflow Manager Configuration). In the next section, you will walk through the complete installation and configuration of the Workflow Manager.

Step-by-Step Install

You have learned about the various installation and configuration options for adding an Azure Workflow Server to your SharePoint 2013 farm. This section now brings it all together with step-by-step installation instructions.

The Environment

This example uses two servers. One server will be an Active Directory domain controller, and the other server will be the SharePoint 2013 server. The SharePoint server was prepared according to the installation instructions described in Chapter 3.

> **WARNING** *Installing Windows Azure Workflow Server on a domain controller is not a supported scenario for a production environment. Although it is possible to install Workflow Manager on a domain controller, it is not recommended. For a SharePoint 2013 production farm with workflow, you need a minimum of two machines.*

ContosoDC

The first server, named ContosoDC, is running Windows Server 2008 R2 (64-bit) with all the latest Windows Updates installed. It has been configured as an Active Directory domain controller for the Contoso domain.

> **NOTE** *If you are building a development and/or test farm and are hardware/resource constrained, you can use Windows Server Core for Windows Server 2008 R2. Server Core has lower memory requirements.*

ContosoServer

The second server, named ContosoServer, is also running Windows Server 2008 R2 (64-bit) with all the latest Windows Updates installed. A supported SQL Server instance has been installed and is hosting the SharePoint 2013 farm. In addition, ContosoServer is a member of the Contoso domain.

The Install

You are ready to perform the installation and configuration. In the sections that follow, you install and configure Workflow Manager, pair the workflow farm with the SharePoint farm, and verify that the environment is functioning properly.

Installing and Configuring Workflow Manager 1.0

Begin by installing and configuring Workflow Manager.

1. Log into ContosoServer as a farm administrator.

2. Download and install the Web Platform Installer using the link provided earlier in the "Web Platform Installer" section. After the prerequisites have been downloaded and installed, the configuration wizard, shown in Figure 16-3, will start automatically.

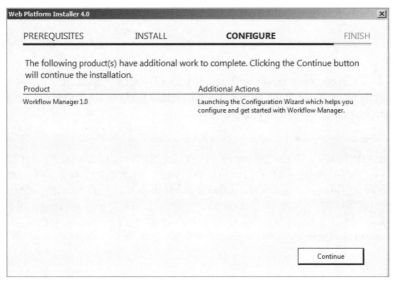

FIGURE 16-3

> **NOTE** *The WPI requires Internet access to complete the installation. If your server does not have Internet access, you can still use the installer by downloading all the required files ahead of time. To do so, use the WebPICmd.exe application, which can be downloaded from* http://go.microsoft.com/fwlink/?LinkId=233753. *After downloading, extract the zip file to your local hard drive. Launch PowerShell using Run as administrator privileges, and execute:*
>
> ```
> ./webpicmd.exe /offline /products:workflow /path:c:\[path]
> ```
>
> *where* c:\[path] *is the location where the installation files will be stored upon download.*

3. Click Continue to proceed with the configuration. You should receive acknowledgment that all required products were successfully installed, as shown in Figure 16-4, and then you can click Exit. The Welcome screen for the configuration wizard, shown in Figure 16-5, should also be displayed. If both windows are open on your desktop, click Exit on the WPI dialog.

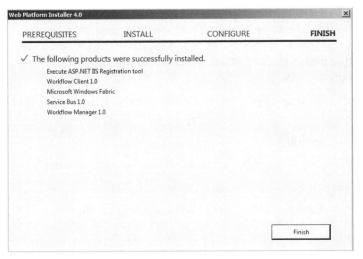

FIGURE 16-4

FIGURE 16-5

4.   Now you need to configure Workflow Manager and the Service Bus. On the Welcome screen, choose Configure Workflow Manager with Default Settings (Recommended). If the Welcome screen is not present for any reason, you can launch the configuration wizard by selecting Start ⇨ All Programs ⇨ Workflow Manager 1.0 ⇨ Workflow Manager Configuration.

You have the option to join an existing farm or, as in this case, create a new farm. In most circumstances it will be sufficient to use the default settings when creating your new workflow farm. If you need to specify the names of the databases created during the process, or change the default ports used for Workflow management over HTTP, then select the With Custom Settings option.

5. On the New Farm Configuration page in the Configure Service Account section, set the credentials as follows:

    ➤   USER ID: sp_workflow@contoso.com

    ➤   PASSWORD: "whatever password this account has been assigned"

> **WARNING** *Make sure the username is entered using the fully qualified UPN format or the domain\username format, not as the default shows in the wizard.*

6. Enable the "Allow Workflow management over HTTP on this computer" option. For a development environment this is permissible, but keep this disabled for a production environment.

7. Click the Test Connection button to verify the connection credentials before proceeding. You should receive a green check mark acknowledging success, as shown in Figure 16-6. If the test fails, you likely forgot to enable remote connectivity, or TCP/IP and named pipes for SQL Server.

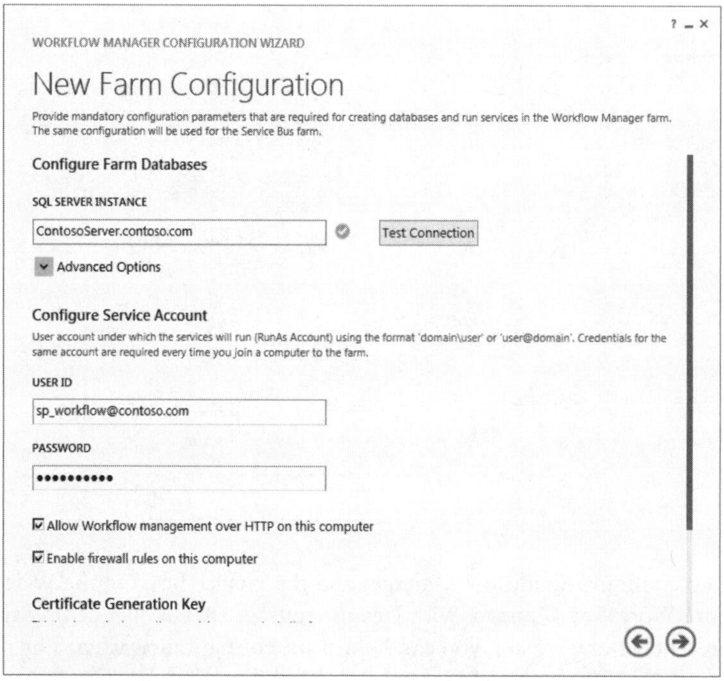

FIGURE 16-6

8. For the certificate generation key, enter a passphrase that you can easily remember. For production, use and document your passphrase because it will be required when additional workflow servers are added to the farm. When you are done, click the right arrow in the lower-right corner.

9. On the Summary page, review your settings. You can copy your configuration settings using the Copy link at the bottom of the page, and you can also get the PowerShell commands for completing the process using the link at the bottom of the Summary page. You should make a copy of the settings, and review the PowerShell cmdlets for future use. When you are done, click the check mark at the bottom of the page to start the configuration process.

10. Upon successful completion of the configuration, you should receive the acknowledgment shown in Figure 16-7 (each step that was successfully completed is followed by a check mark). Go ahead and exit the WPI tool if you haven't already, and exit the Configuration Wizard by clicking the check mark in the right corner.

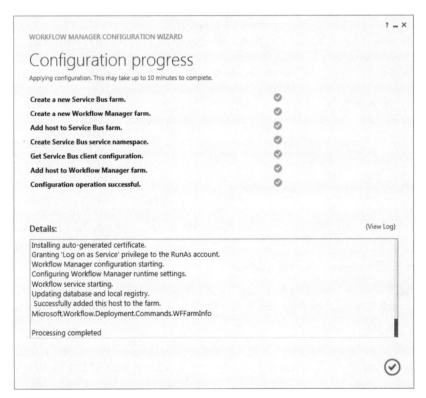

FIGURE 16-7

11. As part of the configuration, the wizard creates a new web application called Workflow Management Site under IIS, which you can browse to at https://localhost:12290, as shown in Figure 16-8, to view the workflow and security configuration.

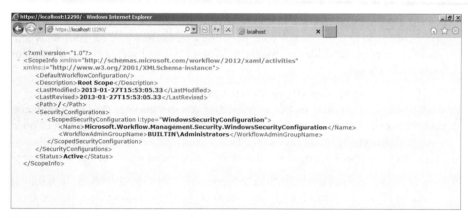

FIGURE 16-8

> **NOTE** *For your production environment and communication over HTTPS, you need to create a digital certificate, configure IIS, export the certificate, and then import and install the certificate on the SharePoint server. This ensures encrypted communication between SharePoint and Workflow Manager. The process is documented at* `http://technet.microsoft.com/en-us/library/jj658589(v=office.15)`.

The next step is to configure SharePoint to use the newly installed workflow farm. This is commonly referred to as "pairing" the farms.

Pairing Workflow Server with SharePoint 2013

In order to get the workflow farm's services operational within your SharePoint farm, you must pair the two farms. This is accomplished using PowerShell; there is no user interface for this. Perform the following steps to pair the farms:

1. Log into ContosoServer as a farm administrator.

2. Open the Workflow Manager PowerShell console (select Start ➪ All Programs ➪ Workflow Manager 1.0 ➪ Workflow Manager PowerShell) and enter the following command:

   ```
   Get-WFFarm
   ```

Note the different ports for HTTP and HTTPS communication, ports 12291 and 12290, respectively. This is how you will access the workflow server, using port 12291 for development and 12290 for production. Be sure to use the FQDN of the workflow farm along with the port number while you are configuring SharePoint. For example, if your web application were `intranet.contoso.com`, then you would use `http://intranet.contoso.com:12291`.

3. When you are ready to pair the farms, execute the following PowerShell cmdlet using the SharePoint 2013 Management Shell window. The command does not return any output if successful, so no news is good news. This script describes how SharePoint and workflow manager will communicate. It essentially "pairs" the site collection with the URL of the workflow server, using HTTP for communication. The value of the SPSite parameter can be any of your SharePoint web applications.

```
Register-SPWorkflowService -SPSite "http://intranet.contoso.com"
  -WorkflowHostUri "http://contososerver.contoso.com:12291"
  -AllowOAuthHttp
```

This installation and configuration process uses a single server for deploying workflow. Just as you can add multiple servers to a SharePoint 2013 farm, you can add multiple workflow servers to a workflow farm to provide fault tolerance and load balancing. If you install the workflow farm on another server, you need to install the workflow client on that server, as it is required to register the workflow service. Be aware that workflow manager currently supports a workflow farm of only one server or three servers. Two-server farms are not supported. Additional servers are added using the same process described previously, except you select Join an Existing Farm during the configuration process. To establish a highly available workflow farm, workflow manager needs a highly available service bus and SQL Server databases. Administrators should refer to the following references for detailed information: http://technet.microsoft.com/en-us/library/jj841106.aspx and http://msdn.microsoft.com/en-us/library/windowsazure/72646b45-646f-4dfb-ab52-e42f187655e7(v=azure.10)#HA.

That completes the pairing of the SharePoint and workflow farms. The next step is to confirm that everything is working properly by creating a workflow using SharePoint Designer 2013.

Testing and Verifying the Workflow Installation

To confirm that the installation went as planned, you are going to use SharePoint Designer 2013.

> **NOTE** *As with previous versions, SharePoint Designer 2013 is available as a free download at* http://www.microsoft.com/en-us/download/details.aspx?id=35491. *Download the 32-bit or 64-bit version, depending on which version of Office 2013 you have installed. For additional information about SharePoint Designer, see Chapter 18, "Working with SharePoint Designer 2013."*

1. Open SharePoint Designer 2013, and click the Open Site button on the Sites page. This is the URL of the site collection you registered previously. You will likely be prompted for credentials, so proceed to log into the site. Once authenticated, you should be ready to use SharePoint Designer 2013 (see Figure 16-9).

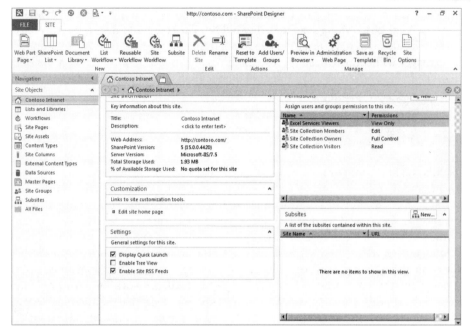

FIGURE 16-9

2. From the Ribbon, click the Site Workflow button to reveal the Create Site Workflow dialog shown in Figure 16-10. Note the two entries under Platform Type: SharePoint 2010 Workflow and SharePoint 2013 Workflow.

3. As long as the SharePoint 2013 Workflow option is visible, you are good to go and can stop there. For skeptical readers who need a little more proof, you can proceed to build your first SharePoint 2013 workflow. This example creates a workflow that reads an item in a custom list and checks for the presence of the word Contoso in the title. If present, it creates a task in the site's task list. It's not anything sophisticated, but it will verify that workflow manager is installed and configured correctly.

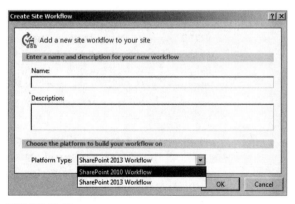

FIGURE 16-10

4. Click the Workflows tab on the left-hand side navigation, and then click the Reusable Workflow button.

5. Name your workflow **MyFirstWorkflow,** and ensure that the SharePoint 2013 Workflow option is selected in the Platform Type box, as shown in Figure 16-11.

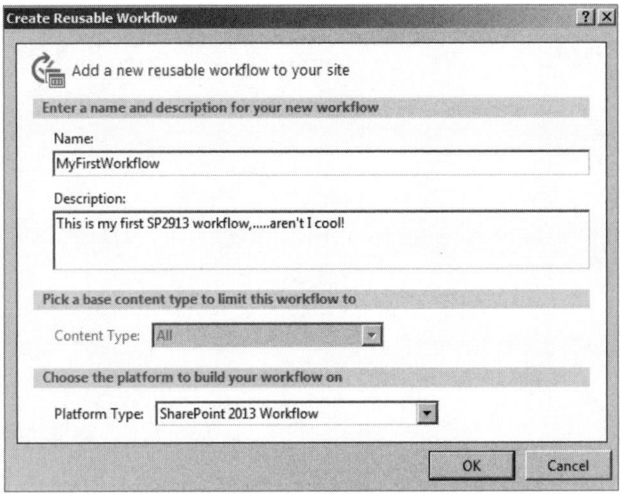

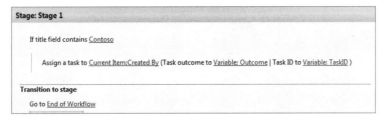

FIGURE 16-11

6. Next, you are going to create a workflow that assigns a task to the current user when they add a new item to a list with the word "Contoso" in the title. The SharePoint Designer code is shown in Figure 16-12. Once you have added the code, click the Save button on the SharePoint Designer Ribbon, followed by clicking the Publish button on the SharePoint Designer Ribbon.

Stage: Stage 1

If title field contains Contoso

    Assign a task to Current Item:Created By (Task outcome to Variable: Outcome | Task ID to Variable: TaskID)

Transition to stage

Go to End of Workflow

FIGURE 16-12

7. Navigate to your SharePoint site and click the Site Contents link on the left-hand side.

8. Click the Add an app option, and then click the Custom List tile. You can call the list whatever you like, such as My Custom List.

9. Navigate to the list and add your workflow to it by selecting the workflow on the Add a Workflow page, as shown in Figure 16-13. You can choose any name you like, but leave all the other default values.

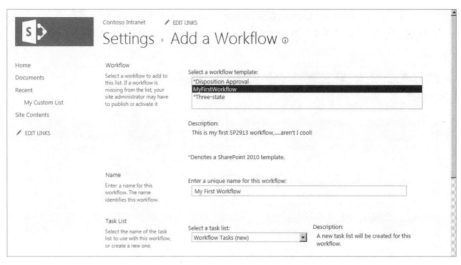

FIGURE 16-13

10. Add a new item to the list and make sure the title contains "Contoso." After you add the item, launch the workflow and browse to the Workflow Tasks page, where you should see that a new task was created by your very fancy, powerful workflow, as shown in Figure 16-14. Hopefully, you're convinced that everything is working properly.

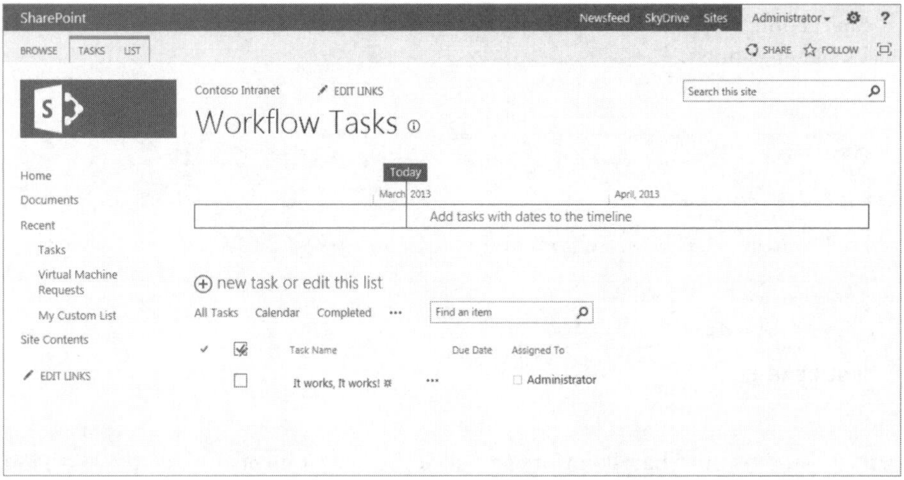

FIGURE 16-14

11. Do one last check by verifying the functionality from Central Administration. This is a quicker way to verify everything is connected properly, but using SharePoint Designer 2013 demonstrates definitively that workflow is working. Open Central Administration and click the Manage service applications link under Application Management. Scroll to the bottom of the page, and click the Workflow Service Application entry. You should see "Workflow is Connected" on the Workflow Service Status page, as shown in Figure 16-15.

FIGURE 16-15

Managing Web Application Settings

Administrators can manage how SharePoint 2013 interacts with the Workflow Server. These settings are configured using the Manage web applications link in the Application Management section of Central Administration. On the web application page, choose the web application to govern, click the General Settings button, and select the Workflow option, which will take you to the dialog shown in Figure 16-16. The following options can be enabled:

➤ **Enable user-defined workflows for all sites on this web application?** — Use this setting to enable or disable user-defined workflows (created by SharePoint Designer 2013). This is enabled by default.

➤ **Alert internal users who do not have site access when they are assigned a workflow task?** — Sometimes, users may be assigned a task within a site to which they do not have access. Use this setting to toggle alert notifications on or off. This is enabled by default.

➤ **Allow external users to participate in workflow by sending them a copy of the document?** — When enabled, this allows a copy of the document to be sent to external users. This is disabled by default.

FIGURE 16-16

You can also configure these settings via PowerShell:

```
Set-SPWorkflowConfig -webapplication http://sitename
    DeclarativeWorkflowsEnabled $true
    -EmailNoPermissionParticipantsEnabled $true
    -SendDocumentToExternalParticipants $false
```

CREATING SHAREPOINT 2013 WORKFLOWS

Before getting into the details of creating a more elaborate SharePoint 2013 workflow, it is important to have a good understanding of the basic workflow concepts. As with anything else, you need to be able to walk before you can run. Each of the following sections discuss the terminology and description of key aspects of a SharePoint workflow.

Templates

A workflow template is a reusable workflow solution that has been deployed and installed in your SharePoint environment. This solution can be available upon installation or it can be a custom workflow solution created using SharePoint Designer or Visual Studio. The workflow templates that are available upon installation need to be enabled, or activated. Upon site provisioning, some of the workflow templates are activated. For example, a team site provides the Disposition Approval Workflow and the Three-state Workflow templates. The provisioning of a publishing site activates the Publishing Approval Workflow template. You can also enable these workflow templates by activating their corresponding features at the site collection or site level.

SharePoint Designer workflows are installed upon creation and don't need to be activated. Custom workflows created using Visual Studio may be deployed using a feature, and therefore may require activating before use. Use the following steps to check the feature settings in your site collection (you must be the administrator of either the site collection or the farm):

1. From the top-level site in your site collection, click Site Actions ⇨ Site Settings.

2. Under the Site Collection Administration section, click Site Collection Features.

3. Ensure that the workflow features have a status of Active.

Associations

A workflow association is a specific connection between a workflow and a target list, library, content type, or site. For example, when you add an out-of-the-box workflow to a document library, you are taking the existing workflow template and creating a workflow association between the workflow and the document library.

Workflows can be associated at the following levels in SharePoint 2013:

➤ **Lists/Libraries** — By creating the association at this level, the workflow will run only on items created within the specified list or library. If you were to save this list or library as a template, any out-of-the-box workflow templates used would be associated with the template, making them part of anything created from the template.

➤ **Content types** — By associating the workflow with a content type, the workflow will run on all items created with this content type. This enables a reusable workflow solution if you were to use the specified content type in multiple lists or libraries.

➤ **Sites** — Some workflows aren't associated with a list or library, and are triggered by a different mechanism. Workflows of this nature can be associated at the site level. The capability to associate workflows with sites means workflow authors are no longer required to use list and library items. Possible scenarios for this would be for the workflow to run when the home page of the site was edited or a new Web Part was added to the page. Only workflows created with SharePoint Designer 2013 and Visual Studio 2012 can be associated at the site level.

> **NOTE** *You must have the Manage Lists permission to add a workflow to a list, library, or content type. In most cases, the site administrators or individuals who manage specific lists or libraries perform this task.*

Instances

A workflow instance is an individual workflow process running on a specific item or site, based on a specific workflow association. For example, suppose you are using an approval workflow on a list, and the workflow is set to start on item creation. When an item is created, the new workflow instance is created.

Forms

Workflow forms enable users to pass information to a workflow. Examples include prompting the user who starts the workflow for necessary information in order for the workflow to run properly. There are essentially two types of forms in SharePoint 2013 workflows:

➤ **Association form** — This type of form provides the opportunity to collect information when the workflow template is associated with a site, list, document library, or content type. Only reusable or site workflows will have an association form. List and document library workflows have no need for an association form, as they are already associated with a list or document library.

➤ **Initiation form** — This type of form allows for the collection of parameters when a new workflow instance is started.

SharePoint Designer 2013 makes it very easy to create these forms for your workflow. Basically, you tell SharePoint Designer what parameters you wish to collect, and the rest is taken care of for you.

Tasks

Workflow tasks are the primary means by which a user can interact with a running workflow instance. Tasks are typically assigned to one or more users, and when the user completes a task, there is a definable outcome. For example, an outcome for an approval task might be *approved* or *rejected*. Workflow tasks have changed significantly in SharePoint 2013, which provides two task actions:

➤ **Assign a Task** — Used to assign a task to a single participant

➤ **Start a Task Process** — Used to assign a task to multiple participants

Workflow tasks are implemented architecturally as a content type. In previous versions of SharePoint, a new custom content type was created each time you created a task. This tended to clutter up the Content Type gallery, and it was difficult to determine which content type was your custom task. In SharePoint 2013, there is a new content type for workflow tasks that greatly simplifies task creation. The *SharePoint 2013 Workflow task* content type derives from the Task content type, and provides a column called *Task Outcome* that can be used to provide options for completing a task. You can extend this content type to provide additional options, including custom task outcomes.

History

Workflow history is a special list that contains information about what occurred during the execution of a workflow instance. SharePoint writes information to this list during execution, and you can too, using the provided Log to History List workflow action. Writing information to the History list can provide valuable insight into what happened while your workflow executed.

> **WARNING** *There is a SharePoint Timer Job that periodically deletes older workflow history items. Although you can disable this job, it is not recommended, as the Workflow History list can grow very quickly and cause performance problems if not purged. If you need to keep an audit trail of what happens during the workflow, create a separate list and use the Create List Item workflow action to log important workflow information. Another option is to keep information on the item itself: If your workflow is associated with a document library, list, or content type, you can also create a multi-line text column and write information there. Finally, a tip for you: Be sure to select the Append Changes to Existing Text option.*

Creating a Custom Workflow Using SharePoint Designer 2013

The goal of this section is to provide the administrator with an overview of the workflow capabilities in SharePoint Designer 2013. The focus is on illustrating how a workflow is created, the capabilities of the design tool, and how a business process is modeled. It is not intended to educate you about the general capabilities of SharePoint Designer, which is covered in Chapter 18, "Working with SharePoint Designer 2013."

A very common scenario in most organizations is some type of change request. This is a good candidate for a SharePoint workflow. For example, suppose an employee needs new computer hardware and software for a project. Typically this involves some type of paper or digital request, followed by an approval process, and then fulfillment of the request. The following example models such a process with a custom workflow.

Virtual Machine Provisioning Scenario

The IT department has decided to implement a process for managing user requests for infrastructure to be provisioned using virtual machines. Although an InfoPath forms library would provide a much richer form authoring experience, for the purpose of this exercise you will create a simple SharePoint list to capture user input. The initial input form will contain fields to capture required information, such as the number of virtual machines, desired RAM, number of CPUs, and justification and/or reasoning for the new virtual machine.

The following roles will participate in the workflow:

➤ **requestor** — The person making the request

➤ **operations manager** — The person who approves/rejects a request

➤ **operations team** — The person(s) involved with fulfilling the request

The workflow will contain the following stages:

➤ **Started** — During this stage, the workflow will start and perform any necessary initialization functions.

➤ **In Review** — During this stage, an operations manager will evaluate the request and determine whether it should be fulfilled.

    ➤ Upon entering this stage, the Requestor should be notified via e-mail.

    ➤ The Operations Manager should be notified that a new request is awaiting approval via e-mail.

    ➤ If the Operations Manager approves the request, it moves into provisioning of the new machines.

    ➤ If the Operations Manager rejects the request, it moves to the Rejected stage.

➤ **Approved** — During this stage, a member of the operations team attempts to provision the virtual machine(s).

    ➤ Upon entering this stage, the Requestor should be notified via e-mail.

    ➤ Entering this stage is allowed only if the Operations Manager approves the request.

➤ **In Triage** — During this stage, the operations team works to resolve issues that occurred while provisioning the virtual machine(s).

    ➤ Upon entering this stage, the Requestor should be notified via e-mail.

    ➤ If the issue can be resolved, the request moves back into provisioning.

    ➤ If the issue cannot be resolved, the request moves to the Rejected stage.

➤ **Rejected** — This stage indicates that the request has been rejected.

    ➤ Upon entering this stage, the Requestor should be notified via e-mail why the request was rejected.

➤ **Deployed** — Provisioning has completed successfully.

➤ **Canceled** — This stage is used to inform the requestor and operations personnel that issues occurred during provisioning that could not be resolved.

➤ **Finished** — During this stage, the workflow performs any finalization functions and then ends.

Figure 16-17 illustrates the example workflow.

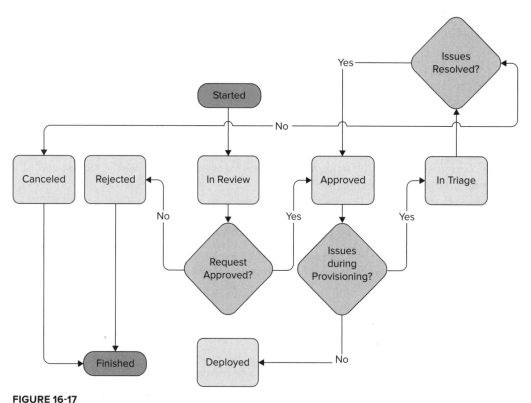

FIGURE 16-17

If during the In Review stage the administrator rejects the request, the workflow will notify the requestor. If the administrator approves the request, it moves to the *Provisioning* stage.

During provisioning, the request is assigned to an operations manager who can create the new virtual machine(s). If the virtual machine(s) are created with no issue, then the workflow completes, and the requestor is notified. If issues are encountered during the provisioning of the virtual machine(s), the request enters a *Triage* stage, during which issues(s) can be resolved by the team. Once the issues are resolved, it will move to provisioning.

Creating Workflow Roles As SharePoint Groups

Before beginning, you need to implement the Operations Managers and Team roles as SharePoint groups. Perform the following steps within your site:

1. Create a SharePoint group called Operations Managers and assign the group Contribute and Edit permissions. Add members to the group as appropriate.

2. Create a SharePoint group called Operations Team and assign the group Contribute permissions. Add members to the group as appropriate.

Creating the Virtual Machine Request List

Before you create your Virtual Machine Request Approval workflow, you need to create a list to capture information for the request. To create the list, perform the following steps:

1. Navigate to the site that will host your custom workflow.

2. Click the Site Actions icon and choose the Add an app option.

3. On the Site Contents page, choose Custom List.

4. Enter **Virtual Machine Requests** for the Name of the custom list, and click Create.

5. After the list has been created, hover over the tile until you see the ellipses (...). Click the ellipses to reveal a flyout menu, and choose the SETTINGS option. This takes you to the list's Settings page.

6. Under Columns, click Create Column.

7. Type **Requested By** for the Column Name.

8. Select Person or Group for the column's data type.

9. For "Require that this column contains information," select Yes.

10. Leave the remainder of the settings for the column at their defaults, and click OK.

11. Repeat the same process to create four additional columns:

    ➤ **Reason** — Type: Multiple Lines of Text, Required.

    ➤ **Amount of Storage** — Type: Number, Required.

    ➤ **Amount of Memory** — Type: Number, Required.

    ➤ **Number of CPUs** — Type: Number, Required.

Now that you have a list to capture the Virtual Machine Request information, the next step is to create the workflow to approve the requests.

Creating the Virtual Machine Request Approval Workflow

Each of the following subsections creates the different stages of the workflow.

Creating the Workflow and Initial Stages

To create the Virtual Machine Request Approval workflow, perform the following steps:

1. Open your site in SharePoint Designer 2013 (SPD).

2. From the navigation pane, click Lists and Libraries.

3. Find the Virtual Machine Requests list you created in the previous section, and select it.

4. From the Ribbon, click the List Workflow button. This will create a new workflow that is associated with the list. The key limitation of this type of workflow is that it cannot be reused.

5. In the Create List Workflow dialog that appears, enter **Virtual Machine Request Approval** for the name of the workflow.

6. Enter a brief description, if desired.

7. Ensure that the SharePoint 2013 Workflow option is the selected Platform Type, and click OK. After the new workflow has been created, SharePoint Designer will display an empty stage, as shown in Figure 16-18. SPD uses stages to model the steps in a business process. You can use the Condition and Action buttons on the Ribbon to define the different checks and actions during the workflow process.

FIGURE 16-18

8. Click the number 1 to the right of Stage, and a text box will appear in which you can rename the stage. Rename it **Start**, and press Enter.

9. From the Ribbon, click the Stage button to insert a new stage. If the Stage button is grayed out, click the Stage: Start banner to enable the Stage button.

10. Rename the new stage **In Review**.

11. Create the following stages using the same process, and be sure to save your work when you are done:

➤ Approved

➤ Deployed

➤ In Triage

➤ Rejected

➤ Cancelled

➤ Finished

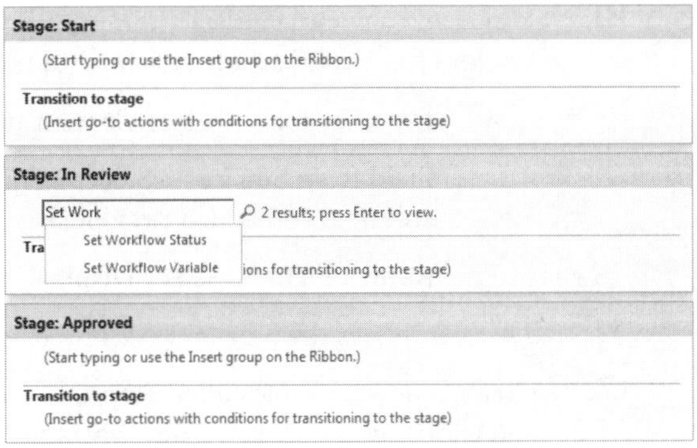

FIGURE 16-19

Configuring the In Review Stage

Recall that during the In Review stage, a task to approve the request is assigned to the Operations Managers group you created in previous steps. If a person in this role approves the request, it moves to the Approved stage. Otherwise, the request moves to the Rejected stage.

1. Hover your mouse over the stage In Review until you see a thin, horizontal orange bar.

2. Start typing the words **Set Work**, and then press Enter. As shown in Figure 16-19, select Set Workflow Status from the drop-down menu to insert the Set Workflow Status action.

> **NOTE** *You can also insert workflow actions from the Ribbon by clicking Action and choosing the desired workflow action.*

3. In the Set Workflow Status action, click the hyperlink labeled "this message" and enter the following text: **In Review.** Now that you have set the status of the workflow, you will create a new task and assign it to the Operations Managers group.

4. Hover your mouse over the stage In Review until you see a thin orange bar under the Set Workflow Status action you created in the previous steps, enter the word **Start**, and then press Enter. From the four items on the menu, select "Start a task process," which will insert the Start a Task Process workflow action.

5. In the Start a Task Process action, click the hyperlink labeled "these users." This will launch the Start a Task Process dialog.

6. To specify the Participants for the task process, click the ellipses (...) to launch the Select Users dialog. Find the Operations Managers group, click Add, and then click OK.

7. Type **New Virtual Machine Request** for the Task Title.

8. Under the Description text box, click the "Open editor for body" button. This will launch the String Builder dialog.

9. In the text box, type **Please approve the virtual machine request for.** Insert the caret after the text "for" and click Add or Change Lookup. This will launch the Lookup for a String dialog.

10. You need to complete the different options to perform the data lookup, so configure the Lookup for String dialog as follows, clicking OK when you are done:

> ➤ **Data Source** — Select Current Item.

> ➤ **Field from Source** — Select Requested By. Note that this was one of the custom columns you added previously.

> ➤ **Return Field** — Select Display Name.

11. That completes the Start a Task Process configuration, so you can click OK.

12. Create a new variable called ApprovalOutcome by clicking the Variable:Outcome hyperlink and choosing the Create a new variable... option. Click OK. Now it is time to determine the outcome of the task and the next stage.

13. Hover your mouse over the stage In Review until you see a thin, orange bar, and click the bar. Then click the Condition button on the Ribbon and choose the "If value equals value" option.

14. The condition statement includes two different **value** options, both of which are actually hyperlinks. Click the first hyperlink that is labeled **value,** and it will launch the Define Workflow Lookup dialog. If the dialog doesn't open, click the **fx** button. Select Workflow Variables and Parameters for the Data Source, and for Field from Source, select Variable: ApprovalOutcome. Click OK when you are done.

15. Click the second hyperlinked that is labeled **value,** and choose Approved from the menu.

16. Within the If branch, hover your mouse until you see the thin orange bar, and click the bar. From the Action button menu, choose the "Go to a stage" option.

17. Within the Go to a stage action, click the "a stage" hyperlink, and select Approved.

18. Add a Go to a stage action to the Else branch. Within the Go to a stage action, click "a stage" and select Rejected. At this point, the In Review stage should resemble Figure 16-20.

Hopefully that wasn't too painful, and by now you should have the basics down. The next sections are much briefer, as the concepts are very similar.

Configuring the Approved Stage

During this stage, a task to approve the request is assigned to the Operations Managers group you created in previous steps. If a person in this role approves the request, it moves to the Deployed stage. Otherwise, the request moves to the In Triage stage.

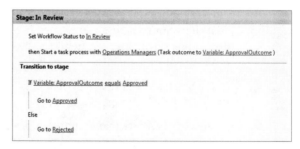

FIGURE 16-20

1. Insert a Set Workflow Status action and choose Approved from the menu as the status value.

2. Insert a Start a Task Process action. This is the task that will prompt the Operations Team to deploy the new virtual machines.

3. Under Transition to Stage, insert an "If value equals value" condition.

4. Configure the If branch to go to the Deployed stage if the DeploymentOutcome variable equals Approved.

5. Configure the Else branch to go to the In Triage stage. The completed stage should resemble Figure 16-21.

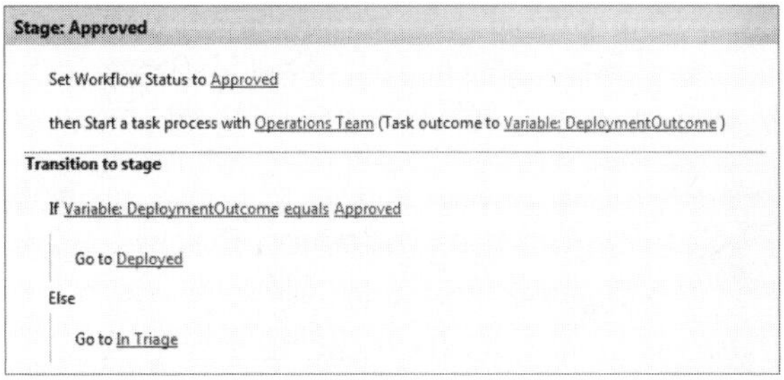

Stage: Approved

Set Workflow Status to Approved

then Start a task process with Operations Team (Task outcome to Variable: DeploymentOutcome)

Transition to stage

If Variable: DeploymentOutcome equals Approved

    Go to Deployed

Else

    Go to In Triage

FIGURE 16-21

Configuring the Deployed Stage

In this stage, the status of the workflow is changed to reflect the current stage, and an e-mail is sent to the requestor to notify them of the request's status. The workflow then moves to the final stage, which is Finished.

1. Insert a Set Workflow Status action, and enter Deployed as the status value.

2. You need to notify the Requestor that the request has been deployed. Insert a Send an Email action, and configure the e-mail to be sent to the User who created the current item, notifying them of the deployment.

3. Under Transition to stage, configure the workflow to go to the Finished stage, and save your work. The completed stage should look like what is shown in Figure 16-22.

Stage: Deployed

Set Workflow Status to Deployed

then Email Current Item:Created By

Transition to stage

Go to Finished

FIGURE 16-22

Configuring the Rejected Stage

In this stage, the status of the workflow is changed to reflect the current stage, and an e-mail is sent to the requestor to notify them that the request for virtual machines has been rejected. In the e-mail, the manager will have outlined the reasons for the rejection. The workflow will then move to the Finished stage. Once your SPD entries are made, your complete Rejected stage should resemble what is shown in Figure 16-23. Be sure to save your work.

Stage: Rejected

Set Workflow Status to Rejected

then Email Current Item:Created By

Transition to stage

Go to Finished

FIGURE 16-23

Configuring the In Triage Stage

In this stage, the status of the workflow is changed, and an e-mail is sent to the requestor to notify them of the current stage of the request. The workflow is in this stage because of issues encountered during provisioning of the virtual machines. Therefore, a task to resolve any issues, and approve the request, will be assigned to the Operations Team group you created in previous steps. If the issues are resolved and the request is approved, the request moves to the Approved stage. Otherwise, an e-mail is sent to the requestor informing them that issues associated with their request could not be resolved, and the workflow moves to the Cancelled stage. The configured In Triage stage is shown in Figure 16-24. Be sure to save your work.

Configuring the Cancelled Stage

As you have done in every other stage, the status of the workflow is changed to reflect the current stage. You send the requestor an e-mail to notify them of the stage of the request, and this time you should notify (cc:) the Operations Managers and the Operations Team members as well. You could include an explanation regarding why the workflow has completed unsuccessfully, at least from the requestor's point of view. The workflow then moves to the final stage, which is Finished. Your completed stage should resemble what is shown in Figure 16-25. Be sure to save your work.

FIGURE 16-24

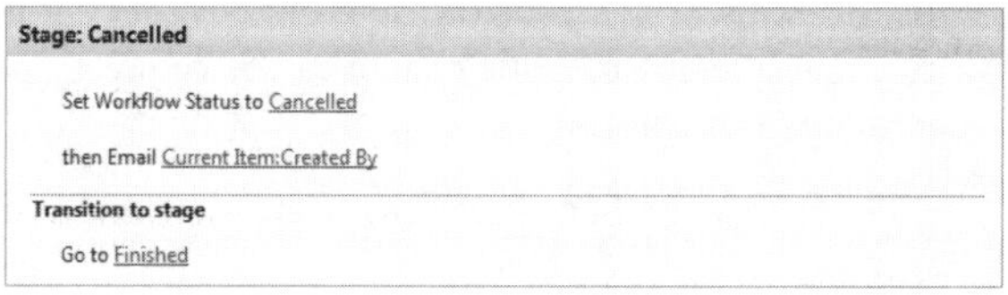

FIGURE 16-25

Configuring the Finished Stage

This simple stage merely provides a reusable and consistent exit mechanism from the workflow. You could also use the Log to History List to write any information you would like to the history information of the workflow. The completed stage is shown in Figure 16-26.

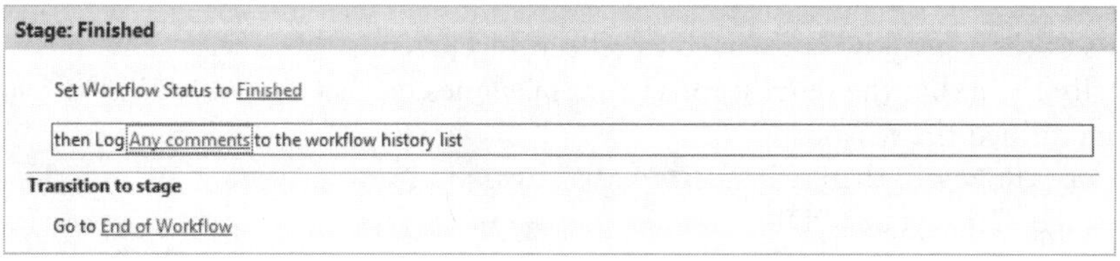

FIGURE 16-26

Configuring the Start Stage

You thought we forgot about this one, didn't you? To begin the process, you notify the requestor that the request has been received, and then you proceed to the In Review stage. Although this stage may not seem very useful, you could use it for a number of purposes, such as writing information to the history list or to a separate list to ensure that the information is retained long-term. The completed stage is shown in Figure 16-27.

You can also configure your workflow to start automatically when a new list item is created. To do so, select the Workflows tab, click the Virtual Machine Request Approval link, and enable the check box "Start workflow automatically when an item is created." Be sure to save your work and publish your workflow. You can test your new workflow by creating a new list item and watching the process as each stage is approved or rejected.

This completes the process for creating your custom workflow using SPD. It should have given you a feel for what is involved in modeling a business process with an SPD workflow.

FIGURE 16-27

Workflow Visualization Using Visio 2013

SharePoint Designer 2013 and Visio 2013 Premium Edition are integrated in a number of ways. SharePoint Designer 2010 and Visio 2010 also provided some integration that enabled Visio process designs to be imported into SharePoint Designer, and exported from SharePoint Designer into Visio, but the two applications were clearly separate. In Visio 2013, the two products are now fully integrated, so you can have two different views of your custom workflow. You need both SharePoint Designer 2013 and Visio 2013 Premium in order to have this capability.

The intent of this section is not to discuss Visio's capabilities, but rather to emphasize the value of this new integration capability when creating custom workflows. For a quick peek, click the Views button on the Ribbon on the design page of the workflow you created previously in SharePoint Designer 2013. Note that there are two options: Text-Based Designer and Visual Designer, as shown in Figure 16-28. Click the Visual Designer option, and you should see what is shown in Figure 16-29.

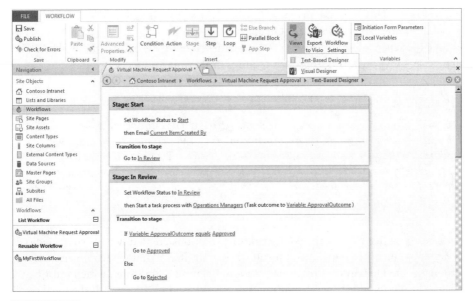

FIGURE 16-28

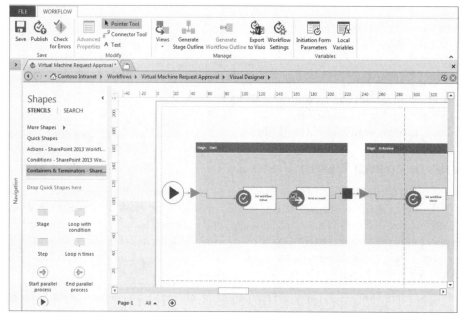

FIGURE 16-29

Creating Custom Workflows Using Visual Studio 2012

Visual Studio 2012 is another option for creating custom workflows, but this option is targeted at professional developers. This is by far the most flexible option, and it can be used to create almost any type of workflow organization could need. Creating a custom workflow in Visual Studio requires an experienced developer, and typically a developer with quite a bit of SharePoint development expertise. Obviously, this approach requires more time and money versus the SharePoint Designer approach.

> **NOTE** *Workflows created with Visual Studio 2012 do not allow the use of .NET code — all workflows are declarative. This is a big change from creating SharePoint 2010 custom workflows using Visual Studio 2010, which did allow .NET code. If you need to utilize .NET code in your custom workflow, you must create a separate web service to host your code, and call the web service using the Call Web Service action.*

In addition, it is a best practice to package your workflow solutions created with Visual Studio 2012 .wsp files. They are subsequently deployed and installed to your SharePoint environment as features by the farm administrator. This process requires additional planning and time, which must be taken into account when considering this type of solution, but Visual Studio 2012 is still the ideal method for creating complex, reusable workflow solutions.

SUMMARY

A successful SharePoint 2013 collaborative solution effectively incorporates workflow into its strategic plans. By utilizing the capability to automate various business processes, your organization can reap the benefits of consistency and efficiency without the negative costs related to process management.

SharePoint 2013 enables the creation of powerful and scalable workflows by integrating with the new Azure Workflow Server. By moving workflow to dedicated application servers, SharePoint 2013 can finally provide the performance and scalability that was lacking in previous versions.

SharePoint 2013, Office 2013, Visio 2013, SharePoint Designer 2013, and Visual Studio 2012 all contain several new and improved toolsets that can be leveraged to create workflow solutions. From creating flowcharts and defining processes through the building of workflows, users have the tools needed to implement successful solutions.

17

Integrating Office Clients with SharePoint

WHAT'S IN THIS CHAPTER

➤ What Office 2013 and SharePoint 2013 share in common

➤ Integrating the various Office clients

➤ Managing Office 2013 through Group Policy

Although technologies like SkyDrive and other cloud-sharing systems are being used by an increasing number of organizations, some workers are still sending documents over e-mail. Even though it is better than using "sneakernet," this practice still creates confusion. With multiple versions of a document floating around, who has the latest version? Who is working on the document? Who made changes? Sending documents this way also causes wasted space on e-mail servers. Consider the cumulative effect of a few people sending a document back and forth four or five times. That is a significant amount of wasted space and efficiency. Compare all that effort to having one, version-controlled copy of the file that anyone can edit and easily track, in one place, and the answer is clear. SharePoint integration with Office can save you time and money.

One of the biggest advantages that SharePoint has over any other collaboration platform is its integration with Microsoft Office; and as long as Office reigns supreme over the information worker's desktop, SharePoint will be king of the collaboration platforms. Interestingly, although most users know that this integration exists, very few can identify exact integration points or take the time to explore the depths of this integration. This chapter provides a close look at the fun and helpful things you can do when you combine Office 2013 and SharePoint 2013.

WHAT OFFICE 2013 AND SHAREPOINT 2013 SHARE IN COMMON

With the exception of the Backstage view, the look of Office has largely remained the same since 2007. The Ribbon interface provides a common set of menus that apply to all applications in the Office suite. Once you are familiar with it, you can use any of the products with ease. Simply put: learn it once, use it everywhere. To that end, many of the SharePoint collaboration features reside in the same place across the Office applications. There are also a multitude of points where Office and SharePoint interact with each other. If a user would like to upload a document, edit a document, or tag an existing document, these tasks can easily be done without ever leaving the client application.

Office 2013 also includes the Office Upload Center. As its name suggests, Upload Center acts as the intermediary between Office and SharePoint. When you save a file destined for SharePoint, Upload Center handles the transfer and alerts you to any errors.

SkyDrive Pro users have the capability to click the Sync button in SharePoint libraries, making the documents available offline in Windows Explorer. Office 2013's Backstage view is also integrated with SkyDrive Pro, enabling users to save documents to their SharePoint MySite, for example.

> **NOTE** *SkyDrive Pro is the replacement for SharePoint Workspaces in Office 2010 and has nothing to do with the SkyDrive you know and love. It allows you to take SharePoint list and libraries offline and access that data. It is installed as part of Office 2013.*

This section describes how you can get the most out of Office 2013 collaboration and integration. The first part covers connecting to SharePoint from within Office, and the second covers connecting to Office from within SharePoint 2013.

Connecting to SharePoint from within Microsoft Office 2013 Applications

For many employees, working with Office documents is a fundamental part of doing their job — they are living inside of Word and Excel documents. When those documents reside inside of a SharePoint document library, the burden of managing and storing them is eliminated. Better yet, with Office 2013 (and to a lesser extent Office 2010), users can enjoy the added advantage of *live co-authoring*. No more worrying about who currently has "the document" — everyone can do their part at the same time.

Live Co-Authoring

Introduced in Office 2010, live co-authoring enables multiple users to work on the same document in near real time without having to check it in or out. Checking out a document can be a work stopper because it locks the document exclusively for the user who checked it out, preventing anyone else from editing it. Because live co-authoring bypasses checkouts, it can greatly increase productivity. It also offers a number of collaboration features. For example, a handy Send a Message feature enables a user to send an e-mail or instant message to everyone working on the document, making it easy to share ideas or corrections. When a collaborator saves the document it is saved back to SharePoint, and shortly after that all the other collaborators will see an updated icon, letting them know the document has been updated. Each user's changes are saved back to SharePoint and reflected in the open version of the other users.

To understand how this looks in the real world, suppose your department is responsible for writing a section of a Microsoft Word document that describes the process of adding new employees to the company's IT systems. Your section of the document deals with adding the new hire's personal information into the company's Active Directory, while your co-worker's section covers granting the proper permissions in the company's SharePoint site collections. When either of you starts typing, a dotted outline bracket appears on the left side of the paragraph you have started. This indicates that the paragraph is locked, and other users will see the locked paragraph on their documents.

Your locked paragraph will appear as a solid bracket, with your username next to it for the other editors. See Figure 17-1 for an example of what the editor sees and Figure 17-2 for what the other author(s) sees. When the document is saved and refreshed, all changes from other users will be highlighted, so you can easily identify what changed. Changes can also be reviewed with Word's comparison feature, which is covered in detail later in the chapter.

FIGURE 17-1

FIGURE 17-2

Determining When a Document Is Being Actively Co-Authored

When a document is being edited from a SharePoint document library, the Save button changes. The icon will include a pair of green "refresh" arrows, as shown in Figure 17-3. This means the document is being co-authored.

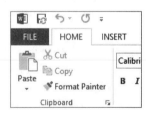

FIGURE 17-3

An icon also appears in the status bar at the bottom of the screen, indicating the number of users currently editing the document, as shown in Figure 17-4. Clicking the people icon will display a list of the users' names. Each name is clickable and can be expanded to display more information about the person, with various ways to contact them. Figure 17-5 shows Grant Young expanded.

FIGURE 17-4

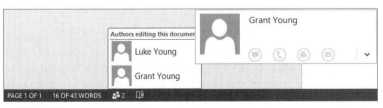

FIGURE 17-5

When a user clicks Save, all other collaborators are notified in the lower-right corner that updates are available. Clicking the notification shown in Figure 17-6 refreshes the document to the newest version.

FIGURE 17-6

As users have the updates added to their document, they are highlighted in green so the changes are easily located. (Hopefully you are a fan of green.)

Live Co-Authoring Compatibility with Other Office Versions

The release of Office 2013 means that there could now be users accessing documents with Office 2007, Office 2010, and Office 2013. Users with Office 2007 should definitely upgrade if possible; otherwise, they will be missing out on a key feature of SharePoint. In fact, lacking this capability can actually hinder users of Office versions prior to Office 2010. When a user opens a document from SharePoint with Office 2007, SharePoint creates a lock on the document that prevents other users from using co-authoring or editing that document. Additionally, documents saved in an Office 2007 format and uploaded to SharePoint cannot be co-authored either.

> **NOTE** *While Office 2007 renders co-authoring completely useless, note that Office 2010 enables co-authoring but only in a reduced functionality mode. For example, the Live Layout feature is disabled if Office 2010 is used for co-authoring. The best-case scenario is for everyone in the organization to upgrade to Office 2013 at the same time.*

Backstage View

Retained from Office 2010, all Microsoft Office 2013 applications offer what is called the *Backstage view*. This feature replaced the old "File" menu from Office 2007. It includes a ton of extra information about the file as well as a few buttons for interacting with SharePoint.

Of the many tabs it offers, the most useful for SharePoint users is the Info tab. The Info tab stores vital information about the file, including the file's name and location. Most of the information on this tab either interacts with or consumes data from SharePoint. Figure 17-7 shows the Info tab while not connected to SharePoint, whereas Figure 17-8 shows the Info tab while connected. Notice that while connected to SharePoint you get much more information, including the list of current editors if co-authoring, and additional metadata properties. The Department and Status properties pull their data directly from the SharePoint document library columns. To get all of the properties to show, click the text Show All properties at the bottom of the screen. The following list describes the sections of the Info tab:

➤ **People Currently Editing** — This section is displayed only if the document is being actively co-authored. The names of any users working on the document are displayed here.

➤ **Send a Message** — This section is displayed only if the document is being actively co-authored. Selecting the drop-down provides two options: one to send an e-mail message to the other editors, and another to start an instant messaging session with everyone editing the document.

FIGURE 17-7

FIGURE 17-8

➤ **Protect Document** — This section contains a number of features. Mark as Final lets readers know the document is done with the editing process. The status for the document is set to final, and all typing, editing commands, and proofing marks are turned off. The document is also set to read-only. When a user opens the document, a notification in the upper-left-hand corner indicates that the document has been marked final. Restrict Editing allows document authors to limit what types of edits can be made to a file. Restrict Access is an option related to SharePoint's support of digital rights management (DRM) through Active Directory Services. DRM is outside the scope of this book; but if you have set it up, SharePoint will honor the settings specified here.

➤ **Versions and Check Out** — This provides a quick date- and time-stamped list of the last 10 local versions of the document. An expanded list can be accessed by clicking the link Show All Versions at the bottom. Clicking Manage Versions will retrieve the latest version information from SharePoint and compare the open document with the last version on the SharePoint server, or the most recent major version. Note that document library versioning must be turned on in order to look at previous versions of the document.

The Share tab offers various methods to publish the document without necessarily using SharePoint. This is useful for collaborating with individuals who might not have access to the SharePoint farm:

➤ **Invite People** — With this option you can save your document out to your SkyDrive. Once saved, you will be prompted to provide the information for people with whom you would like to share the document. The sharing functionality that is native to SkyDrive Office is just taking advantage of it.

➤ **E-mail** — When this option is selected, a number of additional options are displayed, explaining the difference between sending the file as an e-mail attachment versus sending a link to the SharePoint document. As stated at the beginning of the chapter, when users understand the benefit of keeping files inside SharePoint, collaboration becomes much more efficient.

➤ **Present Online** — This feature allows you to share Word and PowerPoint documents across the internet using the Office Presentation Service. The great thing is, assuming you have a Microsoft account, it just works. Once you begin presenting you just need to share the provided link.

➤ **Publish as Blog Post** — This option provides the capability to publish the document to a SharePoint blog. It is covered in more detail later in the chapter in the "Blogging with Microsoft Word" section.

Taking a Look at the Document Panel

In Microsoft Word, Excel, and PowerPoint, the document panel enables you to view the metadata associated with the file, from within the application. Metadata refers to the properties associated with each file in a document library. Columns in document libraries are considered metadata, and contain information about each file, such as Created, Created By, and Modified (just three of several standard metadata columns associated with a default document library). You can add custom metadata to libraries simply by creating new columns.

For an example of the use of metadata, consider a document library that contains company policies. This document library has a metadata column called "Department." When a file is added to the library, it can be associated with a department by picking the appropriate department name in the column. This information can also be added in the document panel in Microsoft Word.

Figure 17-9 shows the Document Properties panel for a document titled, A neat document title. The metadata fields associated with the document library "Title", "Department", and "Status" are shown, and are editable from within Word.

FIGURE 17-9

If the current user does not have at least Contributor permissions on the target document within SharePoint, the document information panel will be displayed in read-only mode.

By default, the document information panel is not displayed when documents are opened. To view it, follow these steps:

1. Open a document from a SharePoint document library.

2. Click the File tab.

3. The Info tab will be the first highlighted tab in the list. On the right-hand side, click Properties.

4. Click Show Document Panel.

When the Document Panel window is shown on the main screen, you can click the Document Properties drop-down in the upper-left corner to switch between different views of the properties. Each view contains different data about the document.

To enable the document panel to display automatically when a document is opened, you can modify the settings for the SharePoint document library. This can be done either through SharePoint Designer 2013 or from a browser by editing the document library's settings. Both methods are discussed next.

Displaying the Document Panel Using the Browser

The following steps illustrate how to use the browser to configure the document panel to appear. You will need the appropriate SharePoint permissions (most likely designer level or greater) to do the following tasks. If you are using the default SharePoint groups you would need to be in the Owners group:

1. In the document library's Library tab, click Library Settings in the Settings section.

2. In the General Settings section, click Advanced Settings.

3. In the Content Types section, change the "Allow management of content types" option to Yes. Click OK.

4. The Document Library Settings page will now contain a section called Content Types. It may be necessary to scroll down the page a little bit to view this section.

5. All the content types for the library are listed here. By default, the only content type is Document. Click this.

6. In the Settings section for this content type, click Document Information Panel settings.

7. Enabling the check box in the Show Always section forces the document information panel to be displayed each time files of this content type are opened.

Displaying the Document Panel Using SharePoint Designer 2013

These steps require that SharePoint Designer 2013 has been downloaded and installed on a client machine that can access the SharePoint farm via the Internet. For more information on SharePoint Designer, see Chapter 18. The price still hasn't changed (free), so you might as well embrace it. As with the previous section you need the appropriate permissions to perform the following steps:

1. In the document library's Library tab, click Edit Library in the Customize Library section. Clicking Edit Library will launch SharePoint Designer 2013. You may be prompted to allow the connection.

2. After loading, SharePoint Designer should automatically take you to the document library page. This can be confirmed by looking at the List Information box. Ensure that the Web Address and Name values are correct for the document library you are editing.

3. Click Administration Web Page in the Ribbon.

4. In the General Settings section, click Advanced Settings.

5. In the Content Types section, change the "Allow management of content types" option to Yes. Click OK.

6. The Document Library Settings page will now contain a section called Content Types. It may be necessary to scroll down the page a little bit to view this section.

7. All the content types for the library are listed here. By default, the only content type is Document. Click this.

8. In the Settings section for this content type, click Document Information Panel settings.

9. Enabling the check box in the Show Always section forces the document information panel to be displayed each time files of this content type are opened.

Connecting to Office 2013 from SharePoint 2013

Each library and list in SharePoint 2013 can be connected to the logged-in user's Office client software. From a library, there is a Connect & Export section of the contextual Ribbon inside the Library tab, as shown in Figure 17-10.

FIGURE 17-10

Depending on the current type of list or library, different options will appear in this area:

➤ **Sync Library to Computer** — This option enables users to create a synchronized copy of the library on their local workstation using SkyDrive Pro 2013, which is a desktop application included with Office 2013. The library will appear under Favorites in Windows Explorer on the user's local workstation. This option should be used with caution; document libraries can become very large, so syncing large document libraries could potently fill user hard drives. Another consideration is bandwidth; a user attempting to sync over a VPN, for example, could bog down the network for other users.

➤ **Connect to Office** — This option creates shortcuts inside Office applications such as Word, Excel, and PowerPoint, enabling users to quickly save files into connected document libraries. This is very similar to bookmarking a page in a browser. The shortcuts appear in the Backstage view inside the Office application. This option is grayed out unless the User Profile Sync Service and My Sites have been configured in the farm, both of which are covered in Chapter 14, "Configuring User Profiles and Social Computing."

➤ **Connect to Outlook** — In SharePoint, certain types of lists and libraries can be added to Outlook. This means that the item will be added as a linked location inside the Outlook client. Once connected, items appear under the heading "SharePoint Lists" at the bottom of Outlook's folder view. Document libraries, task lists, contacts, calendars, and discussion boards are a few examples of what can be connected. You can access and edit connected list items without ever leaving Outlook. If you need to get to the SharePoint document library, you can do so by right-clicking the list and selecting Open in Web Browser.

> **NOTE** *This feature doesn't always work smoothly. For instance, in order to avoid having to log in each time Outlook attempts to sync you may have to add the SharePoint site to your trusted sites. If you are using single sign-on you might have to create a custom security level to force the "Automatic Logon with current user name and password" authentication option. In general, adjustments on the browser side may be needed to smooth out the process and allow you to get the most out of the feature.*

➤ **Export to Excel** — This option enables you to export the current list to an Excel spreadsheet. It takes both the data in the list and the column values as well. This is useful when you want to perform a deeper analysis of the data, or when a static list needs to be sent outside the organization.

➤ **Open in Project** — This option is available in task lists. It enables you to schedule tasks and create reports in Microsoft Project. Changes made inside of project will be synced to the list.

➤ **Open with Access** — This handy integration functionality enables you to connect a SharePoint list to Microsoft Access. When this is done, the live SharePoint list data is available as a table in an Access database.

Now that some of the more common integration features have been covered, the rest of this chapter details each of the Microsoft Office 2013 applications as they relate to SharePoint.

INTEGRATING SHAREPOINT 2013 WITH WORD 2013

Microsoft Word 2013 is used for document creation and editing, and it has its own set of unique integration points with SharePoint. This section covers the following Word capabilities:

➤ Comparing document versions

➤ Document barcodes

➤ Quick Parts

➤ Blogging

Comparing Document Versions

From the Review tab in Word, you can compare various versions of a document to one another. In order to make use of this feature, versioning must be enabled on the document library. By default, versioning is not enabled. Follow these steps to enable versioning:

1. Select the document library from the SharePoint site.

2. Click the Library tab.

3. In the Ribbon, click Library Settings in the Settings section.

4. In General Settings, click Versioning settings.

5. In Document Version History, choose Create major versions. That way, each time the file is saved, it becomes a new version number. You can create major and minor (draft) versions if necessary to work on drafts and then publish each file when it is ready only for public consumption as a major version. In this section you can also specify the number of major and minor versions to keep in the history.

6. Click OK.

To view the file's version information from within SharePoint, click the ellipsis next to a document. In the fly-out menu, click the ellipsis and choose Version History. The version history shows file version numbers with the dates and names of the users who modified them. Previous versions can be opened, but sometimes it's hard to tell exactly what was changed in the document, especially if it's a large document or only minor changes were made. In situations like this, Word's compare feature can be used to view both versions side by side, which makes finding the changes easy.

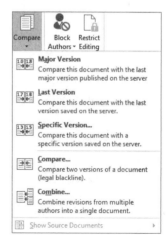

In Word, open a document from a SharePoint document library. Click the Review tab, and select Compare. Figure 17-11 shows the options to compare specific versions to each other, or even combine versions.

When versions are compared side by side, the differences are indicated in red, making it readily apparent what the differences between the two versions are. You would have to look at who saved a given version to find the culprit for those changes you don't like.

FIGURE 17-11

Working with Document Barcodes

The Information Management Policy settings in SharePoint have several capabilities, but the main one related to Office integration is the capability to insert barcodes into documents. Barcodes are often part of a records management strategy, and are used when your document management solution requires that unique barcodes must be associated with, and inserted into, each document.

Barcodes are one aspect of records management. Many companies still need to have hard copies of documents, such as a law office. In this case, documents are created using Word and uploaded to SharePoint for storage. Assuming both the court and the client need copies for their records, how can the law office link the physical document, which can be moved from one file cabinet to another, while at the same time keep track of its electronic counterpart? Barcodes can be a good solution, by assigning a unique barcode to any document uploaded to SharePoint. The assigned barcode can be configured to display on the document when it's printed out.

Barcodes policies can be set up at the site collection level, or on an individual document library. Follow these steps to enable the barcode functionality for a library:

1. Select the document library from the SharePoint site.

2. Click the Library tab.

3. In the Ribbon, click Library Settings in the Settings section.

4. In the Content Types section, change "Allow management of content types" to Yes. Click OK.

5. Back on the Document Library Settings page, under Permissions and Management, click Information management policy settings.

6. Under Content Type, click Document.

7. In the Barcodes section, click Enable Barcodes. Optionally, select the option to prompt users to insert a barcode before saving or printing.

8. Click OK.

Now that you have barcodes enabled you can view them from Word using the Info tab. There is a section called Information Management Policy where you will find relevant information.

Using Quick Parts

Quick Parts in Word are fields that you can insert into your document that will display document metadata from SharePoint within your document. This is really useful when data needs to stay with the document, especially when printed. To put it another way, Quick Parts add context to documents. Let's say you are in charge of training new hires. Typically, such employees receive some sort of handbook with a printed list of policies or other information. Policies can change quickly, so how can you tell if a policy in the handbook is outdated and needs to be reprinted? Quick Parts can help solve this problem.

Using Quick Parts, you can add a field to the document that will display the last date and time the document was modified. This can be done anywhere in the document. For this example, the footer section in a Word document is used:

1. Open a Word document from a SharePoint document library.

2. Scroll to the bottom of the document, right-click in the footer area, and select Edit Footer.

3. Type a word or phrase to give the Quick Part some context — for example, "Last Updated:".

4. Click the Insert tab.

5. Click Quick Parts in the Text section.

6. From the drop-down click Field.

7. Under Field Names, select SaveDate.

8. Select a format in which the date should be displayed and click OK.

The date will be refreshed automatically from SharePoint the next time the document is opened. If you wanted to take this a step further, you could also include the full name or username of the last person to update the document. Follow the same procedure just outlined and select LastSavedBy as the field name. Figure 17-12 shows an example of a useful footer you can easily construct using this technique.

FIGURE 17-12

The Quick Parts feature opens the door to a nearly unlimited number of automation options and the creation of custom solutions. Unfortunately, a deep dive into their use is outside the scope of this book.

Blogging in Microsoft Word

Microsoft Word can be used to easily create and post blog entries right into SharePoint and other types of blogging software. This section covers the Word 2013 blog integration with SharePoint 2013. Here is a list of some blogging terminology to be aware of:

➤ **Blog post** — A post is your content, which can be about anything. Some posts are personal, some are educational, and sometimes they are just a simple rant. Typically, posts are displayed chronologically, with the most recent entry displayed first.

➤ **Blog site** – This is the location on the web where the blog resides and the posts can be viewed. A uniform resource locator (URL) is associated with the blog; for example, `http://portal.contoso.com/sites/IT-Blog`. SharePoint provides a template that enables you to quickly and easily get your own blog up and running.

➤ **Blog account** – The account is the URL and user account information associated with the blog site. Out of the box, Word supports the following blog provider options: Blogger, SharePoint blog, Telligent Community, TypePad, WordPress, and Other. If you choose Other, you need to provide the connection information and then cross your fingers that Word can handle it.

To quickly create a new blog site in SharePoint, follow these steps:

1. From a SharePoint site, click the gear icon.

2. Select View Site Contents.

3. Under Subsites, click New subsite.

4. Add a title for your blog.

5. Add a website address — for example, http://yourservername/myblog.

6. Select the Blog template in the Collaboration tab.

7. Click Create.

Once the blog is set up, you're ready to add your first blog post. Open Word and create a new document. When the post is ready, go to Backstage view and click the Share tab. Select Publish as a Blog Post. If this is your first blog post from Word, you'll be prompted to register your blog account.

To set up your account, follow these steps:

1. Click the Publish as Blog Post button.

2. The document will reload in the Web Layout view, and you will be prompted to register a blog account. Click Register Now.

3. Use the drop-down menu to select "SharePoint blog" as the blog provider.

4. Click Next.

5. Enter the URL of the blog.

6. Click OK. Add your username and password if prompted.

7. Once registration is completed, you will be able to add a post title. After entering the post title, click Publish in the Ribbon.

A confirmation date and time stamp will be displayed on the document to let you know publishing was successful. Congratulations on your first blog post! Go to the SharePoint site and check it out.

There is yet another way to create a new SharePoint blog post in Word. On the blog site in SharePoint, there is a set of links called Blog tools on the right side of the page, which is visible only to content owners and editors. Click Launch blogging app and Word will open in Web Layout view with a blank blog post.

If you have an existing Word document that was not created as a blog post, it can still be published to a blog. Follow these steps:

1. Open the document in Word.

2. In Backstage view, click the Share tab.

3. Select Publish as Blog Post under Share.

4. Click the Publish as a Blog Post button from the panel on the right.

Now that you see how easy it is to blog, thanks to the power of SharePoint and Word, you have no excuses. Start blogging. No matter how trivial you might think the information you are sharing is, chances are someone else out there doesn't know it and would like to. Even just blogging all the error messages you encounter in a day and the fix you used makes for great information and could save someone trouble.

INTEGRATING SHAREPOINT 2013 WITH EXCEL

This section describes the ways in which Excel 2013 is integrated with SharePoint 2013. You will learn about importing from and exporting to SharePoint 2013, displaying charts, and a little bit about Excel Services. You can find additional details about Excel Services in Chapter 8, "Configuring SharePoint for Business Intelligence."

Importing Spreadsheets into SharePoint

The capability to import spreadsheet data into SharePoint is very powerful, enabling workers to be more efficient in their daily tasks. Any properly formatted Excel spreadsheet can be imported into SharePoint as a new custom list. If you can simply upload a spreadsheet into a document library and take turns with other users checking it out and working on it, why would you want to import the spreadsheet? What is the difference?

The difference is quite significant. Consider a scenario in which managers are tasked with entering their sales figures in a shared spreadsheet every day. If that spreadsheet is in a document library, the managers must take turns checking it out, adding their sales numbers, and remembering to check it back in. Conversely, when the spreadsheet is imported as a custom list in SharePoint instead, users are simply creating new items in the same list. Besides the obvious efficiency gain, a benefit of working in a SharePoint list is the capability to use SharePoint alerts. Once the data has been collected, it can still be exported back out to spreadsheet format if needed.

> **WARNING** *A spreadsheet must be properly formatted in order for it to be imported using the Import Spreadsheet App from within a SharePoint site. Each column heading becomes a new column in the SharePoint list, so ensure that row 1 (and only row 1) contains the column headings. The list data must begin at row 2, and there should be no blank rows among the data portion of the spreadsheet.*

Because column headings will become SharePoint list column names, it's a good idea to keep these short. Keep in mind that if a more descriptive column heading is needed, there is a Description field associated with each SharePoint column that can be used for further clarification to end users. Column A in the spreadsheet will become the Title column in the SharePoint list, so it is a good idea to use a Text field as this first column before importing.

Another way to move data from Excel to SharePoint is from within Excel. Select the spreadsheet's data region, click the Format as Table button, and pick a style. From this new table, click the Design tab in the Ribbon. The Export button provides the option to Export Table to SharePoint List.

Exporting to Excel

As mentioned earlier in the section, "Connecting to Office 2013 from SharePoint 2013," lists and libraries contain an Export to Excel button that you can use to export the current view to Excel. To access this feature, click the List or Library tab in SharePoint's Ribbon. Export to Excel is located in the Connect & Export section of the Ribbon. This feature provides a convenient way to do a deeper analysis of items contained in the list or library. The way this works is a new spreadsheet is created with a link back to the SharePoint list. This way the data in the spreadsheet can be refreshed with the latest SharePoint data at any time.

Displaying Charts

The Chart Web Part from SharePoint 2010 is no longer available. If you used the Chart Web Part in SharePoint Server 2010, you will need to use an other SharePoint functionality, such as Excel Services (see next section) or the new PowerView, to display a chart in a SharePoint site.

Using the Excel Web Access Web Part

Users of SharePoint Enterprise Edition have access to the Excel Web Access Web Part as part of Excel Services. This Web Part can be used to display data from within a spreadsheet that has been uploaded to a SharePoint document library, as shown in Figure 17-13.

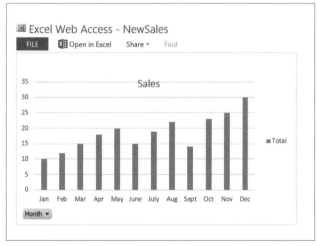

FIGURE 17-13

You can display the entire spreadsheet or just specific portions of it such as ranges and charts. When interactivity is enabled in the Web Part properties, users can work with the spreadsheet directly in the browser. Some interactivity functions include sorting and filtering.

INTEGRATING SHAREPOINT 2013 WITH POWERPOINT

PowerPoint. No other Microsoft application has ever evoked more feelings of fear and dread, in everyone from college students to CEOs. Nearly all of us are familiar with the annoying experience of watching someone bring up a PowerPoint slide with three paragraphs worth of text and then proceed to read every word verbatim.

However, a well-done presentation in PowerPoint links individual slides together into a cohesive flow of information that complements what is being discussed. This section covers the ways in which PowerPoint 2013 and SharePoint 2013 are integrated. Live co-authoring, which is covered earlier in the chapter, is also available in PowerPoint presentations, enabling multiple users to work on the same presentation. Each user's currently edited slide is locked from editing by the other users, which helps prevent three unwanted paragraphs of text from turning up on the slide you're working on, at least until the next user gets hold of it.

Working with Slide Libraries

Slide libraries were introduced in SharePoint 2007 and continued to be awesome in 2010 but like those parachute pants from your youth they went out of style. Thankfully, unlike parachute pants, Microsoft pulled them off the shelf. This feature has been removed from SharePoint 2013 with no ready replacement to suggest. Sorry.

Broadcasting Slides

This feature has been discontinued in SharePoint 2013. The reasoning from Microsoft is that hosting and broadcasting PowerPoint presentations can be done more effectively outside of SharePoint 2013. They recommend using other applications, such as Lync 2013. PowerPoint is still capable of broadcasting presentations over the public web using the Office Presentation Service, which is free but requires a Live ID. If you look under the Share tab of Backstage view, you will see the Present Online option.

INTEGRATING SHAREPOINT 2013 WITH OUTLOOK

As nearly all readers will know, Outlook is Microsoft's e-mail management program, integrating e-mail with personal lists such as contacts, calendars, and tasks. With Outlook 2013, you can find and view information, customize your user interface, and connect to SharePoint and other social media networks. This section focuses specifically on the ways in which Outlook 2013 is used with SharePoint 2013.

In particular, it describes how to manage SharePoint alerts from Outlook, the types of SharePoint lists and libraries that can be connected to Outlook, and how you can integrate Exchange calendars with SharePoint calendars in the browser.

Managing SharePoint Alerts

In SharePoint, *alerts* are e-mail notifications that are set up by end users, in document libraries and lists. When alerts are set up, automatic e-mails arrive when list items are added or changed, and at the frequency that the user specifies. Users can manage all of their own alerts on various SharePoint sites from a single location in Microsoft Outlook.

To view and/or create an alert, execute the following steps:

1. In Outlook, on the Home tab of the Ribbon, click the Rules button in the Move section.

2. Click Manage Rules & Alerts, and then choose the Manage Alerts tab. This screen displays a list of all your existing alerts, which can each be viewed and modified.

3. To create a new alert, click the New Alert button.

Connecting SharePoint Lists and Libraries to Outlook

Many types of SharePoint lists and libraries can be connected to Outlook for interactivity from within the Outlook client software. Using Outlook for e-mail is a standard part of life for many people, so the convenient accessibility of SharePoint data in Outlook is yet another way that Office and SharePoint integration drives efficiency. The following types of lists and libraries can be connected to Outlook:

➤ Calendars

➤ Tasks

➤ Project tasks

➤ Contacts

➤ Discussion boards

➤ Document libraries

➤ Individual document sets

➤ Picture libraries

In the Library or List tab in the Ribbon (depending on whether it's a library or a list), each of these types of lists has a Connect to Outlook button. Users can click this button to link their own Outlook client to SharePoint. When this is done, a new PST file is automatically created on the client hard drive, called `SharePoint Lists.pst`. Take a look at Outlook's Folder view, which usually has this file as the last PST at the bottom. Items in these SharePoint lists are synchronized and editable from either SharePoint or Outlook 2013.

> **NOTE** *Editing files offline from Outlook can get users in trouble with versioning. Also, SharePoint doesn't support merging changes; instead the user needs to decide how to deal with any conflicts that may occur during offline editing. It is recommended that they check the file out before going offline to avoid any conflict.*

All lists and libraries connected to Outlook are actually full, offline copies of the libraries in their entirety. From a client support perspective, this could be a nightmare. Imagine end users clicking the Connect to Outlook button for document libraries with hundreds of files in them. Those hundreds of files are then copied to the PST on that client hard drive. SharePoint 2013 enables site administrators to avoid this scenario by setting Offline Client Availability. Follow these steps to disable the offline availability of a library:

1. In the Library tab in the library's Ribbon, click the Library Settings button.

2. In the General Settings section, click Advanced Settings.

3. Scroll down to the section called Offline Client Availability. The default setting is Yes. Change it to No and click OK.

When offline availability is turned off, the Connect to Outlook button in the library is grayed out and disabled. If clients have already created offline copies of the library, they will still exist as disconnected but they will not receive any further updates from the library.

Other than completely blocking users from downloading offline copies of the libraries to Outlook, two other options are available, although they entail giving a bit of guidance to library owners and contributors:

➤ Teach users the practice of setting up multiple document libraries on each site, as opposed to one large one. A good way to carry this out would be when the site is provisioned. Create new sites with no default document libraries, and instruct the new site owner to create new, separate libraries for different topics.

➤ Use document sets, which enable you to group similar documents together. Multiple document sets can be created in each document library. One of the great things about document sets is that the set itself can be connected to Outlook.

Connecting Calendars and Meetings to Outlook

As discussed previously in this chapter, SharePoint calendars can be connected to Outlook clients. Using an Overlay view, you can add and combine Outlook calendars to SharePoint calendars in the browser, enabling a quick visual comparison of the team's personal calendar with the appointments in a SharePoint calendar:

1. In the Calendar tab, click Calendars Overlay in the Manage Views section.

2. Click New Calendar.

3. Click Exchange in the Type of section.

4. Fill out your Exchange information and click OK.

INTEGRATING SHAREPOINT 2013 WITH INFOPATH

InfoPath is used for the creation and filling out of forms. This powerful program enables business users to easily create and customize their own forms. A lot of time and money can be saved by using InfoPath forms, as no programming knowledge is required, and the interface and form publishing process are simple and familiar.

Consistent with the changes in Office 2010, InfoPath remains divided into Microsoft InfoPath Designer 2013 and Microsoft InfoPath Filler 2013. Because designing a form and filling out a form are two distinct tasks, typically performed by different types of users, it is logical to provide two different entry points to the program.

When forms are created, one of the first choices to make is whether the form will be browser-based — that is, whether it can be opened and filled out in the browser. If a form has not been set up as browser-based, it must rely on client software. The latter option requires that all client computers have InfoPath software installed as part of the Microsoft Office suite. However, at the same time, in order to browser-enable a form, you must have SharePoint 2013 Enterprise. Different types of controls and capabilities within InfoPath forms are compatible with different versions of the InfoPath client, so compatibility with clients is a consideration that is best tackled at the beginning of the form creation process.

When a new form is created for use in a SharePoint form library, you have three different options for publishing the form to SharePoint:

➤ **Form Library** — This method is for publishing the form to a single library on a SharePoint site. Use this option when you know that the form will not be needed in other sites or libraries. Browser-based forms are optional here. Note that at the SharePoint library level, there is a setting that enables administrators to force the manner in which the client machine opens forms.

➤ **Site Content Type** — The form is published to a SharePoint site as a content type. This type of form can then be used in multiple libraries and subsites, and the content type is managed from one location.

➤ **Administrator-approved Form Template** — These types of forms are to be uploaded to InfoPath Forms Services in Central Administration, and they can be globally available in the organization. This option requires selecting the browser-based option. This does not mean that the form can be only browser-based, but that it at least must be available in that format. The next section describes how to manage these administrator-approved forms.

By default, all libraries will be set to use the server default to open documents in the browser, but since that could be changed globally by an administrator to something other than opening documents in the browser, it is possible to set the setting for a specific library. To force an individual library to open documents in the browser:

1. In a SharePoint forms library, click the Library tab. (If you don't have a Form Library created you create it the same way you create all other apps, using the gear icon in the top right-hand corner.)

2. Click Library Settings in the Settings section.

3. Click Advanced Settings.

4. Choose Open in the browser under the Opening Documents in the Browser section.

The following sections describe the administrator-approved templates in relation to InfoPath Forms Services, which entails some Central Administration settings, and step-by-step instructions on how to carry out the form deployment process. A few other concepts covered are the InfoPath Form Web Part, customizing the document information panel using InfoPath, and customizing SharePoint list forms.

Deploying InfoPath Forms Services in Central Administration

In Central Administration, click General Application Settings on the left side of the screen. Figure 17-14 shows the InfoPath Forms Services section.

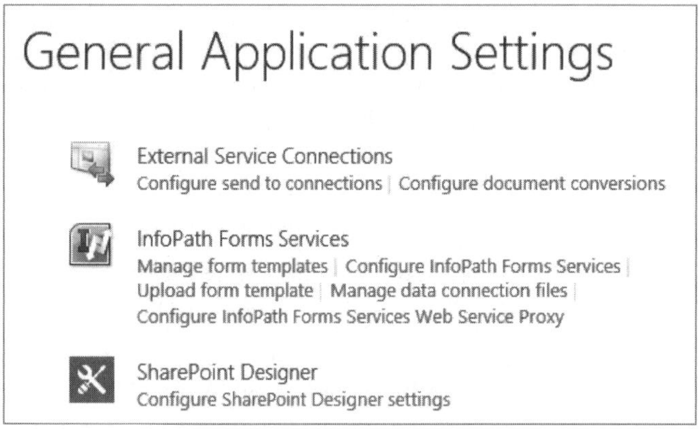

General Application Settings

 External Service Connections
Configure send to connections | Configure document conversions

 InfoPath Forms Services
Manage form templates | Configure InfoPath Forms Services |
Upload form template | Manage data connection files |
Configure InfoPath Forms Services Web Service Proxy

 SharePoint Designer
Configure SharePoint Designer settings

FIGURE 17-14

The following list is a breakdown of the options available for managing InfoPath Forms Services:

➤ **Manage form templates** — This is the master list of all templates that exist in InfoPath Forms Services. Several are provided by default, which are associated with some out-of-the-box workflows in SharePoint 2013.

➤ **Configure InfoPath Forms Services** — This page contains general settings such as time-outs, authentication, and postback thresholds.

➤ **Upload form template** — After an administrator-approved template has been created as described in the previous section, it can be uploaded to InfoPath Forms Services from this screen.

➤ **Manage data connection files** — Upload existing data connection files here so that they can be globally accessed from multiple InfoPath forms.

➤ **Configure InfoPath Forms Services Web Service Proxy** — Use this page to enable the web service proxy for forms.

Deploying a form template to InfoPath Forms Services is done by a SharePoint Farm administrator. This section covers the steps required to take a form from inception to "going live" on a SharePoint site.

What you will need:

➤ **The template file** — The person who has created the InfoPath form sends the form template to the administrator as an XSN file.

➤ **Site Collection URL** — To which site collection(s) will this form need to be deployed? The form creator should also supply this information.

Once the form template and site collection URL have been obtained, take the following steps:

1. On the General Application Settings page in Central Administration, click Upload Form Template.

2. Browse to the form template, which is the XSN file supplied by the form creator.

3. Optionally, click the Verify button, to confirm that the form does not contain any errors.

4. Click the Upload button. After the process has completed, a Form Template Status screen will indicate success.

5. On the Manage Form Templates dialog, hover over the name of the template that was just uploaded. Click Activate to a Site Collection.

6. Select the site collection that the form creator specified from the drop-down menu and click OK.

After the template has been deployed to the site collection, it is available as a content type that can be added to libraries in the site collection.

InfoPath Form Web Part

The InfoPath Form Web Part enables the insertion of any browser-based InfoPath form right onto a Web Part page. A good use of this would be to add a survey to the homepage of a departmental site collection.

Follow these steps to add the Web Part:

1. On a SharePoint page, click the Page tab.

2. Click Edit and choose Edit from the drop-down menu.

3. Click the Insert tab.

4. Click Web Part in the Parts section.

5. In the Categories section, choose Forms.

6. In the Parts section, choose InfoPath Form Web Part.

7. On the bottom-right side, click Add.

8. With the Web Part now on the page, click the link that says, "Click here to open the tool pane."

The tool pane is where you configure your options for the InfoPath Form Web Part. The options include the location of the form to be displayed, as well as what to do once the form has been submitted. After setting your preferences, click OK at the bottom of the tool pane.

Customizing the Document Information Panel

An earlier section of this chapter, "Connecting to SharePoint from within Microsoft Office 2013 Applications," introduced the document panel. To change the appearance of the document information panel, such as inserting a company logo or other graphics, you can use InfoPath to perform these customizations.

DOCUMENT PANEL VS. DOCUMENT INFORMATION PANEL

Ha! There is no vs. with these two. They are the same thing; Microsoft calls it both quite regularly. In 2007 or 2010 it was always called just the document information panel or DIP. This chapter calls it the document panel unless the UI for a given feature specifically calls it the document information panel. Such is the case with InfoPath 2013.

Inherently, a document information panel is associated with a content type in SharePoint. When a custom document information panel is created, the process involves InfoPath communicating with a specific document library in order to obtain information about the content types and meta data (columns) associated with the library. Therefore, before the form is created, obtain the URL of the target document library. Once you have the URL, use the following steps to customize the look and feel of the document information panel using InfoPath 2013:

1. In the Backstage view in InfoPath Designer 2013, click the New tab. Figure 17-15 shows some of the available Form Template Options when you are creating new forms.

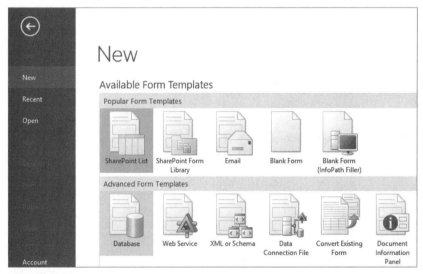

FIGURE 17-15

2. In the Advanced Form Templates section, choose Document Information Panel, and click Design Form on the right.

3. On the first dialog of the Data Source Wizard, enter the URL to the target document library, and then click Next. The URL would be similar to http://portal.contoso.com/shared documents.

4. Choose the Document content type and click Next.

5. Click Finish. At this point, a new form will be displayed in Design view in InfoPath, with all the library fields already inserted. You can customize this form by adding a company logo or rearranging the form fields.

6. It is recommended that you save your own local copy of the form template as a backup, so click the Save button at the top of the screen.

7. Click the File menu to display the Backstage view. On the Info tab, click the Quick Publish button, which publishes the custom document information panel back to the document library specified in step 3.

From this point on, files in the target document library will display the new custom document information panel, rather than the default.

DOCUMENT PANEL MIGHT NOT UPDATE

As of this writing when you click Quick Publish, you get an error message and a success message. If your new document panel doesn't show up, go to plan B. Use the browser to edit the list settings. From there you can modify the Document content type and manually upload your saved XSN file to the Document Information Panel section. Hopefully by the time you read this the error has been worked out but just in case a work-around is always helpful.

Customizing SharePoint List Forms

By default, lists in SharePoint have a standard look and feel. With SharePoint 2013 and InfoPath, you can make advanced customizations to list forms. This is especially useful when you want to highlight information. For example, say you have a Monthly Sales Totals list that has two columns: Month and Units Sold. When entering a new month's information to the list, both titles are a very small font and gray. You can make the fields stand out more by using Customize Form to increase the font size, make the font bold, change the font entirely, or update the background color.

A typical SharePoint list has three associated forms:

➤ **NewForm.aspx** — This is used when a new item is created in a list.

➤ **DispForm.aspx** — After a list item has been created and it is opened to view, this form is used.

➤ **EditForm.aspx** — When the Edit Item button is used on a list item, this is the form that is filled out.

The form customization process starts with first navigating to the desired list. On the List tab in the Ribbon, look in the Customize List section for the button called Customize Form. If the Customize Form button is missing, then the current form cannot be customized.

Follow these steps to customize a SharePoint list form:

1. Navigate to the target SharePoint list.

2. Click the List tab.

3. In the Ribbon, click Customize Form, in the Customize List section. The Microsoft InfoPath Designer 2013 application will start running. You may be prompted for permission to run the application.

4. A very basic version of the current list form will be displayed in InfoPath Designer, with a Fields pane displayed on the right side of the screen.

5. Once you have made your changes, publish them back to the SharePoint server by clicking the File tab in the upper-left corner. Clicking File will take you to the Backstage view. In the Info section, click the Quick Publish button in the Publish your form section.

6. A notification will pop up, indicating that the form was published successfully. Click OK and close InfoPath Designer.

Now to see the fruits of your labor, navigate to the list using your browser and click New. Look at that beautiful form you created; aren't you proud?

INTEGRATING SHAREPOINT 2013 WITH VISIO

Microsoft Visio is an application for the creation of advanced visuals such as charts, diagrams, flow-charts, network diagrams, and even floor plans. This section covers several ways that you can use Visio with SharePoint.

The Visio Graphics Service is a service application in Central Administration. When a Visio diagram has been created on a client machine and published to the server, it eliminates the need for the client software. Once the diagram has been published to the Visio Graphics Service, the server itself knows how to refresh the diagram and maintain the data connections inside of it. It is important to keep in mind that the Visio Graphics Service service application is part of SharePoint 2013 Enterprise. It is also covered in Chapter 8, "Configuring SharePoint for Business Intelligence," in more detail as part of its BI capabilities.

Setting Up the Visio Graphics Service

Getting the Visio Graphics Service set up is easy:

1. In Central Administration, click Manage Service Applications, and confirm that the Visio Graphics Service is listed.

2. Click the Visio Graphics Service link to access the Visio Graphics Service Management page. Two links provide service customization options here:

   ➤ **Global Settings** — This page contains settings for maximum web drawing size, maximum and minimum cache age, maximum cache size, and the maximum recalc duration. Also, if external data connections are to be used in Visio graphics, there is a section here for an unattended service account's application ID.

➤ **Trusted Data Providers** — This page contains a list of default data providers, with databases such as SQL and Oracle. You can add new, custom trusted data providers here.

Adding a Visio Web Access Web Part

When added to a page in SharePoint, the Visio Web Access Web Part is used to display Visio files that have been saved to SharePoint as a Visio Drawing (VSDX) file. Follow these steps to insert a Visio Web Access Web Part on a page and configure it:

1. Navigate to a SharePoint page and click the Page tab.

2. Click Edit in the Edit section.

3. Click the Insert tab, and click Web Part in the Parts section.

4. In categories, choose Business Data.

5. In Parts, choose Visio Web Access and then click Add.

6. After you add the Web Part will get an error. This is because you need to point the Web Part at a Visio diagram. Click the Web Part and from the Ribbon click the WEB PART tab.

7. Click Web Part Properties.

8. Now on the right-hand side of the screen you should see the Web Part properties box. Click the ... for Web Drawing URL. Now you can navigate your site and choose the Visio drawing you want to display in your Web Part.

Figure 17-16 shows an example of a Visio Drawing being displayed in a Visio Web Access Web Part. You can make further customizations in the Web Part tool pane. In addition to the settings displayed in Figure 17-17, there are sections to configure the toolbar and user interface, and web drawing interactivity.

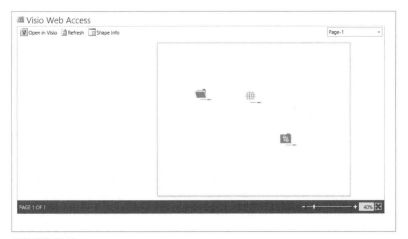

FIGURE 17-16

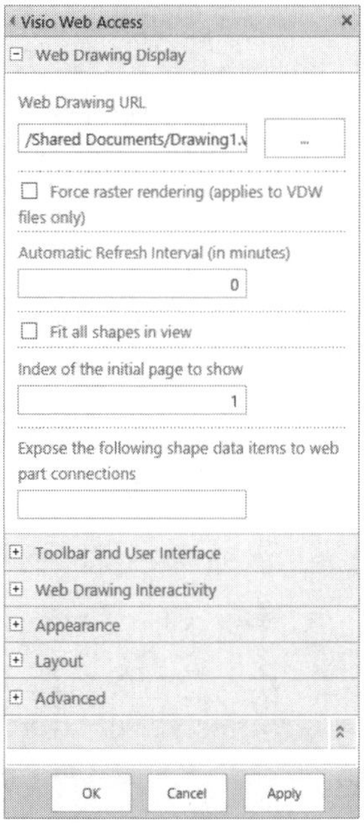

FIGURE 17-17

INTEGRATING SHAREPOINT 2013 WITH ONENOTE

OneNote is an Office application that is used to quickly take notes and organize them. If you have never used OneNote, then you are truly missing out. It is a gem in the Microsoft Office toolbox that doesn't get enough praise. Not only are there note-typing and writing capabilities, you can insert many different types of objects into OneNote files, such as images, links, and even video or voice clips. Putting notes in OneNote gives you a visually clear and easily searchable solution.

OneNote's capability to be shared and integrated with SharePoint and the other Office applications makes it a very useful and easily accessible tool. The live co-authoring feature discussed at the beginning of this chapter also applies to Office OneNote.

A PERSONAL PERSPECTIVE ON ONENOTE

If you aren't a fan of OneNote you don't know what you are missing. I personally use it for so much it makes my head spin. I used to keep everything scattered in text files on my computer, or worse yet post-it notes on my actual desk. Talk about a recipe for disaster! Instead today I now use OneNote for all of it.

I keep all of my SharePoint PowerShell on a page. I have a whole notebook dedicated to clients. Each client has a page with all of the notes of my interactions with them. I have another notebook for all the meetings I go to. On a personal level, I keep my task lists and notes for later all in OneNote.

Additionally, I store my OneNote notebooks on SkyDrive so I can access them from my laptop, Windows Phone, or Surface without having to worry about which one is right. They all point to the same place. Even cooler? Co-author Todd Klindt and I have a shared notebook on his SkyDrive that have all of our farm deployment scripts on them so we can both look at the same source. It even has embedded files. I can't encourage you enough to give it a try. There are even iPhone/Android apps now, so you have no excuse.

To create a new shared notebook for collaboration from a document library in SharePoint, follow these steps:

1. From within OneNote, click the File tab to open the Backstage view.

2. Click New.

3. Click Computer.

4. Click Create in a different folder.

5. Navigate to your SharePoint Document library. If you are having trouble the best way is to type in **http://portal.contoso.com** for your Notebook Name. After you authenticate then you can double-click on your document library.

6. With your document library open type in a name for Notebook Name:. In this example use **Demo Notebook**.

7. Click Create.

8. Once the new file is created, OneNote will prompt you to invite people. Click Invite people to send an e-mail link to the new notebook.

From this point on, users who have at least Contribute permissions on the document library will be able to open the file and make notes. To sync OneNote back to SharePoint after changes are made, follow these steps:

1. From within OneNote, click the File tab to open Backstage view.

2. On the Info tab, select the Settings box next to your notebook's name.

3. Click Sync from the drop-down.

If there are multiple notebooks, clicking the View Sync Status button will show all notebooks and their most recent sync information. There is also a button in this window that enables you to sync all your notebooks at once.

INTEGRATING SHAREPOINT WITH ACCESS 2013 AND ACCESS SERVICES

Microsoft Access is a small-scale relational database management system (RDBMS) that has a somewhat checkered past. Although the earliest versions suffered from some limitations that hindered its widespread adoption, subsequent versions addressed these early issues and the product evolved into a respectable RDBMS; and with SharePoint 2013 a corner has clearly been turned. Microsoft's investment in Access Services makes it clear that Access 2013 has a major role to play.

Access has historically been used to create relatively simple solutions; and in most cases, database creators need not have any programming knowledge. Access provides the capability to connect to any external data sources, such as SQL Server or other databases. Before delving into how this application relates to SharePoint, you should know about some basic Access objects:

➤ **Tables** — Tables are the location where the data itself is stored. Everything that you do in Access is based upon information in your tables.

➤ **Queries** — Queries provide ways to look at or interact with the data in one or more tables. For example, using a query you can filter and refine information, reference information from various tables, sort data, group data, and define the way that common fields relate to each other.

➤ **Forms** — Forms are the means by which end users interact with data in the tables. These generally consist of text boxes, drop-down menus, and other types of controls, such as buttons. Forms are the user interface for adding or modifying table data.

➤ **Reports** — Reports are used to display or print the Access data. Business users generally view reports in order to quickly assess numbers, using tables or graphs.

Access is not generally multi-user friendly, so in scenarios where multiple users are attempting to access and modify the data within Access database tables, SharePoint integration provides a solution. If you think of lists and libraries in SharePoint as tables in a database, it is easy to understand its natural integration with Microsoft Access.

This section describes how to use SharePoint lists as tables in Access databases, how to create Access views in SharePoint lists, and the new concept of Access Services in SharePoint 2013.

SharePoint Data as a Table

The data in SharePoint can easily be connected to serve as live table data in an Access database, which can be queried and reported on. There are a couple of ways to accomplish this. In this section, you'll learn the methods that you can use to establish communications between SharePoint and Access.

Connecting to Access from SharePoint

From a SharePoint 2013 list, select the List tab in the Ribbon. Click the Open with Access button in the Connect & Export section. Figure 17-18 shows the Open in Microsoft Access dialog that appears.

FIGURE 17-18

If the desired database already exists, navigate to it; otherwise, customize the name of the new database to be created. The option to link to the dynamic data is the default, but the data can optionally be exported statically from SharePoint.

Connecting to SharePoint from Access 2013

You can create a dynamic connection to SharePoint from within the Access 2013 application. This section describes the various ways to go about this.

As shown in Figure 17-19, in the External Data tab of Access 2013, both the Import & Link section and the Export section have a drop-down menu called More, which contains an option for SharePoint lists.

FIGURE 17-19

Data can be imported from SharePoint into Access, and it can even be exported from Access, to become a table in SharePoint.

Using the Create tab in Access, you can create several different types of SharePoint lists from within Access. The Database Tools tab contains a button called SharePoint, which you can use to move the tables to a SharePoint list and create linked tables in the database.

USING SHAREPOINT AND ACCESS TOGETHER: AN EXAMPLE

A project management department at a small company has an Access database on a file share, which they have always used to enter new projects. Some fairly complex Access reports are run on the project data. These reports are based on multiple tables and queries, are full of advanced calculations, and need to be shown to the company president every month.

The problem with this archaic solution is that it is not easy for multiple people to enter data at the same time. This is a good scenario in which the tables can be added to SharePoint as lists, and connected to Access. The Access database itself can then be uploaded to a document library, and the original copy on the file share can be deleted. Multiple users can access the Project Management SharePoint site and enter and edit project data, and those monthly reports can still be run from within the Access database in the document library.

Note that changes to the database design itself (not the data) require that the database file be downloaded, changed, and then uploaded to the document library again. When multiple users change the database design simultaneously, a user's version of the file can be overwritten.

Creating Microsoft Access Views in SharePoint

The default SharePoint lists are not very visually exciting. SharePoint site users appreciate both the ease with which data can be displayed and the capability to create custom views of list, but they often ask how they can make it look nicer. One way to visually enhance a SharePoint list is to create an Access view of it. However, the prerequisite is that the view creator and anyone else who will be looking at the view must have Microsoft Access installed on their client computers, and in many cases this prerequisite is prohibitive. This makes Access views a little-known gem.

Follow these steps to create an Access view of a list:

1. On a SharePoint list, click the List tab.

2. Click Create View in the Manage Views section.

3. Under Choose a view type, click Access View.

4. A wizard will guide you through the type of Access object to create, such as a report.

5. Microsoft Access will open with the report in Design mode, to be modified as desired.

6. When you are finished, save and upload the view back to the SharePoint server, using the Save to SharePoint button.

Access Services Overview

Access Services has undergone significant changes since SharePoint 2010. Access Services 2013 for SharePoint 2013 now requires SQL Server 2012. SharePoint itself can still run on an earlier version of SQL, but Access 2013 has some special requirements. Previously, in SharePoint 2010, if you published an Access database to a SharePoint site, the data inside the Access database was stored as part of the site's content database. Now, however, any Access 2013 application created for SharePoint 2013 will generate a dedicated SQL server database. Data input into the new Access app will be pushed into the generated database, keeping the data separate from the site's content database. The databases generated by an Access 2013 application can only reside on SQL Server 2012. It's recommended that these databases be created on a separate dedicated SQL server that does not contain any other SharePoint databases. The database server can be specified in the Access Services Service Application, discussed in the next section.

It's also worth mentioning that Access can create its app as an individual SharePoint site. To extrapolate, this means that an Access database created specifically for publishing to SharePoint is technically considered an app. The Access 2013 client application in this case acts as an abstraction layer for the end user; therefore, even with these changes, no actual coding is necessary, as you can use Access in Designer view.

Access Services is now divided into two different service applications, as explained in the next section. For a much deeper dive into Access Services, including how to configure the service applications, please check out Chapter 8.

Access Services Web Service Application

The Access Services Web Service Application acts as a middle-tier service that handles communication between the Access application, end users, and SharePoint's back end. As mentioned previously, there are now two service applications: Access Services and Access Services 2010.

Access Services

This service application is specifically for settings related to Access 2013. One thing you will notice immediately is that you have fewer configuration options relative to SharePoint 2010. This is because the heavy lifting is done in the background on the SharePoint server Access host. Specifically, this is where you can define the application database server, which must be a SQL Server 2012 server. You will also find a number of options related to session control, such as maximum sessions per user, maximum request duration, cache timeout, and query timeout.

In order to use Access Services you must go through a very difficult battle to get everything configured behind the scenes. That battle is detailed in Chapter 8. You will need to follow the steps for creating an Access Services service application before performing the steps. Use the following steps to create your Access 2013 application:

1. Open Access and choose Custom web app.

2. Add a name in an App Name field.

3. Specify the URL, of SharePoint where the app will reside. You can also choose a location from the Locations list if it is populated.

4. Click the Create button.

5. Choose from a number of existing table templates or create your own.

6. After adding some tables and views, click Launch App in the Home tab, to open the application in the browser.

7. From the browser, you can add, edit, and view the data in your app.

Access Services 2010

This service application now exists for backward compatibility with Access 2010 databases. Here you will find settings to optimize the performance of Access Services, including several query settings such as maximum columns per query, maximum sources (lists) per query, and maximum calculated columns per query. The setting called Maximum rows per query enables you to control how many rows can be viewed at once. For instance, if there are 2 million rows, a default of 50,000 rows per query is an appropriate setting.

> **NOTE** *Another setting for the access services 2010 service application is Maximum records per table. This setting enables you to set a limit on the table's size. For example, the IT department may want to reassess the use of a database when it reaches a certain size. At that point, it can be further evaluated to determine whether the data may be better suited to another type of database, such as a new Access 2013 database or a SQL Server database.*

PUBLISHING LINKS TO OFFICE CLIENT APPLICATIONS

Training users to save documents to SharePoint can be a difficult task. Saving to a web location can be daunting for users who are trained to save to conveniently mapped drives on file shares. You can make it easier for your users by publishing links to common SharePoint locations; that way, when users use Save As in Office, they don't have to manually type a URL. Instead, they just click the link, and Office redirects to a SharePoint site, list, or document library. Publishing links can also utilize the SharePoint audience feature, which enables specific links to be targeted to different user groups. This is a great feature, especially if you have site collections set up for departments. For example, using Audience Targeting, a link to the Human Resources site collection can be pushed out only to members of the Human Resources site, whereas engineers would only see the Engineering site collection link, and so on.

Figure 17-20 shows published links as they would appear to users.

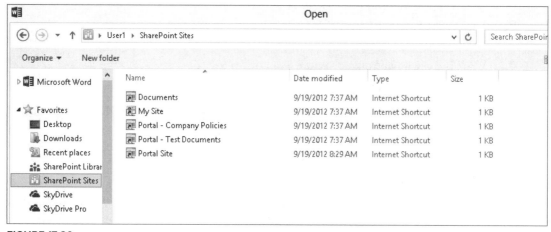

FIGURE 17-20

To configure personal site links:

1. In Central Administration, in the Application Management section, click Manage Service Applications.

2. Scroll down and click User Profile Service Application.

3. Under My Site Settings, click Publish Links to Office Client Applications.

4. Click New Link. Figure 17-21 shows the Properties page for the new link page, which will become available to all clients in their Office applications.

5. Fill out the required fields and click OK.

FIGURE 17-21

MANAGING OFFICE 2013 AND SHAREPOINT THROUGH GROUP POLICY

Active Directory and Group Policy administrators will be excited to learn that they can easily customize a plethora of SharePoint and Office 2013 settings across a large organization by utilizing Group Policy administrative template (.adm) files. Registry-based policy settings (located under the Administrative Templates category in the Group Policy Object Editor) are defined using an XML file format known as ADMX. These files enable you to configure client registry settings in a central location and deploy them in Active Directory containers. To learn more about managing Group Policy, step by step, refer to http://technet.microsoft.com/en-us/library/cc748955(v=ws.10).aspx. The following tables show a sampling of group policy settings you may want to explore further. Table 17-1 is focused on Office as a whole, while Table 17-2 is specific to Outlook. Table 17-3 helps with InfoPath and 17-4 is all about Word. Remember: These are just a small subset — there are plenty more where those came from. TechNet has lots more fun reading at http://technet.microsoft.com/en-us/library/cc179176(v=office.15).aspx.

TABLE 17-1: Office 2013 Configuration Settings

POLICY	GPO PATH	DESCRIPTION
Places Bar Location	software\policies\ microsoft\office\15.0\ common\open find\ adminaddedplaces	Configures the list of items displayed in the Places Bar of the Common File dialogs
Disable Document Information Panel	software\policies\ microsoft\office\15.0\ common\documentinforma tionpanel!disable	Controls whether users can view the Document Information Panel

continues

TABLE 17-1 *(continued)*

POLICY	GPO PATH	DESCRIPTION
Maximum number of items to scan from today to determine the user's colleagues for recommendation	`software\policies\ microsoft\office\15.0\ common\portal\ colleagueimport`	Maximum number of items to scan in the Outlook mailbox to determine the user's colleagues. The larger the number, the more accurate the recommendation. The smaller the number, the faster the recommendations are generated.
Home Workflow Library	`software\policies\ microsoft\office\ common\workflow\home`	Allows administrators to make workflows from a specified list or library available within the workflow-enabled Office applications.

TABLE 17-2: Outlook 2013 Configuration Settings

POLICY	GPO PATH	DESCRIPTION
Default SharePoint Lists	`software\policies\microsoft\ office\15.0\outlook\options\accounts`	Deploys specific SharePoint lists to Outlook
Default servers and data for meeting workspaces	`software\policies\microsoft\ office\15.0\meetings\profile`	Defines up to five servers to be listed when meeting workspaces are created

TABLE 17-3: InfoPath 2013 Configuration Settings

POLICY	GPO PATH	DESCRIPTION
Control behavior for Microsoft SharePoint Foundation gradual upgrade	`software\policies\microsoft\ office\15.0\infopath\security`	Controls whether forms and form templates follow URL redirections provided by Microsoft SharePoint Foundation during a gradual upgrade
Turn off InfoPath Designer mode	`software\policies\microsoft\ office\15.0\infopath\designer\ disabledesigner`	Controls whether InfoPath users can design new or modify existing form templates

TABLE 17-4: Word 2013 Configuration Settings

POLICY	GPO PATH	DESCRIPTION
Control Blogging	`software\policies\microsoft\office\common\blog`	Controls whether users can compose and post blog entries from Word
Default File Location	`software\policies\microsoft\office\15.0\word\options`	Defines the default path to documents

This is just a small sampling of the options that can be deployed. Consider using some of these settings to encourage users to save Office documents to SharePoint, or to automatically view a list of data from SharePoint in Outlook. Integration should be as seamless as possible; you don't want users to have to "find" SharePoint when it is time to upload a document for collaboration.

SUMMARY

Microsoft Office 2013 and SharePoint 2013 are highly integrated. The commonalities of the Ribbon interface and the detailed information stored in both applications enables users to communicate and collaborate with more efficiency. As demonstrated in this chapter, while SharePoint is impressive on its own, it truly shines when you add Office 2013 to the mix.

18

Working with SharePoint Designer

In order to learn and work with SharePoint Designer (SPD), you first have to be willing to accept change. SharePoint Designer is synonymous with the word change and for a good reason: Each new version has undergone major changes, and SharePoint Designer 2013 continues this pattern.

In order to understand the direction in which SPD is headed, however, it's helpful to know something about its past. Back in the early days of SharePoint 2003, users didn't have an officially branded version of Designer that they could use to customize SharePoint. Instead, SharePoint users had to take advantage of the tools currently available, using Microsoft FrontPage to edit SharePoint 2003 sites.

At the time this seemed like a good idea and there was much rejoicing throughout the land. It wasn't until organizations started trying to upgrade to SharePoint 2007 that they saw the error of their ways. FrontPage had so drastically changed the code of SharePoint 2003 sites that in many cases upgrading the site to SharePoint 2007 was impossible.

With SharePoint 2007, Microsoft attempted to make a peace offering to the SharePoint community, releasing SharePoint Designer 2007 as the official product to use to customize SharePoint 2007 sites. Not only was it free, but as an added bonus SharePoint 2007 provided power users and information workers with the capability to create workflows and sophisticated no-code solutions that were previously possible only with code written by trained developers.

However, because SharePoint 2007 marked the first official version of SharePoint Designer, it had some shortcomings, odd bugs, and governance issues. These eventually led most administrators to lovingly refer to SharePoint Designer as "SharePoint Destroyer."

SharePoint 2010 also offered a new version of SharePoint Designer. Changes to this version required SharePoint Designer to be attached to an online SharePoint site before you could do anything; the Office Ribbon was added; and, as a gift to SharePoint administrators, options were added to control who could use SharePoint Designer and how much control they had with the product.

SharePoint 2013 also provides a new version of SharePoint Designer, and again change is the key word, as Microsoft has clearly shaken things up quite a bit with this newest release: *At the time of this writing, SharePoint Designer 2013 has no Design View.* For those of you who are new to SharePoint Designer, the Design View was a handy window that enabled you to see, in real time, what the changes you were making to your SharePoint site would look like in SharePoint — without having to go through the tedious process of checking in and approving your changes first. Microsoft's decision to remove Design View has caused a fair amount of heated drama in the SharePoint community, as many users are understandably upset to lose this useful time-saving feature, which for some users represents the only reason to use SharePoint Designer. Of course, Microsoft hopes that removing Design View will result in a faster and more stable version of the product, but there is no doubt that it will take some getting used to.

Now that you have a sense of SharePoint Designer's history, it's time to look at where it is headed. This chapter provides a high-level overview of the features, changes, and capabilities of SharePoint Designer 2013. It takes you on a tour of its user interface, and includes examples demonstrating how to perform many common tasks.

INTRODUCTION TO SHAREPOINT DESIGNER 2013

One would assume that with a name like SharePoint Designer it would be a tool to design SharePoint sites, and, as described in the preceding section, that is exactly the use for which it was originally intended. Although SharePoint Designer 2013 is still a tool for designing SharePoint sites, it has been definitely enhanced to do much more. One could easily say that SharePoint Designer has become the go-to tool for SharePoint information workers more than people who work as SharePoint branders, aka the people who make it pretty for a living.

In fact, Microsoft provides the following official list of new features, which highlights just how focused SharePoint Designer 2013 is on "no-code solutions":

➤ **2013 Workflows** — New, more advanced workflows are built off of .NET 4 and Windows Azure, while still maintaining the capability to create SharePoint 2010 workflows.

➤ **Visual Designer** — Workflows still have a visual interface that enables users to create workflows based on Visio and by using drag and drop.

➤ **Packaging** — You can now package your workflows to move to different farms or sites, similar to how solution packages work in SharePoint.

➤ **Web Services** — Rest services can now be called from within SharePoint 2013 workflows.

And much, much more....

> **NOTE** *Information about SharePoint Designer 2013 is continuously updated by Microsoft, which has even devoted a separate blog site to all things SharePoint Designer. Be sure to check out the blog from time to time at* http://blogs.msdn .com/b/sharepointdesigner/. *Microsoft also uses this blog to showcase SharePoint Designer's awesome capabilities.*

Of course, just as there is more to SharePoint than websites there is more to SharePoint Designer than workflows. You can also use SharePoint Designer 2013 to manage or create forms, create and manage data sources from within SharePoint or from external sources, and interact with external content types and line-of-business systems. The following sections get you started.

Requirements for Using SPD 2013

Luckily, one important thing hasn't changed since SharePoint Designer 2007/2010: SharePoint Designer 2013 is 100% free. When you consider all the features you get with this full-fledged product, SharePoint Designer is indeed very attractive freeware. You can download SharePoint Designer 2013 at the following location:

http://www.microsoft.com/en-us/download/details.aspx?id=35491

Following are the necessary prerequisites for installing and using SharePoint Designer 2013:

➤ **Supported operating systems** — Windows Server 2008 R2, Windows Server 2012, Windows 7, and Windows 8. with .NET 4.0 Framework or higher installed.

➤ **Computer and processor** — Other than the supported operating systems, Microsoft has not released any system requirements for SharePoint Designer 2013; but the SharePoint Designer client itself is not very hardware intensive and any machine built in the last five years should be able to run the software without issues.

Note that in order to install SharePoint Designer 2013, .NET Framework 4 or later must be installed on the computer on which you are installing SharePoint Designer. Not to worry, though, as the .NET Framework will install on any OS from Windows XP SP3 to Windows Server 2012, and it is available in both 32-bit and 64-bit versions. You can download the .NET Framework here:

```
http://www.microsoft.com/en-us/download/details.aspx?id=17851
```

In terms of compatibility, SharePoint Designer 2013 is backwardly compatible; that is, you can use it to open both SharePoint 2010 sites and SharePoint 2013 sites. You can also open SharePoint 2013 sites with SharePoint Designer 2010, but you lose all of the new features and functionality.

> **NOTE** *Similar to the adage "You can teach a bear to dance but that doesn't make it a good idea," experience has shown that you are better off not trying to do anything across versions; SPD is challenging enough as it is. You should try to always use SPD 2010 with SharePoint 2010, and SPD 2013 with SharePoint 2013.*

While on the subject of compatibility it is important to note that the version of Office you have installed on your computer determines which version of SharePoint Designer you must install. Technically, SharePoint Designer is an Office product (and even has the same interface), so the version installed must match. For instance, if you have the 64-bit version of Office 2010 installed, you must download and use the 64-bit version of SharePoint Designer 2013. Likewise, if you have the 32-bit version of Office 2007 installed, you must use the 32-bit version of SharePoint Designer.

If you have the luxury of choosing, it is recommended that you use SharePoint Designer 2013 along with Office 2013 to safeguard against any compatibility issues. In addition, when in doubt, it is generally a safe bet to go with the 32-bit version of Office and SharePoint Designer 2013. Microsoft has echoed this message as well. The 64-bit version is available if you must use it, but at the end of the day you will find better compatibility with add-ins and other components if you are using 32-bit.

The version of Office you are using is not the only factor limiting which version of SharePoint Designer 2013 you install. If you have previous versions of SharePoint Designer installed, the version of SharePoint Designer 2013 you download must match as well. For example, if you previously downloaded and installed the 32-bit version of SharePoint Designer 2007 and SharePoint Designer 2010 and don't even have Office installed, you must download the 32-bit version of SharePoint Designer 2013 to match your earlier versions of the product. Otherwise, you must uninstall the previous versions of the product before you can install the 64-bit version of SharePoint Designer 2013.

Integrating SP 2013 and SPD 2013

There are two main issues to confront when integrating SharePoint and SharePoint Designer: authentication and system resources. Both will be considered in this section.

The computer on which you will run SharePoint Designer is not your only consideration before installing it. You also need to consider the SharePoint server to which you plan to connect.

Along with ensuring that the SharePoint site and the SharePoint web application allow the use of SharePoint Designer (discussed shortly), you need to determine which authentication method is used by the SharePoint site.

Although this is not fully documented, previous versions of SharePoint Designer work best when connecting to a SharePoint site that uses Windows NTLM authentication. Changing the authentication method to Basic authentication caused odd bugs when you used external content types and tried to use other more advanced features of SharePoint Designer.

In SharePoint Designer 2010, it was not at all uncommon for things to work just fine until you came across a weird error that resulted in wasted time chasing down the source, thinking it was an issue with SharePoint Designer only to discover that the site was using Basic authentication. In fact, at the time of this writing, if your SharePoint site only uses Basic authentication, SharePoint Designer 2013 will not even connect to the SharePoint site. However, sometimes a site is required to use Forms-Based authentication or Basic authentication, so how should you deal with this compatibility issue?

Whenever you plan to use a form of authentication other than NTLM on a web application, the widely accepted workaround is to first create the web application in the default zone using NTLM authentication and then extend the site into another zone using your authentication method of choice. This enables you to connect SharePoint Designer to the fully qualified domain name of the default zone and work without issues.

The last issue in terms of compatibility is system resources. In this regard, SharePoint is smarter than it is sometimes given credit for because it knows when system resources are getting low on the machine that it is running on. Instead of just letting the machine lock up, taking down SharePoint and making your users angry, SharePoint can terminate the functionality of capabilities that it determines are not mission critical. As you might have guessed, one of these capabilities is SharePoint Designer. For example, when the memory usage of the server on which SharePoint is running exceeds 95%, opening SharePoint Designer will result in the not very descriptive error: "The Server could not complete your request."

Although this message can result in you blaming your SharePoint Designer woes on your computer, yourself, the server, or your cat, the cause is actually quite simple: Your SharePoint server is out of RAM. Therefore, before you start using SharePoint Designer 2013, make sure your SharePoint server is adequately equipped to do what you require, especially when it comes to the new SharePoint workflow platform, which is covered shortly.

SPD 2013 and SPD 2010 Interoperability

During our walk down SharePoint memory lane earlier in this chapter, it was mentioned that you couldn't open SharePoint 2010 sites with SharePoint Designer 2007, and likewise you couldn't open SharePoint 2007 sites with SharePoint Designer 2010. Thankfully that trend is now over! With SharePoint Designer 2013, you can open a SharePoint 2010 site and manage it as if you were using SharePoint Designer 2010.

Of course, this means you won't be able to take advantage of SharePoint Designer 2013 features with your SharePoint 2010 sites; but if you are doing something such as trying to add a new subsite to a SharePoint 2010 site, and the functionality hasn't changed between the two products, SharePoint Designer 2013 will let you do that.

Likewise, you have the option to open SharePoint 2013 sites with SharePoint Designer 2010, but this is not recommended and could corrupt your sites. Similarly, before you entertain the idea of using SharePoint Designer 2010 to brand your SharePoint 2013 sites in order to use the Design View, be aware that this doesn't work. The SharePoint Designer 2010 Design View cannot handle SharePoint 2013 master pages, and you will just get errors.

In short, you should match your version of SharePoint to the same version of SharePoint Designer, although you won't be entirely locked out of the gate if you try to use another version.

SharePoint Server 2013 Workflow Platform

Continuing with the theme of change, perhaps one of the biggest changes with SharePoint Designer 2013 is that this is the first version of the product to require that certain software be installed and configured on the SharePoint server before the full feature set of SharePoint Designer becomes available.

The SharePoint 2013 Workflow Platform is a new service that uses a powerful and robust workflow engine. It's built on Windows Azure workflow, which is built on Windows workflow and the .NET Framework. If you don't install and configure the SharePoint 2013 Workflow platform, SharePoint 2013 includes the installation of the same SharePoint 2010 Workflow platform that was included with SharePoint 2010. This provides a level of backward compatibility so that all the workflows you created in SharePoint 2010 can be moved over to SharePoint 2013. It also enables you to create workflows based on SharePoint 2010 in SharePoint 2013 without all of the options that you would have with a SharePoint 2013 workflow.

Because this is a book that focuses on SharePoint administration, it explains the process of installing and configuring the SharePoint 2013 Workflow platform because these are tasks for which you, as the SharePoint administrator, will be responsible to ensure that it is fully and correctly implemented. This in turn ensures that your power users and information workers have the full set of tools they need to create the most robust workflows possible.

> **NOTE** *Instead of diving into the depths of workflow here in the SPD chapter, workflow has been given its own chapter. Please refer to Chapter 16, "Workflows in SharePoint" for everything including how to install the 2013 Workflow platform.*

Enabling SharePoint Designer Restrictions

Given that SharePoint Designer is a very powerful tool, as a SharePoint administrator you may not want all your users to have so much control at their fingertips.

This capability is one of the few things that has not changed in SharePoint Designer 2013; you can still limit its use just as you could with SharePoint 2010. For those of you who are new to the product, this section describes how to restrict who can use SharePoint Designer.

The following options are available to limit how SharePoint Designer is used in an organization:

➤ **Enable SharePoint Designer** — Determines whether SharePoint Designer can be used at all

➤ **Enable Detaching Pages from the Site Definition** — Allows edited pages to be customized and detached from the site definition

➤ **Enable Customizing Master Pages and Layout Pages** — Removes the Master Page link from the Navigation pane and prevents the ability to update master pages and layout pages

➤ **Enable Managing of the Web Site URL Structure** — Removes the All Files link from the Navigation pane

These options enable an organization to control SPD 2013 at whatever level is deemed appropriate. SharePoint 2013 allows access to SPD to be controlled at two different levels:

➤ **Central Administration** — Accessed from Manage Web Applications. A drop-down menu specific to SharePoint Designer can be found under the General Settings menu. It enables farm administrators to control SPD at the web application level. Disabling the options here prevents site collection administrators from enabling the functionality.

➤ **Site Collection** — Accessed from the Site Collection Administration section in Site Settings, this option enables site collection administrators to control SPD access for designers and site owners.

Updating SPD permissions

The following example walks you through the process of updating the SPD settings from Central Administration:

1. Open Central Administration from your SharePoint server.

2. Click the Application Management link in the left-hand navigation.

3. Select Manage web applications underneath the Web Applications section.

4. Select the web application whose setting(s) you want to change.

5. In the Ribbon, click General Settings located on the top left-hand side.

6. From the SharePoint Designer section, click the link for Configure SharePoint Designer Settings. The dialog shown in Figure 18-1 appears.

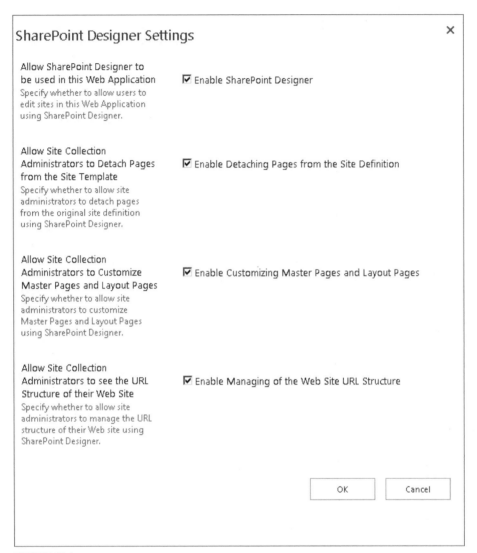

FIGURE 18-1

7. Leave the first box checked, which enables the use of SPD, but remove the checks from the other boxes, as shown in Figure 18-2. Click OK.

8. To test the changes, navigate to the URL of the site collection in your web browser to be used for testing and log in as a site collection administrator. In this case, you will be using http://portal.contoso.com in order for the example to work, and it is important that the account that is used is a site collection administrator. If a farm administrator account is used, the changes to the permissions will not have any effect.

FIGURE 18-2

9. From the Site Actions menu, choose Edit in SharePoint Designer.

10. When SharePoint Designer opens, notice that the Master Page, Page Layouts (only displayed in sites with Publishing enabled), and All Sites links are missing from the left-hand Navigation pane, as seen in Figure 18-3. If the links are still there, verify that you are logged in as a site collection administrator, not a farm administrator. You can check by clicking the icon in the bottom left corner of the SPD window, which displays the name of the logged-in user.

Also, if you were to click Site Pages and try to edit the home.aspx file by right-clicking on it (see Figure 18-4), you would see that there is no option to edit in advanced mode. The page can only be edited in normal mode, which means that only content in Web Part zones can be edited.

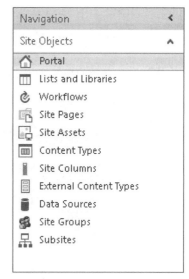

FIGURE 18-3

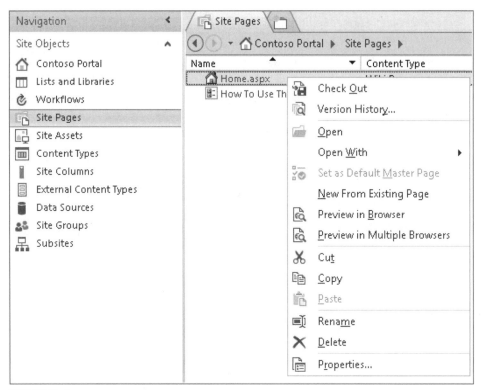

FIGURE 18-4

11. For this step, you are going to test what happens when you completely disable SPD access. Close out the instance of SPD that you were using for the last example. It's OK to leave your web browsers open.

12. Repeat steps 5–7 and remove the check from the Enable SharePoint Designer box. Click OK.

13. Repeat step 9. This time when you try to open SPD you should see the prompt shown in Figure 18-5.

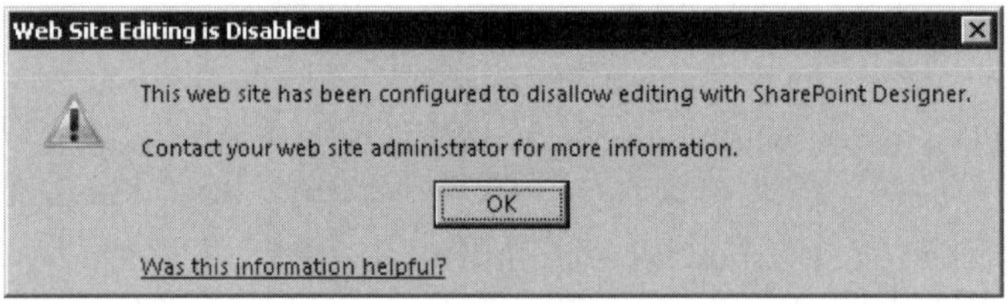

FIGURE 18-5

OVERVIEW OF THE NEW USER INTERFACE

Installation of SharePoint Designer is a very easy process. Once you have downloaded the version of SharePoint Designer that is applicable for your environment, be it the 32-bit version or the 64-bit version, just double-click the SharePoint Designer executable to begin the installation process.

If the installer determines that .NET Framework 4 is not installed, you are prompted to download and install it before continuing with the installation of SharePoint Designer. The installer then asks whether you want to do a default install (Install Now) or a custom install (Customize). For most purposes, selecting Install Now will be fine.

When the installer finishes you can open SharePoint Designer by clicking Start ⇨ All Programs ⇨ SharePoint ⇨ SharePoint Designer 2013. You will notice immediately another change in SharePoint Designer. The logo has the new design of Office 2013 (recall that technically SharePoint Designer is a part of the Office 2013 suite); and unlike previous versions, SharePoint Designer is now much more closely integrated with the Office ecosystem. When SharePoint Designer 2013 starts up for the first time, you are asked a serious of questions about how to configure it. The first thing you need to specify is how updates should be handled. You have three options:

➤ **Use recommended settings** — This option instructs Windows Update to download and install new updates for SharePoint Designer 2013 and to offer optional software and Microsoft diagnostic software.

➤ **Install important updates only** — This is a less intrusive option that tells Windows Update to download only those updates that patch possible security threats.

➤ **Ask me later** — This turns off all automatic downloading for SharePoint Designer 2013, but you can still change this setting later in the options menu.

Next, SharePoint Designer 2013 gives you the option to customize its appearance a little by selecting from several built-in themes (see Figure 18-6).

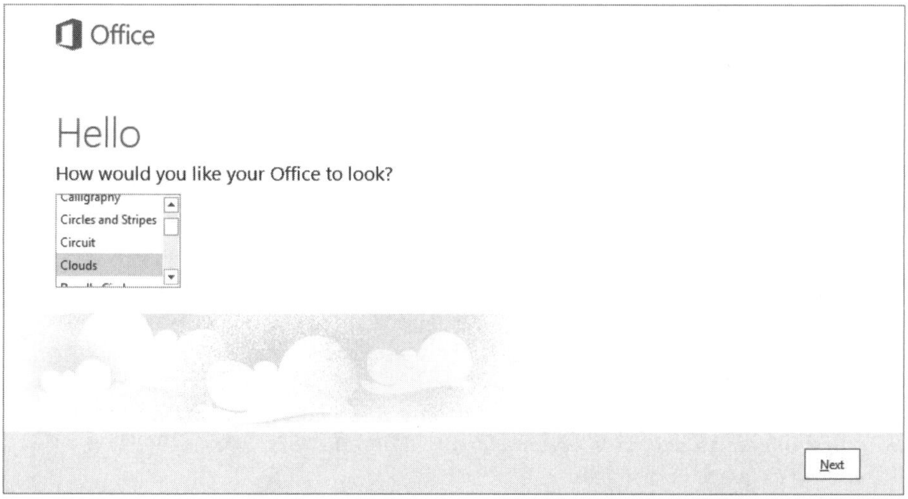

FIGURE 18-6

After selecting a theme, you will be in the actual "lobby area" of SharePoint Designer 2013. From a functional standpoint, nothing has changed since SharePoint Designer 2010: The first screen that opens is referred to as the Sites place. This screen is divided into four self-explanatory areas: Open SharePoint Site, New SharePoint Site, Recent Sites, and Site Templates.

In the Site Templates section, shown in Figure 18-7, by default you'll see three options: Blank Site, Blog, and Team Site. Clicking one of these templates will open a dialog that enables you to create a new site once you specify a URL. If you want to create a new site based on a template that isn't specified, you can click the More Templates button and type in the URL of a site that has more options. For example, typing in the URL for a site created using the Enterprise Wiki template would enable you to choose from additional templates such as Enterprise Wiki, Publishing Site, and others.

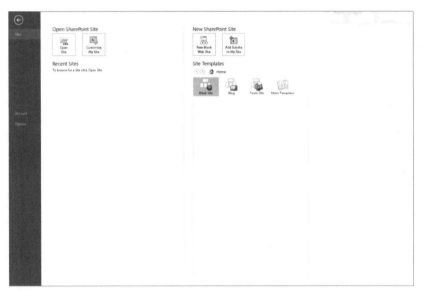

FIGURE 18-7

Because this is the first time you've opened SharePoint Designer, the Recent Sites area will be blank. You need to click the Open Site button. When the Open Site dialog appears, you can type in the address of your site or subsite in the format of "`http://portal.contoso.com`" or "`http://portal.contoso.com/subsite`," and then click Open.

> **NOTE** *In SharePoint Designer 2007 it was possible to do offline editing of files such as master pages or page layouts. With SPD 2013, as with SPD 2010, it is possible to do offline editing but you must first connect to a SharePoint site. In other words, if you don't have access to a SharePoint site you won't be able to use SPD even if someone were to send you the file. If you do try to edit a file without first opening a site, you'll get the error "You must first open a Web site before editing external Web pages."*

What has changed, however, is that SharePoint Designer 2013 now has the look of the new Windows 8 user interface. In fact, as you work with SharePoint 2013, you will notice that the entire product has the look and feel of the Windows 8 UI, including fonts, logos, color schemes, and icons.

The first area that you should focus your attention on is the Account tab, located in the lower left corner. By selecting this link you will see just how integrated SharePoint Designer 2013 is with Office 2013. Along with the capability to select a theme when you first install SharePoint Designer 2013, you can change the account you are logged in with and add connected services. Connected services enable you to add things such as your Office 365 account or SkyDrive account, which can then be used, for example, to access files and images that are saved on those accounts and import them into the SharePoint site that you are customizing with SharePoint Designer 2013. To add a service, follow these steps:

1. From the Account tab, select the Add a service drop-down and select from the three options: Storage, Other Sites, or Office Store (see Figure 18-8). For this example, select Storage ➪ SkyDrive.

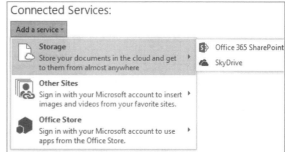

FIGURE 18-8

2. A form dialog will open requesting your Microsoft account name and password. If you have a Windows Live account, type your username and password and select Sign in. You now will have access to your SkyDrive from within SharePoint Designer.

3. Repeat the same process if you have an Office 365 account or if you use Windows Live Essentials with your Windows Live Connect account.

MANAGING SHAREPOINT SITES WITH SHAREPOINT DESIGNER

At this point, you have installed SharePoint Designer and configured it to work with your SharePoint Server, and you are finally connected to your SharePoint site collection. Now the only thing left to do is get to work. One of SharePoint Designer's least talked about features is its ability to manage (for the most part) your SharePoint site collections and subsites.

After connecting to your SharePoint site collection, you are brought to the Site Information page. From here you can get a high-level overview of the site. For instance, you can quickly determine the total storage used and what percentage of available storage is used if you have a quota set on your site collection. You can also quickly add users or groups to your site under the Permissions pane, create subsites in the Subsites pane, and enable various settings in the Settings pane.

Granted, these are all things you can do from within the SharePoint site, but not without a lot of clicking through different screens. SharePoint Designer provides you with quick, one-stop access to all the settings from within this one page, as shown in Figure 18-9.

FIGURE 18-9

Unchanged from SPD 2010 is access to the Ribbon user interface. As with other Windows products, the available Ribbon options vary according to where your mouse is clicked in SharePoint Designer 2013. For example, if you click the Manage area of the Ribbon inside the Site Information pane (see Figure 18-10), you will see icons for Preview in Browser, Administration Web Page, Save as Template, Recycle Bin, and Site Options.

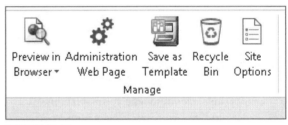

FIGURE 18-10

Clicking any of the options doesn't do anything in SharePoint Designer but instead opens your web browser and takes you to the corresponding section of your SharePoint site for administrating these settings. This may not be as handy as controlling these features from within SharePoint Designer but it does provide you with quick access to all these options.

The Navigation Pane

On the left-hand side of SharePoint Designer 2013 is the Navigation pane, shown in Figure 18-11, which provides access to the different areas of its functionality. From here you can browse the content of your site by selecting the All Files site object, start down your branding path by selecting the Master Pages site object, or manage and create workflows by selecting the Workflows site object all just as you did in SPD 2010.

It is from the Navigation pane that you access SharePoint and work with SharePoint Designer. The list of site objects is self-explanatory, and by exploring each site object you can discover how to manage all aspects of your SharePoint site. Pay close

FIGURE 18-11

attention to the Ribbon as you click each site object, as the available options vary according to what you have clicked. For example, from the List and Libraries area, the Ribbon will give you the option to create a new document library.

Note also that as you hover over each site object, a pushpin appears on the right. By selecting the pushpin you can pin the site object, marking it as a favorite, which causes the contents of that site object to be displayed in the Navigation pane for quick access. For example, if you find yourself frequently browsing over to the Master Pages section to manage them, you can pin the area for quick and easy access (see Figure 18-12). Note that you can only pin one area at a time.

Creating Subsites with SharePoint Designer 2013

The following steps describe how to create a new subsite with SharePoint Designer 2013:

1. Open SharePoint Designer and click the Open Site button. When the Open Site dialog appears, type in the address of your site in the format of `http://portal.contoso.com`, and then click Open.

2. From within the home page, click inside the Subsites pane and select the New icon in the top-right corner. The New Web Site dialog will appear, as shown in Figure 18-13.

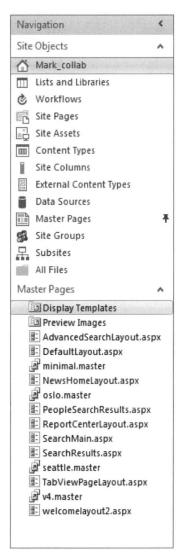

FIGURE 18-12

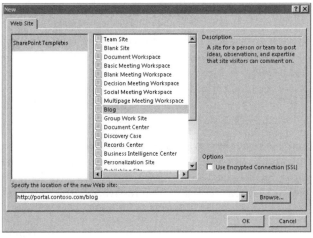

FIGURE 18-13

3. From here you can select among the available templates. For the purpose of this example, select the Blog template, which will cause the description to update.

4. You also have the option to select Use Encrypted Connection (SSL) if you have a site collection that uses HTTPS.

5. After selecting the template, you can provide the name of the subsite. For this example use the URL `http://portal.contoso.com/blog`. SharePoint Designer will open a new home page for the blog subsite you just created (see Figure 18-14).

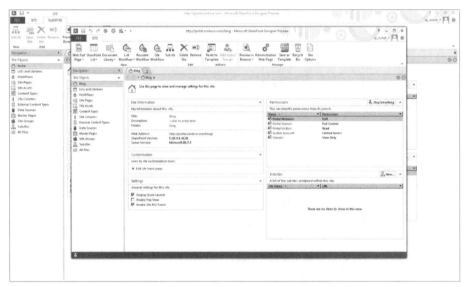

FIGURE 18-14

BRANDING WITH SHAREPOINT DESIGNER 2013

In general, *branding* refers to the process of using a combination of colors, fonts, and logos for company or product brand recognition. Consider Coca-Cola, for example. Even when you see a sign that doesn't include the words "Coca-Cola," if it uses that iconic red and white or includes writing using the Cola-Cola font, you will recognize it as Cola-Cola. That, in a nutshell, is branding. Branding in SharePoint serves a similar purpose. It uses colors, logos, fonts, and layout to create a unique and consistent appearance for your company's site.

From SharePoint's first release, users have sought ways to customize its look and feel to better suit their needs. It is both human nature and good business sense to distinguish a site's appearance. Although there is nothing wrong with SharePoint's look and feel out of the box, the skill of personalizing it is in high demand, as companies want a collaboration tool that shares its colors and logos, and meets the usability needs of its users.

With the loss of Design View in SharePoint Designer 2013, the state of SharePoint branding and SPD's role in branding is currently in a state of flux. However, it's not all gloom and doom. Although Microsoft may have closed the door on one feature, they have opened another with a new feature that will drastically change the way you brand in SharePoint 2013: the capability to map a network drive to your master page gallery via WebDAV. This section covers the basics of SharePoint branding as it relates to SharePoint Designer. For a deep dive into branding, please check out Chapter 12, which is entirely focused on all things branding in SharePoint.

In previous versions of SharePoint, the only supported way to customize your master pages was with SharePoint Designer. Now, however, you can map a network drive to your master page gallery and edit your SharePoint site directly with the design software of your choice. This means you can brand your SharePoint site using something as basic as Notepad or as advanced as professional designer software such as Adobe's Dreamweaver, which does have a design view and does work with SharePoint 2013.

Versioning

At this point you may be wondering why you should use SharePoint Designer for branding if SharePoint 2013 enables the use of other products, including those dedicated to that purpose. That's easy to answer: SharePoint Designer is a fully functional and capable design tool that is also free, whereas tools like Dreamweaver are most definitely not. SharePoint Designer is also built from the ground up with SharePoint, and only SharePoint, in mind. Using it, you can still manage and upload all your code and branding assets; analyze CSS properties, including the capability to change CSS from within SPD; add ASP.NET controls; create new content types for your page layouts; and quickly and efficiently manage versioning by checking in or overriding check-outs. In fact, SharePoint Designer is probably the best way to quickly upload and check in a large number of assets — including images and code, such as master pages and CSS files — without having to check in each item separately.

Typically, when you are branding you are likely working with a site that has the SharePoint publishing feature activated, and when the publishing feature is activated the version controls are usually activated as well. Under most circumstances, versioning is a good thing, requiring users to check out a file before editing it so that multiple users can't make changes at the same time. Of course, it also requires that pages be checked back in before the changes are reflected on your SharePoint site. Versioning is also useful when files should be approved by someone else in your team, which can be great for quality assurance and content deployment. Indeed, these versioning controls are an absolute must when it comes to branding on a production SharePoint site.

Conversely, versioning can be a hassle when you are branding on a test or deployment site, especially now that Design View is no longer available and you cannot see what your changes will look like in real time without first checking in your page each time. Therefore, before you get any further using SharePoint Designer 2013, this section demonstrates how versioning can be turned off so that as soon as you save your site, you can refresh your browser to see any changes.

For the purpose of this example, you will be making these changes on a site created with the Publishing Portal template, which has the SharePoint Server Publishing Infrastructure site collection feature and the SharePoint Server Publishing site feature activated by default.

1. From within your site, click the gear icon in the top right corner and select Site contents.

2. Select the Style Library, which is the recommended location for storing your created code and assets.

3. From the Ribbon, select the Library tab to display all your options for this library. Select Library Settings in the Settings section of the Ribbon.

4. Select Versioning settings and you will see that versioning is indeed turned on for this library. Feel free to turn off versioning here if you like, but the main area of concern is the "Require documents to be checked out before they can be edited?" option.

5. Select No for this option, as shown in Figure 18-15, and click OK.

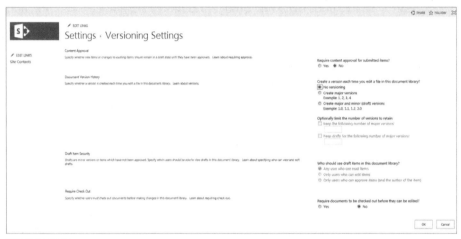

FIGURE 18-15

Now you will no longer be prompted to check in and check out your custom CSS page each time you make a change or load a new image.

Doing this for your master pages is very similar, but the library that contains your master pages is located in Site Settings under the Web Designer Galleries section and is opened by clicking the master pages and page layouts.

In SharePoint 2013, versioning is not turned on by default for the master page gallery, so if you want to enable it you would just repeat the preceding steps but check the box requiring that documents be checked out before editing. As mentioned earlier, turning off the versioning requirement is not recommended for your production farm, but it can save you time on your test farm.

SharePoint Master Pages

Master pages provide the shell of your website, containing your HTML, pointers to your CSS, ASP. NET controls, and your navigation. Master pages enable you to provide a consistent look and feel to all your SharePoint pages. With a master page you can do a little or a lot. You can tweak certain things or totally change the entire structure of your SharePoint site.

Without master pages, SharePoint could not be the massive enterprise collaboration tool that it currently is. Master pages make it possible for every page in your site or site collection to maintain the same look and feel, regardless of whether you have a small site collection with a few subsites and pages or a massive 200GB site collection with hundreds of unique sites. SharePoint Designer provides the capability to customize master pages, enabling you to make a change only once and have it replicated to every appropriate page in your site.

Editing the Master Page

One of the best pieces of advice when it comes to SharePoint branding is to never ever edit SharePoint default files. Whether it's an image file in the SharePoint root or hive, the main CSS file that SharePoint uses, or the master pages that ship with SharePoint, making changes to these files directly can be disastrous.

You never know when an update for SharePoint may overwrite one of the files you have customized or a mistake in your file prevents your site from loading at all. In scenarios such as these you will be very happy that you are using and can point SharePoint to a customized file that you have created — one that is based off of one of SharePoint's default files. Fortunately, when using SharePoint Designer, it is very easy to do just that:

1. Navigate to the URL of the site collection in SharePoint Designer and open your site collection, `http://portal.contoso.com/sites/branding` in this example. The site collection should have been created with the publishing portal template.

2. In the Navigation pane, double click the Master Page site object, and then select the master page that your SharePoint site is using, which in most cases will be `seattle.master`. Right-click the master page and select Copy.

3. Place your mouse in an empty area of the screen, right-click, and select Paste. As shown in Figure 18-16, this will create a new master page called `seattle_copy(1).master` that contains all the same code as `seattle.master` but can be customized as you see fit. Rename the file `custom.master` by right-clicking and select `rename`. When you are done, you can tell SharePoint to use your new master page.

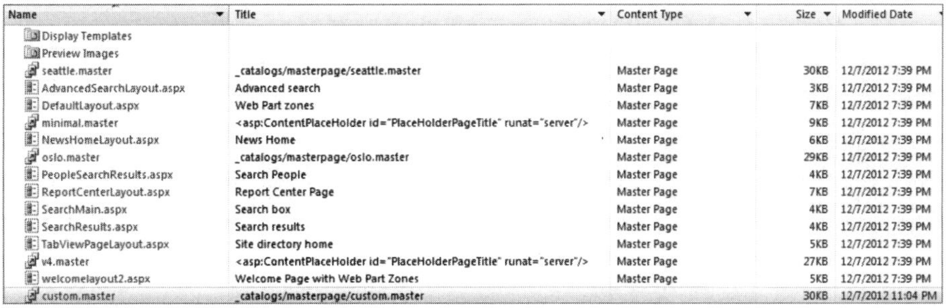

FIGURE 18-16

Now, if for any reason your customized master page ever causes issues, you can tell SharePoint to use one of the default master pages and regain functionality while you troubleshoot your customized master page.

The following example demonstrates how to edit a master page to make a simple change to your site collection. To illustrate the steps involved, it uses a site collection created with the Team Site template.

The new Team Site template in SharePoint 2013 is very different from what you may be used to with SharePoint 2007 or SharePoint 2010. It makes heavy use of the Windows 8 user interface and is similar in style to what you have seen in SharePoint 2013. Something that you may have noticed at the top of the page is a blue bar that stretches across much of the screen and contains the word SharePoint. You are going to change the color of this bar.

1. Navigate to the URL of your site collection in SharePoint Designer and open your site collection — `http://portal.contoso.com/sites/branding` in this example.

2. In the Navigation pane, select the Master Page site object. Then select the master page copy you created in the previous example, `custom.master`. Right-click the file and select Edit File in advanced mode.

3. What you will see now is more than 650 lines of code that make up your SharePoint site's master page. If this looks overwhelming, don't worry. That's why you made, and are working from, a copy of the master page. The line of code that you are looking for is on line 80:

   ```
   <div id="suiteBarLeft">
   ```

4. Click in this area of code and change the line to the following:

   ```
   <div id="suiteBarLeft" style="background-color:gray;">
   ```

5. This is called an inline CSS style and although there are other ways to make CSS changes, this will work for the purpose of the example. Save your master page by selecting the save icon in the top left corner.

6. Switch back over to the Master Pages tab to the right of the tab you were just working in (see Figure 18-17).

FIGURE 18-17

7. Select your `custom.master` file, right-click it, and select Set as Default Master Page. This instructs SharePoint to use your newly created master page and not the default.

8. In a web browser, navigate to the site collection and log into `http://portal.contoso.com/sites/branding`.

Now all the pages in this site will have a gray bar, rather than blue. Granted, this is a very simple change to the master page but it illustrates how changes are made. Now you have the ability to make changes to other facets of your SharePoint site.

Page Layouts

Page layouts are a part of publishing templates. They enable power users and administrators to create web page-quality layouts for their pages with greater ease and flexibility than text layouts, which are what you must use when publishing features are not activated. Page layouts are also extendable, and you can create your own page layouts in SharePoint designer for even more customization. Page layouts are generally used for an Internet-facing portal, an extranet portal, or a heavily branded SharePoint farm.

It is page layouts that truly enable SharePoint to provide an enterprise with a full-featured content management system, making it possible for content authors to create new articles and pages from within SharePoint that all adhere to one common look and feel.

The out-of-the-box page layouts are a good starting point, but you can also create your own page layouts and make changes to the default layouts. This is where page layouts really start to show their power. This section walks through an example that demonstrates how to make changes to the Blank Web Part page layout. The Blank Web Part page layout contains a page content section and eight zones to which you can add a Web Part. You will remove one of these Web Part zones to constrain users to a total of seven Web Part zones.

In order to follow along with the example, you need to create a site collection based on a publishing template, which is available only with SharePoint Server 2013 Standard and Enterprise Editions. For the purpose of this example, the site collection `http://portal.contoso.com/sites/branding` will be created from the Publishing Portal Site template.

1. Navigate to the URL of the site collection in SharePoint Designer and open your site collection.

2. In the Navigation pane, select the Page Layouts site object. Select the `BlankWebPartPage` `.aspx` page layout. Then, just as you did with your master page in the previous example, right-click and copy and paste in an empty area of the screen to create a copy of the Blank Web Part Page page layout.

3. Right-click on the newly created `BlankWebPartPage_copy(1).aspx` file and rename it `DemoPagelayout.aspx`.

4. Right-click on `DemoPagelayout.aspx` again and select Properties. Change the title to **Demo Page Layout**, as shown in Figure 18-18. Click Apply, and then OK.

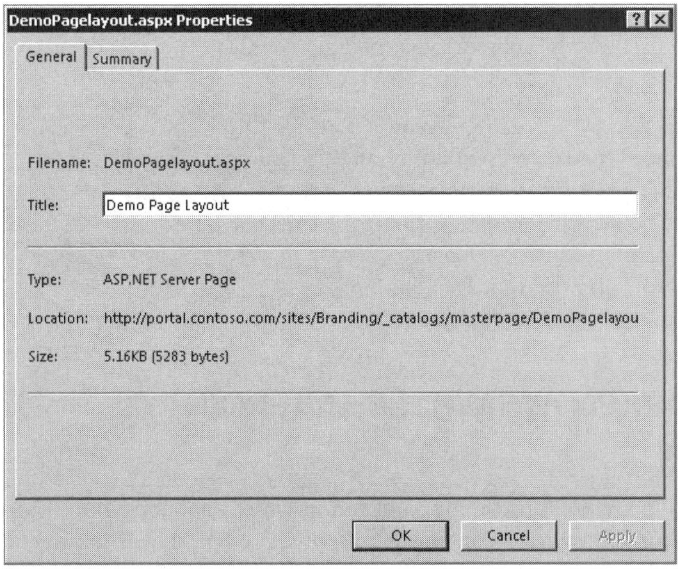

DemoPagelayout.aspx Properties

General | Summary

Filename: DemoPagelayout.aspx

Title: Demo Page Layout

Type: ASP.NET Server Page

Location: http://portal.contoso.com/sites/Branding/_catalogs/masterpage/DemoPagelayou

Size: 5.16KB (5283 bytes)

OK Cancel Apply

FIGURE 18-18

5. Right-click on `DemoPagelayout.aspx` and select the Check Out option. After doing that, right-click and select Edit File in advanced mode.

6. Remove the footer Web Part zone by deleting the code located on line 59.

7. Save the file and select Check In for the file from the Page Layouts section. Be sure the Publish a Major Version option is checked.

8. In a web browser, navigate to the site collection and log into `http://portal.contoso.com/sites/branding`.

9. In the top right corner, click the gear icon and select Add an page. Call the new page **Demo**.

10. From the Ribbon, select the Page tab. In the Page Actions section, select Page Layout. Underneath the Welcome Page section of your Page Layouts, you will see the Demo Page Layout you just created (see Figure 18-19). Select this page layout to apply it to the page you just created.

FIGURE 18-19

You will now see that you have a page content area with seven Web Part zones. Go through step 10 again and select the Blank Web Part page to see how your page layout differs.

Of course, customizing page layouts isn't limited to removing items; you can add them as well and even create your own page layouts based on the content types of the default page layouts.

If you go back into the `DemoPageLayout.aspx` file you just created and edit in advanced mode, you will notice an Insert tab in your Ribbon. Located here are various controls that you can add to your own page layouts, including HTML form controls or navigation controls such as a menu. Simply select the control you want to insert and the required code will be inserted into your page layout.

IMPLEMENTING WORKFLOWS WITH SHAREPOINT DESIGNER 2013

When you think about what companies use SharePoint for, obviously collaboration comes to mind, along with file sharing and for some even a content management system. However, in companies all over the world, one of SharePoint's most useful and powerful features is the capability to automate business tasks with workflows. Workflows are the heart and soul of SharePoint for many organizations, enabling users to accomplish numerous tasks, such as travel request approvals, help desk submissions, and even payroll applications.

In keeping with the theme of change discussed earlier, SharePoint Designer 2013 workflows now include functionality specifically for Windows Azure Workflow, a change that greatly increases the robustness and feature set of workflows in SharePoint 2013. Indeed, when you consider the large number of new features related to workflows, it's clear that Microsoft has given them a lot of attention in SharePoint Designer 2013. This section takes a deeper look at these new features.

Recall that when you first install SharePoint, the workflow engine included with SharePoint 2010 is also installed. When you install and integrate the new workflow engine for SharePoint 2013 workflows, you now have full compatibility between SharePoint 2010 workflows and SharePoint 2013 workflows. This is important, as many organizations will have numerous SharePoint 2010 workflows that they want to move over to SharePoint 2013 without having to rewrite them. To be clear, when you install SharePoint 2013, you get the 2010 engine, which may help with compatibility issues. However, if you want the 2013, you can install it by executing the steps suggested earlier.

With SharePoint Designer 2013, the tools available to you when you begin to write your workflows greatly transcend those available previously, enabling you to do things that were only possible for developers using Visual Studio in SharePoint 2010. Workflows are now stage-based, meaning they no longer have to execute steps one right after the other. You can now jump to any stage in your workflow. Loops are also available and variables have been enhanced to support arrays.

Also enhanced is the capability to make web service calls from within SharePoint Designer, including better support for web services such as REST, SOAP, and HTTP. You can also package your workflows in SharePoint Designer 2013 to deploy to a remote farm without having to use Visual Studio to create a solution; and using what is one of the biggest improvements over SharePoint Designer 2010, you can now cut, copy, and paste your code in the text-based designer!

> **NOTE** *For readers who are new to workflows and may feel a little overwhelmed by all the developer speak in the past couple of paragraphs, the new Visual Designer in SharePoint 2013 provides the capability to draw workflows with the same canvas you use to draw workflows in Visio. With SharePoint 2010 and Visio 2010, workflows could be drawn within Visio and then imported into SharePoint Designer. Now this functionality is included within SharePoint Designer 2013 as long as you have Visio 2013. However, this level of integration is outside the scope of this book. For more information, Visual Designer and Visio 2013 please see* `http://msdn.microsoft.com/en-us/library/share-point/jj670177(v=office.15).aspx`.

Of course, for some code junkies of the world, SharePoint Designer will not meet all their requirements, and the next step for them is to write their workflows in Visual Studio. If this describes you, I recommend taking a look at the following link to read about the differences and similarities governing what you can do with workflows between SharePoint Designer 2013 and Visual Studio: `http://msdn.microsoft.com/en-us/library/sharepoint/jj163199(v=office.15).aspx#bkm_Comparing`.

As noted earlier, you can now save workflows created in SharePoint Designer as a template that bundles the workflow as a .wsp package, which you can then deploy as a solution in a remote farm. With SharePoint Designer 2010 it was possible to do this with a reusable workflow, but now you have the same feature for your List and Site workflows as well. Please note that in order for this example to work, you need to have installed and configured the SharePoint 2013 Workflow platform covered previously in this chapter.

1. Create any List workflow or Site workflow but ensure that you specify it is a SharePoint 2013 workflow. If you need an example of creating a workflow, please see Chapter 16.

2. In the Navigation pane in SharePoint Designer, select the Workflows site object.

3. You will now see a list of the workflows that have been created in your
site. Select the workflow that was
just created, and in the Manage
section of the Ribbon, select the
Save as Template option shown in
Figure 18-20.

FIGURE 18-20

4. You will receive a prompt that the
.wsp package was saved to the Site Assets library. Navigate to the Site Assets site object in the Navigation pane to access the demo.wsp package. From the Ribbon, select the option to export the file and save it to a convenient location.

5. Log on to a SharePoint site other than the one from which your workflow was created and select Site Settings. Click the Solutions link beneath Web Designer Galleries.

6. Select the Upload Solution option and browse to the .wsp file you just created. Choose the option to activate the solution (see Figure 18-21).

FIGURE 18-21

7.   Now return to the Site Settings page and under the Site Actions section, click Manage Site Features. A feature for the Workflow template for the workflow you just created will appear. Activate the feature to make the workflow accessible to the new site.

Of course, this example only scratches the surface of workflows and how you can use SharePoint Designer to create and manage them. To learn more about workflows, please see Chapter 16, which covers them in detail.

SUMMARY

SharePoint Designer is a full-featured management suite for SharePoint whose features and capabilities extend far beyond editing your SharePoint pages. With SharePoint Designer 2013, you can create no-code solutions that previously could only be created with programs such as Visual Studio. In addition, you can create branding that previously could only be accomplished with full-fledged design software such as Adobe Dreamweaver, quickly and efficiently manage your SharePoint sites, and even design solutions that utilize your external line-of-business applications.

Like SharePoint itself, SharePoint Designer is a robust piece of software that serves multiple purposes. Entire books have been written about SharePoint Designer 2007 and 2010, and SharePoint Designer 2013 will be no exception. Obviously, one chapter can only provide a high-level overview of SharePoint Designer 2013, but hopefully from an administrator's point of view you now have some insight into its power, and it has piqued your curiosity enough to get you started.

19

Troubleshooting SharePoint

WHAT'S IN THIS CHAPTER?

➤ The Unified Logging Service

➤ The Correlation ID

➤ The Developer Dashboard

➤ Additional tools and resources

For a product that provides so many options and functions, SharePoint is remarkably stable. That being said, SharePoint isn't perfect. Sometimes things don't work the way you might expect, and sometimes they may not work at all. Even a great administrator won't know everything about a system as complex as a SharePoint farm, so it is important to understand the basics of getting to the root of SharePoint issues. This chapter demonstrates a wide range of ways in which SharePoint speaks to you about its problems. Before digging into the details, however, remember that your brain is your best troubleshooting tool. Find out as much information about the error as possible before you even touch the server. When does the error occur? Does it happen to everyone, or only to certain users? Does the problem occur only in certain scenarios or does it seem to be random? Finally, not to be forgotten, what was the last thing that changed? Did you just add a patch or install a farm solution? Did all your users just upgrade their browser version? Things that are new or things that were old and eliminated are always good places to start when looking for the cause of a problem. If none of the basics give you an idea of what went wrong, have no fear; there are plenty of other places to look.

THE UNIFIED LOGGING SERVICE

The Unified Logging Service (ULS) is the system that drives two of the diagnostic logs in your farm, the trace log, often referred to as the ULS log, and the SharePoint-related errors that surface in the Windows Event Log system. The trace log wasn't created strictly for troubleshooting. On the one hand, although you can configure the amount of information that is captured by the ULS, generally the service tracks a lot of events, big and small, as they occur and logs them in the trace log. On the other hand, messages that actually are sent to the Windows Event Logs from the ULS are much more likely to be areas of concern for troubleshooting. Because it can become confusing having things logged in two places, SharePoint has tried to make it a bit easier. Every error that is logged in the Windows Event Logs will always have a corresponding entry in the ULS logs. This is a welcome change from earlier versions of SharePoint (I'm looking at you SharePoint 2003 and SharePoint 2007), for which some events would be in the ULS logs and others would be in the Windows Event Logs. Trying to find all the log entries associated with a problem was like looking for Blackbeard's treasure.

The amount of data provided by the ULS can be overwhelming; and as mentioned earlier, it is possible to configure it to report with more or less detail. However, if you have spent a lot of time and effort configuring the logging for general monitoring purposes, it might not be a great idea to change those settings for a short troubleshooting window, especially if other people use the trace logs for other purposes.

> **NOTE** *As you go through this and other chapters, remember that the Unified Logging Service is the service that sends messages to the Windows Event Logs and to the SharePoint trace logs. Sometimes you will hear or see the trace logs referred to as the ULS logs. There is nothing incorrect about calling the trace logs ULS logs but for the purposes of clarity, when discussing the service and the logs in a conversation, it is useful to be a little picky and remember the trace log is the only place ULS information surfaces.*

Windows Event Logs

Because the ULS tends to send messages to the Windows Event logs only when something serious happens, they are a good place to start looking for clues. To open the Event Viewer for Windows Server 2012, go to the Start panel that has all the Windows tiles and begin typing **Event Viewer** until it appears in the apps list; or if you are in the desktop view put your mouse cursor in the lower left-hand corner and click the right mouse key, or press Windows+X. This will open a command menu that includes the Event Viewer, as shown in Figure 19-1.

While some strictly informational items for SharePoint might appear in the Event Viewer, typically the event level will be either Critical or Warning if it is of interest to a troubleshooter. To help separate the wheat from the chaff, you can put the Windows Event Viewer into a "bad news

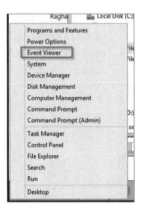

FIGURE 19-1

only" view that strips out all the events in the Information and Verbose categories, showing only events that are Critical, Warning, or Error. This makes it much easier to find problems when you're troubleshooting. To experience this nirvana, select a log in Event Viewer, such as the Application log. On the right-hand side of the screen, under Actions, click Filter Current Logs... When the Filter Current Log dialog appears, click the check boxes next to Critical, Warning, and Error. After you click OK, this log will only show errors. Figure 19-2 shows the dialog with the correct boxes checked.

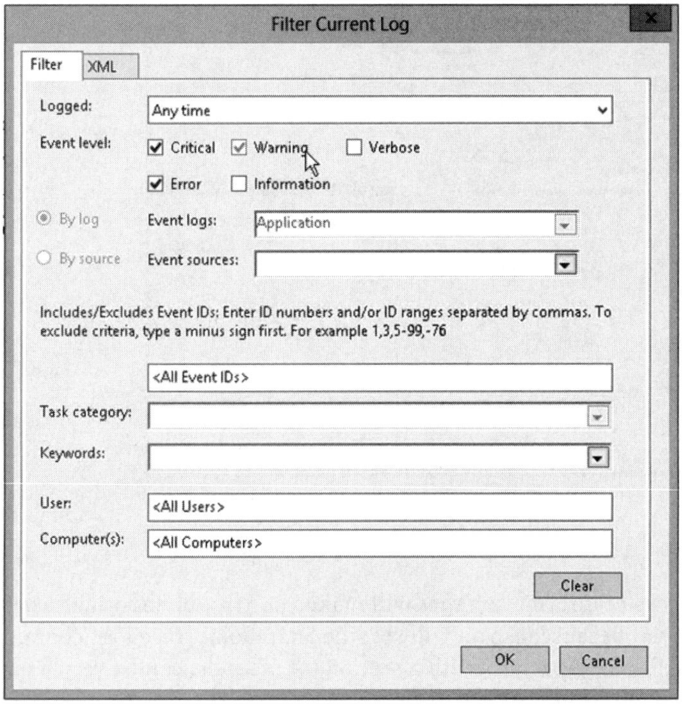

FIGURE 19-2

You can take this one step further to filter out events that you don't care about. As you're troubleshooting a problem, you may see error events that don't pertain to the issue you're currently doing battle with. While you're certainly welcome to fix other problems too, those errors are just getting in the way for the moment. You can use that same filter to filter out unwanted events. Click the Filter Current Log action again to return to the filter settings. In the box that is populated with "<All Event IDs>" type a minus sign (-) and then the Event ID of the event you want to filter out. You can filter out multiple events by separating them with commas. After you've shown that particular SharePoint problem who's boss, you can remove the filters by clicking Clear Filter under Actions, or access the Filter Current Log dialog and click Clear.

Figure 19-3 gives you an idea of what a typical SharePoint error looks like in the Event Viewer when no filters are applied.

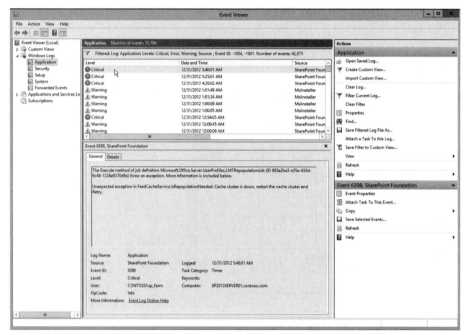

FIGURE 19-3

Immediately you can see several pieces of information that will make your troubleshooting easier. The Date and Time column is essential because, as you will see, the SharePoint trace logs contain a lot of information. Having a time column, especially with a section for seconds, can be very handy, as one minute of trace logs can be several pages long.

For example, if a user presents a problem and says, "It happened about lunch time," that gives you a rough idea of where you need to begin looking in the Event Log. When you see a red Critical error at 12:13:27 with the word SharePoint in the Source column, you now have a specific time to search for even if the rest of the information in that log entry isn't helpful.

Very often, the Source column of the error will show SharePoint Foundation, SharePoint Server, or make some other direct reference to SharePoint, which helps separate SharePoint errors from other issues on the server.

The Task Category column will sometimes reference a SharePoint service or service application, such as Health (the Usage and Health Data Collection service application) or Timer (the SharePoint Timer Service), so remember to check that column to get an idea of where SharePoint is having the problem. It is also likely that the same category will appear in the corresponding trace log column described in the next section.

The Event ID can be one of the most immediately useful pieces of information you have. The nice thing about having Event IDs in the Event Viewer is that you can easily find more information about each event by doing an Internet search. Referring back to Figure 19-3, note the Critical SharePoint Foundation errors with an Event ID of 6398. An Internet search for "SharePoint Event ID 6398" will return hundreds, if not thousands, of articles. In this particular case, you will find that many different problems may be attached to Event ID 6398 because it is the standard Event ID for SharePoint timer jobs that fail. For this type of error, the Event ID isn't enough; you have to look at the specifics of the error itself. Figure 19-4 shows the Details tab that is displayed when you double-click on a particular Event Viewer entry.

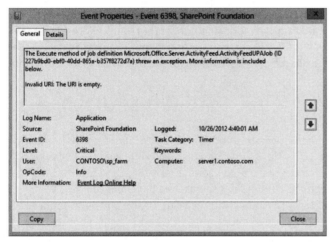

FIGURE 19-4

This tab contains a lot of information. In addition to doing an Internet search on the text of the error, you can see the user under whom the error happened — in this case the farm account, because that is usually the user under whom the SharePoint Timer job runs. You also have a handy Copy button that enables you to copy the entire text of the error, both from the General tab and the Details tab, so you can paste the information into a support ticket or your personal notes. Not a bad start for the first log you have looked in! Just in case you are curious, this particular error was caused because the User Profile Synchronization service application was not fully configured. If only all SharePoint problems were this easy to solve.

Although you can find SharePoint-specific issues in the Event Viewer, remember that SharePoint runs in Windows and uses IIS to serve information. Any critical errors in the Event Viewer are worth examining. Windows and IIS are key partners in making SharePoint work, so don't ignore them when they beg for help. SharePoint-specific errors are a good place to start looking for the answer to a specific problem, but they may not be the only place you need to look.

This also means that you'll have to venture outside of the Application log and look in the System and Security logs. It's not uncommon for a Windows issue or a security issue to be the cause of SharePoint misbehaving. It's not enough to just to poke around in the Application logs and hope for the best. You have to get your junior detective magnifying glass and sniff around in the other logs, too, in order to piece all the clues together.

While you are looking at this stuff, give some thought to managing your Event Logs. By default, Windows saves 20 megabytes of Event Log data, and once that limit is met new events will overwrite the oldest events. In a way that's nice, the log never gets larger and will never accidently fill your hard drive, and the logs don't take quite as long to open remotely. Unfortunately, this default setting also means that when there are serious issues, 20 megabytes may only hold a day or two of information and the beginning of your problem may be overwritten before you get a chance to look for it. Microsoft has lots of information about managing the event logs at `http://technet.microsoft.com/en-us/library/cc766178.aspx`. This link includes information such as how to change log retention settings, clearing and archiving the data, as well as reading archived logs that are no longer in the current Event Log. Consider a retention strategy that allows you to archive and keep logs for a set number of days to avoid losing important troubleshooting data. Every organization has different requirements, but a good general target is to make sure you have Event Logs from the last week copied off of the SharePoint servers on a nightly basis in case of a serious failure.

Trace Logs

Trace logs contain only SharePoint-specific information, but much of it is about normal operations, not specifically errors. By default, the trace logs are found in `%CommonProgramFiles%\Common Files\microsoft shared\Web Server Extensions\15\LOGS`, and `%CommonProgramFiles%` is typically the `C:\Program Files` directory. The log files themselves have names like `SERVERNAME-20121026-1200.log`. Notice 2012, indicating the year; 10, for the tenth month; 26, for the 26th day; 12, for the 12th hour; and so on. This naming convention helps you find the right log to look in if you know the date and time of the event you are looking for. By default, a new log file is created every 30 minutes. The trace logs can be overwhelming even when the ULS is set to collect only moderate amounts of information. At the very least you want to have a specific time or error message to look for in the logs, as each log file may be hundreds of megabytes or more in size. The data in the trace logs is laid out in columns, so it is easily parsed using an Excel spreadsheet or similar tool, but it can also be read with `notepad.exe`. Because the listings are usually quite lengthy, they would not fit nicely on a printed page in this book, so Table 19-1 summarizes a typical trace log entry.

TABLE 19-1: Trace Log Entries

COLUMN HEADINGS	EXAMPLE LOG DATA
Timestamp	10/26/2012 12:16:09.21
Process (the process that generated the log entry)	w3wp.exe (0x00F4)
TID (Thread ID)	0x16A8
Area	SharePoint Foundation

Category	Topology
EventID	e5mc
Level	Medium
Message	WcfSendRequest: RemoteAddress: 'http://server:32843/e7560c95030343e08f2ff3e3ed7f70c9/MetadataWebService.svc' Channel: 'Microsoft.SharePoint.Taxonomy.IMetadataWebServiceApplication' Action: 'http://schemas.microsoft.com/sharepoint/taxonomy/soap/IDataAccessReadOnly/GetChanges2' MessageId: 'urn:uuid:18a9aac5-894d-4370-8b2d-95e42caeb137'
Correlation (the Correlation ID)	6d951f7e-7796-44e5-907a-11f59cf974c6

The data shown in Table 19-1 is nothing exciting; in fact, the log it was pulled from had literally hundreds of lines that were nearly identical, representing a normal process that the Metadata service application goes through every day. This is why it is important to use other sources of information such as the Windows Event Log to narrow down your search in the trace log using things like error message text or timestamps.

Powerful PowerShell Tweaks

Just like the Event Logs, the trace logs have certain default settings that may or may not be appropriate for your organization's needs. Chapter 20 has two sections about configuring the ULS, creatively named Configuring ULS via Central Administration and Configuring ULS via PowerShell. There is no need to repeat everything in those sections here, but a quick overview might be helpful so you don't have to skip around too much. PowerShell is cooler than Central Administration so that is what the examples will use.

Open the SharePoint 2013 Management Shell, type `Get-SPDiagnosticConfig`, and hit enter. The output of the cmdlet will be something like this:

```
PS C:\Users\administrator.CONTOSO> Get-SPDiagnosticConfig


AllowLegacyTraceProviders                       : False
AppAnalyticsAutomaticUploadEnabled              : False
CustomerExperienceImprovementProgramEnabled     : True
ErrorReportingEnabled                           : True
ErrorReportingAutomaticUploadEnabled            : True
DownloadErrorReportingUpdatesEnabled            : True
DaysToKeepLogs                                  : 14
LogMaxDiskSpaceUsageEnabled                     : False
LogDiskSpaceUsageGB                             : 1000
LogLocation                                     : %CommonProgramFiles%\Microsoft
                                                  Shared\Web Server
                                                  Extensions\15\LOGS\
LogCutInterval                                  : 30
```

```
EventLogFloodProtectionEnabled                 : True
EventLogFloodProtectionThreshold               : 5
EventLogFloodProtectionTriggerPeriod           : 2
EventLogFloodProtectionQuietPeriod             : 2
EventLogFloodProtectionNotifyInterval          : 5
ScriptErrorReportingEnabled                    : True
ScriptErrorReportingRequireAuth                : True
ScriptErrorReportingDelay                      : 60
```

Remember, the trace logs aren't just for troubleshooting, so don't jump straight into changing these settings without giving the results some thought. There are a few settings that could be tweaked, either for convenience or the safety of your farm. First there is LogLocation, the location you see in the preceding code snippet, and %CommonProgramFiles%\Microsoft Shared\Web ServerExtensions\15\LOGS\ is the default location for the ULS logs. If you prefer the logs to be on a separate drive than the operating system, a quick change is in order. Maybe you want the ULS logs in a new directory on a different drive such as D:\. To make things easy to find for anyone else that gets on your server, don't change the path, just the drive letter. Use the following command to move the ULS logs to the same path, but on the D: drive:

```
. Set-SPDiagnosticConfig -LogLocation "D:\ Program Files\Common Files\
microsoft shared\Web Server Extensions\15\LOGS".
```

This won't move or copy the existing log files though so be sure to move or delete those manually.

Unlike the Event Logs, the trace logs are set to keep 14 days' worth of log data by default, not a set number of megabytes. Combined with the fact that the -LogMaxDiskSpaceUsageEnabled parameter is set to False, this means that your logs could use all of the available hard drive space. Even setting -LogMaxDiskSpaceUsageEnabled to True would only limit the logs to 1000 gigabytes of space as defined in the -LogDiskSpaceUsageGB setting. Does that D: drive even have a terabyte free? Settings like this are trouble waiting to happen. If you move the trace logs to the D drive, but it is only a 500GB volume, you will want to change the Set-SPDiagnosticConfig parameters appropriately. To protect your server and still capture as much data as possible, you would use the following commands:

```
Set-SPDiagnosticConfig -LogDiskSpaceUsage 450
Set-SPDiagnosticConfig -LogMaxDiskSpaceUsageEnabled True
```

Why use 450 for the disk space usage instead of 500? As a rule of thumb, a minimum of 10% of a disk volume should be free if at all possible to prevent running out of space and causing data loss. A couple of quick changes using Set-SPDiagnosticConfig and you have given yourself easier access to the trace logs and protected yourself from possible data corruption. Not bad for one PowerShell cmdlet.

Set-SPDiagnosticConfig has other options that may be especially useful when troubleshooting. In the output for Get-SPDiagnosticConfig, the LogCutInterval is 30 minutes by default. That means the ULS will spend 30 minutes filling a single trace log file before it creates another. In situations where there are lots of errors, a single trace log file may get very large in half an hour. Later in the "Using PowerShell to Tame the ULS Logs" section, you will see information about the New-SPLogFile cmdlet, but to use it effectively it helps to know when an error happens or how to cause it on demand. If you just want to make sure the logs are smaller so you can open and read them in notepad, it might be enough just to limit the amount of time the ULS spends putting data into each file. For example, changing the `LogCutInterval` to 5 means that only 5 minutes of data is contained in each trace log file. To make this change use the cmdlet below.

```
Set-SPDiagnosticConfig -LogCutInterval 5
```

This won't cause the ULS to capture less data, it just causes it to put the information in 12 trace log files an hour instead of just 2. Each file will be smaller and more manageable.

Once you are finished troubleshooting you probably want to set the `-LogCutInterval` back to 30 just to cut down on the clutter of generating so many trace logs per hour.

More information about the parameters of the `Set-SPDiagnosticConfig` cmdlet can be found at `http://technet.microsoft.com/en-us/library/ff607575.aspx` and there are more examples of its use in the Monitoring SharePoint 2013 chapter ahead.

Another way you may be able to prevent future troubleshooting problems is to encourage your developers to use the trace logs in their project. This is an administration book, not a developer guide, but at very least you can provide `http://msdn.microsoft.com/en-us/library/ee535537(v=office.14).aspx` as an introduction if they have no idea where to begin.

Viewing the ULS Logs with the ULS Viewer

While the ULS logs are simple, well-formatted text files, trying to look through them with a garden-variety text editor can be maddening. Trying to investigate the problem may end up being worse than the problem itself. Fortunately, however, there is a tool written expressly for the purpose of opening ULS log files and displaying them in such a way that humans can actually make sense of them. Called the ULS Viewer, the best part about this tool is that it's a completely free download at MSDN: `http://archive.msdn.microsoft.com/ULSViewer`. This tool should exist on every SharePoint server in your environment; it's that handy. It's a mere 500KB in size and doesn't require any kind of install. When you need it, you just fire it up and bask in its efficiency. (Note that if you download it directly from the Internet to your server, you may need to "unblock" it before you can run it.)

The ULS Viewer can view ULS logs from a couple of different locations, but this chapter focuses on the live logs. To watch the ULS logs in real time, start the ULS Viewer on your server by selecting File ➪ Open From, as shown in Figure 19-5. Alternately, just select Ctrl+U.

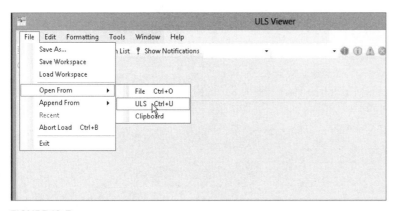

FIGURE 19-5

By default, the ULS Viewer opens the logs from SharePoint's default log directory. In most cases you can just click OK at the File Location dialog that appears. If you want to watch the ULS logs from another server, you can also enter the UNC path to its ULS logs in that dialog. This enables you to monitor the logs from several servers from one location.

If you get an "access denied" error when the ULS Viewer tries to open the logs, make sure the user you're logged in as has permission to that location. If you're trying to view the logs on the local server, you need to run the ULS Viewer with the "Run as administrator" option.

Once the ULS Viewer is open and doing its job, it can be a little intimidating, especially on a busy server, but it provides quite a few methods for slicing and dicing log entries to make it easy to find what you're looking for. Probably the most helpful is the capability to format log entries based on common criteria. For example, the User Profile Service can be a bugger to work with sometimes, so it often provides the reason to start the ULS Viewer. Figure 19-6 shows how you can format all the lines that pertain to the User Profile Service to the same color, making them easy to identify.

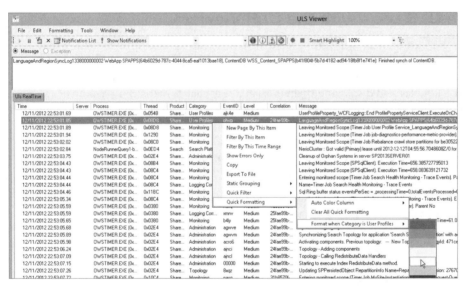

FIGURE 19-6

After that's done, all the events within the User Profile Service category will be highlighted in the chosen color, as shown in Figure 19-7.

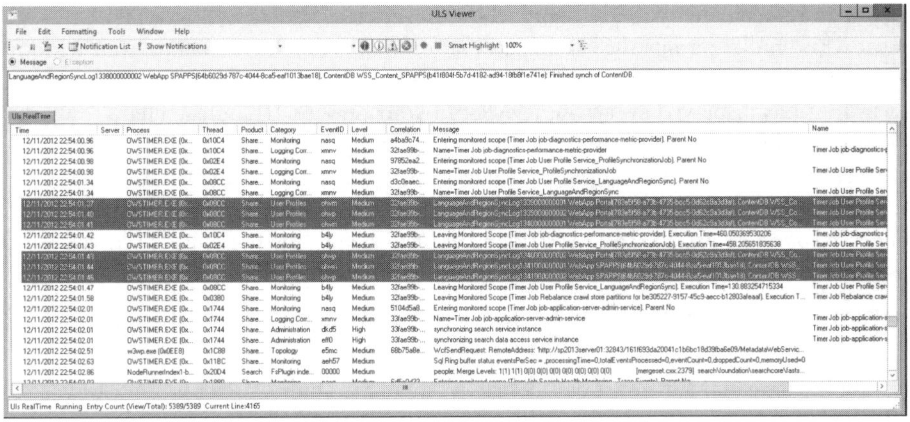

FIGURE 19-7

This capability makes it very easy to follow a specific issue without the pertinent log entries getting lost in all the other traffic. It's very flexible; you can format based on any column, filtering the entries to whatever you're trying to track down. You can also have multiple formatting statements in place at once. Using formatting to highlight the log entries you want is usually better than filtering out the ones you don't want. You never know if something unexpected is causing the issue you're trying to resolve.

For most troubleshooting you should pay special attention to four areas of a log message. The Message column contains text that usually provides specific information. If the text doesn't get you closer to an answer by itself, you can search the Internet for similar problems. The Process column can help isolate which services, and therefore which service accounts, are involved in the error. As noted earlier, the Category column is also a good one to watch. Finally, the Correlation ID column, which is discussed in more detail in the section "The Correlation ID: Your New Best Friend," can help you hone in on the exact area of the log relevant to your problem.

Using PowerShell to Tame the ULS Logs

While the ULS Viewer is a fine tool, it's useful to know other ways of getting the same information. We all have different work preferences, so this section shows you how to reign in those ULS logs with PowerShell. Anytime you find yourself in a position where you need to use PowerShell with SharePoint, you should ensure that the logged-in user meets a few requirements:

➤ The user should have the `securityadmin` fixed role in the SQL Server instance(s) where your SharePoint databases reside.

➤ The user should have the `db_owner` fixed role on all the databases with which you hope to interact.

➤ The "Run as Administrator" option should be used when starting the SharePoint 2013 Management Shell.

With those three requirements met you are ready to start. The first cmdlet to discuss is `Get-SPLogEvent`. This cmdlet pumps the trace log event data into the PowerShell output window faster than you can probably read it, and generally the data is too wide to display in the window. It also won't stop until it has displayed every single event in your server's ULS logs. That's probably not helpful, and will probably result in you falling asleep at your desk before it is finished. Fortunately, `Get-SPLogEvent` has numerous parameters, as do most PowerShell cmdlets. Chapter 7, "Administering SharePoint 2013 with PowerShell," contains all the details about how to get the most out of it, but here are a couple of brief examples. The following cmdlet returns all the log events in a time range (using United States date and time formatting):

```
Get-SPLogEvent -StartTime "10/25/2012 12:00" -EndTime "10/25/2012 13:00"
```

Because formatting the date and time part can be tricky, there are some shortcuts you can use. The following PowerShell command will return all the events that occurred in the last 10 minutes:

```
Get-SPLogEvent -StartTime ((Get-Date).addminutes(-10))
```

With this statement we're being sneaky. The `Get-Time` cmdlet returns the current date and time. To specify a start time that occurred 10 minutes ago, you add a negative 10 minutes to the current time. Be careful using `Get-SPLogEvent` without the `-StartTime` parameter, otherwise it will pull data starting from the first trace log available to it, which may be days or weeks old.

The following line shows how to use PowerShell to view log events from trace logs in a specific location:

```
Get-SPLogEvent -Directory "C:\Logfiles"
```

This enables you to view only the files you think are relevant to your problem, rather than the entire default log location. If you have multiple servers in your farm, you can copy their ULS logs to one location and use this technique to view them. Later in this section you'll see another option for dealing with multi-server farms.

Unfortunately, when you use a cmdlet like this in the PowerShell command window, your output is limited by the size of the PowerShell window itself. The same problem exists if you try to use other PowerShell commands to sort the data, such as the following:

```
Get-SPLogEvent | Where-Object {$_.Level -eq "High"}
```

This command takes the `Get-SPLogEvent` cmdlet and pipes it through a loop that examines each line, looking for and then outputting only those trace log events for which the `Level` (from Table 19-1) equals `High`. The syntax is perfectly valid, but unfortunately the output looks something like this:

```
Timestamp    Area                    Category                   EventID  Level
---------    ----                    --------                   -------  -----
08:47:39.93 SharePoint Server        Unified Logging Service    b8fx     High
08:47:40.88 SharePoint Foundation    SQM                        8zn7     High
08:47:42.51 SharePoint Foundation    Unified Logging Service    b8fx     High
08:47:42.58 SharePoint Foundation    SQM                        8zn7     High
08:47:42.60 SharePoint Foundation    Unified Logging Service    b8fx     High
08:47:42.66 SharePoint Foundation    SQM                        8zn7     High
08:47:53.46 SharePoint Foundation    Upgrade                    fbv7     High
```

No message, no Correlation ID; in short, most of the information you probably want will be chopped off the end. Don't despair, however; there is one more trick you need to see and it is a good one! The following `Out-GridView` cmdlet sends the PowerShell output to an interactive table viewer, as shown in Figure 19-8:

```
Get-SPLogEvent | Where-Object {$_.Level -eq "High"}|Out-GridView
```

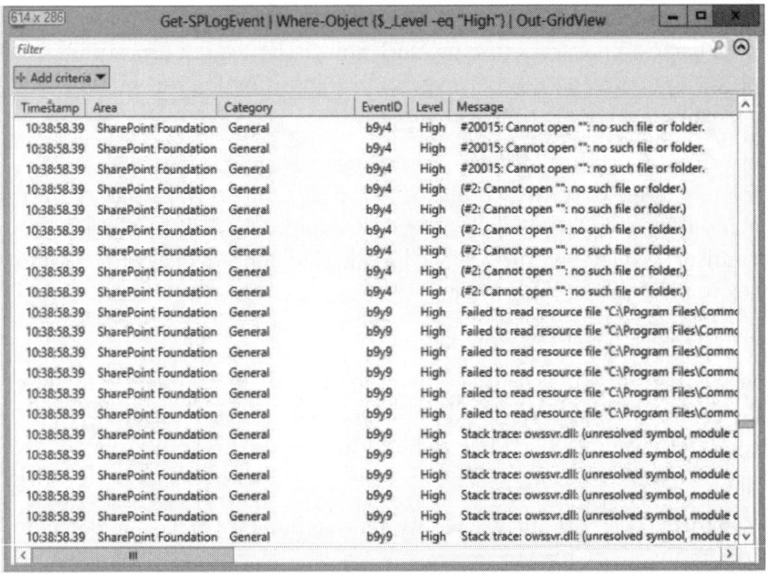

FIGURE 19-8

HAVING TROUBLE WITH OUT-GRIDVIEW?

PowerShell can be a harsh mistress, and using `Out-GridView` is one way to anger it. You might get an error that the cmdlet isn't found when you try to run `Out-GridView`. That's because `Out-GridView` isn't included with the out-of-the-box PowerShell configuration. You only get it if you have PowerShell's Integrated Scripting Environment (ISE). This ISE is included with Windows, but it isn't always installed. For instructions on how to install the ISE, refer to Chapter 7.

First, notice that this table viewer doesn't chop off any data you want to see. Even better, this interactive table viewer also includes a number of additional options for sorting the output using the Add criteria button and filter line you see. The `Out-GridView` view is also a good tool to use for copying data to be pasted into spreadsheets and other applications. You can get the same output shown in Figure 19-8 by using `Get-SPLogEvent | Out-GridView` and adding a criteria of "and Level equal High" in the interactive grid viewer; but like many graphical tools, the viewer can be slow when sorting through very large amounts of data. Simplifying the output by using PowerShell will give you faster results.

Sometimes all this complex sorting isn't necessary. Remember that the best time to use the trace logs is when you have some idea of where to look. If you are troubleshooting an issue you can reproduce, there are other ways to narrow down your search using PowerShell, such as the `New-SPLogFile` cmdlet. `New-SPLogFile` causes the creation of a new trace log file, making it much easier to search through the entries using Notepad or the ULS Viewer. To use `New-SPLogFile` you simply issue the cmdlet in a PowerShell session, perform the steps to reproduce your issue, wait a few minutes for everything to get logged, and then run `New-SPLogFile` again. The resulting log file will contain only the events that are happening around the same time as your error.

In larger SharePoint farms it can be difficult to determine which server an error is occurring on. It could be happening on the search index server, or on one of two web front ends. Rather than trying to reproduce the issue on each server several times and search their individual trace logs, you can use the `Merge-SPLogFile` cmdlet to create one super trace log file that contains data from all the farm members. Here is one example of using this cmdlet:

```
Merge-SPLogFile -Path C:\Logs\Superlog.txt
```

After you run this command, SharePoint will schedule a timer job to run on each server in your farm to copy the last hours' worth of ULS logs to the file you specified — in this case, `c:\logs\Superlog.txt` on the local system. It might take a few minutes for that file to be completely populated.

If you run this on a farm of any size, you will quickly realize that an hour's worth of logs from all your servers results in a pretty unwieldy file. There are a few methods to make the merged file a little less comically large. For one, you can restrict the time frame during which it merges. `Merge-SPLogFile` supports the same `-StartTime` and `-EndTime` parameters that `Get-SPLogEvent` supports. This makes it easy to retrieve only the last few minutes' worth of events in your merged file. You can also filter the events on many of the fields, such as level, message, and area. That's not ideal, though. You never know what surrounding events might help you figure out the cause of a problem. It's better to get all the events during the given time. You can view the merged file with the ULS view described earlier, so consider filtering and formatting inside of that if necessary.

> **NOTE** *For more information about* `Merge-SPLogFile` *and other cmdlets, see Chapter 20 and Chapter 7, "Administering SharePoint 2013 with Windows PowerShell."*

THE CORRELATION ID: YOUR NEW BEST FRIEND

This section could have been called "Correlation ID Love and Appreciation," as the Correlation ID really is that helpful when it comes to troubleshooting SharePoint. Unfortunately, some users are confused about what exactly Correlation IDs are, so this section has been set aside in order to clear things up.

If you are unfamiliar with Correlation IDs, they are the GUIDs (A Globally Unique Identifier that's 32 hexadecimal characters long) that sometimes appear when an error occurs, as shown in Figure 19-9.

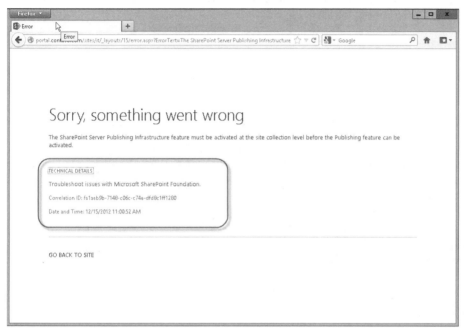

FIGURE 19-9

To get to the meat of the error message, you have to click the Technical Details link. When you do, you are rewarded with a Correlation ID as well as the exact time of the error. Both of these details can be used to hone in on all the log events that led up to the error. In this case, you also received an error message indicating exactly what the problem is, but SharePoint isn't always that generous.

When speaking with SharePoint administrators and users, it is common to hear things like "I searched the Internet for an hour looking for that Correlation ID, and I couldn't find a single answer." The reason people can't find Correlation IDs in an Internet search is because they aren't error codes like Event ID numbers from the Windows Event Viewer. Instead, the Correlation ID is a GUID that is applied to every "conversation" that SharePoint has with either users or itself. You can think of it as a fingerprint for all events that happen on your farm. You can use Correlation IDs to correlate events that are part of the same conversation.

Referring to Table 19-1, note that the Correlation ID is in a column of its own. If you replicate an error that displays an error message like this 10 times, each time you will get a different Correlation ID; and each time the ID will be found in the trace logs associated with the time and server on which the problem occurred. If you are lucky enough to have this ID, it can greatly reduce your troubleshooting time. By paying close attention to the time when a message like this appears, you can go straight to the trace log from that time period, open it in the ULS Viewer, and search for the

Correlation ID to get to the exact spot in the log where your problem occurs. Figure 19-10 shows the ULS Viewer displaying the error shown in Figure 19-9, with all the correlated events highlighted. These events were all formatted according to Correlation ID. You can watch the entire process as it happens, culminating with the surprise ending when you get the failure. Although the error in these figures is easy to diagnose, that's not always the case. Seeing all the events that led up to an error can be important in determining why it occurred.

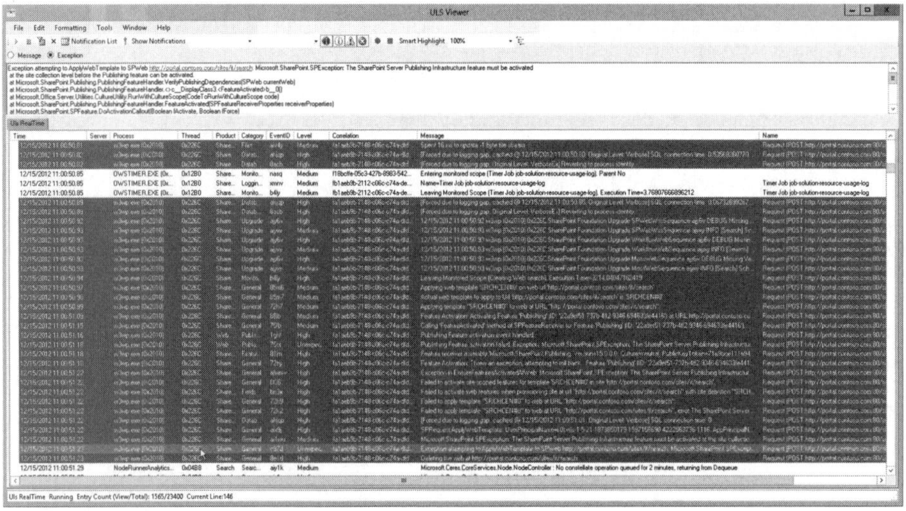

FIGURE 19-10

You can also use some of the PowerShell tricks previously covered to search for the Correlation ID you want to match. This eliminates a lot of effort associated with narrowing down your search of the trace logs. Correlation ID messages are one of the few ways in which SharePoint will make a direct reference to the trace logs and assist you with finding the cause of an issue.

Remind the users of your SharePoint farm that when they are reporting problems, a few key pieces of information can help you resolve the issue more efficiently. Writing down Correlation IDs or providing screen shots will be helpful, but the URL of the page they were accessing and the date and time of the error could be just as important.

THE DEVELOPER DASHBOARD

Administrators and developers of SharePoint 2010 may be familiar with the SharePoint Developer Dashboard. In SharePoint 2013 this tool has been extensively reworked, making it an even more useful and usable addition to your troubleshooting toolbox. The 2010 version of the Developer Dashboard made some design choices that may have prevented it from being widely used as a general troubleshooting tool. Certain configurations created performance problems; and attaching the Dashboard data to the bottom of pages sometimes created problems, rather than help resolve them. The SharePoint 2013 Developer Dashboard has received a promotion, now enjoying its own window. The new window loads a page that's located at /_layouts/15/devdash.aspx in the web you're browsing. It no longer changes how the SharePoint pages look when they load.

The Developer Dashboard can't be activated from SharePoint Central Administration. Instead, the best method is to use PowerShell. To enable the Developer Dashboard, open the SharePoint 2013 Management Shell and enter the following commands:

```
$devdash = [Microsoft.SharePoint.Administration.SPWebService]::ContentService.

DeveloperDashboardSettings
$devdash.DisplayLevel = "On"
$devdash.Update()
```

To disable the Dashboard after you are finished using it, simply use the preceding commands but replace `$devdash.DisplayLevel = "On"` with `$devdash.DisplayLevel = "Off"`.

You can also use the following stsadm commands if you insist on doing things the uncool way:

```
stsadm -o setproperty -pn developer-dashboard -pv on
stsadm -o setproperty -pn developer-dashboard -pv off
```

> **NOTE** *Whereas the SharePoint 2010 version of the Developer Dashboard had three different options for* DisplayLevel *(On, Off, and* OnDemand*), in 2013 the* OnDemand *option has been deprecated and replaced with* On.

Enabling the Developer Dashboard adds the icon shown in Figure 19-11 to SharePoint pages. It looks like a piece of medical equipment, which isn't a bad analogy. The Developer Dashboard isn't displayed to all users, only users who have the AddAndCustomizePages permissions level in that web. This makes sense, as it isn't useful to show users what's wrong with a page if they can't actually do anything to fix it. Because only privileged users can see it, you might be tempted to just leave the Developer Dashboard on all the time. However, don't forget that users often get all kinds of elevated permissions in their site collections; and if your farm has MySites, all users are the site collection administrator for their own MySite, so they'll always see it when they go there. To avoid a lot of "What does this icon do?" and "What's this scary page I get when I click it?" type of questions, only turn the Developer Dashboard on when you're actively troubleshooting a problem.

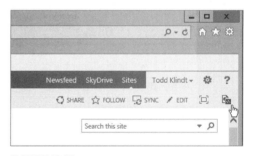

FIGURE 19-11

CHANGING PERMISSIONS NEEDED FOR THE DEVELOPER DASHBOARD

In some scenarios, the default permissions needed to see the Developer Dashboard (AddAndCustomizePages) might be either too high or too low. You can modify the RequiredPermissions property of the Developer Dashboard to change the permissions needed to see it. The following example enables everyone to see the Developer Dashboard:

continues

continued

```
$devds = [Microsoft.SharePoint.Administration.SPWebService]::
 ContentService.

DeveloperDashboardSettings
$devds. RequiredPermissions = "EmptyMask"
$devds.Update()
```

Now any user, regardless of his or her permissions in the web, will see the icon for the Developer Dashboard and be able to open it. You can use any permissions level listed at http://msdn.microsoft.com/en-us/library/microsoft.sharepoint .spbasepermissions(v=office.15).aspx. Be careful with this, as the Developer Dashboard provides a lot of information, and poorly written web parts or controls might expose back-end usernames and passwords. As a best practice, don't expose the Developer Dashboard to any users who don't need it.

When you open the Developer Dashboard you might notice that most of the fields are blank. Only one URL is available in the Requests tab for the Dashboard to analyze. If you load or reload another SharePoint page after the Dashboard is open, the page will appear in this list; and clicking on its URL will populate the Dashboard with information, as shown in Figure 19-12.

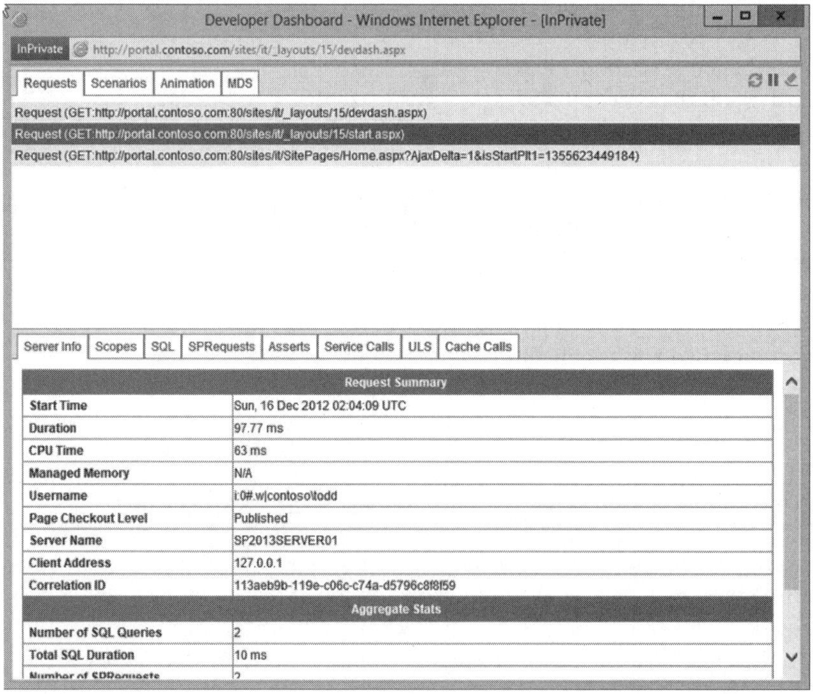

FIGURE 19-12

In Figure 19-12 you see three icons in the upper right-hand corner. The circle made of arrows is used to refresh the data in the window. The pause icon appears as two parallel bars and is similar to the pause button on many audio players. If you click on the pause icon it will be replaced by a right-pointing arrow icon similar to the play button on many devices. This right-pointing arrow is the resume button, which enables you to control when pages are captured in the Dashboard. The eraser icon enables you to clear all the current request URLs and their information from the Dashboard window when it starts to look cluttered.

As you can see, several items might be useful almost immediately for troubleshooting or performance tuning, such as Duration (of the page loads) and Page Checkout Level. How often have you heard "SharePoint is slow!" but without any concrete definition of what "slow" really is? Now you can easily get objective numbers that reflect exactly how long a page takes to load. If a page does take a long time to load, you can determine why using the Scopes tab, which shows all the steps that went into building and displaying the page, as well as how long each step took. It isn't necessary to read through every step, but you can quickly look down the list for outliers, steps that took longer than the rest. If you're troubleshooting a slow page load, that's a good place to start. An unpublished page will take longer to load than a published page and may also throw unexpected "Access Denied" errors, so knowing the Page Checkout Level is also good information.

The Server Info page also has another useful bit of information on it — the Correlation ID for the page request. You know that when something fails entirely, SharePoint provides the Correlation ID on the error page; but what if only part of the page fails, such as a web part? You can use the Developer Dashboard to get the Correlation ID to start your troubleshooting.

Speaking of troubleshooting, the Developer Dashboard has another trick up its sleeve. The ULS tab exposes the section of the standard trace logs that pertains to the given page load. This enables you to avoid digging through a large text file and go straight to the information you need. No PowerShell, no ULS Viewer — how handy is that?

The Developer Dashboard does put a little extra demand on the SharePoint farm. If you have problems with the Dashboard not populating with data, there may not be enough memory free on one of the members of your farm. By default you need at least 5% of your memory free to get usable results in the Developer Dashboard so use it sparingly if your servers are under a heavy load.

MORE TROUBLESHOOTING TECHNIQUES

As you spend more time troubleshooting SharePoint, you pick up little techniques here and there that help you get to the bottom of an issue. This section describes a few of the techniques you can add to your troubleshooting toolbox.

Using Fiddler to Watch Your Web Traffic

Fiddler is one of the most unknown and underused tools for troubleshooting SharePoint. It is a web page debugging tool that enables you to watch both incoming and outgoing web traffic and even "fiddle" with it if necessary. Used with SharePoint, it's a great way to troubleshoot slow page loads, Access Denied errors, Kerberos errors, pages that look wrong, and all kinds of problems. Fiddler is a free tool that can be downloaded at `http://www.fiddler2.com`. Fiddler works by setting itself as a proxy between the browser and the web server to which you are connecting. If your organization uses a proxy server already you may have to go through some extra steps to get Fiddler working in your environment. Luckily the Fiddler website has videos and documentation to help you out. For most users this isn't an issue but it was worth the warning. Figure 19-13 shows what a typical Fiddler session looks like once you have everything up and running.

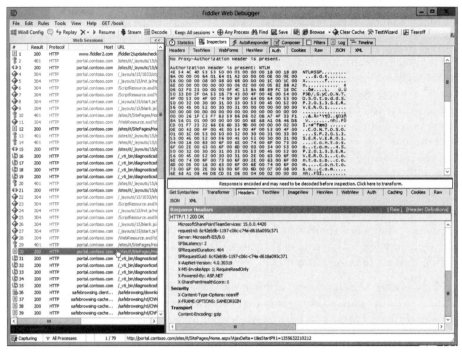

FIGURE 19-13

Fiddler has a lot of useful tabs, but Figure 19-13 shows two of the handiest. In the top pane, Inspectors has been selected, followed by Auth, which displays authentication information about this session. You can see that this web application is configured to use NTLM. If you're having troubles with Kerberos, this tab is a great way to ensure that everything is using it. If you see NTLMSSP here, then the session is not. If you see "this session looks like it's using Kerberos," then it probably is.

The bottom pane is showing the HTTP headers for the session. There's a lot of good information there, but three pieces are especially relevant to troubleshooting:

➤   **SPRequestGUID** — Where might you have seen that before? That's right, it's the Correlation ID for the current session. This is another good way to discover the Correlation ID so you can jump right to the ULS events that are pertinent to your session.

➤   **X-SharePointHealthScore** — This is a number from 0 to 10 that exposes how busy the SharePoint server is. The lower the number, the less stressed the server is. As the Health Score rises, SharePoint will start to shut off functionality in order to save resources for important tasks, such as answering page requests. If you're getting flaky behavior from SharePoint, make sure the Health Score is low. Your server might just be overworked.

➤ **MicrosoftSharePointTeamServices** — This header exposes a SharePoint build number. For a lot of technical reasons involving DLLs, IIS, and various account permissions during patching operations and installations, this number might not always match the build number of your farm or site collection. In fact it might not even be the same on different members of your farm. The best advice is just not to trust this number as anything more than a rough estimate of what build your farm is on.

Fiddler can also allow you to troubleshoot HTTPS secured traffic, but doing so requires some extra configuration. Instructions for decrypting HTTPS encrypted traffic can be found at `http://www.fiddler2.com /fiddler/help/httpsdecryption.asp`. There are plenty of other things to discover in Fiddler; don't just limit it to troubleshooting. The timeline tab can be used in troubleshooting by helping you spot resources that are taking a long time to load, but it can also be used to give your designers and programmers feedback on how they are impacting load times. Knowledge is power and Fiddler can serve up a lot of knowledge for the low price of nothing.

Creating a New Web Application

Sometimes a SharePoint problem defies logic. What is completely broken on one system will work everywhere else in the SharePoint farm. When that's the case, it's good to know whether your entire farm is broken or only some portion of it. To determine whether it's only a portion, you can create a new web application. When a new web application is created, a fresh site is created in IIS, and along with that a new `web.config` file, not to mention all the objects in SharePoint and SQL Server. If something has become corrupted in SharePoint, creating a new web application gives you a blank slate to test with. If whatever was broken is working, then you can start slowly adding pieces back until something breaks. If there were `web.config` changes, add them. If features were applied to the broken web app, apply them to the new web app. You can also restore site collection or database backups to the new web application to test the content. As you do this, don't forget to either make a DNS entry for your new web application or manually add it to your HOSTS file so it resolves.

Making All Your Service Accounts Local Administrators

A wise man once said about SharePoint, "It's always permissions." Quite often that's true. If everything looks right but things still don't work, make all the service accounts local administrators on all the SharePoint servers, and then reboot all around. If the problem you're troubleshooting was caused by a service account not having enough permissions, this should fix it. If that works, start moving accounts back to see which one needs the extra permissions. You read that correctly. If making the accounts local administrators *does work*, start moving accounts back out of the local administrators group. Just because it made things work doesn't mean you have your whole answer. It is still necessary to figure out which specific account didn't have the permissions it needed and to figure out the lowest permission level it can have and still work correctly. Be sure to reboot between permissions changes. A related technique is to give all your service accounts the SYSADMIN role on your SQL servers. Sometimes a service account doesn't have access to something in SQL that it needs, which breaks some functionality. Making all the service accounts SYSADMINs gives them access to everything. If global SYSADMIN rights fixes the problem, then you can investigate which account needs access to what.

DIFFERENT USERS FOR DIFFERENT RESULTS

"It's always permissions." The quote cuts both ways, and as a SharePoint administrator, your personal account might have a few more permissions than it really needs
on a daily basis. Have a few other accounts to use during troubleshooting. Often
things that don't work for anyone else will work for a Site Collection Administrator.
Obviously you can't bump up all the users to have that kind of access in SharePoint,
but knowing the point where things go wrong might lead you to the cause. A couple
of test accounts can be a big help in troubleshooting problems that only some users
are seeing. Match the test account as closely as possible to the people who are seeing an issue and maybe you can avoid having to work around the schedule of a busy
user who doesn't have time to troubleshoot a SharePoint issue all day. At least one
of your test users should be as real as possible, fill out their profile, upload a picture,
upload files into their Skydrive Pro, all the things your real users do. SharePoint
2013 has a lot of interrelated parts, and having a test account that accurately simu-
lates your real users can be a big help.

Checking for Failed Timer Jobs

A lot of things in SharePoint are driven by timer jobs. If the Timer Job service becomes gummed
up, a lot of unexpected collateral damage can result. Starting and stopping the SharePoint Timer
Service Windows Service that runs the timer jobs is often enough to kick-start things. You can do
that in the Services MMC console or with the `Restart-Service` PowerShell cmdlet. In rare cases,
you may have to flush the Timer Job cache. You can find instructions for doing so in the KB article
at `http://support.microsoft.com/kb/939308`.

Starting Fresh with IISReset

Doing an IISReset is sort of like giving SharePoint some flowers and a box of nice chocolates. If you
are unfamiliar with *IISReset*, it is a command-line utility that stops and restarts all the IIS worker
processes (w3wp.exe in Task Manager) and lets everything start fresh; all the IIS cache information
is dropped as well. Like a good night's sleep and a cup of coffee, IISReset just puts SharePoint in a
better mood. In the name of good performance, SharePoint caches a lot of information. Sometimes
all that caching bites you as bad things are cached or corrupted in RAM. Doing an IISReset lets
SharePoint take a deep breath and start from a blank slate. It's amazing how often that clears things
up. IISReset has some downsides; for instance, all the existing sessions will be dropped and the
sessions state will be cleared. That means if people are filling in a form or editing a list entry, data
may be lost, so try to make sure you warn users or perform this step when they aren't around to
bug you. Some articles will advise using the `/noforce` parameter to avoid losing information that
is being entered by users. This might be good advice if you are forced to try a reset on a production
farm that is being actively used, but the `/noforce` option isn't as complete in clearing things out of
IIS so it sometimes doesn't work as well. IISReset also drops all the cached data IIS is holding, so
the first pages loaded after the reset will be slow to load (30 to 60 seconds is not unusual) so have
some patience.

Reboots for Everyone!

Rebooting your computer to fix a problem is such a common suggestion it's almost a cliché. There's a reason for that: It works! Much like an IISReset helps get IIS's brain straight; a reboot helps get the whole server's head straight. Rebooting a server might feel like a cop-out, but its purpose isn't to fix the problem, but rather to help diagnose the problem. If a reboot reliably fixes the problem, then you can focus your troubleshooting on what is happening that makes things break. Another benefit of the reboot is that it gets things up and running quickly, so users can get back to work. That way, when things are less busy you can troubleshoot the problem.

Shoot Trouble Before It Happens!

Strictly speaking this isn't a troubleshooting tip as much as it is a tip for preparing for the day something goes wrong. Ideally all SharePoint administrators would know their farm so well they would immediately notice any changes made by someone else. In that world of sunshine and rainbows, administrators would also have perfect memories. In the world you probably live in, things aren't so easy. Documenting your farm while things are working properly will make finding troublesome changes a lot easier. There are lots of third-party tools available for creating a record of all the services, web applications, and solution packages being utilized in a farm. Microsoft has even provided a PowerShell script for documenting configurations in SharePoint 2013. You can find it at `http://technet.microsoft.com/en-us/library/ff645391.aspx`. Another tool available to every administrator is notepad. Take notes when you make changes to your farm, especially changes that are supposed to be temporary or for "testing" purposes. Little things tend to accumulate over time and be forgotten in complex systems like SharePoint. Temporary changes become permanent; tests become production. Good documentation will give you a place to look when you are wondering which services should be running, or what accounts they are supposed to be using. Documentation will also help you realize things that looked out of place at first were really changes you made months ago and forgot about.

Along with basic documentation, don't forget to put important information like the install files and license keys for third party solutions or passwords for important accounts in a safe place.

See the Bigger Picture: IIS and SQL

One of the challenges of SharePoint is that it doesn't stand alone. Without IIS and SQL, SharePoint can't function. To your users it doesn't matter if the problem is SQL Server, IIS, or Active Directory, in their eyes it is SharePoint that isn't doing what they want. If you have a Database Administrator, hopefully they are aware of tools like SQL Profiler and have experience with using them. If not you might start with a basic overview like the one found at `http://msdn.microsoft.com/en-us/library/ff650699.aspx`. SQL Server is an important part of your SharePoint farm; if you aren't lucky enough to have a Database Administrator on staff, you might benefit from some research dedicated to its care and feeding.

IIS is another essential component to getting the most out of SharePoint. Like SharePoint, IIS has logs that may be helpful for troubleshooting. Typically IIS logs are located at `%SystemDrive%\inetpub\logs\LogFiles\` (c:\inetpub\logs\LogFiles for most installations). Also like SharePoint IIS logs can be difficult to read so you might want to look for a tool like Microsoft's Log Parser at `http://www.microsoft.com/en-us/download/details.aspx?id=24659` to help you out.

IIS logs display the time in Coordinated Universal Time (UTC) not your local time zone so be careful to remember that when you are trying to find a specific entry. While IIS logs are typically not as large as SharePoint trace logs, they are not automatically purged over time. Make sure you put it on your "to-do" list to go in and clean them up occasionally, especially if you have a small storage volume.

Windows Server is the operating system that all of these technologies reside within. As you work your way through Event logs and error messages, pay attention to any signs of distress in the operating system itself. The Window Task Manager is the easiest way to look at what is running on your system and what resources it is consuming. If you aren't very familiar with Task Manager, there is a good Microsoft support article at `http://support.microsoft.com/kb/323527`.

If you find something in Task Manager that makes you think there is a problem but you can't quite figure it out, try Perfmon.exe, also known as Performance Monitor. Perfmon is very flexible and can be a little hard to get started with, but a quick Internet search can give you a lot of good tips. One of the major advantages is that you can set it to capture information about specific things at intervals over time. For example you can use Perfmon to collect data processor activity on your system and run that collection overnight to see when the highest and lowest processor load occurs. Perfmon essentially allows you to create your own log files looking specifically at the information you want. Doesn't that sound handy?

ADDITIONAL TOOLS AND RESOURCES

This chapter contained several references to Internet searches. Troubleshooting SharePoint is sometimes too big of a job for one person to take on alone. Fortunately, there are discussion forums, blogs, and technical documentation from Microsoft to guide your way, so be sure to use them. The following two resources are a good starting place when you are looking for help:

➤ MSDN Forums: `http://social.msdn.microsoft.com/Forums/en-US/category/sharepoint`

➤ SharePoint Stack Exchange: `http://sharepoint.stackexchange.com`

When asking your question, be sure to provide as much information as possible. This includes the SharePoint build, how many machines are in your farm, what was the last thing that was changed before the problem started, what you've already tried, and so on. Also, be respectful to the people trying to help you. In most cases they are unpaid volunteers who are giving you their most valuable resource — their time. You can also take your problem to Twitter, if you want to wade into that pool. There are a lot of SharePoint professionals there willing to help you out. If you want to cast a wide net with your questions, include the hashtag `#sphelp`.

Also available are many tools to assist in managing and troubleshooting your SharePoint farm; some are free, and some are available for purchase. They range from simple applications that parse and search the ULS logs to complex solutions that completely change how SharePoint works. All of these tools should be evaluated on a test farm first, and some of them can be very helpful.

Don't overlook the most common tool for troubleshooting any website, the web browser. Almost every modern web browser has some developer tools built in and many have extensions that can add additional debugging features. Even if they aren't in the same league as something like Fiddler, having them available on every machine makes it worth knowing how to use them. SharePoint 2013 supports Internet Explorer versions 8 through 10 and the most recent versions of Google Chrome, Firefox, and Safari so often you can use the one you are most comfortable with. Just be sure not to forget that some settings for Internet Explorer, especially those around authentication and the network zones (Local Intranet, Trusted sites, Internet, and Restricted sites) can have an influence on how other applications, such as Microsoft Office, interact with SharePoint.

> **TRUST BUT CONFIRM!**
>
> Speaking of test farms, never use PowerShell or registry keys that you find on the Internet in your production farm without testing them first. Even little things like punctuation can completely change what a script does, and usually not in a good way. Another thing you might see recommended as a solution to problems in SharePoint is SQL scripting. *Never* use a SQL script or command that queries or alters data to fix problems with your production farm without getting approval from Microsoft. SharePoint content and configuration databases are strictly no-touch items according to Microsoft; even running a query against them might techni-cally take you out of a supportable state. Just don't do it. The one exception is the SharePoint_Logging database, which you can query as an information source, but even that database shouldn't be changed via SQL commands.

SUMMARY

This chapter described several tools and other resources you can use when you are seeking a solution to a SharePoint problem. As you wade through these sources of information, however, it bears repeating that your brain, at least the parts not devoted to quoting lines from movies and remembering where your car keys are, is your best troubleshooting tool. Keep in mind that SharePoint exists inside of a whole range of technologies and physical requirements. Active Directory, DNS, networking, and even the offices where the cleaning crew unplugs servers to free up a plug for the vacuum can all influence how your SharePoint farm functions.

Although facing a problem may seem daunting, this chapter has outlined several guidelines for troubleshooting. Look for things that have changed, either in the farm or in the general environment. Look for repetition and patterns (does it happen every four hours, every night at 1:44 A.M., etc.), and any common denominators among the people and places where the error occurs. In a world of VPNs, firewalls, bring-your-own-device policies, and different browser updates daily, not all SharePoint problems are related to SharePoint. Another trap administrators sometimes fall into is concentrating on *why* a problem exists in a production farm. Every administrator would like to know the root cause of an issue, but on a production server the highest priority is getting things working again. If recreating the web application gets everyone back to work, you can look for the cause in the trace logs later. Happy hunting!

20

Monitoring and Analytics

WHAT'S IN THIS CHAPTER?

➤ Using the Unified Logging System

➤ Configuring the Usage and Health Data Collection service

➤ Monitoring the Search service application

As with any complex system, monitoring and maintenance are necessary to keep SharePoint running happily. SharePoint's monitoring functions are comprised of four components: the Unified Logging Service (ULS), the Health Analyzer engine, the Usage and Health Analysis reporting system, and Timer Job monitoring. The ULS system provides active (and potentially extremely detailed) logging data of the various requests being processed, the Health Analyzer engine runs periodic checks of the environment against an established baseline, the Usage and Health Analysis reporting system collects data about usage patterns of various SharePoint resources, and Timer Job monitoring reports on the run history and success or failure of SharePoint Timer Jobs.

From an IT management perspective, these components can be roughly categorized as reactive (ULS, Timer Job monitoring), proactive (Health Analyzer), and predictive (Usage and Health Analysis). Proper monitoring of a SharePoint farm involves using all four forms of monitoring in concert.

CONFIGURING MONITORING IN CENTRAL ADMINISTRATION

Most of the monitoring configurations for SharePoint can be done via Central Admin under the aptly named Monitoring section, but some additional health and usage reports are provided as part of the Search Service Application (more on that later), and some settings are cleverly hidden only in PowerShell. Under the Monitoring section in Central Admin, the locations of the Health Analyzer and Timer Job sections are obvious; but for unknown reasons, the ULS configuration and Usage and Health Analysis settings are lumped together under the general Reporting heading. It's like a Monitoring scavenger hunt that's gone horribly awry.

Unified Logging Service

The lowest-level monitoring system is called the Unified Logging Service. This service records information about each operation that occurs inside of SharePoint, and it provides the most direct and detailed view into SharePoint's operation. It gives insight into the processing of specific events and requests, regardless of whether or not an error was observed. The level of detail provided in the ULS logs, while of great value, can be both a blessing and a curse, as it can generate a large quantity of data to evaluate. However, with the right configuration and the right tools, you can strike a balance that provides the information you need without inundating you with mountains of irrelevant data.

If you are familiar with the ULS system introduced in SharePoint 2010, you will find that it is mostly unchanged in SharePoint 2013. The ULS engine can log events into both the Windows Event Log system and SharePoint's own trace logs, with independent control available for the reporting level of each, but these are not simply two different channels for reporting the same data. The types of events typically sent to the Windows Event Log are critical errors (e.g., failure to connect to a database, service account errors) or general informational events (e.g., farm topology changes, search index replication status), whereas the entries made in the trace logs go much deeper, tracking the actions (and sometimes errors) of individual requests as they are processed.

Configuring ULS via Central Admin

Initially, the ULS appears to be very straightforward to configure, but you will quickly see that it is not quite so simple. First, you will look at the ULS configuration options inside of Central Admin. Here are the steps:

1. Browse to the Monitoring section of Central Admin.

2. Select Configure Diagnostic Logging.

3. You will see a screen like the one in Figure 20-1. The first block of settings, Event Throttling, enables you to select, for a large number of categories and subcategories, the least critical events to be sent to either the Event Log or the trace log.

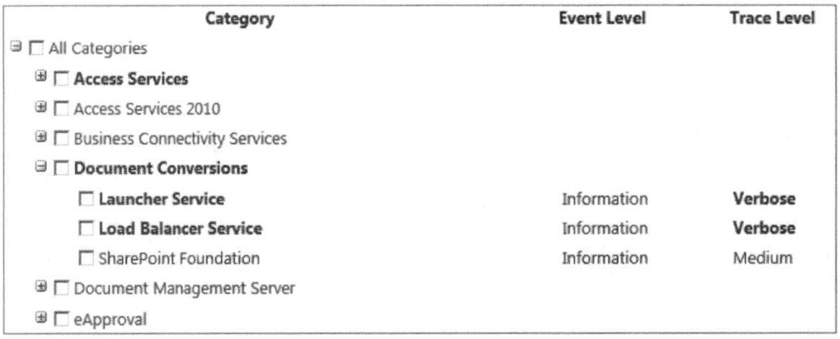

Category	Event Level	Trace Level
⊟ ☐ All Categories		
⊞ ☐ **Access Services**		
⊞ ☐ Access Services 2010		
⊞ ☐ Business Connectivity Services		
⊟ ☐ **Document Conversions**		
☐ **Launcher Service**	Information	**Verbose**
☐ **Load Balancer Service**	Information	**Verbose**
☐ SharePoint Foundation	Information	Medium
⊞ ☐ Document Management Server		
⊞ ☐ eApproval		

FIGURE 20-1

As you expand the items in the tree, you will find that the ULS provides a nearly overwhelming amount of granularity for controlling the logging of various elements of SharePoint. Unfortunately, there is no built-in explanation of what exactly is included in any given category, and little or no documentation elsewhere on the topic. Some are fairly obvious (e.g., SharePoint Foundation ⇨ Alerts), while others wouldn't necessarily mean anything to a systems administrator and might very well be made up (e.g., SharePoint Server ⇨ Command Base Validators).

Beneath the list of categories is a pair of drop-down menus used to select the *least* critical event to be reported to either the Event Log or the Trace Log. Note that the boxes do not use exactly the same severity settings, but rather each uses the severity nomenclature for its target log. Both boxes list the logging options in order of decreasing severity; therefore, the further down the list you go, the more verbose the ULS will be in its reporting. The most verbose options can be quite verbose. Before asking the ULS to give you more logging, be careful what you wish for, you just might get it. It's a good idea to move down the list slowly, or select a few categories at a time. It is possible to crank the logging up so high that the overhead affects performance.

The check boxes in the category list allow you to set a specific severity level for multiple categories or subcategories simultaneously, but you cannot set multiple different severity levels simultaneously; every item checked is set to the values selected in the drop-down boxes. To set more than one severity value for various categories, you need to make your selections, click OK, and then return to Configure Diagnostic Logging for each severity level that you wish to set.

SharePoint 2010 introduced a great improvement over MOSS 2007 with the capability to easily set logging categories back to their default severity level, and that capability has been carried over to SharePoint 2013. (In SharePoint 2007 the only want to reset a category's logging level was with STSADM, and there was no easy way to determine which categories were not at their default levels.) In SharePoint 2010 and SharePoint 2013, if any category's logging severity level has been changed from the default, then the new value is displayed in bold text, making it obvious what has changed. Before SharePoint 2010, you could only see the currently set values; there was no indication whether that setting was the default.

The next option to look at on the page is the Event Log Flood Protection setting. The goal, of course, is to keep the farm running in an error-free state, but when SharePoint starts reporting errors, it becomes very chatty indeed. This isn't really a problem for SharePoint's trace logs, as we expect all errors to be reported there. Where it becomes problematic, however, is in the server's event logs. These logs are used for the server's own reporting and for other applications, so it would be rude for SharePoint to commandeer the logs and flood them with hundreds or thousands of identical error messages. In fact, such a log flood could actually make it more difficult to notice system-level error messages that might be the root cause of an issue. The Event Log Flood Protection option is enabled by default, which causes SharePoint to watch for repetitive error messages; when detected, it switches to creating occasional messages summarizing how many times the error has occurred and when it was last seen.

If you're using any third-party monitoring tools that comb through your application logs looking for events, make sure they are capable of handling flood prevention. Otherwise, they may not recognize a problem if one exists.

Moving right along, we come to the Trace Log configuration options. These options are, for the most part, self-explanatory, but that is not to say that some thought shouldn't be put into them. The first option is the path for storing the logs. By default it is set to `%CommonProgramFiles%\Microsoft Shared\Web Server Extensions\15\LOGS\`, which is typically the C:\ drive of the SharePoint server(s). It is recommended that you change this path to a drive other than the system drive to avoid the possibility of the log files growing to the point of exhausting the system drive's free space. Windows gets very upset if the boot drive runs out of space — and if Windows ain't happy, nobody's happy.

However, two points must be considered when relocating the trace logs. First, the path specified must exist on all servers that are members of the farm. This is easy enough to ensure when the farm is set up, but you must also consider whether any additional servers may be added to the farm, as they too must have the same path available. When you move your logs, don't try to be overly clever with the new path. If they're in the same path as the 15 hive but on a different drive, they're very easy for other administrators to find. Conversely, if they're buried under `E:\Logs\SharePoint Logs\ULS Logs\` they're tougher to find without looking for their location in Central Admin or PowerShell. `E:\Program Files\Common Files\Microsoft Shared\Web Server Extensions\15\Logs` might be a mouthful, but it's a very obvious place to look if there are no ULS logs on the C drive. Second, the writing of the trace logs can potentially be a very disk I/O-intensive operation, so it is important to ensure that you don't slow down SharePoint by putting the logs on excessively slow storage, and that you don't inadvertently slow down other applications that might be running off the same drive you select for your trace logs.

Following the trace log path setting are two options controlling retention for the logs, according to both age and total space consumed. By default, the logs are retained for 14 days and the option to restrict log disk space usage is disabled. However, note that the box for specifying maximum storage size uses GB as its unit of measure; therefore, if you enable the size restriction without changing the size value, you have effectively just configured a "restriction" of 1TB! When processing log retention, SharePoint uses the more restrictive of the two configurations to determine which files to keep and which to delete. For instance, if you set a retention age of 10 days and a maximum storage space of 5GB, SharePoint will delete logs older than 10 days even if the 5GB limit hasn't been reached; conversely, it will delete the oldest logs if the 5GB limit is exceeded, even if those logs are younger than 10 days old. Figure 20-2 shows the Restriction Settings page.

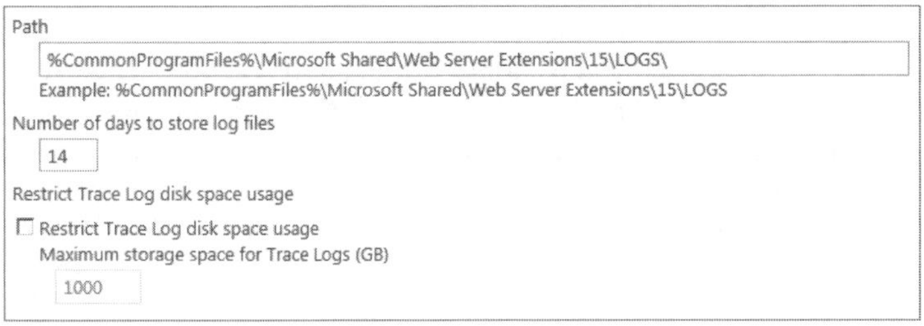

Path

%CommonProgramFiles%\Microsoft Shared\Web Server Extensions\15\LOGS\

Example: %CommonProgramFiles%\Microsoft Shared\Web Server Extensions\15\LOGS

Number of days to store log files

14

Restrict Trace Log disk space usage

☐ Restrict Trace Log disk space usage

Maximum storage space for Trace Logs (GB)

1000

FIGURE 20-2

Configuring ULS via PowerShell

The options for ULS configuration provided by Central Admin are great, but a few additional options are not available in the browser, and configuring each filtering category manually can be frustrating. Fortunately, PowerShell comes to the rescue! All of the options available via Central Admin (and then some) are exposed in PowerShell cmdlets, opening up the possibility of scripting, remote management through PowerShell, and more.

The PowerShell cmdlets for managing ULS are divided into two groups of commands. The first group of cmdlets is for managing the ULS event filtering categories and is fairly straightforward. Get-SPLogLevel will display the current severity filters for the various logging categories, but be prepared for this command to return several screens of data. You can filter the results down to only what you are looking for by using the command's Identity parameter, passing it a string in the "Area:Name" format. For instance, if you wanted to see only the setting for the Administration subcategory of area Access Services, the command would be as follows:

```
Get-SPLogLevel -Identity "Access Services:Administration"
```

Figure 20-3 shows the output of that command. You can also use an asterisk to specify all the subcategories of a given area, such as the following:

```
"Access Services:*"
```

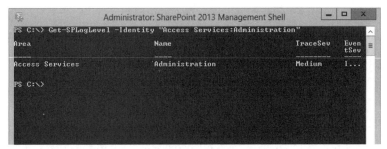

FIGURE 20-3

Notice that, unlike the corresponding Central Admin page, the output from this cmdlet doesn't indicate whether any values have been changed from their defaults, so you still have to rely on the Central Admin page for that information. You can set a new logging level for one or more categories with Set-SPLogLevel and reset a category to the default level with Clear-SPLogLevel. Both of these cmdlets accept the same type of Identity filtering shown earlier for Get-SPLogLevel.

The second group of commands enables additional control of the Event Log flood protection, and of the trace log path and retention options. The cmdlet Get-SPDiagnosticConfig will return the currently configured values. You may recognize a few of the values (such as LogLocation or LogDiskSpaceUsageGB) from the Central Admin configuration, but additional options are exposed as well. For instance, LogCutInterval specifies the number of minutes that ULS will use a log file before starting a new one, and there are additional threshold and interval values to tune the Event Log flood protection.

Now that you know what options are available, you can set them with the `Set-SPDiagnostic Config` cmdlet. For instance, `Set-SPDiagnosticConfig -LogCutInterval 15` would cause ULS to move to a new log file every 15 minutes, and `Set-SPDiagnosticConfig -EventLog FloodProtectionTriggerPeriod 3` would cause ULS to look for five of the same events within a three-minute window, rather than the default two-minute window.

Two additional cmdlets can be very useful for troubleshooting. `New-SPLogFile` manually triggers the creation of a new log file, which can be useful when you want to re-create an issue but not have to sort through hundreds of previous log entries. This is very helpful if you want to isolate the events from a specific operation into a known ULS log file. This might be for your own use or if you've been asked to send the ULS log to someone who is helping you troubleshoot a problem. You can run `New-SPLogFile` right before reproducing the issue. After you've reproduced it, and it has spewed some events in the ULS log, wait a couple of minutes for everything to flush out, then run `New-SPLogFile` again.

Because SharePoint 2013 servers work as a team, you never know for sure if the key to solving the issue you're fighting lies in a log file on another server in your farm. `Merge-SPLogFile` is used to merge all the ULS logs from all the machines in your farm into one large, trouble-finding file. With no parameters, it will schedule a timer job on each member of the farm to take its last hours' worth of logs and copy them to a single file on the machine where you ran `Merge-SPLogFile`. Because it's timer job-based, you have to be patient; it takes a couple of minutes to be completely populated. Once it is full you can open it and follow all the events in the farm on all the servers. In most cases, an hour is way too many events. You really only need the last five or ten minutes' worth. Fortunately, you have several ways to prune the results of Merge-SPLogFile. You can filter by user, category, level, or time. One of the handiest ways is to get the last 10 minutes' worth of events. To do that you would use the following command:

```
Merge-SPLogFile -Path E:\Logs\BigFile.txt –StartTime (Get-Date).AddMinutes(-10)
```

You will discover other `Merge-SPLogFile` tricks in Chapter 7, "Administering SharePoint with Windows PowerShell."

CORRELATION ID: WHAT IT IS (AND IS NOT)

When an error occurs that results in an error message being sent back to the browser, it usually includes a value named "correlation ID" along with the error. There is a common misconception that a correlation ID value (as shown on an error message) is a form of error number or error code that inherently means something; and end users often ask SharePoint administrators what the error means based on this value. However, correlation IDs are not error codes, but rather GUIDs assigned by SharePoint to every conversation, allowing that request to more easily be tracked through the logs. This enables you to correlate or group events together, making it easy to find the whole series of events that led up to the issue you're looking at.

When ULS writes entries into the trace logs, it also includes the correlation ID value of the request that caused that log entry to be generated, so if you know the correlation ID of the request that generated an error, you can filter the log for all entries that are tagged with that correlation ID, enabling you to see the full history of the request from start to finish. Note that it is also important to have the date and time at which the error was received, so that you know which log file to look in when searching for the correlation ID.

USING AND CONFIGURING THE HEALTH ANALYZER

The ULS logs can help you figure out what happened after an issue has already occurred, but the Health Analyzer is a trustworthy (albeit sometimes overzealous) sidekick that wants to keep you out of trouble in the first place. Whether you realize it or not, you've probably already seen the Health Analyzer at work if you've ever opened Central Admin and seen a yellow or red bar warning that serious or critical issues have been detected and require attention. Central Admin just doesn't seem right without those bars at the top. Figure 20-4 shows your old friend. However, Health Analyzer is capable of doing much more than just reporting on issues; in some cases it can even fix them for you!

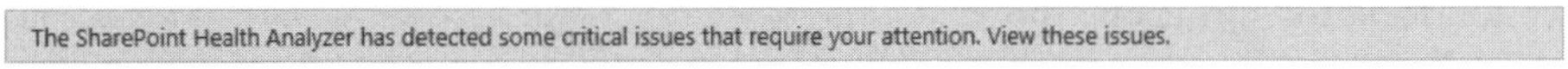

The SharePoint Health Analyzer has detected some critical issues that require your attention. View these issues.

FIGURE 20-4

If you are familiar with Health Analyzer in SharePoint 2010, then you will notice that it remains basically unchanged for 2013. The Health Analyzer's role is to run a whole series of predefined checks against various portions of the farm, looking for potential problems before they become serious enough to affect it. These checks can run the gamut from service account permissions checks to available server disk space to database index fragmentation. SharePoint 2013 increases the number of out-of-the-box rules to 68 (from SharePoint 2010's 52), and spending a few moments looking through the list of checks and how they are done is certainly a worthwhile use of time, as it will familiarize you with what Health Analyzer does and does not check, and how often those checks are run. To view the list of configured Health Analyzer rules, go to the Monitoring section of Central Admin, and under the Health Analyzer section, you will see Review Rule Definitions.

The rules are divided into sections based on the type of check that is done, and include a short description of the rule, its run schedule, enabled/disabled status, and whether or not it is permitted to attempt an automatic repair of the issue. Figure 20-5 shows some of the rule definitions under the Security heading. While technically this is just another SharePoint list to which you can add new items, simply typing up a description of a new rule and adding to this list doesn't make a functional rule. This list is really just a configuration front end for a series of timer jobs that actually execute the check. Without the corresponding timer job, these list items have no effect whatsoever. To get a feel for the issues the Health Analyzer is watching for, you can page through the list of job definitions.

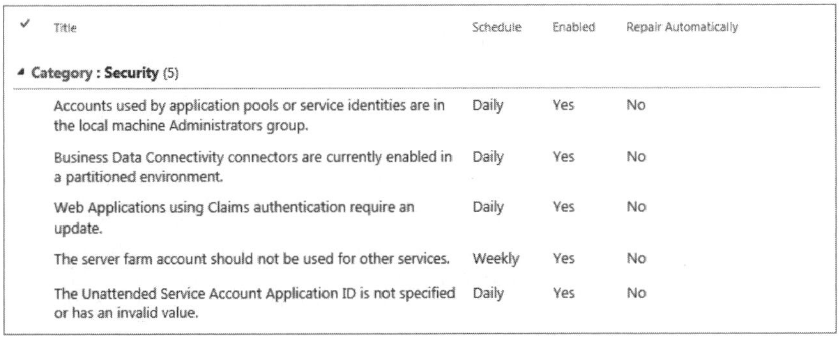

✓	Title	Schedule	Enabled	Repair Automatically
◢ Category : Security (5)				
	Accounts used by application pools or service identities are in the local machine Administrators group.	Daily	Yes	No
	Business Data Connectivity connectors are currently enabled in a partitioned environment.	Daily	Yes	No
	Web Applications using Claims authentication require an update.	Daily	Yes	No
	The server farm account should not be used for other services.	Weekly	Yes	No
	The Unattended Service Account Application ID is not specified or has an invalid value.	Daily	Yes	No

FIGURE 20-5

To view the current list of triggered warnings, from Central Admin select Monitoring ⇨ Health Analyzer ⇨ Review Problems and Solutions. Alternately, just click the ever-present red or yellow bar at the top of Central Admin. If some of the rules have triggered warnings, you can also reach this page by clicking a link provided on the yellow or red Health Analyzer warning bar. Here you will see a list of the outstanding problems, along with the last time that the check was run and found to still be failing. Clicking the item description for a rule brings up more details about the failure, and in many cases the Explanation field will indicate precisely what caused the check to fail. Figure 20-6 shows the description for the rule that checks for an outbound SMTP server.

Title	Outbound e-mail has not been configured.
Severity	1 - Error
Category	Configuration
Explanation	A default SMTP server has not been configured. One or more web applications do not have SMTP servers configured. Because of this, features such as alerts will not function properly.
Remedy	Configure an outgoing e-mail server from the central administration site or execute the following command: C:\Program Files\Common Files\Microsoft Shared\Web Server Extensions\15\bin\stsadm.exe-o email -outsmtpserver <SMTP server> -fromaddress <someone@example.com> -replytoaddress <someone@example.com> -codepage <codepage> For more information about this rule, see "http://go.microsoft.com/fwlink/?LinkID=142684".
Failing Servers	
Failing Services	SPTimerService (SPTimerV4)
Rule Settings	View

FIGURE 20-6

Some of the Health Analyzer rules have unrealistically high standards, which do not necessarily apply to all scenarios. For instance, one of the rules triggers a warning if a SharePoint server's free disk space drops below an amount equal to five times the server's total RAM. This is a well-intentioned rule, but it doesn't take into account high-powered SharePoint Web Front End servers, which could easily be equipped with 32GB of RAM or more. Thus, it is necessary to take Health Analyzer's warnings with a grain of salt, and evaluate any warning against the usage scenario of the farm. If you determine that the rule does not apply to your farm, you can disable that rule from the Review Rule Definitions page. You should look at the Health Analyzer the same way you look at the GPS in your car. It's just one of the things you take into consideration when making decisions. Your GPS can be helpful, but it can also tell you to turn right when there is no road to turn right onto. Just as you don't blindly follow your GPS off a cliff, you shouldn't blindly follow the Health Analyzer when it tells you to shrink your databases.

Some failures can be fixed automatically by Health Analyzer; and in fact, some are configured to do so by default. For instance, if it is detected that databases being used by SharePoint have excessively fragmented indexes, then Health Analyzer will launch a re-indexing stored procedure inside the database. Other alerts, such as, "Outbound e-mail has not been configured," can't be automatically fixed by Health Analyzer, as the "fix" requires information that it does not have — namely, the mail server host name and the sender and reply-to addresses. In addition, some alerts, such as, "Drive is out of space," shouldn't be fixed automatically by SharePoint, unless it will call your storage vendor and order more drives. Moreover, you don't want it to free up space by deleting all the Justin Bieber MP3s that you have hidden on your SharePoint server.

Unlike the ULS, control over the Health Analyzer with PowerShell is quite limited; there is a grand total of three cmdlets related to Health Analyzer, and they don't really do a whole lot. You can use the cmdlet `Get-SPHealthAnalysisRule` to retrieve the full list of Health Analyzer rules, or you can provide the optional `-Identity` parameter to retrieve a single rule by its name or GUID. However, the only information returned is the rule's system name, GUID, enabled/disabled status, category, and summary. Notably absent are the options for Scope, Server, and Repair Automatically. In addition, while it may appear that you can set the `Enabled` property of a Health Analyzer Rule, you cannot. You can try setting it to either `$true` or `$false`, but even if you call the `Update()` method, the new setting won't stick. To change the `Enabled` state of a Health Analyzer Rule, you have to use one of the other two cmdlets: `Enable-SPHealthAnalysisRule` and `Disable-SPHealthAnalysisRule`, which are self-explanatory.

Earlier you learned about the Health Analyzer Rule that triggers an alert if the free space on any of your SharePoint server drives drops below five times the amount of RAM in the system. You also learned that in systems with a lot of RAM, that alert is not practical. You can use `Get-SPHealthAnalysisRule` to view a list of all rules and their names. Then you can use `Disable-SPHealthAnalysisRule` to disable that rule and get that monkey off your back:

```
Get-SPHealthAnalysisRule AppServerDrivesAreNearlyFullWarning | Disable
-SPHealthAnalysisRule
```

PowerShell will ask you to confirm that you really want to disable this rule. You do. Now that unhelpful alert will no longer sully your Central Admin pages.

USAGE AND HEALTH DATA COLLECTION

By now it should be fairly obvious that SharePoint is capable of collecting a very large amount of information about how it is running. However, we're about to tumble down the rabbit hole and see just how broad its data collection capabilities truly are. The Usage and Health Data Collection system not only provides basic SharePoint information such as web app statistics, feature use, and page requests within the scope of its reporting umbrella, but also extends its reach to InfoPath, the State Service, the Windows Event Log, and even SQL Server performance.

Collecting large quantities of data can potentially have a very significant performance impact on the farm, but fortunately you can enable, disable, and schedule each data category individually. This enables the collection to be distributed across low-usage times and restricted to only the data you want, minimizing the impact to the farm.

It's great to have a lot of data; but if it were stored in log files only, then trying to extract any kind of useful information from the data set would be unwieldy and frustrating at best. Thankfully, the Usage and Health Data Collection system is capable of aggregating all the collected information into a SQL Server database. Microsoft has explicitly stated that SharePoint databases should *never* be directly queried or edited. As the saying goes, however, there's an exception to every rule, and this database is the exception to that rule. It exists solely to allow administrators to query performance and usage data about the farm in order to generate their own reports. How do you configure this amazing database? What is the name of this rule-breaking, renegade database? You'll plumb all these mysteries and plenty more in this section.

Configuring Usage and Health Data Collection

Like many parts of SharePoint, the Usage and Health Data Collection settings can be modified both in the Central Admin UI and with PowerShell. Each place has things it does better than the other. The following sections cover the options you have with both approaches.

Configuration in Central Admin

Configuration of the Usage and Health data collection process is handled, conveniently enough, on the Configure Usage and Health Data Collection page under the Monitoring section of Central Admin. The first option available is "Enable usage data collection." Despite its name, this is actually only the first step in enabling usage data collection. It is not fully functional until a timer job that handles the collection is changed from its default state of Disabled, but that is discussed shortly. Figure 20-7 shows some of the events you can log.

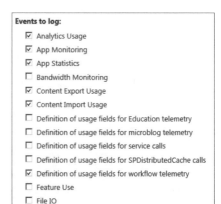

FIGURE 20-7

Immediately following the Enable/Disable option is a large block of check boxes for selecting which events should be logged as part of the usage data collection. Again, some of these options can result in a large performance impact on the farm, so only enable the options you truly need. For instance, if your environment seems slow, the SQL IO Usage and SQL Latency Usage options could provide valuable information. If you need to see which features are being used at what times, you can enable the Feature Use option.

Next is a field titled Log File Location, which you might notice is the same location as the default path set for the ULS logs. This is the location where SharePoint stores the collected usage data; and, as with the ULS logs, the specified location must match on all SharePoint servers in the farm. Also like the ULS log, it's a good idea to move this to a drive other than your Windows system drive. You don't want Windows and SharePoint fighting for IOPS on that drive. Even worse, you don't want SharePoint filling it up. SharePoint 2013 differs from SharePoint 2010 in that there was previously a field where you could specify, in GB, the maximum space to be utilized by the logs. However, you can still use PowerShell to modify the value from its default of 5GB.

The second function of this service is health data collection. Unlike the usage collection, which gathers information about how various functions are being used, the health data collection periodically captures information about lower-level resources such as blocking reports or deadlocks in SQL Server, timer service-recycling, password management, and much more. You can configure the data collection schedule for each of the gathering categories by clicking Health Logging Schedule. Note that the health logging collection processes are really nothing more than SharePoint timer jobs; and like any other timer job, you can enable, disable, or set a custom schedule for these. Figure 20-8 shows some of the timer jobs that can be changed.

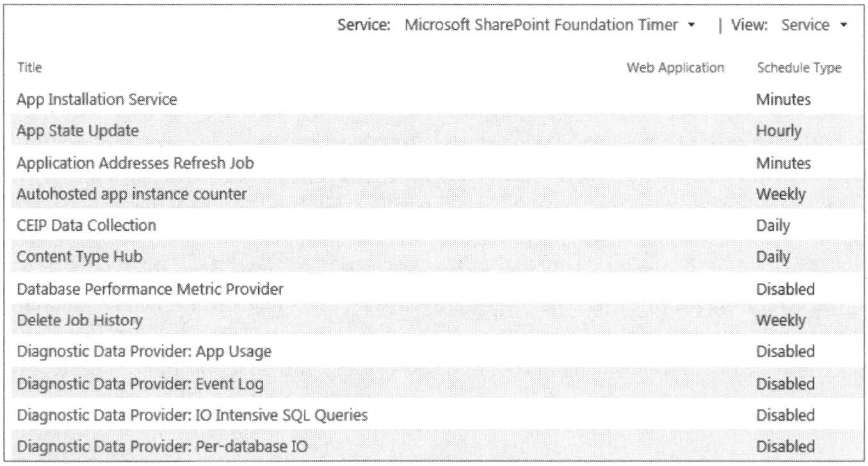

	Service: Microsoft SharePoint Foundation Timer ▼		View: Service ▼
Title		Web Application	Schedule Type
App Installation Service			Minutes
App State Update			Hourly
Application Addresses Refresh Job			Minutes
Autohosted app instance counter			Weekly
CEIP Data Collection			Daily
Content Type Hub			Daily
Database Performance Metric Provider			Disabled
Delete Job History			Weekly
Diagnostic Data Provider: App Usage			Disabled
Diagnostic Data Provider: Event Log			Disabled
Diagnostic Data Provider: IO Intensive SQL Queries			Disabled
Diagnostic Data Provider: Per-database IO			Disabled

FIGURE 20-8

Configuration with PowerShell

As with ULS, some elements of Usage and Health data collection can also be configured via PowerShell, and in fact a few are *only* accessible through PowerShell. The cmdlet `Get-SPUsageService` will return information roughly equivalent to the Usage Data Collection and Health Data Collection sections in Central Admin. Of note in the output are two values that are absent from the Central Admin page: UsageLogMaxSpaceGB and UsageLogCutTime. Recall that UsageLogMaxSpaceGB is the value that was accessible through Central Admin in SharePoint 2010 but is hidden in SharePoint 2013, although the default value is still unchanged, at 5GB. UsageLogCutTime specifies how long SharePoint will use the current usage log file before it rotates to a new file. Its default value of five minutes coincides with the log collection import time cycle (covered later), but you can change that. In fact, if the log collection import cycle is increased to an hour or longer, changing UsageLogCutTime to match might result in log files large enough to slow SharePoint down.

You can set UsageLogMaxSpaceGB and UsageLogCutTime, as well as LoggingEnabled and UsageLogLocation, by passing them to the `Set-SPUsageService` cmdlet.

Log Collection and Processing

The settings thus far have all been related to how each individual SharePoint server handles the collection of its own log data. However, one of the greatest benefits of the Usage and Health data collection service is that it can aggregate the logging information of all the servers in a farm into a single SQL database, and generate reports based on that data. Once again, you can pick your weapon of choice, either Central Admin or PowerShell to change these settings.

Configuration with Central Admin

The final group of options on the "Configure usage and health data collection" page is for the log collection schedule and the logging database configuration.

This section looks at the Logging Database Server options first, as they must be properly configured for the log collection to work. Depending on whether or not this service was set up previously, you may find that the Database Server and Database Name fields are disabled, preventing you from editing them. If so, then it is because either the "Enable usage data collection" or the "Enable health data collection" boxes (or both) are checked. When either of these functions is enabled, the service assumes it can use the configured values for the logging database, thus it prevents you from changing them. If you wish to change either the database server or the logging database name, you need to disable both usage and health data collection, change the values, and then enable the collection again. SharePoint will then begin using the newly configured values for all log collection.

DON'T CHANGE THE DATABASE NAME

By default, this database is named WSS_Logging, as shown in Figure 20-9; and unless you have a good reason, don't change it. As mentioned earlier, this is the only database that Microsoft has officially blessed to be queried or updated outside of SharePoint. Renaming it can cause confusion and result in querying or updating the wrong database. Imagine how disappointed in you Microsoft will be if this happens.

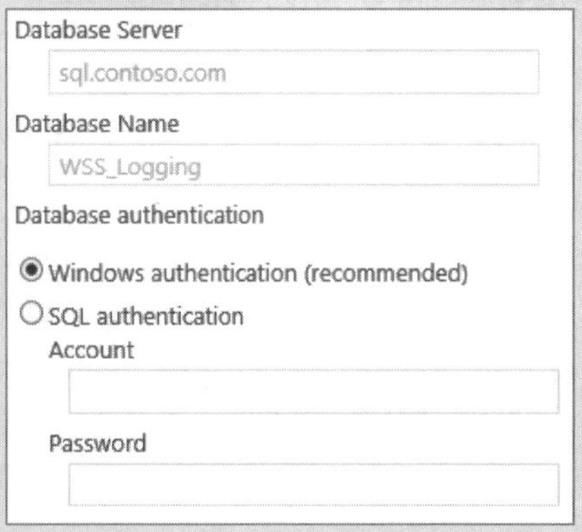

Database Server

    sql.contoso.com

Database Name

    WSS_Logging

Database authentication

⦿ Windows authentication (recommended)
◯ SQL authentication
    Account

    Password

FIGURE 20-9

Returning to the Log Collection Schedule section, click the Log Collection Schedule link to access the Timer Job Configuration page, which is filtered down to just two timer jobs: the Microsoft SharePoint Foundation Usage job for Data Import, and for Data Processing. Figure 20-10 shows the two timer jobs as they appear in Central Admin. The Data Import timer job is responsible for collecting the log data stored on each server and merging it into the logging database. In order to prevent massive import jobs that can degrade server performance, the Data Import job is configured to run at a five-minute interval, which prevents the quantity of not yet imported data from getting too large.

Service:	Microsoft SharePoint Foundation Usage ▾		View:	Service ▾
Title		Web Application	Schedule Type	
Microsoft SharePoint Foundation Usage Data Import			Minutes	
Microsoft SharePoint Foundation Usage Data Processing			Daily	

FIGURE 20-10

The Data Processing timer job's role is to process the data that has been imported to the logging database throughout the day and generate meaningful reports from it. By default, the timer job is configured to run between 1:00 AM and 3:00 AM, but it also defaults to a disabled state. Therefore, unless you manually enable the timer job, the log data will only be collected in the database; no reports will be generated from it.

Configuration with PowerShell

The enabled/disabled status of logging and the name of the logging database can be retrieved with the cmdlet `Get-SPUsageApplication`, but in most cases the rest of the information returned is of little use. You can change the logging database server, database name, database login user name, and (if necessary) the database login password with the `Set-SPUsageApplication` cmdlet. One advantage to changing this information with PowerShell, rather than in Central Admin, is that the change can be made without having to disable the usage and health data collection first! Plus changing it in PowerShell is just cooler than in Central Admin, so you get that added feeling of superiority over people that don't do it in PowerShell.

TIMER JOBS IN SHAREPOINT 2013

The SharePoint Timer Service is the conductor for all of SharePoint's automated systems, responsible for everything from workflows to server configuration synchronization to e-mail notifications, making it one of the most critical components that sets SharePoint apart from a basic data-driven website. As a matter of fact, the Timer Service is responsible for executing the Health Analyzer rule-checks and for initiating the creation of the Usage and Health Analysis reports discussed previously.

The various responsibilities of the Timer Service are defined as *timer jobs*, which are typically a set of instructions to carry out, and these timer jobs are deployed to the farm as solutions, not created in Central Admin. Timer jobs can be scoped at the farm level, or they can be scoped specifically to a web application or SharePoint service. Due to this scoping, it is quite possible to see multiple copies of the same timer job configured in the same farm, but with associations to different web applications or services.

Despite the fact that the Timer Service itself is responsible for running most of the other monitoring processes, the timer jobs themselves must be monitored in case one or more of them begins to fail to complete its set of instructions. Depending on the environment, the failure of some timer jobs, such as Outgoing E-mail Alerts, may not pose an immediate problem; but if a timer job responsible for pushing farm configuration changes out to the SharePoint servers begins to fail, the results could be catastrophic for the farm if the issue isn't dealt with immediately.

Managing Timer Jobs in Central Admin

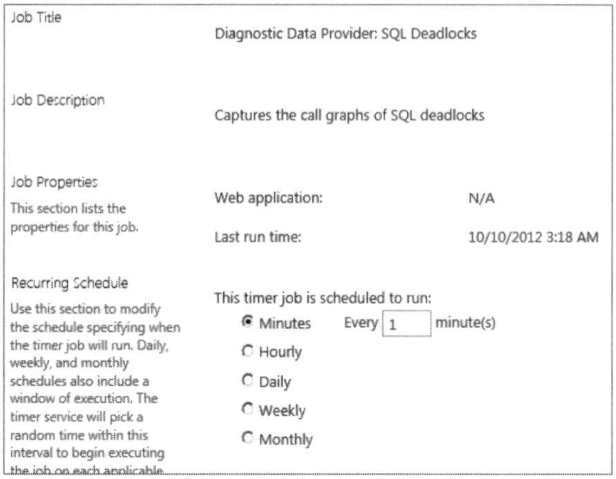

You can find the timer job definitions in Central Admin by selecting
Monitoring ➪ Timer Job Definitions. On your
first visit, you will be shown all the configured
timer jobs, and there are pages and pages of
them. You can use the top-right View menu
of the dialog to filter the contents to a specific
web application or SharePoint service if you
wish. Once you've found the timer job you're
looking for, clicking it brings up the configuration and details screen for that timer job.
Figure 20-11 shows the options that can be
changed on a timer job.

FIGURE 20-11

The "Last run time" information is quite valuable, as it tells you whether the job is actually being
executed according to its schedule. You can use the schedule options to change the execution schedule for timer jobs, but make sure that you are aware of both the impact that changing the schedule
may have on the farm's resources and any requirements that SharePoint or other systems may have
in terms of when or how often the jobs run.

The Run Now and Disable buttons were important changes related to timer jobs introduced
with SharePoint 2010. Prior to SharePoint 2010, both manually executing and disabling a timer
job required writing code that would make calls against the SharePoint API. Now that these functions are available directly, you can disable a timer job before a potentially destructive change, or
you can manually run a timer job immediately after deploying new code, or any number of other
scenarios.

Aside from the timer job definitions and the timer job details, you will find four additional Timer
Links:

➤ Timer Job Status

➤ Scheduled Jobs

➤ Running Jobs

➤ Job History

As per their names, the last three pages show lists of upcoming jobs to be run, currently running
jobs, and recently completed jobs, respectively. The View menu can be used to filter these lists not
only by service and web application, but also by the server on which the job is to be executed, or by
the job definition. Take a quick hop back to the first link, Timer Job Status. Figure 20-12 is a single-
page summary of the three status pages you just looked at.

FIGURE 20-12

One easy-to-miss detail on both the Job History and Timer Job Status pages is that the job status is a clickable link. Clicking this link not only takes you to a job history list filtered by the status value you clicked (success, failure, etc.), but also provides details about the error encountered if the job failed. This is a great way to start troubleshooting a failed timer job.

Managing Timer Jobs in PowerShell

Several very useful, if not particularly deep, cmdlets are available for working with timer jobs in PowerShell. The basic cmdlet to retrieve timer job entries is Get-SPTimerJob. This will return *all* timer jobs configured in the farm, so it is wise to do a bit of filtering to only retrieve the job or jobs with which you wish to work. This alone exposes a great deal of information about the timer job(s).

After retrieving the timer job, you can then disable it with Disable-SPTimerJob, enable it with Enable-SPTimerJob, manually launch it with Start-SPTimerJob, or change its schedule with Set-SPTimerJob.

One handy way to use these cmdlets is to manipulate the Health Analyzer Rules, which run at different intervals — some hourly, some daily, some weekly, and some monthly. Some might even run completely randomly, but there's no proof of that. Because of these intervals, Health Analyzer Rule warnings show up at various times after SharePoint 2013 has been installed. You can use PowerShell to sift through all the timer jobs, pick out the ones that execute the Health Analyzer Rules, and run them all at once. It looks like the following:

```
Get-SPTimerJob | Where-Object { $_.name -like "*health-analysis*" } | Start
-SPTimerJob
```

The preceding example gets all the timer jobs in the farm, filters out the ones with "health-analysis" in their name, and then starts each of them. Don't worry if you don't understand the exact syntax of that PowerShell command. You can become a virtual PowerShell expert by reading Chapter 7.

If you go back to the Timer Job Status page, you'll see a whole slew of new running timer jobs in the list, and with any luck in a few minutes you'll have the familiar red or yellow bar welcoming you at the top of your SharePoint Central Admin page.

SEARCH SERVICE APPLICATION MONITORING

SharePoint 2013 has introduced some truly impressive new capabilities for monitoring the Search service application. The extent of SharePoint 2010's Search monitoring was a crawl log to report crawl failures, and the rather ambiguously named "Recent crawl rate" and "Recent query rate" metrics. Together this provided only the most basic troubleshooting capability, and almost any search-related issue would land you knee-deep in log files with little clue of what you were looking for.

SharePoint 2013 has completely revamped the Search service application and its monitoring, and it now provides a wealth of information on the current and historical performance of the Search service application. The same crawl log information is still available, but it has now been supplemented with filterable, sortable data that SharePoint can plot out into extremely helpful graphs. Additionally, reports are generated that go beyond evaluating the performance of the search engine and move into evaluating the accuracy and effectiveness of the search results that are generated.

If you browse to the Search Administration page of your farm's Search service application, the page initially looks almost identical to the 2010 version. However, immediately noticeable is the redesigned Search Application Topology section. It has been reformatted into an icon-based view that makes it easier to quickly identify which search components are running on which servers, and their status. Figure 20-13 shows the different roles in the Search topology as they appear in Central Admin.

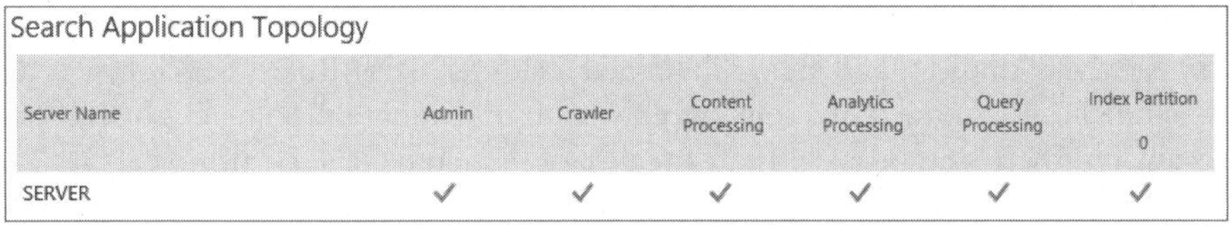

Search Application Topology						
Server Name	Admin	Crawler	Content Processing	Analytics Processing	Query Processing	Index Partition 0
SERVER	✓	✓	✓	✓	✓	✓

FIGURE 20-13

The Crawl Log

The second thing you may notice is that the navigation menu to the left now has a dedicated Diagnostics section. Hurray! Starting with the Crawl Log subsection, it also looks almost identical to its counterpart in SharePoint 2010. However, there are some subtle changes that are of exceptional value. Figure 20-14 shows the new Crawl Log screen.

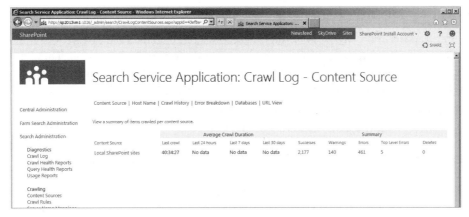

FIGURE 20-14

Views you can see from the Crawl Log include:

➤ As in SharePoint 2010, the Content Source view shows a summary of recent successes, warnings, errors, and deletes as organized by content source. New in SharePoint 2013, it also tracks average crawl durations over three periods of time: the last 24 hours, the last 7 days, and the last 30 days. As in previous versions, the numbers in the columns (e.g., Success, Warning, etc.) can be clicked to see a detailed report of each item that was crawled.

➤ The Host Name view shows a similar summary of crawl results, but in this case grouped by host name of the items, rather than content source. This page is unchanged from SharePoint 2010; you don't mess with perfection.

➤ The Crawl History view arranges the logs according to recently completed crawls, not only showing successes, warnings, errors, and deletes, but also including numbers for items that were not modified, items with security updates, and items with security errors. New to SharePoint 2013 are the additional values of Crawl Rate (in documents per second) and Repository Latency. Both of these new items are clickable links leading to graphs, which are discussed in subsequent sections.

➤ The Error Breakdown view (called Error Message in SharePoint 2010) enables you to easily view the errors for a specific content source, or a specific host inside of that content source. As with Host Name, this view is unchanged from SharePoint 2010.

➤ New to SharePoint 2013 is the Databases view. This view offers visibility into the usage of the crawl store databases associated with the Search service application. This information is not likely to be useful in most scenarios, but in an environment that utilizes multiple SQL servers, it could be used to identify load on a given server.

➤ The URL view enables you to filter crawl logs based not only on host name, but also on other portions of the URL, as well as status, message, and start and end time. The options are the same as those available in SharePoint 2010, but the layout of the dialog has been rearranged a bit, and Content Source was changed from being an alternative to the URL box to now being grouped with the other filters.

Crawl and Query Health Reports

The Crawl Health Reports and Crawl Query Reports sections of Diagnostics are entirely new for SharePoint 2013, and entire chapters could be written on just these two sections alone. They expose a wealth of detailed information about the performance of the Search service application, using a straightforward interface that presents the information in an easily understood format.

Your best bet here is to explore the various reports and consider various scenarios in which they could be useful. For instance, if crawls are taking a long time to complete, you can check the Crawl Rate report to determine whether one content source is crawling slower than the others, or whether the service takes longer to process certain types of updates. If your users are complaining about slowness while a crawl is running, use the CPU and Memory Load report to see how many system resources the crawl is consuming, and which element of the crawling processes is having the greatest impact. If your users are reporting slowness in search results, use the Overall view of the Query Health Reports section to see if there has been a recent spike in latency for the processing of server rendering, object model, or back-end requests. Similarly, you could check the SharePoint Search Provider view to determine whether the delay is related to security trimming.

Usage Reports

The last of the new additions to SharePoint 2013's search monitoring capabilities are the Usage Reports. These reports move beyond Search service performance, and into the realm of search result accuracy and search trending. From these reports you can pull information about the top queries by day or by month, or track abandoned queries, which could indicate that users are not finding what they're looking for in the results.

SharePoint 2013 introduces the Query Rule into search as a means of improving the search experience. *Query Rules* are rules that enable Search administrators to control how results are ordered. They allow content that matches a rule to be promoted or grouped with other results. The Query Rule reports are intended to guide you first in shaping your search design to improve accuracy and usefulness using Query Rules, and then in evaluating the effectiveness of your changes.

Chapter 13, "Configuring and Managing Enterprise Search," covers these monitoring topics and other search-related topics in more detail.

SUMMARY

SharePoint 2013 is a great product that works remarkably well. To get the most out of it, though, you need to keep an eye on it, using the well-known "trust, but verify" philosophy. SharePoint 2013 offers numerous ways you can look under the hood to see how things are running, in many cases enabling you to address an issue before it becomes a problem (and users interrupting your engrossing game of Spider Solitaire because SharePoint is down). you can peek in on SharePoint by looking at the ULS logs and Event Logs, as well as the Search service application's reports. You can also let SharePoint do some of the heavy lifting for you by looking at the Health Analyzer to see if any problems are cropping up there. You have many ways to keep SharePoint at the top of its game.

21

Configuring and Managing Web Content Management and Internet Sites

WHAT'S IN THIS CHAPTER?

➤ What's new with WCM?

➤ Architecting Internet sites

➤ Configuring and creating WCM Internet sites

➤ Cross-site publishing

➤ Authoring content improvements

SharePoint 2013 delivers the biggest leap forward in web content management (WCM) functionality in the history of the product. Although SharePoint 2007 was a major development with its introduction of true WCM capabilities, SharePoint 2013 web content management has ironed out any remaining wrinkles. For example, you can say goodbye to the /pages directory showing up in the URL, and to the single site-collection constraints that have hindered developers in the past. You can say welcome to friendly URLs, cross-site content publishing, and adaptive experiences. The new release of SharePoint delivers new capabilities and features in the WCM space for everyone: web designers, developers, content authors, and, of course, SharePoint administrators. These major new enhancements to WCM capabilities enable an organization to leverage its SharePoint expertise to build web content publishing solutions for either internal sites or public, Internet-facing sites.

This chapter begins with a brief overview of what's new with WCM in SharePoint 2013. Then it digs deeper from an administrative point of view and looks at architecting Internet sites, deployment considerations, building out a WCM Internet-facing solution, and monitoring your Internet-facing site after it has launched. Keep in mind that an entire book would be necessary to cover WCM and Internet site creation in complete detail, so this chapter focuses on the most significant new SharePoint 2013 capabilities affecting administrators.

WHAT'S NEW WITH WCM?

If you are new to web content management (WCM), think of it as a set of features and functionality in SharePoint 2013 that organizations can use to build, manage, publish, and monitor site collections, sites, and web pages. For those with SharePoint experience, this section provides a quick overview of each of the many new capabilities that affect the management and configuration of the SharePoint farm. While not all the new features specifically apply to SharePoint administrators, it is important that administrators understand the new functionality at a high level. This overview also introduces a lot of new terminology that is used throughout the chapter.

Cross-Site Publishing

At the heart of the new web content management features in SharePoint 2013 is *cross-site publishing*. You might see this functionality described in a number of different ways, including adaptive experience, content by search, dynamic publishing, or search-driven publishing. Regardless of the terminology, cross-site publishing is incredibly powerful, removing barriers and opening up several new possibilities for publishing content. This new publishing capability relies on the new search architecture in SharePoint 2013, which is discussed in Chapter 13, "Configuring and Managing Enterprise Search." Cross-site publishing enables an organization to author content in one or more site collections and then dynamically expose that content through search to other publishing site collections, each potentially with unique branding and a mix of content from authoring sites and the current site collection. When the content in an authoring site is changed, the publishing site collections are automatically updated. You will take a deeper look at cross-site publishing in the Configuring Cross-Site Publishing section later in this chapter.

Catalogs and Category Pages

The catalog is a new capability in SharePoint 2013 that, when used together with cross-site publishing, enables easy access to content in other site collections across the farm. You enable this capability by designating any library or list within a site collection as a catalog, and then this content can be easily reused by any publishing site collections. This new feature removes the content publishing barriers across site collections or farms that have been a challenge with past versions of SharePoint. Catalog data can be displayed using *category pages*, which are new forms of page layouts for displaying content from a product catalog or list catalog.

Just as page layouts provide a structured way to organize and display content, category pages provide a very powerful way to aggregate and display content that requires a specific format. Site designers can manage the overall page design, such as text formatting and images, and then each product or category can use this same design and same page for product display. For example, most organizations issue numerous announcements that they want to publish in a consistent way. Category pages provide a structure to ensure that all the announcements are displayed in the same way, versus creating individual pages for each announcement. For a more comprehensive discussion on ways to implement and control how content is presented, the reader is referred to Chapter 12, "Branding SharePoint."

Managed Navigation

SharePoint 2010 introduced managed metadata and term sets. SharePoint 2013 introduces *managed navigation,* which allows the administrator to configure and manage site navigation using term sets. Site collection administrators can use the traditional navigation based on website structure or the new managed navigation. Managed navigation is created by adding terms to term sets in the Term Store Management tool. Managed navigation and category pages are often used together, as you can associate a category page with a specific term in a term set used for managed navigation. This means that you can create more user-friendly and more contextually relevant URLs using managed navigation and category pages, rather than URLs that are based on complex site structure and numerous characters that have little to no meaning to end users.

Content Search

You read earlier that search drives the new cross-site publishing model for building WCM sites. Several new features and capabilities make this possible:

➤ **Content Search Web Part** — Central to the new search-driven site model is the new Content Search Web Part. Administrators specify a query value for this Web Part. There is a new Query Builder tool that allows the administrator to visually create their query, as opposed to learning complex syntax. For example, you could create a query to display all the web sites the user has access to, or display all the tasks assigned to a user. When users browse to the page that contains the Content Search Web Part, the query is automatically executed and the results from the search query are displayed. When used with capabilities such as managed navigation and category pages, this Web Part becomes very powerful.

➤ **Item details pages** — Item details pages are similar in nature to category pages. They retrieve search content, finding a single item in the catalog, and display it following a predefined format. One page can be used for multiple items and URLs.

➤ **Friendly URLs** — When category pages are used in conjunction with managed navigation, you can build a friendly URL to content by designating a particular value or term from the term set to use with the navigation. Category pages and item details pages can automatically display this content.

➤ **Refiners and faceted navigation** — These features enable site designers to build category pages that provide site users with a way to reduce the number of search results based on a particular value. Refiners are based on managed properties and can be included on a page via the Refinement Panel Web Part. Faceted navigation enables site designers to use different refiners for each term in a term set if desired.

➤ **Query Rules** — Search result sets are processed through query rules in SharePoint 2013. Query Rules are managed at the site collection level, and enable site designers to specify conditions, actions, and publishing values. Query Rules can also be used to fine-tune the ranking or promote specific results based on defined business results. For example, you could create a Query Rule that promotes all of the results that contain an Excel spreadsheet.

➤ **Analytics Processing** — SharePoint 2013 includes a new analytics processing component that looks at search index content and bubbles up content that seems more relevant to site users. This information is surfaced through the Recommended Items Web Part or the Popular Items Web Part. Including this type of information on the page helps to point users in the right direction based on what other previous users found helpful or interesting.

Internet Site Improvements

Before digging deeper into what makes a public Internet site unique, it is worth mentioning several improvements to the web content management capabilities that are targeted at public-facing Internet sites.

SEO Site Maps and Improvements

SharePoint 2013 provides several search engine optimization (SEO) improvements over the previous versions. SEO includes a number of different approaches that are designed to improve your sites visibility to potential visitors. For example, SharePoint no longer has 302 redirects, something that has made SEO difficult in the past. Friendly URLs also help with SEO significantly, as well as country code top-level domains (enabled via cross-site publishing). SEO properties such as meta HTML tag description and keywords are now built in to the managed navigation; and SharePoint 2013 can be configured to auto-generate an XML sitemap and register with robots.txt greatly enhances SharePoint's ability to play nice with Internet search engines such as Bing or Google. Finally, SharePoint 2013 comes with webmaster tools integration that help site administrators register their site with Internet search companies and go through the owner verification process.

Custom Error Pages

Another new feature in SharePoint 2013 is the capability to include custom error pages in publishing sites. In cases where 404 errors occur, users are now redirected to a custom error page in the site collection. This page is created by default in the publishing site Pages Library (PageNotFoundError .aspx) and can be set via the `PageNotFoundURL` property at the site collection level. For Internet websites, this important capability provides users with the best possible navigation experience, even when something doesn't go as planned.

Performance Improvements

The HTML markup has been redesigned from the ground up to keep it as simple and clean as possible. This enhancement supports the overall minimal download strategy, making every effort to minimize bits on the wire. Another major aspect of the performance improvements is the Distributed Cache service. Based on Windows Server AppFabric, the Distributed Cache service manages caching throughout the farm. This includes managing the Content Search Web Part cache, which is an important part of search-driven publishing sites. Finally, image renditions and channels are brand-new capabilities that can significantly reduce the amount of data sent over the wire. You'll learn more about image renditions and channels later in this section.

Variations and Translation Services

Variations is a SharePoint feature that provides a structure for copying content from a source site to one or more target sites based on specific settings and scenarios. The Variations feature was first introduced in SharePoint 2007, but several new enhancements to Variations and translation are included in SharePoint 2013. The Variations feature set is now targeted solely at creating multi-language sites. Users who visit a site where Variations are in use will be redirected to the correct variations site based on their browser language settings. Variations has also been improved with an integrated translation service. Content authors can either make their content available for third-party human translation via a standard XLIFF file format or send content off for machine translation. In addition, variations plays nicely with cross-site publishing scenarios as well. Variations also includes several administrative enhancements and reliability improvements, including improved logging data, the capability to export logs to Excel, and bulk page export capabilities.

Design Manager

Master pages provide the capability to deliver the specific navigation and look and feel to the website. Web designers typically are not familiar with creating custom master pages, and therefore have struggled to convert their website design into a usable master page. *Design Manager* is a new capability that enables web designers to create a design package using their editor of choice, upload it into SharePoint, and have a master page created for them. This is a powerful capability, converting what used to be an extremely laborious and technical process into a fully automated end-to-end tool that caters to web designers. Any web designer is now a SharePoint branding guru as well. For a more comprehensive discussion of Design Manager and the branding process, refer to Chapter 12, "Branding SharePoint."

Snippet Gallery

The *Snippet Gallery* is actually part of the Design Manager but it plays such an important role that it is worth calling it out separately. This gallery contains SharePoint components such as controls and Web Parts that designers can quickly add to their pages. In the past, web designers didn't have the knowledge or patience necessary to incorporate these elements into the page design. Typically, a developer was required to make these types of changes.

The gallery provides an easy way to select a component, configure its properties, copy the generated HTML, and then add it to the design. For example, web designers can add to their design the SharePoint-specific page elements from the snippet gallery such as the top global navigation or a search box, or the main placeholder control. In addition, designers can continue to use their preferred HTML editor to update their design.

Device Channels

Device Channels are also a part of the Design Manager that warrant separate discussion because of their importance. Device Channels enable SharePoint sites to be targeted to a particular device in a whole new way. Through the Design Manager, administrators or designers can define different device channels for each device or browser they wish to target. Device Channels can be ranked so that certain channels take precedence over others. This way, if a particular browser matches two different channels, the rankings can be used to determine which channel to apply.

With each channel, designers can specify a different master page and CSS. Page layouts are used with all Device Channels, but within the page layout, designers can leverage the new *Device Channel Panel control* to designate page layout content that is unique for a particular channel. For example, the control can be used on a page layout when a designer wishes to remove a column of content for smartphone rendering.

Channels and device channels give designers much better control over the user experience for each targeted mobile platform, making SharePoint 2013 a much more mobile-friendly experience than previously. Chapter 12 also takes a deeper look at Device Channels and how they can be used to enhance a site's user experience across a variety of devices.

Content Authoring Improvements

The authoring experience in SharePoint is also extremely important. Several improvements to SharePoint 2013 will be welcomed by content authors and contributors:

➤ **Text editor improvements** — Clean copy from Microsoft Word, whereby formatting is kept but all the extra Microsoft Word HTML is removed. Authors are presented with options for pasting content based on their individual needs.

➤ **Iframe support** — Using a built-in method, authors are able to easily and quickly embed iframe code. From an administrative perspective, this can be enabled, disabled, or enabled for specific sites via a new *HTML Field Security* setting.

➤ **Navigation configuration** — Global and current navigation are also much easier to configure and utilize. Links to add new menu items are available in edit mode, while authors and designers can now drag and drop these items to set a desired order in cases where such navigation is required.

➤ **Image renditions** — Image renditions enable authors to upload one image and then display different versions or renditions of this image within the site based on a specified size, width, or crop. When you create a rendition you specify the dimensions, and then every image that uses that rendition will adhere to the specified size. Image renditions are especially valuable for mobile device performance or when bandwidth is a premium, because you can have one very large image in the site and then use renditions to display smaller versions of the image throughout the site.

➤ **Video enhancements** — There is a new built-in video content type. The video upload process is improved for authors, and video thumbnail previews are automatically generated. Playing video uses HTML5 by default whenever possible, reverting to Silverlight if the browser doesn't support HTML5. Also introduced is a new concept known as *video sets*, whereby authors can upload multiple videos with different bandwidth renditions, and SharePoint will pick the lowest resolution set to display by default.

As you can see, there are numerous exciting additions to the WCM feature set in SharePoint 2013. With these features in mind, the following sections look at how they can be used to build and deploy an Internet website using SharePoint 2013. Keep in mind that all of these features (and the discussion about them) apply to building an intranet website as well.

ARCHITECTING INTERNET SITES

Clearly, there are a lot of exciting new WCM capabilities in SharePoint 2013. The administrator must be able to combine all of these great new features to architect and implement a public-facing Internet website that meets business requirements.

The rest of the chapter dives deeper into how to meet this challenge. It focuses on key considerations in architecting and implementing Internet publishing sites, but a lot of the content applies to internal sites as well, such as an intranet portal for an organization.

What Is SharePoint for Internet Sites?

At this point, it would be useful to examine the key factors that distinguish SharePoint Internet sites from other sites. How should administrators view an Internet-facing SharePoint environment versus the typical internal-facing SharePoint environment? Table 21.1 below highlights a few of the differences between an Internet website and an internal site.

TABLE 21.1 Internal versus Internet SharePoint Sites

INTERNAL SHAREPOINT SITE	PUBLIC INTERNET SITE
Internal — "behind the firewall"	Available on the Internet
Authentication required	Typically anonymous access
Users read and contribute data	Users read, seldom contribute
Branding important but not critical	Branding is critical
Loosely controlled publishing Web page content changes infrequently Loosely controlled navigation	Tightly controlled publishing Web page content changes frequently Tightly controlled navigation
Control of devices and browser types	No control of devices and browsers
Internal content Search engine optimization (SEO) not important	Public content SEO very important

These differences affect how the site is architected, the functionality, and the overall configuration and management. Because the Internet site content is public, and the web page content changes much more frequently, tighter controls are typically in place for authoring, reviewing, and publishing of content, as well as the navigation of the site. Because SharePoint WCM is all about the authoring, publishing, and managing of content, this chapter focuses on the Internet website and the use of WCM for those sites; but content publishing can be equally important to an intranet site or an extranet site, so the discussion also pertains to any site for which this capability is important.

Preparing the Farm for WCM

Typically, the purpose of Internet sites is to publish articles and content, or to promote products and services to prospective customers, partners, investors, or potential employees. Before discussing how to create sites and configure the WCM capability, this section looks at the key services and functionality required to support WCM and Internet sites. This can be referred to as *preparing the farm* for WCM.

A few core platform improvements in SharePoint 2013 significantly impact the function and performance of Internet websites. These include search and the new Distributed Cache service. As discussed in Chapter 13, "Configuring and Managing Enterprise Search," SharePoint 2013 now combines the best of SharePoint 2010's search capability and the best of the separate search product FAST Search for SharePoint 2010 into a single search platform. No longer available as a separate product, FAST Search is now fully integrated and provides the core functionality of SharePoint 2013 search. This significant change has paved the way for search-driven websites and capabilities that play critical roles in WCM.

The Distributed Cache service is a new service for SharePoint 2013. It provides farm-level caching capability for a number of features, including page load performance and security trimming of content. Because SharePoint's social features, such as microblogging and newsfeeds, rely heavily on this cache, it is covered in more detail in Chapter 14; but pertinent to our discussion, the Distributed Cache service manages the Content Search Web Part cache, which is a key part of the search-driven publishing sites infrastructure. We'll revisit this service later in the chapter in more detail as part of the discussion about the new publishing model and search-driven content.

Other platform-level improvements in SharePoint 2013 include the Machine Translation Service. This new service application is responsible for automatic translation of content in cases where you want to localize your Internet website and rely on the automated translation. The Machine Translation Service connects to the Microsoft Translator online service via SSL.

Over the course of the chapter, you'll set up a SharePoint publishing site and create new content using many of the new features just described in order to familiarize yourself with all of SharePoint's WCM capability. As part of preparing the farm for WCM, you will learn which services are critical, and then verify their existence and configuration.

Distributed Cache Service

You need to verify that the Distributed Cache service is installed and running on your farm. This service is configured and started automatically on every web front end and application server when the configuration wizard is executed to join the server to the farm. Administrators can manage this service or offload the functionality to a single server (also called a *host*) or to a set of dedicated servers referred to as a *cache cluster*. For this exercise, you'll simply verify that the service has been started. Keep in mind that the following steps apply to a Distributed Cache host that is not part of a cache cluster. If you have implemented a cluster, then refer to Chapter 14 for guidance or see the reference at `http://technet.microsoft.com/en-us/library/jj219613.aspx`.

1. Open Central Administration.

2. Under System Settings, click Manage Services on Server. If you have several servers in your farm, note the server drop-down section in the top right of the list. Be sure to select a server that is either a web front end or an application server.

3. In the list of services, verify that the Distributed Cache service is "Started" by reviewing the value in the Status column, as shown in Figure 21-1.

4. If the service is stopped, click Start in the Action column to start it.

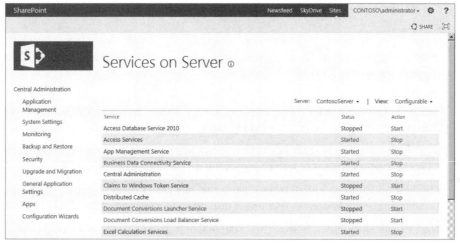

FIGURE 21-1

Search Service Application

The details about creating and configuring the Search Service Application are covered in Chapter 13. The following discussion ensures that the minimum search configuration has been completed to enable cross-site publishing functionality, and to enable you to update your settings if necessary. Use the following steps to verify that the service application is started, that all web applications are being crawled, and that a crawl configuration has been completed.

1. Open Central Administration. Under Application Management, click Manage service applications and verify that the Search Service Application has been created and is started. If it has not been created or has not been started, refer to Chapter 13 for details on performing this configuration.

2. Click the Search Service Application name, which will take you to the Search Service Application: Search Administration web page, shown in Figure 21-2.

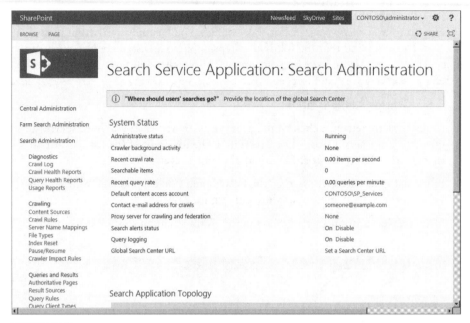

FIGURE 21-2

3. On the left, under the Crawling heading, click Content Sources. You want to confirm that SharePoint content is being crawled regularly.

4. By default, you should see a Local SharePoint site's content source listed on the Manage Content Sources page. Click the drop-down arrow and select Edit.

5. On the Edit Content Source page, ensure that the URLs for all your web applications are listed in the Start Addresses section. If not, add the missing URLs.

6. Under Crawl Schedules, ensure that Enable Continuous Crawls is selected or a crawl schedule has been created if Enable Incremental Crawls has been chosen. Now is also the time to update the incremental crawl schedule if necessary.

7. Click OK if you made any changes.

There are several other configuration options and settings in the Search Service Application, but for now it is sufficient to confirm that the SharePoint content is being crawled regularly, as it ensures that search-driven sites work as expected.

Creating and Configuring the Machine Translation Service Application

The Machine Translation Service provides the capability to automatically translate documents. This application will likely not have been created and configured, so this section will spend a little more time on it, rather than just verification. This exercise guides you through the process of creating a new Machine Translation Service application if one isn't already created, and applying the necessary settings. Before you begin, you must ensure the following:

➤ The App Management service application must be configured and started (discussed in Chapter 11).

➤ Server-to-server authentication and app authentication must be configured (discussed in Chapter 11).

➤ A User Profile service application must be created and configured (discussed in Chapter 14).

➤ Internet access must be available from the server providing the machine translations.

1. Using the Manage Service Applications page in Central Administration, verify that the Machine Translation Service application has been created and is started. You may want to review the settings on the Machine Translation Service page by clicking the service application name to ensure the settings are appropriate for your requirements.

2. If the service application does not exist, click the New button in the Ribbon and select Machine Translation Service. The Create New Machine Translation Service dialog will appear (see Figure 21-3). Give the new service application a name, and choose an existing application pool or create a new one. Keep in mind that the account used by the application pool must have Full Control permissions on the User Profile service application.

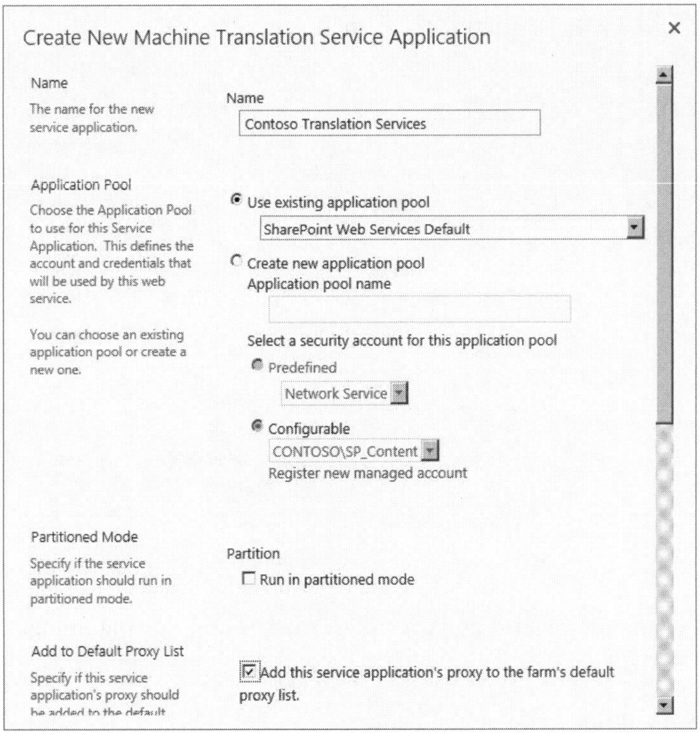

FIGURE 21-3

3. Select the "Add this service application's proxy to the farm's default proxy list" check box, unless you have multiple web applications that will be using different translation services.

4. In the Database section, enter the appropriate information based on your company's naming conventions and security protocol.

5. Leave the Partitioned Mode option disabled. This option configures the application for multitenancy. You would choose Run in partitioned mode if you were hosting translation services for multiple tenants. For the purposes of this chapter, you can leave this option disabled.

6. Click OK to save your configuration and create the service application.

7. Once the new service application has been created, click the service application name to bring up the configuration settings page. Review each of the configuration settings but don't make any changes for now. Of particular interest are the Enabled File Extensions options shown in Figure 21-4. Also available are Item Size Limits, Proxy Settings, Throughput, Translation Attempts, and Online Translation Connection settings.

FIGURE 21-4

8. Leave the default configuration as is and click OK. You will validate the configuration settings in a later exercise.

Creating a Publishing Site Collection

Now that the key services and service applications are confirmed to be operational, you'll create a publishing site collection using the Publishing Portal site template. This has several important site collection WCM publishing features activated by default. The publishing features can also be enabled manually for any nonpublishing site. Keep in mind that a site collection that has the publishing features enabled is critical to implementing the WCM capability.

> **NOTE** *If you are already familiar with creating a new SharePoint 2013 site collection, you can skip this exercise.*

1. Open Central Administration. Under Application Management, click Create site collections.

2. On the Create Site Collection page, note the Web Application selector at the top of the page. Be sure to select the correct web application because this is where the new site collection will be hosted.

3. Fill in the fields for Title, Description, and Web Site Address (the URL of the site collection).

4. For Template Selection, click the Publishing tab and then select Publishing Portal. An example of this page and the template options is shown in Figure 21-5. Note that there are three different publishing site collection templates: Publishing Portal, Enterprise Wiki, and Product Catalog. Review the descriptions for each of the templates. You will use the Product Catalog template later in the chapter.

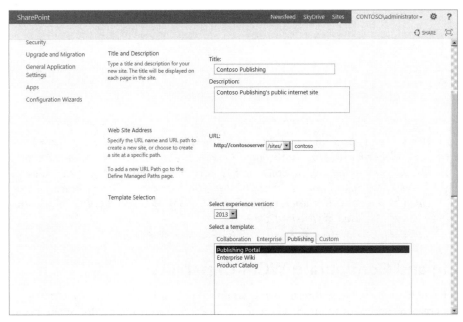

FIGURE 21-5

5. Enter the name of a Primary Site Collection Administrator and a Secondary Administrator. You could select a Quota Template if you wish, but it is not relevant for this exercise.

6. Click OK. After a few seconds the new site collection will be created and you are presented with a link to open it in a new browser window.

Figure 21-6 shows the newly created Publishing Portal site collection. You can see that many of the important features associated with creating a publishing portal have been provided, separated into categories pertinent to the designer and architect.

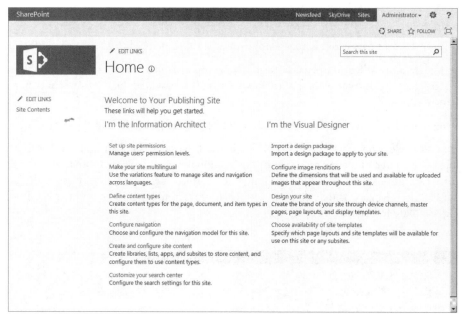

FIGURE 21-6

> **NOTE** *The publishing capability that is enabled automatically by creating the site collection using the Publishing Portal template can also be enabled manually for any nonpublishing site collection. To do so, you must activate two separate features; the SharePoint Server Publishing Infrastructure feature must be activated at the site collection level, and the SharePoint Server Publishing feature must be activated at the site level.*

Planning and Configuring WCM Capability

As you begin to architect your Internet sites, you need to consider several different topics to ensure that you create a successful solution. These topics are summarized in the following list and then discussed in more detail in the following sections:

➤ SharePoint architecture and site hierarchy

➤ Variations and multilingual support

➤ Publishing methods and site content

This broad overview includes planning, so some of the following material is theoretical, but you will also walk through some necessary configuration steps as well. Rather than provide an in-depth planning review, this combination of discussion and action gives you hands-on experience with key topics and issues pertaining to WCM and Internet sites.

SharePoint Architecture

You need to determine how many different public-facing websites you require. These different sites may represent different geographic regions of your company or different products. In addition, you need to determine what types of sites to provision and your site hierarchy. Just like SharePoint 2010, SharePoint 2013 websites exist in a site collection, so you need to know whether your different Internet sites will be provisioned as site collections or sites contained in a site collection (also known as subsites). Conceptually, this is referred to as the *site hierarchy*.

Site Hierarchy

The site hierarchy in SharePoint 2010 still exists in SharePoint 2013 and can be used just as it was in previous versions. This hierarchy includes the following logical architecture components:

➤ Server farm

➤ Service applications

➤ Web applications

➤ Site collections

➤ Sites

➤ Lists and libraries

➤ Items

There are additional logical architecture components such as zones, web application policies, and content databases, but the preceding list serves as a simplified outline. Because of its similarity to the SharePoint 2010 logical hierarchy, you can follow a similar process to plan and administer your environment in SharePoint 2013. However, because SharePoint 2013 introduces a number of new features, such as cross-site publishing, you need to consider how these new features impact your architecture. Another such feature important to Internet sites is caching, which is discussed in the next section.

> **NOTE** *For a refresher on site planning, see the following articles:*
> http://technet.microsoft.com/en-us/library/cc263267.aspx,
> *and* http://technet.microsoft.com/en-us/library/cc262410.aspx. *For a discussion of the SharePoint 2010 logical architecture components, check out the article here:* http://technet.microsoft.com/en-us/library/cc263121.

Caching

SharePoint 2013 includes both old and new caching capabilities. The new Distributed Cache service was discussed earlier. This service supports the social features in SharePoint 2013, as well as Content Search Web Part caching. Because search plays such a prominent role in cross-site publishing, this caching service is important. The service is on by default, but you can configure and modify it to maximize performance. Refer to Chapter 14 for more information about configuring the Distributed Cache service.

Several other caching methods still available from previous SharePoint versions need to be a part of solutions in SharePoint 2013. The different caching options are summarized here:

➤ **ASP.NET output cache** — Also known as the page output cache, this caches frequently accessed compiled pages in web front-end memory. Multiple device channels means more memory is required to cache this content now.

➤ **BLOB caching** — This is also known as disk-based caching. Frequently accessed BLOB content such as images is stored in this cache. The introduction of image renditions ensures that the BLOB cache is better utilized.

➤ **Object cache** — The object cache reduces the amount of chatter between the SharePoint servers and SQL servers by caching frequently accessed content such as tables or lists on the web front ends.

Because BLOB and object caching play critical roles, the following exercise demonstrates how to ensure that they are properly configured.

> **NOTE** *Experienced administrators are likely familiar with this, so you can skip this section if you already know this information.*

The following steps configure object and BLOB cache settings on your publishing portal web application:

1. Click Start and go to Administrative Tools ➪ Internet Information Services (IIS) Manager.

2. Click the plus (+) sign in the Connections pane, and then click the plus sign next to Sites to drill into the specific web application.

3. Right-click the name of the web application for which you want object and BLOB caching enabled, and choose Explore, revealing the virtual directory and specifically the web.config file.

4. It is strongly suggested you make a backup copy of the web.config file before making any changes. Right-click web.config and choose Open or Open With.

5. Select Notepad (you might need to expand the Other Programs section to see this option) or any other text editing tool you prefer.

6. Find the line in the file containing `<ObjectCache maxsize="100" />`. The value is in megabytes. Update the value to "200." For WCM sites, increasing the size of the object cache helps reduce traffic between the web server and the SQL Server database, which will render the pages more rapidly. You may want to increase the `maxsize` to greater than 200, depending on your desired performance.

7. Find the line containing `<BlobCache location=`… and update the BlobCache with a path name.

> **WARNING** *It is recommended that you choose a different path from the server operating system swap files or server log files.*

8. Update BlobCache file types if desired, separating each file type with a pipe (|) character.

9. Update the size of the cache (units are in gigabytes). This should be 10GB at a minimum.

10. Change the enabled attribute from false to true in order to turn on BLOB caching.

11. Save and close Notepad to commit the changes.

> **WARNING** *The web application in IIS automatically recycles when saving changes.*

Variations and Multilingual Sites

You should consider whether your site needs require providing content in more than one language, or to more than one locale. Even if your initial assessment suggests you only have to support a single language, you should strongly consider supporting multiple languages in case this may be necessary in the future. The reason is that multilingual support affects your site structure, and it is much simpler to design this into your solution up front than to add it later. It also saves time and resources later if language requirements change because SharePoint 2013 uses *variations* to provide multilingual support, and adding variations can impact site URLs, resulting in more work.

Whereas Variations in SharePoint 2010 could be used to target different groups based on various criteria, SharePoint 2013 uses Variations only for providing multilingual support. Earlier in the chapter, the "What's New with WCM" section briefly described improvements to the variations feature in SharePoint 2013. Using Variations, you can copy content from a source site or variation to one or more target Variations sites, providing a multilingual content targeting capability. Users who browse to a site where Variations is in use will be redirected to the correct Variations site based on their browser language settings. Variations also tracks the relationships between source and target content to ensure they remain synchronized.

Before jumping into the architectural considerations related to multilingual site development and how to configure variations, it would be useful to take a quick look at how variations and multilingual site considerations have changed with SharePoint 2013 in more detail. As mentioned earlier, Variations existed in earlier versions of SharePoint, but the feature was targeted for much broader usage scenarios, including supporting multiple types of devices. Table 21-2 compares how Variations were used in SharePoint 2010 to how they are used in SharePoint 2013.

TABLE 21-2: Variations

SOLUTION REQUIREMENT	SHAREPOINT 2010	SHAREPOINT 2013
Target content based on language	Variations	Variations
Target content based on mobile device/browser	Variations	Mobile channels and device targeting
Target content based on location or geography	Variations	Cross-site publishing
Target content based on corporate branding needs	Variations	Cross-site publishing

In addition to this new multilingual-only focus with variations, SharePoint 2013 provides several other improvements over SharePoint 2010 variation capabilities:

➤ **Performance improvements and redundancy elimination** — The Variations hierarchy creation process takes half the time to process in cases where a new language and target variation is added; and in cases for which the variation process is interrupted, the content propagation process picks up where it left off. List items and documents are decoupled from web pages, so this content propagates independently. For example, if only a document that is linked from a page is updated in the source, only the document is sent to the target, not the entire page.

➤ **Improved flexibility** — Content propagation can be centrally managed or adhere to more of a distributed model, whereby targets can opt in to updates and view differences in variations before deciding to pick up any changes.

➤ **Translation capability** — Content can be targeted for human translation or machine translation, and used in combination with cross-site publishing to target content across site collections.

Setting Up Variations in a Site Collection

This example walks you through the process of setting up variations, as well as integration with Translation Services. You can either use the same site collection you created earlier in this chapter or create a new one using the Publishing Portal template.

1. Navigate to the site collection you created previously using the Publishing Portal template or create a new one. This will be used for authoring new content.

2. Click on the configuration button represented by the gear icon at the top of the screen and select Site Settings. Because this is the root site in the site collection, the Site Collection Administration section should be visible.

3. Under Site Collection Administration, select Variation Labels. Note that because this site was created as a Publishing Portal, a link to this location is also available on the main page, as previously shown in Figure 21-6. The link is called "Make this site multilingual."

4. To create a source label, click New Label. Select English as the value for the Language and English (United States) for the Locale sections, and choose the root site collection as the Variations Home by entering a / in the box. Figure 21-7 shows an example of how your page should look.

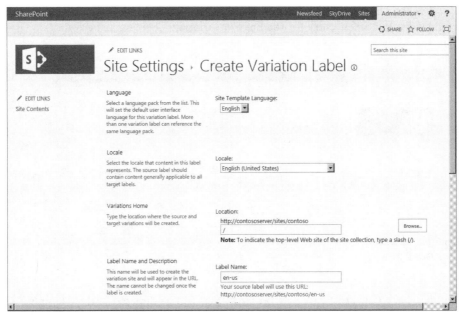

FIGURE 21-7

5. Choose Publishing Site as the Publishing Site Template in the drop-down and specify the current account you are logged in with as the Label Contact. Click OK to finish. Upon successful creation of the new label, you should be redirected to the page shown in Figure 21-8, indicating label creation was successful. Review the text on the page. Note that SharePoint 2013 uses the terminology variation *label* synonymously with a variation website.

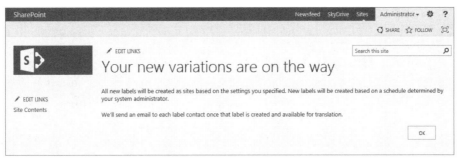

FIGURE 21-8

Now that you've created your source variation label, create one target label as well.

1. Click the OK button to return to the Variation Labels page shown in Figure 21-9, which now displays a new entry for the English variation label you just created.

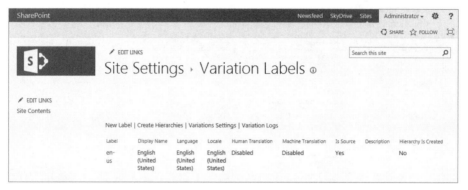

FIGURE 21-9

2. Click New Label to create a target label. You will be directed to the Configure Your Target Label page, shown in Figure 21-10. If you've used variations in the past, you'll notice immediately that the setup page is very different. Rather than one long form, it is now a wizard-like experience.

FIGURE 21-10

3. The Site Template Language options are based on the language packs you have installed. Variations don't require language packs, but for all practical purposes you will need them. For example, without the Spanish language pack, the text "Configure Your Target Label" will appear in English to Spanish-speaking users, as opposed to Spanish if you have the Spanish language pack installed. Thus, the "site chrome" appears in the target variation language the way it should with the language pack installed. For this exercise, it isn't necessary to have language packs installed, but if you have one feel free to select it. Otherwise, use default English as the site template language.

4. For Locale, choose Spanish (Mexico) and click Continue.

5. For the Name Your Target Label page, review the options but keep the default settings. Note that Hierarchy Creation has a few options. Click Continue.

6. On the Translation Options page, note the options to allow or disallow human and machine translation. Use the default settings of Spanish (Mexico) for human translation, and use Spanish for machine translation, as shown in Figure 21-11. Click Continue.

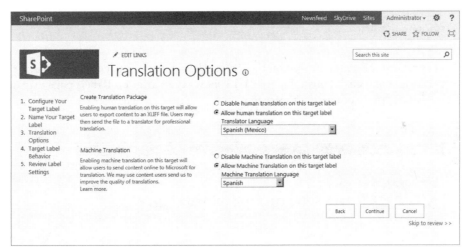

FIGURE 21-11

7. On the Target Label Behavior page, shown in Figure 21-12, you can see the new flexibility provided by the content synchronization behavior. For this exercise you can keep the default settings, but in practice you would want to make this selection based on how much control you want to give content owners on the target label. The label contact will receive an e-mail whenever the source content has changed.

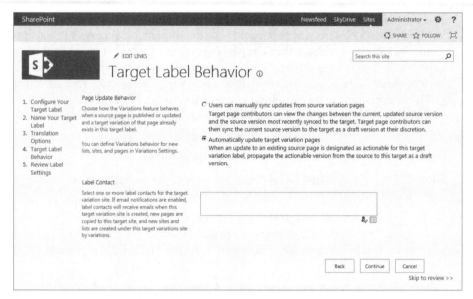

FIGURE 21-12

8. Let's review the configuration on the Review Label Settings page. Verify that the settings are correct and click Finish. Figure 21-13 shows the Variation Labels page displaying the two labels after completing these steps.

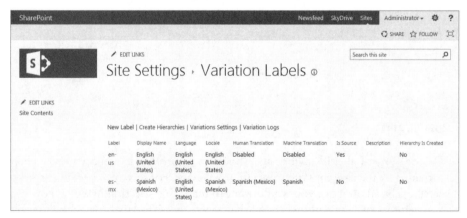

FIGURE 21-13

9. On the Variation Labels page, click Create Hierarchies to create content in the target location. Click OK.

10. Click Variations Settings on the Variation Labels page. The page shown in Figure 21-14 will appear. Note the new options to choose whether to publish selectively or everywhere, as well as how to manage Web Part translation and deleted target content. Keep the default values for this exercise.

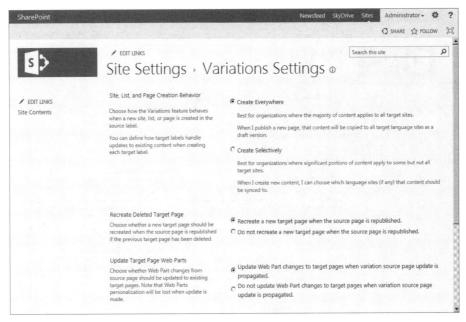

FIGURE 21-14

11. Browse to the home page at the root of the site collection, where you will notice that the URL has now changed, with the variation label added to it. You may also see a yellow banner indicating that the page has not been published yet. Click the Publish it link. On the English variation site, click the Follow button in the upper-right corner to add this site to the list of sites you are following.

This completes the configuration of variations. The next few steps illustrate how Machine Translation Services integrate with Variations. Recall that you previously configured the Machine Translation Service earlier in the chapter.

1. Browse to the Spanish variation site. If you're not sure how to do that, there are several options, but for this example you can browse to the English variation site and then navigate to the Site Settings page.

2. On the Site Settings page, click the "Go to top level site settings" hyperlink in the Site Collection Administration section. Now you are at the root of the site collection.

3. Click the Sites and workspaces link. On the Sites and Workspaces page, you will see the two variation sites listed under the Sites heading. Both the variations were created in the same site collection as the original publishing portal site.

4. Click the Spanish site hyperlink, which should take you to the Variations home page, as shown in Figure 21-15. The yellow banner indicates that this page has not yet been published. Click the Follow button to add it to your Sites list; you can also bookmark the web page for future reference as well. Next you'll take a closer look at the integration of the Translation Services capability with variations.

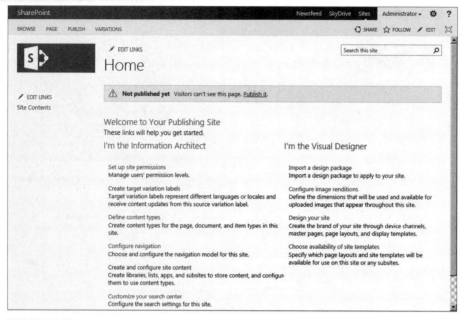

FIGURE 21-15

Translation Services Integration with Variations

One new capability that goes hand-in-hand with variations is Translation Services. During the configuration of variations, you saw that an organization has two built-in translation options:

➤ **Machine translation** — This option connects to Microsoft Online Translation Service via SSL. Content is automatically translated. Machine translation may not be as accurate, especially with any cultural or colloquial syntax, as human translation, but it is obviously cheaper and quicker than human translation. Machine translation can be disabled by administrators.

➤ **Human translation** — SharePoint 2013 now provides a way for source content to be packaged in an industry-standard XML format known as *XLIFF*. Large translation companies and translation tools support this format, making it much easier for an enterprise to get content translated and imported back in to their SharePoint environment.

An organization can choose whichever option is most suitable for translation content. In many cases, leveraging both translation options is appropriate — using human translation for mission-critical, high-visibility sites, and machine translation for less critical, internal sites. SharePoint will translate SharePoint fields, terms and term properties, and Word and text documents (rtf, txt, html, etc.). There are also term store improvements. Language packs are no longer required to translate content in a term store. Tagging term sets can now be translated as well. Once Machine Translation is configured, the actual process is straightforward. The following exercise walks through the translation options in a little more detail:

1. On the Spanish variation site, click the Variations tab in the Ribbon to reveal the four different options associated with content translation, as shown in Figure 21-16. If the Ribbon is not visible, you can enable it from the configurations drop-down menu by clicking the gear icon. Review each of the four different options on the Variations tab.

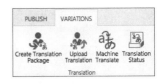

FIGURE 21-16

2. Mouse over Create Translation Package to review the description. This option exports the current page as an XLIFF file to be sent for human translation.

3. Repeat the process for each option to become familiar with its capabilities. When you are done, click the Publish link.

4. (Optional) To illustrate the content propagation process, modify the English variation home page by editing the page and changing the content. For example, Figure 21-17 shows changes made to the English variation site. After making your changes, click the Publish tab and then click the Update all targets button. You should receive an acknowledgment in the top-right corner that propagation has been initiated.

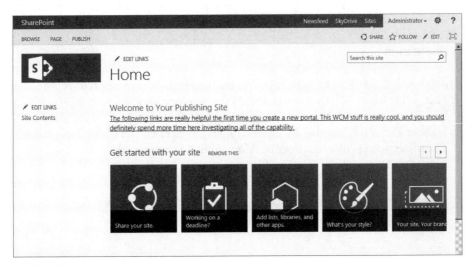

FIGURE 21-17

5. (Optional) Navigate to the Spanish variation site and click the Sync from Source button on the Variations tab to initiate content propagation. The content propagation process is controlled by several timer jobs. For the purpose of this exercise, you can manually initiate these jobs to see the effects immediately. Browse to the Job Definitions page by going to the Monitoring page in Central Administration and clicking the Review job definitions link. You will see several different Variations Propagate Timer Jobs associated with the web application that is hosting your Variations site collection. You may see Variations Propagate Timer jobs for other web applications, such as the My Site host, but you are only interested in those for your web application. For each of the Variation Propagate Timer jobs pertinent to your web application, click on the timer job name hyperlink, and select Run Now to manually initiate the content

propagation. Return to the Spanish variations site and refresh the page if necessary, and you should see the content changes fully propagated, as shown in Figure 21-18.

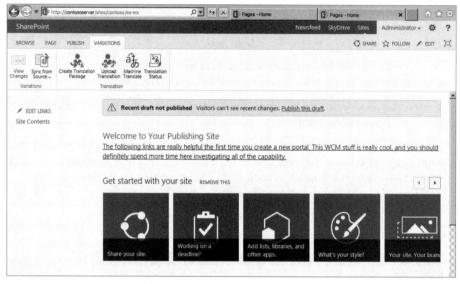

FIGURE 21-18

6. (Optional) Click the Machine Translate button on the Variations tab from the Spanish site. This will submit a job for translation. Make sure you have Internet access. Return to the Job Definitions page and execute two timer jobs: the Machine Translation Service - Language Support Timer Job, and the Machine Translation Service - Machine Translation Service Timer Job, to expedite the process. After about 15 minutes, the text on the page should be automatically translated into Spanish, as shown in Figure 21-19.

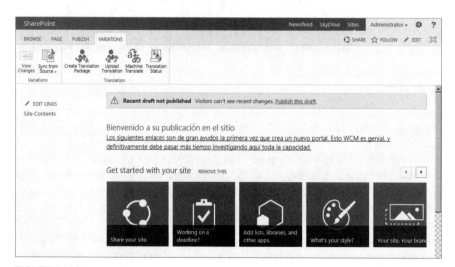

FIGURE 21-19

Site Publishing Models

SharePoint 2013 introduces a new publishing model called *cross-site publishing*. This supplements the author-in-place model available in previous versions, making WCM content publishing much more flexible and versatile. Prior to choosing the best model, you should have a good understanding of what type of content is going to be published, how frequently, and whether the content will be reused across multiple sites. For Internet sites, choosing the best publishing model is arguably one of the most important architecture decisions you are going to make. The two publishing models can be briefly described as follows:

➤ **Author-in-place** — In this model, content authoring and publishing occurs in a single site collection. Authors and administrators can control publishing via workflow and version control. Author-in-place is the best choice for architectures that don't require you to author content on more than one site, or publish content to more than one site, or where content reuse is minimal. This would include single-farm deployments for which authors are creating new content inside the production environment, instead of authoring in a testing environment and publishing to the production environment.

➤ **Cross-site publishing** — Content authoring can occur in one or more site collections, and the published content can be viewed in one or more site collections using the Search and Content Search Web Parts. Clearly, the capability to separate the authoring and publishing environments is a key new feature. Keep in mind that the publishing sites can also have a different look and feel relative to the authoring sites. Cross-site publishing enables a broad set of new architecture options in SharePoint 2013, some of which are covered later in this section.

Benefits of Cross-Site Publishing

Both publishing models are available and fully supported in SharePoint 2013, but the new cross-site publishing model provides a number of key benefits over the traditional author-in-place approach:

➤ It enables several architecture options that were never before possible, including multiple authoring sites, and multiple published sites sharing content. This includes multiple authoring sites publishing content to a single site, and a single authoring site simultaneously publishing to multiple sites.

➤ It provides a separation between authoring and publishing sites, including branding differences.

➤ It removes site collection boundaries, working across sites, web applications, and even farms.

➤ It provides the capability to mix authored content and published content easily on the same site.

➤ It offers more flexibility in terms of site hierarchy and navigation.

As you can see, there are several reasons to consider the cross-site publishing model. SharePoint 2013 provides a number of ways to build your site with this model, while recognizing that not every site requires it.

Organizations that have used previous versions of SharePoint for an Internet site have an advantage when determining which model to use, as they already have a handle on what is working well (and not so well) with the older SharePoint publishing model. Using this information, they can quickly determine whether they want to adopt the same author-in-place publishing model or re-architect their site to follow the new cross-site publishing model.

> **NOTE** *You can use a simple flowchart tool that is aimed at helping architects and administrators select the right publishing model. See the publishing method decision flowchart at* `http://technet.microsoft.com/en-us/library/jj635878.aspx`.

Cross-Site Publishing Architecture

The search-driven cross-site publishing model is a significant change from previous SharePoint versions. With cross-site publishing in SharePoint 2013, there are some key architectural differences. The following list describes the components of a typical Internet site built with the cross-site publishing model:

> ➤ **Authoring site collections** — Site collections to which authors contribute content. Typically not exposed broadly to end users.

> ➤ **Publishing site collections** — Public-facing Internet sites or internal publishing portals accessible to a broad audience

> ➤ **Search** – Centralized search functionality that enables cross-site publishing. It must be accessible by both the authoring site collections and the publishing site collections.

> ➤ **Asset libraries** — Asset libraries contain picture and video content for the publishing sites. In Internet sites, the asset library must be separate from the authoring site in a web application that allows anonymous access. The asset library must also be available to content authors.

> ➤ **Term store** — The term store is used by both the authoring sites, for tagging content, and the publishing site collections, for managed navigation and publishing tagged items.

Most cross-site publishing solutions have at least two site collections: an authoring site and a publishing site. Your specific solution might have additional site collections depending on the number of catalogs, authoring sites, and publishing sites. If you have requirements for multilingual sites with country code top-level domains (e.g., contoso.com, contoso.mx, contoso.ca), then this could increase the number of publishing site collections. Search, site assets, and metadata configuration can also impact the number of site collections used.

In the case of Internet sites, authoring typically happens on an organization's internal network. Publishing site collections and asset libraries are typically in the perimeter network, exposed to the Internet, with search able to crawl the authoring content. They are accessible to the Internet publishing site collection for search-driven content.

Content Deployment

For those who have utilized SharePoint's content deployment capability in the past, you may be wondering what role it plays in SharePoint 2013. In previous versions of SharePoint, the majority of Internet sites used a process known as *content deployment* to copy content from an authoring environment to the public-facing publishing site. Content deployment did a good job of separating authoring from publishing but it had a few limitations:

➤ **Limited content publishing** — Only certain content could be propagated. It was more of an all-or-nothing approach.

➤ **Stability** — Stable propagation was a challenge, especially for larger sites. Editing of content on the target sites would quickly lead to problems during content propagation.

➤ **Inflexibility** — Fewer configuration options were available.

In SharePoint 2013, content deployment still exists and can be used as a means for getting content from one site to another, but this feature is obviously less relevant now that the power of cross-site publishing is available. As a general rule, if you need to author content and then publish content to another site, you should be using cross-site publishing. Cross-site publishing is a major new capability, and one of the features this chapter spends much more time on; you actually create and implement an Internet site with WCM capability in the next section.

> **NOTE** *If you are a die-hard content deployment advocate, you'll be happy to know that in SharePoint 2013, content deployment is truer to its name. In earlier versions of SharePoint, content deployment was actually site deployment, propagating the entire site, including workflows, permissions, and other site-wide settings. Content deployment in SharePoint 2013 is now just about the content. This more limited scope, along with the true content-only deployment changes, will make content deployment a faster and more reliable experience in Internet site scenarios.*

CONFIGURING AND CREATING WCM INTERNET SITES

You have looked at many of the new WCM capabilities, reviewed key considerations that need to be a part of your planning, and configured many services and components to prepare your farm for hosting Internet sites and using WCM capability. In this section, you'll learn more about the specific steps to actually build out an Internet site and leverage the new WCM capabilities. This includes many more exercises and examples related to building and administering Internet sites. At this point, you have completed the following steps to build an example publishing site with cross-site publishing:

➤ Created a new authoring publishing portal

➤ Validated the Distributed Cache service

➤ Configured the Search service

➤ Created and configured the Machine Translation Service

➤ Configured variations on the authoring site

➤ Configured machine translation and validated on the authoring site

➤ Configured BLOB cache and object cache on the web application

Several additional exercises in this chapter build on the preceding configuration steps. Each exercise focuses on how to set up and administer new WCM capabilities in SharePoint 2013.

Configuring Cross-Site Publishing

In order to create and configure the new cross-site publishing capability, you need an authoring site collection and a publishing site collection. Typically, the first step is to create site collections using the Publishing Portal site template, which is used for authoring and publishing. Because you have already created the authoring site collection, you can reuse that for this exercise. You will create another site collection that serves as your publishing site collection and your Internet site. Then you will activate the necessary features to enable cross-site publishing.

1. Create a new site collection that will represent your Internet site and the publishing site collection. For the sake of this exercise, you can use the same web application as before. In typical production instances, organizations use a separate web application or possibly even a separate farm.

2. Navigate to Site Settings on the authoring site collection.

3. Under Site Collection Administration, click Go to top level site settings, if you aren't already at the top level.

4. Under Site Collection Administration on the root site, choose Site Collection Features.

5. Activate the Cross-Site Publishing feature.

You will configure the rest of the cross-site publishing settings in the next section, after a brief look at SharePoint's new catalogs capability.

Using the New Catalogs Capability

Simply put, catalogs provide a way for content to be easily reused across site collections. Catalogs can be HTML-based content from a Pages library, a list, a library of documents, or site assets. SharePoint 2013 provides two ways to create a catalog of information:

➤ Designate a new or existing list or library as a catalog. To do this, the Cross-Site Collection Publishing feature must be activated, as described in the previous section.

➤ There is a new type of site collection site template called the Product Catalog. This site collection template was built to include everything an organization needs to author and work with content in a catalog scenario. The site template has all the required features activated, and central to the site is a Product Catalog list as a starting point for managing catalog content.

It is easy to get hung up on the term catalog or product catalog and not see how it is connected to your specific solution. The important thing to note about working with a catalog is that it doesn't have to contain product information. You can use catalogs for knowledge-based articles, FAQs, services you provide, or any other relevant list of data that you want to expose for consumption via the cross-site publishing model.

Sharing an Existing Library As a Catalog

Earlier in this section you activated Cross-Site Collection Publishing on the authoring site. With this feature activated, you can share any list or library on the site as a catalog. The following example takes you through the process of sharing the Pages library:

1. On the authoring site collection, click the gear icon button in the upper-right corner and select Site Contents.

2. On the Site Contents page, locate the Pages app icon, and click the ellipses (...) button in the top-right corner of the Pages app icon. This brings up information about the Pages library and a link to the library settings, as shown in Figure 21-20.

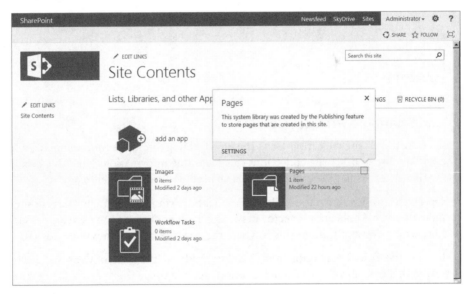

FIGURE 21-20

3. Click the Settings link to view the Pages library settings. Under General Settings, you'll see a new library option called Catalog Settings.

4. Click Catalog Settings to open the Catalog Settings configuration page.

5. Check the box that says, "Enable this library as a catalog." This makes the library content available to other sites and site collections.

6. Add ID as one of the Selected Fields, as shown in Figure 21-21. Note the additional options on the Catalog Settings page. Catalog Navigation is discussed later in the chapter.

7. Click OK. The Pages library is now a catalog.

FIGURE 21-21

Creating and Sharing a Product Catalog

Next, you create a new site collection using the new Catalog Site Collection template, and then share the Product list so other site collections can reuse this information. For this example, you can continue to use the existing web application you've used with the previous exercises.

1. Open Central Administration. Under Application Management, click Create site collections. Note the Web Application selector in the upper-right corner of the screen. Be sure to select the correct web application; this is where the new site collection will be hosted.

2. Provide the Title, Description, and Web Site Address (the URL of the site collection). The rest of this example uses "Product Catalog" for the title.

3. For Template Selection, click the Publishing tab and then select Product Catalog.

4. Enter the name of a Primary Site Collection Administrator and a secondary one if desired. You could select a Quota Template too, but for this exercise you can leave this blank.

5. Click OK. After a few seconds the new site collection will be created and you are presented with a link to open it in a new browser window. Figure 21-22 shows part of the home page of the newly created Product Catalog site collection. Catalog-specific configuration settings are available on the main page. Note that the Products list is also visible.

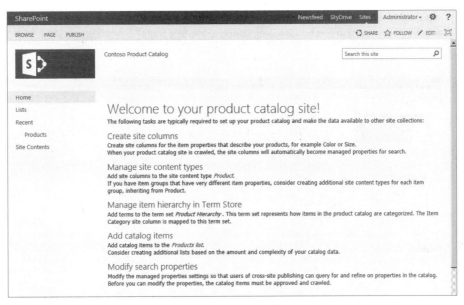

FIGURE 21-22

6. The next step is to share the Products list. You can navigate to the list and share it just as you did for sharing the Pages library, or you can click the Products link on the left side of the home page.

7. From the Products list page, click the LIST tab, and then click the List Settings button on the far-right side of the Ribbon.

8. Select Catalog Settings, and check the box that says "Enable this library as a catalog."

9. Add Item Number as a Selected Field, and select Item Category in the Catalog Navigation drop-down.

10. Click OK. The Products library is now available to other sites as a catalog.

Connecting to a Catalog from a Publishing Site

As a refresher, the examples in this chapter take you through the process of creating a basic cross-site publishing architecture. At this point you have two different catalogs configured, the Products library and the authoring site's Pages library. Use the following steps to connect to this content in the publishing site:

1. Go to the Site Settings page for the publishing Internet site you created earlier.

2. Click the Manage Catalog Connections link under the Site Administration section.

3. In the Manage catalog connections page, click the Connect to a catalog link.

4. The Pages and Products catalogs should both be displayed in the list. In some cases, you may not see the catalogs listed, and instead see a yellow banner indicating that a search crawl is necessary, as shown in Figure 21-23. After performing a full crawl, your two catalogs should be listed, as shown in Figure 21-24. Click Connect for the Products catalog, which will take you to the Catalog Source Settings page.

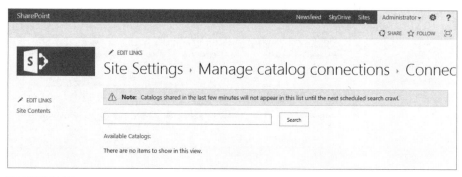

FIGURE 21-23

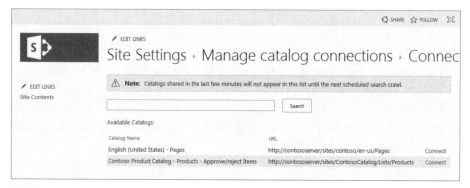

FIGURE 21-24

5. On the Catalog Source Settings page, you can see that there are several different configuration settings. Many of these are associated with navigation hierarchy and how the content in the catalog will integrate into the site. Review all the different settings, but for now leave these at their defaults. You will return to this page in subsequent examples and update these settings to build the site out more fully. Click OK to connect the catalog.

Branding

As illustrated earlier in the first table of this chapter, branding is typically a mission-critical part of creating an Internet site. It is also a very important aspect of the overall publishing experience, and one of the main design decisions in the process of building an Internet site. Chapter 12 focuses entirely on branding, so be sure to read or review the capabilities it describes in depth, and then return to this chapter. However, because branding plays such a prominent role in Internet sites, this section briefly highlights the Design Manager, device channels, and the Snippet Gallery, as well as special branding considerations for Internet sites.

Design Manager

Web designers typically build out site designs using a tool such as Adobe Dreamweaver or another HTML-type editor; and they generally use HTML, CSS, and JavaScript as the key building blocks during the design phase. The challenge with previous versions of SharePoint is that once an organization agreed on a particular look and feel, the process to convert it from an HTML-based design to a working SharePoint-based solution was tedious and relied heavily on .NET developers. A new tool in SharePoint 2013 called the Design Manager greatly simplifies this process.

The Design Manager is more than just a design import utility; it walks the designer through several steps to build and tweak custom branding for the site. From the site's home page, you can browse to the Design Manager tool, shown in Figure 21-25, by clicking the gear icon and choosing the Designer Manager option on the drop-down menu. Using the Design Manager, designers can make ongoing changes to their design using the HTML editor of their choice. This includes an easy way to update master pages, page layouts, and display templates. A completed design can be packaged using the Design Manager as well.

A key component of the Design Manager is the capability to create device channels, which can be used to display content geared specifically to the device that is being used to browse the site. The different channels can be ranked such that certain channels take precedence over others. This way, if a particular browser matches two channels, the rankings can determine which channel to apply. With each different channel, designers can specify a different master page and CSS. Page layouts are used with all device channels, but within the page layout designers can leverage the new Device Channel Panel container control to designate page layout content that is unique for a particular channel. For example, the Device Channel Panel container can be used on a page layout when a designer wishes to remove a column of content for smartphone rendering.

FIGURE 21-25

> **NOTE** *The SharePoint Server Publishing Infrastructure site collection feature must be activated in order for the Design Manager capabilities to be available.*

Once a design is imported via the Design Manager, the site designer can use a tool in Design Manager called the Snippet Gallery to insert or replace specific design elements with the proper SharePoint 2013 markup. For example, Web Part zones, top navigation, or the top page controls can be configured through wizard-like pages, and then the correct markup is provided to the designer.

Using the Snippet Gallery and device channels in combination with the Design Manager gives designers much better control over the user experience for each targeted mobile platform, which makes browsing SharePoint 2013 websites a mobile-friendly experience. After a brief detour for a look at branding considerations specific to Internet sites, you'll configure a device channel.

Branding Considerations for Internet Sites

Internet sites should be designed with a few unique branding considerations in mind. First, to ensure the best user experience, SharePoint websites must load rapidly to display information. Because optimum performance is critical, careful attention needs to be paid to things such as caching, downloading the minimum amount and types of content, and using minimal CSS. Fortunately, SharePoint 2013 has a complete set of tools to configure a SharePoint site this way. Image renditions, a new CSS model, and caching tools are beneficial for these purposes.

Second, an organization has very little control over the types of browsers and devices used to access its Internet site. Therefore, channels and device targeting (and testing with those devices!) provide a huge benefit for tailoring and optimizing the user experience.

Finally, branding an Internet site typically includes unique security requirements. In earlier versions of SharePoint this often meant that two separate farms and content deployment was part of the architecture. In those cases, authoring farms would have similar but slightly different branding from the production Internet site. With cross-site publishing, the authoring environment can look significantly different from the publishing site's branding.

Configuring Device Channels

While this section won't dig too deeply into branding, it does spend a little time looking at the channels feature in the Design Manager and walks you through the steps to create a channel. From an administration standpoint, this will give you some high-level hands-on experience with the Design Manager.

1. Go to the publishing Internet site you created earlier, and navigate to the Design Manager page by clicking the gear icon and choosing the Design Manager option.

2. Select option 2, Manage Device Channels.

3. By default, one device channel is available. Click the link Create a channel to display the Device Channels - New Item dialog.

4. Fill in the form, targeting a specific browser or device. In the example, the Firefox browser is used. For the alias, create a short descriptive string without any spaces. The most important section here is Device Inclusion Rules. This must be a substring from a user agent value. In this case, "Firefox" is used. Be sure to activate it only when the channel is fully configured in production. Click Active for this exercise to test the channel process. Click OK. Figure 21-26 shows a completed form.

FIGURE 21-26

5. To customize your new channel, click option 7 in the Design Manager, the Publish and Apply Design link.

6. In the center text on this page, click the link "Assign master pages to your site based on device channel," which will take you to the Site Master Page Settings dialog.

7. Note the Firefox option in this section. In the drop-down menu next to the Firefox entry, change the value to **oslo**, which is one of the choices in the drop-down menu.

8. Using the Firefox browser, browse to the Internet site and verify that the Oslo master page is invoked.

This exercise took you through the process of setting up a channel and selecting a different master page, but channels can also be used to update the master page and page layouts to target content to specific channels only. This is done in the Design Manager using a new snippet feature called Device Channel Panels, and site designers can use different image renditions for specific channels using JavaScript in the page designs, providing a more optimized mobile experience. Image renditions are discussed in more detail later in this chapter.

Navigation

SharePoint 2013 provides some powerful new capabilities and options for site navigation. With previous versions of SharePoint, the only option available when using out-of-the-box navigation controls and settings was structured navigation. The site navigation was built from the site structure and pages in the site collection. Brand new in SharePoint 2013 is the capability to create managed navigation, based on a specific managed metadata term set.

The new navigation option provides several important benefits. Menu options can be updated quickly and easily through the Term Store Management tool. Administrators have the ability to copy the term set and translate it into other languages for multilingual sites, or even build navigation by combining multiple navigation term sets across different site collections. Using managed navigation, an organization can build SharePoint sites with friendly, intuitive URLs in a new way, enabling new scenarios and removing barriers that existed in previous SharePoint versions.

One new navigation approach in SharePoint 2013 is the capability to combine parts of different term sets across sites. This is particularly interesting in scenarios in which an organization uses a product catalog to surface content through cross-site publishing. The following examples build on previous exercises in this chapter, walking you through the process of combining term sets to form a single navigation for the Internet site.

Setting Up Managed Navigation in a Publishing Site

The following steps walk you through configuring managed navigation.

1. Go to the publishing Internet site you created earlier. Click the option Configure navigation, which is located on the main page. Alternatively, on the Site Settings page, click the Navigation link.

2. On the Navigation Settings page, select Managed Navigation for both the Global Navigation and Current Navigation settings.

3. You haven't configured a navigation term set yet, so under Managed Navigation: Term Set, select Create Term Set.

4. When you receive an acknowledgment in green text stating "Successfully created term set...," click the link to open the Term Store Management tool.

5. Locate your new term set in the navigation tree, click on the name, and in the drop-down menu select Create Term. Assign the value "Home" to the term.

6. Repeat the process two more times, creating terms for About Us and Careers.

7. Note the additional tabs across the top for the term set, surfacing property settings specific to navigation. Click the Intended Use tab and ensure that "Use this Term Set for Site Navigation" is checked, as shown in Figure 21-27.

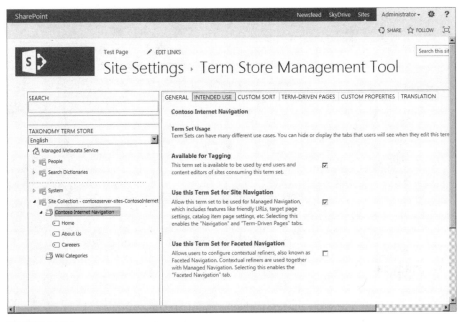

FIGURE 21-27

8. Click the Translation and Term-Driven Pages tabs to see additional options.

9. Click on a term such as Home and then note the change in the tabs specific to this term. Click Navigation and Term-Driven Pages to view the different options.

10. Under the Term-Driven Pages tab, check the box next to "Change target page for this term."

11. Browse to `default.aspx` in the Pages library and select it as the target page. Click the Save button.

12. Click the About Us term and repeat the process, but choose the `PageNotFoundError.aspx` file in the Pages library.

13. Click the Careers term. Under the Navigation tab, select the radio button Simple Link or Header and leave the text box blank. This will leave Careers as an item on the navigation but without a hyperlink.

14. Return to the Navigation settings (see step 2) and ensure that Managed Navigation is selected for global navigation and your newly created term set is selected in the Managed Navigation: Term Set section (see Figure 21-28). Click OK to save the configuration.

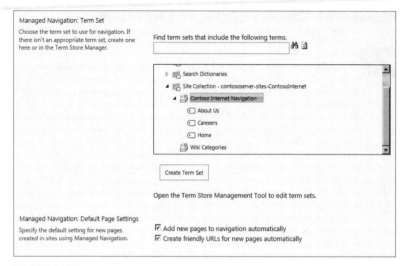

FIGURE 21-28

15. Return to the Internet site and note the new global navigation. Click the Home link and verify the managed navigation and the friendly URL, as shown in Figure 21-29. Also confirm the managed navigation for About Us, as shown in Figure 21-30, and confirm that Careers is not hyperlinked. This step verifies the new managed navigation settings you configured.

FIGURE 21-29

FIGURE 21-30

> **NOTE** *To access the Term Store Management tool, you can always go to Site Settings, and then click Site Administration ⇨ Term Store Management.*

Building a Term Set for Product Catalog Tagging

In this next exercise you will quickly build up a term set for the Product Catalog site, and populate the catalog site with a few items to make it more interesting. For this example, assume you are a travel agent, and the products in this case are vacation packages:

1. Go to the Product Catalog site you created previously. Navigate to Site Settings and click the Term store management link.

2. The Product Hierarchy term set should already exist. If not, create a new term set.

3. Click the Product Hierarchy term set and choose Create Term, and specify **Vacation Packages** for the new term.

4. Continue building out your term set until it looks like the hierarchy shown in Figure 21-31. This is only an example; you can choose to build any hierarchy you choose.

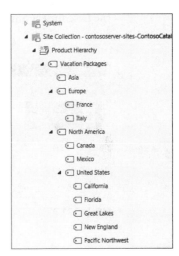

Now that you have created a simple term set that loosely correlates to your product categories, you will associate it with the catalog list.

1. From the Internet site home page, click the Site Contents link.

2. Move your mouse over the Products icon and click the ellipses (...) to view more information. Click the Settings link to bring up the Products list settings.

3. Scroll down to the Columns section and click the column named Item Category, which will take you to the Edit Column page. This is a managed metadata column, and you want to verify that the Term Set Settings area is pointing to the Product Hierarchy term set you just built.

FIGURE 21-31

4. Once confirmed, click OK to save the changes.

5. Create content for the Products list that you will use for demonstration purposes. Feel free to choose your own pictures and information, or just enter the data without images. Images can be uploaded into the Images document library on the site. For each new item, select an Item Category from the term set you just created.

6. Content approval is turned on for the Products list by default. Go through the list and approve any new items you create. In SharePoint 2013 you can select multiple items and approve in bulk. Return to Central Administration and the Search Service Application, and activate an Incremental Crawl to ensure that all the new content you just added has been indexed. You will use the Products catalog in the next exercise.

Configuring Combined Navigation Using Cross-Site Publishing

The final example in this section walks you through the process of using managed navigation to combine navigation elements from multiple sources to build a complete managed navigation solution. First you built a simple managed navigation solution with three items. Then you built a term set and a Products catalog. Now, using the following steps, you integrate that catalog term set into the site navigation, and consume that content via search:

1. Go to the publishing Internet site and navigate to the Site Settings page. Select Manage Catalog Connections.

2. Previously, you set up a catalog connection to the Products catalog, as shown in Figure 21-32. Click the Disconnect link on the page so you can start fresh again. Then click the Disconnect button on the Disconnect Catalog dialog when prompted.

FIGURE 21-32

3. Click the Connect to a catalog option and select the Products catalog from the list of available catalogs.

4. Under Connection Integration, choose "Integrate the catalog into my site." This integrates the catalog contents into the site.

5. Under Navigation Hierarchy, leave the value as Item Category and click the Tag icon to bring up the term set. Select Vacation Packages as the root term set to use and leave the "Include root term in site navigation" check box disabled.

6. Leave the additional settings as is, scroll down to the bottom of the page, and click OK. When the catalog connection process is complete, the term set from the Products catalog should be displayed on the global navigation, as shown in Figure 21-33.

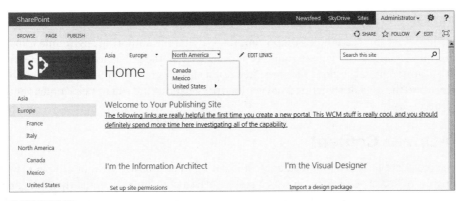

FIGURE 21-33

7. Click on one of the terms in the hierarchy, such as California, and you'll navigate to a dynamically created page displaying the image that is mapped via the Item Category value to the California term, as shown in Figure 21-34. Note that this page is in draft mode and has not yet been published. If you don't see an image, ensure that you choose a term that you added to one of your items in the Products list when you populated the list with content. Also note the URL containing the term-set hierarchy, and the left-hand side navigation, which has been updated. Choose another term in the hierarchy to view a different page, and you'll see that the URL and left-hand side navigation are updated dynamically.

FIGURE 21-34

You have successfully published content in one site collection to another site collection while creating friendly URLs based on managed navigation. Anytime the content is updated in the Products catalog, your web pages will be automatically updated after the new content has been crawled by the search service. This illustrates some of the power of cross-site publishing.

Authoring Site Navigation

Before concluding this section, it is important to note that the authoring environment in the cross-site publishing model is often a separate site collection from the published Internet site. As a result, it often has different navigation. The two sites could share a common term set, but in most cases it is better to use the default structured navigation for the authoring site to help content authors create content more easily.

Search-Driven Content

With the cross-site publishing model, content is delivered to Internet sites, or any sites, via search. You already looked at some ways in which search-driven content is delivered through configuring catalog connections and managed navigation. This section covers some additional methods for surfacing search-driven content in SharePoint 2013.

From an administrative perspective, several new search settings are available at the site collection level. One important capability is *Query Rules*. Query Rules are SharePoint's attempt to return results that users *intended*, as opposed to what they actually requested. That's correct — search is attempting to understand intent. To create a Query Rule, you specify one or more conditions and correlated actions. If any of the conditions are met, then the actions are implemented with the purpose of improving the relevance of the search results. Query Rules can also be used to fine-tune the ranking of results or to promote specific results, similar to what Best Bets did in SharePoint 2010.

Chapter 13 covers Query Rules in much more detail, but their capability is also covered here for completeness. Search result sets are processed through Query Rules in SharePoint 2013. Query Rules, which are managed at the site collection level, enable site designers to specify conditions, actions, and publishing values.

To access the Query Rules feature, go to the Site Collection Administration section on the Site Settings page. The Search Query Rules link takes you to the Manage Query Rules page shown in Figure 21-35.

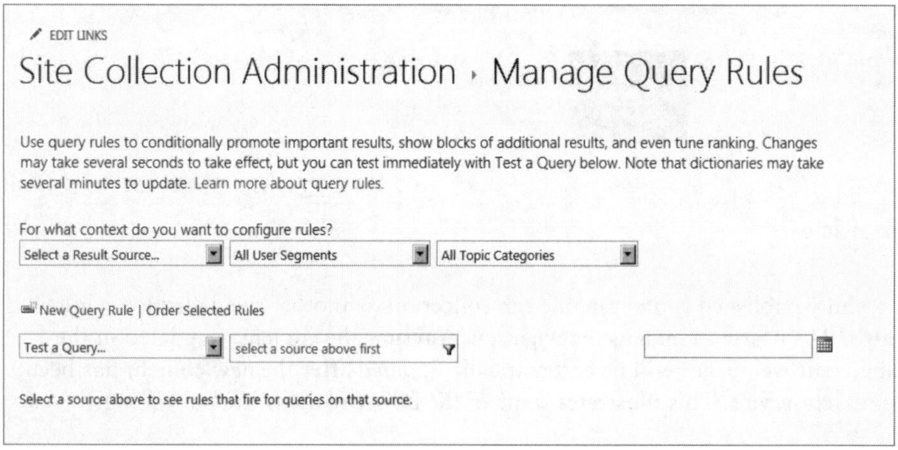

FIGURE 21-35

Another aspect of search-driven content is the use of *refiners* and *faceted navigation*. In the past, these elements have been a part of search solutions or on the search center site. But in SharePoint 2013, these capabilities are now a design element that can be reused on WCM sites to help deliver rich, dynamic navigation, and provide site users with the most relevant content. For example, if a user were navigating a site and wanted to filter vacation packages based on specific amenities, the specific amenities could be a refinement option on the category page. The Refinement Panel Web Part or Search Navigation Web Part can be used throughout an Internet site to provide a compelling and dynamic navigation experience.

Content Search Web Parts

The new Content Search Web Part is incredibly powerful, returning results from any site collection. Yes, that's correct, any site collection. After content has been crawled, it becomes available to any site collection throughout the farm.

Display templates are an important part of the Content Search Web Part. There are two types of display template. The *control display template* determines the overall container design for the Web Part. The *item display template* defines the look and feel for an individual item (think in terms of catalog items). When you add a Content Search Web Part to a page, the configuration settings include the option to choose both the control and item display templates. You can easily update or create new templates using HTML and JavaScript.

You can also use the Content Search Web Part in conjunction with other search capabilities, such as managed navigation and category pages. In fact, in the previous example, Content Search Web Parts were delivering the real-time content to both the category page and the item page. This content publishing was established by connecting the catalogs and managed navigation. This all happened automatically as part of the catalog connection process, but this section takes you behind the scenes to understand this process a bit better.

Finally, administrators can control some aspects of the overall performance of the Content Search Web Parts, such as enabling client-side rendering using HTML and JavaScript templates. Administrators should also understand this feature's limitations. For example, Content Search Web Parts execute in batches of five. This means that if you add a sixth Content Search Web Part to the page, it might render significantly slower.

Adding and Configuring a Content Search Web Part

The following steps describe how to add a Content Search Web Part to your publishing site and configure it:

1. Return to your Internet site that you connected to the Products catalog.

2. On the main page, click Edit in the upper right-hand corner of the page to go into edit mode.

3. For this exercise, you'll add a Content Search Web Part to the main page. While still in edit mode, click a location in the Page Content section at the top, and then click Insert on the Ribbon and choose Web Part. If you haven't already, explore the Web Part categories and options. You'll notice a category called Search-Driven Content that contains several Web Parts that enable you to build search-driven sites. This includes Video, Items Matching a Tag, and the adaptive-site capabilities surfaced through Recommended Items and Popular Items. More information on adaptive sites is included later in the chapter.

4. The Content Search Web Part is actually in the Content Rollup category. Click on this category and select the Content Search Web Part. Click Add to add the Web Part to the page.

5. You will update the Web Part properties to show vacation packages. On the right side of the Web Part, click the drop-down menu and select Edit Web Part. This brings up the Content Search Web Part properties.

6. Under Search Criteria, select Change query. This opens a wizard with which you can build your query.

7. In the Select a query section, click the drop-down menu, and choose Products Catalog - Product Results. You are going to pull data from the Products catalog that you set up earlier in the chapter. Search Result Preview shows the expected results for the query. Initially you'll see a list of all the Products catalog items in your list. In this example you will filter this down to items tagged with California.

8. Click the Refiners tab at the top of the window. On the left side is a list of potential refiners. Scroll down and choose California, and then click the Add button. The Search Result Preview window will be updated with the item that was tagged with the California term.

9. Click OK to select the query settings, and return to the main page. Click Apply in the properties dialog for the changes to show up on the left.

10. Next, you want to change how the results are displayed on the page. Under Display Templates in the Properties dialog, you'll see an option for Control (the overall display of the content in the Web Part) and Item (the individual item display).

11. Choose Slideshow in the Control drop-down, and Large picture from the Item drop-down.

12. Click OK in the Web Part properties panel to apply the changes, and close the dialog.

13. Click the Save and Publish buttons, successively, on the Ribbon. Now you should see your new home page with the Content Search Web Part, as shown in Figure 21-36.

FIGURE 21-36

Now you have seen two different ways to achieve cross-site publishing, but both approaches utilize the search services. Hopefully, at this point, you are convinced of the power of this new publishing capability.

Analytics Processing Engine

The Analytics Processing Engine in SharePoint 2013 isn't completely new. It has some of the same capabilities as the Web Analytics service application from SharePoint 2010, but it has been redesigned and significantly improved to deliver a lot more value.

The Analytics Processing Engine tracks data and clickstream events that occur in the SharePoint farm, generating reports that are accessible to administrators. It does much more than just usage processing with data delivered as reports, however. The processing engine is also able to mine data from your SharePoint sites and surface these findings right back in your site dynamically. Organizations can easily build a SharePoint 2013 site that recommends related content on the fly with special Web Parts.

Two types of data or analysis are available with the Analytics Processing Engine:

➤ **Search analytics** — Content that is added to the system via search

➤ **Usage analytics** — Usage information such as related content, user actions, clickstream activity, or viewed items

The processing engine builds reports with data about general SharePoint usage, popularity of content, and popularity trends. It will generate recommendations and then capture whether those recommendations are viewed. The event model is extensible too, so custom usage events can be added and tracked. In Site Settings, under the Site Collection Administration section, there is an option called Popularity and Search Reports that will take you to the View Usage Reports page, shown in Figure 21-37. You should familiarize yourself with each type of report available.

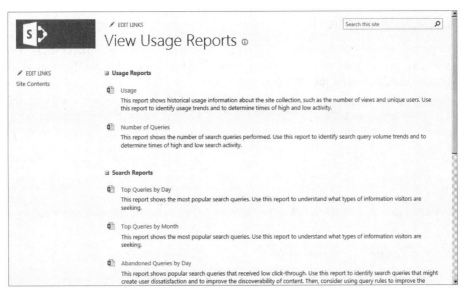

FIGURE 21-37

There are also new features and capabilities whose sole purpose is to aggregate the dynamic, mined data and display it immediately on a page for viewing, such as the Recommended Items Web Part or the Popular Items Web Part. Administrators can also use the data to determine the most popular items on a list or library, as shown in Figure 21-38, which shows the Products catalog. Note on the Ribbon there is a button called Popularity Trends. You should review this capability, as it is new to SharePoint 2013.

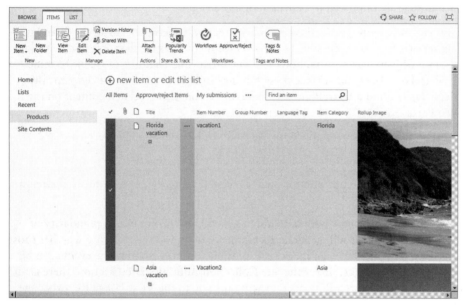

FIGURE 21-38

Search Engine Optimization

SharePoint 2013 provides several improvements related to search engine optimization (SEO), which is news that will excite any Internet website administrator. The following table highlights new capabilities in SharePoint 2013 from the SEO point of view:

CAPABILITY	SHAREPOINT 2010	SHAREPOINT 2013
Clean URLs	/pages library	Clean URLs everywhere
XML sitemaps	None	Automatically generated
SEO properties	None	Meta keywords and descriptions
Country code top-level domains	Very difficult custom code	Cross-site publishing and search-driven sites
Webmaster tools integration for SEO	None	Yes

Webmaster Tools and SEO Site Settings

From an administrative perspective, site collection owners now have a Search Engine Optimization Settings link under the Site Collection Administration heading in Site Settings. This dialog, shown in Figure 21-39, provides guidance to site administrators about how to register their site with Bing or Google to validate site ownership. This dialog also provides site administrators with options for managing link consolidation in specific scenarios. Review the ownership verification and link consolidation sections so you understand these new features.

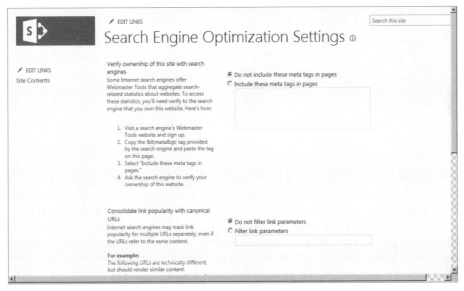

FIGURE 21-39

Generating a Search Engine Sitemap

Another important way to improve SEO on Internet sites is to provide search engines with an up-to-date sitemap. Administrators can enable this capability for their Internet sites by activating the Search Engine Sitemap feature at the site collection level. You should ensure that anonymous access is enabled on the Internet site, which is usually the case, but it is worth emphasizing.

That's all there is to it. The map will be built regularly and public search engines can consume it to understand URL and site structure for better crawling.

AUTHORING CONTENT IMPROVEMENTS

For an Internet site to be successful, it is important to consider the authoring experience and how content is added and updated. This next few sections provide a brief discussion of some of the authoring improvements in SharePoint 2013, looking at the new features in the context of Internet sites.

Rich Text Editor Improvements

SharePoint content can be copied directly from Microsoft Word and pasted into a Rich Text Editor Web Part or directly on the page, now with significant improvements in the HTML. Content contributors who have used previous versions of SharePoint are familiar with all the extra HTML markup that was copied over in this scenario. With SharePoint 2013, text formatting, tables, and headings remain intact, without the extra markup that used to be included in this copy/paste scenario. The Paste Clean option shown in Figure 21-40 copies content from the clipboard and removes unnecessary markup. In addition, on the far right side of the Ribbon, note the option to convert HTML to XHTML-compliant markup.

FIGURE 21-40

SharePoint 2013 also provides authors with a built-in method for adding iframe code to their page, making it very easy to add external videos or maps to a page. To provide governance of this feature, a new site setting was added, called HTML Field Security. This is configured at the site collection level using the HTML Field Security link under the Site Collection Administration section of the Site Settings page. The HTML Field Security dialog is shown in Figure 21-41. From here, administrators can enable and disable the iframe insertion capability, or specify that iframes can only be contributed from a list of approved source sites.

FIGURE 21-41

Using Video Support Enhancements

It is becoming increasingly common for Internet sites to leverage video, including simple getting-started videos, how-to guides, product announcements, and more. This rapid adoption of video as a central component of Internet sites is expected to increase.

SharePoint 2013 provides a new video content type, and the process for uploading video is improved over previous SharePoint versions. There is also much better support for embedded videos, and video preview is built in as well. SharePoint 2013 defaults to the HTML5 video player whenever possible and reverts to Silverlight only when necessary. Authors also have the capability to use a new video set content type that can store multiple video files with different renditions. The built-in video player defaults to the lowest bandwidth rendition.

SharePoint 2013 also provides richer templates for displaying video, and it offers an improved video experience in search as well. Finally, SharePoint 2013 automatically generates thumbnail preview images when a video is uploaded into SharePoint. Together, these improvements in video support provide content authors and site administrators with an improved set of tools to deliver content-rich websites.

> **NOTE** *The Desktop Experience feature must be installed on the web front-end servers in SharePoint for the automatic thumbnail creation to work. For more information about the Desktop Experience feature, see the Desktop Experience Overview on Microsoft TechNet at* `http://technet.microsoft.com/en-us/library/cc772567.aspx.`

Image Renditions

The image renditions feature is an important new content authoring capability in SharePoint 2013. Image renditions enable authors to upload one image and then display different versions, or renditions, of the image within the site based on a specified size, width, or crop configuration. For example, an author might upload one image from a digital camera and then use this image in two locations across the site — one location requiring a fairly large image and the other a thumbnail display. The author can use different image renditions of that single image, which are automatically generated when the file is uploaded. The author can also edit a particular rendition to choose a particular section of the image to display.

When you create a rendition you can specify the dimensions, and then every image that uses that rendition will adhere to the specified size. Image renditions provide a simple yet highly efficient way to create and use multiple smaller versions of one very large image throughout the site.

> **NOTE** *BLOB cache must be enabled for image renditions to work.*

Creating a New Image Rendition Template

You can easily configure the image renditions that will be generated on the site. Four rendition templates are created by default. The following steps describe the process to create a new template:

1. Go to the Products catalog site you created earlier. You should create the renditions in the site where your image assets are stored. This might be a separate site collection or part of an existing site collection such as the product catalog.

2. Go to Site Settings, and under the Look and Feel section of the Site Settings page click Image Renditions.

3. You should see four image rendition templates. If BLOB cache is not enabled, you'll see a warning on this screen as well. See details earlier in the Caching section on how to enable this cache.

4. Click the Add New Item link.

5. On the New Image Rendition page, fill in the Name, Width, and Height sections, and then click Save to generate your new rendition template. You'll see the new image rendition template displayed on the Image Renditions page.

In the next exercise you'll take a look at an asset library to verify that the new image rendition is being generated for images in the site.

Customizing the Image Rendition

In the previous exercise you added a new image rendition template. Now you will look at an asset library to view the renditions that are produced, editing any as desired.

1. Go to the Images asset library that is part of the Product Catalog website, or choose any other asset library you prefer.

2. Add images to this library if it is empty. This example uses the same images used previously for the managed navigation exercise.

3. Choose an image to view, and then click the ellipses (...) to open a dialog for that specific image, as shown in Figure 21-42.

4. Click the Edit Renditions link to view the generated renditions for this image. You should see five different renditions, including a rendition based on your new template created in the last exercise. Review the different renditions and the additional information on the page.

5. Choose a rendition to edit, and click the Click to change hyperlink.

6. Edit the rendition in the pop-up by selecting the portions of the image you wish to display. Click the Save button when you are finished.

As you can see, it is extremely easy to configure image renditions, define templates, and then customize the generated image renditions. Once renditions are generated, site designers and administrators can use the RenditionID value and URL to choose a specific rendition for a display template. This is especially helpful when creating experiences targeted at mobile devices.

FIGURE 21-42

SUMMARY

In this chapter you looked at the new WCM features and functionality in SharePoint 2013, and then reviewed these capabilities in the context of architecting and implementing an Internet website. You learned what key considerations were important as you architect, create, and administer your site. We also looked at WCM authoring improvements in SharePoint 2013. Cross-site publishing provides capability to publish content from a single site to multiples sites, and from multiple sites into a single site. The Content Search Web Part plays a significant role for aggregating content across sites collections. In general, the search architecture and functionality plays a very big role in the WCM capability. There are so many new capabilities and options available for WCM and creating Internet sites that administrators should consider utilizing SharePoint 2013 as their platform for such sites.

INDEX

H

X

Z